D0154464

D
16
G5

36492

Gilbert

Historical Studies today.

LIBRARY
SOLANO COMMUNITY COLLEGE
P. O. BOX 246
SUISUN CITY, CALIFORNIA 94585
(707) 422-4750

Historical Studies Today

Essays by

E. J. Hobsbawm
John Habakkuk
François Furet
Emmanuel Le Roy Ladurie / Paul Dumont
Lawrence Stone
Felix Gilbert
Thomas S. Kuhn
John E. Talbott
Frank E. Manuel
Robert Darnton
M. I. Finley
Pierre Goubert
Lawrence Stone
Stephan Thernstrom
Jacques Le Goff
Gordon A. Craig
Peter Paret
Arthur Schlesinger, Jr.
Jan Vansina
Benjamin I. Schwartz

Historical Studies Today

Edited by FELIX GILBERT *and* STEPHEN R. GRAUBARD

 W · W · NORTON & COMPANY · INC · *New York*

Copyright © 1972, 1971 by the American Academy of Arts and
Sciences. All rights reserved. Published simultaneously
in Canada by George J. McLeod Limited, Toronto. Printed in the
United States of America.

Library of Congress Catalog Card No. 70-163367

SBN 393 05453 5 Cloth Edition

SBN 393 09402 2 Paper Edition

1 2 3 4 5 6 7 8 9 0

CONTENTS

D
16
G5

36492

Preface   vii

Introduction   xi

E. J. HOBSBAWM · From Social History to the History of Society   1

JOHN HABAKKUK · Economic History and Economic Theory   27

FRANÇOIS FURET · Quantitative History   45

EMMANUEL LE ROY LADURIE AND PAUL DUMONT · Quantitative
   and Cartographical Exploitation of French Military
   Archives, 1819-1826   62

LAWRENCE STONE · Prosopography   107

FELIX GILBERT · Intellectual History: Its Aims and Methods   141

THOMAS S. KUHN · The Relations Between History and History
   of Science   159

JOHN E. TALBOTT · Education in Intellectual and Social History   193

FRANK E. MANUEL · The Use and Abuse of Psychology in
   History   211

ROBERT DARNTON · Reading, Writing, and Publishing in
   Eighteenth-Century France: A Case Study in the
   Sociology of Literature   238

M. I. FINLEY · Archaeology and History   281

PIERRE GOUBERT · Local History   300

LAWRENCE STONE · English and United States Local History   315

STEPHAN THERNSTROM · Reflections on the New Urban History   320

JACQUES LE GOFF · Is Politics Still the Backbone of History?   337

GORDON A. CRAIG · Political and Diplomatic History   356

PETER PARET · The History of War   372

ARTHUR SCHLESINGER, JR. · The Historian as Participant   393

JAN VANSINA · Once Upon a Time: Oral Traditions as History
   in Africa   413

BENJAMIN I. SCHWARTZ · A Brief Defense of Political and Intellectual History . . . with Particular Reference to Non-
Western Countries   440

Notes on Contributors   455

Index   459

·THE historical profession, like any other, needs periodically to review itself, to consider with whatever objectivity it can muster both its strengths and weaknesses. To do so at the present time would seem to be imperative: many, correctly or incorrectly, perceive a "crisis" in the profession, and are concerned for its future.

C. Vann Woodward, for instance, detects unmistakable evidences of a diminished interest in history; he warned the 1969 meeting of the American Historical Association of a growing antihistorical bias in contemporary culture, and stated that the turning away from historical studies both in schools and colleges only confirms what other warning systems also announce. A "crisis" in the historical profession is occurring because the "market" for its product and the taste for its methods is declining.

While many would draw attention to the altered intellectual climate, with its influence on historical as well as other disciplines, others believe that a change has taken place not only in society, but in the historical profession itself. Oscar Handlin, for example, in speaking to the American Historical Association meeting in 1970, blamed the historical profession itself; it had lost its "unifying purpose" and raised expectations largely "unfulfilled," and there had been, he said, a "decline of craftsmanship" since the time he entered the profession in the 1930's.

Is this adverse judgment on the profession justified? It is difficult to say. Not one of the more than two dozen historians who have written for this volume would appear to share his view, though several are critical of scholarship in their respective fields. Why do they appear so sanguine when their colleague is so alarmed?

Clearly, they do not see the profession as he does. They do not judge the 1930's (or the 1960's) in the way that he chooses to. The 1930's are not, for them, the golden years of historical scholarship. While no one of them is interested in disparaging his "masters"— there are innumerable references to the "founders" of methods and disciplines which, in some instances, are only now beginning to make a deep impression on the historical profession as a whole—they do not feel themselves to be epigones, standing on the shoulders of giants. Few think it necessary to make excuses for the scholarship of the 1960's.

Clearly, certain trends in historical research that first became apparent in the inter-war years have gained greater importance since 1945. Thus, for example, it is impossible to deny the increased interest in social history. While it would be wrong to say that credit for this development belongs solely to the *Annales* school, it would be difficult to find any international influence that has been more pervasive. The United States may have produced social historians of great distinction in the 1930's; they did not become the "teachers" of a whole generation of historians in several countries. Marc Bloch's fame, and the fame of his journal, in this regard, is of a different order than anything produced elsewhere.

So long as the *Annales* school was on the outside, looking in on a historical establishment largely formed by other traditions, there was no great incentive to attack its methods or premises. Now, when, as in France, the "school" has captured many university chairs, and is so obviously influential, there is greater reason to raise questions about its orientations.

Social history may best be viewed as a discipline still in its infancy. The development of sophisticated techniques, as in historical demography, does not extend over into other areas where equal precision is required. Almost every author who has chosen to dwell on some aspect of social history has insisted on the modesty of the results so far achieved. This, however, does not prevent Eric Hobsbawm from saying: "But it would be wrong to conclude without noting, and welcoming, the remarkably flourishing state of the field. It is a good moment to be a social historian. Even those of us who never set out to call ourselves by this name will not want to disclaim it today."

This spirit may be said to be the dominant one of the volume, whether the subject is prosopography, intellectual history, local history, the history of education, the history of science, or urban history. There is no crude celebration of accomplishment in any of these fields, and no disinclination to conceal the insufficiencies of research in many of them, but there is little or no sense of disillusion with the profession or with the enterprises its practitioners have selected for themselves.

Is it possible, then, that professional historians are excited by their research, fully confident of its intrinsic worth, and not at all inclined to disparage it, while society as a whole gives less heed to their findings? This, in fact, is precisely the situation of the moment. Many of the developments of recent years have helped those who have viewed history as a science—not a science in the sense that its data may be said to have predictive utility, but a science in François Furet's sense: "of substituting for the elusive 'event' of positivist history the regular repetition of data selected or constructed by reason of their comparability." History, constructed along such lines, can never serve the purposes of a public that still craves narrative accounts. Inevitably, such history will be meaningful only to other historians and to scholars who will have some special reason for being interested.

Historians who have chosen to travel this route have not driven out others who prefer the more conventional narrative approach; in some countries—the United Kingdom, for example—the latter may still be in the ascendancy. There are many who do not believe that all history should become social history; fidelity to the traditional historical categories is not at all uncommon. What is interesting, however, is that even many of the traditionalists approach their tasks in a new spirit. Within the historical profession itself—in the universities of many countries—those who are thought most creative are those who experiment with new methods and new kinds of inquiry. Such historical writing is rarely "popular."

So long as history could be viewed as the prologue to the present, so long as its most accomplished practitioners accepted national frames—writing about the political, cultural, and diplomatic experiences of particular states, to educate their fellow-citizens— history was *the* humanistic discipline. Whether the subject was Greece, Rome, the Catholic Church, the Reformation, the Renaissance, the development of science, the Enlightenment, the French Revolution, or Romanticism, all were thought relevant to what Europe (and America) had been or had become. When the past ceased to be viewed in such a way, when the presuppositions of such work were dismissed as narrowly Whig or scientifically imprecise, there was less incentive to study history for such purposes. Clearly, the change came very gradually; even today, the idea of a Western Civilization or an American Civilization is not entirely dead. University courses, departments, and divisions attest to their "reality." Yet, there is a growing reluctance to think in such categories. It is not only in America that the conventional lines separating disciplines are questioned. Time and space are both being thought of in new ways.

This volume tells of new archives that are being formed, based on materials that were until very recently ignored by historians. It tells also of new methods being experimented with. Much of what is being done has made no great impression on the larger public that once thought it needed to know history. This may be the greatest shortcoming of the research that is going on. Perhaps history ought never to become "exclusive" in the way that economics, philosophy, and physics have. Perhaps it will soon turn from its present preoccupations. If it does, it will not, however, be a return to the narrative history of the nineteenth century—however brilliant that accomplishment may have been.

The professional historian of the 1970's, less concerned about the "completeness" of his archive than his nineteenth-century predecessor, realizing that he is himself in part the creator of that archive, shows a hospitality to the study of near-contemporary events that would have been inconceivable fifty years ago. While he still has a long distance to traverse before he reclaims whole fields that have fallen into the hands of sociologists and political scientists—because no historical claim was ever made for these fields—this may in fact increasingly be his purpose. If he succeeds in this, he will inevitably be led to do again what historians from the time of Thucydides were always prepared to do: interpret the contemporary world to their generation. The opportunities for comparative history are today unequaled. The appetite for such study, and for learning from it, may bring a new educated public to recognize the unique values that such historical research affords.

Stephen R. Graubard

Present-day historical scholarship differs from that of previous years. That is the assumption—actually a fact rather than an assumption—which gives interest and value to an investigation of the status of historical scholarship in the present world. The question whether traditional fields of history are studied in a novel manner and whether new fields have appeared on the historian's horizon can be answered only through an analysis of the work that today's historians are doing; the essays in this volume attempt such an analysis. The historian, however, becomes aware of these changes not only through a study of the works that scholars have written, but also through personal experience. A note in personal terms might therefore introduce some of the themes that follow.

When I first climbed the steep steps of the Uffizi which led to the Archivio di Stato in Florence I was frightened at beginning work in a foreign country, and when I entered the reading room I sat down quickly at a table nearest the entrance. Immediately an official appeared who told me severely that ladies and gentlemen worked at separate tables and that I had sat down at a table *per le signorine*. After this incident things went smoothly. I received the documents I ordered and got busy copying those that seemed of interest to my work. After the siesta hour the Archivio was closed, so I would go to the private archives of the Guicciardini family. Usually I found there an archivist and an Italian scholar who was preparing a revised edition of Francesco Guicciardini's works. When any of us found a word or a passage incomprehensible—and I should say that this happened much more frequently to me than to the two others—we put our heads together and puzzled over the difficult passage; the reading on which we agreed was adopted in the manuscript being written or the edition being prepared.

That was forty years ago. Now when I go to the Archivio there is no longer a separate table for ladies. But more important changes have taken place as well. First, the tempo of work has changed. If in my younger years I was happy to get through one volume of documents in a day, I am now annoyed if the number of volumes a reader is allowed to have on his desk is limited to three or four. The usual procedure is to look quickly through the documents, mark with a slip of paper those that seem important and relevant, and send them to the photocopying office of the Archivio; after they have been microfilmed or photostated a careful study can be done at home—wherever that is.

The introduction of new techniques of facsimile reproduction— photostats, xerox, microfilm, microfilm printer-readers—has altered the nature of historical work in many respects. As more files can be examined in less time, research can extend more readily from one field to another—from politics to taxation, public safety, economic regulations, and so on. If earlier historians seem to have been less aware of the social implications of political issues than we are, one reason was the difficulty in finding time for venturing beyond the volumes containing the basic political documents. Today, facsimiles of documents can be examined at home with unhurried care; photostats of passages difficult to read or to understand can be sent to experts; if determination of an individual's handwriting is important, all the material needed for comparison can be easily assembled.

Similarly, all the existing copies of a manuscript needed for the reconstruction of its lost original text can be brought together from different libraries or archives. Modern technology has been instrumental in raising the standards for the production of critical editions of the writings of important figures. Facsimiles of all manuscripts can be assembled in one place making possible a previously unknown exactitude in establishing the relation among various drafts of a manuscript, in placing a fragment in its appropriate context, and in the dating of letters or memoranda. Julian Boyd's edition of the Jefferson papers, probably the model of the many great editorial enterprises underway at present, would scarcely have been possible without modern means of facsimile reproduction. The correspondence of Lorenzo Magnifico is being edited in both Florence and London because photostats of the material have been assembled in each city. Modern technology has influenced not only editorial techniques, but historical writing as well. Historians working in the last century usually based their publications chiefly on sources in one particular archive, frequently the central archive of the historian's own country, which could be reached most easily; this dependence on national sources certainly had its influence in determining the nationally bound character of nineteenth-century historiography. Relative ease of travel and modern techniques of reproduction now facilitate use of collections from a great number of archives. One of the somewhat astounding examples of this development is that Italian foreign affairs in the second part of the fifteenth century can quite as well if not better be studied in Amherst, Massachusetts, where microfilms of all the diplomatic reports of the Italian states from this period have been collected, than in any other place.

Are we at the end of the road down which modern technology has led us, and have its possibilities been fully utilized? Frankly, it seems likely that we are only at the beginning of a new approach to historical source materials. The collection of microfilms from the late Quattrocento just mentioned is an example of what can be done in assembling reproductions of all the material pertaining to a particular problem or period. A beginning has been made in microfilming manuscript collections in the event the originals are destroyed. The same could be done for purposes of research; libraries with special collections might add archives in which microfilms of basic documentary material relating to the subject of their special collections can be assembled. Perhaps the notion of what an archive is begins to change; at least we should recognize that there are different kinds of archives. Originally, archives were established to house the accumulating mass of official papers; although collections of private papers were added to it, the storing of government material remained the main purpose of an archive. However, one can well imagine a historian or team of historians assembling an archive to suit the purposes of the research they pursue. They might isolate the various issues that form part of the problem of their investigation and try to collect microfilms and photostats of all the documents, books, manuscripts, and pamphlets that deal with the various aspects of that problem. François Furet, in his essay here on "Quantitative History," is discussing a new kind of archive in reference to the newly developed field of serial history, but his demand for "new archives" probably has bearing on most fields of history. In contrast to governmental archives set up according to the business which the documents served, archives on tapes or of photographically reproduced material could be organized according to the problem the material might solve or clarify. This is not an original suggestion; but it might serve to place on a more systematic basis what many historians are beginning to do for themselves.

It is more attractive to envisage the possibilities technical inventions have opened than to discuss whether we have habits or customs which technology has made obsolete. But the question whether or not there are areas in which technical innovations have made continuation of traditional procedures inappropriate is unavoidable. The customary manner of publication of historical source materials is one of these issues. Certainly photographic techniques have greatly assisted in the task of editing and have improved its quality, but the mass of documents and the explanatory notes have resulted in editions of thirty, forty, fifty, or more volumes. They are no longer suitable for private libraries and are not read by the non-professional but historically interested person; they are bought by libraries for the use of scholars. Would it not be possible to achieve the same purpose if microfilms of the collected and edited materials were accessible to libraries, or if, in the case of texts difficult to read, microfilms containing facsimiles, their transcriptions, and notes were made available? The scholarly usefulness of such editorial work, even if it does not result in books but remains on microfilm, would not be diminished; expenses would be lowered and the funds would be available for other research purposes. Such suggestions will not please booklovers, nor will they please those for whom daily work in archives with scholars from other countries working on the same subject constitutes a gratifying experience. But it seems impossible to deny that new techniques require new forms.

Perhaps I should add that my reflections on the changed nature of archival research are not meant to diminish the importance of archives as they exist or of research in them. In order to use sources or to microfilm them one has to find them, and many can be found only by searching in archives. As everyone who has done archival research knows, archives are inexhaustible and concentrating on the few central series with which one's research inevitably begins does not do justice to their richness; innumerable volumes—largely because of the slowness of research in former times—have hardly been looked into and certainly have never been carefully studied or analyzed. Moreover, documents frequently allude to facts or names that a search in the registers of the archives can quickly identify and that, at any other place, might involve lengthy, often futile investigations. Finally, the search in an archive gives to the historian one of his most important experiences: a shock of recognition. I still remember the start I received when at the beginning of my studies in the Florentine Archivio I looked through a volume of documents and found a message signed in big letters: Cesare of France, Duke of Romagna and Valence. I doubt that before I saw this writing I had ever really believed that the man about whom Burckhardt and Nietzsche had written had really existed.

In the first decades of the twentieth century reflections on history and on historical scholarship would have started with Ranke, the guide and master; the attainments of historical scholarship would have been measured in relation to Ranke's work. If in the essays of this volume dedicated to history Ranke's name occurs at all, it is to emphasize that the aims which he set are no longer valid and that the fields on which he focused—political and diplomatic history —have neither the interest nor the significance he ascribed to them.

This almost unanimous rejection of the historian whom fifty years ago everyone acknowledged to be the father of modern historiography cries for a few words in Ranke's defense. Whoever reads his writings—the chapter on Henry IV's budget in his *French History*, the long discussion of the peasant war in the *History of the Reformation*, or his volume on the structure of the *Spanish Monarchy*—is simply unable to accept the view that Ranke was exclusively concerned with political and diplomatic history; he was much more aware of the issues of social and intellectual history than his critics allow. It is frequently stated in the following essays that around the turn of the last century historical scholarship became increasingly compartmentalized and rigidified. It was the rather sterile generation following Ranke which asserted that in focusing exclusively on political and diplomatic history they were doing what Ranke had taught; Ranke's present critics are in revolt against the view of Ranke's principles as spread by his disciples rather than against those derived from a study of Ranke's works. But the frequency with which this misinterpretation occurs is characteristic and significant; it shows that Ranke is a name, a concept rather than a clearly seen personality. The conclusion is unavoidable: he is hardly read any longer.

Historians who entered the profession in the twenties had no difficulty in drawing up a list of those whom they regarded as the great masters of their profession. The list included Ranke, Mommsen and Treitschke, Michelet, Sorel and Taine, Macaulay, Seeley and Maitland; the more sophisticated might have added Tocqueville and Burckhardt. The works of these great historians were read and the issues they had raised—whether it was Macaulay's Whig interpretation of English history or Mommsen's evaluation of Caesar as fulfillment of Roman history—were taken into account and debated.

Different names appear when we prepare a list of the historians whom the authors of the following essays praise as models: Marc Bloch, Namier, Chabod, Hintze. Of the great figures of nineteenth-century historiography, only the outsiders—Tocqueville and Burckhardt—are still mentioned. This changing of the guards is not caused merely by the passing of time. The great historians of the nineteenth century were already removed in time from those who entered upon the study of history after the First World War. One generation at least intervened. But the members of this generation were judged to be inferior to their elders, whose standards and works remained the great models. Meinecke, perhaps the outstanding historian of the intervening generation, frankly confessed that he felt himself to be an epigone. The passing of time therefore is not the reason that the names present-day historians recognize as their masters are different from those mentioned fifty years ago. The change has significance and points to the new trends that have developed in historical scholarship.

This is evident if we look more closely at these two lists of names. Michelet and Ranke were also great literary figures and Mommsen, in fact, received the Nobel Prize. None of those we now consider great historians can be thought of as literary figures and many would find the application of such a criterion inappropriate. The historians of the nineteenth century presented the finds they had made at the archives in multivolume histories, frequently covering long stretches of time. These volumes contained the historians' new contributions to scholarship: their discoveries. But they were addressed to the educated public, and in their form of presentation they were intended to be works of art. In contrast, the writings of the leading historians of the last decades usually dealt with events in a narrow compass. They analyzed the structure of society in a given period; investigated the interaction between economic and political organization; related intellectual attitudes and beliefs to social and political action. They did not provide long narratives; they did not describe great events. They dealt with problems and were analytical. Although some of their new theories might be presented in monographs, most of their discoveries are found in scholarly journal articles. These writings contain tables and statistics; they are heavily documented; they are criticisms of the view of others. The meaning of these products is difficult for the educated layman to understand. Although history might not be a science, historians now are inclined to be scientific. The leading historians of more recent vintage are "historians' historians." It must be mentioned that we are only beginning work in quantitative history and in the use of the computer for historical research. If one asks, therefore, what the future holds the answer I think must be that the present tendencies will continue and perhaps accelerate. The results of research will emerge in the form of an internal dialogue among scholars. The gap between the products of historical scholarship and the educated public will widen. History will undergo a development from which it was believed to be exempt, the same development that has taken place in most other fields of knowledge.

After this has been said a few reservations ought immediately to be made. When in the nineteenth century historians produced their histories, they were usually concerned with developments which were only vaguely known and surrounded by myth. One of the great tasks and achievements of nineteenth-century historical scholarship was to establish the main features of the history of European nations from the ancient world to the eighteenth century and to place the story of their development on a sound and reliable foundation. This basic work has not yet been done for large parts of the non-European or non-Western world. Historians dealing with these areas of history might still produce lengthy narratives with appeal to the general public. It should also be mentioned that the historical presentation of recent events, especially if the scholar's own country is involved, will aim at basic factual clarifications of interest to the wider public. Finally, it seems unlikely that the educated public will lose interest in reading history. General histories will continue to be written and they might even become more important because, at least in the United States, the old style textbook is losing ground as its readership demands a more sophisticated approach. There is no reason why this work should not be undertaken by experts, by historical scholars. Although such works might present a topic of history in the light of recent scholarship, they will not be the place, however, where historical discoveries are first presented to the public, or where historical theses are advanced and defended.

One will have to accept that understanding of the scholarly discussion by which historical knowledge is advanced will be limited to "professionals." We do not need to assume that this trend will go as far as it does in some theoretical fields of the natural sciences where experts write only for experts in the same field. History is so closely connected with the work of scholars in other areas of the humanities and the social sciences—economics, political science, languages, linguistics—that the communication of the historian will have to be couched in a form which keeps open the possibility of discussions with scholars in other fields. Still, this will not alter the fact that a fundamental change in the relation between the historian and the educated general public has taken place.

Many might regret such a development and might fear that we accelerate it by stressing it. It seems necessary, however, to bring the issue out into the open, because it concerns the editorial policy of the scholarly periodicals and has bearing on the question how historical work ought to be presented to the outside world. Many pitfalls derive from the fact that an author is urged—by his publisher or by his own notion of history—to provide a sound but limited scholarly investigation with a meretricious "general appeal." But the issue is important too because it establishes criteria for judging historical work, and confusion about such criteria can do and is doing damage.

In 1930—around the time of the above-mentioned visit to the Florentine archives—the annual meeting of the American Historical Association took place in Boston.[2] The program offered two sessions on Latin America, one on the Far East, and one on Europe in Africa. There were no sessions on American foreign relations, on the Near East, on Russia, or on India. European history formed the center of the meeting, but not one of the sessions was concerned with European history after the French Revolution; the Middle Ages and early European history were the focus of attention.

It is illuminating to compare this program with that of another American Historical Association convention in Boston held forty years later, in 1970. Not even half of the sessions treated topics of European history, and of these the sessions concerned with events since the French Revolution were twice as numerous as those that discussed developments of ancient, medieval, or early modern European history. On the other hand, the number of sessions devoted to the history of areas outside Europe and the United States was as great as the number of sessions in modern European history. This is a rough estimate[3] which gives some indication of the rapidity with which new fields and new interests have developed in recent years. The turning away from European history to the history of other areas of the world is probably more pronounced in the United States than in Europe, but there too this trend can be noticed. Moreover, today's European historical scholarship concentrates on recent history, which is particularly significant because in the past the study of medieval history, of the Renaissance and the Reformation, was a prominent feature of European historiography.

The general trend is clear. Scholars show increasing interest in the historical developments of those areas that do not belong to the Western world (to use a popular expression); within European history they tend to emphasize the nineteenth and the twentieth centuries.

Reasons for these changes in emphasis are not difficult to find. Politics, economics, and modern means of communication have brought the various parts of the world closer together and whatever happens in one region has repercussions in others. These developments have drawn attention to the non-Western nations, to variations in the levels of their economic development, and to ethnic differences. Awareness of distinctions among different ethnic groups has increased all over the world. The history of many of these nations—previously barely known in the West—has become important to investigations of ethnic differences as revealed in traditions and behavior in basic social relations. The chief stimulus for the rapid expansion of Western historical interest over wider areas came from contemporary politics; explanation of the present has remained an aim of these investigations. These are mainly recent studies and are therefore conducted with the instruments of modern technology which, as Jan Vansina's essay shows, are particularly appropriate for investigations in these areas. Statistical materials and data which permit a quantitative analysis are—perhaps not exclusively but certainly more readily—available for the history of the last two or three hundred years.

Nevertheless, the emphasis on the history of recent times and of non-Western nations could not have occurred if a profound change in historical outlook had not taken place. The historical process is no longer seen as a continuum. The notion of the continuity of the historical process was Europe-centered; it was the story of a development that began in the ancient world and the

Mediterranean area, spread over the whole of Europe creating various nations with a common legacy, and issued in the domination of the world by the European nations. Because of the coherence which this Europe-centered notion of history seemed to possess there could be no doubt about the relevance of the past for the present. The decline of European power and the rise of the importance of the non-European peoples has shaken this belief. These doubts have been strengthened by the experiences of our own times. The scientific discoveries made in the twentieth century and the resulting changes in the external circumstances of life have been so far-reaching and so fundamental that we seem separated from the past rather than linked to it.

When the past is no longer relevant to the present, occupation with the past becomes antiquarianism, a threat that always hangs over the historian's head, especially today. With the emphasis on recent history, ancient and medieval history have been neglected; their separation from the main body of historical work is reinforced by the difficulty in using the methods of modern technology in these areas. As always happens in such situations, isolation becomes a conscious withdrawal and breeds rigid traditionalism. But antiquarianism can also permeate work in modern history. The emergence of specialists for every new area on the globe and the concern of social historians with endless details fills the observer with some foreboding; enthusiasm for a new approach is no guarantee against antiquarianism. Moreover, even these areas have remained somewhat separated from what was and is, in sophisticated intensity, still the main body of historical work. Language barriers are beginning to restrict the appreciation and evaluation of work done in other fields of history; as long as the historian was exclusively concerned with European and American history he was expected to—and could—read all the most important languages. With the expansion of the scope of history over the entire globe this is no longer the case, and historical work becomes compartmentalized according to regions.

The reader of the following essays will be aware that the danger of antiquarianism, although it exists, is not great. In almost all fields there is a concern for comparative history, for the study of relationships, for the analysis of structure. There is an agreement about the questions that need to be asked and this serves to tie historical work together and to maintain the unity of history.

But agreement on the questions the historian ought to ask disappears if it is not invested with a theoretical foundation. Theorists of history have not tackled these questions. Forty years ago young historians had a lively interest in theoretical and philosophical questions, and although the discussions on relativism and historicism now seem obsolete, they opened doors to an understanding of a wider world—to that non-Western world which has now become a center of interest. But the next stage for historical theorists was philosophy rather than history—that is, analysis of the logic of historical narrative and causation—a consideration remote from the work historians are doing today. It is still more astounding that some of the handbooks summarizing the principles of historical method are the same as they were forty years ago.

All this has increased misunderstandings about the work of the historical scholar and has given rise to the strange situation to which allusion is made in the Preface: that a major turning away from historical study seems to occur just at a time when professional historians believe that historical investigation is flourishing. To remove misconceptions—to fill the gap which exists between what people believe the historian is doing and what he is really doing—is a task which not only concerns the historical profession but is important for an understanding of the role of scholarship in the modern world. This task is a purpose of this volume.

Felix Gilbert

REFERENCES

1. See Vincent Ilardi, "Fifteenth-Century Diplomatic Documents in Western European Archives (1450-1494)," *Studies in the Renaissance,* 9 (1962), 64-112.

2. See the report about "The Boston Meeting of the American Historical Association," *American Historical Review,* 36 (1930-1931), 495-509.

3. It is difficult to be precise because some sessions deal with issues on a comparative basis, others discuss the status of the historical profession; but the general trend described above is incontestable.

4. *L'Histoire et Ses Méthodes,* a volume in the Encyclopédie de la Pléiade, published in 1961, is excellent as a well-informed survey of relevant facts but does not enter upon a discussion of the influence of new developments in method on historical research and writing. The problems which have arisen in recent times because of the incompatability of traditional approaches with new demands are interestingly discussed in P. J. Lee, "History at the Universities: The Consumer's View," *History,* 55 (1970), 327-336.

Historical Studies Today

E. J. HOBSBAWM

From Social History to the History of Society

THIS ESSAY is an attempt to observe and analyze, not to state a personal credo or to express (except where this is clearly stated) the author's preferences and value judgments. I say this at the outset in order to distinguish this essay from others which are defenses of or pleas for the kind of history practiced by their authors—as it happens social history does not need either at the moment—but also to avoid two misunderstandings especially common in discussions heavily charged with ideology. All discussions about social history are.

The first is the tendency for readers to identify authors with the views they write about, unless they disclaim this identification in the clearest terms and sometimes even when they do so. The second is the tendency to confuse the ideological or political motivations of research, or its utilization, with its scientific value. Where ideological intention or bias produces triviality or error, as is often the case in the human sciences, we may happily condemn motivation, method, and result. However, life would be a great deal simpler if our understanding of history were advanced exclusively by those with whom we are in agreement or in sympathy on all public and even private matters. Social history is at present in fashion. None of those who practice it would care to be seen keeping ideological company with all those who come under the same historical heading. Nevertheless, what is more important than to define one's attitude is to discover where social history stands today after two decades of unsystematic if copious development, and whither it might go.

I

The term social history has always been difficult to define, and until recently there has been no great pressure to define it, for it has lacked the institutional and professional vested interests which

1

normally insist on precise demarcations. Broadly speaking, until
the present vogue of the subject—or at least of the name—it was in
the past used in three sometimes overlapping senses. First, it
referred to the history of the poor or lower classes, and more specifically to the history of the movements of the poor ("social movements"). The term could be even more specialized, referring
essentially to the history of labor and socialist ideas and organizations. For obvious reasons this link between social history and the
history of social protest or socialist movements has remained strong.
A number of social historians have been attracted to the subject
because they were radicals or socialists and as such interested in
subjects of great sentimental relevance to them.[1]

Second, the term was used to refer to works on a variety of
human activities difficult to classify except in such terms as "man-
ners, customs, everyday life." This was, perhaps for linguistic reasons, a largely Anglo-Saxon usage, since the English language lacks
suitable terms for what the Germans who wrote about similar subjects—often also in a rather superficial and journalistic manner—
called *Kultur-* or *Sittengeschichte*. This kind of social history was
not particularly oriented toward the lower classes—indeed rather
the opposite—though the more politically radical practitioners
tended to pay attention to them. It formed the unspoken basis of
what may be called the residual view of social history, which was
put forward by the late G. M. Trevelyan in his *English Social
History* (London, 1944) as "history with the politics left out." It
requires no comment.

The third meaning of the term was certainly the most common
and for our purposes the most relevant: "social" was used in combination with "economic history." Indeed, outside the Anglo-
Saxon world, the title of the typical specialist journal in this field
before the Second World War always (I think) bracketed the two
words, as in the *Vierteljahrschrift fuer Sozial- u. Wirtschaftsge-
schichte*, the *Revue d'Histoire E. & S.*, or the *Annales d'Histoire E.
& S.* It must be admitted that the economic half of this combination
was overwhelmingly preponderant. There were hardly any social
histories of equivalent caliber to set beside the numerous volumes
devoted to the economic history of various countries, periods, and
subjects. There were in fact not very many economic and social
histories. Before 1939 one can think of only a few such works,
admittedly sometimes by impressive authors (Pirenne, Mikhail
Rostovtzeff, J. W. Thompson, perhaps Dopsch), and the mono-

graphic or periodical literature was even sparser. Nevertheless, the habitual bracketing of economic and social, whether in the definitions of the general field of historical specialization or under the more specialized banner of economic history, is significant.

It revealed the desire for an approach to history systematically different from the classical Rankean one. What interested historians of this kind was the evolution of the economy, and this in turn interested them because of the light it threw on the structure and changes in society, and more especially on the relationship between classes and social groups, as George Unwin admitted.[2] This social dimension is evident even in the work of the most narrowly or cautiously economic historians so long as they claimed to be historians. Even J. H. Clapham argued that economic history was of all varieties of history the most fundamental because it was the foundation of society. The predominance of the economic over the social in this combination had, we may suggest, two reasons. It was partly owing to a view of economic theory which refused to isolate the economic from social, institutional, and other elements, as with the Marxists and the German historical school, and partly to the sheer headstart of economics over the other social sciences. If history had to be integrated into the social sciences, economics was the one it had primarily to come to terms with. One might go further and argue (with Marx) that, whatever the essential inseparability of the economic and the social in human society, the analytical base of any historical inquiry into the evolution of human societies must be the process of social production.

None of the three versions of social history produced a specialized academic field of social history until the 1950's, though at one time the famous *Annales* of Lucien Febvre and Marc Bloch dropped the economic half of its subtitle and proclaimed itself purely social. However, this was a temporary diversion of the war years, and the title by which this great journal has now been known for a quarter of a century—*Annales: économies, sociétés, civilisations*—as well as the nature of its contents, reflect the original and essentially global and comprehensive aims of its founders. Neither the subject itself, nor the discussion of its problems, developed seriously before 1950. The journals specializing in it, still few in number, were not founded until the end of the 1950's: we may perhaps regard the *Comparative Studies in Society and History* (1958) as the first. As an academic specialization, social history is therefore quite new.

What explains the rapid development and growing emancipation of social history in the past twenty years? The question could be answered in terms of technical and institutional changes within the academic disciplines of social science: the deliberate specialization of economic history to fit in with the requirements of the rapidly developing economic theory and analysis, of which the "new economic history" is an example; the remarkable and worldwide growth of sociology as an academic subject and fashion, which in turn called for subsidiary historical service-branches analogous to those required by economics departments. We cannot neglect such factors. Many historians (such as the Marxists) who had previously labeled themselves economic because the problems they were interested in were plainly not encouraged or even considered by orthodox general history, found themselves extruded from a rapidly narrowing economic history and accepted or welcomed the title of "social historians," especially if their mathematics were poor. It is improbable whether in the atmosphere of the 1950's and early 1960's someone like R. H. Tawney would have been welcomed among the economic historians had he been a young researcher and not president of the Economic History Society. However, such academic redefinitions and professional shifts hardly explain much, though they cannot be overlooked.

Far more significant was the general historization of the social sciences which took place during this period, and may retrospectively appear to have been the most important development within them at this time. For my present purpose it is not necessary to explain this change, but it is impossible to avoid drawing attention to the immense significance of the revolutions and struggles for political and economic emancipation of colonial and semicolonial countries, which drew the attention of governments, international and research organizations, and consequently also of social scientists, to what are essentially problems of historic transformations. These were subjects which had hitherto been outside, or at best on the margins of, academic orthodoxy in the social sciences, and had increasingly been neglected by historians.

At all events essentially historical questions and concepts (sometimes, as in the case of "modernization" or "economic growth," excessively crude concepts) have captured even the discipline hitherto most immune to history, when not actually, like Radcliffe-Brown's social anthropology, actively hostile to it. This progressive infiltration of history is perhaps most evident in economics, where an initial field of growth economics, whose assumptions, though much more sophisticated, were those of the cookery book ("Take the following quantities of ingredients *a* through *n*, mix and cook, and the result will be the take-off into self-sustained growth"), has been succeeded by the growing realization that factors outside economics also determine economic development. In brief, it is now impossible to pursue many activities of the social scientist in any but a trivial manner without coming to terms with social structure and its transformations: without the history of societies. It is a curious paradox that the economists were beginning to grope for some understanding of social (or at any rate not strictly economic) factors at the very moment when the economic historians, absorbing the economists' models of fifteen years earlier, were trying to make themselves look hard rather than soft by forgetting about everything except equations and statistics.

What can we conclude from this brief glance at the historical development of social history? It can hardly be an adequate guide to the nature and tasks of the subject under consideration, though it can explain why certain more or less heterogeneous subjects of research came to be loosely grouped under this general title, and how developments in other social sciences prepared the ground for the establishment of an academic theory specially demarcated as such. At most it can provide us with some hints, at least one of which is worth mentioning immediately.

A survey of social history in the past seems to show that its best practitioners have always felt uncomfortable with the term itself. They have either, like the great Frenchmen to whom we owe so much, preferred to describe themselves simply as historians and their aim as "total" or "global" history, or as men who sought to integrate the contributions of all relevant social sciences in history, rather than to exemplify any one of them. Marc Bloch, Fernand Braudel, Georges Lefebvre are not names which can be pigeonholed as social historians except insofar as they accepted Fustel de Coulanges' statement that "History is not the accumulation of events of all kinds which occurred in the past. It is the science of human societies."

Social history can never be another specialization like economic or other hyphenated histories because its subject matter cannot be isolated. We can define certain human activities as economic, at least for analytical purposes, and then study them historically. Though this may be (except for certain definable purposes) artificial or unrealistic, it is not impracticable. In much the same way, though at a lower level of theory, the old kind of intellectual history which isolated written ideas from their human context and traced their filiation from one writer to another is possible, if one wants to do that sort of thing. But the social or societal aspects of man's being cannot be separated from the other aspects of his being, except at the cost of tautology or extreme trivialization. They cannot, for more than a moment, be separated from the ways in which men get their living and their material environment. They cannot, even for a moment, be separated from their ideas, since their relations with one another are expressed and formulated in language which implies concepts as soon as they open their mouths. And so on. The intellectual historian may (at his risk) pay no attention to economics, the economic historian to Shakespeare, but the social historian who neglects either will not get far. Conversely, while it is extremely improbable that a monograph on provençal poetry will be economic history or one on inflation in the sixteenth century intellectual history, both could be treated in a way to make them social history.

II

Let us turn from the past to the present and consider the problems of writing the history of society. The first question concerns how much societal historians can get from other social sciences, or indeed how far their subject is or ought to be merely the science of society insofar as it deals with the past. This question is natural, though the experience of the past two decades suggests two different answers to it. It is clear that social history has since 1950 been powerfully shaped and stimulated, not only by the professional structure of other social sciences (for example, their specific course requirements for university students), and by their methods and techniques, but also by their questions. It is hardly too much to say that the recent efflorescence of studies in the British industrial revolution, a subject once grossly neglected by its own experts because they doubted the validity of the concept of industrial revolution, is due primarily to the urge of economists (doubtless in turn echoing that of governments and planners) to discover how industrial revolutions happen, what makes them happen, and what sociopolitical consequences they have. With certain notable exceptions, the flow of stimulation in the past twenty years has been one way. On the other hand, if we look at recent developments in another way, we shall be struck by the obvious convergence of workers from different disciplines toward sociohistorical problems. The study of millennial phenomena is a case in point, since among writers on these subjects we find men coming from anthropology, sociology, political science, history, not to mention students of literature and religions—though not, so far as I am aware, economists. We also note the transfer of men with other professional formations, at least temporarily, to work which historians would consider historical—as with Charles Tilly and Neil Smelser from sociology, Eric Wolf from anthropology, Everett Hagen and Sir John Hicks from economics.

Yet the second tendency is perhaps best regarded not as convergence but as conversion. For it must never be forgotten that if nonhistorical social scientists have begun to ask properly historical questions and to ask historians for answers, it is because they themselves have none. And if they have sometimes turned themselves into historians, it is because the practicing members of our discipline, with the notable exception of the Marxists and others— not necessarily *Marxisants*—who accept a similar problematic, have not provided the answers.[5] Moreover, though there are now a few social scientists from other disciplines who have made themselves sufficiently expert in our field to command respect, there are more who have merely applied a few crude mechanical concepts and models. For every *Vendée* by a Tilly, there are, alas, several dozen equivalents of Rostow's *Stages*. I leave aside the numerous others who have ventured into the difficult territory of historical source material without an adequate knowledge of the hazards they are likely to encounter there, or of the means of avoiding and overcoming them. In brief, the situation at present is one in which historians, with all their willingness to learn from other disciplines, are required to teach rather than to learn. The history of society cannot be written by applying the meager available models from other sciences; it requires the construction of adequate new ones— or, at least (Marxists would argue), the development of existing sketches into models.

This is not, of course, true of techniques and methods, where the historians are already net debtors to a substantial extent, and will, or at least ought, to go even more heavily and systematically into debt. I do not wish to discuss this aspect of the problem of the history of society, but a point or two can be made in passing. Given the nature of our sources, we can hardly advance much beyond a combination of the suggestive hypothesis and the apt anecdotal illustration without the techniques for the discovery, the statistical grouping, and handling of large quantities of data, where necessary with the aid of division of research labor and technological devices, which other social sciences have long developed. At the opposite extreme, we stand in equal need of the techniques for the observation and analysis in depth of specific individuals, small groups, and situations, which have also been pioneered outside history, and which may be adaptable to our purposes—for example, the participant observation of the social anthropologists, the interview-in-depth, perhaps even psychoanalytical methods. At the very least these various techniques can stimulate the search for adaptations and equivalents in our field, which may help to answer otherwise impenetrable questions.[6]

I am much more doubtful about the prospect of turning social history into a backward projection of sociology, as of turning economic history into retrospective economic theory, because these disciplines do not at present provide us with useful models or analytical frameworks for the study of long-run *historical* socio-economic transformations. Indeed the bulk of their thinking has not been concerned with, or even interested in, such changes, if we except such trends as Marxism. Moreover, it may be argued that in important respects their analytical models have been developed systematically, and most profitably, by abstracting from historical change. This is notably true, I would suggest, of sociology and social anthropology.

The founding fathers of sociology have indeed been more historically minded than the main school of neoclassic economics (though not necessarily than the original school of classical political economists), but theirs is an altogether less developed science. Stanley Hoffmann has rightly pointed to the difference between the "models" of the economists and the "checklists" of the sociologists and anthropologists.[7] Perhaps they are more than mere checklists. These sciences have also provided us with certain visions, patterns of possible structures composed of elements which can be permuted and combined in various ways, vague analogues to Kekulé's ring glimpsed at the top of the bus, but with the drawback of unverifiability. At their best such structural-functional patterns may be both elegant and heuristically useful, at least for some. At a more modest level, they may provide us with useful metaphors, concepts, or terms (such as "role"), or convenient aids in ordering our material.

Moreover, quite apart from their deficiency as models, it may be argued that the theoretical constructions of sociology (or social anthropology) have been most successful by excluding history, that is, directional or oriented change.[8] Broadly speaking, the structural-functional patterns illuminate what societies have in common in spite of their differences, whereas our problem is with what they have not. It is not what light Lévi-Strauss's Amazonian tribes can throw on modern (indeed on any) society, but on how humanity got from the cavemen to modern industrialism or postindustrialism, and what changes in society were associated with this progress, or necessary for it to take place, or consequential upon it. Or, to use another illustration, it is not to observe the permanent necessity of all human societies to supply themselves with food by growing or otherwise acquiring it, but what happens when this function, having been overwhelmingly fulfilled (since the neolithic revolution) by classes of peasants forming the majority of their societies, comes to be fulfilled by small groups of other kinds of agricultural producers and may come to be fulfilled in nonagricultural ways. How does this happen and why? I do not believe that sociology and social anthropology, however helpful they are incidentally, at present provide us with much guidance.

On the other hand, while I remain skeptical of most current economic theory as a framework of the historical analysis of societies (and therefore of the claims of the new economic history), I am inclined to think that the possible value of economics for the historian of society is great. It cannot but deal with what is an essentially dynamic element in history, namely the process—and, speaking globally and on a long time-scale, progress—of social production. Insofar as it does this it has, as Marx saw, historical development built into it. To take a simple illustration: the concept of the "economic surplus," which the late Paul Baran revived and utilized to such good effect,[9] is patently fundamental to any historian of the development of societies, and strikes me as not only more objective and quantifiable, but also more primary, speaking in terms of analysis, than, say, the dichotomy *Gemeinschaft-Gesellschaft*. Of course Marx knew that economic models, if they are to be valuable for historical analysis, cannot be divorced from social and institutional realities, which include certain basic types of human communal or kinship organization, not to mention the structures and assumptions specific to particular socioeconomic formations or cultures. And yet, though Marx is not for nothing regarded as one of the major founding fathers of modern sociological thought (directly and through his followers and critics), the fact remains that his major intellectual project *Das Kapital* took the form of a work of economic analysis. We are required neither to agree with his conclusions nor his methodology. But we would be unwise to neglect the practice of the thinker who, more than any other, has defined or suggested the set of historical questions to which social scientists find themselves drawn today.

III

How are we to write the history of society? It is not possible for me to produce a definition or model of what we mean by society here, or even a checklist of what we want to know about its history. Even if I could, I do not know how profitable this would be. However, it may be useful to put up a small and miscellaneous assortment of signposts to direct or warn off future traffic.

(1) The history of society is *history;* that is to say it has real chronological time as one of its dimensions. We are concerned not only with structures and their mechanisms of persistence and change, and with the general possibilities and patterns of their transformations, but also with what actually happened. If we are not, then (as Fernand Braudel has reminded us in his article on "Histoire et Longue Durée"[10]) we are not historians. *Conjectural* history has a place in our discipline, even though its chief value is to help us assess the possibilities of present and future, rather than past, where its place is taken by *comparative* history; but actual history is what we must explain. The possible development or nondevelopment of capitalism in imperial China is relevant to us only insofar as it helps to explain the actual fact that this type of economy developed fully, at least to begin with, in one and only one region of the world. This in turn may be usefully contrasted (again in the light of general models) with the tendency for other systems of social relations—for example, the broadly feudal—to develop much more frequently and in a greater number of areas. The history of society is thus a collaboration between general models of social structure and change and the specific set of phenomena which actually occurred. This is true whatever the geographical or chronological scale of our inquiries.

(2) The history of society is, among other things, that of specific units of people living together and definable in sociological terms. It is the history of societies as well as of human society (as distinct from, say, that of apes and ants), or of certain types of society and their possible relationships (as in such terms as "bourgeois" or "pastoral" society), or of the general development of humanity considered as a whole. The definition of a society in this sense raises difficult questions, even if we assume that we are defining an objective reality, as seems likely, unless we reject as illegitimate such statements as "Japanese society in 1930 differed from English society." For even if we eliminate the confusions between different uses of the word "society," we face problems (a) because the size, complexity, and scope of these units varies, for example, at different historical periods or stages of development; and (b) because what we call society is merely one set of human interrelations among several of varying scale and comprehensiveness into which people are classifiable or classify themselves, often simultaneously and with overlaps. In extreme cases such as New Guinea or Amazon tribes, these various sets may define the same group of people, though this is in fact rather improbable. But normally this group is congruent neither with such relevant sociological units as the community, nor with certain wider systems of relationship of which the society forms a part, and which may be functionally essential to it (like the set of economic relations) or nonessential (like those of culture).

Christendom or Islam exist and are recognized as self-classifications, but though they may define a *class* of societies sharing certain common characteristics, they are not societies in the sense in which we use the word when talking about the Greeks or modern Sweden. On the other hand, while in many ways Detroit and Cuzco are today part of a single system of functional interrelationships (for example, part of one economic system), few would regard them as part of the same society, sociologically speaking. Neither would we regard as one the societies of the Romans or the Han and those of the barbarians who formed, quite evidently, part of a wider system of interrelationships with them. How do we define these units? It is far from easy to say, though most of us solve—or evade— the problem by choosing some outside criterion: territorial, ethnic, political, or the like. But this is not always satisfactory. The problem is more than methodological. One of the major themes of the history of modern societies is the increase in their scale, internal homogeneity, or at least in the centralization and directness of social relationships, the change from an essentially pluralist to an essentially unitary structure. In tracing this, problems of definition become very troublesome, as every student of the development of national societies or at least of nationalisms knows.

(3) The history of societies requires us to apply, if not a formalized and elaborate model of such structures, then at least an approximate order of research priorities and a working assumption about what constitutes the central nexus or complex of connections of our subject, though of course these things imply a model. Every social historian does in fact make such assumptions and hold such priorities. Thus I doubt whether any historian of eighteenth-century Brazil would give the Catholicism of that society analytical priority over its slavery, or any historian of nineteenth-century Britain would regard kinship as central a social nexus as he would in Anglo-Saxon England.

A tacit consensus among historians seems to have established a fairly common working model of this kind, with variants. One starts with the material and historical environment, goes on to the forces and techniques of production (demography coming somewhere in between), the structure of the consequent economy— divisions of labor, exchange, accumulation, distribution of the surplus, and so forth—and the social relations arising from these. These might be followed by the institutions and the image of society and its functioning which underlie them. The shape of the social structure is thus established, the specific characteristics and details of which, insofar as they derive from other sources, can then be determined, most likely by comparative study. The practice is thus to work outwards and upwards from the process of social production in its specific setting. Historians will be tempted—in my view rightly—to pick on one particular relation or relational complex as central and specific to the society (or type of society) in question, and to group the rest of the treatment around it—for example, Bloch's "relations of interdependence" in his *Feudal Society,* or those arising out of industrial production, possibly in industrial society, certainly in its capitalist form. Once the structure has been established, it must be seen in its historical movement. In the French phrase "structure" must be seen in "conjuncture," though this term must not be taken to exclude other, and possibly more relevant, forms and patterns of historical change. Once again the tendency is to treat economic movements (in the broadest sense) as the backbone of such an analysis. The tensions to which the society is exposed in the process of historic change and transformation then allow the historian to expose (1) the general mechanism by which the structures of society simultaneously tend to lose and reestablish their equilibria, and (2) the phenomena which are traditionally the subject of interest to the social historians, for example, collective consciousness, social movements, the social dimension of intellectual and cultural changes, and so on.

My object in summarizing what I believe—perhaps wrongly— to be a widely accepted working plan of social historians is not to recommend it, even though I am personally in its favor. It is rather the opposite: to suggest that we try and make the implicit assumptions on which we work explicit and to ask ourselves whether this plan is in fact the best for the formulation of the nature and structure of societies and the mechanisms of their historic transformations (or stabilizations), whether other plans of work based on other questions can be made compatible with it, or are to be preferred to it, or can simply be superimposed to produce the historical equivalent of those Picasso portraits which are simultaneously displayed full-face and in profile.

In brief, if as historians of society we are to help in producing— for the benefit of all the social sciences—valid models of sociohistoric dynamics, we shall have to establish a greater unity of our practice and our theory, which at the present stage of the game probably means in the first instance to watch what we are doing, to generalize it, and to correct it in the light of the problems arising out of further practice.

IV

Consequently, I should like to conclude by surveying the actual practice of social history in the past decade or two, in order to see what future approaches and problems it suggests. This procedure has the advantage that it fits in both with the professional inclinations of a historian and with what little we know about the actual progress of sciences. What topics and problems have attracted most attention in recent years? What are the growing-points? What are the interesting people doing? The answers to such questions do not exhaust analysis, but without them we cannot get very far. The consensus of workers may be mistaken, or distorted by fashion or— as is obviously the case in such a field as the study of public disorder

—by the impact of politics and administrative requirements, but we neglect it at our peril. The progress of science has derived less from the attempt to define perspectives and programs a priori—if it did we should now be curing cancer—than from an obscure and often simultaneous convergence upon the questions worth asking and, above all, those ripe for an answer. Let us see what has been happening, at least insofar as it is reflected in the impressionistic view of one observer.

Let me suggest that the bulk of interesting work in social history in the past ten or fifteen years has clustered around the following topics or complexes of questions:

(1) Demography and kinship
(2) Urban studies insofar as these fall within our field
(3) Classes and social groups
(4) The history of "mentalities" or collective consciousness or of "culture" in the anthropologists' sense
(5) The transformation of societies (for example, modernization or industrialization)
(6) Social movements and phenomena of social protest.

The first two groups can be singled out because they have already institutionalized themselves as fields, regardless of the importance of their subject matter, and now possess their own organization, methodology, and system of publications. Historical demography is a rapidly growing and fruitful field, which rests not so much on a set of problems as on a technical innovation in research (family reconstitution) that makes it possible to derive interesting results from material hitherto regarded as recalcitrant or exhausted (parish registers). It has thus opened a new range of sources, whose characteristics in turn have led to the formulation of questions. The major interest for social historians of historical demography lies in the light it sheds on certain aspects of family structure and behavior, on the life-curves of people at different periods, and on intergenerational changes. These are important though limited by the nature of the sources—more limited than the most enthusiastic champions of the subject allow, and certainly by themselves insufficient to provide the framework of analysis of "The World We Have Lost." Nevertheless, the fundamental importance of this field is not in question, and it has served to encourage the use of strict quantitative techniques. One welcome effect—or side effect— has been to arouse a greater interest in historical problems of kinship structure than social historians might have shown without this stimulus, though a modest demonstration effect from social anthropology ought not to be neglected. The nature and prospects of this field have been sufficiently debated to make further discussion unnecessary here.

Urban history also possesses a certain technologically determined unity. The individual city is normally a geographically limited and coherent unit, often with its specific documentation and even more often of a size which lends itself to research on the Ph.D. scale. It also reflects the urgency of urban problems which have increasingly become the major, or at least the most dramatic, problems of social planning and management in modern industrial societies. Both these influences tend to make urban history a large container with ill-defined, heterogeneous, and sometimes indiscriminate contents. It includes anything about cities. But it is clear that it raises problems peculiarly germane to social history, at least in the sense that the city can never be an analytical framework for economic macrohistory (because economically it must be part of a larger system), and politically it is only rarely found as a self-contained city state. It is essentially a body of human beings living together in a particular way, and the characteristic process of urbanization in modern societies makes it, at least up to the present, the form in which most of them live together. The technical, social, and political problems of the city arise essentially out of the interactions of masses of human beings living in close proximity to one another; and even the ideas about the city (insofar as it is not a mere stage-set for the display of some ruler's power and glory) are those in which men—from the Book of Revelation on—have tried to express their aspirations about human communities. Moreover, in recent centuries it has raised and dramatized the problems of rapid social change more than any other institution. That the social historians who have flocked into urban studies are aware of this need hardly be said.[11] One may say that they have been groping toward a view of urban history as a paradigm of social change. I doubt whether it can be this, at least for the period up to the present. I also doubt whether many really impressive global studies of the larger cities of the industrial era have so far been produced, considering the vast quantity of work in this field. However, urban history must remain a central concern of historians of society, if only because it brings out—or can bring out—those specific aspects of societal change and structure with which sociologists and social psychologists are peculiarly concerned.

The other clusters of concentration have not so far been institutionalized, though one or two may be approaching this stage of development. The history of classes and social groups has plainly developed out of the common assumption that no understanding of society is possible without an understanding of the major components of all societies no longer based primarily on kinship. In no field has the advance been more dramatic and—given the neglect of historians in the past—more necessary. The briefest list of the most significant works in social history must include Lawrence Stone on the Elizabethan aristocracy, E. Le Roy Ladurie on the Languedoc peasants, Edward Thompson on the making of the English working class, Adeline Daumard on the Parisian bourgeoisie; but these are merely peaks in what is already a sizeable mountain range. Compared to these the study of more restricted social groups—professions, for instance—has been less significant.

The novelty of the enterprise has been its ambition. Classes, or specific relations of production such as slavery, are today being systematically considered on the scale of a society, or in intersocietal comparison, or as general types of social relationship. They are also now considered in depth, that is, in all aspects of their social existence, relations, and behavior. This is new, and the achievements are already striking, though the work has barely begun—if we except fields of specially intense activity, such as the comparative study of slavery. Nevertheless, a number of difficulties can be discerned, and a few words about them may not be out of place.

(1) The mass and variety of material for these studies is such that the preindustrial artisan technique of older historians is plainly inadequate. They require cooperative teamwork and the utilization of modern technical equipment. I would guess that the massive works of individual scholarship will mark the early phases of this kind of research, but will give way on the one hand to systematic cooperative projects (such as the projected study of the Stockholm working class in the nineteenth century)[12] and on the other hand to periodic (and probably still single-handed) attempts at synthesis. This is evident in the field of work with which I am most familiar, the history of the working class. Even the most ambitious single work—E. P. Thompson's—is no more than a great torso, though it deals with a rather short period. (Jürgen Kuczynski's

titanic *Geschichte der Lage der Arbeiter unter dem Kapitalismus,* as its title implies, concentrates only on certain aspects of the working class.)

(2) The field raises daunting technical difficulties, even where conceptual clarity exists, especially as regards the measurement of change over time—for example, the flow into and out of any specified social group, or the changes in peasant landholdings. We may be lucky enough to have sources from which such changes can be derived (for example, the recorded genealogies of the aristocracy and gentry as a group) or from which the material for our analysis may be constructed (for example, by the methods of historical demography, or the data on which the valuable studies of the Chinese bureaucracy have been based). But what are we to do, say, about Indian castes, which we also know to have contained such movements, presumably intergenerational, but about which it is so far impossible to make even rough quantitative statements?

(3) More serious are the conceptual problems, which have not always been clearly confronted by historians—a fact which does not preclude good work (horses can be recognized and ridden by those who can't define them), but which suggests that we have been slow to face the more general problems of social structure and relations and their transformations. These in turn raise technical problems, such as those of the possibly changing specification of the membership of a class over time, which complicates quantitative study. It also raises the more general problem of the multidimensionality of social groups. To take a few examples, there is the well-known Marxian duality of the term "class." In one sense it is a general phenomenon of all post-tribal history, in another a product of modern bourgeois society; in one sense almost an analytical construct to make sense of otherwise inexplicable phenomena, in another a group of people actually seen as belonging together in their own or some other group's consciousness, or both. These problems of consciousness in turn raise the question of the language of class— the changing, often overlapping, and sometimes unrealistic terminologies of such contemporary classification[13] about which we know as yet very little in quantitative terms. (Here historians might look carefully at the methods and preoccupations of social anthropologists, while pursuing—as L. Girard and a Sorbonne team are doing—the systematic quantitative study of sociopolitical vocabulary.[14])

Again, there are degrees of class. To use Theodore Shanin's

phrase,[15] the peasantry of Marx's 18th Brumaire is a "class of low classness," whereas Marx's proletariat is a class of very high, perhaps of maximal "classness." There are the problems of the homogeneity or heterogeneity of classes; or what may be much the same, of their definition in relation to other groups and their internal divisions and stratifications. In the most general sense, there is the problem of the relation between classifications, necessarily static at any given time, and the multiple and changing reality behind them.

(4) The most serious difficulty may well be the one which leads us directly toward the history of society as a whole. It arises from the fact that class defines not a group of people in isolation, but a system of relationships, both vertical and horizontal. Thus it is a relationship of difference (or similarity) and of distance, but also a qualitatively different relationship of social function, of exploitation, of dominance/subjection. Research on class must therefore involve the rest of society of which it is a part. Slaveowners cannot be understood without slaves, and without the nonslave sectors of society. It might be argued that for the self-definition of the nineteenth-century European middle classes the capacity to exercise power over people (whether through property, keeping servants, or even—via the patriarchal family structure—wives and children), and of not having direct power exercised over themselves, was essential. Class studies are therefore, unless confined to a deliberately restricted and partial aspect, analyses of society. The most impressive—like Le Roy Ladurie's—therefore go far beyond the limits of their title.

It may thus be suggested that in recent years the most direct approach to the history of society has come through the study of class in this wider sense.[16] Whether we believe that this reflects a correct perception of the nature of post-tribal societies, or whether we merely put it down to the current influence of *Marxisant* history, the future prospects of this type of research appear bright.

In many ways the recent interest in the history of "mentalities" marks an even more direct approach to central methodological problems of social history. It has been largely stimulated by the traditional interest in "the common people" of many who are drawn to social history. It has dealt largely with the individually inarticulate, undocumented, and obscure, and is often indistinct from an interest in their social movements or in more general phenomena of social behavior, which today, fortunately, also includes an interest in those who fail to take part in such movements—for example, in the conservative as well as in the militant or passively socialist worker.

This very fact has encouraged a specifically dynamic treatment of culture by historians, superior to such studies as those of the "culture of poverty" by anthropologists, though not uninfluenced by their methods and pioneering experience. They have been not so much studies of an aggregate of beliefs and ideas, persistent or not —though there has been much valuable thought about these matters, for example, by Alphonse Dupront[17]—as of ideas in action and, more specifically, in situations of social tensions and crisis, as in Georges Lefebvre's *Grande Peur,* which has inspired so much subsequent work. The nature of sources for such study has rarely allowed the historian to confine himself to simple factual study and exposition. He has been obliged from the outset to construct models, that is, to fit his partial and scattered data into coherent systems, without which they would be little more than anecdotal. The criterion of such models is or ought to be that its components should fit together and provide a guide to both the nature of collective action in specifiable social situations and to its limits.[18] Edward Thompson's concept of the "moral economy" of preindustrial England may be one such; my own analysis of social banditry has tried to base itself on another.

Insofar as these systems of belief and action are, or imply, images of society as a whole (which may be, as occasion arises, images either seeking its permanence or its transformation), and insofar as these correspond to certain aspects of its actual reality, they bring us closer to the core of our task. Insofar as the most successful such analyses have dealt with traditional or customary societies, even though sometimes with such societies under the impact of social transformation, their scope has been more limited. For a period characterized by constant, rapid, and fundamental change, and by a complexity which puts society far beyond the individual's experience or even conceptual grasp, the models derivable from the history of culture have probably a diminishing contact with the social realities. They may not even any longer be very useful in constructing the pattern of aspiration of modern society ("what society ought to be like"). For the basic change brought about by the Industrial Revolution in the field of social thought has been to substitute a system of beliefs resting on unceasing *progress* toward aims which can be specified only as a *process,* for one resting on the assumption of permanent order, which can be described or illustrated in terms of some concrete social model, normally drawn from the past, real or imaginary. The cultures of the past measured their own society against such specific models; the cultures of the present can measure them only against possibilities. Still, the history of "mentalities" has been useful in introducing something analogous to the discipline of the social anthropologists into history, and its usefulness is very far from exhausted.

I think the profitability of the numerous studies of social conflict, ranging from riots to revolutions, requires more careful assessment. Why they should attract research today is obvious. That they always dramatize crucial aspects of social structure because they are here strained to the breaking point is not in doubt. Moreover, certain important problems cannot be studied at all except in and through such moments of eruption, which do not merely bring into the open so much that is normally latent, but also concentrate and magnify phenomena for the benefit of the student, while—not the least of their advantages—normally multiplying our documentation about them. To take a simple example: How much less would we know about the ideas of those who normally do not express themselves commonly or at all in writing but for the extraordinary explosion of articulateness which is so characteristic of revolutionary periods, and to which the mountains of pamphlets, letters, articles, and speeches, not to mention the mass of police reports, court depositions, and general inquiries bear witness? How fruitful the study of the great, and above all the well-documented, revolutions can be is shown by the historiography of the French Revolution, which has been studied longer and more intensively perhaps than any period of equal brevity, without visibly diminishing returns. It has been, and still remains, an almost perfect laboratory for the historian.[19]

The danger of this type of study lies in the temptation to isolate the phenomenon of overt crisis from the wider context of a society undergoing transformation. This danger may be particularly great when we launch into comparative studies, especially when moved by the desire to solve problems (such as how to make or stop revolutions), which is not a very fruitful approach in sociology or social history. What, say, riots have in common with one another (for example, "violence") may be trivial. It may even be illusory, insofar as we may be imposing an anachronistic criterion, legal, political, or otherwise, on the phenomena—something which historical students of criminality are learning to avoid. The same may or may not be true of revolutions. I am the last person to wish to discourage an interest in such matters, since I have spent a good deal of professional time on them. However, in studying them we ought to define the precise purpose of our interest clearly. If it lies in the major transformations of society, we may find, paradoxically, that the value of our study of the revolution itself is in inverse proportion to our concentration on the brief moment of conflict. There are things about the Russian Revolution, or about human history, which can only be discovered by concentrating on the period from March to November 1917 or the subsequent Civil War; but there are other matters which cannot emerge from such a concentrated study of brief periods of crisis, however dramatic and significant.

On the other hand, revolutions and similar subjects of study (including social movements) can normally be integrated into a wider field which does not merely lend itself to, but requires, a comprehensive grasp of social structure and dynamics: the short-term social transformations experienced and labeled as such, which stretch over a period of a few decades or generations. We are dealing not simply with chronological chunks carved out of a continuum of growth or development, but with relatively brief historic periods during which society is reoriented and transformed, as the very phrase "industrial revolution" implies. (Such periods may of course include great political revolutions, but cannot be chronologically delimited by them.) The popularity of such historically crude terms as "modernization" or "industrialization" indicates a certain apprehension of such phenomena.

The difficulties of such an enterprise are enormous, which is perhaps why there are as yet no adequate studies of the eighteenth-nineteenth century industrial revolutions as social processes for any country, though one or two excellent regional and local works are now available, such as Rudolf Braun on the Zurich countryside and John Foster on early nineteenth-century Oldham.[20] It may be that a practicable approach to such phenomena can be at present derived not only from economic history (which has inspired studies of industrial revolution), but from political science. Workers in the field of the prehistory and history of colonial liberation have naturally been forced to confront such problems, though perhaps in an excessively political perspective, and African studies have proved particularly fruitful, though recent attempts to extend this approach to India may be noted.[21] In consequence the political science and political sociology dealing with the modernization of colonial societies can furnish us with some useful help.

The analytical advantage of the colonial situation (by which I mean that of *formal* colonies acquired by conquest and directly administered) is that here an entire society or group of societies is sharply defined by contrast with an outside force, and its various internal shifts and changes, as well as its reactions to the uncontrollable and rapid impact of this force, can be observed and analyzed as a whole. Certain forces which in other societies are internal, or operate in a gradual and complex interaction with internal elements of that society, can here be considered for practical purposes and in the short run as entirely external, which is analytically very helpful. (We shall not of course overlook the distortions of the colonial societies—for example, by the truncation of their economy and social hierarchy—which also result from colonization, but the interest of the colonial situation does not depend on the assumption that colonial society is a replica of noncolonial.)

There is perhaps a more specific advantage. A central preoccupation of workers in this field has been nationalism and nation-building, and here the colonial situation can provide a much closer approximation to the general model. Though historians have hardly yet come to grips with it, the complex of phenomena which can be called national(ist) is clearly crucial to the understanding of social structure and dynamics in the industrial era, and some of the more interesting work in political sociology has come to recognize it. The project conducted by Stein Rokkan, Eric Allardt, and others on "Centre Formation, Nation-Building and Cultural Diversity" provides some very interesting approaches.[22]

The "nation," a historical invention of the past two hundred years, whose immense practical significance today hardly needs discussion, raises several crucial questions of the history of society, for example, the change in the scale of societies, the transformation of pluralist, indirectly linked social systems into unitary ones with direct linkages (or the fusion of several preexisting smaller societies into a larger social system), the factors determining the boundaries of a social system (such as territorial-political), and others of equal significance. To what extent are these boundaries objectively imposed by the requirements of economic development, which necessitate as the locus of, for example, the nineteenth-century type industrial economy a territorial state of minimum or maximum size in given circumstances?[23] To what extent do these requirements automatically imply not only the weakening and destruction of earlier social structures, but also particular degrees of simplification, standardization, and centralization—that is, direct and increasingly exclusive links between "center" and "periphery" (or rather "top" and "bottom")? To what extent is the "nation" an attempt to fill the void left by the dismantling of earlier community and social structures by inventing something which could function as, or produce symbolic substitutes for, the functioning of a consciously apprehended community or society? (The concept of the "nation-state" might then combine these objective and subjective developments.)

The colonial and ex-colonial situations are not necessarily more suitable bases for investigating this complex of questions than is European history, but in the absence of serious work about it by the historians of nineteenth- and twentieth-century Europe, who have been hitherto—including the Marxists—rather baffled by it, it seems likely that recent Afro-Asian history may form the most convenient starting-point.

V

How far has the research of recent years advanced us toward a history of society? Let me put my cards on the table. I cannot point to any single work which exemplifies the history of society to which we ought, I believe, to aspire. Marc Bloch has given us in *La société féodale*, a masterly, indeed an exemplary, work on the nature of social structure, including both the consideration of a certain type of society and of its actual and possible variants, illuminated by the comparative method, into the dangers and the much greater rewards of which I do not propose to enter here. Marx has sketched out for us, or allows us to sketch for ourselves, a model of the typology and the long-term historical transformation and evolution of societies which remains immensely powerful and almost as far ahead of its time as were the Prolegomena of Ibn Khaldun, whose own model, based on the interaction of different types of societies, has of course also been fruitful, especially in pre-history, ancient, and oriental history. (I am thinking of the late Gordon Childe and Owen Lattimore.) Recently there have been important advances toward the study of certain types of society—notably those based on slavery in the Americas (the slave-societies of antiquity appear to be in recession) and those based on a large body of peasant cultivators. On the other hand the attempts to translate a comprehensive social history into popular synthesis strike me so far as either relatively unsuccessful or, with all their great merits, not the least of which is stimulation, as schematic and tentative. The history of society is still being constructed. I have in this essay tried to suggest some of its problems, to assess some of its practice, and incidentally to hint at certain problems which might benefit from more concentrated exploration. But it would be wrong to conclude without noting, and welcoming, the remarkably flourishing state of the field. It is a good moment to be a social historian. Even those of us who never set out to call ourselves by this name will not want to disclaim it today.

REFERENCES

1. See the remarks of A. J. C. Rueter in *IX congrès international des sciences historiques* (Paris, 1950), I, 298.

2. R. H. Tawney, *Studies in Economic History* (London, 1927), pp. xxiii, 33-34, 39.

3. J. H. Clapham, *A Concise Economic History of Britain* (Cambridge, Eng.: University Press, 1949), introduction.

4. Two quotations from the same document (Economic and Social Studies Conference Board, *Social Aspects of Economic Development,* Istanbul, 1964) may illustrate the divergent motivations behind this new preoccupation. By the Turkish president of the board: "Economic development or growth in the economically retarded areas is one of the most important questions which confronts the world today . . . Poor countries have made of this issue of development a high ideal. Economic development is to them associated with political independence and a sense of sovereignty." By Daniel Lerner: "A decade of global experience with social change and economic development lies behind us. The decade has been fraught with efforts, in every part of the world, to induce economic development without producing cultural chaos, to accelerate economic growth without disrupting societal equilibrium; to promote economic mobility without subverting political stability" (xxiii, 1).

5. Sir John Hicks's complaint is characteristic: "My 'theory of history' . . . will be a good deal nearer to the kind of thing that was attempted by Marx . . . Most of [those who believe ideas can be used by historians to order their material, so that the general course of history can be fitted into place] . . . would use the Marxian categories, or some modified version of them; since there is so little in the way of an alternative version that is available, it is not surprising that they should. It does, nevertheless, remain extraordinary that one hundred years after *Das Kapital,* after a century during which there have been enormous developments in social science, so little else should have emerged." *A Theory of Economic History* (Oxford: Clarendon Press, 1969), pp. 2-3.

6. Thus Marc Ferro's sampling of the telegrams and resolutions sent to Petrograd in the first weeks of the February revolution of 1917 is plainly the equivalent of a retrospective public opinion survey. One may doubt whether it would have been thought of without the earlier development of opinion research for nonhistorical purposes. M. Ferro, *La Révolution de 1917* (Paris: Aubier, 1967).

7. At the conference on New Trends in History, Princeton, N. J., May 1968.

8. I do not regard such devices for inserting direction into societies as "increasing complexity" as historical. They may, of course, be true.

9. P. Baran, *The Political Economy of Growth* (New York: Monthly Review Press, 1957), chap. 2.

10. For an English version of this important article, see *Social Science Information,* 9 (February 1970), 145-174.

11. Cf. "At stake in a broader view of urban history is the possibility of making the societal process of urbanization central to the study of social change. Efforts should be made to conceptualize urbanization in ways that actually represent social change." Eric Lampard in Oscar Handlin and John Burchard, *The Historians and the City* (Cambridge, Mass.: M.I.T. Press, 1963), p. 233.

12. This work is in progress under the direction of Professor Sven-Ulric Palme at the University of Stockholm.

13. For the possible divergences between reality and classification, see the discussions about the complex socioracial hierarchies of colonial Latin America. Magnus Mörner, "The History of Race Relations in Latin America," in L. Foner and E. D. Genovese, *Slavery in the New World* (Englewood Cliffs, N. J.: Prentice-Hall, 1969), p. 221.

14. See A. Prost, "Vocabulaire et typologie des familles politiques," *Cahiers de lexicologie,* XIV (1969).

15. T. Shanin, "The Peasantry as a Political Factor," *Sociological Review,* 14 (1966), 17.

16. Class has long been the central preoccupation of social historians. See, for example, A. J. C. Rueter in *IX congrès international des sciences historiques,* I, 298-299.

17. A. Dupront, "Problèmes et méthodes d'une histoire de la psychologie collective," *Annales: économies, sociétés, civilisations,* 16 (January–February 1961), 3-11.

18. By "fitting together" I mean establishing a systematic connection between different, and sometimes apparently unconnected, parts of the same syndrome—for example, the beliefs of the classic nineteenth-century liberal bourgeoisie in both individual liberty and a patriarchal family structure.

19. We look forward to the time when the Russian Revolution will provide historians with comparable opportunities for the twentieth century.

20. R. Braun, *Industrialisierung und Volksleben* (Erlenbach-Zurich: Rentsch, 1960); *Sozialer und kultureller Wandel in einem ländlichen Industriegebiet . . . im 19. und 20. Jahrhundert* (Erlenbach-Zurich: Rentsch, 1965). J. O. Foster's thesis is being prepared for publication.

21. Eric Stokes, who is doing this, is conscious of applying the results of work in African history. E. Stokes, *Traditional Resistance Movements and Afro-Asian Nationalism: The Context of the 1857 Mutiny-Rebellion in India* (forthcoming).

22. *Centre Formation, Nation-Building and Cultural Diversity: Report on a Symposium Organized by UNESCO* (duplicated draft, n.d.). The symposium was held August 28–September 1, 1968.

23. Though capitalism has developed as a global system of economic interactions, in fact the real units of its development have been certain territorial-political units— British, French, German, U. S. economies—which may be due to historic accident but also (the question remains open) to the necessary role of the state in economic development, even in the era of the purest economic liberalism.

J O H N   H A B A K K U K

Economic History and Economic Theory

ECONOMIC THEORY characteristically proceeds by building a model, a simplified, abstract version of the real world. A model is more than a hypothesis; it is a series of functional relations between the various elements of which an economy is composed. The major economic elements are isolated—wages, capital, investment, consumption, and so forth—and certain relationships between them are postulated. For the purpose of any particular exercise, certain of the factors are assumed to be constant and the consequences of the postulated relations between the variables are worked out on a variety of different assumptions. The notion that underlies this procedure is that the multitudinous facts of economic life constitute a system.

Since its origin in the late seventeenth century, this method has proved a very powerful instrument of thought about the problems of economic life. The concepts have been multiplied and refined and a vast number of exercises have been conducted on a great variety of assumptions. Thus models have been adapted to analyze the effects of random shocks on a system. In view of its power one should perhaps be surprised at the little use made of this method (and its results) in the explanation of past economic events, either by economists or historians.

Among economists, Adam Smith did have a model in mind when he wrote his account of European economic history in *The Wealth of Nations*. A good deal of this account belongs to the category of "hypothetical history," that is, it is an attempt to explain how the forces of natural liberty "must have" operated under primitive conditions. The model is not a complicated one and it is not specified clearly, but its main elements are clear enough. Smith relied on it when he was interpreting the established facts

27

and even more when no such facts were available and he had to guess what "must have" happened. Smith's account was *histoire raisonné*, that is, it described the way in which the relationships in his model implied events happened. Even more clearly, Marx's interpretation of economic history—and of history in general— was governed by the working of his model of capitalist development. Implicit in the writings of the other classical economists there was a theory, or, more accurately, a number of theories of economic development which would have lent themselves to an interpretation of the past, but I cannot recall any major classical writer who made systematic use of his theory for this purpose. The classical economists made systematic use of their theory in their examination of current problems, but not of the past. Perhaps they would have done so had they been more interested in explaining the past; but most of them regarded the past merely as a storehouse of instances.

Malthus, Ricardo, and Mill had models that could have been adapted to the explanation of the past, but they were not interested in such interpretation. Alfred Marshall had highly developed historical interests and made several ventures on to historical ground. But his most substantial historical exercise, Book 1 of *Industry and Trade* in which he examined some origins of current problems, makes little use of the theories worked out in his *Principles*, except possibly for the notion of "economies of massive production." His persistent emphasis on development as a slow and gradual process may have been derived in some measure from his "marginalist" economic theory, but one could read his account of the process without realizing that the author was an eminent theorist. Marshall's explanations, when they are not political, are usually sociological ("a man's energies are at their best when he is emerging from poverty and distress into the command of great opportunities," p. 87) or biological (Spain's "best industrial qualities were largely due to Saracenic blood," p. 107).

In only three fields was there some marriage of history and economics in the early decades of this century in the writings of economists: business cycles, international trade, and money. Early attempts to analyze economic fluctuations were prompted by specific business cycles, and theory was intertwined with accounts of specific fluctuations. There is, for example, a great deal of economic history in D. H. Robertson's *A Study of Industrial Fluctuations* (1915) along with elements of a "model." J. A. Schumpeter's

Business Cycles (1939) was essentially an attempt to explain a historical process: "a quantitative and carefully dated account of a period of 250 years may be called the minimum of existence of the student of business cycles." International trade theory did produce propositions on relationships between economic variables about which a good deal of statistical data was available, and Frank W. Taussig and his pupils in a number of studies attempted to test theory against history. Taussig himself, in his *History of the American Tariff*, did try to write substantive history in the light of the current state of the relevant theory. The inflation after the First World War also gave rise to attempts to harness theory to explain a specific historical episode, most notably in the work of Bresciani-Turroni.[1]

In these fields some contact was made between theory and historical fact. But in the main, history was used by economists, when they used it at all, to *illustrate* theory. There is, of course, a narrow line between the use of history to *illustrate* theory and its use to *test* the hypotheses derived from theory; and, in turn, the use of history to test hypotheses is often not clearly to be distinguished from the interpretation of particular historical episodes in the light of a theory. Knut Wicksell, in *Interest and Prices,* used the evidence of the period 1850–1895 to illustrate his hypotheses about the relationships between interest rates and prices, but he was also concerned to establish the plausibility of the hypotheses by showing that they explained actual behavior over a historical period. Keynes, in the historical chapters of the *Treatise on Money,* went further and recounted a number of historical episodes in the light of his theory. But I cannot recall any economist before the Great Depression of the 1930's who attempted to explain a particular economic situation or development by drawing on the full range of economic techniques.

If one turns from economists to economic historians—that is, scholars whose primary interest was to give an explanatory account of past economic events—one finds their use of economic theory, in the sense of economic models, was negligible. I can think of very few economic historians before 1945 who made any systematic use of economic theory. J. H. Clapham, who was a pupil of Marshall and a friend of Arthur C. Pigou, almost entirely eschewed theory in his *Economic History of Modern Britain.*

It is sometimes suggested that lack of contact between history and theory in the late nineteenth and early twentieth centuries was owing to the state of theory. Neoclassical theory was concerned primarily with problems of market equilibrium; the techniques developed in analyzing these problems were not well adapted to explaining change over time. Sometimes propositions emerged which, in principle, were capable of being verified by reference to fact, for example, Henry Schulz's work on demand. But most of the propositions of, for example, price theory could not be—and, in some sense, did not need to be—checked against empirical data.[2] The villains of the piece, on this view, are William S. Jevons, Carl Menger, and Léon Walras, who shunted theory off the track of economic dynamics. There is obviously some truth in this suggestion. If economists in the age of Walras had been preoccupied with models of growth and accumulation, they would have turned to historical change to a much greater extent and economic historians would have been able to borrow from economists' techniques appropriate for the explanation of change over time.

This cannot, however, entirely explain why so little use was made of economic theory, if only because many of the concepts which the recent econometric historians have used derive from static equilibrium theory and not from theories of economic growth. If economists did not pay much attention to economic history, it was not only because of the particular nature of the theory that preoccupied them; it was also because there were few of them and they just did not have enough time. So far as the economic historians are concerned, they did not neglect theory from a conviction that the theory was inappropriate; they consciously rejected theory, whether classical or neoclassical, out of an explicit conviction that it was not useful in the explanation of economic history. This was the attitude of the German school of "historical" economists which powerfully influenced the development of economic history in the United States and the United Kingdom.

In the last two decades there has been a systematic attempt to reunite history and theory, the result mainly of the "new" economic historians who have applied econometric methods to historical data.[3] Though their work has antecedents and in this sense is not "new," it does represent a substantial departure in the history of the subject. To put it in perspective I find it useful to distinguish five stages at which economic theory can be employed.

1. In the first stage the relevant concepts or elements are identified and defined. A decision has to be made that certain phenomena of real life have enough in common to be grouped together in a single category called, for example, labor.

2. Certain of these categories are chosen for study, that is, one decides which phenomena one wants to explain or understand and which elements are likely to be relevant to the task.

3. Quantitative evidence about these elements is obtained.

4. The relations between the elements so quantified are explored.

5. The relations so established are interpreted.

To put the matter in terms of equations: the elements of the economic system have to be defined; the problem identified; the equations set up; the relations established which determine the values of the elements, that is, the problem "solved"; and the properties of the solution investigated and assessed.

The distinctive feature of the new economic history is not that it uses theory to derive new hypotheses or pose new problems. Many of the problems tackled by the new economic historians are, in fact, those posed by the assertions of the historians of an earlier generation. Was slavery profitable? Were the railways built ahead of demand? Were the railways a necessary condition for the exploitation of new lands? How important was technical progress to the growth of productivity? As Robert Fogel has observed (see note 3), "Some of the most important revisions of the new economic history have arisen from nothing more than the discovery that the simple functions assumed in the past are poor descriptions of the relationships on which arguments were anchored."

The distinctive feature of the new economic history is that it uses theory (a) to identify the elements about which, for explanatory purposes, it is necessary to obtain quantitative evidence, that is, the elements in the equations and (b) to deduce evidence about these elements when direct evidence is lacking. Most of the attention of the new economic historians has been devoted to (b).

Even for periods where a great deal of direct evidence is available, it is rarely sufficient to enable the historian to make a direct measurement of the variables in which he is interested. He has therefore to deduce the information he wants from the known facts, which are rarely quite what he wants, by using relations derived from a model. For example, a historian may need to know the marginal social costs of a particular activity. No direct estimate of these is available, so he uses the observed prices of the relevant product as an indicator of marginal social costs because of relations derived from a study of the properties of competitive markets.

In a general sense, this is merely a particular form of the activity which all historians undertake when they do more than publish the documents. We all draw inferences from our sources about phenomena for which the sources themselves are not explicit. In a more restricted sense the use of the known as surrogate for the unknown is a practice of long standing. As Professor Fogel points out, economic historians have used the rate of growth of pig iron as a substitute for the rate of growth of the output of the iron industry, miles of main line as a substitute for the investment of railways, and so on.

What is new in the new economic history is that the move from the known to the unknown is based explicitly upon a chain of economic reasoning which is derived from the working of a theoretical model. (The attempts to move from the known to the unknown are also more strenuous and ambitious than any earlier attempts.) What are the problems which arise from operating in this way? The first is simply that the calculations are often complicated and the chain-of-reasoning linking of the known to the unknown is very elaborate. This is not, of course, invariably true. Sometimes the calculations are simple and the reasoning immediately apparent (whether valid or not)—for example, the derivation of all classes of freight from the statistics relating to the carriage of one class. More commonly, however, it is necessary to build up an estimate by a cumulative process of argument each stage of which is elaborate, even when the models underlying the argument are not themselves particularly novel or sophisticated.

A good deal of the underlying theory is in fact old. In the studies which attempt to assess the relative contribution of various factors to the expansion of American industries, "the theory required for the desired measurements follows rather directly from the economists' traditional analytic tools of supply and demand."[4] The very fruitful work on the profitability of slavery has been done with relatively few concepts—for example, a consumption goods sector and a capital goods sector and the notion of a rate of return as the rate which equates the price of the capital good (slaves) to the discounted value of the stream of earnings derived from their employment. The point is that, even where the underlying theory is simple, the reasoning necessary to derive the desired information may be very intricate, and each step depends on a series of succeeding steps in a way which is exceedingly difficult to hold in mind. For this reason it requires a great deal of effort on the part of the reader, particularly the noneconometric reader, to assess the validity of the "conclusions" of any piece of new economic history. It is particularly difficult to see readily the full range of assumptions that have been made and identify those which are crucial to the conclusion. Also, an implausible assumption or faulty reasoning at one point may vitiate the whole process.

This difficulty is, of course, inherent in any attempt to reconstruct data. It is probably less difficult to deal with when mathematical reasoning is used, for when the assumptions are made explicit it is easier to check on their consistency. But the fact that the chain of reasoning behind the data of the new economic history is often complicated does make the conclusions of such history particularly difficult to handle.

Much more important, it is difficult to check on the *empirical validity* of the assumptions made in the course of the reasoning. The criterion which economists apply when they make assumptions in model building is not solely or even mainly the correspondence between these assumptions and reality. In order to frame a model that is "workable," that is, the logic of whose operations can be systematically explored, it may be necessary for the theorist to include some assumptions evidently not in accord with the facts. For example, he may assume perfect foresight on the part of the businessmen or a situation of pure competition. The fact that businessmen do not in fact have perfect foresight does not prevent models containing this assumption from providing one with some useful clues about particular economic situations. But when a model is used to construct data, that is, to *describe* actual situations, then the empirical validity of the assumptions becomes a crucial matter. Of course, it is precisely in these circumstances that it is most difficult to check the empirical validity of the assumptions; for it is where the data is sparsest that one has to rely most heavily on reasoning based on a model.

The assumption, for example, that prices represent marginal costs may be made because there is no useable evidence about costs; but precisely for this reason it may be impossible to provide an entirely satisfactory check on the empirical validity of the assumption. This is an important point, because it is even more difficult in this type of work than in other forms of historical inquiry to avoid the temptation to cut the corners fine and to make a heroic assumption if it is necessary to arrive at a quantitative estimate of some variable believed to be crucial for the problem in hand.

To use theory effectively in order to quantify, one has to limit the equations to a manageable number and include in them only those factors for which some sort of quantification is possible, that is, to specify the problem in terms of characteristics for which, directly or indirectly, data can be provided. It is only thus that statements can be made amenable to confirmation or contradiction. But the need to limit the variables for these reasons may compel one to include an assumption that greatly limits the utility of the model to someone interested in explaining actual events. As R. M. Solow has observed: "While there is something foolish about a theory of capital built on the assumption of perfect foresight, we have no equally precise and definite assumption to take its place."[5] Or, consider the theory of imperfect competition from the point of view of someone who wishes to derive from it a model of the working of an industry. "The trouble," writes N. Kaldor, "is that existing theories of imperfect competition . . . are largely micro-theories; they concern the equilibrium of an individual firm faced with a given market situation. When it comes to considering the equilibrium of a *group* of firms, they all assume (explicitly or implicitly) that all firms are identical with respect to their cost and demand functions—a procedure which assumes away all the interesting (and important) aspects of the competitive process."[6]

By definition a model contains assumptions which depart from reality. This is precisely what models are for; they are attempts to understand reality by simplifying it. The model builder can make his own choice of the degree and nature of the simplification. But more is involved than the fact of abstraction. The point is that a great deal of economic theory is based upon particular types of abstraction.

Thus, in the first place, most economic reasoning is rooted in or makes use of the notion of equilibrium—roughly speaking the state of affairs which would be reached if all the forces worked themselves out. The economic system is seen as consisting of a number of quantitative relations between economic variables which simultaneously determine one another. If the relations are such as to determine a set of values of the variables that displays no tendency to change under the sole influence of the facts included in these relations, the system is said to be in equilibrium.[7] Second, a significant part of the corpus of economic theory—and a part which has been used by econometric historians—derives from attempts to establish relations between elements of the economic system all of which refer to the same point of time, for example, simple demand and supply theory. Third, a good deal of economic theory has been built on the assumption that perfect competition is the normal case.

Propositions derived from economic reasoning of these kinds, when used in the construction of quantitative data, are particularly liable to give rise to false conclusions, because they are based on assumptions which do not correspond to reality. Econometric history raises the same difficulties as econometrics itself.

I now turn to a different use of theory—not to quantify the variables but to identify those which are crucial for whatever problem is in hand and to specify the nature of the relations between them. In this task the empirical validity of the assumptions underlying the model seems to me to matter less than it does when the model is used to quantify the variables. But it is still important, particularly when an attempt is made to specify the relationships with some precision. Here again difficulties are likely to arise not only from the high degree of abstraction necessary in any model, but also from the use which economic reasoning characteristically makes of the notion of equilibrium. The difficulty is not only that a crucial variable may be left out of the model, but also that it is difficult to operate a model without making some use of the notion of equilibrium. For example, P. Temin's model of the American economy in the nineteenth century is based on the assumptions that returns to scale were constant and that the economy was in equilibrium. In reply to a critic he very fairly pointed out that "these assumptions are the assumptions that economists usually make."[8] The case for using them is that their logical implications have been exhaustively explored. "Little is known," Temin writes, "about the behaviour of an economy not in equilibrium." This highlights the problem because historians spend all their time dealing with economies which are not in equilibrium; that is the only sort of economy they know about. If, therefore, the model of an economy is set up on the assumption that the economy is in equilibrium, then the real problems presented by historical phenomena may be assumed away, or conclusions about historical situations may be reached which, in fact, are simply the logical deductions from the initial assumptions. Of course, this danger is latent in the use of any model, but it is particularly likely to be present when it is a state of equilibrium that is assumed.

Apart from all these difficulties, there is the danger that use will be made of a bad, that is, logically defective, model, or of a model which is imperfectly specified, or of one which is not relevant to the purpose in hand.

There are evidently a great many dangers in using economic theory to interpret and explain the past. Many of these are not dangers that can be avoided simply by refraining from the use of theory. Theory of some sort is implicit in even the most rudimentary attempts to explain events. The great merit of making the model explicit is that the assumptions can be argued about and, in some degree, tested by the collection of additional data.

This has happened in the case of most of the major contributions to the new economic history. Each contribution has been followed by a long argument about the logical and empirical validity of the assumptions (for example, the controversies following Alfred Conrad and John Meyer and Fogel); and substantial progress has been registered. Models can be adapted and assumptions made less restrictive.[9] There are probably some assumptions the validity or even plausibility of which cannot be verified either because of their nature or because of lack of data. But it is too early to be pessimistic and suppose that there are many such assumptions. Although we are not likely to be able to measure the extent to which a whole economy is "in equilibrium," it should often be possible to say something about the degree of perfection in particular markets from a study of the behavior of prices. It may prove, also, that a series of studies, each with a weak or tentative conclusion, will strengthen each other.

There are a great many problems where the relevant variables can be quantified, a great deal of work to be done on the Fogel lines. But how far will theory be able to interpret the relations between the variables when they have been quantified? This question is relevant to a much wider field than economic history. For models are now used also in attempts to explain political behavior. Economic theorists have, for example, devoted a great deal of attention to analyzing problems of choice in terms of tastes, resources, and costs. There need be nothing specifically economic about these elements. "The tastes do not necessarily have to be for marketable goods; the resources and costs do not have to be financial. I can have a taste for peace, consider time as a resource, and injustice as a cost."[10] The models of economic choice have been applied to problems of political choice, for example, in Professor Brian Barry's *Political Argument* (1965). There is in principle no reason why they should not be used in the analysis of political choice in the past.

In one respect, high hopes are warranted, for since the war a great deal of intellectual effort has been applied to elaborating models of economic growth. There is now a whole galaxy of models which deal with the growth of the economy. They deal precisely with those problems of economic change over time which, in a quite different way, economic historians also suppose they are concerned with. Some of the models have provided their builders (for example, Professor Kaldor) with insights into economic history in a way which suggests that the model could be used to interpret the past. So far very little use has been made of them for historical purposes. Even Sir John Hicks does not make great use of recent growth theory when he writes economic history. In his recent "A Theory of Economic History" there is certainly much theory, but it is more the economics of his *Value and Capital* than of his *Theory of Economic Growth*. The potentialities are there; in principle, these models could be used for historical purposes.

Developments in econometrics may also have more revolutionary effects on economic history than they have yet had. In recent years there have been attempts to construct models of the United Kingdom and of the United States economies and of sectors within them—for example, labor markets and the monetary sector—partly for the purpose of forecasting and analyzing the effect of changes in government policy.[11] As a means of forecasting, the record has not been very successful, but the exercises help to improve understanding of how the economy works. The extent to which the economic relationships specified in the model are derived from economic theory, rather than from closeness of statistical fit, varies according to the model. Econometric methods have not yet been applied on any significant scale to the *history* of substantial sectors of the economy, still less to the history of the whole economy. But there are some who believe that there is no reason in principle why they should not be, that is, that if the relevant data was available all economic history would be econometrics.

The scope for the use of theory in the explanation of human behavior depends essentially on the nature of the behavior in question. In any situation there are systematic elements and elements which are fortuitous (from the point of view of the particular situation). For example, in analyzing the demography of the fourteenth century, the Black Death may reasonably be regarded as a fortuitous element and any relations between mortality and income as systematic. There are some situations which are dominated by the fortuitous; they consist of relations which it is not fruitful to regard as corresponding to a self-determining system, for example, the relations between two highly idiosyncratic diplomats. There are other cases where most of the salient features of a situation or development can be explained in terms of the systematic relationship between a small number of variables, for example, the growth of a closed population. There is no a priori way of knowing how the systematic and the fortuitous are distributed among the situations available for historical study. The first inclination is to suppose that the systematic elements are most prominent in situations involving large numbers of people, and that the smaller the numbers the more important are the fortuitous elements. But while this may be a reasonable expectation, the correspondence is by no means exact. The most restricted of situations may be illuminated by a model, and the proceedings of a small committee may be made more intelligible by the application of decision theory. At the other extreme, a situation involving large numbers may be dominated by fortuitous factors, for example, medieval population in the instance already mentioned. The traditional instinct of most historians is to suppose that the area of human behavior dominated by the "contingent and the unforeseen" is very large indeed. Most economists on the other hand—and most sociologists and anthropologists—regard the relations they examine as in some degree constituting a system; this is increasingly becoming the habit of professional students of politics. To some extent this difference is the result of the fact that, by tradition, historians have concentrated on the relations between individuals rather than between groups, that is, on the areas where it may reasonably be expected that the fortuitous elements are of greatest importance. But, even when a historian is dealing with relationships similar in nature (and different only because they are in the past) to those dealt with by sociologists and anthropologists, the assumptions about the relative significance of fortuitous and systematic elements implied in his method of approach are radically different from those of the scholar studying the relationships in their current context. Only a large number of attempts to apply theory will show how much truth there is in the traditional instincts of historians.

Similar considerations apply to the use of the notion of equilibrium, that is, to the notion that there are not only systematic elements in a situation but that they are systematic elements of a particular kind. This notion is not only the basis of a good deal of theory, sociological as well as economic, but has been fruitfully applied to a number of actual situations (for example, Neil Smelser's well-known work on social change in the Industrial Revolution). The notion has been criticized by an economic theorist,[12] but whatever the merits of that particular comment it is obvious that, in a general sense, the idea can be a useful one for historians. It is evident that when a state of affairs is disturbed, *some* systematic forces will accentuate the effect of the disturbance while others will make for a restoration of the situation that existed before the disturbance. Or, if we are considering the growth of an area or of an economy, there are forces making for instability in the rate of growth and forces counteracting the causes of instability. The crucial problem in each case is whether the latter are sufficiently strong to make it useful and sensible to think of the process in terms of an equilibrium, whether a static or a dynamic equilibrium.

The notion of a system or an equilibrium is, of course, to be found in the work of traditional historians. A large part of diplomatic history has been discussed in terms of a "balance of power," that is, on the assumption that the actions of statesmen were dominated by a desire to maintain an equilibrium. Or, again, the traditional account of technical progress in cotton textiles during the Industrial Revolution is written in terms of the disturbance and restoration of a balance between spinning and weaving. There is therefore nothing inherently abhorrent in the notion. But I think it is fair to say that many historians have instinctively felt that, in most of the situations with which they dealt, the systematic factors were so overshadowed and the forces making for equilibrium so weak, that it was not sensible to attempt to make strenuous and rigorous use of these notions.

The traditional historians' hunch about theory can perhaps be put in another way. Granted that a particular historical situation can be approached by examining the relationships between a number of variables. The difficulty in going far with this approach may be (1) that the number of relevant variables is very large, or that the major part of the variance cannot be ascribed to a small number of variables; (2) that the relations do not determine a single value or sequence of values, that is, there may be no unique set of values to which the relations have to conform.

Cases when the number of variables relevant to the problem is very great and when the relations between them determine a range of values and not a unique set may well, in fact, be the situations most commonly faced by historians. There is something in the feeling that an intuitive approach and the infinite nuances and flexibilities of prose may arrive at less misleading conclusions than a more rigorous and formal treatment.

The econometric historian starts by framing a hypothesis and then considers those facts that are relevant to the question of its validity. In the past most historians proceeded in quite a different way. They absorbed a large number of miscellaneous facts relating to the period in which they were interested or to problems very loosely defined. Their taste was catholic and they did not accept or reject on any rigorous test of relevance to a hypothesis. They retained in their minds an accumulating stock of information, as it were a compost heap, on which in due course ideas and generalizations burgeoned, as a result of reflection, flair, and intuition. This process is very haphazard—it is rather like that which according to A. E. Housman creates poetry—but it has produced a great many penetrating insights, and it keeps the mind open to a wide range of considerations. These two ways of proceeding are not likely to be compatible; one man cannot think in two ways. A capacity for analysis may impair memory and imagination. One may have to make a choice, and a good judgment informed by wide reading of history, by long practical experience of how men behave in a wide variety of circumstances, and by detailed inside knowledge of particular institutions and situations *may* for many historical problems produce a more accurate interpretation of events than analysis in terms of a rigorously specified system. Such analysis may throw a powerful beam on certain places, but one which distorts or leaves in darkness the surrounding landscape; informed judgment, though less powerful, may shed a more equable and dependable light on the full range of human activities.

There is a similar though logically distinct point which expresses the misgivings of historians about *quantification,* rather than about the use of theory per se. When all the elements that can reasonably be quantified have been quantified, there will still remain influences that cannot be measured. We have to rely on "good judgment" or "common sense" to take account of them. In principle there is no necessary contradiction between a taste and capacity for measurement on the one hand and common sense on the other. Indeed, it might be argued that men who have grappled with problems of measurement are for that reason better able to weigh the influences which cannot be measured, since every stage in the creation of a statistical estimate involves a measure of judgment. But I suspect that, in practice, there is some conflict between the capacities for quantitative judgment and those for qualitative judgment. A continually exercised taste for measurement may breed an impatience with those considerations that do not lend themselves to measurement. Writing of the forecasters in the British Treasury, Harold Lever, a former Labour minister, wrote: "If something likely to happen, something that common sense tells you *will* happen, is not computable, the Treasury forecasters are apt to leave it out of count. At some point it becomes almost a rule that if you cannot quantify commonsense you do not use it." Sometimes econometric historians have been suspected of the same disposition.

The real question at present is the number and type of problems which prove amenable to treatment by the methods of the econometric historians. So far the methods have had a high degree of success and have advanced thought about and knowledge of a surprisingly wide range of problems. It may well be that as econometric historians extend their attempts into less promising fields, they will be less successful. If this proves to be true, it will not be simply a limitation of econometric history. It will have implications for all forms of history. For it will suggest that there are severe limitations of the statements that can be reliably made about the past. Almost any book of history contains a large number of statements which cannot in fact be verified or disproved. They are often the result of the historian's hunch after submerging himself in the documents, the product of a process of subconscious inference. If in fact the econometricians turn out in the next twenty years to be very unsuccessful in their attempts to reconstruct data, the greater part of economic history—and possibly of other forms of history as well—will continue to consist of conclusions that are essentially no more than well-informed guesses, and controlled conjectures.

I have been considering primarily the use of rigorous theory in economic history, that is, the use of models in which the relations between the variables are specified with precision to identify the critical relationships and to give numerical values to the variables. Theory can also be used in a less rigorous fashion. By less rigorous I do not mean *implicit* as opposed to *explicit* theory. The distinction I have in mind is that between the use of theory in Fogel's *Railroads and American Economic Growth* and that in Charles Kindleberger's *Economic Growth in France and Britain, 1851-1950*. Though I find it difficult to define the distinction, it seems clear to me that the difference is more than a matter of degree. In a sense, there is much more theory in Kindleberger than in Fogel, and the use of theory is quite explicit. But the theory is much more loosely related to the history and the relations between the variables are not specified with precision. Theory is used to suggest hypotheses, pose questions, offer clues, and provide a test of logical consistency for explanations. The use of theory for these purposes seems to have limitless possibilities.

For this purpose it does not matter so much if the assumptions of the models depart from reality. The model provides a source of expectations and it may be as illuminating to the historian when the expectations are confounded as when they are confirmed. If we construct a very simplified model and examine how it would work, we can see which of the phenomena of the real world would exist in it, and which would not. We are provided with some clues to the causes of the real phenomena which are lacking in the working model as well as those which appear in it. It becomes easier to see what needs to be explained, or what points need to be established before an explanation can be accepted. From this point of view, very simple or highly abstract theory can be fruitful. Thus the idea of a competitive market and simple supply and demand analysis can illuminate a variety of situations. For example, some of the characteristics of the cultural institutions of a community can be explored by regarding the institutions as competitors for members and by invoking the theory of consumer choice. Cultural institutions are not, of course, primarily competitors for members, but an analysis in these terms will suggest questions which would not otherwise occur to the historian and the attempt to answer them may shed new light on the structure of these institutions, their subscription rates, and the facilities they offer. Even the analysis of the properties of a "stationary state," of an economic process which merely reproduces itself, can help one to think about the problems of a growing economy.

The use of theory and the attempt to measure—even if it proves impossible to quantify precisely—increase the precision of "literary" economic history. They illuminate cases where what is apparently one proposition in fact conceals two distinct propositions. They also make writers more careful of the implications of what they write. A great deal of "literary" economic history consists of statements which logically imply that the writer has evidence on points about which, in fact, he knows nothing.

At the very least, theory can provide a test of the internal consistency of an explanation. It is common to find in traditional economic history mutually incompatible explanations of a given phenomenon, sometimes presented by the same historian. Theory will not indicate which explanation corresponds to the facts, but it can establish the incompatibility of the assumptions.

REFERENCES

1. Costantino Bresciani-Turroni, *The Economics of Inflation*, trans. Millicent E. Sayers (London: Allen and Unwin, 1937).

2. H. Schulz, *Statistical Laws of Demand and Supply* (Chicago: University of Chicago Press, 1928).

3. Robert W. Fogel, "The New Economic History: Its Findings and Methods," *Economic History Review* (1966). There is now a very large body of economic history of this kind. The most notable examples are Robert W. Fogel, *Railroads and American Economic Growth* (Baltimore: Johns Hopkins University Press, 1964); Albert Fishlow, *American Railroads and the Transformation of the Ante-Bellum Economy* (Cambridge, Mass.: Harvard University Press, 1965); Peter Temin, *Iron and Steel in Nineteenth-Century America* (Cambridge, Mass.: M.I.T. Press, 1964).

4. Robert W. Fogel and S. L. Engerman, "A Model for the Explanation of Industrial Expansion During the Nineteenth Century," *Journal of Political Economy*, 77 (1969), 307.

5. R. M. Solow, "The Production Function and the Theory of Capital," *Review of Economic Studies*, 23 (1955-1956), 102.

6. N. Kaldor, "Some Fallacies in the Interpretation of Kaldor," *Review of Economic Studies*, 37 (1970), 3.

7. Joseph A. Schumpeter, *History of Economic Analysis* (New York: Oxford University Press, 1954), 963-972.

8. Peter Temin, "Labour Scarcity and the Problem of American Industrial

Efficiency in the 1850's: A Reply," *Journal of Economic History,* 28 (1968), 124-125.

9. Thus Fogel and Engerman adapt their model to deal with industries whose expansion leads to an increase in the price of inputs. "A Model for the Explanation of Industrial Expansion During the Nineteenth Century," p. 307.

10. G. Hawthorn, "The Morals of Sociology," *Twentieth Century,* 177 (1969).

11. Z. Griliches, "The Brookings Model Volume: A Review Article," *Review of Economics and Statistics,* 50 (1968), 215-240.

12. J. Robinson, "The Production Function and the Theory of Capital," *Review of Economic Studies,* 21 (1953-1954), 85. "A space metaphor applied to time is a very tricky knife to handle, and the concept of equilibrium often cuts the arm that wields it."

FRANÇOIS FURET

Quantitative History

QUANTITATIVE HISTORY is fashionable just now both in Europe and
in the United States. Since the 1930's historical research has been
making rapidly increasing use of quantitative sources and of calculation and quantification procedures. But like all fashionable
phrases, "quantitative history" has come to be used so sweepingly
that it covers almost everything, from critical use of the simple
enumerations of seventeenth-century political arithmeticians, to
systematic application of mathematical models in the reconstruction of the past. Sometimes quantitative history refers to a type of
source, sometimes to a type of procedure; always, in some way or
other, explicit or not, to a type of conceptualization of the past.
It seems to me that if one goes from the general to the particular
and tries to pinpoint the specific nature of historical knowledge in
relation to the other social sciences, one can distinguish three groups
of problems relating to quantitative history.

(1) The first group concerns the methods of treating the data:
problems to do with the formation of different families of data,
the geographical unity of each family, and its internal subdivisions;
with correlations between different series; with the values, in relation to the data, of different models of statistical analysis; with
the interpretation of statistical relationships; and so on.

These problems belong to the *technology* of research in the social sciences. It is true they may also include questions of methodology. For ultimately they are bound to raise the problem of whether,
and to what extent, historical or sociological knowledge is compatible with, or can be dealt with exhaustively by, mathematical
conceptualization of a probabilistic kind. But neither the technical
nor the theoretical debate is specific to history: both arise in connection with all the social sciences. In this respect quantitative history is no different from, for example, what is now called "em-

pirical sociology," which in this context is simply contemporary quantitative history.

(2) Quantitative history also refers, at least in France, to the aims and researches of certain economic historians,[1] who attempt to turn history into a kind of retrospective econometrics, or in other words, on the basis of modern national accounting, to fill in all the columns of an imaginary input-output table for past centuries. The champions of this econometric history advocate total and systematic quantification, in their view indispensable both for the elimination of arbitrariness in selecting data and for the use of mathematical models in their processing. This processing is based on the concept of general equilibrium as imported into economic history from political economy.

According to this argument, genuine quantitative history would be the result of a two-fold reduction of history: first, at least provisionally, the reduction of its field to economics, and secondly the reduction of its descriptive and interpretative system to the one worked out by the most rigorously constituted of the social sciences today, political economy. The same analysis could be applied to demography and demographic history: here again a conceptually constituted science indicates the data and supplies the methods for a particular historical discipline, the latter thus becoming a sort of by-product of the other discipline, whose questions and concepts it merely transposes into the past.

Of course, there have to be data for the past just as for the present; or at least it has to be possible to work them out with a sufficient degree of accuracy, or to reconstruct or extrapolate them. This necessity sets the first limit to the complete quantification of historical data. Complete quantification, even if possible at all before the nineteenth century, could not go back beyond the introduction of the statistical or proto-statistical recording of data, which coincides with the centralization of the great European monarchies. But history did not begin with William Petty or Sébastien Vauban.

Moreover, there is no reason why the historian should agree, even provisionally, to have his field of research reduced to economics or demography. There are two alternatives. Either history is only the study of a previously determined, limited sector of the past, into which mathematical models established by certain social sciences are imported in order to be tested. In which case, we come back again to contemporary political economy, which seems to me the only one of the social sciences with such models at its disposal. History then becomes nothing more than an additional field of data. Or—the second alternative—one takes history in the widest sense, that is, as a discipline not strictly reducible to a set of concepts and with countless different levels of analysis, and then addresses oneself to describing these levels and establishing simple statistical connections between them on the basis of hypotheses which, whether original or borrowed, depend on the intuition of the researcher.

(3) This is why, even if one qualifies history as "quantitative," one cannot escape what is the specific object of historical research: the study of time, of the diachronic dimension of phenomena. But, looked at from this point of view, quantitative history's most general and elementary object is to form historical fact into temporal series of homogeneous and comparable units, so that their evolution can be measured in terms of fixed intervals, usually years. This fundamental and logical operation constitutes what Pierre Chaunu[2] has called "serial history," a necessary though not sufficient condition of strictly quantitative history as defined above. For serial history offers the conclusive advantage, from the scientific point of view, of substituting for the elusive "event" of positivist history the regular repetition of data selected or constructed by reason of their comparability. It does not, however, claim to give an exhaustive account of the whole body of evidence, nor to be an over-all system of interpretation, nor to be a mathematical formulation. On the contrary, the division of historical reality into series leaves the historian confronted with his material broken down into different levels and subsystems, among which he is at liberty to suggest internal relationships if he chooses.

Defined in this way, quantitative and serial history emerge as at once connected with and distinct from each other. But they share an elementary basis in that both substitute the series for the event, both make a construction from historical data in terms of probabilistic analysis. To the classic question "What is a historical fact?" they both give a new answer which transforms the historian's raw material—time. It is about this internal transformation that I should like to put forward a few ideas.

To avoid any misunderstanding, let me say at once that this essay does not set out to prescribe quantitative history as the only kind permissible. During the last ten or twenty years serial history has turned out to be one of the most fertile approaches in the advancement of historical knowledge. It has also the immense advantage of introducing into the ancient discipline of history a rigor and efficiency superior to those of qualitative methodology. But it is nevertheless true that there are important sectors of historical reality which it is by nature unable to treat or even to approach, either for circumstantial reasons such as irremediable lack of data, or for fundamental reasons such as the irreducibly qualitative nature of the phenomenon concerned. This explains why, for example, historians of antiquity, who work with data very discontinuous in time, or specialists in intellectual biography, concentrating particularly on what is unique and incomparable in creativeness, are usually less attracted by serial history than, say, historians of the industrial take-off of modern Europe.

But the fact that serial history has limits—a subject which might be discussed on another occasion—does not excuse intellectual indolence or absolve the historian from reflecting on the transformation which has taken place in his knowledge. Because of serial history he is now confronted with a new panorama of data and a new awareness of the premises of his profession.

The Historian and His Sources

Quantitative history presupposes the existence and elaboration of long series of homogeneous and comparable data, and the first problem which presents itself in new terms is that of sources. In general, European archives were formed and classified in the nineteenth century, in accordance with procedures and criteria reflecting the ideological and methodological preoccupations of the period. This meant, on the one hand, that national values predominated and that priority was given to politico-administrative sources. It also meant that documents were preserved and classified in accordance with the special and limited purpose of a particular inquiry: archives were built up to witness to events rather than to time. They were constituted and criticized in themselves and not as factors in a series; the point of reference was external. What was in question was the historical "fact" of the positivists, the naïve mind's illusory sheet-anchor in what is supposed to be real, as distinct from mere testimony—a particular, discontinuous, elusive sequence within either an indefinite flux or a chronology preestablished in terms of centuries, reigns, and ministers. In short, archives are the memoirs of nations, just as the letters a person keeps show what an individual has chosen to remember.

But the data of quantitative history refer not to some external, vaguely outlined "fact" but to internal criteria of consistency. A fact is no longer an event selected because it marks a high spot in a history whose meaning has been predetermined, but a phenomenon chosen and sometimes constructed by reason of the recurrence which makes it comparable with others in terms of some unit of time. The whole conception of history based on archives is radically transformed at the very time when its technical possibilities are multiplied by the electronic processing of information. This simultaneous and interconnected revolution in methodology and technique enables us to think in terms of a new kind of archive preserved on perforated tapes. Such archives would not only be built up according to a deliberately planned system; their criteria would also be quite different from those of the nineteenth century. Documents and data exist no longer for themselves but in relation to the series which in each case precedes or follows: it is their comparative value which becomes objective instead of their relation to some elusive "real" substance. Thus, incidentally, the old problem of the *critique* of historical documents moves on to different ground. "External" criticism is no longer based on credibility as derived from contemporaneous texts of another kind, but on consistency with a text of the same kind occurring elsewhere in the temporal series. "Internal" criticism is simplified inasmuch as many of the necessary cleaning-up operations can be entrusted to the memory of the computer.

Consistency is introduced at the outset, when the data are first sorted out, by a minimal formalization of each document which makes it possible to retrieve, over a long period and for each unit of time, the same data in the same logical order. From this point of view the historian's use of computers is not only an enormous practical advance in the time it saves (especially when the sorting is done verbally by tape-recording, as in the Couturier method[3]); it is also a very useful theoretical discipline, in that the formalization of a documentary series which is to be programmed forces the historian from the very beginning to abandon epistemological naïveté, to construct the actual object of his research, to scrutinize his hypotheses, and to make the transition from implicit to explicit. The second critical process, this time an internal one, consists in testing the consistency of the data themselves in relation to those which come before and after—in other words, in eliminating errors. It thus emerges as a sort of consequence of the first process, and can in fact be done largely by automation through programmed methods of verification.

Naturally enough, serial history in its manual form began by using those historical series which were easiest to handle, that is, economic, fiscal, and demographic documentation. The revolution introduced by the computer into the collection and processing of data has steadily multiplied the extent to which such numerical series can be explored. The technique can now be applied to any kind of historical data reducible to a language that can be programmed—not only fiscal and legal rolls, but also series of relatively homogeneous literary collections such as medieval chartularies or the cahiers of the states-general of monarchical France.

Thus emerges the first task of serial history, the imperative of its development: the constitution of its subject matter. Classical historiography was constructed from archives worked on and processed according to the critical rules bequeathed to us by the Benedictines of the age of Enlightenment and the German historians of the nineteenth century. The serial history of today has to reconstruct its archives in terms of the dual methodological and technical revolution which has transformed the rules and procedures of history.

This being so, the question arises of the problematical nature of history's subject matter, the hazards of its survival, its partial destruction and sometimes total disappearance. I am not sure this question distinguishes history as much as is sometimes alleged from the other human sciences whose objects are more specifically defined. The characteristic feature of history is the extraordinary and almost unlimited elasticity of its sources. As the researcher's curiosity roves further and further, huge dormant areas of documentation are revealed. What nineteenth-century historian bothered with the parish registers which have now become, especially in England and France, one of the surest sources of our knowledge of preindustrial society?

Moreover, if the researcher invests them with a new significance, sources already exploited once can be used again for other purposes. Descriptions of price movements can lead to sociological or political analyses; Georges d'Avenel is followed by Ernest Labrousse. Demographic series studied from the point of view of, for example, the use of contraception by married couples can also throw light on problems of mental attitude or religious practice. Signatures to legal documents can give statistics about the spread of literacy. Biographies systematically grouped in terms of common criteria, on the basis of a given working hypothesis, can build up documentary series imparting an entirely new life to one of the oldest kinds of historical narrative.

Hitherto history has been almost exclusively based on the written traces of men's existence. No doubt live interrogation, which provides empirical sociology with so much of its data, will always be beyond the reach of the historian except for the period in which he lives. But how much unwritten evidence there is still to be catalogued and systematically described. The physical conditions of rural life, the divisions of the land, iconography sacred and profane, the lay-out of early towns, what the houses were like inside—one could go on forever listing the elements of civilization which once catalogued and classified in detail would make it possible to establish new chronological series, and put at the historian's disposal the new subject matter which the conceptual enlargement of history demands. For it is not the sources which determine the approach, but the approach which determines the sources.

Of course, this type of argument must not be pressed too far. To the documentary demands of certain contemporary social sciences history can only answer with irreparable gaps. It is difficult to see what substitutions or extrapolations could ever fill in the columns of an input-output table for the French economy in the time of Henry IV, not to mention periods even more distant. But all this means really is that, conceptually, history is not reducible to political economy. The problem of sources, for the historian, lies not so much in absolute lacunae as in series which are incomplete, and this not only because of the difficulties of inter- and extrapolation, but because of the chronological illusions they may lead to.

Take the classic example of popular revolts in France at the beginning of the seventeenth century. Because of the great abundance of administrative documents relating to the subject at that time, this period has become the best-known chronological sector in the history of peasant risings between the end of the Middle Ages and the French Revolution. The hazards of survival have even seen to it that a large part of these archives, the *fonds Séguier,* ended up in Leningrad, enabling Soviet historians to advance a Marxist interpretation of France's Ancien Regime. The subsequent controversy has enhanced the interest of the documents still further. But another problem arises before that of interpretation, and this concerns the presupposition common to both interpretations here: that is, that there really was, during the period when the absolutist state was coming into being and there was probably a rapid increase in taxation, a special chronological concentration of that classic phenomenon in French history, the "jacquerie." The existence of such a concentration could only be definitely established by the study of a long homogeneous series and comparison between this section of it and those before and after. But for several reasons such a series cannot be constructed; in the first place because there is no unique and homogeneous source for such revolts over a long period. Moreover, there is every reason to believe that the survival of such a collection as the *fonds Séguier* in Leningrad, a collection especially rich in this respect, but limited to the papers of one family and thus subject to the hazards and possible distortions of individuals' careers, falsifies our chronological perception of the subject. In any case, a jacquerie is a story without direct sources, a rising of illiterates. We can glimpse it today through the medium of administrative or legal archives, but by this very fact, as Charles Tilly has remarked, every revolt which escapes repression escapes history. The relative richness of our sources during a given period may be a sign of changes which are institutional (reinforcement of the apparatus of repression) or purely individual (special vigilance on the part of a particular official), rather than of any unusual frequency in the phenomenon itself. The difference between the number of peasant risings under Henry II and under Louis XIII may reflect first and foremost the progress of monarchical centralization.

Therefore, in handling serial sources the historian is forced to think carefully about the influence that the way they were constituted may have on their quantitative application. I think we may distinguish between such sources as follows, in order of increasing complexity in their conversion into series.

(1) Structurally numerical sources, grouped together as such and used by the historian to answer questions directly connected with their original field of investigation: for example, French parish registers for the demographic historian; prefectoral inquiries into industrial or agricultural statistics in the nineteenth century for the economic historian; the data on American presidential elections for the specialist in sociopolitical history. These sources sometimes need standardizing (as when there is a variation in local units or a modification of the classifying criterion); also, when there are gaps in the

documentary sequence, one may have to extrapolate certain elements. But in such cases both operations are carried out with the minimum of uncertainty.

(2) Sources which are structurally numerical but used by the historian substitutively, to find the answers to questions completely outside their original field of investigation. For example, the analysis of sexual behavior on the basis of parish registers, the study of economic growth through price series, the socioprofessional evolution of a population through a series relating to taxes. Here the historian encounters a double difficulty. He has to define his questions all the more meticulously because the documentary material was not assembled with them in mind, and the question is constantly before him of the relevance of such material to such questions. He usually has to reorganize the material completely in order to make it usable, and in so doing makes it more arbitrary and so more open to objection.

(3) Sources which are not structually numerical but which the historian wants to use quantitatively, by a process involving two substitutions. In such cases he has to find in his sources a univocal significance in relation to the question he is asking. He also has to be able to reorganize them in series, that is, in comparable chronological units, and this demands an even more complex process of standardization than in (2). Data of this third type, which become more and more frequent the farther one goes back into the past, can be subdivided into two classes. First, nonnumerical sources which are nevertheless serial and thus easily quantifiable, as for example modern European marriage contracts drawn up by notaries, which, according to the historian's choice, can give evidence about endogamy, social mobility, income, literacy, and so on. Secondly there are the sources which are strictly qualitative and therefore not serial, or at least particularly difficult to standardize and arrange in series, as for example the administrative and legal series referred to above, or iconographical survivals of forgotten faiths.

But whichever kind of source he is dealing with, the historian of today has to rid himself of any methodological naïveté and devote a good deal of thought to the way in which his knowledge is to be established. The computer gives him the leisure to do so by freeing him from what used to take up most of his time—the recording and card-indexing of data. But at the same time it demands from him rigorous preliminary work on the organization of series and their meaning in relation to the inquiry. Like all the social sciences, but perhaps with a slight time-lag, history is passing from the implicit to the explicit. The encoding of data presupposes their definition; their definition implies a certain number of choices and hypotheses, made all the more consciously because they have to conform to the logic of a program. And so the mask finally falls away of that historical objectivity which was supposed to lie concealed in the facts and to reveal itself at the same time as them. Henceforward the historian is bound to be aware that he has constructed his own facts, and that the objectivity of his research resides in the use of correct methods for elaborating and processing them, and in their relevance to his hypotheses.

So serial history is not only, or even primarily, a transformation of the raw material of history. It is a revolution in the historiographical consciousness.

The Historian and His Facts

The historian, working systematically on chronological series of homogeneous data, is really transforming the specific object of his knowledge—time, or rather his conception and representation of it.

(1) The so-called *histoire événementielle* is not to be defined by the preponderance it gives to political facts. Nor is it made up of a mere narrative of certain selected "events" along the time axis. First and foremost it is based on the idea that these events are unique and cannot be set out statistically, and that the unique is the material par excellence of history. That is why this kind of history paradoxically deals at one and the same time in the short term and in a finalistic ideology. Since the event, a sudden irruption of the unique and the new into the concatenation of time, cannot be compared to any antecedent, the only way of integrating it into history is to give it a teleological meaning. And as history, especially since the nineteenth century, has developed primarily as a mode of interiorizing and conceptualizing the sense of progress, the "event" usually marks some stage in the advent of a political or philosophical ideal—republic, liberty, democracy, reason, and so forth. The historian's ideological consciousness can assume very subtle forms. It may group knowledge relating to a certain period around unifying schemas not directly linked to political options or values: for example the spirit of an age, its *Weltanschauung*. But basically the same compensating mechanism is at work: in order to be intelligible the event needs a general history apart from itself and independently determined.

Hence the classic conception of historical time as a series of discontinuities described in the mode of continuity—that is, as narrative.

Serial history, on the other hand, describes continuities in the mode of discontinuity: it is a problem-history instead of a narrative one. Because it has to distinguish between the levels of historical reality, it breaks down all previous conceptions of general history, calling in question the old postulate that all the elements of a society follow a homogeneous and identical evolution. The analysis of series only has meaning if it is done on a long-term basis, so as to show short or periodic variations within trends. The series reveals a time which is no longer the mysterious occasional spurt of the event, but an evolutionary rhythm which is measurable, comparable, and doubly differential in that it can be examined within one series or as between two or more.

A wedge has thus been driven into the old carefully enclosed empire of classical historiography, and this by means of two distinct but connected operations. First, by the analytical breakdown of reality into different levels of description, serial history has opened history in general to concepts and methods imported from the more specifically constituted social sciences such as political economy, which has probably been the operative factor in the recent historical revival. Secondly, by quantitatively analyzing the different evolutionary rhythms of the different levels of reality, it has at last turned into a scientifically measurable object the dimension of human activity which is history's raison d'être—time.

(2) Now that the historian's hypothesis has shifted from the level of the philosophy of history to that of a series of data both particular and homogeneous, it usually reaps the advantage of becoming explicit and formulable. But at the same time historical reality is broken down into fragments so distinct that history's classic claim to give a universal view of things is endangered. Must the claim be abandoned?

I would say it may probably be kept as a goal on the horizon, but that if history wants to go forward it should abandon this ambition as a point of departure. Otherwise it might fall once more into the teleological illusion described above. Present-day historiography can only progress insofar as it delimits its object, defines its hypotheses, and constitutes and describes its sources as carefully as possible. This does not mean it has to restrict itself to microscopic analysis of one chronological series. It can group several series together and put forward an interpretation of a system or subsystem. But today a

comprehensive analysis of the "system of systems" is probably beyond its power.

We may take as examples demographic and economic history,
the most advanced sectors now in France and probably elsewhere.
It so happens that for the past twenty years or so the period which
in France is called "modern"—that is, the period between the end of
the Middle Ages and the beginning of the nineteenth century—has
been the subject of the largest number of studies in serial history,
both demographic and economic. So it is the one we are least
ignorant about from this point of view. French historiography,[4]
starting out from legal records and reconstructed prices, has compared these with the evolution in the number of people as shown in
demographic series. Thus there has gradually been built up the concept of an "economic Ancien Regime," based on the preponderance
of a cereal production exposed to the vagaries of meteorology, and
on the periodical purging of the system by recurrent crises. These
crises are indicated by sudden steep rises in price curves and the
collapse of those indicating size of population.

But the price series, the meanings of which can be quite varied
and ambiguous, have been supplemented by more specific indicators concerning volume of production, and by the use of series suggesting the evolution of supply and demand, itself a factor in the
evolution of prices. On the subject of production, though the tithe
records concern the same percentage of the harvest every year and
so tell us nothing absolute, they are valuable because of their relative comparability. For production we also have the proto-statistical
sources brought together by the administration of the Ancien Regime and possibly reorganized on a national scale. On the subject of
demand, in addition to general demographic records, we can also
turn to the reconstruction of the great masses of liquid money: the
treasuries of communes and seigneuries, tithes, rents, profits, wages.

The combination of many demographic and economic series has
recently enabled Professor E. Le Roy Ladurie to make a wider analysis of the old agrarian economy.[5] His book gives a sampling of data
covering the whole of the Languedoc, a long-term chronology (from
the fifteenth to the eighteenth century), and a rich and varied quantitative documentation. Thanks to the cadastral surveys, the latter
makes possible a study of rural property-owning. The fifteenth to the
eighteenth centuries are the story of a very long agrarian cycle
characterized at once by a general equilibrium and by a series of
states of disequilibrium. The general equilibrium roughly corre-

sponds to the Malthusian model—the model which Malthus discovered and made immortal at the very moment it ceased to be true, at the time of England's take-off. The economy of early rural Languedoc is dominated in the long term by the relation between agricultural production and the number of men. Society's inability to raise agrarian productivity and the absence of an unlimited reserve of cultivable land, together with the famous "monetary famine" beloved of the price historians, all presented structural obstacles to decisive growth. Though the monetary explanation loses its central role, it is integrated into a multiple and unified interpretation.

The structure of the old economy acted in the long term as an internal regulator. Nevertheless, within the system, the different variables—number of men, evolution of property, distribution of income from rents, fluctuations in productivity and prices, and so on—make it possible to distinguish separate periods in accordance with the position each variable occupies in relation to the whole, in terms of the annual rhythms and cycles of each particular curve. The complete structure thus chronologically comprises several types of combinations of series, that is, several different situations. And in fact it is through the careful examination of these successive situations, and the features they have in common or in which they differ, that the structure itself emerges. This, incidentally, may shed some light on the dispute over synchronic and diachronic which often divides anthropologists and historians, and which at present is at the heart of the evolution of the social sciences. The short- or medium-term periodic movement which constitutes an "event" on the economic plane does not necessarily clash with the theory of general equilibrium. On the contrary, an empirical description of such movements may make it possible to define the theoretical conditions of the equilibrium, the elasticity of which indicates the limits within which it operates.

(3) But the Languedoc example quoted above is a special case in that the correlation there between the different demographic and economic series is made within a comparatively homogeneous region and a limited sphere of human activity (agrarian economy). The sectional application of serial history to different areas usually leads to the analysis of regional or national disequilibria. And general, or would-be general, serial history, even when restricted to a limited geographical area, tends to lead to the analysis of disequilibria in time between the different evolutionary rhythms of different levels of human activity.

(3a) The first point is now well known, thanks to the increasing number of studies on regional economic history. The specialist is used to the idea of there being measurable differences between different countries, and between areas influenced in different degrees by the same situation or reacting in different ways to similar situations occurring at different times. There are countless examples, some of which raise problems which have become classic in European history. Such, for instance, are the recently revived question of comparative growth as between France and England in the eighteenth century;[6] the antithesis between the rise of agriculture in Catalonia in the eighteenth century and its decline in Castile, which has been shown by P. Vilar;[7] or the contrast in seventeenth-century France between the Beauvaisis revealed by Goubert,[8] poor, and seriously stricken by the middle of the century by economic and demographic recession, and the Provence described by Baehrel,[9] comparatively fortunate, or at least not affected by the turndown of expansion until appreciably later. More generally, the date of this reversal, this plunge into the "tragedy" of the seventeenth century, varies considerably according to region and to the nature of the local economy. It becomes increasingly unlikely that there is only one economic *conjoncture* obtained for both urban and rural economies.[10]

Thus serial history opens out at once into the analysis of situations either differential or simply separated from one another in time (in other words, into what might be called the geography of serial history's chronology), and into the study of structural differences which may indicate chronological discrepancies. Cycles occurring at different times in the same or different regions, but fundamentally comparable internally, only exhibit geographical variations of the same theme. Contradictory developments, on the other hand, whether within the same geographical area (for example, as between town and country), or between two different areas, may present the historian with differences in economic structure.

(3b) But history cannot be reduced just to the description and interpretation of economic activity. If it has a specific character distinguishing it from the other social sciences, this consists precisely in having no specific character, and in claiming the right to explore time in all its dimensions. It is easy to see why economics has been the primary sphere of quantitative history—because of the necessarily measurable character of its indicators; by the preciseness of the concepts it makes available; and by its theoretical approach in terms of growth, the favorite image for historical change in Western thought today. But man is not merely an economic agent. The contemporary world offers too many examples of cultural resistance to the general adoption of growth on the Western model for the historian not to mistrust the Manchester school approach to progress (or its Marxist inversion). He is bound to want to analyze the societies of the past in terms of politics and ideology as well as economics.

But even so he does not and cannot revert to the old teleological history of progress, which extrapolates into cultural life the rhythms of economic development, whether this is supposed to occur by a kind of peaceful, natural adaptation or through the necessary medium of revolution. These ideological postulates of another age are useless now; it is not by clinging to them that the historian can preserve the universality of history. The only way to do so is by setting out to list and describe by the methods of serial history the other levels of human activity besides the objective processes of economics; by starting from the hypothesis that chronological rhythms, the researcher's attitude to time, may vary according to the different levels of reality or to the particular part of the system being analyzed.

On the practical plane almost everything still remains to be done. The historian must examine what may be the indicators, quantifiable or otherwise, of what may be called a "politico-ideological" society; he must establish its documentation and what constitutes representativity and comparability from one period to another. For all this there are sources as abundant and series as homogeneous as in the field of economics or demography: they exist for popular literacy;[11] the sociology of education and religious sentiment; the absorption of ideas by elites; the manifest or latent contents of political ideologies; and so on. On the theoretical plane the main thing of course is to build up gradually the components of a comprehensive history, but first and above all to analyze the different rhythms of development at various levels of a historical complex. This is the only way to achieve two of the priorities of historiography today. These are:

(1) To revise the traditional general periodizations, which are mainly an ideological inheritance from the nineteenth century, and which presuppose precisely what is still to be demonstrated, that is, the roughly concomitant development of the most diverse components of a historical complex within a given period. Instead of

beginning from a set of periodizations, it is probably more useful to start by examining the components concerned. It is probable, for example, that while the concept of the Renaissance is relevant to many of the indicators of cultural history, it is devoid of meaning in relation to the data for agricultural productivity.

(2) The problem then is to define, within a complex of data of different kinds, which levels are developing rapidly or changing decisively, and which in the medium or long term are in a state of inertia. It is not clear, for example, that the dynamism of French history from, say, the great expansion of the eleventh–twelfth centuries is economic in character: it may be that educational, cultural (in the broad sense), and state investment (the latter through the various public offices), play a more fundamental role here than increase in the national product. Perhaps I shall be allowed to conclude on this bold hypothesis if I add that it will remain unverifiable until general history has sat at the feet of serial history.

This article was translated from the French by Barbara Bray.

REFERENCES

1. J. Marczewski, general ed., *Histoire quantitative de l'économie française,* 10 vols. to date (Paris: I.S.E.A., 1961-1968), esp. vol. I, *Histoire quantitative—buts et méthodes,* by J. Marczewski.

2. See especially *Histoire quantitative ou histoire sérielle,* Cahiers Vilfredo Pareto (Geneva, 1968).

3. Marcel Couturier, "Vers une nouvelle méthodologie mécanographique: la préparation des données," *Annales: économies, sociétés, civilisations* (July-August 1966).

4. The bibliography is too vast even to be summarized.

5. E. Le Roy Ladurie, *Les paysans du Languedoc* (Paris: Flammarion, 1969). The account I give here is a shorter version of my article "Sur quelques problèmes posés par le développement de l'histoire quantitative," *Social Sciences Information* (1968).

6. F. Crouzet, "Angleterre et France au XVIIIe siècle: essai d'analyse comparée de deux croissances économiques," *Annales: économies, sociétés, civilisations* (1966).

7. P. Vilar, *La Catalogne dans l'Espagne moderne* (Paris: S.E.V.P.E.N., 1962), esp. vol. II.

8. P. Goubert, *Beauvais et le Beauvaisis de 1600 à 1730* (Paris: Imprimerie nationale, 1960).

9. R. Baehrel, *Une croissance: la Basse-Provence rurale, fin du XVIe siècle–1789* (Paris: S.E.V.P.E.N., 1961).

10. D. Richet, "Croissance et blocage en France du XVe au XVIIIe," *Annales: économies, sociétés, civilisations* (July-August 1968).

11. M. Fleury, "Les progrès de l'instruction élémentaire de Louis XIV a Napoléon III," *Population* (1957). See also L. Stone, "Literacy and Education in England, 1640-1900," *Past and Present* (February 1968), pp. 69-139.

EMMANUEL LE ROY LADURIE AND PAUL DUMONT

Quantitative and Cartographical Exploitation of French Military Archives, 1819-1826

FRENCH MILITARY archives,[1] particularly those concerning recruitment, raise various specific problems in the context of the new trends in history. In the first place—and this is what initially aroused our interest—they show regional differences between young Frenchmen of military age from which emerge interesting contrasts between underdeveloped and more advanced parts of the country.[2] About 1820, when detailed national statistics covered only such basic sectors as demography and agricultural production, the individual records made by the *conseil de révision* (recruitment board) provide a comprehensive account, although a fairly cursory one, of every conscript. They cover his occupation, height, physical defects, literacy, ecclesiastical vocation if any; they even— though here one could go on indefinitely discussing the implications—report on his "delinquency" in the national sense, that is, his cooperativeness in the matter of conscription. If we add together all these data and compare them, by means of maps and other correlations, in terms of administrative or "ecological" units (cantons, arrondissements, departments), we arrive at statistical criteria which make it possible to determine the comparative level and quality of development in the various regions. Both level and quality can be approached through the indexes derived from the files of the recruitment boards (economic, social, professional, medical, cultural, and so on).

Approached from this point of view the recruitment archives naturally suggest the need for a corresponding anthropology. This was felt by those first in the field, the sociologists of the 1830's— d'Angeville, Dupin, and Guerry.[3] They constructed models relating the degree of civilization reached in a given region to various

62

factors revealed by the statistics of the period, which they themselves had discovered and pressed into service with pioneering ardor.
They adopted a general and systematic approach, and tried to
describe the masses and youth of France as a whole, deriving
the relevant information from "general statistics" and military
archives, respectively. For this purpose they proposed what was in
effect a physical anthropology (relating to stature and illness); a
cultural and social one (dealing with education, delinquence
against persons and property, and suicide); and also an economic
and social analysis. They never dealt with these various aspects
separately. Later Durkheim,[4] led in this direction by a particular
problem, made similar inquiries. He, like others, had been struck by
the coincidence that regions where the people were tall also tended
to have a high suicide rate. He began by making fun of the genetico-
racialist theories which said this was owing to the fact that the tall-
ish inhabitants of northern France were descendants of "big blond
Aryans" and suffered from the incurable romantic melancholy characteristic of all Germanic ethnic groups. Durkheim had little difficulty exploding this nonsense, and the positive part of his refutation contained something new and fruitful. Turning social reality
the right way up again, he implied in his demonstration that tallness
of stature and a tendency to suicide each in its own way reflected
the relatively high standard of living and civilization in the northern half of France. In this case it was not biology that determined
culture, but exactly the reverse.

This brief methodological excursion, in the course of which
Durkheim tried to bring together elements as various as the physical, mental, and socioeconomic, unfortunately ended there for the
time being for both sociology and history. There are several reasons. With Vacher de Lapouge,[5] who unfortunately had some followers in Germany, physical anthropology, in France at least, got
sidetracked into racialist byways, and for a long while the other
social sciences shrank from any rapprochement with it. On the other
hand, the influence of Marxism caused particular stress to be laid
on social and economic factors, and in our own day many of the
other variables of human activity—biological and cultural ones,
for example—have been neglected by social history, and to a certain extent by serial history as well.[6] Such omissions are understandable enough in the early days, but they should not be prolonged.
Here and there attempts have no doubt been made to find ways of
remedying this neglect, and among these may be included the study

of the recruitment archives, with their multiple approach. Their chief advantage is that they allow us to see the individual—hundreds of thousands of young individuals—at various levels (biological, professional, educational, behavioral). Each of these levels is studied both in itself and in all its correlations.

The following account is the result of a joint inquiry into the recruitment files for the French army between 1819 and 1826. It is meant mainly as an introduction to the subject, presented partly in the form of comparative maps, and is of course an essay in quantitative history.

The basic document (Archives Nationales, series F 9/150 to F 9/161) is in the form of statistical tables grouped in boxes, one for each department. In theory there is a separate set of statistics for each department for each year. Although the period covered is in fact 1816 to 1832, we have restricted ourselves, for the moment at least, to the period 1819 to 1826, as there are many lacunae before and after these two dates.[7] Each set of statistics—known in administrative language as "concise numerical accounts"—consists of four tables for the department and year in question: (1) military data about the draft, (2) height of the conscripts, (3) their occupations, (4) physical defects justifying exemption.

The first table gives figures for the number drafted, those who are dispensed from military service, those declared fit for service, those who are given exemption, absentees, and *remplaçants* (paid substitutes). Each of these groups is subdivided. The table for height puts the young men into fourteen categories, from those who are under five feet three inches to those who are over six feet four inches. The data concerning occupation is given in terms of professions directly or indirectly useful in the army (for example, tailor or shoemaker). The officials who drew up these concise numerical accounts left out entirely the large group employed in the textile trade proper: weavers and so on must, one assumes, have been entered under the heading "exercising professions other than those indicated in the preceding columns." Physical defects or diseases justifying exemption are represented by such headings as goiter, loss of fingers or teeth, scabies, ringworm, hernia, stuntedness, and so on. Mostly, but not entirely, these headings relate to the visible and external parts of the body. Sometimes however the terminology is archaic, and such descriptions as "diseases of the chest" are difficult to interpret.

After 1827 information is also given on the conscripts' elementary education: whether they are illiterate or have some skill in reading and writing. But this is after our *terminus ad quem,* so we shall limit ourselves to a few maps on this subject and go into it further at another time.

All the above-mentioned information is set out in columns in the concise summary accounts. Horizontally the tables show the various arrondissements and cantons into which each department is divided and the number of conscripts possessing the variable in question. We thus have a very detailed set of statistics reaching right down to cantonal level, and it is this which gives the material particular interest.

For the present we have restricted ourselves to the broader ecological units and maps broken down into departments. But of course this is only a provisional stage, the ultimate intention being to convert information at the cantonal level into maps and correlative tables. At the present stage of the inquiry the departmental maps help us to pose certain problems but they cannot provide us with exhaustive answers.

In the majority of cases it has been possible to base our statistics, means, percentages, and maps on the whole eight-year period, 1819-1826, or at least on six or seven years. But for a certain number of departments we have figures for only about four or five years. For the Ain and the Vendée the statistics are based on only two or three. (In the case of the Ain one wonders whether d'Angeville, deputy for the department and a great connoisseur of statistics, may not have abstracted the missing files for his own archives.)

Not surprisingly, either the prefect or the clerks working under him sometimes made mistakes in adding up the figures. Fortunately, these are easy to detect. For example, if one adds together all the categories of different professions the total should be the same as for "young men appearing on the departmental draft list." Our team has discovered several errors in this way.

Method of Calculation

For each variable (for example, shoemaker) the number of conscripts concerned is given as a percentage of a larger total. Thus:

(1) The percentages relating to height are given in terms of the total number of those measured.[8]

(2) The percentage of conscripts belonging to various profes-

sions is calculated in relation to the total given in column 32 of the table, headed "recapitulation of different professions." In theory the recruitment board registered the professions of all the young men "appearing on the departmental draft list."

(3) The conscripts exempted because of physical defects are given as a percentage of the "total number of young men examined" (column 4 of the table headed "general state of class").

(4) The percentages of conscripts replaced by (paid) *remplaçants* or (unpaid) substitutes are calculated in relation to the total number of men "finally declared fit for service" (column 14 of table "general state of class").

(5) Percentages relating to the various categories dispensed from military service as conscripts (those enrolled as volunteers, those entered for the navy, those studying for the Church, the various "elites") have been calculated as a percentage of the whole draft (column 16 of table "general state of class"). This group was in fact made up after and on the basis of the formation of the draft as a whole.

The following are examples of the methods followed in this study.

First, for the total figures in the department of the Ain, 1819-1826, we worked on only three complete years (1819, 1820, 1826). Our calculations were based on in all 9,850 men, who represent the total "strength of the class" for these three years. After the drawing of lots, 3,508 conscripts were examined, 70 of whom were eliminated and 1,972 of whom were for various reasons exempted; 1,466 were declared fit for service. The draft required of the department was 1,527, and the difference between this and the number judged fit for service is 61. This difference of 61 is accounted for by the fact that there were 31 volunteers, 26 dispensed from military service because they were studying for the Church, and 4 members of the "elite."

Some of the maps were drawn up by using several columns of the original document. The map for "woodworkers" represents the total for the columns "carpenters," "joiners," "cartwrights," "sawyers," and "boatbuilders." Of course, these groupings (we adopted the terminology used by the army authorities in 1820) are open to certain criticisms, and in any case a few decades later they would no longer be entirely valid. For example, at the end of the nineteenth century the work of a cartwright still involved using wood, as it had in 1820, but it was coming to imply working in metal as well.

In the maps we have adapted the method of M. Bertin to the needs of this particular study. France is divided into squares of 5 millimeters by 5 millimeters. The center of each square is also the center of the "point Bertin."[9] The diameter of each circle is proportional to the percentage of that particular department for the variable in question; the scale is of course different for each variable. For example, in the case of carters the percentages range from .06 per cent to 1.93 per cent; for laborers *(laboureurs)* from 7.94 per cent to 79.83 per cent. Extremely small percentages are shown by a blank; if there is no percentage at all the map shows a zero. Maximum percentages are shown by shading the whole department black, with a circle in the middle of which the radius is proportional to the percentage. This direct borrowing of M. Bertin's techniques enabled us to deal with the problem of mapping maxima and minima.[10]

Elite and Priests

We begin with two maps which put us on the track of two different geographical structures (see maps 1 and 2 at the end of the essay). We have followed the convention of including as members of the "elite" all those conscripts who are "members of the teaching profession, students at the Polytechnique or special army or naval colleges, students at establishments preparing for entry into the public service, and young men who have won outstanding distinctions."[11] It should be noted that this group includes all teachers whose qualifications correspond to current state regulations.

The map shows this elite to be fundamentally concentrated in northwest France, that is, in the part most developed and best educated[12]—in just those regions which, from the end of the seventeenth century at least, are known to have had more schools and a higher degree of literacy than the less developed areas of the west, the center, and the south.[13] Several small islands of elite can be seen, however, in some departments of the center (Puy-de-Dôme) and the southwest (the Hautes-Pyrénées, and especially the Basses-Pyrénées).

The map showing the distribution of ecclesiastical students foreshadows those drawn up by Canon Boulard on religious practice in France in the twentieth century.[14] The map of clerical France—or of clerical vocation—arrived at in the present study shows three main zones, two essential and one less marked. First come the traditionally pious areas of the Massif Armoricain: no one will be surprised to see Brittany almost highest among the priest-producing departments. No less foreseeable are the high percentages of ecclesiastical students for the southern fringes of the Massif Central, and in general for a number of poor and mountainous regions in the south: the Hautes-Pyrénées, the Massif Central, the Hautes- and Basses-Alpes, and Corsica. There are smaller but still comparatively high percentages in certain regions of the Ain, especially the Bas-Rhin, the Vosges, and the Jura, which can be related to local intensity of religious practice.

Certain methodological adjustments and distinctions need to be made in this map, however, to avoid oversimplification. There is no doubt, for example, that the Breton bishops were lavish in dispensing the certificates of ecclesiastical vocation which enabled the recipients to escape military service. But this does not mean they all went into the Church. Still, it cannot be denied that the main masses of clerical influence are truly represented on our map. It also shows, conversely, a big gap of declericalization along a diagonal running from Paris to the Gironde, disemboweling, so to speak, and separating the two ecclesiastically productive blocs of Armorica and the southern Massif Central. Another, less marked gap seems to emerge toward the east central regions of the Ain, Saône-et-Loire, Allier, Nièvre, and Yone.

The big declericalized strip from Paris to Bordeaux or the Charente is partly to be explained in terms of migration movements, of which more later. Another problem is that in certain regions (Brittany and the south of the Massif Central) there is a marked contrast between the variables "elite" and "ecclesiastical students." There seems to be a difference here between the traditional type of social mobility which consists in pushing a gifted child toward clerical studies, and the more modern kind which forms lay elites: at all events, the Bretons on the one hand and the Aveyronnais on the other have few elite but many future priests. But this contrast is not found everywhere by any means. The Ain and the Haut-Rhin, for example, produce both a numerous elite and a large number of ecclesiastical students. More striking still is the case of the Hautes-Pyrénées, which wins the record for the highest number both of elite (2.92 per cent) and of priests (8.26 per cent).

These two maps showing the whole of France introduce us to two different types of distribution: in the case of the elite, the classic contrast between north and south, or more precisely between the

northeast and the rest of the country; that is, between the developed
and the less developed parts. In the case of ecclesiastical students
there is a more complex kind of distribution, the interpretation of
which raises more problems than it solves.[15]

Laborers (Laboureurs)

As one would have expected, the percentages showing an overwhelming majority of agricultural workers belong to the departments of the center, the west, and the south (see map 3). The
extreme north was already affected by a certain diversification of
professional activities which reduces relatively, though not absolutely, the numbers employed in purely agricultural occupations.

Yet from this point of view the best map, even more relevant than
that showing "laborers," is the one showing "those employed in
rural occupations" (see map 4). This description covers various
purely agricultural occupations ("laborers," "those employed in
rural occupations") and others connected more or less with agriculture ("carters"). On this map the prevalence of agriculture appreciably fades only north of a line from Evreux to Haguenau.

The significance of the "laborers" map is as much semantic as
economic or socioprofessional. It includes (1) regions where the
word "laborer" has a restricted sense and applies chiefly to an important but minority group of farmers—hence, paradoxically, the
low percentage of "laborers" in areas where the social group has
been most studied, as in the Paris region;[16] and (2) regions where it
means an agricultural worker in general, because it has been mis-
translated from the langue d'oc *laurador*, or some other reason.

Of course, the whims of army and prefectoral officials and of
semantic geography result in considerable variations from one
province to another. Thus for several years the compilers of the
concise numerical accounts in the Aveyron systematically avoid
the word "laborer" and speak instead of those "rurally employed."
So the most significant map from the point of view of geographical
distribution is the comprehensive one entitled "those employed in
rural occupations," which adds together all the agricultural and
para-agricultural categories mentioned in the recruitment files.

The predominance of "those employed in rural occupations" in
departments like the Landes, Aveyron, Vendée, and the Hautes-
and Basses-Alpes is not surprising, as they are basically rural departments without diversified activities.[17]

Artisans

The map showing "workers in wood, leather, iron, and other metals" (see map 5) exhibits a geography which is both artisanal and industrial but not agricultural (though a certain number of young men included under this heading may have been both artisans and part-time farmworkers). But even from the artisanal and industrial point of view it is incomplete: it does not show the textile professions that have no specific reference to recruitment (only tailors, in the textile group, are directly useful to the army).

But the map is still significant. It shows industrial-artisanal types of activity (building and textile trades apart) clearly concentrated in the northern half of France (excluding the Massif Armoricain). The concentration is densest in the Oise, the Ardennes, and the Haute-Marne. There are, however, several lesser centers in the south (in the Loire, because of the availability of iron; in the Cantal, because of the use of leather and copper; in the Gironde, because of the availability of wood).

Lameness

Map 6 shows only small percentages in comparison with the total number of conscripts examined in each department. The minimum is 0.10 per cent (Seine); the maximum 1.32 per cent (Vendée). There is nothing surprising about the lowness of the figures, but it may be worth putting forward a hypothesis which may or may not be confirmed by finer analysis at cantonal level. It appears that lameness is more prevalent in regions where there is an overwhelming majority of young men in rural occupations. On the face of it this would seem reasonable enough: if you are a peasant it is not unlikely you may fall out of a barn or off a cart or a rick and break your leg. A certain number of these cases may also be owing to congenital dislocation of the hip, a defect common in endogamous regions such as Brittany, the Vendée, and the south of the Massif Central, all rural areas into the bargain.

Carters

Here, as in the case of "laborers," the word itself is somewhat ambiguous. It can mean agricultural workers who drive ploughs or wagons on the farm, or full-time carriers, or agricultural workers who work part-time as carriers. All kinds of combinations are possible. But a certain pattern of geographical distribution is clear (see map 7). The map brings out a concentration in the Paris region, where the volume of road transport is considerable, horses and carts numerous, roads well developed, and oats grown in quantity. The farms are large and well equipped. All these different but complementary factors increase the number of carters.

There are also blank areas. The backward regions of the Massif Central have few horses and roads which are inadequate or even nonexistent. In mountainous parts like this, transport is by packhorse or mule as often as by cart or coach.

It is worth raising a last and purely methodological point concerning carters. Some regions present a high density which can only be explained by military semantics. An example is the department of the Cotentin, where the recruiting authorities seem to have included many conscripts as carters just because they were capable of driving, so that the category is unnaturally inflated by the inclusion of ordinary agricultural workers.

Cartwrights

From the point of view of classification, map 8 is less ambiguous than the one for carters, as a cartwright was by definition professionally qualified to make or repair carts, coaches, agricultural implements, and so on. But there is an ambiguity, as mentioned above, in the fact that a cartwright, although considered by the army authorities as a worker in wood, was probably in some cases a specialist in iron as well. With this reservation, the map shows several points clearly enough. Cartwrights are particularly numerous in a large area in the northeast, that is, where roads are developed and horses widely used. There is a minor concentration in the Aquitaine basin.

Harnessmakers and Saddlers

Here the distribution is fairly similar to that for cartwrights, which is not surprising as far as the northeast of France is concerned (see map 9). The comparative scarcity of harnessmakers in central, southern, and western France is no doubt owing to the fact that saddles and carts were not in such common use there. Curious variations occur, however, within the Aquitaine basin, which has a comparatively large number of cartwrights but comparatively few harnessmakers and saddlers. The documents do not yet enable us to say why.

Shoemakers

There is an interesting comparison here (see map 10) with the previous map, which also concerns workers in leather. Shoemakers tend to be concentrated on the one hand in the extreme northeast (Ardennes, Alsace, Doubs), and on the other hand, though less densely, in the south. There is of course a big concentration in the Cantal, which specialized in shoemaking. There are relatively few shoemakers in western France, where people wore sabots.

The map showing "leatherworkers" (see map 11), which groups together all the relevant categories, does not add much to the information already given by the map for "shoemakers," as these far outnumber all other workers in leather and hides.[18]

Tailors

Here the regional grouping is somewhat various (see map 12). On the one hand, as in the case of shoemakers, there is a major concentration in the extreme northeast. Tailors are also numerous in the southwest. Recent traditions appear to confirm this pattern. Until quite recently the village tailor was a widespread, important, and popular figure in the department of the Gers. Specialists in this region, such as P. Wolff and Pierre Féral,[19] have stressed the importance of clothes as a form of conspicuous consumption in the civilization of Aquitaine in the old days. (There are certain parallels here with Spain which might be considered.)

Brittany, which in general has few artisans, produces a large number of tailors, a fact confirmed by historical and ethnographical evidence. A study of Plouzevet has revealed the sociological and numerical importance of tailors in Breton civilization in the nineteenth century, when they acted both as promoters of regional costume and conveyors of new political ideas.[20]

Wood

With tailors and shoemakers we left our north-south distribution a long way behind, but with woodworkers we make a partial return to it (see map 13). This map was made by adding together several categories of workers in wood: joiners, sawyers, carpenters, cartwrights, boatbuilders, and "other woodworkers." Generally speaking, as one might expect, working in wood was one of the basic activities. In certain areas (Gironde, Ain) as many as 10 per cent of the conscripts come into this category. The map shows a big northern concentration extending unevenly from the Haute-Marne in the east to the Indre-et-Loire and the Sarthe in the west. A minor area stands out in the Gironde around Bordeaux, probably because of certain local industries such as caskmaking. Some areas, such as Brittany and the departments in the south of the Massif Central, have few woodworkers or even none at all. This could of course be taken as a sign of underdevelopment, but it should not be forgotten, in the case of Brittany for example, that in many areas the peasants often practice do-it-yourself carpentry.

Metalworkers

The maps showing workers in iron and other metals includes locksmiths, blacksmiths, makers of edge-tools, cutlers, gunsmiths, farriers, and other metalworkers (see maps 14, 15, 16). So the group includes both genuine industrial workers in enterprises of some size and village artisans. The maps indicate on the one hand departments where metalworking is relatively developed or industrial (Ardennes, Haute-Marne, Loire—and, surprisingly, Cantal, probably because of the copperworkers), and, on the other, departments which are less industrial but which differ from other parts of France in having a fairly large number of farriers and other artisans working in metal. This indicates a certain diversification of activity and a higher degree of development than in departments with lower percentages.

Rentiers

Somewhat paradoxically, the map showing young men of independent means (see map 17) exhibits the largest concentrations in the west of France and above all in the south in the broad sense of the term—the Vendée, Burgundy, the Aquitaine basin, the south of the Massif Central. But this does not necessarily reflect a greater wealth per capita than in other regions. In these southern areas small landowners and especially owners of moderate-sized properties, who in more prosaic parts of the country would have called themselves "laborers" or "rural workers," tend to emphasize the fact that theoretically they are of independent means. This emerges particularly clearly in Corsica, a poor department with a backward outlook where manual work comes very low in the scale of values and prestige. Many young Corsicans who are probably the sons of quite poor small landowners declare proudly that they live on their income. This attitude seems characteristic of those southern regions generally less economically developed than those of the north and northeast. North of a line from Caen to Besançon even quite well-off conscripts are more likely to describe themselves as having a definite occupation (for example, "laborer") than as landowners or persons of independent means. The northern attitude is more modern and in conformity with the professional outlook in regions which are active and expanding.

Absentees

The map showing absentees (see map 18) can be taken as illustration of a certain form of resistance to military service. Absentees are the young men who have neither presented themselves before the recruitment board nor bothered to arrange for anyone else to appear for them. They seem to be mainly the countries of the langue d'oc, that is, south of the Loire, where, according to d'Angeville's maps, there is similar widespread resistance to taxation.

Of course, certain features of this map are influenced by the political situation. The Vendée, for example, a Catholic and royalist department which was hostile to conscription in 1793, has become very docile in this respect under the "good governments" of the Restoration. But there are also more general factors. It is relevant to wonder whether the large number of absentees in the Languedoc regions, which were inhabited by linguistic minorities, does not reflect a certain lack of integration into the nation as a whole.[21] Deserters could easily slip across the Spanish frontier. Certain departments, such as the Creuse, had a traditional reputation for being resistant to military service, and the gendarmerie were not keen on hunting for absentees in this wooded and mountainous area.

Loss of Fingers

Map 19 is juxtaposed with the one showing absentees because, as numerous texts indicate, self-inflicted mutilation was another common way of avoiding military service. Young men would cut off thumb or forefinger so as not to be able to use a gun; sometimes it was the conscript's mother who performed the operation on the chopping-block, rather than let her son be called up. Other conscripts would have teeth pulled out or filed, or say they had a stammer, and then, once they had been given exemption, come and harangue the army authorities on behalf of their friends. At all events, the map for missing fingers shows important parallels with that for absentees, especially in the Languedoc. This is especially clear in the Haute-Loire and neighboring departments. In northern France, on the other hand (the Paris region, Normandy, and the northern departments), the situation is less clear, and the many missing fingers may be either self-inflicted or the result of accidents at work.

Height

The maps showing height (see maps 20, 21, 22, 23) more than confirm the existence of two well-differentiated areas. Three maps show those who were exempted because they were too short (under five feet three inches); those who were not very tall (between five feet three inches and five feet four inches); and those who were over five feet six inches. A fourth map shows the average height for each department, calculated from the height of all the conscripts there.

All these maps show a bloc of taller men to the north of a line from St. Malo to Geneva, and a bloc of shorter men in the west, the center, and the south. Of course, this distribution may be explained by a number of purely genetic factors. But it is obvious that in certain areas it is also a reflection of poverty, sometimes extreme want, with resulting lack of physical development. This is clearly true in the case of the poorer parts of Brittany and the Massif Central.[22] In the twentieth century, as the work of M. C. Chamla has shown,[23] the rise in the standard of living was to cause a veritable revolution in the physical anthropology of French conscripts: the stature of those from the south, and particularly from the southwest, became equal to that of the traditionally tall men from the north and northeast. In other words, the low statures which emerge from the south in the 1820's are not merely owing to permanent genetic factors but also to socio-economic factors susceptible of change and improvement.[24]

Exemptions

To start by looking at this question as a whole (see map 24), the departments with most exemptions—sometimes with such incredibly high proportions as 53 per cent—generally belong to the part of France south of the Loire (for example, Corrèze, the Hautes-Pyrénées, Haute-Garonne, and the Allier). Of course these groupings may partly reflect the geography of wire-pulling and bribes. Some doctors were corrupt, and this made it possible for many young men, in the Allier for instance, to appear with faked wounds and hernias[25] which made the prefect tear his hair.[26]

General

A certain number of our maps present, in differing degrees, a contrast between a southern France which is underdeveloped, more particularist, and perhaps less integrated into the nation, and a northern (sometimes northeastern) France in which activities are more diversified and modern. In some cases the disparities in regional development may even have repercussions on physical anthropology: for reasons which are not only genetic, the average conscript from northeast France in the period in question is taller than those from the center, south, and west. Among the maps which show this northern concentration are those relating to the elite, transport (harnessmakers, saddlers, carters, cartwrights), nonagricultural activities, and tallness. Those showing concentration in the south include the maps for laborers (localized mainly in the south and west), those employed in rural occupations, the lame, those of low stature, and (though this reflects semantics and mental attitudes rather than social realities) young men of independent means. The map showing absentees also illustrates in its own fashion the particularism of the south.

All this seems to show a marked geographical variation: the various and apparently heterogeneous factors linked to development and modernization are predominantly localized in the north of France. (Similar distributions are found in the geography of elementary education.) Sociologists of the first half of the twentieth century, such as d'Angeville and Baron Dupin, were quite well aware of these cultural contrasts. They drew a line of demarcation between the developed and less developed areas which they called the St. Malo-Geneva line. As our maps show, this line is overschematic, but the existence of north/south (or north/west, center, and south) contrasts is undeniable. Some variables, however, cannot be reduced to this simplification. The map for ecclesiastical students shows two blocs of traditionalism—one the Massif Armoricain, the other the south of the Massif Central, and the mountainous areas of southern France in general. But there is a third and much less marked clerical bloc right in the middle of a region which is comparatively developed technically —that is, in the east (Jura, Haute-Marne, Alsace, Lorraine). Moreover an area of anticlerical modernization, characterized by a low number of ecclesiastical vocations, emerges in the economically underdeveloped regions of the center and the southwest, about an axis running roughly from the Paris region to the Gironde.[27]

Another very important professional category, that of the masons and stonecutters (see map 25), shows an entirely unique distribution which corresponds to well-known data on the migration of masons (often called *limousins* because many used to come from the region of Limoges) to the capital. Masons and stonecutters seem to be specially concentrated in areas stretching from the Paris region through the Indre, Indre-et-Loire, and Eure-et-Loir, to the Creuse and Haute-Vienne. These migrations were sometimes seasonal and sometimes involved several journeys there and back. They could therefore spread cultural influences originating in Paris (see, for a later period, the memoirs of Martin Nadaud, a mason from the Creuse[28]). This radiation from the capital was not necessarily favorable to the Church. At all events, there is a striking parallel, which may or may not be fortuitous, between the regions where there are many young men who are masons and the regions where there are few young men training to be priests.

The map of ecclesiastical students shows two extremely traditionalist areas in the Massif Central and the Massif Armoricain. Other signs of archaism can also be detected: for example, the fact that these same regions produce very few makers of edge-tools, blacksmiths, and farriers, indicates a certain lack of rural crafts and even, probably, a scarcity of metal agricultural implements. Another shortage characteristic of these areas occurs in the category of professional "writers": clerks, bookkeepers, sometimes public letter-writers who would compose love letters and other necessary correspondence for the illiterate.

In addition to these patterns of contrasting degrees of development (north or northeast/rest of France), and the patterns showing extreme backwardness (Brittany and the south of the Massif Central), there are other geographical distributions which involve fewer variables and are often completely predictable. For example, the map for boatmen and watermen (see map 26) shows them concentrated near the coast and to a lesser degree in the river basins (Loire, Rhone, Garonne, Rhin). Similarly, the conscripts who are set down as sailors live, naturally enough, by the sea (see map 27). Nevertheless a huge proportion of these categories occurs in the Armorican peninsula. In Finistère, more than 15 per cent of the draftees are naval conscripts and more than 10 per cent are boatmen. At Ouessant, the four conscripts who are called up every year are all drafted to the navy. Brittany and Cotentin have many more naval conscripts than other maritime departments, such as the Landes, Calvados, and Bas-Languedoc. But Brittany's outlet to the sea did not cure the backwardness it suffered from at this time.

The maps for "volunteers" and *remplaçants* (see maps 28 and 29) complement each other in certain ways. There are many volunteers in the poor and mountainous departments of the Hautes- and Basses-Pyrénées; while in the rich, urbanized, vine-growing department of the Gironde many of the conscripts supply *remplaçants*. These distributions reveal a definite trade.[29] The demand occurs in the Bordeaux region; the supply is found in the mountains. But taking the country as a whole the maps showing volunteers and *remplaçants* do not show the spacial complementarities one might expect—that is, a rich France of those who provide themselves with *remplaçants* contrasted with a poor France of the volunteers. The fact is that volunteers are particularly numerous on the northern and eastern frontiers and the Mediterranean and Pyrenean borders. The concentration in the northeast frontier area conforms to the traditional picture of "our valiant peoples in the east." A more concrete factor is that men from these parts tend to be tall, so that when they volunteer they are liable to be snapped up by recruiting officers for the show they will make on parade.[30] The central departments and Brittany, where "the physical type is poor," are a less successful breeding ground than the northeast, where according to our sources "the physical type is excellent." The proximity of the frontier may also be a factor. Barracks are numerous on the borders, and parades frequent. Young men can see the attractions of a career in the army, whereas these sociocultural factors are less active in central departments where barracks are uncommon. One may also ask oneself whether the concentration of volunteers along the frontiers did not create a market and stimulate the practice of *remplacement* in the same areas. Nevertheless, the geographical distribution of those who supplied themselves with *remplaçants* still brings out quite clearly the existence of certain specific zones of poverty, as in the center and the Pyrenean areas, where there are relatively few families with enough money to provide their son with a *remplaçant*.

The map showing substitutions (see map 30) reveals certain likenesses to those for volunteers and *remplacés*. The sort of relationship implied in one young man's offering himself as a substitute for another is interesting but unexplored. The fact that many of the substitutions took place in the Bas-Rhône, Jura, and Haut-Rhine areas offers intriguing matter for speculation on the ethnography of nineteenth-century France.

I have kept till last certain fascinating but enigmatic maps relating to health. The map showing goiters (see map 31) brings out factors already well known: occurrences are in mountainous areas, like the Alps, where the water has iodine deficiency, and poor areas, particularly those far from the coast, where less fish is eaten than in western France. Brittany, where a lot of fish is eaten, has very few conscripts with goiter, though it has distressingly high percentages of other physical defects.

The maps of scrofulous and chest diseases (see maps 32, 33, 34) give an idea—approximate, naturally—of the geography of tubercular affections in the early nineteenth century (scrofula, like pulmonary tuberculosis, is caused by Koch's bacillus). Apart from the clear case of the tuberculosis area around Marseilles, which can be explained in terms of urban poverty, it is difficult to determine the underlying causes of this distribution. The map remains an open subject for a historical study in epidemics, urbanization, and poverty.

The map for missing teeth (see map 35) probably incorporates many different factors: lack of fluorine in drinking water; in Normandy, cider-drinking; in certain cases, as under other headings above, self-inflicted loss.

Skin diseases (see map 36) theoretically include ringworm, scabies, leprosy, and "other skin diseases." (There are four headings in all.) In fact, most of the conscripts with skin diseases, true or false, are entered under the headings "ringworm" or "other skin diseases." Scabies is rare, and leprosy, of course, even rarer —in Paris, fifteen cases of leprosy in eight years.

In these circumstances the map for skin diseases is somewhat difficult to interpret. D'Angeville, who was interested in the problem, thought the fundamental factor was cleanliness, and on the basis of a map similar to ours made a bold distinction between regions where conscripts did, and regions where they did not, perform adequate ablutions. Needless to say, this is a mere hypothesis which may turn out to be partly or even largely false. Moreover, skin diseases are comparatively easy to simulate. Many texts describe how the appearance of ringworm may be produced by applying plasters to the scalp, and so on.

Curiously enough, the map for hernias (see map 37) shows two large blanks for the most backward regions, Brittany and the Massif Central. Conversely, Seine-Maritime and Bouches-du-Rhône have a lot of conscripts with ruptures. It is tempting to draw a parallel here with the heavy work in which some of them may have been employed in ports such as Rouen and Marseilles. The relative absence of hernias in extremely backward areas like Brittany and the Massif Central may perhaps be explained by the low percentages employed there in strenuous professions involving working in wood, iron, or stone. But in fact all this is still a matter of unverified hypothesis. Hernia is one of the most frequently simulated defects and many must have gotten away with the deception. The texts speak of dozens of cases of simulated hernia ("insufflated through the scrotum," and so on). In some instances the cases reported may reflect a real medical geography, but in others they may belong to the category of jests and japes, or, as the prefects more loftily put it, "self-inflicted mutilations and hoaxes."[31]

So the main patterns revealed by these maps (see also maps 38-42 on literacy) are the contrast between development and underdevelopment (northeast/east, center, and south) and, within this fundamental pattern, zones of extreme traditionalism such as Brittany and the Massif Central. There are other less important patterns, such as the influence of frontiers and the sea. Our research, when extended down to cantonal level, may make it possible to throw light on a number of questions raised by an inquiry which at this stage naturally raises more problems than it resolves.

Among these questions are certain problems of method which it may be worth considering by way of conclusion. The classical technique of the historian faced with a document of any kind is to begin by considering it critically. The next stage is to force it to disgorge its meaning, first by extracting all its inherent significance, then by juxtaposing it with other sources which confirm or contradict it. But in this case the documentation is far too extensive to be subjected to exhaustive criticism before having its content extracted. It consists of some hundreds of thousands of pieces of evidence derived from the adding together of three thousand cantons and over two million individual examinations. In fact the cart had to be put before the horse and the usual critical procedure had to be reversed. We began by assuming what we think is undeniable, namely that the "concise numerical accounts" possess a certain historiographic value. So as a first stage we started to apply the material, first by deriving from it the series of maps which is the subject of the present essay. The internal criticism so justly beloved of traditional historiography was thus made possible; it sprang spontaneously from analysis and comparison of the maps. It was evident from the outset that certain variables, and certain maps, had little significance or interest, either from a national or from a departmental point of view. Examples are the categories "those employed in other rural occupations" and "epilepsy," which exhibit no useful cartographical pattern. The map showing "carters" is of no use in the special case of the Cotentin. But most of the other maps do refer to concrete facts which can be checked by reference to other evidence, as in the cases of literacy and ecclesiastical students. Of a third group of maps it could be said they are semantic rather than realistic. Examples are the ones showing "laborers" or "young men of independent means," which refer not to a genuine social or professional situation but, in the first case, to a word which varies in connotation from one part of the country to another, and, second, to the lofty ideas nourished by certain conscripts themselves.

All this brings out both the advantages and the inadequacies of our method. The main advantage is that this approach has enabled us to explore and scan comprehensively (though not yet exhaustively) the mass of data contained in the "concise numerical accounts." The inadequacy is due to the obvious fact that the subdivision into departments gives a net with too wide a mesh. We are at present completing a set of maps drawn up at the level of cantons, which will make possible more accurate differentiations and distinguish urban cantons from rural ones. Another drawback is that although the comparison of maps as practiced so far is a convenient and effective method of analysis, it is limited and needs to be supplemented by rigorous calculation of the correlations between variables. This, however, cannot be adequately done until we have finely calibrated data at the cantonal level.[32] We shall present these calculations in a second phase of this inquiry.

A last objection is that our maps are open to the serious and well-known accusation of subscribing to the "ecological fallacy."[33] The comparisons we have based on the maps do not really rest on the most certain interconnections between variables—those which are established as fundamentally as possible, at the level of the individuals themselves. Ours start off from statistical groups which necessarily smother information by treating the conscripts in terms of "ecological" administrative divisions.[34] We are well aware of this objection, and so in another article have made a detailed prosopographic study based on individual dossiers also taken from the military archives.[35] The two approaches, ecological and individual, thus complement each other.

Apart from these considerations of method, and whatever the later developments of this inquiry may produce, it is still true to say that the image or series of images proposed on the basis of a few dozen variables relating to the conscripts of 1819 to 1826 has a definite significance outside itself. It gives a concrete representation, a "local habitation and a name," to a nation which is still a traditional one, with its masses of rustics and small craftsmen, its problems of health, unequal regional development, and crass ignorance. In spite of the vast political and social changes which had taken place thirty years earlier, the young men of the reign of Louis XVIII are still scarcely emerging from the *Ancien Régime* which however they never knew. What can be glimpsed through these maps of the 1820's, still surviving at the fundamental levels of geography and commonalty, is the peasant and popular France of a backward eighteenth century resisting its own demise.

This article was translated from the French by Barbara Bray.

REFERENCES

1. See A. Corvisier, *L'armée française de la fin du XVIIe siècle au ministére de Choiseul* (Paris: Presses Universitaires de France, 1964).

2. A. D. d'Angeville, *Essai statistique sur la population française* (Bourg-en-Bresse, 1837, republished, The Hague: Mouton, 1969), with an introduction by E. Le Roy Ladurie.

3. C. Dupin, *Forces productives et commerciales de la France* (Paris: Bachelier, 1827); A. Guerry, *Essai sur la statistique morale de la France* (Paris: Chez Crochard, 1833).

4. Emile Durkheim, *Suicide* (New York: The Free Press, 1968), pp. 90-93 and n. 8.

5. See, for example, his articles in the *Bulletin* of the Geographical Society of the Hérault, 1894 and 1898.

6. There are happy exceptions. See Fleury and Valmary in *Population* (1957).

7. The boxes also contain other documents, including prefectoral reports and administrative correspondence. But as this article aims chiefly at presenting an essay in quantitative history, we shall deal only with the statistical tables.

8. That is, the total as calculated for the present study, arrived at by adding together columns 3 to 16 inclusive of the table giving height.

9. Jacques Bertin, *Sémiologie graphique* (Paris: Gauthier-Villars, 1968).

10. A good example of the way this method deals with maximum values can be seen on the "masons" map, for the Creuse.

11. See article 659 of the *Manuel de recrutement*, 2d ed. (Paris: Imprimerie royale, June 1825).

12. See d'Angeville, *Essai statistique*.

13. See Fleury, *Population* (1957), p. 57.

14. See his map in Georges Duby and Robert Mandrou, *Histoire de la civilisation française* (Paris: A. Colin, 1958), pp. 360-361.

15. The data for ecclesiastical students refer mainly to Catholics. Protestant students exert some influence, a very small one, on the percentages for such departments as the Gard, Haut-Rhin, Bas-Rhin, and Charente-inférieure.

16. M. Vénard, *Bourgeois et paysans au XVIIe siècle* (Paris: S.E.V.P.E.N., 1957).

17. We leave aside the problem of *terrassiers* (literally diggers; "navvies") who must, in certain departments, such as the Aude, have been agricultural workers. We shall return to this in a later study.

18. For example, in the Ardèche for the period 1819-1826 there are 2 harness-makers, 3 saddlers, 107 shoemakers, and 6 "other leatherworkers."

19. Philippe Wolff, *Commerce et marchands de Toulouse* (Paris: Plon, 1954); Pierre Féral, *Approches* (Auch: Imprimerie Cocharaux, 1957).

20. Edgar Morin, *Commune en France* (Paris: Fayard, 1967).

21. Conversely the departments of the northeast show strong evidence of such integration. See, for example, the letter written by the prefect of the Ardennes on January 14, 1831 (A.N. F 9/157): "The spirit of the department of the Ardennes is too good for me to have the least fear of mischief-makers . . . or of the way in which recruiting operations will be carried out. I can assure you in advance that not only will there be no disturbance, but the Ardennes will seize this opportunity of demonstrating its patriotism."

22. On the link between low stature and the "culture of poverty" see, for example, for the Dordogne, A.N. F 9/92. The prefect writes to the minister for war on March 4, 1830, with reference to the physical decline of the population: "out of 2,556 men called up, nearly half had to be exempted, 304 because they were not tall enough and 971 because of infirmity or weak constitution . . . The main reasons for the physical deterioration in the arrondissements of Ribérac and Nontron are poor nutrition and the marshiness of the locality. The absence of roads makes communications sometimes difficult in hilly country where civilization is still so backward that many young soldiers cannot tell you their surname, and only know their parents' Christian names. [There is] urgent need for by-roads and schools. In certain communes the mayor is the only person who can read and write."

23. M. C. Chamla, "L'accroissement de la stature en France, 1880-1960," *Bulletin* of the Société d'anthropologie of Paris, 11th series (1964), pp. 261-278.

24. Changes occur even within the framework of the present documentation. See, for example, the Basses-Pyrénées (A.N. F 9/236, 8/80), year 1827, letter from the prefect to the minister: "As regards the class of 1826, the physical standard is not up to that of previous years. Nevertheless the average height is 2mm more than that for 1825." In 1828 (*ibid.*, 8/83) "the number . . . of exemptions is less than for the preceding class (628 instead of 677), and the draft consists in general of *good physical specimens:* they are healthy and strong and their average height is about 4mm more than that of the young men of 1826."

25. See F 9/152, Allier, year 1822.

26. Hautes-Pyrénées, F 9/209, Lozere, 19.1.1819, report to the minister (9/3): "Several diseases are equivocal, such as for example myopia, deafness, stomach pains, asthma and epilepsy, and can only be proved by long acquaintance with the person who claims to suffer from them."

27. The apparent lack of ecclesiastical students in the Vendée may seem surprising, but this may be owing to the fact that we possess documents relating to only two years.

28. M. Nadaud, *Les mémoires de Léonard, ancien garçon maçon* (Paris: Librairie C. Delagrave, 1912).

29. B. Schnapper, *Le remplacement militaire en France au XIXe siècle* (Bourganeuf, 1895).

30. For an aesthetic criterion of a slightly different kind see, for example, A.N. F 9/209, Lozère, 19.1.1819, report to the minister (9/3): "It seems in accordance with the laws of equity and in the interest of the government to choose only healthy men, without any infirmities which are unsightly or repulsive: and with this in mind the board rejected men with only one eye, although under the old rule only men lacking the right eye were deemed unfit for service."

31. See, for example, A.N. F 9/153 (14/4), Basses-Alpes, May 9, 1822, self-inflicted mutilations by application of blisters of nitric acid or other caustics; F 9/229 (9/76), Oise, December 4, 1828, self-inflicted mutilations relating to teeth. A.N. F 9/229 (9/54), March 1823, Oise, refers to simulated or self-inflicted mutilations such as amputation of the right forefinger, insufflated scrotum, and simulated ringworm; see also Oise, *ibid.*, 30.1.1824 (9/89); 9.6.1825; 19.10.1827 (9/74). Similarly F 9/238 A (1/129), year 1825, Hautes-Pyrénées, shows the prefect writing to the minister for war about a "doubtful hernia" in the canton of Castelnau. The inhabitants of the district were genuinely of poor physique: this part of the department has the most cases of goiter and cretinism. For the Hautes-Pyrénées again, see A.N. F 9/238 A, year 1823 (1/114): "The number of young men called up was almost a third larger than the class of 1822. The board was able to choose some fine men among whom some might go into the special services . . . Simulated wounds and induced hernias were almost entirely absent (only one case of each)." And *ibid.* (1/127), year 1825, Bagnères: "one insufflated hernia, one self-inflicted defect (top joint of right forefinger missing)."

32. In France a canton is an administrative unit larger than a commune and smaller than an arrondissement or a department.

33. W. S. Robinson, "Ecological Correlations and the Behavior of Individuals," *American Sociological Review,* 15 (1950), 351-357.

34. The original material creates these divisions by dividing conscripts according to canton, arrondissement, and department.

35. E. Le Roy Ladurie, N. Bernageau, Y. Pasquet, "Le conscrit et l'ordinateur: Perspectives de recherche sur les archives militaire du XIXe siècle français," *Studi storici,* X (April-June 1969).

ELITE

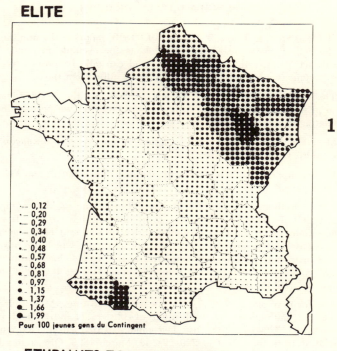

- 0,12
- 0,20
- 0,29
- 0,34
- 0,40
- 0,48
- 0,57
- 0,68
- 0,81
- 0,97
- 1,15
- 1,37
- 1,66
- 1,99

Pour 100 jeunes gens du Contingent

1

ETUDIANTS ECCLESIASTIQUES

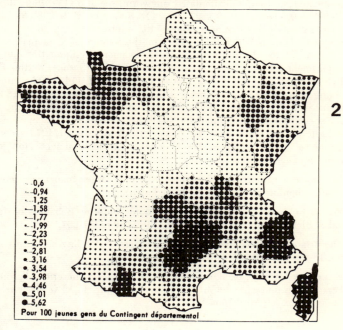

- 0,6
- 0,94
- 1,25
- 1,58
- 1,77
- 1,99
- 2,23
- 2,51
- 2,81
- 3,16
- 3,54
- 3,98
- 4,46
- 5,01
- 5,62

Pour 100 jeunes gens du Contingent départemental

2

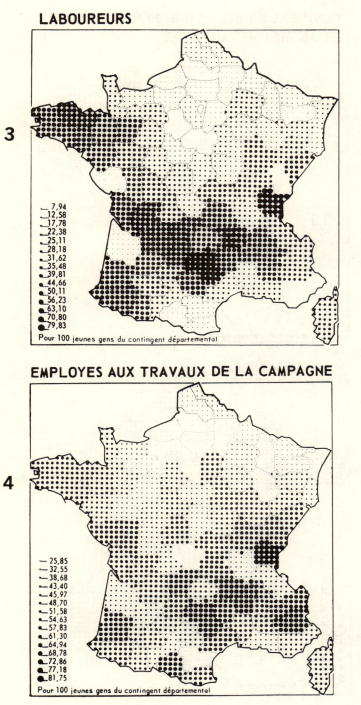

LABOUREURS

3

— 7,94
— 12,58
— 17,78
— 22,38
— 25,11
— 28,18
— 31,62
— 35,48
— 39,81
— 44,66
— 50,11
— 56,23
— 63,10
— 70,80
— 79,83

Pour 100 jeunes gens du contingent départemental

EMPLOYES AUX TRAVAUX DE LA CAMPAGNE

4

— 25,85
— 32,55
— 38,68
— 43,40
— 45,97
— 48,70
— 51,58
— 54,63
— 57,83
— 61,30
— 64,94
— 68,78
— 72,86
— 77,18
— 81,75

Pour 100 jeunes gens du contingent départemental

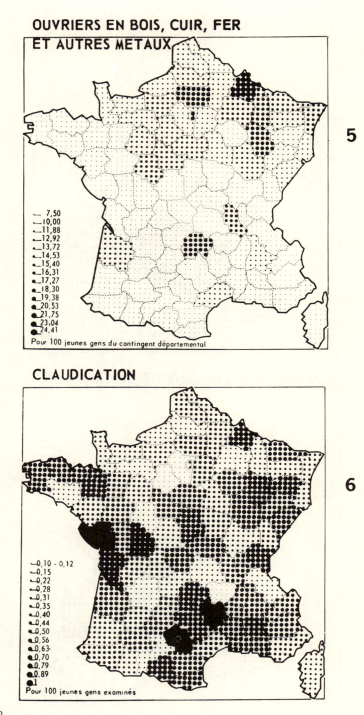

OUVRIERS EN BOIS, CUIR, FER ET AUTRES MÉTAUX

5

— 7,50
—10,00
—11,88
—12,92
—13,72
—14,53
—15,40
—16,31
—17,27
—18,30
—19,38
—20,53
—21,75
—23,04
—24,41

Pour 100 jeunes gens du contingent départemental

CLAUDICATION

6

—0,10 - 0,12
—0,15
—0,22
—0,28
—0,31
—0,35
—0,40
—0,44
—0,50
—0,56
—0,63
—0,70
—0,79
—0,89
—1

Pour 100 jeunes gens examinés

CHARRETIERS

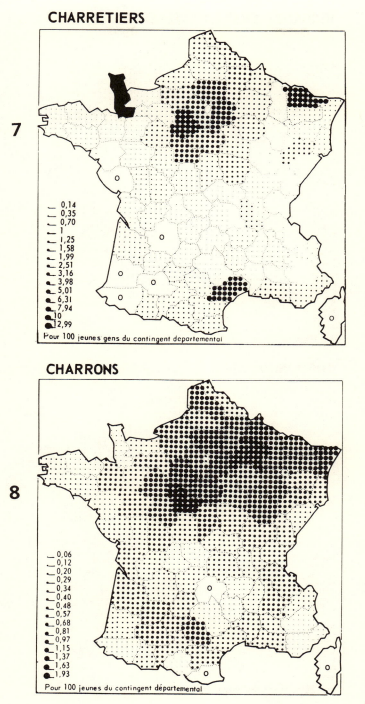

7

_ 0,14
_ 0,35
_ 0,70
_ 1
_ 1,25
_ 1,58
_ 1,99
_ 2,51
_ 3,16
_ 3,98
_ 5,01
_ 6,31
_ 7,94
_ 10
_ 12,99

Pour 100 jeunes gens du contingent départemental

CHARRONS

8

_ 0,06
_ 0,12
_ 0,20
_ 0,29
_ 0,34
_ 0,40
_ 0,48
_ 0,57
_ 0,68
_ 0,81
_ 0,97
_ 1,15
_ 1,37
_ 1,63
_ 1,93

Pour 100 jeunes du contingent départemental

89

"BOURRELIERS" ET "SELLIERS"

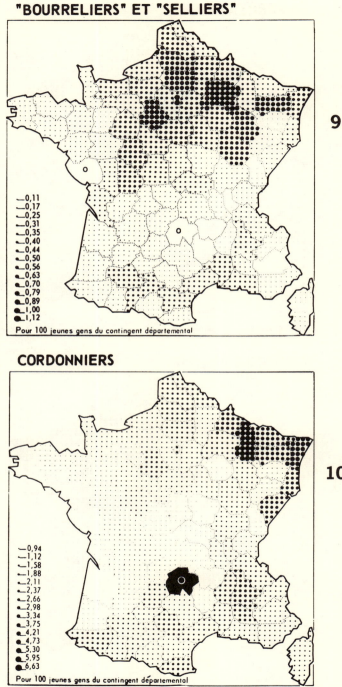

9

Legend (map 9):
— 0,11
— 0,17
— 0,25
— 0,31
— 0,35
— 0,40
— 0,44
— 0,50
— 0,56
— 0,63
— 0,70
— 0,79
— 0,89
— 1,00
— 1,12

Pour 100 jeunes gens du contingent départemental

CORDONNIERS

10

Legend (map 10):
— 0,94
— 1,12
— 1,58
— 1,88
— 2,11
— 2,37
— 2,66
— 2,98
— 3,34
— 3,75
— 4,21
— 4,73
— 5,30
— 5,95
— 6,63

Pour 100 jeunes gens du contingent départemental

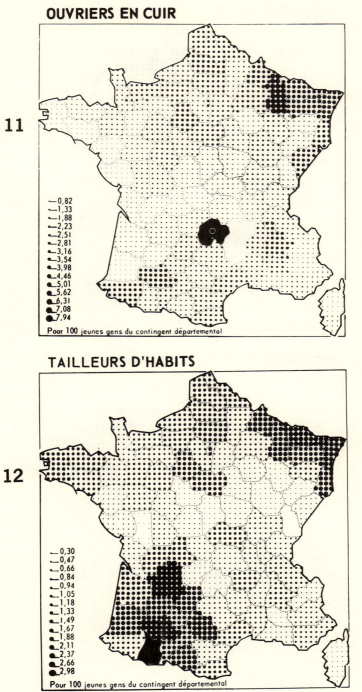

OUVRIERS EN CUIR

11

—0,82
—1,33
—1,88
—2,23
—2,51
—2,81
—3,16
—3,54
—3,98
—4,46
—5,01
—5,62
—6,31
—7,08
—7,94

Pour 100 jeunes gens du contingent départemental

TAILLEURS D'HABITS

12

—0,30
—0,47
—0,66
—0,84
—0,94
—1,05
—1,18
—1,33
—1,49
—1,67
—1,88
—2,11
—2,37
—2,66
—2,98

Pour 100 jeunes gens du contingent départemental

OUVRIERS EN BOIS

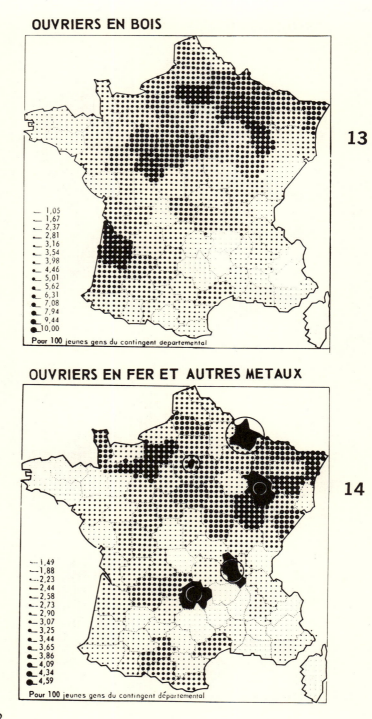

13

1,05
1,67
2,37
2,81
3,16
3,54
3,98
4,46
5,01
5,62
6,31
7,08
7,94
9,44
10,00

Pour 100 jeunes gens du contingent départemental

OUVRIERS EN FER ET AUTRES METAUX

14

1,49
1,88
2,23
2,44
2,58
2,73
2,90
3,07
3,25
3,44
3,65
3,86
4,09
4,34
4,59

Pour 100 jeunes gens du contingent départemental

92

TAILLANDIERS ET FORGERONS

15

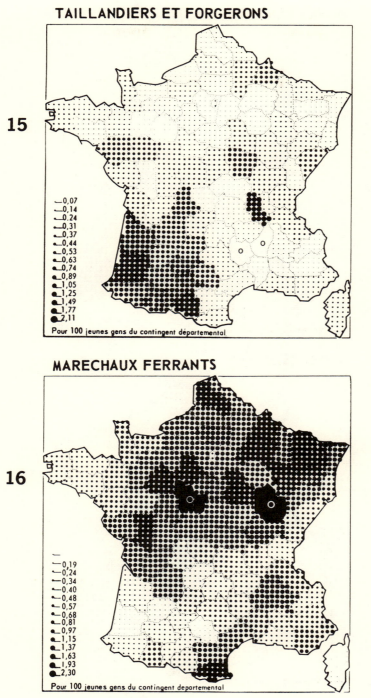

−0,07
−0,14
−0,24
−0,31
−0,37
−0,44
−0,53
−0,63
−0,74
−0,89
−1,05
−1,25
−1,49
−1,77
−2,11

Pour 100 jeunes gens du contingent départemental

MARECHAUX FERRANTS

16

−
−0,19
−0,24
−0,34
−0,40
−0,48
−0,57
−0,68
−0,81
−0,97
−1,15
−1,37
−1,63
−1,93
−2,30

Pour 100 jeunes gens du contingent départemental

JEUNES GENS...VIVANT DE LEURS REVENUS

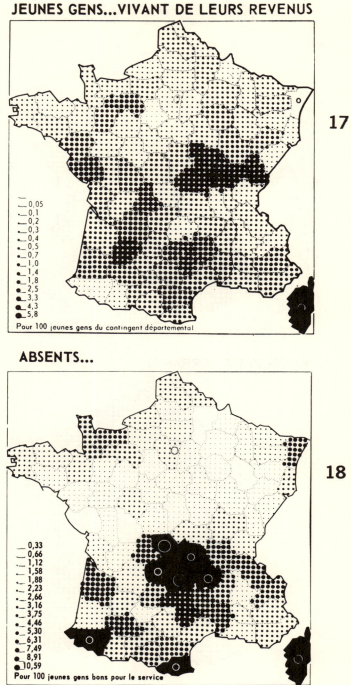

17

— 0,05
— 0,1
— 0,2
— 0,3
— 0,4
— 0,5
• 0,7
• 1,0
• 1,4
• 1,8
• 2,5
• 3,3
• 4,3
• 5,8

Pour 100 jeunes gens du contingent départemental

ABSENTS...

18

— 0,33
— 0,66
— 1,12
— 1,58
— 1,88
• 2,23
• 2,66
• 3,16
• 3,75
• 4,46
• 5,30
• 6,31
• 7,49
• 8,91
• 10,59

Pour 100 jeunes gens bons pour le service

PERTE DES DOIGTS

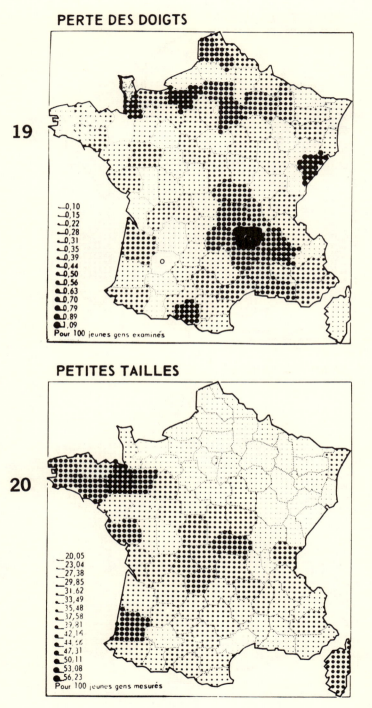

19

0,10
0,15
0,22
0,28
0,31
0,35
0,39
0,44
0,50
0,56
0,63
0,70
0,79
0,89
1,09

Pour 100 jeunes gens examinés

PETITES TAILLES

20

20,05
23,04
27,38
29,85
31,62
33,49
35,48
37,58
39,81
42,16
44,56
47,31
50,11
53,08
56,23

Pour 100 jeunes gens mesurés

95

DEFAUT DE TAILLE

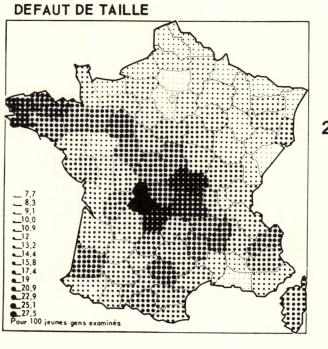

7,7
8,3
9,1
10,0
10,9
12
13,2
14,4
15,8
17,4
19
20,9
22,9
25,1
27,5

Pour 100 jeunes gens examinés

21

GRANDES TAILLES

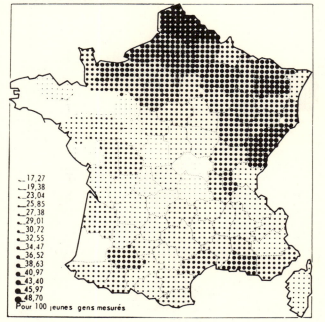

17,27
19,38
23,04
25,85
27,38
29,01
30,72
32,55
34,47
36,52
38,63
40,97
43,40
45,97
48,70

Pour 100 jeunes gens mesurés

22

MOYENNE DES TAILLES

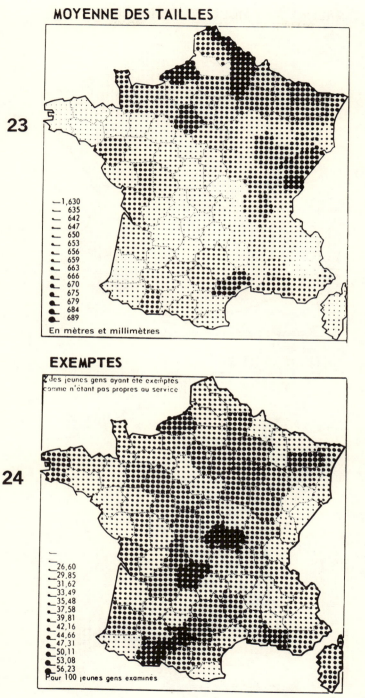

23

— 1,630
— 635
— 642
— 647
— 650
— 653
— 656
— 659
— 663
— 666
— 670
— 675
— 679
— 684
— 689

En mètres et millimètres

EXEMPTES

% des jeunes gens ayant été exemptés
comme n'étant pas propres au service

24

— 26,60
— 29,85
— 31,62
— 33,49
— 35,48
— 37,58
— 39,81
— 42,16
— 44,66
— 47,31
— 50,11
— 53,08
— 56,23

Pour 100 jeunes gens examinés

MACONS ET TAILLEURS DE PIERRE

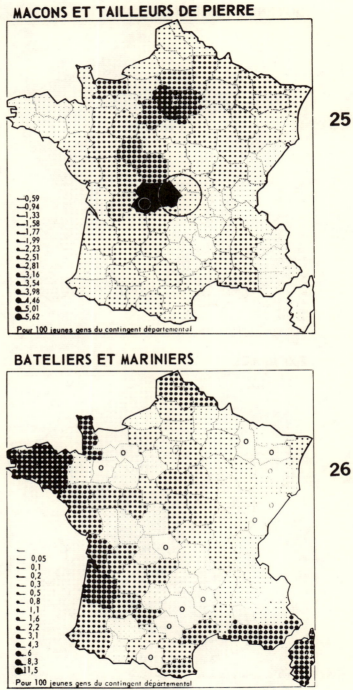

25

—0,59
—0,94
—1,33
—1,58
—1,77
—1,99
—2,23
—2,51
—2,81
—3,16
—3,54
—3,98
—4,46
—5,01
—5,62

Pour 100 jeunes gens du contingent départemental

BATELIERS ET MARINIERS

26

— 0,05
— 0,1
— 0,2
— 0,3
— 0,5
— 0,8
— 1,1
— 1,6
— 2,2
— 3,1
— 4,3
— 6
— 8,3
—11,5

Pour 100 jeunes gens du contingent départemental

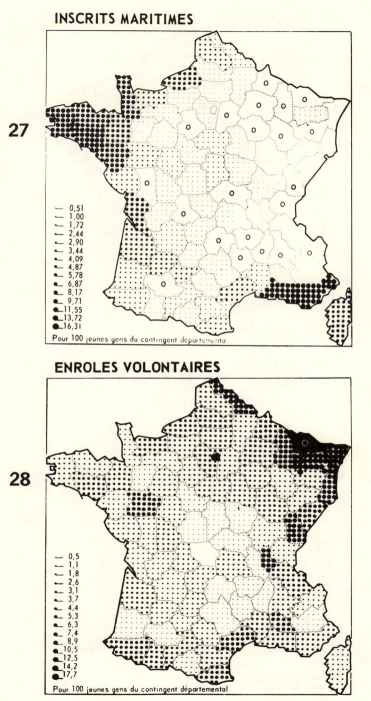

INSCRITS MARITIMES

27

— 0,51
— 1,00
— 1,72
— 2,44
— 2,90
— 3,44
— 4,09
— 4,87
— 5,78
— 6,87
— 8,17
— 9,71
— 11,55
— 13,72
— 16,31

Pour 100 jeunes gens du contingent départemental.

ENROLES VOLONTAIRES

28

— 0,5
— 1,1
— 1,8
— 2,6
— 3,1
— 3,7
— 4,4
— 5,3
— 6,3
— 7,4
— 8,9
— 10,5
— 12,5
— 14,2
— 17,7

Pour 100 jeunes gens du contingent départemental

REMPLACEMENTS

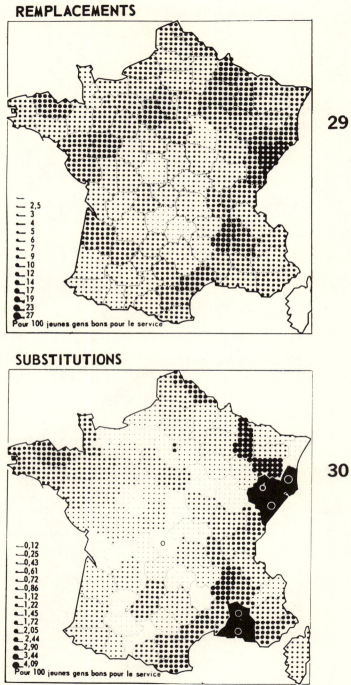

29

—— 2,5
—— 3
—— 4
—— 5
—— 6
—— 7
—— 9
—— 10
—— 12
—— 14
—— 17
—— 19
—— 23
—— 27
Pour 100 jeunes gens bons pour le service

SUBSTITUTIONS

30

—0,12
—0,25
—0,43
—0,61
—0,72
—0,86
—1,12
—1,22
—1,45
—1,72
—2,05
—2,44
—2,90
—3,44
—4,09
Pour 100 jeunes gens bons pour le service

GOITRES

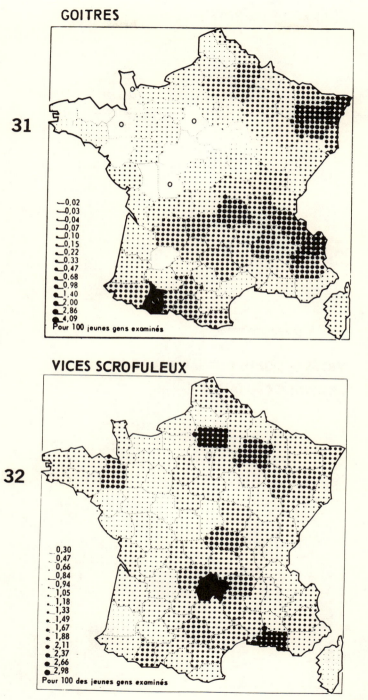

31

—0,02
—0,03
—0,04
—0,07
—0,10
—0,15
—0,22
—0,33
—0,47
—0,68
—0,98
—1,40
—2,00
—2,86
—4,09

Pour 100 jeunes gens examinés

VICES SCROFULEUX

32

0,30
0,47
0,66
0,84
0,94
1,05
1,18
1,33
1,49
1,67
1,88
2,11
2,37
2,66
2,98

Pour 100 des jeunes gens examinés

101

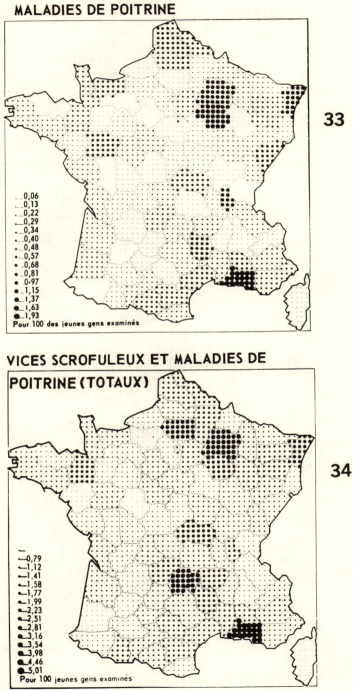

MALADIES DE POITRINE

33

- — 0,06
- — 0,13
- — 0,22
- — 0,29
- — 0,34
- . — 0,40
- . — 0,48
- . — 0,57
- . — 0,68
- ● — 0,81
- ● — 0,97
- ● — 1,15
- ● — 1,37
- ● — 1,63
- ● — 1,93

Pour 100 des jeunes gens examinés

VICES SCROFULEUX ET MALADIES DE POITRINE (TOTAUX)

34

- —
- — 0,79
- — 1,12
- — 1,41
- — 1,58
- — 1,77
- — 1,99
- ● — 2,23
- ● — 2,51
- ● — 2,81
- ● — 3,16
- ● — 3,54
- ● — 3,98
- ● — 4,46
- ● — 5,01

Pour 100 jeunes gens examinés

102

PERTE DES DENTS

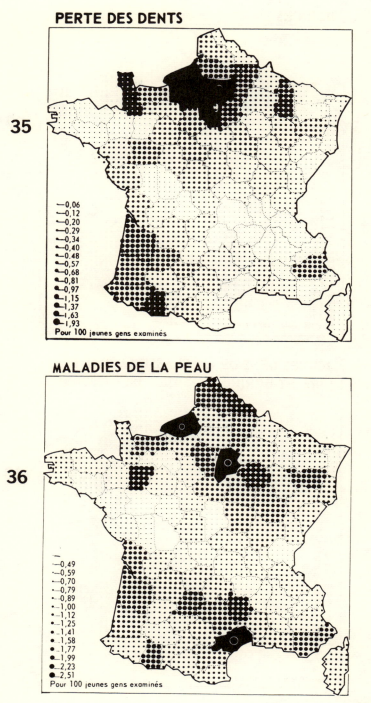

35

—0,06
—0,12
—0,20
—0,29
—0,34
—0,40
—0,48
—0,57
—0,68
—0,81
—0,97
—1,15
—1,37
—1,63
—1,93

Pour 100 jeunes gens examinés

MALADIES DE LA PEAU

36

—
—0,49
—0,59
—0,70
—0,79
—0,89
—1,00
—1,12
—1,25
—1,41
—1,58
—1,77
—1,99
—2,23
—2,51

Pour 100 jeunes gens examinés

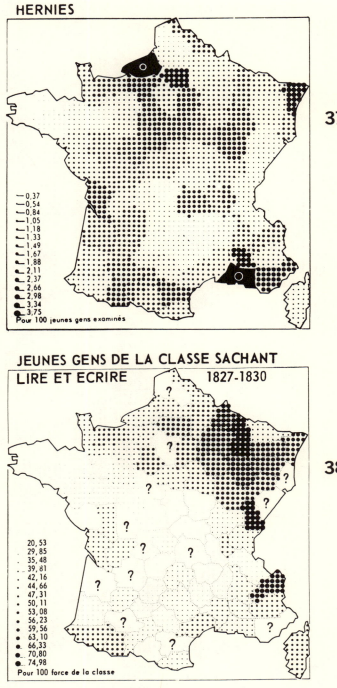

HERNIES

—0,37
—0,54
—0,84
—1,05
—1,18
—1,33
—1,49
—1,67
—1,88
—2,11
—2,37
—2,66
—2,98
—3,34
—3,75
Pour 100 jeunes gens examinés

37

JEUNES GENS DE LA CLASSE SACHANT
LIRE ET ECRIRE   1827-1830

20,53
29,85
35,48
39,81
42,16
44,66
47,31
50,11
53,08
56,23
59,56
63,10
66,33
70,80
74,98
Pour 100 force de la classe

38

104

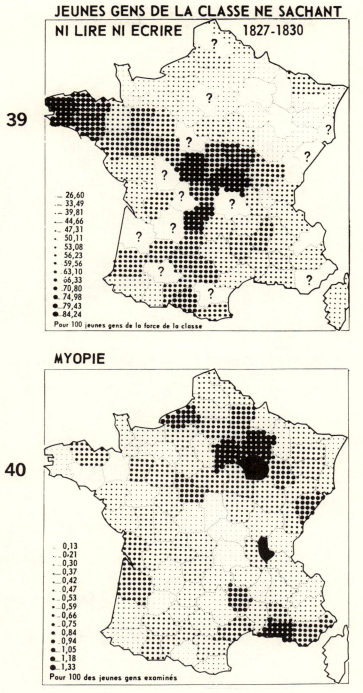

JEUNES GENS DE LA CLASSE NE SACHANT NI LIRE NI ECRIRE 1827-1830

39

- 26,60
- 33,49
- 39,81
- 44,66
- 47,31
- 50,11
- 53,08
- 56,23
- 59,56
- 63,10
- 66,33
- 70,80
- 74,98
- 79,43
- 84,24

Pour 100 jeunes gens de la force de la classe

MYOPIE

40

- 0,13
- 0,21
- 0,30
- 0,37
- 0,42
- 0,47
- 0,53
- 0,59
- 0,66
- 0,75
- 0,84
- 0,94
- 1,05
- 1,18
- 1,33

Pour 100 des jeunes gens examinés

MYOPIE ET AUTRES MALADIES DES YEUX

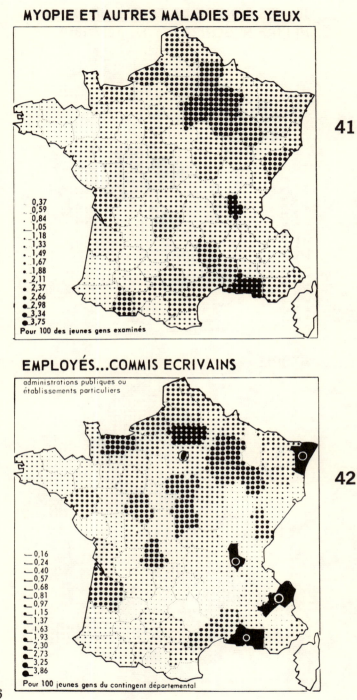

41

0,37
0,59
0,84
1,05
1,18
1,33
1,49
1,67
1,88
2,11
2,37
2,66
2,98
3,34
3,75

Pour 100 des jeunes gens examinés

EMPLOYÉS...COMMIS ECRIVAINS

administrations publiques ou
établissements particuliers

42

0,16
0,24
0,40
0,57
0,68
0,81
0,97
1,15
1,37
1,63
1,93
2,30
2,73
3,25
3,86

Pour 100 jeunes gens du contingent départemental

LAWRENCE STONE

Prosopography

Origins

IN THE last forty years collective biography (as the modern historians call it), multiple career-line analysis (as the social scientists call it), or prosopography (as the ancient historians call it) has developed into one of the most valuable and most familiar techniques of the research historian. Prosopography[1] is the investigation of the common background characteristics of a group of actors in history by means of a collective study of their lives. The method employed is to establish a universe to be studied, and then to ask a set of uniform questions—about birth and death, marriage and family, social origins and inherited economic position, place of residence, education, amount and source of personal wealth, occupation, religion, experience of office, and so on. The various types of information about the individuals in the universe are then juxtaposed and combined, and are examined for significant variables. They are tested both for internal correlations and for correlations with other forms of behavior or action.

Prosopography is used as a tool with which to attack two of the most basic problems in history. The first concerns the roots of political action: the uncovering of the deeper interests that are thought to lie beneath the rhetoric of politics; the analysis of the social and economic affiliations of political groupings; the exposure of the workings of a political machine; and the identification of those who pull the levers. The second concerns social structure and social mobility: one set of problems involves analysis of the role in society, and especially the changes in that role over time, of specific (usually elite) status groups, holders of titles, members of professional associations, officeholders, occupational groups, or economic classes; another set is concerned with the determination of the degree of social

107

mobility at certain levels by a study of the family origins, social and geographical, of recruits to a certain political status or occupational position, the significance of that position in a career, and the effect of holding that position upon the fortunes of the family; a third set struggles with the correlation of intellectual or religious movements with social, geographical, occupational, or other factors. Thus, in the eyes of its exponents, the purpose of prosopography is to make sense of political action, to help explain ideological or cultural change, to identify social reality, and to describe and analyze with precision the structure of society and the degree and the nature of the movements within it. Invented as a tool of political history, it is now being increasingly employed by the social historians.

The major contributors to the development of prosopography can be divided into two fairly distinct schools. Those of the elitist school have been concerned with small-group-dynamics, or the interaction, in terms of family, marriage, and economic ties, of a restricted number of individuals. The subjects of study have usually been power elites, such as Roman or United States senators or English M.P.'s or cabinet members, but the same process and model can be and have been applied to revolutionary leaders as well.[2] The technique employed is to make a meticulously detailed investigation into the genealogy, business interests, and political activities of the group, the relationships being displayed by means of detailed case studies, supported to only a secondary and relatively minor degree by statistical underpinnings. The purpose of such research is to demonstrate the cohesive strength of the group in question, bound together by common blood, background, education, and economic interests, to say nothing of prejudices, ideals, and ideology. When the main problem is political, it is argued that it is this web of purely social and economic ties which gave the group its unity and therefore its political force, and to a considerable extent also its political motivation, inasmuch as politics is a matter of the ins against the outs. This school has owed little or nothing to the social sciences, despite the fact that it could have learned much from them, and has been largely innocent of conscious sociological or psychological theory. Its assumptions, however, are clearly that politics is a matter of the interplay of small ruling elites and their clients rather than mass movements, and that self-interest, meaning a fierce Hobbesian competition for power and wealth and security, is what makes the world go round.[3]

The second is the more statistically-minded mass school, which deliberately draws its inspiration from the social sciences. The members of this school have mostly, but by no means entirely, concerned themselves with large numbers, about all—or indeed sometimes any—of whom in the nature of things nothing very detailed or very intimate can be known, since they are dead and therefore unavailable for an interview. The members of this school have a sense that history is determined by the movements of popular opinion rather than by the decisions of so-called "great men," or by elites, and they have been aware that human needs cannot usefully be defined exclusively in terms of power and wealth. They have necessarily been more concerned with social history than political history, and have therefore tried to ask a wider, if inevitably more superficial, set of questions than those usually posed by the members of the elitist school. They have also been far more concerned with testing the statistical correlations of the many variables than with conveying a sense of historical reality by a series of detailed case studies. Insofar as they have tried to describe the past they have tended to do so more by the construction of Weberian ideal-types than by presenting a series of concrete examples. Much of their work has been concerned with social mobility, but some of it has looked for statistically meaningful relationships between environment and ideas, and between ideas and political or religious behavior. The two schools therefore differ significantly in their subjects of study, and somewhat in their presuppositions, means, and end, but they are similar in their common interest in the group rather than in the individual or the institution.

Both the elitist and the mass schools first became clearly identifiable in the profession in the 1920's and 1930's, when a number of works appeared that had a profound effect on all subsequent development. The raw materials from which these prosopographical studies were and are constructed are mostly of three broad kinds: bare lists of names of holders of certain offices or titles, or professional or educational qualifications; family genealogies; and full biographical dictionaries, which are usually built up in part from the first two categories and in part from an infinitely wider range of sources. The collection of biographical materials of this kind had been in progress for a very long time before the first professional prosopographers appeared on the scene. To take the case of English history (although Roman history would be an equally good example),[1] throughout the late eighteenth, nineteenth, and early twentieth centuries, diligent antiquaries, clergymen, and scholars had been producing biographical information of all kinds in quite astonishing quantities. From public and private presses there poured a flood of biographical collections of every description and every quality: M.P.'s, peers, baronets, gentry, Archbishops of Canterbury, London clergy, lords chancellor, judges, sergeants at law, army officers, Catholic recusants, Huguenot refugees, Oxford and Cambridge alumni—the list is almost endless.[5]

The purpose of this outpouring—which was matched in the United States, Germany, and elsewhere—is not at all clear, since prosopography as a historical method had not been invented, and these publications were not used by professional historians except as quarries from which to dig out chunks of information about particular individuals. In terms of psychological motivation, these obsessive collectors of biographical information belong to the same category of anal-erotic males as the collectors of butterflies, postage stamps, or cigarette cards; all are by-products of the Protestant Ethic. But part of the stimulus came from local or institutional pride and affection, which took the form of a desire to record the past members of a corporation, college, profession, or sect. Part also derived from that inexhaustible passion for genealogy and ancestor-hunting which has gripped large sections of the English upper classes since the sixteenth century. With the huge expansion of the educated middle class in the nineteenth century, and with the growth of university and public libraries, there was at last a large enough market to justify the publication of these rather esoteric and unreadable volumes.

The supreme achievement of this century-long English movement for collective biography was the undertaking of the great *Dictionary of National Biography,* which is an enduring monument to the drive and dedication of the Victorians in the pursuit of information about the individual dead. When the first historical prosopographers got down to work after the First World War, they therefore found at hand a mass of biographical information already collected and in print, and merely waiting to be analyzed, collated, and used to construct an intelligible picture of society and politics.

The first historian to adopt the elitist method of prosopography to attack a major historical problem was Charles Beard, who as early as 1913 offered an explanation of the establishment of the American Federal Constitution by a close analysis of the economic and class interests of the Founding Fathers.[6] In the key chapter, "The Economic Interests of the Members of the Convention," he asked him-

self whether they represented "distinct groups whose economic interests they understood and felt in concrete, definite forms through
their own personal experience with identical property rights, or
were they working merely under the guidance of abstract principles
of political science." His conclusion was unambiguous: "The first
firm steps towards the formation of the Constitution were taken by
a small and active group of men immediately interested through
their personal possessions in the outcome of their labors," a conclusion reached through an economic biography of all those connected
with its framing. This remarkable and brilliant pioneering work
seems to have had curiously little influence on postwar developments, perhaps because of the dogmatically rigid framework of
economic determinism within which it was constructed. In his
preface of 1935 Beard attempted to deny that his attitude to economic determinism was all embracing, that he was deeply influenced
by Marxist thought, or that he was attributing sordid and self-
interested motives to the Founding Fathers. But his disclaimers are
not altogether convincing.[7] What Beard contributed to elitist
prosopography was a suspicious curiosity about the finances of a
political actor and the hypothesis that they are important. What he
missed was the role of social and kinship ties which were to bulk
so large in the later studies of Sir Lewis Namier and others. On the
other hand, Beard's work should have been familiar to Namier, who,
however much he may have been repelled by the Marxist economic
determinism, must surely have been impressed by the interpretive
power of the method.

A year later another American scholar, A. P. Newton, published a less well-known book which carried the method a little
further.[8] He carefully tracked down kinship relationships and economic connections in order to demonstrate the formation of the
Puritan opposition leadership to Charles I in the 1630's. His book
was clearly a modest forerunner of Namier, but for some reason,
perhaps because of the rather forbidding title, it never attracted
much general attention.[9]

The real breakthrough into general acceptance by the profession
did not come until the publication of Namier's *Structure of Politics
at the Accession of George III* (London, 1929), Sir Ronald Syme's
Roman Revolution (Oxford, 1939), and R. K. Merton's *Science,
Technology, and Puritanism in Seventeenth Century England*
(*Osiris*, IV, 1938). All three were able to draw on the store of biographical information which had been accumulated and published

over the previous century. Merton used the *Dictionary of National Biography* for his work, Syme was indebted to two German historians, M. Gelzer and F. Münzer,[10] and Namier could exploit 130 years of data-collection about the lives of M.P.'s. The pioneer work of the prewar German school of historiography was of considerable importance for the later development of classical—and possibly also of modern—prosopography, but its achievements have been overshadowed by the more arresting and ambitious work of Namier and Syme. Apart from Beard and Newton, the two latter were the first historians of outstanding capacity to use this kind of approach to attempt a major reinterpretation of a critical political development which had been studied ad nauseam by more conventional historians over a very long period. Both worked impressionistically through case studies and personal vignettes, which they used to build up a picture of elitist personal interests, mainly kinship groupings, business affiliations, and a complicated web of favors given and received.

The third study, by R. K. Merton, was rather different in both its objectives and its method. As befitted an American sociologist rather than a British historian, what he produced was a statistically based group biography, rather than a group portrait pieced together from a series of case studies. The problem he set himself was also different, since he was not trying to account for specific political actions but for a state of mind, and was explaining a mental set not by family ties or economic interests but by ideological affiliations: he was attempting to link a favorable attitude toward natural science with allegiance to what he loosely described as Puritanism. On the other hand, his work was similar to that of Namier and Syme in that he was examining, although at a much shallower depth of research, the behavior of an elite rather than a mass.

Both Syme and Namier, but particularly the latter, were to have an enormous influence on the next generation of scholars in their fields of specialty. Some years ago a reviewer surveyed the recent and current work of historians of eighteenth-century British politics, and from the problems they set themselves and the methods they used for resolving them, concluded that they were all members of a single corporation: "Namier, Inc."[11] Today both the case-study and the statistical methods—and especially the latter—have spread to other fields and time periods, and are being applied on an ever-widening scale to every aspect of the historical process, at every time and in every place. The mass school now has a flourishing political subbranch called psephology, or the analysis of the voting behavior of the electorate; and the elitist school has spawned a more scientific subbranch, roll-call analysis of the legislature. Both these new special fields are absorbing increasing amounts of time, money, and attention from historians and political scientists.[12]

Intellectual Roots

That these developments occurred at the same period in the writings of scholars working entirely independently (Sir Ronald Syme assures me that he had not read Namier) proves that there is more to them than mere serendipity. Prosopography would not have flourished the way it did in the 1920's and 1930's had it not been for a crisis in the historical profession, which was already discernible to the more perceptive young men of the coming generation.[13] This crisis stemmed from the near-exhaustion of the great tradition of Western historical scholarship established in the nineteenth century. Based on a very close study of the archives of the state, its glories had been institutional, administrative, constitutional, and diplomatic history. But the major advances in these areas had all been made by the race of giants of the late Victorian and Edwardian periods, the outstanding figures for English history being C. W. Stubbs, T. F. Tout, F. W. Maitland, and S. R. Gardiner. In their search for new and more fruitful ways to understand the working of the institutions, some young historians just before and after the First World War began to turn from the close textual study of political theories and constitutional documents or the elucidation of bureaucratic machinery to an examination of the individuals concerned and the experiences to which they had been subjected. Exasperated by the windy pieties of a generation of historical interpreters of the framing of the American Constitution, Beard introduced his own book with the acid remark that "The Constitution was of human origin, immediately at least, and it is now discussed and applied by human beings who find themselves engaged in certain callings, occupations, professions and interests." In his challenging introductory statement a quarter of a century later, Syme also declared open war upon the elder generation of historians.[14] When dealing with the attitudes of Parliament toward the American colonies before the Revolution, Namier did not bother himself with the political theory of no taxation without representation. Instead he asked: "What acquaintance with the American Colonies had the house in which the Stamp Act was passed and repealed, and in which the Townshend Duties were enacted? How many of its Members had been to the American Colonies, had connections with them, or had an intimate knowledge of American affairs? Were any of them American born?"[15]

Following this example similar questions about who rather than what have been asked about such diverse questions in English historiography as Magna Carta, the House of Commons, riots, the civil service, and the Cabinet.[16] The unstated premise is that an understanding of who the actors were will go far toward explaining the workings of the institution to which they belonged, will reveal the true objectives behind the flow of political rhetoric, and will enable us better to understand their achievement, and more correctly to interpret the documents they produced.

The direction in which this attack on the conventional approach to political institutions and policies would develop was powerfully influenced by other important trends in the intellectual climate of the period, of which the first and most important was cultural relativism. Greater familiarity with foreign countries through travel combined with the growing volume of anthropological studies to reveal the extraordinary range of cultural patterns that have been adopted by different societies around the world. The educated public became uneasily aware that morals, laws, constitutions, religious beliefs, political attitudes, class structures, and sexual practices differ widely from one society to another, and this awareness in time led to a recognition that there are few universal norms of human behavior or social organization. The stress on environmental conditioning as the determining factor in creating this variety was all the greater because the 1920's and 1930's was a period when genetic explanations of cultural differences were not treated with the seriousness it now begins to appear that they may possibly deserve.[17] Social Darwinism, which was a powerful influence around the turn of the century, laid far more stress on nurture than nature. Moreover, the Freudian psychologists, who soon afterwards began to come into their own, also laid great stress upon the role of nurture, with particular emphasis on childhood and early sexual experience. It must be admitted, however, that Freudian psychology has not been much use to the historian, who is usually unable to penetrate the bedroom, the bathroom, or the nursery. If Freud is right, and if these are the places where the action is, there is not much the historian can do about it. The subsequent modification of Freudian ideas by Erik Erikson, according to which character formation continues through childhood and adolescence, and crystallizes in an "identity crisis" just before maturity, opens up new possibilities for the historian, who can sometimes discover a little about the thoughts and feelings of his subject in adolescence, even if he knows little or nothing about his infancy and early childhood. Up to now, however, Eriksonian psychology has been very little used by historians, and a far more important influence upon the profession has been behaviorist theories of challenge and response to environmental pressures.

The third influential element in the intellectual climate of the age was the decay of confidence in the integrity of politicians, and the decline of faith in the importance of constitutions. Much of this cynicism was generated by the political and moral disaster of the First World War, followed by the collapse of hopes of a better world order. Many people came to believe that this was the time when millions died and European civilization disintegrated, while politicians jockeyed for place and power by outbidding each other in the jingo rhetoric of hate. The result was the penetration into intellectual circles and into the upper classes of the ancient folklore of the poor, that all politicians are crooks. This was the muckraking era, in which the top was blown off the nineteenth century by books like Lytton Strachey's *Eminent Victorians* (1918) and Matthew Josephson's *The Robber Barons* (1934). Nor should it be forgotten that the events of the period did nothing to redress the balance; it was the era of Teapot Dome, Jimmy Thomas, and Stavisky. These popular assumptions and actual discoveries about the moral, and in particular the financial, laxity of politicians, led historians to think that if only one could get access to the private papers of past political actors, similar motives would be revealed as a driving force in history.

Apart from Fascism (which had little intellectual appeal), Marxism was the only powerful ideology of the period. Marxism gave many historians a somewhat naïve belief in economic determinism, which strongly reinforced these dark suspicions about human motivation. Beard thus declared that "the direct compelling motive" behind the framers of the American Constitution "was the economic advantages which the beneficiaries expected would accrue to themselves first from their action." [18] In its early stages, therefore, prosopography reflected a deeply pessimistic attitude toward human affairs, and was conducted either by radicals under Marxist influence, like Beard, or by men like Sir Lewis Namier and Sir Ronald Syme, who are ostensibly of a conservative frame of mind. Syme frankly admitted of his own work that "The design has imposed a pessimistic and truculent tone, to the almost complete exclusion of the gentler emotions and the domestic virtues," while an early reviewer commented with dismay of Namier's book that "The political system which it describes is certainly not attractive, based as it was upon a possibly enlightened but a certainly sordid self-interest." [19]

Nor was this cynicism confined to attitudes toward individual politicians; it also covered political systems. If revolutions mean no more than substitution of one grasping and self-centered ruling elite for another, if a handful of unscrupulous men steer the ship of state the way they want, whatever the constitutional flag under which they sail, then the difference between tyranny and democracy becomes blurred, to say the least. From this point of view the elitist school of historical prosopographers of the 1930's was deeply affected by the contemporary crisis of confidence in democracy. Namier deliberately set out to destroy theories about a tyrannical conspiracy by George III against the British constitution, and Syme appeared to remove any basis for moral judgments about the destruction of the Roman republic by Augustus. In 1939 A. Momigliano applied to Syme his own description of Tacitus: "a monarchist from perspicacious despair of human nature." [20] Robert Dahl has rightly observed, however, that "for individuals with a strong strain of frustrated idealism, it [elite theory] has just the right touch of hard-boiled cynicism."[21] The elite theorist and the elite historian tend to be disappointed egalitarians, whose misanthropy springs directly from outraged moral sentiment.

The attitude toward the workings of politics taken by the early prosopographers appears to owe little to the writings of political theorists. Marx himself stressed the role first of the feudal lords and then of the bourgeoisie, and directed attention to the self-interest that guided their actions. But the first fully-fledged elitist political theories came out of Europe in the early twentieth century, with the writings of R. Michels, G. Mosca, and V. Pareto. Although Michels was available in French, Pareto and Mosca were not translated into English before the 1930's, and there is no evidence that they had the slightest influence in historical circles in the Anglo-Saxon world until that time. Namier, Merton, and Syme were strongly anti-Marxist, and yet only Merton appears to have been familiar with these non-Marxist elitist models. What we have, therefore, is the development by political scientists of a full-blown theory of rule by elites a generation before the historians set to work. But apart from Merton the historians carried out their empirical studies based on their own semiconscious assumptions about political behavior, without the benefit of the political theory which would have provided them with the framework they needed. It is one of the more bizarre episodes of intellectual history, a consequence of the slowness of the great European social scientists to be translated into English, and of the isolation of history from the other social sciences in the early twentieth century.

A key feature of the elitist interpretation of the historical process is the deliberate and systematic removal of both party programs and ideological passions from the center of the political stage, and their replacement by a complex web uniting patrons with their clients and dependents. For Roman history, this is expressly stated by Professors L. R. Taylor and E. Badian.[22] For English history Namier substituted the "connection" for the party as the central organizing principle of mid-eighteenth-century politics, K. B. McFarlane invented the phrase "Bastard Feudalism" to represent not dissimilar patron-client relationships which he believed could explain the fifteenth century, while Sir John Neale borrowed the word "clientage" from the classical historians to make sense of the Elizabethan political system. In a key passage the latter wrote, "most of the gentry seem to have grouped themselves in close or loose relationships around one or other of the few great men of the country . . . The grouping and interdependence of the gentry, with its accompanying and constant struggle for prestige and supremacy, permeated English life. It assumed the part played by politics in our modern society, and in the country, is the main clue to parliamentary elections." [23] For some scholars, prosopography was not merely a way of ignoring passions and ideas, it was adopted for the specific purpose of neutralizing these disturbing and intractable elements.

A fourth stimulus to elitist prosopography, which in turn reinforced the new awareness of the essential role played in politics by associations of dependents, was the almost obsessive concern of the anthropologists for the family and kinship, the full impact of which is only just beginning to make itself fully felt in the historical profession today. It was Namier's work on mid-eighteenth-century English politics which first drew the attention of historians to the potentialities of family arrangements and kinship links as political bonds.[24] It is perhaps not too farfetched to see a parallel between the preoccupation with such linkages of the elitist school of historians and similar preoccupations in contemporary fiction, notably Proust's *A la recherche du temps perdu* and Antony Powell's more recent *Music of Time.*

These intellectual trends are sufficient in themselves to explain the rise of the elitist school between the wars. The more scientifically-orientated mass school obviously owed something to all of them, but much more to the concurrent rise of the social sciences. From Weber to Merton the most intelligent and most successful of the social scientists have limited themselves to advancing middle-range hypotheses about such things as suicide or bureaucracy or receptivity to right-wing political views. Historical prosopography is obviously immensely valuable as a source of material for such investigations, and it is no coincidence that Marx and Weber and Merton have all had strong historical interests. The main inspiration for the type of questions asked and the methods employed to solve them by Merton and by a host of subsequent historical investigators of the mass school was the development of social survey techniques. From them comes the confidence in the sampling method and the habit of asking a very wide range of questions, many of which turn out to be wholly irrelevant, in the hope of picking out the significant variables by statistical manipulation later on.

Given these many converging trends in the intellectual life of the period between the two World Wars, it is hardly surprising that it was then that prosopography grew up. Indeed in retrospect what is surprising is rather the slowness of its advance upon the historical stage, for it was not until the 1950's or even the 1960's that significant numbers of students began to use the method, and that a steady stream of useful findings began to be published.

Limitations and Dangers

Sufficient experience has now accumulated to make it possible to appreciate both the potentialities and the limitations of prosopographical studies. Some of the errors and deficiencies are inevitable consequences of pioneering in a new method, and can be avoided in the future by learning from the mistakes of the past. Others, however, go deeper, and arise from some political and psychological presuppositions which are embedded in the foundations upon which prosopography rests.

Deficiencies in the Data

It is self-evident that biographical studies of substantial numbers of persons are possible only for fairly well-documented groups, and that prosopography is therefore severely limited by the quantity and quality of the data accumulated about the past. In any historical group, it is likely that almost everything will be known about some members of it, and almost nothing at all about others; certain items will be lacking for some, and different items will be lacking for others. If the unknowns bulk very large, and if with the seriously incompletes they form a substantial majority of the whole, generalizations based on statistical averages become very shaky indeed, if not altogether impossible. Studies which have to be confined to that tenth or twentieth part of the group about which enough is known depend for their reliability on the recorded minority being a genuinely random sample of the whole. But this is an unlikely assumption, since the very fact that more than usual has been recorded about the lives and careers of a tiny minority indicates that they were somehow atypical. To a degree which cannot be measured, studies based on such fragmentary evidence will tend to exaggerate, and perhaps hopelessly to distort, the status, education, upward mobility, and so forth of the group under examination. For most social groups in most areas prosopography cannot usefully be employed before the explosion of record materials in the sixteenth century, caused by the invention of the printing press, the spread of literacy, and the growth of the bureaucratic, record-keeping nation-state.

The only exception to this generalization is when there exists a single detailed census-type survey, such as the Florentine *catasto* of 1427. These rare documents allow the historian to make a cross section through a society at a given moment, but they cannot answer any questions about change over time, since there is usually nothing before or after with which to compare them. They also need to be handled with care, since they may silently omit certain classes of persons, such as beggars, their categories may be vague or erratic, and their financial statistics are likely to underestimate the affluence of the rich relative to the poor.

The second limitation imposed by the record evidence is that of status. At all times and in all places, the lower one goes in the social system the poorer becomes the documentation. As a result, most studies that have already been made or are in progress today have been devoted to elites. The most popular subject for prosopography has been and still is political elites, but other groups which lend themselves most readily to such treatment are members of certain high status categories, such as civil servants, army officers, upper clergy, intellectuals and educators, lawyers, doctors, members of other professional bodies, and industrial and commercial entrepreneurs. The only elements of the lower classes about whom something can be done in anything more than a highly impressionistic way are persecuted minorities, since police reports and legal records often supply much of the necessary information, especially in societies with a long tradition of heavy bureaucratic and police control like France. The odd result is that the only groups of poor and humble about whom we can sometimes find out a good deal are minority groups, which are by definition exceptional since they are in revolt against the *mores* and beliefs of the majority.

The third limitation imposed by the evidence arises from the fact that it is abundant for some aspect of human life and almost nonexistent for others. The surviving records are concerned first and foremost with the amount, type, ownership, and transmission of property. It is this which is the prime concern of official and private legal records, official tax records, and public and private administrative records, which together form the vast bulk of the written material of the past. There is thus a strong bias toward treating the individual as *homoeconomicus,* and to study him primarily in the light of his financial interests and behavior, since this is what the records illuminate in the greatest clarity and detail. But economic interests may conflict, and even when the interest is clear, it is impossible to be sure that this is the overriding consideration. Moreover the split between the compromisers and the last-ditchers is often more important politically than the split between clearly defined economic interest-groups.[25]

After economic interests, the second item of information that is relatively easy to discover about a person is his family background and connections. Among the upper classes marriage has been used in the past to provide young men with useful friends and contacts, as well as to merge properties and so create great territorial estates. Family ties have also played an important part in the construction of political groups and parties at all times from the Middle Ages to the eighteenth century and beyond. One has only to think of the Howards and Dudleys in sixteenth-century England, the Villiers in the early seventeenth century, the Pelhams in the eighteenth, and

the Cecils and Cavendishes in the late nineteenth and early twentieth, to recognize the continuing importance of this factor. But this
does not answer the question of how far it is safe to pursue this line
of reasoning, for the cementing role of kinship clearly varies from
place to place, from time to time, and from social level to social
level. There are countless examples in history of members of the
same family who have disagreed among themselves, often with extreme violence. Moreover, even when kinship ties were strong and
can be shown to have been so, there are limits to the meaningful
pursuit of genealogical links. Two diligent prosopographers working
on the Long Parliament of 1640 tracked down genealogical connections which related the radical John Hampden to eighty fellow
M.P.'s, but unfortunately these kin turned out to be of widely varying political and religious opinions. When the authors found that
by going back far enough they could find a kinship connection between Charles I and Oliver Cromwell, they realized that they had
perhaps passed beyond the outer limits of utility of this particular
line of inquiry. Similar doubts have been recently expressed about
the role ascribed by the prosopographical school to kinship in classical Rome.[26]

Errors in the Classification of the Data

Meaningful classification is essential to the success of any study,
but unfortunately for the historian every individual plays many
roles, some of which are in conflict with others. He belongs to a
civilization, to a national culture, and to a host of subcultures—
ethnic, professional, religious, peer-group, political, social, occupational, economic, sexual, and so on. As a result, no one classification
is of universal validity, and a perfect congruence of classifications is
quite rare. Status categories may bear little relation to wealth, and
also may vary in their importance over time. Class categories based
on wealth may not reflect social realities, may be almost impossible
to identify, and may be even more impossible to compare over time;
professional categories may cut through both status and class lines
and run vertically up and down the social system; power categories,
such as political offices, may vary over time in the social status attached to them, in the power they wield, and in the income they
produce.

The second danger which threatens every prosopographer is
that he may fail to identify important subdivisions, and may thus be

lumping together individuals who differ significantly from one another.[27] Good research depends on a constant interplay between the hypothesis and the evidence, the former undergoing repeated modification in the light of the latter. But if a subdivision which later turns out to be of critical importance has not been noted at the time, it is usually too late to go back and do the work all over again, a difficulty which is particularly acute in computer-aided studies, since the code book determines the questions that can later be asked.[28]

Errors in the Interpretation of the Data

Even if his documentation is adequate and his system of classification is properly designed, the unwary prosopographer is still liable to draw erroneous conclusions from his data. One common hazard which faces him is the possibility that that portion of the total population about which he can discover reliable information does not represent a random sample of the whole. If the unknowns mostly fall into a single slanted category, the figures taken from the sample of the known will give a distorted picture of reality. Thus Theodore Rabb himself provides reason to think that his sample of seventeenth-century English investors is biased, since it is quite likely that most of the unidentified 38 per cent of investors, both named and unnamed, were petty merchants.[29] This is a problem which affects all work which used this methodology, and against which the only defense is the most careful assessment of the probabilities, and the application where necessary of an index error to correct the statistics. Another mistake which often occurs in prosopographical studies springs from a failure to relate the findings about the composition of the group under study to that of the population at large. A good example of the difficulties into which the historian may stumble if he neglects this point is the dispute about the social composition of the victims of the Terror in the French Revolution. Professor D. Greer discovered that the great majority of the victims were drawn from the lower or middle class rather than the nobility. It has since been pointed out that the proportion of noble victims may have been very small, but since the proportion of nobles in the population at large was even smaller, there is still a correlation of noble birth with execution. One can still say that a nobleman had "X" times more chances of being killed in the Terror than a member of the bourgeoisie or a peasant.[30]

Another type of error which arises from neglecting the relationship between the part and the whole springs from the assumption that because a majority of members of a certain group comes from a particular social class or occupation, that therefore they are representative, in the sense that a majority of members of their class or occupation belongs to the group. Hugh R. Trevor-Roper pointed out that the men who seized power in England in the late 1640's and early 1650's were mostly drawn not from the old landed elite who had ruled England before the war but from the poor gentry, mere gentry, or parish gentry, who had hitherto played no significant part in national and only a minor role in local affairs. Inspired by this discovery, he proceeded to generalize that the downwardly mobile mere gentry were the principle dissatisfied elements in the country and the main supporters of radicalism. In fact, however, it now seems fairly clear that a far larger number of the mere gentry— indeed the majority in the heartland of the class in the north and the west—were loyal church-and-king men who fought for King Charles. The Independent gentry who supported Cromwell were merely an untypical minority, goaded into taking a position so much at variance with that of most of their class by motives which at present we can only very dimly perceive, but one of which was certainly religious conviction.[31]

Limitations of Historical Understanding

So far, the errors which have been discovered have all been ones which can be avoided by learning the harsh lessons of experience, but there are others which will be more difficult to eradicate. In the first place, the concentration upon the study of elites has been part cause and part effect of a tendency to see history exclusively as a story of the ruling class, in which popular movements play little or no part. Syme claimed that "In all ages, whatever the form and name of government, be it monarchy, republic, or democracy, an oligarchy lurks behind the facade."[32] This is true enough as far as it goes, but one may reasonably question whether it goes far enough. Close study of the political maneuverings of the elite may conceal rather than illuminate the profounder workings of the social process. Major changes in class relationships, social mobility, religious opinions, and moral attitudes may be occurring among the lower strata, changes to which the elite will eventually be obliged to respond, if it is not to be swept away in violent revolution.[33]

If we look at the three most brilliant examples of prosopographical research on political elites, Syme's *Roman Revolution,* Namier's
Structure of Politics, and Sir John Neale's great trilogy on the Elizabethan House of Commons, published in the 1950's, we can see the
same narrowing of focus. Syme interpreted the transformations of
the Roman republic into an empire as the consolidation of a new
elite around Augustus, the result of a complex factional in-fighting
at the top. He proved his point, but he ignored the urgent demands
of the nameless client masses upon their patrons which supported—
and perhaps dictated—this shift of power. Political movements, and
revolutions or counterrevolutions in particular, can hardly be satisfactorily explained by exclusive study of the leadership. Namier's
picture of wheeling and dealing in the eighteenth-century House of
Commons shattered conventional theories beyond repair, but his
explanatory model could not include the springs of popular feeling
generated by John Wilkes or the American War of Independence.
Similarly, Sir John Neale's description of the relations between
Queen Elizabeth and her Parliaments needs modification through
greater appreciation of the deep roots that Puritanism was sinking
into the society. This was an ideology which both cut across and
exploited the nexus of aristocratic clientage which Sir John so brilliantly and convincingly described.

The second great intellectual weakness of prosopographers has
been their relative unwillingness to build into their perspective of
history a role for ideas, prejudices, passions, ideologies, ideals, or
principles. Intimate personal correspondence is a rarity among
historical records. It usually got destroyed during life or at death,
since, unlike genealogical, legal, or business records, nobody among
the family or friends had any incentive to preserve it. Even in the
rare cases when such material exists, it is often not very illuminating, since men rarely commit their deepest convictions to paper,
even with their friends. Moreover, since in most periods in history
it has been positively dangerous to express minority views about
religion or politics, such written comments as survive about basic
issues tend to be confined within the accepted norms of the society.
The systematic bias in the historical record in favor of material
interests and kinship ties and against ideas and principles fitted
in well with the explicitly stated presupposition of the greatest of the
early elitist scholars.[34] "Spiritual interests of people are considered
much less than their marriages," complained Momigliano as soon as
Syme's book appeared. Sir Herbert Butterfield protested with ref-

erence to Namier that "human beings are the carriers of ideas, as well as the repositories of vested interests."[35]

Despite some later disclaimers, there can be little doubt that in practice both Namier and Syme attached little importance to any ideal or prejudice which ran counter to the calculations of self-interest. The attention paid by these historians to the tactics rather than the strategy of politics presupposes a society without conviction in which manipulation and wire-pulling are more important than issues of principle or policy. It so happened that the mid-eighteenth century, upon which Namier first focused his attention, was a period in English history unusually devoid of major issues of controversy, and a period when the political actors formed an unusually homogeneous group: he thus chose, by accident or design, a period and a class which were especially susceptible to analysis by the methods he adopted. But some of his followers have found, to their cost, that it is not always safe to carry the same assumptions forwards and backwards in time. Robert Walcott tried to use the model for the reign of Queen Anne, with results that are now generally recognized to have been little short of disastrous.[36] One may also wonder whether Oliver Cromwell's failure successfully to manage his Parliaments can really be explained by his lack of tactical skill, as Professor Trevor-Roper argues, or whether disagreement over fundamental constitutional and religious issues between the military and the civilians, and between Independents, Presbyterians, and Anglicans, put a settlement quite out of reach of even the most shrewd and assiduous manipulator of men.[37] One may therefore conclude that the explanatory power of the interest-group theory of politics, which has tended to be associated with the elitist prosopographical approach, is much greater at some periods and in some places than it is at and in others. The fewer the major political issues, the lower the ideological temperature, the more oligarchic the political organization, the more likely it is to provide a convincing historical interpretation.

Another limitation of the prosopographical school of historians is that its members sometimes unduly neglect the stuff of politics, the institutional framework within which the system functions, and the narrative of how political actors shape public policy. "We are given a story that becomes silent or curiously neglectful as it touches the very things that government and Parliaments exist to do," complained Sir Herbert Butterfield. He concluded harshly that: "There is little interest in the work of ministers within their departments; in

the springs of policy and the origins of important decisions; in the
actual content of the political controversies of the time; in the attitude of the public to measures and men; and in the thrust and
counter-thrust of parliamentary debate . . . Such tendencies are
calculated to raise the question whether the new form of structural
analysis is not capable of producing in the practitioners of the craft
its own kind of occupational disease."[38] The disease of which Sir
Herbert complains is a form of colorblindness which prevents its
victims perceiving the political content of politics.

Many elitist prosopographers instinctively opt for a simplistic
view of human motivation, according to which the springs of action
are either one thing or another. We all of us ask our students to
distinguish religious from political motives in the foreign policies of
Gustavus Adolphus, or Oliver Cromwell, or whomever. In real life,
human nature does not seem to function this way. The individual
is moved by a convergence of constantly shifting forces, a cluster
of influences such as kinship, friendship, economic interest, class
prejudice, political principle, religious conviction, and so on, which
all play their varying parts and which can usefully be disentangled
only for analytical purposes. Moreover there is reason to think that
the relative importance of the various background characteristics
will vary from culture to culture and nation to nation and time to
time; that some attitudes can be more closely related to identifiable
background characteristics than others; and that some background
characteristics are moderately influential over a large range of attitudes while others are highly influential over a single attitude.[39]

In any case it is essential to distinguish sharply between relatively minor matters over which a politician is ready enough to favor
a relative or client or to receive a bribe, and major issues of principle, over which he is likely to follow the dictates of his head and his
heart rather than those of his blood or his pocketbook.

Achievements

Nothing which has so far been said should be interpreted to
mean that elitist prosopography is by its nature either useless or misleading. Red flags have been put up around the main danger spots
where lie the bones of many pioneers in the method, and a case has
been made for reducing the claims of prosopography generally as an
explanatory tool. If past errors can be avoided, and if the limitations
of the method are recognized, the potentialities are very great. In-

deed, provided that it is accepted—as it surely must be—that values and behavior patterns are strongly influenced by past experience and upbringing, the power of the method can hardly be denied. All that is needed is more willingness to recognize the baffling complexity of human nature, the power of ideas, and the persistent influence of institutional structures. Prosopography does not have all the answers, but it is ideally fitted to reveal the web of sociopsychological ties that bind a group together. For example, to identify such ties among the leaders of the parliamentary opposition to Charles I in the late 1630's and early 1640's does not help us to decide whether economic or constitutional or religious issues caused the Civil War. But it does most powerfully illuminate the process of radical party formation, and in the end makes any such question seem redundant, for the simple reason that men do not tear up their political institutions by the roots unless all these influences are working together to form an overwhelming incentive for change.

The best way to illustrate the full range of the contribution which prosopography has made to historical understanding in the last twenty years is to focus on some particular time and place, for which the religious, social and political history of England between 1500 and 1660 will serve as well as any. The first major problem which has been enormously enriched by these studies is the English Reformation. Although during the 1950's and 1960's the dominant textbook interpreted this event in primarily political terms, as an act of state carried out by a handful of determined men at the top, there was at the same time in train a whole series of monographs which were to shatter this simple picture. Examination of the educational, moral, and financial condition of the pre-Reformation clergy has shown up their many shortcomings, but has also indicated that what was happening was not so much a decline in the quality and zeal of the clergy as a rise in the demands made upon them by the laity.[40] Viewed in this light, the Reformation becomes yet another "revolution of rising expectations." The monks have also been studied prosopographically, with similar results, and it has been established that there was a decline in numbers in the pre-Reformation period, and a massive voluntary flight from monastic seclusion in the early 1530's. Monasteries and nunneries can be seen trying desperately to adapt themselves to the needs of the upper class lay society by serving as old age homes for pensioned retainers and servants, as hotels for traveling gentlemen and noblemen, and as institutions for the deposit of unwanted children.[41] The fate of the monks after the Dissolution was early subjected to prosopographical analysis, which proved beyond doubt the fallacy of the hoary legend of the sufferings of the dispossessed.[42] The behavior of the bishops during the Reformation crisis has been elucidated and the divisions of opinion convincingly related to different education training—in theology or law—and to different career lines—in the church or the state bureaucracy.[43]

Even more important in its historical consequences than these valuable studies of members of the official hierarchies within the church has been the uncovering of the roots of religious radicalism in secular society. The great advance here came with the publication of Professor A. G. Dickens' pioneering work on *Lollards and Protestants in the Diocese of York* (1959), which used hitherto unexplored sources, and raised a whole range of new problems, which have since been further worked on by students and followers. Thanks to the patient tracking of Protestant heretics through secular and religious court records of prosecutions, the size, influence, social composition, occupational characteristics, and geographical spread of these persecuted minority groups have at last begun to emerge from the shadows. No serious scholar any longer dismisses the survival of Lollardy as of no consequence in the spread of radical religious ideas, and we can now see the dissemination of Protestant ideas not merely through the activities of a handful of scholars at Cambridge, but also through the penetration of imported Lutheran pamphlets, translated Bibles, and other subversive literature from the seaports to the inland areas via traders, cloth workers, dissident friars, and the like.[44]

The subsequent religious history of England has also benefited enormously from prosopography. The Marian exiles, who fled abroad to escape Catholic persecution between 1553 and 1558, have been shown to be an intellectual and social elite for which there is hardly any parallel before the flight of the Jews from Hitlerite Germany in the 1930's, and their role in determining the shape of the Anglican Settlement of 1558-1559 is now recognized to have been of the greatest importance.[45] Our understanding of why the Anglican church failed in its early years to win greater acceptance and to gain more converts has been illuminated through clerical prosopography, which has revealed the many shortcomings in numbers, education, zeal, and economic independence of the early Elizabethan parish clergy.[46] On one flank of the Established Church we are beginning to have a better picture of the growth of Puritanism through greater knowledge of who the Puritans were, though much work still remains to be done on Puritan merchants, dons, schoolmasters, clergy, and nobles.[47] On the other flank a very careful statistical and geographical comparison of Catholics in the 1560's and Catholics in the 1580's has proved conclusively, as no other method could, that the late Elizabethan development of Catholicism was a gentry-based revival stimulated by the missionary activities of the seminary priests, and not a survival of popular pre-Reformation Catholicism.[48]

Social history, which is concerned with groups rather than individuals, ideas, or institutions, is a field to which prosopography probably has most to contribute. Attempts to generalize about social change in advance of either detailed local studies or global statistics based on serious archival research lead to the kind of impasse into which the famous "gentry controversy" got itself stuck twenty years ago, during which rival hypotheses about broad social movements between 1540 and 1640 and their relationship to the revolution were bandied about on the basis of craftily selected examples whose typicality was altogether unknown. Since that time there have appeared several local studies of groups of gentry, and one general study on the aristocracy, which together go some way to eliminate certain hypotheses and to put statistical weight behind some others.[49]

For example, as a result of many years of very careful work upon the gentry of Yorkshire, it has been shown that of those gentry of the country who were in economic decline before the war and who took sides, three quarters joined the royalists and only one quarter the parliamentarians.[50] If this is true across the country, it disproves Professor Trevor-Roper's hypothesis that the radicals on the parliamentary side represented the declining "mere gentry." The same study also brings out the importance of Puritanism among so many parliamentarians and of Catholicism among a significant number of royalists. It adds one more nail to the coffin of the old Marxist theory, tentatively supported by R. H. Tawney and J. E. C. Hill, that the civil war was a conflict between capitalist entrepreneurial landlords and old-fashioned *rentiers*. In this case, detailed prosopographical analysis has put to the test—as nothing else could—the many theories of the social causes of the revolution, and has begun to sift truth from falsehood among them.[51]

As one might expect, the greatest concentration of prosopographical energy has been directed toward the political elite, and in particular toward the M.P.'s. The late nineteenth- and early twentieth-century historians had established the key role played in English political history by the increasingly independent and powerful House of Commons, and it had long been known that it was here that the basic issues were fought out. But it was not until after the Second World War that scholars began to ask what sort of people it was who made this history. Today we have studies of the M.P.'s of almost every Parliament between 1559 and 1660, and a much richer and more convincing picture has emerged as a result.[52] Through comparative statistics and a series of detailed case studies, we can watch the expansion in the numbers of M.P.'s and trace its cause in a desire by Elizabethan magnates to extend the range of their patronage, and in the willingness of Elizabeth to make concessions, however politically unwise in the long run, which did not cost her money in the short run. Statistical inquiries have revealed the striking growth in the educational training and administrative experience of M.P.'s and the persistent rise in the proportion of gentry. We know now how the members were elected and how electoral contests were fought and won, and we are beginning to learn a little about the changing relationship between the electors and their representatives. We can trace the decline in the electoral influence of the great court magnates before 1640, as it gave way to that of local gentlemen, and even of townsmen themselves for borough seats.

Prosopographical studies of local elites outside Parliament in the counties and the cities are just beginning to be even more helpful in illuminating the social and economic factors behind the party line-ups in the Civil War. They have already revealed that in some counties and towns—but not in all—there was a withdrawal from positions of authority in the late 1640's of members of the greater gentry and the old urban oligarchies, and their replacement by men drawn from the lesser gentry and small merchants, as more radical policies were adopted for the prosecution of the war and achievement of a political settlement.[53]

The principal conclusion which emerges from this survey of the literature is that the method works best when it is applied to easily defined and fairly small groups over a limited period of not much more than a hundred years, when the data is drawn from a very wide variety of sources which complement and enrich each other, and when the study is directed to solving a specific problem. Lollards and Protestants in the early sixteenth century, Captain Swing rioters in the early nineteenth, make ideal subjects. Ambitious surveys of many thousands of individuals over very long time-spans, using only the most easily accessible printed source materials, and applying a shotgun scatter approach to the problems which may be answered, are far less likely to produce worthwhile results.

Conclusion

Prosopography is today in the process of coming of age. It has passed through the follies and excesses of adolescence and is now settling down to the humdrum routine of responsible early middle age. If the elitist school had its origins in Germany and the United States, it was first developed in England, both in classical and in modern history, and a good deal of the best work still comes from there. But this early pioneering is now being overtaken, both in quantity and quality, by the scholarly outpourings from America. The latter has always been the main center of the mass school, the scale of whose output and the sophistication of whose methods is now increasing fast.[54] The principal causes of this proliferation of scientific historical prosopography in the United States has been the great influence of sociology and political science and the advanced training in the use of, and easy access to, the computer. The most impressive institutional achievement of this school has been the creation of the Inter-University Consortium for Political Research at the University of Michigan. Here there is being collected and put into machine-readable form information about the voting behavior, as recorded in congressional roll calls, of every congressman since 1789. In addition, the psephologists are being supplied with data about popular voting at the county level in every election since 1824, correlated with information from the census returns since 1790 about income, race, religion, and other key variables for each county and state.[55] A beginning is now being made in collecting machine-readable statistical data for earlier periods of American history and also for other countries.

It is indicative of the parting of the ways between British and American scholarship in the 1960's that the parallel monument to prosopography on the eastern side of the Atlantic takes the rather different form of the postwar History of Parliament project. Initiated and planned by Sir Lewis Namier, this began in 1951 and will result in a multi-volume biographical dictionary of all M.P.'s, linked by introductory volumes which use this personal information to provide illuminating case studies, to put together statistical comparisons, and to draw political conclusions. It is characteristic of the British approach that this project is paid for by the government and not by universities or foundations, that the biographical information it assembles is not being prepared in machine-readable form (except for one period under the editorship of an American), and that more emphasis is placed on the biographies and case studies than on the statistics.[56]

France is the third major center of historical research in the world, but for the last thirty years the best French historians have been preoccupied with some dazzlingly successful explorations of other new techniques of research. They have pioneered some brilliant environmental studies of local societies seen as a totality and examined in great depth, they have produced some massive statistical time-series about prices, foreign trade, and industrial output, and they have pioneered the scientific study of historical demography. Only in the last few years have French historians begun to take to prosopography, and in conformity with their long-standing emphasis upon quantification they are now embarked upon some very large-scale projects of the mass school, using the most sophisticated computer gadgetry.[57] These are being supported by the VI Section of the Ecole Pratique des Hautes Etudes in Paris, which for decades has been the center of statistical historical inquiry in France.

One of the reasons—although a poor and irrelevant one—why prosopography will continue to develop on both sides of the Atlantic is because it is so ideally suited to the requirements of research papers and doctoral dissertations. It introduces the novice student to a very wide range of sources, it teaches him to evaluate his evidence and to apply his judgment to resolve contradictions, it demands meticulous accuracy and the arrangement of information on a methodical basis, and it offers a topic which can readily be expanded or cut down by modifying the size of the sample in order to meet the requirements of available time and resources. Some of this research undoubtedly contributes to the New Antiquarianism—data collection for data collection's sake—but under skilled and organized leadership the projects can be fitted together by the director to produce a useful contribution to the sum of historical knowledge.

A second powerful—but equally irrelevant—reason for a further expansion of prosopography is the arrival of the computer, the full significance of which is only just becoming apparent. As historians slowly and timidly began to explore the potentialities of this new technological tool, they began to realize its almost limitless capacity for handling just the sort of material that prosopography throws up. The correlation of numerous variables affecting large masses of data, assembled on a uniform basis, is precisely what the computer can do best; it is also what is most laborious, and in many cases virtually impossible, for even the most mathematically-minded of historians working without electronic aids. It is painful to admit that the advent of a technical gadget should dictate the type of historical questions asked and the methods used for solving them, but it would be adopting the posture of the ostrich to pretend that this is not happening now, and will not happen on an even greater scale in the years to come.

It must be admitted that there are some serious dangers inherent in the very success and popularity of prosopography. The first is that the really large undertakings, like Sir John Neale's work on Elizabethan Parliaments, Professor W. K. Jordan's on charitable giving, or Sir Lewis Namier's even grander History of Parliament project, must be carried out by teams of researchers, assembling data on the lines laid down by the director. This material is then studied, collated, and eventually published by the director, to whom alone the credit goes.[58] Collective research is already fully accepted by the physical scientists as a familiar and necessary process, but it involves a degree of intellectual peonage by students and junior faculty to the professor, which many scholars bred in the older individualistic and independent tradition of historiography find disturbing. The second danger is that instead of coming together, the mass and the elitist schools will specialize more and more on their different approaches, the one becoming more scientific and quantitative and the other more impressionistic and devoted to individual examples inadequately controlled by random sampling. This would be a disaster for the profession, since it would spell the end of fruitful cross-fertilization. The danger has been greatly increased by the advent of the computer, which has been embraced by the more statistically-minded with all the undiscriminating enthusiasm of the nymphomaniac, and rejected by the less scientific partly from intellectual prudery, and partly from complacent ignorance of what pleasures they are missing. The availability of the computer will increasingly tempt some historians to concentrate their energies on problems that can be solved by quantification, problems which are sometimes—but by no means always—the most important or interesting ones. It will also tempt them to abandon sampling techniques, which are frequently perfectly adequate for their purposes, and to embark on very time-consuming statistical investigations of total populations, which in many cases is a wholly unnecessary procedure. Other historians may increasingly come to regard the computer as a threat to their intellectual predominance, and may retreat still further into the dark recesses of impressionistic methodology. To make matters worse, there are strong national overtones to the split, since the American and the French have far greater access to and confidence in the computer than their English colleagues, strong cultural overtones, with threats of a new war between the Ancients and the Moderns, the Humanities and the Sciences, and even philosophical overtones, with a clash between Fact and Fancy, Mr. Gradgrind and Sissy Jupe. As a result, it may be a long while before there is a full meeting of minds.

Prosopography nevertheless contains within it the potentiality to help in the re-creation of a unified field out of the loose confederation of jealously independent topics and techniques which at present constitutes the historian's empire. It could be a means to bind together constitutional and institutional history on the one hand and personal biography on the other, which are the two oldest and best developed of the historian's crafts, but which have hitherto run along more or less parallel lines. It could combine the humane skill in historical reconstruction through meticulous concentration on the significant detail and the particular example, with the statistical and theoretical preoccupations of the social scientists; it could form the missing connection between political history and social history, which at present are all too often treated in largely watertight compartments, either in different monographs or in different chapters of a single volume. It could help reconcile history to sociology and psychology. And it could form one string among many to tie the exciting developments in intellectual and cultural history down to the social, economic, and political bedrock. Whether or not prosopography will seize all or any of these opportunities will depend on the expertise, sophistication, modesty, and common sense of the next generation of historians.

REFERENCES

1. The word prosopography has a long history; its first known use is in 1743. C. Nicolet, "Prosopographie et histoire sociale: Rome et Italie a l'époque republicaine," *Annales: économies, sociétés, civilisations*, no. 3 (1970), n. 3 (I am indebted to the editors of *Annales* for a sight of this article

in proof). It provides a concise and accurate term for an increasingly common historical method, and is already in standard use by one group in the profession. It therefore seems very desirable that it should pass into everyday use among modern historians.

2. H. D. Lasswell and D. Lerner, *World Revolutionary Elites: Studies in Coercive Ideological Movements* (Cambridge, Mass.: M.I.T. Press, 1965).

3. D. A. Rustow, "The Study of Elites," *World Politics*, 18 (1966).

4. Nicolet, "Prosopographie et histoire sociale."

5. Joshua Wilson, *Biographical Index to the Present House of Commons* (London, 1806); A. Collins, *The Peerage of England* (London, 1714); A. Collins, *The Baronetage of England* (London, 1720); J. Burke, *The Commoners of Great Britain and Ireland* (London, 1833-1838); W. F. Hook, *Lives of the Archbishops of Canterbury* (London, 1860-1876); G. Hennessy, *Repertorium Ecclesiasticum Parochiale Londinense* (London, 1898); J. Campbell, *Lives of the Lord Chancellors* (London, 1845-1847); J. Campbell, *Lives of the Chief Justices* (London, 1849); E. Foss, *Biographia Juridica, A Biographical Dictionary of the Judges of England . . . 1066-1870* (London, 1870); H. W. Woolrych, *Lives of Eminent Sergeants-at-Law* (London, 1869); C. Dalton, *English Army Lists, 1661-1714* (London, 1892-1904); C. Dalton, *George the First's Army, 1716-1727* (London, 1910); J. Campbell, *Lives of the Admirals* (London, 1742-1744); J. Charnock, *Biographia Navalis* (London, 1794-1798); W. Munk, *Roll of the Royal College of Physicians of London* (1861); A. B. Beaven, *Aldermen of the City of London* (London, 1908-1913); J. Gillow, *Bibliographical Dictionary of English Catholics, 1534-1902* (1885-1902); D. C. A. Agnew, *Protestant Exiles from France in the Reign of Louis XIV* (Edinburgh: Huguenot Society, 1886); J. and J. A. Venn, *Alumni Cantabrigienses* (Cambridge, Eng., 1922-1954); J. Foster, *Alumni Oxonienses* (Oxford, 1891-1892).

6. Charles A. Beard, *An Economic Interpretation of the Constitution of the United States* (New York: Macmillan, 1913).

7. *Ibid.* (1935), pp. 73, 324, xii-xiv.

8. A. P. Newton, *The Colonising Activities of the English Puritans* (New Haven: Yale University Press, 1914).

9. It was not followed up until the publication of J. H. Hexter, *The Reign of King Pym* (Cambridge, Mass.: Harvard University Press, 1941).

10. M. Gelzer, *Die Nobilität der römischen Republik* (Leipzig-Berlin: B. G. Teubner, 1912); F. Munzer, *Römische Adelsparteien und Adelsfamilien* (Stuttgart, 1920).

11. John Raymond, *New Statesman* (October 19, 1957), pp. 499-500.

12. Some examples are published in D. K. Rowney and J. Q. Graham, *Quantitative History* (Homewood, Ill.: Dorsey Press, 1969), part VI.

13. The leaders of this intellectual revolution were the French, Marc Bloch and Lucien Febvre.

14. Beard, *Economic Interpretation of the Constitution,* p. xiv; R. Syme, *The Roman Revolution* (Oxford: Oxford University Press, 1939), p. vii. For a description of this historiographical sea-change in Roman history, see Nicolet, "Prosopographie et histoire sociale," n. 4.

15. L. B. Namier, *England in the Age of the American Revolution,* 2d ed. (London: Macmillan, 1961), p. 229.

16. J. C. Holt, *The Northerners* (Oxford: Oxford University Press, 1961); J. E. Neale, *The Elizabethan House of Commons* (London: Cape, 1949); M. F. Keeler, *The Long Parliament, 1640-1641* (Philadelphia: American Philosophical Society, 1954); L. B. Namier and J. Brooke, *The House of Commons, 1754-1790* (London: Oxford University Press, 1964); E. J. Hobsbawm and G. Rudé, *Captain Swing* (London: Lawrence and Wishart, 1969); G. E. Aylmer, *The King's Servants: The Civil Service of Charles I, 1625-1642* (London: Routledge and Paul, 1961); W. L. Guttsman, *The British Political Elite* (London: Macgibbon and Kee, 1963).

17. For a suggestive, if highly speculative, survey of the possibilities of genetic influence see C. D. Darlington, "The Genetics of Society," *Past and Present,* 43 (1969).

18. Beard, *Economic Interpretation of the Constitution,* pp. 17-18.

19. Syme, *Roman Revolution,* p. viii; D. A. Winstanley, reviewing Namier in *English Historical Review,* 44 (1929), 660.

20. A. Momigliano reviewing Syme in *Journal of Roman Studies,* 30 (1940), 75.

21. As quoted in D. A. Rustow, "Study of Elites," p. 713.

22. L. R. Taylor, *Party Politics in the Age of Caesar* (Berkeley: University of California Press, 1949), p. 23; E. Badian, *Foreign Clientelae* (Oxford: Oxford University Press, 1958), p. 1.

23. K. B. McFarlane, "Bastard Feudalism," *Bulletin of the Institute for Historical Research,* 21 (1945); Neale, *Elizabethan House of Commons,* pp. 24, 27.

24. Namier, *England in the Age of the American Revolution,* p. 19. See also Syme, *Roman Revolution,* p. vii; Holt, *The Northerners;* Neale, *Elizabethan House of Commons;* N. Annan, "The Intellectual Aristocracy," in J. H. Plumb, ed., *Studies in Social History* (London: Longmans, Green, 1955).

25. For example, W. O. Aydelotte, "The Country Gentlemen and the Repeal of the Corn Laws," *English Historical Review,* 82 (1967); "Voting Patterns in the British House of Commons in the 1840's," in Rowney and Graham, *Quantitative History.*

26. D. Brunton and D. H. Pennington, *Members of the Long Parliament* (London: Allen and Unwin, 1954). For a convincing refutation of the theory "that genealogical and political links would normally coincide" in the early eighteenth century, see G. Holmes, *British Politics in the Age of Anne*

(London: Macmillan, 1967), pp. 327-334. C. Meier, *Res Publica Amissa* (Wiesbaden: Steiner, 1966), and a review of it by P. A. Brunt in *Journal of Roman Studies*, 58 (1968), 229-232.

27. For an example which has been criticized on these grounds, see L. Stone, *The Crisis of the Aristocracy: 1558-1641* (Oxford: Oxford University Press, 1965). D. C. Coleman, "The 'Gentry' Controversy and the Aristocracy in Crisis, 1558-1641," *History*, 51 (1966); E. L. Petersen, "The Elizabethan Aristocracy Anatomized, Atomized and Reassessed," *Scandinavian Economic History Review*, 16 (1968); S. J. Woolf, "La Transformazione dell'Aristocrazia et la Revoluzione Inglese," *Studi Storici* (December 1968); J. H. Hexter, "The English Aristocracy, Its Crises, and the English Revolution, 1558-1660," *Journal of British Studies*, 8 (1968). The failure to work out sufficiently detailed subcategories seriously reduced the usefulness of Brunton and Pennington's study of the Long Parliament.

28. J.-Y. Tirat, "Problèmes de méthode en histoire sociale," *Revue d'Histoire Moderne et Contemporaine*, 10 (1963), 217.

29. T. K. Rabb, *Enterprise and Empire: Merchant and Gentry Investment in the Expansion of England, 1575-1630* (Cambridge, Mass.: Harvard University Press, 1967). For a review that makes this and other points, see J. J. McCusker in *Historical Methods Newsletter*, 2 (June 1969), 16-17. Another example of this problem is David Pottinger's claim that the writers of Old Regime France were drawn predominantly from the *noblesse d'épee* and the high bourgeoisie—a conclusion reached after the elimination of 48.5 per cent of all writers because their social background could not be discovered. D. Pottinger, *The French Book Trade in the Ancien Regime, 1500-1791* (Cambridge, Mass.: Harvard University Press, 1958). I owe this criticism to Professor Robert Darnton.

30. D. Greer, *The Incidence of the Terror During the French Revolution: A Statistical Interpretation*, 3d ed. (Cambridge, Mass.: Harvard University Press, 1964), pp. 385-387. A slightly different example of the same fallacy is D. Lerner's attempt to show that the Nazi leaders were "marginal men," when his definition of marginality clearly comprised over half the population (Rustow, "Study of Elites," p. 702).

31. H. R. Trevor-Roper, *The Gentry, 1540-1640* (*Economic History Review* Supplement I [1953]); W. G. Hoskins, "The Estates of the Caroline Gentry," in W. G. Hoskins and H. P. R. Finberg, eds., *Devonshire Studies* (London: Cape, 1952); J. T. Cliffe, *The Yorkshire Gentry* (London: Athlone Press, 1969), chap. 15; A. Everitt, *The Community of Kent and the Great Rebellion, 1640-1660* (Leicester: Leicester University Press, 1966), pp. 143-144, 243-244. For another example of the same error, see D. Donald, "Towards a Reconsideration of Abolitionists," in his *Lincoln Reconsidered* (New York: Knopf, 1956); R. A. Skotheim, "A Note on Historical Method: David Donald's Towards a Reconsideration of Abolitionists," *Journal of Southern History*, 25 (1959).

32. Syme, *Roman Revolution*, p. 7.

33. See P. A. Brunt's remarks in *Journal of Roman History*, 58 (1968), 230-231.

34. Namier, *England in the Age of the American Revolution*, p. 18; Beard, *Economic Interpretation of the Constitution*, p. 13.

35. Momigliano reviewing Syme in *Journal of Roman Studies*, 30 (1940), p. 76; H. Butterfield, *George III and the Historians* (London: Collins, 1957), p. 211.

36. R. Walcott, *English Politics in the Early Eighteenth Century* (Oxford: Oxford University Press, 1956); J. H. Plumb, *The Origins of Political Stability: England, 1675-1725* (Boston: Houghton Mifflin, 1967), pp. xiv, 44-46, 135-138; Holmes, *British Politics in the Age of Anne*, pp. 2-4, 327-334.

37. H. R. Trevor-Roper, "Oliver Cromwell and His Parliament," in his *Religion, the Reformation and Social Change* (London: Macmillan, 1967).

38. Butterfield, *George III and the Historians*, pp. 208-209.

39. L. J. Edinger and D. S. Searing, "Social Background in Elite Analysis: A Methodological Enquiry," *American Political Science Review*, 61 (1967).

40. Peter Heath, *The English Parish Clergy on the Eve of the Reformation* (London: Routledge and Paul, 1969), pp. 187-196; M. Bowker, *The Secular Clergy in the Diocese of Lincoln, 1495-1520* (Cambridge, Eng.: Cambridge University Press, 1968).

41. G. A. J. Hodgett, "The Unpensioned Ex-Religious in Tudor England," *Journal of Ecclesiastical History*, 13 (1962).

42. G. Baskerville, *English Monks and the Suppression of the Monasteries* (London: Cape, 1937); Hodgett, "The Unpensioned Ex-Religious in Tudor England."

43. L. B. Smith, *Tudor Prelates and Politics* (Princeton: Princeton University Press, 1953).

44. M. Aston, "Lollardy and the Reformation: Survival or Revival?" *History*, 49 (1964); J. F. Davis, "Lollard Survival and the Textile Industry in the South-East of England," *Studies in Church History*, 3 (1966); W. Clebsch, *England's Earliest Protestants, 1520-1535* (New Haven: Yale University Press, 1964).

45. C. H. Garrett, *The Marian Exiles* (Cambridge, Eng.: Cambridge University Press, 1938); M. Walzer, *The Revolution of the Saints* (Cambridge, Mass.: Harvard University Press, 1965), pp. 92-113; J. E. Neale, *Elizabeth I and Her Parliaments, 1559-1581* (London: Cape, 1953), part I.

46. W. G. Hoskins, "The Leicestershire Country Parson in the Sixteenth Century," *Essays in Leicestershire History* (Liverpool: University Press, 1950); F. W. Brooks, "The Social Position of the Parson in the Sixteenth Century," *British Archaeological Society Journal*, 3d ser., 10 (1948); D. M. Barrett, "The Condition of the Parish Clergy Between the Reformation and

1660," Ph.D. diss., Oxford, 1949; P. Tyler, "The Status of the Elizabethan Parochial Clergy," *Studies in Church History*, 4 (1957).

47. There is a good deal of incidental prosopographical material in P. Collinson's great book, *The Elizabethan Puritan Movement* (London: Cape, 1967). P. S. Seaver, *The Puritan Lectureships* (Stanford: Stanford University Press, 1970), chaps. 5, 6.

48. A. G. Dickens, "The First Stages of Romanist Recusancy in Yorkshire, 1560-1590," *Yorkshire Archaeological Journal*, 35 (1941). See also J. Bossy, "The Character of Elizabethan Catholicism," *Past and Present*, 21 (1962); B. Magee, *The English Recusants* (London: Burns, Oates, and Washbourne, 1938).

49. For a summary of the controversy see L. Stone, *Social Change and Revolution in England, 1540-1640* (London: Longmans, 1965), pp. xi-xxvi; M. E. Finch, *The Wealth of Five Northamptonshire Families, 1540-1640* (Oxford: Northamptonshire Record Society, 1956); Cliffe, *The Yorkshire Gentry;* H. A. Lloyd, *The Gentry of South-West Wales, 1540-1640* (Cardiff: University of Wales Press, 1968); Stone, *The Crisis of the Aristocracy.* In the last few years some twenty doctoral theses have been or are being written on groups of gentry in various counties.

50. Cliffe, *The Yorkshire Gentry,* p. 354. These percentages and the conclusions drawn from them are mine, not Dr. Cliffe's.

51. Prosopography has also undermined another hypothesis about the causes of the Civil War, namely H. R. Trevor-Roper's claims about the role of the bureaucracy. G. E. Aylmer, "Office-holding as a Factor in English History, 1625-42," *History*, 44 (1959).

52. Unpublished theses by pupils of Sir John Neale, a brilliant synthesis and interpretation of whose findings is set out in his *Elizabethan House of Commons.* T. L. Moir, *The Addled Parliament of 1614* (Oxford: Clarendon Press, 1958); Keeler, *The Long Parliament;* Brunton and Pennington, *Members of the Long Parliament;* P. J. Pinkney, "The Cromwellian Parliament of 1656," Ph.D. diss., Vanderbilt, 1962; M. E. W. Helms, "The Convention Parliament of 1660," Ph.D. diss., Bryn Mawr, 1963.

53. Everitt, *The Community of Kent,* p. 143; V. Pearl, *London and the Outbreak of the Puritan Revolution* (London: Oxford University Press, 1961), p. 160; R. G. Howell, *Newcastle upon Tyne and the Puritan Revolution* (Oxford: Clarendon Press, 1967), pp. 171-173. The old elite held on in Suffolk. See A. Everitt, *Suffolk and the Great Rebellion, 1640-1660,* Suffolk Record Society, 3 (1960).

54. Distinguished elite studies by American scholars in American history include: J. T. Main, *The Upper House in Revolutionary America, 1763-1788* (Madison: University of Wisconsin Press, 1967); D. J. Rothman, *Politics and Power: The United States Senate, 1869-1901* (Cambridge, Mass.: Harvard University Press, 1966); S. H. Aronson, *Status and Kinship in the Higher Civil Service* (Cambridge, Mass.: Harvard University Press, 1964);

B. Bailyn, *New England Merchants in the Seventeenth Century* (Cambridge, Mass.: Harvard University Press, 1955); C. W. Mills, *The Power Elite* (New York: Oxford University Press, 1956); P. M. G. Harris, "The Social Origins of American Leaders: The Demographic Foundations," *Perspectives in American History,* 3 (1969), pp. 159-346. For bibliographies of the mass school, see n. 12 above.

55. See M. Clubb, "The Inter-University Consortium for Political Research: Progress and Prospects," *Historical Methods Newsletter,* 2 (1969).

56. The first abortive attempt to launch this project was in 1929, when an official committee was set up by the House of Commons to investigate "the materials available for a record of the personnel and politics of past members of the House of Commons from 1264 to 1832, and the cost of desirability of their publication." The committee reported favorably and in the 1930's Colonel Wedgwood produced two volumes on M.P.'s between 1439 and 1509. Unfortunately he failed to publish the third volume of synthesis and in any case his methods were so criticized that further work along these lines was abandoned. J. C. Wedgwood, *History of Parliament, Biographies of Members of the Commons' House, 1439-1509* (London: His Majesty's Stationery Office, 1936-1938). Review by M. McKisack in *English Historical Review,* 53 (1938), 503-506.

57. E. Le Roy Ladurie, N. Bernageau, and Y. Pasquet, "Le conscrit et l'ordinateur: perspectives de recherches," *Studi Storici,* 10 (1969). Recent French studies of elites include: F. Bluche, *Les magistrats du Parlement de Paris au XVIIIe siècle* (Paris: Les Belles Lettres, 1960); A. Corvisier, *L'armée française de la fin du XVIIe siècle au ministère de Choiseul* (Paris: Presses universitaires de France, 1964); L. Girard, A. Prost, R. Gossez, *Les Conseillers Généraux en 1870* (Paris: Presses universitaires de France, 1967).

58. See J. E. Neale, "The Biographical Approach to History," in his *Essays in Elizabethan History* (New York: St. Martin's Press, 1958), pp. 229-234.

Research for this paper was supported by grant GS 1559X from the National Science Foundation.

FELIX GILBERT

Intellectual History: Its Aims and Methods

OVER THIRTY years ago Perry Miller published his *New England Mind*. Hardly noticed at the time of its publication, and perhaps even viewed with some distrust as an audacious synthesis, the book was gradually recognized for its originality and has now become a classic. Miller himself was aware of the nonconformist nature of his undertaking and he justified his project and its method in a long foreword; he said that the book was intended "as the first volume in a projected series upon the intellectual history of New England." Was Miller aware that intellectual history was a novel concept, and by using this term did he want to indicate that his work belonged to a new genre of history?

Miller's reasons for using this term can no longer be established. The fact is that in 1939 the term "intellectual history" had not yet become a household word; it has crept gradually into the scholarly vocabulary. In 1904 James Harvey Robinson, one of the founding fathers of what then was called the "new history," offered a course entitled The Intellectual History of Western Europe, and Robinson referred to intellectual history at various occasions.[1] During the interwar years the term came more and more into use, but Perry Miller's *New England Mind*—and this statement is made with all the reservations with which statements about first occurrences must be made—seems to have been the first serious scholarly work which claimed to be an "intellectual history."

An examination of the history of this term reveals some further surprising facts. *Histoire intellectuelle* is not used by French scholars; nor does the *Oxford English Dictionary* recognize the existence of the term "intellectual history." The practice of the *New Cambridge Modern History* attests to the exactitude of the *Oxford English Dictionary*; none of the chapters of the *Cambridge Modern His-*

141

tory is entitled "intellectual history,"[2] although many of them deal
with subjects for which this term would have been appropriate. In
Italy in 1953 the term *storia intellettuale* was still such an unusual
combination that it was placed in quotation marks to indicate that
these two words might serve best to reproduce the meaning of the
German *Geistesgeschichte*.[3] The German knows only *Geistesgeschichte*[4] or *Ideengeschichte*, not *intellektuelle Geschichte*. The failure of historians of other countries to have an equivalent for what
in the United States is called "intellectual history" does not mean
that the subject matters which come under this heading are disregarded in other countries. In a discussion of the problems of intellectual history the first question, therefore, must be whether Americans have only given a convenient, all-encompassing name to a
number of different but related subject matters that in other countries go under various headings, or whether the new name indicates
the emergence of a new genre of history.

Unquestionably the subject matters which fall into the sphere of
intellectual history have always been concerns of the historian. He
has always studied the progress of scholarship—either by examining the history of universities[5] or by tracing the evolution of different scholarly fields—philosophy, law, economics; he has always
treated with particular attention and care the development of his
own field—the history of history. Works on these subjects have
taken different forms; they have focused on individual scholars;
they have analyzed change and progress in method; or they have
been concerned with the ideas determining these developments—
with the history of political thought, of economic thought, of religious thought, and so on. Such studies can also proceed horizontally, encompassing several or all fields of thought of an epoch; their
results might be presented in a national framework, as Leslie
Stephen did with his *History of English Thought in the Eighteenth
Century*, or such studies might attempt to delineate a movement
which extended over the entire European intellectual scene; the
Enlightenment has been a preferred subject matter of this latter
type.[6] The great intellectual movements which formed the dominant outlook of an entire period tie different ideas together in a
unique combination, but the various strains of this combination can
also be isolated and studied separately. We have had histories of the
idea of rationalism, of the idea of progress or of secularism. Usually,
investigation of the history of an idea has included the further question of its influence; the problem of the relation between thought

and action has been behind all such studies even when such a relation was by no means obvious. For instance, since Max Weber and Ernst Troeltsch raised the issue, the relation of religious thought to social life and economic activities has been a source of scholarly disputes. Because of the central role given to political history the discussion of ideas on politics has been a permanent theme in historical work. This concern has led to somewhat massive attempts to demonstrate that in the course of history man has always been dominated by one idea: for instance, that of extending the realm of freedom; or, on the other extreme, to very detailed and sophisticated investigations like those of Friedrich Meinecke in *Cosmopolitanism and the National State,* which carefully analyzes the intellectual influences that formed the mind of the active statesmen in one brief period of history.

It is evident that, insofar as the subject matter is concerned, intellectual history is nothing new; if the emergence of this term in our language represents a new departure it must be the manner in which it is treated that is new. And—as I shall try to show—this indeed is the case.[7]

The problem with which Perry Miller deals in his *New England Mind* is similar to that which forms the subject of Troeltsch's *Social Teachings of the Christian Churches:* the influence of religious beliefs and attitudes on social life and social action. In both cases the sources are primarily theological writings. Troeltsch examined the statements in these writings that had a direct bearing on social life and conduct. Miller reconstructed the entire system of thought of Puritan writers and teachers. He analyzed the logic with which they argued, their image of the cosmos, and their views on the nature of man; God's commands for the ordering of human society were presented as integral parts of the Puritan world view. Whereas Troeltsch assumed that intellectual developments in one field can be treated independently from those in other areas, Perry Miller demonstrated that a change in one area of thought involves a realignment of thought and action in all other spheres. The assumption on which Miller's "intellectual history" is based and which distinguishes his treatment from previous ones is that of the interconnected character of man's concept of life.

A broadening of the scope of investigation can be noticed also in another field of intellectual history—that of the development of the various branches of scholarship. Studies in the history of history usually focused on great historians. They analyzed the advance-

ment in method from one to the other and explained the progress
in historiography by stressing the influence of the philosophical
ideas of an age on historical writing. A prime example of this approach has been the historiography of the eighteenth century. The
philosophes, as critics of despotism and power politics, stressed the
importance of developments in the fields of thought—in art, philosophy, and science; according to them history ought to be history
of civilization. Belief in man's natural reason provided criteria with
which historians could gauge the defects of political institutions and
could measure progress. The philosophical rationalism of the Enlightenment implied skepticism about Christian legends and classical myths and induced a new critical approach to historical sources.
The views of the philosophes about the task of the historian were
neatly summarized by Voltaire in the statement: "Il faut écrire
l'histoire en philosophe." Indeed, scholars who studied eighteenth-
century historiography—for instance, Wilhelm Dilthey or John B.
Black[8]—chiefly analyzed the influence of the philosophical ideas of
the Enlightenment on the historical writings of the epoch. Briefly,
they tried to show that the eighteenth-century historians had done
what Voltaire had asked them to do. Indeed, this approach reveals
the basic intentions and the methodical innovations of historical
writers like Voltaire, Gibbon, Hume. But it has also become evident
that by focusing exclusively on these great literary figures the picture of the development of historiography in the eighteenth century
has been distorted or at least has remained incomplete.

A quite different side is revealed in Lionel Gossman's book,
Medieval Ideologies of the Enlightenment (1968). This work concentrates on what might be called the internal history of historiography: the relation of a historical work not to philosophy or politics
but to other historical writings of the time. Gossman examined the
great mass of material on historical subjects published by academies, preserved in manuscripts or contained in letters among intellectuals. The book shows that most of the investigations of historical
subjects were undertaken in answer to previous ones with which
they were closely linked; out of these debates methodical progress
and innovations or, as in the case of the subject of Gossman's book,
a new view about the significance of the Middle Ages emerged.
Gossman also shows the extent to which academies and salons—
that is, the places in which scholars exchanged ideas and presented
the results of their inquiries—patterned the content and the form of
their work. Gossman's book suggests that in the developments of

scholarship and intellectual life the means of intellectual communication are of crucial importance.[9]

A tendency to stress the links between the mind of the individual and the thinking of the group from which he comes can be noticed also in works dealing with a subject that has always been a favorite theme of the historian: the influence of ideas on politics. When Meinecke composed his *Cosmopolitanism and the National State* (1906) he seemed to strike out on a new line. He discussed the thought of poets, writers, and philosophers for their contribution to the development of nationalism and he then tried to show how these ideas were reflected in the minds of the political leaders who achieved German unification. But forty-five years later, in Federico Chabod's *Storia della politica estera Italiana dal 1870 al 1896,* the canvas was again enlarged. Chabod, on the basis of newspapers, speeches, and pamphlets, analyzed the impact which recent events—the reorganization of the European state system in 1871— had upon the various groups of Italian society. The result was an all-embracing but extremely differentiated picture of the political concerns in all strata of Italian society around 1870. Then Chabod proceeded carefully to investigate the development of each of the leading Italian statesmen and to establish their position in the spectrum of Italian public opinion—where they might have found political associates and where possible political adversaries; this analysis revealed the road which they might take but also the path which was closed to them. The result is a brilliant description of the mind of a ruling group clearly outlined in its particularity but placed in the framework of thought of the entire society.

Unquestionably, recent scholarly work in the area of intellectual history has stressed aspects which previously received little or no attention: the interconnected structure of thought; the internal self-propelling factors in the progress of scholarship as well as the importance of means of intellectual communication for the nature of an intellectual product and the need to extend analysis beyond prominent individuals to all strata of society. Nevertheless, this does not answer the question whether, and if so in what manner, these developments are connected with each other and whether they indicate a new stage in historiography in which intellectual history is recognized as a particular field of research with its own method, a branch of history equal in importance to the traditional genres of political, diplomatic, and economic history. The question to what extent a change has taken place requires some understanding of the

manner in which topics of intellectual history have been treated in
the past. This is a historiographical question which leads us far back
to the sixteenth century, to the beginnings of modern historiography.[10]

The outstanding historical works of the sixteenth and seventeenth century are lengthy detailed descriptions of political, diplomatic, and military events composed by statesmen or participants
like Francesco Guicciardini, the Earl of Clarendon, or Samuel Puf-
endorf. In the nineteenth century, when attention of the historian
was centered on these subjects, the only historical works of value
produced in these earlier centuries were believed to be the writings
of these statesmen-historians. It is true that when these histories
were published they aroused the interest of rulers and of members
of the ruling group. But students at the universities were taught a
very different, much less colorful brand of history. The subject of
history at the universities remained universal history although the
Reformation had forced some alterations in the medieval outline of
world history. Philipp Melanchthon had set up a new scheme of
world history compatible with the new ideas. He divided history
into two areas: the *historia ecclesiastica* was to focus on the history of the Church as signifying the continued existence of a spiritual world; the *historia ethnica* was to describe worldly events, although the existence of a chain of universal empires within which
profane history evolved served as a sign that God kept his protecting hand over all humanity and wanted to save all of it. Already the
generation following Melanchthon found this two-fold division incomplete and unsatisfactory. In 1583 one of Melanchthon's pupils
demanded that the categories of ecclesiastical and political history
should be complemented by addition of a further category, that of
scholarly history: "Scholasticam historiam dicere possumus, quae
versatur circa litteras, artes, diciplinas earumque originem, incre-
mentum, propagationem ac perfectionem demonstrat." The impetus
which artistic and scholarly endeavors had received in the fifteenth
and sixteenth centuries could not be disregarded. Thus, Francis
Bacon, one of the great synthesizers of the humanist and scholarly
thought of the previous centuries, took up the demand for an enlargement of history to include developments in intellectual life.
For Bacon history which omitted the history of literature and arts
"is not dissimilar to a statue of Polyphemus after his eye had been
removed."[11] But Bacon rejected separate histories of the lives of
scholars or of the development of individual sciences; the *historia*

artium et literarum, as he called it, ought to be treated as an inter-connected whole. He was aware that he asked for a kind of history that did not yet exist and indeed his suggestion found no followers. Perhaps Vico and Voltaire in the eighteenth century based their description of the various epochs of the past on a conviction of the inner unity of all intellectual phenomena. But in general scholars who worked in the field of *historia scholastica* wrote biographies of individual figures of intellectual life or histories of special scholarly fields. Although the importance of the subject was recognized, the historical literature which dealt with the phenomena of intellectual life stood outside the mainstream of historical scholarship.

When finally a closer integration of intellectual developments with the general course of history was attempted, the impulse came from another direction. That part of universal history that was treated in the *historia ecclesiastica* was inevitably drawn into the dogmatic disputes among the Christian churches and sects. Argu-ments from history were used in justification of the particular doc-trines of each of the Christian denominations; ecclesiastical history became imprisoned in the faculties of theology. Universal history now became identical with *historia politica* but the latter had to change its character insofar as it had to take over the most important task which the *historia ecclesiastica* had carried out: it had to endow the historical process with meaning. The developments of history were placed under the rule of ideas; if history had been separated from theology it became allied with philosophy. Philosophers un-dertook the task of elucidating the nature of the ideas that con-trolled the historical process. They demonstrated the logic by which these ideas were linked to each other; because ideas dominated the course of history each period of history was tied to the next in logi-cal succession. The names of Condorcet, Hegel, or Comte show the influence of these notions on the historical thinking of the nine-teenth century. Even Ranke, a more empirical mind, was imbued with this way of thinking. Although he might have felt uncertain about the human capacity to discern and define the logic of the historical process, he was convinced that each period of history was reflection of an individual idea and that this idea molded its various aspects. Politics, religion, literature, and philosophy all were ex-pressions of the same *Zeitgeist.* The age of "Realpolitik" was the time of realism in literature; in the period of Baroque art the con-duct of politics had Baroque features. In most historical works, how-ever, the attempts to establish connections among political, intellectual, and social life remained superficial. It is true that in Jakob Burckhardt's *Civilization of the Renaissance in Italy* the analysis of literature, poetry, and politics is linked together to an unforgettable picture of an entire period. But this is not only a unique work; Burckhardt was aware that his approach, with its emphasis on cultural history, was in opposition to that of the great majority of historians of his time. They shunned incisive analyses of literary, artistic, or philosophic thought, and developments in scholarship and science were hardly touched. They picked out a figure or a quotation which they considered to be characteristic of the pervasive mode of thought so that some of the discussions of the intellectual aspects of a period were highly subjective; a striking example is T. B. Macaulay's moralizing judgment about the authors of the Restoration comedies: "Whatever our dramatists touched, they tainted." Although intellectual developments were regarded to form a part of history, references to them remained spotty and primarily illustrative.

In the nineteenth century historical scholarship underwent not only the influence of philosophical idealism but it was also patterned by the forces struggling against this notion. In the overthrow of an idealistic world outlook the thought of Karl Marx has been the most powerful force. Whatever view one might have about the relation of the material to the ideal world and the degree of their dependence on each other, it is no longer possible to see ideas as determining events or floating freely above them. After Marx the existence of a close relation between ideas and interest can no longer be doubted and only careful analysis can determine the function of ideas in social life—whether they serve progress or rigidify the forces which inhibit development. Although Marx's criticism of the idealistic view of history has been his most significant contribution to the development of historiography, among his other contributions there are two which need to be mentioned in this context. One is the emphasis which he placed on the notion of structure.[12] Marx suggested that a change in one element of a social formation presupposes changes in every other element. This view implied the existence of a basic unity in man's attitude toward the various aspects of life. Furthermore, Marx's theory of the class struggle meant that a fundamental gap existed between the intellectual concerns and the outlook of the ruling class and the outlook of the lower classes, the ruled. Because society consisted of various groups with different interests the existence of a common dominating idea in each historical period could not be maintained, but the outlook of each period had to be conceived as a differentiated structure. Once this thesis had been advanced it became evident that the attention of historians had been exclusively focused on the ruling class and the actions of its members.

> Denn die einen sind im Dunkel
> Und die anderen sind im Licht
> Und man siehet die im Lichte
> Die im Dunkeln sieht man nicht.[13]

Exclusive concern with the upper classes particularly has shaped the historian's interest in intellectual and cultural phenomena. Scholars have concentrated on the various manifestations of high culture literature, painting, music—but those of popular culture or of the culture of the lower classes—popular religion, music, amusements— have hardly been found worth considering. This was more than an omission, it was a distortion because it disregarded the importance of the interaction which continuously takes place among the various levels of intellectual activities. The simultaneous existence of differ- ent levels of intellectual life might lead to modifications of each of them through interpenetration, or it might have the opposite effect of hardening each group in its own position. These questions can be answered only if the past is considered in all its aspects, not only in parts.

Marxism was not the only intellectual movement which under- mined the presuppositions of an idealistic view of history. Positiv- ism and the rise of the natural sciences with its emphasis on empiri- cism worked in the same direction of destroying the assumptions of an ideal reality behind the phenomenological world. By the end of the nineteenth century the notion of history as a process reflect- ing ideas and controlled by them was abandoned. What happened in historical scholarship was a narrowing of the area of scholarly concerns: research focused on documentary sources and history became exclusively political history.

This is a simplifying description of a somewhat more compli- cated development. The names of Oswald Spengler and Arnold Toynbee indicate that interpretations of universal history based on Hegelian foundations were not entirely abandoned. However, such wide-ranging projections had their life now outside profes- sional historical scholarship. Interest in the history of ideas also remained alive although they were considered to exist in wide

distance from the mainstream of history and the investigation of
their history became a special field of study.[14] Severed from the entanglement in metaphysical logic, each idea could be viewed as a
unit in itself and examined in isolation. An idea might broaden or
contract according to the association in which it was placed and
the use to which it was put. Such investigations can show how the
same idea can have distinct meanings in the minds of different
writers; on the other hand insistence on the key importance of the
same idea can serve to establish a common trend among intellectuals working in different fields. But the value of such studies, at
least for the historian, is limited because they do not include those
questions in which he is particularly interested: relation of idea and
interest; impact of thought on action; the connection between intellectual attitudes and social levels; and so on.

The fact is that by the end of the nineteenth century the linkage
between political and intellectual activities which the belief in the
power of ideas over history had established was broken. The professional historian tried to proceed in an almost scientific manner.
His traditional inclination toward political history became reinforced by the conviction that the sources for political history were
almost the only sources which could be scientifically explored. For
political developments, diplomatic actions, constitutional changes
were fixed in written documents. These areas were regarded as the
historian's legitimate concern.

It is a not uncommon error to assume that criticisms of the
narrowness of political and diplomatic history are of recent date.
Actually, they go back to the last decade of the nineteenth century;[15]
since then a discussion has been underway about the historical
significance of the social and cultural factors which, with the decline of historical idealism and the concentration on political history,
had been sloughed off the main body of historical work. The genesis
of the new history in the United States belongs in this context;[16] in
a country in which religious convictions and economic expansion
had been powerful historical forces the limited nature of a politically oriented historiography was particularly noticeable. A further
reason was the importance that the social sciences were gaining in
the United States; by stressing the role of social forces in history,
history would be brought into the orbit of the social sciences. In
any case it was of great significance for the rise of intellectual history in the twentieth century that, because of the exclusiveness
with which the historians practiced political history, the orphaned

fields of social history and intellectual history were coupled together. This relationship greatly influenced the evolution of intellectual history: it served to sharpen questions and to refine methods by directing attention to the methods and advances in the social sciences; it represented a spur to a clear definition of the task of the intellectual historian. The differences between older and more recent studies in the field of intellectual history to which the earlier part of this essay directed attention can now be seen as a result of the increased awareness with which research in this field had to be pursued. Changes took place in all areas of intellectual history—in the investigation of the mind of an individual, of the outlook of a group, or of the origin and the impact of an intellectual product.

The biography of an intellectual figure has always been recognized as a legitimate subject; the changes in this field, therefore, are particularly startling. In earlier times a man's ideas and thoughts were presented as parts of a system which he had formed in his early years and to which he held throughout his life. Early statements could be explained therefore by statements made in later life and vice versa. Or his system could be divided into its component parts and one chapter could summarize his views on moral philosophy, another on economics, and a third one on politics.[17] The scholar who broke with this approach was Dilthey, first in his *Leben Schleiermachers* and then in the *Jugendgeschichte Hegels*. Dilthey regarded mental attitudes as stimulated by external impressions; the mind of a person was nothing constant; it was in flux, changing and developing. Therefore in dealing with the life and the works of an intellectual figure a historian must follow the intellectual evolution of his hero from step to step. The written material from each period of life must be examined separately. No idea ought to be explained by reference to statements made at later times. One can understand the significance of an intellectual choice only if one is aware of the possibilities which existed. All this seems obvious, but if earlier times were not aware of what has now caused an excited debate, the distinction between the humanist Marx of early years and the materialist Marx of later years, the reason is that they did not know the genetic method.

The application of new methods is closely tied up with the opening up of new sources. In the writing of the biography of an intellectual figure, material which had seemed of secondary significance—drafts, fragments, lecture notes, private correspondence—

have gained importance because they might indicate the gradual maturation of ideas.

Any intellectual work is the product of its author's mind, but it is also shaped by its function. It is part of an intellectual debate. It answers questions which have previously been raised. It is presented in the form in which such problems have previously been treated. Consciously or unconsciously the writer has in his mind a model according to which he fashions his work. This has frequently been overlooked in the past. If people are astonished by the moralistic tone in general histories of the nineteenth century the reason is that they are no longer aware that history was taught at the universities as part of moral philosophy; such an original work as Burckhardt's *Weltgeschichtliche Betrachtungen* stills shows the traces of an adjustment to the moral purposes of history teaching. Briefly, it has become clear that no intellectual work can be really evaluated without knowledge of the model according to which it was patterned. Of course, great works and great achievements are those which break through the traditional mold and create a new trend. But an exact appreciation of what is new and has been achieved requires knowledge of the shell that was broken.

In many respects the methods available for the analysis of the evaluation of the mind of an individual and for the establishment of the distinctive intellectual features of a group are the same. But there are also methods particularly appropriate to the one or the other. If the genetic method is especially suited for a biographical study, a chief requirement in the discussion of intellectual developments and trends is the analysis of key concepts. Writings may differ in purpose and content; in order to demonstrate whether their authors have a common intellectual outlook, how one group differs from another, or what constitutes the dividing line between intellectual movements, it is necessary to find out to what extent the key concepts of their conceptual framework were identical. Bernard Bailyn, in his analysis of American pamphlets before the War of Independence, emphasized their common notions about the nature of power and the nature of liberty and concludes that these pamphlets showed an "integrated group of attitudes and ideas which made concerted action against the English rule possible."[18] There are many issues, of course, from which the common outlook of a group or intellectual divisions in a society can be inferred; the positive or negative evaluation of periods of the past—of the classical world, of the Middle Ages—has been frequently and efficiently used as such a touchstone. Probably it would not be right to claim more than that in cases where previous generations of scholars have trusted their intuition the present tendency is to be exact and detailed. The present manner of quoting might serve as an example. If a historian deals with the works of an individual, a striking and concise passage is in place. But when the thought of a group is discussed, the representative statement that can be backed up by a large number of similar statements is necessary and if footnotes with references to this mass of similar passages become too bulky the scholar will have to follow Perry Miller who placed into the library a complete set of notes "in which references are given . . . to other instances of like utterances."[19]

We have said that the interest of the intellectual historian has extended beyond the ruling group to all classes of society; this widening of his field of research requires new methodical procedures. In popular literature the contents, the ideas, are of secondary interest. They are simple and repetitive. The historian wants to know about the influence of this kind of literature and this question requires investigation of the size and number of editions, their regional distribution, and so on. This is a field for statistical investigations and has become more manageable through recent technical inventions. But we are only at the beginning of establishing the possibilities and limitations of statistical methods in this area.

In the case of popular literature it is clear that its contents is determined by the audience to which it is addressed. This can be said, however, about almost any intellectual product. Every intellectual activity wants to make some kind of appeal and is shaped by this need. In the past historians have rather neglected these questions and they have learned about their importance chiefly from studies in the field of sociology and political science. Clearly the decisive change in external conditions of intellectual life was the invention of printing. Whether a manuscript circulated among a small number of people with education and interests similar to those of the writer, or whether a manuscript might be read by a great number of people unknown to the author creates necessarily a great difference in the attitude of an author. The decline of Latin and the rise of the vernacular, the abandonment of a chancellery language in public documents in favor of the spoken language, these consequences of the invention of printing stimulated new developments in literary life and political thought. Moreover, printing was a business and writing became a profession. The invention of printing also placed the question of social control of intellectual and literary activities on a new level. It was the state and the government rather than the Church which by means of licenses and censorship could direct or influence the direction of intellectual work. The institutional aspects of these developments are well known but it is still somewhat *terra incognita* to what extent these developments shaped the course and the tempo of intellectual activities.

Methodical procedures are a scholastic subject; they have entered this discussion because, and insofar as, they reveal a characteristic trend of recent work in the field of intellectual history: search for precision. This tendency is a response to the objection which the intellectual historian frequently encounters: that he operates with vague terms like "influence" or "dominating trend," that his product lacks in precision and is "unscientific." It may have to be admitted that in work of an interpretative character intuition will always have a part, but although there may have been reasons for complaints about the lack of exactitude in intellectual history in the past, this negative attitude is hardly justifiable with regard to recent work done in this field.

Unquestionably the recognition of the need for carefulness and precision in intellectual history owes something to the fact that the intellectual historian wants to be able to compete with the social historian. The development of the relation between intellectual history and social history is interesting and enlightening. In a very general way they are complementary. In their modern form they emerged at the same time and as allies, both struggling against the domination of history by politics. This close relationship is reflected in the fact that at American colleges and universities courses bearing the double title Social and Intellectual History have been frequent.[20] But when their fight for recognition as essential branches of history had been won alliance changed into antagonism. One reason was the opposite nature of their subject matter. The social historian focuses on movements whose driving force frequently remains anonymous: demographic changes, economic growth, technological advances. The work of the intellectual historian remains tied to the human mind and its products. The difference in subject matter has created also a more profound contrast. The social historian tends to imply that a full analysis of the facts with which he is concerned might "explain" history and even indicate future trends. An extreme expression of this attitude is the view that the course of history is determined by laws which can be discovered. In a more cautious form the same idea can be found in the demand that the historian should concentrate on basic structures or forces of long duration like climate and geography; in relation to them a history of events deals with factors that are ephemeral.[21] The implication is that only social history comes to grips with the basic factors of history; only social history is "true history." This claim diminishes the value of all other branches of history and necessarily evokes the opposition of their practitioners.

The contentions of social history are of significance in our context for a special reason. They throw a sharp light on the general position of intellectual history and of the intellectual historian. Intellectual history cannot claim to be the true or only history; modern intellectual history arose after belief in the control of events by ideas had collapsed. It exists only in connection with, and in relation to, the surrounding political, economic, and social forces. The investigation of subjects of intellectual history leads beyond the purely intellectual world and intellectual history per se does not exist. But if this is so, has the intellectual historian a special task, and what is it?[22] The debate on this question has brought forth various suggestions and the answer most frequently given is that intellectual history is concerned with reconstructing the *Zeitgeist* of an epoch. This solution of the problem is questionable because every society consists of various social strata and each has its own intellectual outlook; if we go beyond reconstructing the outlook of the ruling group the picture becomes diffuse.[23] Moreover, there is still a Hegelian flavor in the assumption that each period has its own *Zeitgeist*. It might be more modest to say that the intellectual historian reconstitutes the mind of an individual or of groups at the times when a particular event happened or an advance was achieved. To call this formulation "modest" is probably an understatement because this task, if fully done, will lead very far afield. Moreover, it is a task of great import. Whatever one thinks of the forces that underlie the historical process, they are filtered through the human mind and this determines the tempo and the manner in which they work.[24] It is human consciousness which connects the long-range factors and forces and the individual event and it is at this crucial point of the historical process that the intellectual historian does his work.

REFERENCES

1. On James Harvey Robinson see Luther V. Hendricks, *James Harvey Robinson, Teacher of History* (New York: King's Crown Press, 1946), esp. p. 16. In James Harvey Robinson, *The New History* (New York: Macmillan, 1912), we find on pp. 101-131 an essay entitled "Some Reflections on Intellectual History," and the *Festschrift* devoted to him in 1929 was called *Essays in Intellectual History*, but for Robinson "intellectual history" seems to have been chiefly identical with a history of the progress of scholarship. For the questions connected with the development of this "branch" of history, see John Higham, "The Rise of American Intellectual History," *American Historical Review*, 56 (1951), 453-471, esp. pp. 458-459. Higham calls Carl Becker's *Declaration of Independence* "the first important contribution" of the new school of intellectual history, but it should be noted that Becker himself gave his book the subtitle *A Study in the History of Political Ideas*.

2. The term "intellectual" appears only in one chapter heading of the *New Cambridge Modern History*, in the combination "intellectual tendencies"; see vol. II, chap. XII.

3. See Delio Cantimori, *Studi di Storia* (Torino: Einaudi, 1959), p. 495, in an article which was first published in 1953. An earlier use of the word (see *ibid.*, p. 227) has not the meaning of "intellectual history."

4. *Geistesgeschichte* is used in different ways; for a recent application of this term, see note 23 below.

5. In a broad sense, the history of education falls into the category of intellectual history, but it has its special features which make a more detailed separate treatment desirable, see the essay by John Talbott in this volume; undoubtedly there are many parallels between the problems of modern intellectual history and modern history of education. On the other hand, the history of science seems a field somewhat apart; for a discussion of this problem, see the essay by Thomas Kuhn in this volume.

6. The two volumes of Peter Gay, *The Enlightenment: An Interpretation* (New York: Knopf, 1966-1969) are the most recent examples.

7. I would like to emphasize that the following confrontation of older with more recent works of historical scholarship is not meant to involve judgments of values; there are many factors—above and beyond methodical procedure—which determine the importance of a scholarly work.

8. Wilhelm Dilthey in "Das Achtzehnte Jahrhundert und die Geschichtliche Welt" (now in his *Gesammelte Schriften* [Leipzig: Teubner, 1921-1936], vol. III), and John B. Black in *The Art of History* (New York: Crofts, 1926).

9. For demonstration of this point, I could have also chosen the book by Andreas Kraus, *Vernunft und Geschichte, die Bedeutung der Deutschen Akademien für die Entwicklung der Geschichtswissenschaft im späten 18. Jahrhundert* (Freiburg: Herder, 1963); Kraus places particular emphasis

on the means of scholarly communication, but he follows very much the same lines as Gossmann, with equally startling results.

10. For the following, see Adalbert Klempt, *Die Saekularisierung der univer-sal-historischen Auffassung* (Göttingen: Musterschmidt Verlag, 1960). It is very characteristic that in earlier research the entire issue of the *historia scholastica* has been overlooked; it deserves more study.

11. Bacon, *De Augmentis scientiarum,* bk. II, chap. 4.

12. See R. Bastide, *Sens et usages du terme Structure* ('S-Gravenhage: Mouton, 1962), esp. pp. 100-106.

13. Bertolt Brecht in the film version of the *Dreigroschenoper,* badly trans-lated by Isherwood as:

> Therefore some are in darkness
> Some are in the light, and these
> You may see, but all those others
> In the darkness no one sees.

14. The program of this "school" has been outlined by Arthur O. Lovejoy, in an essay entitled "The Historiography of Ideas," now reprinted in his *Essays in the History of Ideas* (Baltimore: Johns Hopkins University Press, 1948); Lovejoy's program was broader than his interests which were pri-marily aesthetic and philosophical.

15. In Germany, a revolt against the concentration on political history broke out in the nineties, and many of the concepts which are now in the center of theoretical discussion—for instance, type, structure, statistical method, situation—made their appearance in this debate; see Gerhard Oestreich, "Die Fachhistorie und die Anfänge der sozialgeschichtlichen Forschung in Deutschland," *Historische Zeitschrift,* 208 (1969), 320-363. The struggle in Germany ended with a triumph of the political historians, at least in the sense that they were able to keep their opponents out of all influential posi-tions. In France, Henri Berr raised the demand for a *synthèse historique* in 1900, and the line runs from him to Marc Bloch and Lucien Febvre and the foundation of the *Annales.* Similar developments can be observed in Italy; only English history seems to have missed out on this controversy. It is a chapter of historiography which has never been treated in its appro-priate supranational context.

16. Higham's section in John Higham, Leonard Krieger, Felix Gilbert, *History* (Englewood Cliffs, N. J.: Prentice-Hall, 1965), describes in detail these developments in the United States.

17. See, for instance, Leslie Stephen's treatment of Locke in his *History of English Thought in the Eighteenth Century* (New York: G. P. Putnam's Sons, 1876).

18. See Bernard Bailyn, ed., *Pamphlets of the American Revolution,* I (Cam-bridge, Mass.: Harvard University Press, 1965), p. 60.

19. Perry Miller, *The New England Mind: The Seventeenth Century* (New York: Macmillan, 1939), p. ix.

20. See H. L. Swint, "Trends in the Teaching of Social and Intellectual History," *The Social Studies,* 46 (1955), 243-251.

21. On the concept of the *longue durée,* see Fernand Braudel in *Annales: économies, sociétés, civilisations* (1958), now reprinted in Fernand Braudel, *Ecrits sur l' histoire* (Paris: Flammarion, 1969), pp. 41ff. It seems to me that Braudel's emphasis on the importance of factors of *longue durée* has made the gap between structure and event almost unbridgeable. As important and rich as Braudel's *La Méditerranée et le monde méditerranéen à l'époque de Philippe II* is, I agree with Ernesto Sestan, "Storia degli Avvenimenti e Storia delle Strutture," report on the *XIII Congresso Internazionale di Science Storiche* (Moscow, 1970), pp. 24-25, that Braudel never fully succeeds in showing the relevance of the long-range developments for the events of the period of Philipe II. The question, as I shall discuss below, has bearing on the significance of intellectual history.

22. See Franklin L. Baumer, "Intellectual History and Its Problems," *Journal of Modern History,* 21 (1949), 191-203. But see also the review essay of Arthur M. Schlesinger in *History and Theory,* 7 (1968), 217-224, and the article by John Higham, "Intellectual History and Its Neighbors," *Journal of the History of Ideas,* 15 (1954), 339-347, for general considerations of the problem.

23. Hans Joachim Schoeps considers *Zeitgeistgeschichte* as the primary task of *Geistesgeschichte,* but the two volumes in which this notion is supposed to be carried out—*Das Wilhelminische Zeitalter* and *Zeitgeist der Weimarer Republik* (Stuttgart: Klett, 1967-1968)—present essays on various aspects of life, but no synthesis.

24. Marx's statement in his preface to the *Critique of Political Economy* deserves to be quoted: "In considering such transformations a distinction should always be made between the material transformation of the economic conditions of production which can be determined with the precision of natural science, and the legal, political, religious, aesthetic or philosophic forms in which men become conscious of this conflict and fight it out."

THOMAS S. KUHN

The Relations Between History and History of Science

THE INVITATION to write this essay asks that I address myself to
the relations between my own field and other sorts of history. "For
several decades," it points out, "the history of science has seemed
a discipline apart with only very tenuous links with other kinds
of historical study." That generalization, which errs only in sup-
posing that the separation is but a few decades old, isolates a
problem with which I have struggled, both intellectually and
emotionally, since I first began to teach the history of science,
twenty years ago. My colleagues and my students are no less aware
of it than I, and its existence does much to determine both the
scale and direction of our discipline's development. Strangely
enough, however, though we repeatedly gnaw at it among ourselves, no one has previously made the problem a matter for public
scrutiny and discussion. The opportunity to do so here is correspondingly welcome. Historians of science, if they must act alone,
are unlikely to succeed in resolving the central dilemma of their
field.

That perception of my assignment determines my approach.
My topic is one I have lived with rather than studied. The data
I bring to its analysis are correspondingly personal and impressionistic rather than systematic, with the result, among others, that
I shall consider only the situation in the United States. Partisanship
I shall try to avoid, but without hope of entire success, for I take
up the subject as an advocate, a man much concerned with some
central impediments to the development and exploitation of his
special field.

Despite the universal lip service paid by historians to the special
role of science in the development of Western culture during the
past four centuries, history of science is for most of them still

foreign territory. In many cases, perhaps in most, such resistance
to foreign travel does no obvious harm, for scientific development
has little apparent relevance to many of the central problems of
modern Western history. But men who consider socioeconomic development or who discuss changes in values, attitudes, and ideas
have regularly adverted to the sciences and must presumably continue to do so. Even they, however, regularly observe science from
afar, balking at the border which would give access to the terrain
and the natives they discuss. That resistance is damaging, both to
their own work and to the development of history of science.

To identify the problem more clearly, I shall begin this essay
by mapping the border which has heretofore separated the traditional fields of historical studies from history of science. Conceding
that part of the separation is due simply to the intrinsic technicality
of science, I shall next try to isolate and to examine the consequences of the still substantial division which will need to be
explained in other ways. Seeking such explanations, I shall first
discuss some aspects of a traditional historiography of science that
have characteristically repelled and sometimes also misled historians. Since that tradition has, however, been largely out of date
for a quarter of a century, it cannot entirely explain the historians'
contemporary stance. Fuller understanding must depend as well
upon an examination of selected aspects of the traditional structure
and ideology of the historical profession, topics to be examined
briefly in the penultimate sections below. To me, at least, the
more sociological sources of division there discussed seem central,
and it is hard to see how they are to be entirely overcome. Nevertheless, I shall consider in closing a few recent developments,
primarily within my own discipline, which suggest that an at least
partial rapprochement may characterize the decade immediately
ahead.

I

What does one have in mind when speaking of history of
science as "a discipline apart"? Partly that almost no students of
history pay any attention to it. Since 1956 my own courses in history
of science have regularly been listed among history courses under
the masthead of the department of which I was a member. Yet
in those courses only about one student in twenty has been an un-
dergraduate history major or a graduate student of history, except-

ing history of science. The majority of those enrolled have regularly been scientists or engineers. Among the remainder, philosophers and social scientists outnumber historians, and students of literature are not far behind. Again, in both the history departments to which I have belonged, a history-of-science area has been an available minor-field option for historians taking graduate general examinations. I think, however, of only five students who have elected it in fourteen years, a particular misfortune because these examinations provide an especially effective route to rapprochement. For some time I feared that the fault was my own, since my training was in physics rather than history and my teaching probably embodies residues. But all the colleagues to whom I have bemoaned the situation, many of them trained as historians, report identical experiences. Furthermore, the subject they teach appears not to matter. Courses on the Scientific Revolution or on Science in the French Revolution seem no more attractive to prospective historians than courses on the Development of Modern Physics. Apparently the word "science" in a title is sufficient to turn students of history away.

Those phenomena have a corollary which is equally revealing. Though history of science remains a small field, it has expanded more than tenfold in the last fifteen years, especially during the last eight. Most new members of the discipline are placed in history departments, which is, I shall later urge, where they belong. But the pressure to employ them almost always comes from outside rather than from within the department to which they are ultimately attached. Usually the initiative is taken by scientists or philosophers who must persuade the university administration to add a new slot in history. Only after that condition is met may a historian of science be appointed. Thereafter, he is usually treated with complete cordiality within his new department; no group has received me more warmly nor supplied more of my close friends than my history colleagues. Nevertheless, in subtle ways the historian of science is sometimes asked to maintain intellectual distance. I have, for example, occasionally had to defend the work of a colleague or student from a historian's charge that it was not really history of science at all but just history. In ways that are obscure, and perhaps correspondingly important, a historian of science is expected, occasionally even by older historians of science, to be not quite a historian.

The preceding remarks are directed to the social indices of

separatism. Look now at some of its pedagogic and intellectual consequences. These seem to be primarily of two sorts, neither of which can be considered in much detail until I discuss, below, the extent to which they are merely the inevitable results of the intrinsic technicality of scientific source materials. Even a sketchy description at this point will, however, point the direction of my argument.

One over-all consequence of separatism has, I think, been the abdication by historians of responsibility for evaluating and portraying the role of science in the development of Western culture since the end of the Middle Ages. To those tasks the historian of science can and must make essential contributions, at least by providing the books, monographs, and articles which will be the main sources for other sorts of historians. But insofar as his first commitment is to his specialty, the student of scientific development is no more responsible for the task of integration than the historian of ideas or of socioeconomic development, and he has generally been less well equipped than they to perform it. What is needed is a critical interpenetration of the concerns and achievements of historians of science with those of men tilling certain other historical fields, and such interpenetration, if it has occurred at all, is not evident in the work of most current historians. The usual global acknowledgments that science has somehow been vastly important to the development of modern Western society provide no substitute. Taken in conjunction with the few traditional examples used to illustrate them, they often exaggerate and regularly distort the nature, extent, and timing of the sciences' role.

Surveys of the development of Western civilization illustrate the main consequences of the failure to interpenetrate. Perhaps the most striking of these is the almost total neglect of scientific development since 1750, the period during which science assumed its main role as a historical prime mover. A chapter on the Industrial Revolution—the relation of which to science is at once interesting, obscure, and undiscussed—is sometimes succeeded by a section on Darwinism, mostly social. Often that is all! The overwhelming majority of the space devoted to science in all but a very few general history books is reserved for the years before 1750, an imbalance with disastrous consequences to which I shall return in Section III below.[1]

Neglect of science, though less extreme, used also to characterize discussions of European history in the years before 1750. With respect to space allocation, however, that oversight has been generously rectified since the appearance in 1949 of Herbert Butterfield's admirable *Origins of Modern Science*. By now almost all surveys have come to include a chapter or major section on the Scientific Revolution of the sixteenth and seventeenth centuries. But those chapters often fail to recognize, much less to confront, the principal historiographic novelty which Butterfield discovered in the current specialists' literature and made available to a wider audience—the relatively minor role played by new experimental methods in the substantive changes of scientific theory during the Scientific Revolution. They are still dominated by old myths about the role of method, to the consequences of which I shall return below.[2]

Perhaps it is some sense of that inadequacy which often makes historians reluctant to give lectures accompanying the reading on the birth of modern science. Occasionally, if unable to co-opt a historian of science to fill the gap, they simply assign chapters in Butterfield as a supplement and reserve discussion for section meetings. Butterfield or the bomb has persuaded historians that they must take some account of science's role, and they attempt to discharge that obligation with a block of material on the Scientific Revolution. But the chapters they then produce seldom reflect an awareness of the problems with which their subject has confronted recent generations of academic specialists. Students must usually look elsewhere for examples of the critical standards ordinarily defended by the profession.

Neglect of the current specialists' literature is, however, only one part of the problem and perhaps not the most serious. More central is the peculiar selectivity with which historians approach the sciences, whether through primary or secondary sources. Dealing with, say, music or the arts, the historian may read program notes and the catalogues of exhibits, but he also listens to symphonies and looks at paintings, and his discussion, whatever its sources, is directed to them. Dealing with the sciences, however, he reads *and discusses* programmatic works almost exclusively: Bacon's *Novum Organum,* but usually Book I (the Idols) rather than Book II (heat as motion); Descartes' *Discourse on Method,* but not the three substantive essays to which it provides the introduction; Galileo's *Assayer,* but only the introductory pages of his *Two New Sciences;* and so on. The same selectivity shows in the historian's attention to secondary works: Alexandre Koyré's *From the Closed World to the Infinite Universe,* but not his *Études galiléennes* or *The Problem of Fall;* E. A. Burtt's *Metaphysical Foundations of Modern Physical Science,* but not E. J. Dijksterhuis' magistral *Mechanization of the World Picture.*[3] Even within individual works there is a marked tendency, which I shall illustrate below, to skip the chapters that deal with technical contributions.

I do not suggest that what scientists say about what they do is irrelevant to their performance and their concrete achievements. Nor am I suggesting that historians ought not read and discuss programmatic works. But, as the parallel to program notes should indicate, the relation of prefaces and programmatic writings to substantive science is seldom literal and always problematic. The former must, of course, be read, for they are frequently the media through which scientific ideas reach a larger public. But they are often decisively misleading with respect to a whole series of issues that the historian ought, and often pretends, to deal with: Where do influential scientific ideas come from? What gives them their special authority and appeal? To what extent do they remain the same ideas as they become effective in the larger culture? And, finally, if their influence is not literal, in what sense is it really due to the science to which it is imputed?[4] The intellectual impact of the sciences on extrascientific thought will not, in short, be understood without attention also to the sciences' technical core. That historians regularly attempt such a sleight of hand suggests that one essential part of what has to this point been described as a gap between history and history of science might more accurately be seen as a barrier between historians as a group and the sciences. To that point, also, I shall return more concretely below.

II

Before looking more closely at the manner in which historians approach the sciences, I must, however, ask how much may reasonably be expected of them. That question, in turn, demands a sharp separation between the problems of intellectual history, on the one hand, and those of socioeconomic history, on the other. Let me consider them in order.

Intellectual history is the area in which the historian's selectivity with respect to sources has its primary effect, and one may well wonder whether he has an alternative. Excepting historians of science, among whom the requisite skills are also relatively rare, almost no historians have the training required to read, say, the works of Euler and Lagrange, Maxwell and Boltzmann, or Einstein and Bohr. But that is a very special list in several respects. All the men on it are mathematical physicists; the oldest of them was not born until the first decade of the eighteenth century; and none of them, so far as I can see, has had more than the most tenuous and indirect impact upon the development of extrascientific thought.

The last point, which is the crucial one, may be debatable and ultimately wrong with respect to Einstein and Bohr. Discussions of the contemporary intellectual scene often refer to relativity and the quantum theory when discussing such issues as the limitations of science and of reason. Yet the arguments for direct influence—as against the appeal to authority in support of views held for other reasons—have so far been extremely forced. My own suspicion, which provides at least a reasonable working hypothesis, is that after a science has become thoroughly technical, particularly mathematically technical, its role as a force in intellectual history becomes relatively insignificant. Probably there are occasional exceptions, but if Einstein and Bohr provide them, then the exceptions prove the rule. Whatever their role may have been, it is very different from that of, say, Galileo, or Descartes, of Lyell, Playfair, or Darwin, or, for that matter, of Freud, all of whom were read by laymen. If the intellectual historian must consider scientists, they are generally the early figures in the development of their fields.

Not surprisingly, just because the figures he must treat are the early ones, the intellectual historian could handle them in depth if he wished to do so. The job would not be easy: I am not arguing that no significant effort is required—only that there is no other way. Nor would every historian be responsible for undertaking it regardless of his interests. But the man whose concerns include ideas affected by scientific development could study the technical scientific source materials to which he currently only makes reference. Very little of the technical literature written before 1700 is in principle inaccessible to anyone with sound high school scientific training, at least not if he is willing to undertake a modicum of additional work as he goes along. For the eighteenth century the same background in science is adequate to the literature of chemistry, experimental physics (particularly electricity, optics, and heat), geology, and biology—all of science, in short, excepting mathematical mechanics and astronomy. For the nineteenth century most of physics and much of chemistry becomes excessively technical, but men with high school science have access to almost the whole literature of geology, biology, and psychology. I do not suggest that the historian should become a historian of science whenever scientific development becomes relevant to the topic he studies. Here, as elsewhere, specialization is inevitable. But he could in principle do so, and he can therefore certainly command the specialists' secondary literature on his topic. By failing to do even that, he ignores constitutive elements and problems of scientific advance, and the result, as I shall shortly indicate, shows in his work.

The preceding list of topics potentially accessible to the intellectual historian is revealing in two respects. First, as already indicated, it includes all the technical subject matters with which, *qua* intellectual historian, he is likely to wish to deal. Second, it is coextensive with the list of fields which have been most and best discussed by historians of science. Contrary to a widespread impression, historians of science have seldom dealt in depth with the development of the technically most advanced subjects. Studies of the history of mechanics are sparse from the eve of the publication of Newton's *Principia;* histories of electricity break off with Franklin or at most with Charles Coulomb; of chemistry with Antoine Lavoisier or John Dalton; and so on. The main exceptions, though not the only ones, are Whiggish compendia by scientists, sometimes invaluable as reference works, but otherwise virtually useless to the man whose interests include the development of ideas. However regrettable, that imbalance in favor of relatively nontechnical subjects should surprise no one. Most of the men who have produced the models which contemporary historians of science aim to emulate have not been scientists nor have they had much scientific training. Interestingly enough, however, their background has not been in history either, though historians might have done the job and even done it better since their concerns would not have been so narrowly focused on the conceptual. Instead, they have come from philosophy, though mostly, like Koyré, from Continental schools where the divide between history and philosophy is by no means so deep as in the English-speaking world. All of which suggests once more that a central part of the problem to which this paper is addressed arises from the attitudes of historians toward science.

I shall explore these attitudes further near the end of this essay, but must first ask whether they make any difference to the performance of the tasks which intellectual historians undertake. Obviously they do not in the large proportion of cases which involve scientific ideas only marginally or not at all. In numerous other cases, however, characteristic infirmities result from what I have previously described as history derived predominantly from prefaces and programmatic works. When scientific ideas are discussed without reference to the concrete technical problems against which they were forged, what results is a decidedly misleading notion of the way in which scientific theories develop and impinge on their extrascientific environment.

One form which the systematic misdirection takes is particularly clear in discussions of the Scientific Revolution, including many by older historians of science: an excessive emphasis on the role of new methods, particularly on the power of experiment to create, by itself, new scientific theories. Reading the continuing argument over the so-called Merton thesis, for example, I am constantly depressed by the almost universal misstatement of what that debate is about. What is really at issue, I take it, is an explanation of the rise and dominion of the Baconian movement in England. Both proponents and critics of the Merton thesis simply take it for granted that an explanation of the rise of the new experimental philosophy is tantamount to an explanation of scientific development. On that view, if Puritanism or some other new trend in religion increased the dignity of manual manipulation and fostered the search for God in His works, then, ipso facto, it fostered science. Conversely, if first-rate science was done in Catholic countries, then no Protestant religious movements could be responsible for the rise of seventeenth-century science.

That all-or-nothing polarization is, however, unnecessary and it may well be false. A strong case can be made for the thesis that Baconian experimentalism had comparatively little to do with the main changes of scientific theory which marked the Scientific Revolution. Astronomy and mechanics were transformed with little recourse to experiment and none to new sorts of experimentation. In optics and physiology experiment played a larger role, but the models were not Baconian but rather classic and medieval: Galen in physiology, Ptolemy and Alhazen in optics. These fields plus mathematics exhaust the list of those in which theory was radically transformed during the Scientific Revolution. With respect to their practice neither experimentalism nor its putative religious correlate should be expected to make much difference.

That view, if correct, does not, however, render either Baconianism or new religious movements unimportant to scientific development. What it does suggest is that the role of the new Baconian methods and values was not to produce new theories in previously established sciences but rather to make new fields, often those with roots in the prior crafts, available for scientific scrutiny (for example, magnetism, chemistry, electricity, and the study of heat). Those fields, however, received little significant theoretical reordering before the mid-eighteenth century, the time through which one must wait to discover that the Baconian movement in the sciences was by no means a fraud. That Britain rather than Catholic France, especially after the revocation of the edict of Nantes, played the dominant role in bringing order to these newer, more Baconian fields may indicate that a revised Merton thesis will yet prove immensely informative. Perhaps it will even help us understand why one old saw about science continues to withstand close scrutiny: at least from 1700 to 1850, British science was predominantly experimental and mechanical, French mathematical and rationalistic. In addition, it may tell us something about the quite special roles played by Scotland and Switzerland in the scientific developments of the eighteenth century.

That historians have had such difficulty in even imagining possibilities like these is, I think, at least partly due to a widespread conviction that scientists discover truth by the quasi-mechanical (and perhaps not very interesting) application of scientific method. Having accounted for the seventeenth-century discovery of method, the historian may, and indeed does, leave the sciences to shift for themselves. That attitude, however, cannot be quite conscious, for another main by-product of preface history is incompatible with it. On the rare occasions when they turn from scientific methods to the substance of new scientific theories, historians seem invariably to give excessive emphasis to the role of the surrounding climate of extrascientific ideas. I would not argue for a moment that that climate is unimportant to scientific development. But, except in the rudimentary stages of the development of a field, the ambient intellectual milieu reacts on the theoretical structure of a science only to the extent that it can be made relevant to the concrete technical problems with which the practitioners of that field engage. Historians of science may, in the past, have been excessively concerned with this technical core, but historians have usually ignored its existence entirely. They know it is there, but they act as though it were the mere product of science—of proper method acting in a suitable environment—

rather than being the most essential of all the various determinants of a science's development. What results from this approach is reminiscent of the story of the emperor's new clothes.

Let me give two concrete examples. Both intellectual historians and historians of art often describe the novel intellectual currents of the Renaissance, especially Neoplatonism, which made it possible for Kepler to introduce the ellipse to astronomy, thus breaking the traditional hold of orbits compounded from perfect circular motions. On this view, Tycho's neutral observations plus the Renaissance intellectual milieu yield Kepler's Laws. What is regularly ignored, however, is the elementary fact that elliptical orbits would have been useless if applied to any geocentric astronomical scheme. Before the use of ellipses could transform astronomy, the sun had to replace the earth at the center of the universe. That step was not, however, taken until just over a half-century before Kepler's work, and to it the novel *intellectual* climate of the Renaissance made only equivocal contributions. It is an open question, as well as an interesting and important one, whether Kepler might not equally easily have been led to ellipses without benefit of Neoplatonism.[5] To tell the story without reference to any of the technical factors on which the answer to that question depends is to misrepresent the manner in which scientific laws and theories enter the realm of ideas at large.

A more important example to the same effect is provided by countless standard discussions of the origin of Darwin's theory of evolution.[6] What was required, we are told, to transform the static Chain of Being into an ever-moving escalator was the currency of such ideas as infinite perfectability and progress, the laissez-faire competitive economy of an Adam Smith, and, above all, the population analyses of Malthus. I cannot doubt that factors of this sort were vitally important; anyone who does would do well to ask how, in their absence, the historian is to understand the proliferation, particularly in England, of pre-Darwinian evolutionary theories like those of Erasmus Darwin, Spencer, and Robert Chambers. Yet these speculative theories were uniformly anathema to the scientists whom Charles Darwin managed to persuade in the course of making evolutionary theory a standard ingredient of the Western intellectual heritage. What Darwin did, unlike these predecessors, was to show how evolutionary concepts should be applied to a mass of observational materials which had accumulated only during the first half of the nineteenth century and were, quite independently of evolutionary ideas, already making trouble for several recognized scientific specialties. This part of the Darwin story, without which the whole cannot be understood, demands analysis of the changing state, during the decades before the *Origin of Species,* of fields like stratigraphy and paleontology, the geographical study of plant and animal distribution, and the increasing success of classificatory systems which substituted morphological resemblances for Linneaus' parallelisms of function. The men who, in developing natural systems of classification, first spoke of tendrils as "aborted" leaves or who accounted for the different number of ovaries in closely related plant species by referring to the "adherence" in one species of organs separate in the other were not evolutionists by any means. But without their work, Darwin's *Origin* could not have achieved either its final form or its impact on the scientific and the lay public.

One last point will conclude this portion of my argument. I said earlier that, in accounting for the genesis of novel scientific theories, the emphasis on method and the emphasis on extra-scientific intellectual milieu were not quite compatible. I would now add that, at the most fundamental level, the two prove to be identical in their effects. Both induce an apparently incurable Whiggishness which permits the historian to dismiss as superstition all the scientific forebears of the ideas with which he deals. The hold of the circle on the astronomical imagination is to be understood as a product of the Platonic infatuation with geometric perfection, perpetuated by medieval dogmatism; the endurance in biology of the idea of fixed species is to be understood as the result of an excessively literal reading of Genesis. What is missing from the first account, however, is any reference to the elegant and predictively successful astronomical systems built from circles, an achievement on which Copernicus did not himself improve. What is missing from the second is any recognition that the observed existence of discrete species, without which there could be no taxonomic enterprise, becomes extremely difficult to understand unless the current members of each descend from some original pair. Since Darwin the definition of basic taxonomic categories like species and genus have necessarily become and remained relatively arbitrary and extraordinarily problematic. Conversely, one technical root of Darwin's work is the increasing difficulty, during the early nineteenth century, of applying these standard classificatory tools to a body of data vastly expanded by, among other things, exploration of the New World and the Pacific. In short, ideas which the historian dismisses as superstitions usually prove to have been crucial elements in highly successful older scientific systems. When they do, the emergence of novel replacements will not be understood as the consequence merely of good method applied in a favorable intellectual milieu.

III

I have spoken so far of the effect of preface history on the man concerned to place science in intellectual history. Turning now to standard views about the socioeconomic role of science, one encounters a very different situation. What the historian lacks in this area is not so much a knowledge of technical sources, which would in any case be largely irrelevant, as a command of conceptual distinctions essential to the analysis of science as a social force. Some of those distinctions would generate themselves if the socioeconomic historian possessed a better understanding of the nature of science as an enterprise and of its changes over time. Concerned with the role of the sciences, he requires at least a global sense of how men gain membership in scientific communities, of what they then do, where their problems come from, and what they receive as solutions. To this extent, his needs overlap the intellectual historian's, though they are technically far less demanding. But the socioeconomic historian also has needs which the intellectual historian does not: some knowledge of the nature of technology as an enterprise, an ability to distinguish it from science, both socially and intellectually, and above all a sensitivity to the various modes of interaction between the two.

Science, when it affects socioeconomic development at all, does so through technology. Historians tend frequently to conflate the two enterprises, abetted by prefaces which, since the seventeenth century, have regularly proclaimed the utility of science and have often then illustrated it with explanations of existing machines and modes of production.[7] On these issues, too, Bacon has been taken not only seriously, as he should be, but literally, as he should not. The methodological innovations of the seventeenth century are thus seen as the source of a useful as well as sound science. Explicitly or implicitly, science is portrayed as having played a steadily increasing socioeconomic role ever since. In fact, however, despite the hortatory claims of Bacon and his successors for three centuries, technology flourished without significant substantive inputs from the sciences until about one hundred years ago. Science's emergence as a prime mover in socioeconomic development was not a gradual but a sudden phenomenon, first significantly foreshadowed in the organic-chemical dye industry in the 1870's, continued in the electric power industry from the 1890's, and rapidly accelerated since the 1920's. To treat these developments as the emergent consequences of the Scientific Revolution is to miss one of the radical historical transformations constitutive of the contemporary scene. Many current debates over science policy would be more fruitful if the nature of this change were better understood.

To that transformation I shall return but must first sketch, however simplistically and dogmatically, some background for it. Science and technology had been separate enterprises before Bacon announced their marriage in the beginning of the seventeenth century, and they continued separate for almost three centuries more. Until late in the nineteenth century, significant technological innovations almost never came from the men, the institutions, or the social groups that contributed to the sciences. Though scientists sometimes tried and though their spokesmen often claimed success, the effective improvers of technology were predominantly craftsmen, foremen, and ingenious contrivers, a group often in sharp conflict with their contemporaries in the sciences.[8] Scorn for inventors shows repeatedly in the literature of science, and hostility to the pretentious, abstract, and wool-gathering scientist is a persistent theme in the literature of technology. There is even evidence that this polarization of science and technology has deep sociological roots, for almost no historical society has managed successfully to nurture both at the same time.

Greece, when it came to value its science, viewed technology as a finished heritage from its ancient gods; Rome, on the other hand, famous for its technology, produced no notable science. The series of late-medieval and Renaissance technological innovations which made possible the emergence of modern European culture had largely ceased before the Scientific Revolution began. Britain, though it produced a significant series of isolated innovators, was generally backward in at least the abstract and developed sciences during the century which embraces the Industrial Revolution, while technologically second-rate France was the world's preeminent scientific power. With the possible exceptions (it is too early to be sure) of the United States and the Soviet Union since about

1930, Germany during the century before World War II is the only nation that has managed simultaneously to support first-rate traditions in both science and technology. Institutional separation—the universities for *Wissenschaft* and the Technische Hochschulen for industry and the crafts—is a likely cause of that unique success. As a first approximation, the historian of socioeconomic development would do well to treat science and technology as radically distinct enterprises, not unlike the sciences and the arts. That technologies have, between the Renaissance and the late nineteenth century, usually been classified as arts is not an accident.

Starting from this perspective one can ask, as the socioeconomic historian must, about interactions between the two enterprises, now seen as distinct. Such interactions have characteristically been of three sorts, one dating from antiquity, the second from the mid-eighteenth century, and the third from the late nineteenth. The longest lasting, now probably finished except in the social sciences, is the impact of preexisting technologies, whatever their source, on the sciences. Ancient statics, the new sciences of the seventeenth century like magnetism and chemistry, and the development of thermodynamics in the nineteenth century all provide examples. In each of these cases and countless others, critically important advances in the understanding of nature resulted from the decision of scientists to study what craftsmen had already learned how to do. There are other main sources of novelty in the sciences, but this one has too often been underrated, except perhaps by Marxists.

In all these cases, however, the resulting benefits have accrued to science not to technology, a point which Marxist historians repeatedly miss. When Kepler studied the optimum dimension of wine casks, the proportions which would yield maximum content for the least consumption of wood, he helped to invent the calculus of variations, but existing wine casks were, he found, already built to the dimensions he derived. When Sadi Carnot undertook to produce the theory of the steam engine, a prime mover to which, as he emphasized, science had contributed little or nothing, the result was an important step toward thermodynamics; his prescription for engine improvement, however, had been embodied in engineering practice before his study began.[9] With few exceptions, none of much significance, the scientists who turned to technology for their problems succeeded merely in validating and explaining, not in improving, techniques developed earlier and without science's aid.

A second mode of interaction, visible from the mid-eighteenth century, was the increasing deployment in the practical arts of methods borrowed from science and sometimes of scientists themselves.[10] The effectiveness of the movement remains uncertain. It has, for example, no apparent role in the development of the new textile machinery and iron fabricating techniques so important to the Industrial Revolution. But the "experimental farms" of eighteenth-century Britain, the record books of the stock breeders, and the experiments on steam that Watt performed in developing the separate condenser are all plausibly seen as a conscious attempt to employ scientific methods in the crafts, and such methods were on occasions productive. The men who used them were seldom, however, contributors to contemporary science which, in any case, few of them knew. When they succeeded, it was not by applying existing science but by a frontal attack, however methodologically sophisticated, on a recognized social need.

Only in chemistry is the situation significantly more equivocal.[11] Particularly in France, distinguished chemists, including both Lavoisier and C. L. Bertolet, were employed to supervise and improve such industries as dyeing, ceramics, and gunpowder. Their regimens, furthermore, were an apparent success. But the changes they introduced were neither dramatic nor, in any obvious way, dependent on contemporary chemical theory and discovery. Lavoisier's new chemistry is a case in point. It undoubtedly provided a more profound understanding of the previously developed technology of ore reduction, acids manufacture, and so on. In addition it permitted the gradual elaboration of better techniques of quality control. But it was responsible for no fundamental changes in these established industries, nor did it have an observable role in the nineteenth-century development of such new technologies as sulphuric acid, soda, or wrought iron and steel. If one looks for important new processes which result from the development of scientific knowledge, one must wait for the maturation of organic chemistry, current electricity, and thermodynamics during the generations from 1840 to 1870.

Products and processes derived from prior scientific research and dependent for their development on additional research by men with scientific training display a third mode of interaction between science and technology.[12] Since its emergence in the organic dye industry a century ago, it has transformed communication, the generation and distribution of power (twice), the materials both of industry and of everyday life, and also both medicine and warfare. Today its omnipresence and importance disguise the still real cleavage between science and technology. In the process, they make it difficult to realize how very recent and decisive the emergence of this kind of interaction has been. Even economic historians seldom seem aware of the qualitative divide between the forces promoting change during the Industrial Revolution and those operative in the twentieth century. Most general histories disguise even the existence of any such transformation. One need not, however, inflate the importance of history of science to suppose that since 1870 science has assumed a role which no student of modern socioeconomic development may responsibly ignore.

What are the sources of the transformation and how may the socioeconomic historian contribute to their understanding? I suggest there are two, of which he can recognize the first and participate in unraveling the second. No science, however highly developed, need have applications which will significantly alter existing technological practice. The classical sciences like mechanics, astronomy, and mathematics had few such effects even after they were recast during the Scientific Revolution. The sciences which did were those born of the Baconian movement of the seventeenth century, particularly chemistry and electricity. But even they did not reach the levels of development required to generate significant applications until the middle third of the nineteenth century. Before the maturation of these fields at mid-century, there was little of much socioeconomic importance that scientific knowledge in any field could produce. Though few socioeconomic historians are equipped to follow the technical aspects of the advances which suddenly made science productive of new materials and devices, they can surely be aware of these developments and their special role.

Internal technical development was not, however, the only requisite for the emergence of a socially significant science, and about what remained the socioeconomic historian could have a great deal of significance to say. During the nineteenth century the institutional and social structure of the sciences was transformed in ways not even foreshadowed in the Scientific Revolution. Beginning in the 1780's and continuing through the first half of the following century, newly formed societies of specialists in individual branches of science assumed the leadership which the all-embracing national societies had previously attempted to supply. Simultaneously, private scientific journals and particularly journals of individual specialties proliferated rapidly and increasingly replaced the house organs of the national academies which had previously been the almost exclusive media of public scientific communication. A similar change is visible in scientific education and in the locus of research. Excepting in medicine and at a few military schools, scientific education scarcely existed before the foundation of the École polytechnique in the last decade of the eighteenth century. That model spread rapidly, however, first to Germany, then to the United States, and finally, more equivocally, to England. With it developed other new institutional forms, especially teaching and research laboratories, like Justus von Liebig's at Giessen or the Royal College of Chemistry in London. These are the developments which first made possible and then supported what had previously scarcely existed, the professional scientific career. Like a potentially applicable science, they emerged relatively suddenly and quickly. Together with the maturation of the Baconian sciences of the seventeenth century, they are the pivot of a second scientific revolution which centered in the first half of the *nineteenth* century, a historical episode at least as crucial to an understanding of modern times as its older namesake. It is time it found its way into history books, but it is too much a part of other developments in the nineteenth century to be untangled by historians of science alone.

IV

I have so far been describing the historian's neglect of science and its history, repeatedly implying while doing so that the blame lies exclusively with historians, scarcely at all with the specialists who have chosen science as their object of study. Today, for reasons to which I shall return, that allocation of responsibility seems to me increasingly nearly justified, if ultimately unfair. But the current situation is in part a product of the past. If the contemporary gap between history and history of science is to be further analyzed in hope of its amelioration, the contribution to separatism made by the history of the history of science must first be recognized.

Until the early years of this century, history of science, or what little there was of it, was dominated by two main traditions.[13] One of them, with an almost continuous tradition from Condorcet and

Comte to Dampier and Sarton, viewed scientific advance as the triumph of reason over primitive superstition, the unique example of humanity operating in its highest mode. Though vast scholarship, some of it still useful, was sometimes expended on them, the chronicles which this tradition produced were ultimately hortatory in intent, and they included remarkably little information about the content of science beyond who first made which positive discovery when. Except occasionally for reference or the preparation of historiographic articles, no contemporary historian of science reads them, a fact which does not yet seem to have been as widely appreciated as it should be by the historical profession at large. Though I know it will give offense to some people whose feelings I value, I see no alternative to underscoring the point. Historians of science owe the late George Sarton an immense debt for his role in establishing their profession, but the image of their specialty which he propagated continues to do much damage even though it has long since been rejected.

A second tradition, more important both for its products and because, particularly on the Continent, it still displays some life, originates with practicing scientists, sometimes eminent ones, who have from time to time prepared histories of their specialties. Their work usually began as a by-product of science pedagogy and was directed predominantly to science students. Besides intrinsic appeal, they saw in such histories a means to elucidate the contents of their specialty, to establish its tradition, and to attract students. The volumes they produced were and are quite technical, and the best of them can still be used with profit by specialists with different historiographic inclinations. But seen as history, at least from current perspectives, the tradition has two great limitations. Excepting in occasional naïve asides, it produced exclusively internal histories which considered neither context for, nor external effects of, the evolution of the concepts and techniques being discussed. That limitation need not always have been a defect, for the mature sciences are regularly more insulated from the external climate, at least of ideas, than are other creative fields. But it was undoubtedly badly overdone and, in any case, made work in this mode unattractive to historians, excepting perhaps historians of ideas.

Even the purest historians of ideas were, however, repelled and on occasion seriously misled by a second and even more pronounced defect of this tradition. Scientist-historians and those who followed their lead characteristically imposed contemporary scientific categories, concepts, and standards on the past. Sometimes a specialty which they traced from antiquity had not existed as a recognized subject for study until a generation before they wrote. Nevertheless, knowing what belonged to it, they retrieved the specialty's current contents from past texts of a variety of heterogeneous fields, not noticing that the tradition they constructed in the process had never existed. In addition, they usually treated concepts and theories of the past as imperfect approximations to those in current use, thus disguising both the structure and integrity of past scientific traditions. Inevitably, histories written in this way reinforced the impression that the history of science is a not very interesting chronicle of the triumph of sound method over careless error and superstition. If these were the only possible models available, one could criticize historians for little except being too easily misled.

But they are not the only models, nor for thirty years have they been even the ones dominant in the profession. Those derive from a more recent tradition which increasingly adapted to the sciences an approach discovered in late-nineteenth-century histories of philosophy. In that field, of course, only the most partisan could feel confident of their ability to distinguish positive knowledge from error and superstition. As a result, historians could scarcely escape the force of an injunction later phrased succinctly by Bertrand Russell: "In studying a philosopher, the right attitude is neither reverence nor contempt, but first a kind of hypothetical sympathy, until it is possible to know what it feels like to believe in his theories."[14] In the history of ideas, the resulting tradition is the one which produced both Ernst Cassirer and Arthur Lovejoy, men whose work, however profound its limitations, has had a great and fructifying influence on the subsequent treatment of ideas in history. What is surprising and remains to be explained is the lack of any comparable influence, even on intellectual historians, of the works of the men who, following Alexandre Koyré, have for a generation been developing the same models for the sciences. Seen through their writings, science is not the same enterprise as the one represented in either of the older traditions. For the first time it has become potentially a fully historical enterprise, like music, literature, philosophy, or law.

I say "potentially" because that model too has limitations. Though it has extended the proper subject matter of the historian of science to the entire context of ideas, it remains internal history in the sense that it pays little or no attention to the institutional or socioeconomic context within which the sciences have developed. Recent historiography has, for example, largely discredited the myth of method, but it has then had difficulty finding any significant role for the Baconian movement and has had little but scorn for either the Merton thesis or the relation between science and technology, industry, or the crafts.[15] It is time to confess that a few of the object lessons I have read to historians above could be fruitfully circulated in my own profession as well. But the areas to which these object lessons apply are the interstices between history of science and the now standard concerns of the cultural and socioeconomic historian. They will need to be worked by both groups. Given a model of the internal development of science which provides points of entrée, historians of science are now increasingly turning to it, a movement to be discussed in my concluding section. I am aware of no comparable movement within the historical profession at large.

V

Clearly, historians of science must share the blame. But no catalogue of their past and present sins will entirely explain the realities of their current relation to the rest of the historical profession. What currency their work has achieved has come primarily through Butterfield's book, published over twenty years ago, when their discipline was embryonic, and never fully assimilated since. Neglect of their subject matter, science, remains particularly acute for just the years during which it became a major historical force. Though usually placed in history departments, their courses are seldom taken and their books seldom read by historians. About the causes of that situation I can only speculate and part of that speculation must deal with subjects that I know only through conversations with colleagues and friends. Nevertheless, the occasion of this volume may provide an excuse for speculation.

Two sorts of explanations suggest themselves, of which the first arises from what is perhaps a factor unique to history among the learned disciplines. History of science is not in principle a narrower specialty than, say, political, diplomatic, social, or intellectual history. Nor are its methods radically distinct from the ones employed in those fields. But it is a specialty of a different sort, for it is concerned in the first instance with the activity of a special group—the scientists—rather than with a set of phenomena which must at the start be abstracted from the totality of activities within a geographically defined community. In this respect its natural kin are the history of literature, of philosophy, of music, and of the plastic arts.[16] These specialties, however, are not ordinarily offered by departments of history. Instead, they are more or less integral parts of the offering of the department responsible for the discipline of which the history is to be studied. Perhaps historians react to the history of science in the same way that they do to the history of other disciplines. Perhaps it is only the proximity created by membership in the same department which leads to a special sense of strain.

Those suggestions I owe to Carl Schorske, one of the two historians with whom I and my students have interacted most closely and fruitfully since I first began to teach in a history department fourteen years ago. He has persuaded me, though not until this essay was well advanced, that many of the problems discussed under the heading of science-in-intellectual-history, above, have precise parallels in the historian's typical discussion of other intellectual, literary, and artistic pursuits. Historians are, he argues, often quite adept at retrieving from a novel, a painting, or a philosophical disquisition, themes which reflect contemporary social problems and values. What they regularly miss, however, sometimes by explaining them away, are those aspects of these artifacts that are internally determined, partly by the intrinsic nature of the discipline which produces them and partly by the special role which that discipline's past always plays in its current evolution. Artists, whether in imitation or revolt, build from past art. Like scientists, philosophers, writers, and musicians, they live and work both within a larger culture and within a quasi-independent disciplinary tradition of their own. Both environments shape their creative products, but the historian all too often considers only the first.

Excepting in my own field, my competence for evaluating these generalizations is restricted to history of philosophy. There, however, they fit as precisely as they do in history of science. Since they are, in addition, extremely plausible, I shall tentatively accept them. What historians generally view as historical in the development of individual creative disciplines are those aspects which reflect its immersion in a larger society. What they all too often reject, as not quite history, are those internal features which give the discipline a history in its own right.

The perception which permits that rejection seems to me profoundly unhistorical. The historian does not apply it in other realms. Why should he do so here? Consider, for example, the manner in which historians treat geographical and linguistic subdivisions. Few of them would deny the existence of problems which can be treated only on the gigantic canvas of world history. But they do not therefore deny that the study of the development of Europe or America is also historical. Nor do they resist the next step, which finds a legitimate role for national or even county histories provided that their authors remain alert to the aspects of their restricted subject which are determined by the influence of surrounding groups. When, as is inevitable, communication problems arise, for example between British and European historians, these are deplored as historiographic blinders and as likely sources of error. The feelings which are generated sometimes resemble those which historians of science or art regularly encounter, but no one would say *out loud* that French history is by definition historical in some sense in which British is not. Yet that is very often the response when the analytic units shift from geographically defined subsystems to groups whose cohesiveness—not necessarily less (or more) real than that of a national community—derives from training in a special discipline and an allegiance to its special values. Perhaps if historians could admit the existence of seams in Clio's web, they could more easily recognize that there are no rents.

The resistance to disciplinary histories is not, of course, exclusively the fault of the historians who work within history departments. With a few notable exceptions like Paul Kristeller and Erwin Panofsky, the men who study a discipline's development from within that discipline's parent department concentrate excessively on the internal logic of the field they study, often missing both consequences and causes in the larger cultures. I remember with deep embarrassment the day on which a student found occasion to remind me that Arnold Sommerfeld's relativistic treatment of the atom was invented midway through the First World War. Institutional separations depress historical sensitivities on both sides of the barrier they create. Nor is separation the only source of difficulty. The man who teaches within the department responsible for the discipline he studies almost always addresses himself to that discipline's practitioners or, in the case of literature and the arts, to its critics. Usually the historical dimension of his work is subordinated to the function of teaching and perfecting the current discipline. History of philosophy, as taught within philosophy departments, is often, for example, a parody of the historical. Reading a work of the past, the philosopher regularly seeks the author's positions on current problems, criticizes them with the aid of current apparatus, and interprets his text to maximize its coherence with modern doctrine. In that process the historic original is often lost. I am told, for example, of the response of a former philosophy colleague to a student who questioned his reading of a passage in Marx. "Yes," he said, "the words do seem to say what you suggest. But that cannot be what Marx meant, for it is plainly false." Why Marx should have chosen to use the words he did was not a problem worth pausing for.

Most examples of the Whiggishness enforced by placing history in the service of a parent discipline are more subtle but no less unhistorical. The damage they do is no greater, I think, than that done by the historian's rejection of disciplinary history, but it is surely as great. I have already pointed out that history of science displayed all the same unhistorical syndromes when it was taught within science departments. The forces which have increasingly transferred it to history departments in recent years have placed it where it belongs. Though a shotgun was required for the wedding and though the strains characteristic of forced marriages result, the offspring may yet be viable. I cannot doubt that similar compulsory association with the practitioners of other branches of disciplinary history would be equally fruitful. Perhaps, as my first history department chairman, the late George Guttridge, once remarked, we shall soon recognize how badly history fits the departmental organization of American universities. Some transdepartmental institutional arrangement is badly needed, perhaps a faculty or school of historical studies which would bring together all those whose concern, regardless of their departmental affiliations, is with the past in evolution.

VI

I have been considering the suggestion that the relations between history and history of science differ only in intensity, not in kind, from the relations between history and the study of the development of other disciplines. The parallels are, I think, clear, and they carry us a long way toward an understanding of the problem I have been asked to discuss. But they are not complete, and they do not explain everything. Treating literature, art, or philosophy, historians do, I have suggested, read sources as they do not in the sciences. The historian's ignorance of even the main developmental stages of science has no parallel for the other disciplines on which he touches. Even offered in other departments, courses in the history of literature and the arts are more likely to attract historians than courses in the history of science. Above all, there is no precedent in other disciplines for the historian's exclusive attention to a single period when discussing a science. Those historians who consider art, literature, or philosophy at all are as likely to do so when dealing with the nineteenth century as with the Renaissance. Science, on the other hand, is a topic to be discussed only between 1540 and 1700. One reason, I suspect, for the historian's characteristic emphasis on the discovery of method is that it protects him from the need to deal with the sciences after that period. With their method in hand, the sciences cease to be historical, a perception for which there is no parallel in the historian's view of other disciplines.

Contemplating these phenomena and some more personal experiences to be illustrated below, I reluctantly conclude that part of what separates historians from their colleagues in history of science is what, in addition to personality, separates F. R. Leavis from C. P. Snow. Though I sympathize with those who believe it has been misnamed, the two-culture problem is another probable source of the difficulties we have been considering.

My basis for that conjecture is largely impressionistic, but not entirely so. Consider the following quotation from a British psychologist whose tests enable him to predict with some assurance the future specialties of high school students, even though (like I.Q. tests, which he includes) they discriminate scarcely at all between those who will do well and badly after specialization:

The typical historian or modern linguist had, relatively speaking, rather a low I.Q., and a verbal bias of intelligence. He was prone to work erratically on the intelligence test, accurate at times and slap dash at others; and his interests tended to be cultural rather than practical. The young physical scientist often had a high I.Q., and a non verbal bias of ability; he was usually consistently accurate; his interests were usually technical, mechanical, or in life out of doors. Naturally, these rules-of-thumb were not perfect: a minority of arts specialists had scores like scientists, and vice versa. But, by and large, the predictions held surprisingly well, and at the extremes they were infallible.[17]

Together with other evidence from the same source, this passage suggests that historians and scientists, at least those of the more mathematical and abstract sort, are polar types.[18] Other studies, though insufficiently detailed to single out historians, indicate that scientists as a group come from a lower socioeconomic stratum than their academic colleagues in other fields.[19] Personal impressions, both from my own school days and my children's, suggest that the intellectual differences appear quite early, especially in mathematics where they are often obvious before age fourteen. I am thinking now not primarily of ability or creativity, but merely of affection. Though there are both exceptions and a large middle ground, I suggest that a passion for history is seldom compatible with even a developed liking for mathematics or laboratory science, and vice versa.

Not surprisingly, as these polarities develop and are embodied in career decisions, they often find expression in defensiveness and hostility. The historians who read this essay will not need to be told of the often overt disdain of scientists for historical studies. Unless I suppose that it is reciprocated, I cannot account for the stance, described above, of historians toward the sciences. Historians of science ought to be exceptions, but even they often prove the rule. Most of them begin in science, turning to its history only at the graduate level. Those who do frequently insist that their interest is only in history of science not in mere history, a field they conceive as at once irrelevant and uninteresting. As a result, they are more easily attracted to special departments or programs than to regular history departments. Fortunately, it is usually possible to convert them once they are there.

If, however, many historians are hostile to science—as I suppose—it must be admitted that they disguise it well, far better, for example, than their colleagues in literature, language, and the arts, who are often entirely explicit. Yet that difference provides at least no counterevidence, for it could have been expected. Like philosophers and unlike most students of literature and art, historians see their enterprise as somehow cognitive and thus akin to science if not of it. With scientists they share such values as impartiality, objectivity, and faithfulness to evidence. They too have tasted the forbidden fruit of the tree of knowledge, and the antiscientific rhetoric of the arts is no longer available to them. There are, however, subtler ways of expressing hostility, some of which I have suggested above. This part of my argument will therefore conclude with some evidence of a more personal sort.

The first is a memorable encounter with a much-valued friend and colleague, who has from time to time organized and led an experimental seminar at Princeton designed to acquaint first-year graduate students with ancillary methods and approaches for which the future specialist may some day find a use. When appropriate, a local or visiting specialist is asked to manage discussion and to consult about the preparatory reading. Several years ago I accepted an invitation to lead the group in the first of a pair of meetings on the history of science. The central item of the reading, selected after much talk, was an old book of mine, *The Copernican Revolution.* That choice may not have been the best, but there were reasons for it, explicit both in my conversations with my colleague and in the preface. Though not a text, the book was written so that it could be used in college courses on science for the nonscientist. It would not, therefore, present insuperable obstacles to our graduate students. More important, when it was written the book was the only one that attempted to portray, within a single pair of covers, both the technical-astronomical and the wider intellectual-historical dimensions of the revolution. It was thus a concrete example of the point I have argued more abstractly above: the role of science in intellectual history cannot be understood without the science. How many students grasped that point I cannot be sure, but my colleague did not. Midway through a lively discussion, he interjected, "But, of course, I skipped the technical parts." Since he is a busy man, the omission may not be surprising. But what is suggested by his willingness, unsolicited, to make it public?

My second, briefer example is in the public domain. Frank Manuel's *Portrait of Isaac Newton* is surely the most brilliant and thorough study of its subject in a very long time. Excepting those offended by its psychoanalytic approach, the Newtonian experts with whom I have discussed it assure me that it will affect their work for years to come. History of science would be far poorer if it had not been written. Nevertheless, in the present context, it raises a fundamental question. Is there any field but science in which one can imagine a historian's preparing a major biography which omits, consciously and deliberately, any attempt to deal with the creative work which made its subject's life a worthy object of study. I cannot think of a similar labor of love devoted to a major figure in the arts, philosophy, religion, or public life. Under the circumstances, I am not sure that love is the emotion involved.

These examples were introduced by the claim that they would display hostility to science. Having presented them, I confess my uncertainty that "hostility" is altogether the appropriate term. But they are examples of strange behavior. If what they illustrate must for the moment remain obscure, it may nevertheless constitute the central impediment separating history and history of science.

VII

Having by now said more than all I know about the barriers which divide history from history of science, I shall conclude with some brief remarks on signs of change. One of them is the mere proliferation of historians of science and their increasing placement in departments of history. Though both numbers and proximity may be initially a source of friction, they also increase the availability of communication channels. Growth is also responsible for a second encouraging development, the increasing attention now being devoted to periods more recent than the Scientific Revolution and to previously little explored parts of science. The better secondary literature will not for much longer be restricted to the sixteenth and seventeenth centuries, nor will it continue to deal primarily with the physical sciences. The current increase in the study of the history of the life sciences may prove particularly important. These fields have, until recently, been far less technical than the main physical sciences contemporary with them. Studies which trace their development are likely to be correspondingly more accessible to the historian who would like to discover what history of science is about.

Look next at two other developments the effects of which are now observable among many of the history of science's younger practitioners. Led by Frances Yates and Walter Pagel, they are now finding increasingly significant roles for Hermeticism and related movements in the early stages of the Scientific Revolution.[20] The original and exciting literature which results may well have three effects which transcend its explicit subject. First, just because Hermeticism was an avowedly mystical and irrational movement, recognition of its roles should help to make science more palatable to historians repelled by what many have taken to be a quasi-mechanical enterprise, governed by pure reason and cold fact. (It would plainly be absurd to select the rational elements from Hermeticism for exclusive attention as an older generation has done with Neoplatonism.) Second, Hermeticism now appears to have affected two aspects of scientific development previously seen as mutually exclusive and defended by competing schools. On the one hand, it was an intellectual, quasi-metaphysical movement which changed man's ideas about the entities and causes underlying natural phenomena; as such it is analyzable by the usual techniques of the historian of ideas. But it was also a movement which, in the figure of the Magus, prescribed new goals and methods for science. Treatises on, for example, Natural Magic show that the new emphasis on science's power, on the study of crafts, and on mechanical manipulation and machines are in part products of the same movement that changed the intellectual climate. Two disparate approaches to the history of science are thus unified in a way likely to have particular appeal to the historian. Finally, newest, and perhaps most important, Hermeticism now begins to be studied as a class movement with a discernable social base.[21] If that development continues, the study of the Scientific Revolution will become multi-dimensional cultural history of the sort many historians are now also striving to create.

I turn finally to the newest movement of all, apparent primarily among graduate students and the very youngest members of the profession. Perhaps partly because of their increasing contact with historians, they are turning more and more to the study of what is often described as external history. Increasingly they emphasize the effects on science not of the intellectual but of the socioeconomic milieu, effects manifest in changing patterns of education, institutionalization, communication, and values. Their efforts owe something to the older Marxist histories, but their concerns are at once broader, deeper, and less doctrinaire than those of their predecessors. Because historians will find themselves more at home with its products than they have been with older histories of science, they are particularly likely to welcome the change. Indeed they may even learn from it something of more general relevance. Like literature and the arts, science is the product of a group, a community of scientists. But in the sciences, particularly in the later stages of their development, disciplinary communities are both easier to isolate and also more nearly self-contained and self-sufficient than the relevant groups in other fields. As a result the sciences provide a particularly promising area in which to explore the role of forces current in the larger society in shaping the evolution of a discipline which is simultaneously controlled by its own internal demands.[22] That study, if successful, could provide models for a variety of fields besides the sciences.

All these developments are necessarily encouraging to anyone bothered by the traditional chasm between history and the history of science. If they continue, as seems likely, it will be less deep a decade hence than it has been in the past. But it is not likely to disappear, for the new trends described above can have only indirect, partial, and long-range effects on what I take to be the fundamental source of the division. Perhaps the example of history of science can by itself undermine the historian's resistance to disciplinary history, but I would be more confident if I knew the reasons for that resistance in the past. In any case, history of science is, by itself, an unlikely remedy for a social malady so deep and widespread as the two-culture problem. Instead, in my most depressed moments, I sometimes fear that history of science may yet be that problem's victim. Though I welcome the turn to external history of science as redressing a balance which has long been seriously askew, its new popularity may not be an unmixed blessing. One reason it now flourishes is undoubtedly the increasingly virulent antiscientific climate of these times. If it becomes the exclusive approach, history of science could be reduced to a higher-level version of the tradition which, by leaving the science out, ignored the internalities which shape the development of any discipline. That price would be too high to pay for rapprochement, but unless historians can find a place for the history of disciplines, it will be hard to avoid.

In revising this essay I have profited from occasional comments made at the conference for which it was prepared, particularly those of M. I. Finley. Even more helpful have been criticisms of my draft by several colleagues: T. M. Brown, Roger Hahn, J. L. Heilbron, and Carl Schorske. None of them agrees altogether with the views here expressed, but the paper is better for their intervention.

REFERENCES

1. Roger Hahn persuades me that a few very recent textbooks show signs of change. Perhaps I am *merely* impatient. But the progress of the last half-dozen years, if it is real, still seems to me belated, scattered, and incomplete. Why, for example, has J. H. Randall's *Making of the Modern Mind*,

a book first published in 1926 and long out of date, yet to be surpassed as a balanced survey of science's role in the development of Western thought?

2. One aspect of Butterfield's discussion has, in fact, helped to preserve the myths. The historiographic novelties accessible through his book are concentrated in chaps. 1, 2, and 4, which deal with the development of astronomy and mechanics. These are, however, juxtaposed with essentially traditional accounts of the methodological views of Bacon and Descartes, illustrated in application by a chapter on William Harvey. The two resulting versions of the requisites for a transformed science are hard to reconcile, a fact which Butterfield's subsequent discussion of the Chemical Revolution makes particularly apparent.

3. The following observation may strengthen the point at which I aim. In the arts the men who create and those who criticize belong to separate, often hostile, groups. Historians may sometimes rely excessively on the latter, but they know the difference between critics and artists, and they are careful to acquaint themselves with works of art as well. In the sciences, on the other hand, the nearest equivalents to the works of critics are written by scientists themselves, usually in prefatory chapters or separate essays. Historians usually rely *exclusively* on these works of "criticism," failing to note, because their authors were also creative scientists, that that selection leaves the science out. On the significance of the different role of the critic in science and in art see my "Comment [on the Relation of Science and Art]," in *Comparative Studies in Society and History*, 11 (1969), 403-412.

4. For an example of the sort of illumination that can be provided by someone who knows the science and its history see the discussion of science's role in the Enlightenment by C. C. Gillispie, *The Edge of Objectivity* (Princeton: Princeton University Press, 1960), chap. 5.

5. T. S. Kuhn, *The Copernican Revolution* (Cambridge, Mass.: Harvard University Press, 1957), pp. 135-143. N. R. Hanson, *Patterns of Discovery* (Cambridge, Eng.: University Press, 1958), chap. 4. Note that there are other aspects of Kepler's thought to which the relevance of Neoplatonism is beyond doubt.

6. See, for example, R. M. Young, "Malthus and the Evolutionists: The Common Context of Biological and Social Theory," *Past and Present*, no. 43 (1969), 109-145, an essay which includes much useful guidance to the recent literature on Darwinism. Note, however, one irony which illustrates the problems of perception now under discussion. Young opens by deploring the asumptions, widespread among "both historians of science and other sorts of historians . . . that scientific ideas and findings can be dealt with as relatively unequivocal units with fairly sharply defined boundaries . . . [and] that 'non-scientific' factors [have] played relatively little part in shaping the development of scientific ideas." His paper is intended as "a case study which attempts to break down barriers in one small area between the history of science and other branches of history." Obviously, this is just the sort of contribution which I too would particularly welcome.

Yet Young cites almost no literature which has attempted to explain the emergence of Darwinism as a response to the development of *scientific* ideas or techniques, and indeed there is very little to cite. Nor does his own paper make any attempt to deal with the technical issues which may have helped to shape Darwin's thought. Very likely it will be for some time the standard account of Malthus' influence on evolutionary thought, for it is admirably thorough, erudite, and perceptive. But far from being a barrier breaker, it belongs to a standard historiographic tradition which has done much to preserve the very separation Young deplores.

7. The historian's difficulties with science-*cum*-technology are nowhere better illustrated than in discussions of the Industrial Revolution. The long-standard attitude is that of T. S. Ashton, *The Industrial Revolution, 1760-1830* (London and New York: Oxford University Press, 1948), p. 15: "The stream of English scientific thought, issuing from the teaching of Francis Bacon, and enlarged by the genius of Boyle and Newton, was one of the main tributaries of the industrial revolution." Roland Mousnier's *Progrès scientifique et technique au XVIIIe siècle* (Paris: Plon, 1958) takes the opposite position in an even more extreme form, arguing for total independence of the two enterprises. As a corrective to the view that the Industrial Revolution was applied Newtonian science, Mousnier's version is an improvement, but it entirely misses the significant methodological and ideological interactions of eighteenth-century science and technology. For these see below or the excellent sketch in the chapter "Science" in E. J. Hobsbawm's *The Age of Revolution, 1789-1848* (Cleveland: World Publishing Company, 1962).

8. R. P. Multhauf, "The Scientist and the 'Improver' of Technology," *Technology and Culture*, 1 (1959), 38-47; C. C. Gillispie, "The *Encyclopédie* and the Jacobin Philosophy of Science," in M. Clagett, ed., *Critical Problems in the History of Science* (Madison: University of Wisconsin Press, 1959), pp. 255-289. For hints at an explanation of the dichotomy, see my "Comments" in R. R. Nelson, ed., *The Rate and Direction of Inventive Activity*, a Report of the National Bureau of Economic Research (Princeton: Princeton University Press, 1962), pp. 379-384, 450-457, and the epilogue of my paper, "The Essential Tension: Tradition and Innovation in Scientific Research," in C. W. Taylor and Frank Barron, *Scientific Creativity: Its Recognition and Development* (New York: Wiley, 1963), pp. 341-354.

9. W. C. Unwin, "The Development of the Experimental Study of Heat Engines," *The Electrician*, 35 (1895), 46-50, 77-80, is a striking account of the difficulties encountered when attempting to use Carnot's theory and its successors for practical engineering design.

10. C. C. Gillispie, "The Natural History of Industry," and R. E. Schofield, "The Industrial Orientation of the Lunar Society of Birmingham," *Isis*, 48 (1957), 398-407, 408-415. Note the extent to which both authors, while disagreeing vehemently, are nevertheless defending the same thesis in different words.

11. H. Guerlac, "Some French Antecedents of the Chemical Revolution,"

Chymia, 5 (1968), 73-112; Archibald Clow and N. L. Clow, *The Chemical Revolution* (London: Batchworth Press, 1952); and L. F. Haber, *The Chemical Industry during the Nineteenth Century* (Oxford: Clarendon Press, 1958).

12. John Beer, *The Emergence of the German Dye Industry,* Illinois Studies in the Social Sciences, 44 (Urbana: University of Illinois Press, 1959); H. C. Passer, *The Electrical Manufacturers, 1875-1900* (Cambridge, Mass.: Harvard University Press, 1953).

13. A number of the following points are developed more fully in my "History of Science," *International Encyclopedia of the Social Sciences,* 14 (New York, 1968), 74-83.

14. Bertrand Russell, *A History of Western Philosophy* (New York: Simon and Schuster, 1945), p. 39.

15. T. S. Kuhn, "Alexandre Koyré and the History of Science," *Encounter,* 34 (1970), 67-70.

16. M. I. Finley points out that the history of law would provide an even more revealing parallel. The law, after all, is one of the obvious determinants of the sorts of political and social developments which historians have traditionally studied. But, excepting for reference to the expression of society's will through legislation, historians seldom pay attention to its evolution as an institution. Reactions at the conference to Peter Paret's insistance that military history must be in part the history of the military establishment as an institution with a life that is in part its own suggests how deep resistance to disciplinary history sometimes lies. Participants suggested, for example, that what military history ought to be is the study of the social sources of war and of the effects of war on society. But these subjects, though they perhaps provide the main reasons for wanting to have military history done, must not be its primary focus. An understanding of wars, their development and consequences, depends in essential ways on an understanding of military establishments. In any case, the subject war-and-society is as much the responsibility of the general historian as of his colleague who specializes in military history. The parallel to history of science is very close.

17. Liam Hudson, *Contrary Imaginations: A Psychological Study of the English Schoolboy* (London: Methuen, 1966), p. 22.

18. A fuller analysis, to which Hudson's pioneering book provides many fascinating leads, would recognize that there are multiple dimensions of polarization. For example, the same sorts of scientists who are most likely to disdain history are often passionately interested in music though not usually in the other main forms of artistic expression. Neither Hudson nor I is referring to a simple spectrum ranging from the artist, at one extreme, to the scientist, at the other, with the historian and artist at the same end of the spectrum.

19. C. C. Gillispie, "Remarks on Social Selection as a Factor in the Progres-

sivism of Science," *American Scientist,* 56 (1968), 439-450, underscores the phenomenon and provides relevant bibliography.

20. F. A. Yates, "The Hermetic Tradition in Renaissance Science," in C. S. Singleton, ed., *Art, Science, and History in the Renaissance* (Baltimore: Johns Hopkins University Press, 1967), pp. 255-274; Walter Pagel, *William Harvey's Biological Ideas* (New York: Karger, 1967).

21. P. M. Rattansi, "Paracelsus and the Puritan Revolution," *Ambix,* 11 (1963), 24-32, and "The Helmontian-Galenist Controversy in Restoration England," *Ambix,* 12 (1964), 1-23.

22. The penultimate section of the article cited in note 13 elaborates this possibility in theoretical terms. T. M. Brown's "The College of Physicians and the Acceptance of Iatromechanism in England, 1665-1695," *Bulletin of the History of Medicine,* 44 (1970), 12-30, provides a concrete example.

JOHN E. TALBOTT

Education in Intellectual and Social History

HISTORIANS HAVE begun to stake new claims in the history of education. Over the past decade a number of pioneering books and articles have appeared on subjects whose long neglect now seems quite remarkable—from the Spanish universities under the Habsburgs to childrearing practices in colonial America. Despite the great diversity of themes and problems with which these studies are concerned, they share a similarity of approach. Nearly all seek, to use Bernard Bailyn's phrase, "to see education in its elaborate, intricate involvements with the rest of society."[1] This approach has opened new perspectives in a field historians had long ignored.

Not that the history of education has been neglected. The bibliography in the field is enormous. But it is lopsided, mainly concerned with "house history" and the ideas of pedagogical reformers. Countless histories of individual schools and universities have been published, describing aims, organization, faculty, curricula, finances, student life, and so forth; histories of pedagogical ideas have surveyed the views of leading theorists from Plato through Dewey. To be sure, great monuments of historical scholarship stand forth in the field; such studies as Hastings Rashdall's *The Universities of Europe in the Middle Ages* and Werner W. Jaeger's *Paideia* are not likely soon to be surpassed.

But to the contemporary historian much of the older literature seems inadequate—impressive in bulk but insubstantial, seldom addressed to the sorts of questions with which historical scholarship is now concerned. A good share of the institutional history has been the work of antiquaries and devoted alumni, who uncovered much valuable information but rarely sought to interpret it. With the professionalization of schoolteaching and the establishment of teachers' colleges educational history became nearly a separate discipline, isolated from the mainstream of historical study. The educationists

193

who founded and sustained these institutions sought to give prospective schoolteachers a historical sense of mission, certainly a
not unworthy aim. But in the hands of some of them educational
history became a weapon against adversaries living and dead, a
vindication of their own ideas and efforts in the struggle for public
schooling; in the hands of others it became a whiggish chronicle, a
quick guided tour of the past in search of the antecedents of contemporary educational institutions.

If historians were frequently heard to lament the inadequacies
of traditional approaches to the history of education, they were slow
to do anything about them. Only after the Second World War, when
educational issues began to loom larger in the public consciousness,
did they turn in any numbers to the subject. The deepening crisis in
education, charted in issues of *Dædalus*, from the neutral-sounding
"The Contemporary University: U.S.A." of 1964, to "The Embattled
University" of 1970, is likely to accelerate this trend.

Trends in the professional study of history also encouraged the
new interest. Chief among these, perhaps, was what might be called
an increasing concern for the interrelatedness of past experience,
brought on by the pervasive influence of social history, the emphasis
on interdisciplinary approaches to the past, and the collapse of the
internal boundaries that once delineated "areas" of historical study.
Historians began to recognize that education touches upon nearly
all aspects of a particular society. The historical study of education
came to be seen not only as an end in itself but as a promising and
hitherto neglected avenue of approach to an extremely broad range
of problems.

New approaches to the history of education differ from the old
primarily in the attention now being given to the interplay between
education and society. But this is a very great difference indeed.
What was once a narrow specialty is now seen to have such broad
ramifications that it has become hopelessly ill-defined. For if the role
of education in the historical process is to be understood, attention
must be paid to the external influences that shape the educational
arrangements a society has made; to the ways in which these
external influences impinge upon each other at the same time they
are acting upon education; and to the ways in which education itself
influences the society. The social composition of an elite educational
institution, for example, is the consequence of the interaction of
economic factors, of patterns of social stratification, of the conscious
political decisions of the established authorities, and so forth.

It is one thing, however, to recognize all the influences that need to be taken into account in the study of a particular problem in the history of education. It is quite another thing to determine the relative weight that is to be assigned each of them, especially over long periods of time. Research is at an early stage, and has not moved far beyond an enumeration of influences. In some important areas, such as the study of literacy in pre- and early industrial societies, the collection of raw data has scarcely begun; only recently have statistics long available in manuscript form been published and useful manuscript sources rescued from neglect.[2] In advanced industrial societies, where statistics on literacy abound, nearly the entire adult population is formally literate. But these figures conceal the functional illiteracy that is one of the consequences of technological change, and about which very little is now known. The questions that need to be asked in the new educational history are only beginning to be clarified. Conceptual models for dealing with these questions have yet to be devised; the methodological controversies that have enlivened more developed areas of study have yet to take place.

Thus the history of education is an area of study whose potentialities are only beginning to be exploited and the inchoate state in which it now exists is precisely what makes it attractive. So varied are the purposes now brought to the history of education, so patchy is the present state of knowledge, that the field does not lend itself to systematic treatment. Nevertheless, an idea of present concerns and problems can be conveyed by tugging at a few strands in the network of relationships that bind education to society.

I

Conventional histories of education are filled with generalizations about relationships between education and social structure. It has been a common practice, for example, to attach a class label to an educational institution, which is then held to respond to the "needs" or "demands" of a particular social class. Who determines these needs, or whether, if such needs exist, the institution in fact responds to them, is left unclear. Moreover, such static descriptive statements, based on implicit assumptions about how the class system works, explain very little about the dynamics of the interaction between education and the structure of society. Nor do they allow for the possibility that cultural values and styles of education once presumably moored to a particular social class may drift loose from that class and become the common property of an entire society—in which case they are not particularly amenable to class analysis except in its crudest forms. It is hard to see how describing an American university education as "middle class" explains very much about either the American university or American society. To be sure, education and social class have been, and continue to be, intimately connected. But the complexity of the historical connections between them has only begun to receive the carefully nuanced analysis it requires.[3] One would expect to find a large number of aristocrats' sons in an institution labeled "aristocratic." But one would also find some people who were not the sons of aristocrats. Who were they? Furthermore, one might also find aristocrats' sons in fairly large numbers in institutions not traditionally associated with the aristocracy. What were they doing there? Detailed research has only recently begun on who actually received the education a particular society has offered, how this has changed, and what the causes and consequences of change have been.[4]

With more attention being paid to who actually got educated, historians are now beginning to see that relationships between education and social structure have often been different from what the providers of education intended. It is roughly true that, until very recently, the structure of education in most European countries had the effect of reinforcing class distinctions and reducing the flow of social mobility—and was often intentionally designed to do so. Different social classes received different kinds of education in different schools; the upper levels of education were the preserve of the upper classes, a means of maintaining their children in established social positions and of bolstering their own political and social authority. But attempts to make patterns of education conform to the pattern of society have often been frustrated, both by forces the established authorities have been unable to control and by changes in other sectors of society which they have promoted themselves. One example of the latter is an expansion of job opportunities. Lawrence Stone has shown that in early modern England, economic growth and the proliferation of the bureaucracy of the state triggered an educational expansion: "So great was the boom . . . that all classes above a certain level took their part,"[5]—a consequence not entirely welcome to the ruling class of a highly stratified society. Other forces, of which demographic change is one, need to be identified and assessed.[6]

Patterns of social stratification affect the structure of education. But educational arrangements also turn back upon the structure of society and exert their own influences upon it: the relationship between education and social stratification is a two-way street. This process can be seen at work in the history of European secondary education. Elitist patterns that took shape during the sixteenth and seventeenth centuries, when the hereditary ruling classes sent their sons to secondary schools in increasing numbers, persisted well into modern times. Recent studies of the English public school have addressed themselves to some of the consequences of this persistence. Among the most important and far-reaching of these consequences was the preservation of the values and attitudes—and therefore the social ascendancy—of the aristocracy, in a fully industrialized and formally democratic society.[7]

Research into who actually got educated will lend a good deal more precision to statements about the historical role of education in the promotion of social mobility and in the maintenance of established social positions. Until recently, these have possessed all the rigor of the notorious generalizations about the rising middle classes. Such research should shed light on changes and continuities in the recruitment of elites, matters of particular concern to social and political historians. What has been the role of education in this process, in the long movement away from a society in which status was based on birth to a society in which status is increasingly based on achievement? What have been the social and political consequences of the paradoxical principle of the career open to talent, which holds that everyone should have an equal chance to become unequal? To what extent were traditional elites able to adjust themselves to the pressures for meritocratic standards of recruitment which emerged from the economic and political revolutions of the eighteenth century? To what extent did the implementation of such standards truly open the way for new men? For the upper levels of education, which prepared their clientele for elite positions, abundant evidence is available on the social origins of students over long periods of time. University matriculation registers, for example, are waiting to be tapped.

But it is not enough simply to describe with greater precision the role of education in the promotion of social mobility (or in the maintenance of established social positions). It also needs to be asked what the consequences of this form of mobility have been, what it has meant to the individuals who experienced it and the societies in which they lived. Such qualitative questions may be exceedingly difficult to answer.

The education of the lower classes presents the historian with equally difficult problems. What influences have primary schools exerted on the values and attitudes of their clientele? Recent studies of elite institutions offer persuasive evidence of the ways in which education acts upon social structure through the medium of values and attitudes. But for lower levels of education, the kinds of literary evidence that permit one to generalize about the gentlemanly lifestyle of the public school, or the bourgeois ethos of the lycée, rarely exist. So far, historical studies of the impact of popular education on values and attitudes have been mainly concerned with such public issues as the promotion of nationalism and nation building— as in the case of the Third French Republic, whose founders quite consciously undertook a sweeping reform and extension of a state-supported system of primary education in order to provide a new regime with republicans. Comparatively little is known about the role of the school in shaping attitudes toward more ostensibly private matters, such as sex, or toward such divisive questions as social class. Analysis of the content of textbooks would at least suggest what attitudes the authorities sought to inculcate, though the degree to which they succeeded is quite another question.[8]

Attention to the social consequences that educational arrangements have produced, apart from what their designers intended, should help put to rest the largely speculative leaps of the kind which assume an exact correspondence between the structure of a society and the structure of its education. Indeed, given the extraordinarily high incidence of anachronistic features that educational arrangements exhibit (such as the persistence of classical studies in the West), it is hard to see how such a direct correspondence could ever have been drawn. Instead, historical relationships between education and social structure, as one sociologist has perceptively remarked, "are various, involve structural discontinuities and are singularly lacking in symmetry."[9]

Nevertheless, the sons of the rich are usually better educated (or spend more time in school) than the sons of the poor. As soon as education began to confer social, economic, or political benefits, the question of who should be educated became a source of bitter controversy. Some of the involvements of education in politics have received considerable attention: the intervention of the state in the provision of popular education has been one traditional area of concern. State intervention followed on centuries of debate about the wisdom of providing widespread education; seldom has a question been agonized over so long and settled so swiftly. The arguments for and against popular education, the activities of certain reform groups, the legislative aspects of reform, the church-state struggle, have all been treated in a number of studies. These questions fall within the traditional preoccupations of political history. But a vast amount of territory remains to be explored, and older interpretations need to be reexamined.

Older studies, for example, regarded the extension of popular education as an aspect of the process of democratization, a necessary consequence of the implications of liberal political philosophy. More recent work has held that the decisive motive in the drive for public schooling was social control of the lower classes in an industrializing and urbanizing society.[10]

But both interpretations are mainly concerned with the attitudes of the upper-class proponents of widespread schooling; they stress the intentions of the reformers, not the consequences of the reforms. Very little is known about the attitudes toward education of the people whom the upper classes quarreled over. Popular education needs to be studied "from below." and several works have opened the way. E. P. Thompson, for example, has shown how an eagerness for learning and an enthusiasm for the printed word were important elements in the radical culture of the English working class.[11] Inquiry is now moving beyond the confines of the politically-conscious elements of that class. What were the attitudes toward education of the unskilled and illiterate laborers who poured into the factories with their wives and children in the early stages of industrialization? Literary evidence is likely to yield very few answers; such evidence as does exist is likely to be testimony from men who were not themselves workers. An investigation of this kind must rely on indirect evidence: census records, school attendance records, the reports of factory inspectors, and so forth; new methods must be added to those already devised for dealing with the inarticulate.

Traditional governing elites, from their point of view, at least, had reason to fear the possible consequences of widespread literacy. To be sure, there existed conservative arguments in support of popular instruction. In Protestant countries, Christian duty seemed to require that the people be enabled to read the Bible; the idea that popular literacy was one more means of teaching the lowly respect for their betters and resignation to their lot bolstered the moral and religious arguments in its favor. But once people had been taught to read, it was nearly impossible to control what they read, without resort to the extraordinary measures which only twentieth-century dictatorships have been willing, or able, to undertake. Events of our own times provide abundant evidence that education can influence political behavior and the structure of politics in ways that the established authorities by no means intend. This aspect of the relationship between politics and education offers many promising lines of historical inquiry.

In recent studies of revolution, for example, attention has been given to the conditions which produce that ubiquitous revolutionary figure, the alienated intellectual. An oversupply of overeducated and underemployed men seems to be a common plight of countries in the early stages of development.[12] These conditions existed in both seventeenth-century England and eighteenth-century France. In both countries an expansion of enrollments at the upper levels of education produced too many educated men seeking too few places, frustrated in their ambitions and ready to turn against a society that had no use for their talents. All that was needed to create an extremely dangerous situation for the established authorities was an ideology which enabled personal grievances to be elevated into opposition to the regime: Puritanism in the case of England; a radical version of the Enlightenment in the case of France.[13]

If historians have begun to hammer out answers to important questions concerning the relationship between education and politics, in the equally significant area of education's links with the economy they are just beginning their work. Economists since Adam Smith have been interested in the relationship of education to the economy, and particularly to economic development; in the last decade the economics of education has become a vigorous subdiscipline. But historians have their own contribution to make, especially since the vexing question of the ways in which education has influenced economic growth demands historical treatment. As David McClelland has put it, "Did increases in educational investment precede rapid rates of economic growth, or were rapid increases in wealth followed by increased spending on education? Or did both occur together? These are the critical questions of social dynamics that cry out for an answer."[14] Historians are just starting to attempt to break the vicious circle in which such questions have been enclosed.

Take, for example, the problem of literacy—a topic which itself is only beginning to be investigated systematically. R. S. Schofield has remarked, "Today literacy is considered to be a necessary precondition for economic development; but the historian might well ask himself whether this was so in England at the end of the eighteenth century."[15] It would be plausible to argue that the relatively high rate of literacy that had long prevailed in England had much to do with that country's becoming the first industrial power. But on closer examination it is far from clear how literacy and schooling have contributed to rapid growth, especially in the early stages. In the first decades of industrialization, the factory system put no premium on even low-level intellectual skills. Whatever relationships existed between widespread literacy and early industrial development must have been quite roundabout. In one of the best treatments of this problem, Ronald Dore has shown that what was actually learned in school mattered less than the discipline involved in learning anything at all:

But what does widespread literacy do for a developing country? At the very least it constitutes a training in being trained. The man who has in childhood submitted to some process of disciplined and conscious learning is more likely to respond to further training, be it in a conscript army, in a factory, or at lectures arranged by his village agricultural association. And such training can be more precise and efficient, and more nationally standardized, if the written word can be used to supplement the spoken.[16]

Directing his attention to a higher level of training, David Landes has recently argued that the links between technical and scientific education on the one hand and economic development on the other are much more direct than the links between literacy and development.[17] Certainly, the prima facie evidence in the classic comparison between the sluggishness of the British and the explosiveness of the German economies in the late nineteenth century, when industrial processes came increasingly to depend upon scientific innovation, would appear to support Landes's case: German scientific education was undoubtedly superior to British, and German entrepreneurs were more willing to hire and to heed the advice of graduates of scientific and technical institutes than were their British counterparts. But too little is now known about scientific education in the industrial age; historians of science have so far given more attention to the early modern period. When work in progress on scientific education in later times appears, it may well complicate, even if it does not substantially modify, the picture Landes presents.[18]

Such studies, which define education as a process that takes place in specialized institutions, are likely to remain at the center of attention in historical writing. Nevertheless, any definition of education must be broad enough to include learning experiences which take place outside the framework of formal institutions, particularly within the family, whose role in the educational process remains of primary importance. But historical research on the family is now at a rudimentary stage. Very little is known, for example, about the ways in which responsibility for education after the earliest years of childhood shifted over a period of centuries, from the family to specialized institutions, such as the apprenticeship system and schools. Nor have we discovered much about the interaction between changes in the structure of the family and changes in the structure of education, or about how these changes have differed from class to class and among various levels of education. Did changes in family structure make formal educational institutions increasingly important agencies of socialization, or did pressures outside the family, from government or from social and religious institutions, provide the impetus for this shift in educational responsibilities? What have been the social and psychological consequences of these changes? How has submission to the discipline of the school altered the experience of childhood and affected patterns of adult behavior? Only in the last decade have such questions begun to receive the attention they deserve.[19]

II

If the exploration of "the involvements of education with the rest of society" is the new credo, it is a credo not without its own ambiguities and difficulties. The phrase can be interpreted in a variety of ways. It has been employed in a specific critical sense, to suggest the inadequacies of the history of education, old style, without meaning to lay down a program for the new. It has been used superficially, to dress up straightforward descriptions of educational institutions hardly different from older institutional histories.

More significantly, the phrase also lends itself to a quasi-functionalist interpretation which may distort the role of education in the historical process. This interpretation assumes that everything which may be identified with education responds to or fulfills the needs of society; that the structure of an educational system is merely a reflection of the class structure; that the pace of change in education is roughly equal to, indeed responds to, the pace of other changes in the larger society. First of all, it is never easy to decide what constitutes "society," the abstract entity to which education responds. Moreover, the functionalist view runs afoul of empirical evidence which suggests that the pace of change in education has often been widely at variance with the pace of social change. And this view is hard-pressed to allow for the anomalies and anachronisms so frequently found in educational systems. The relationship between change in an educational system and changes in the society of which it is a part is certainly one of the most important and least understood problems confronting the historian of education. An explanatory model which could be applied to this relationship would be an extremely useful tool, but for all its compelling simplicity—indeed, because of it—the functionalist approach is inadequate.[20]

The new credo may also be interpreted too broadly. An undiscriminating concern with relationships between education and society can lead to an emphasis on certain aspects of the role of education in the historical process at the expense of others. If the historical study of education is too preoccupied with relationships and interconnections, it may slight certain problems internal to the process of education itself, problems which may not be very satisfactorily explained in terms of external influences. Along with our attempts to understand how the larger society influences education, perhaps we need to understand the ways it does not.

For this very reason the study of educational institutions remains important—but what is needed is institutional history in a new key. The new studies should indeed take into account the larger social context in which educational institutions are located, but their viewpoints should be from the inside looking out. Only in this way are we likely to understand such matters as the consequences of educational reform as opposed to the intentions of reformers, or such significant topics in intellectual history as the influence which institutional settings exercise on patterns of thought and intellectual creativity.

Sheldon Rothblatt has attacked some of the foregoing problems in his recent book on nineteenth-century Cambridge, an important example of the new institutional history.[21] He argues that two historiographical traditions can be traced in the writing of English university history. The Whig interpretation assumed that university history could be written as an extension of political history: the ancient universities were seen as pliant tools of the Georgian

Establishment. Unable and unwilling to respond to the challenge of industrialism, Oxbridge was forced into the modern world only by pressure administered from the outside, in the form of investigations by royal commissions. Of course the Whig version applauded these nineteenth-century changes. A second historiographical tradition, the class-conflict interpretation, holds that "the function of the university is to serve whichever social class is in power." This view reverses the Whig judgment: it does not regard the nineteenth-century reforms as progressive but as merely the transfer of control of the universities from one class to another. Whatever their respective merits, Rothblatt argues, both the Whig and the class-conflict versions have assumed much too close a fit between society's wishes and the response of educational institutions to them. Especially in a pluralistic society, "it is entirely possible that the university and society will be in subtle and complex states of disagreement as well as agreement with one another, that the direction of university change may not be completely obvious, that surprises will occur."[22] Rothblatt elaborates this thesis by showing how the reform of Cambridge, though quickened by external pressures, sprang largely from within the university, from the reformulation of donnish traditions which had very little to do with either the presumed needs of an industrial society or the "demands" of a rising middle class, and which in fact set itself against them.

The new institutional history is valuable not only as an illustration of the dangers in interpreting the new credo too broadly. There are other good reasons for maintaining institutional history amid the central concerns of the history of education. Despite the wealth of old-style studies of institutions, little is known about most of the problems with which contemporary historians are now engaged. Modeled on the constitutional history that dominated nineteenth-century scholarship, the older studies were preoccupied with formal structures; contemporary historical writing, on the other hand, might be characterized as mainly concerned with processes, with relationships of power and influence and social interaction that may have been widely at variance with the dictates of formal institutional structures. There are many histories of individual American universities, for example, but there is not even a handful of trans-institutional, comparative studies of the caliber of Laurence R. Veysey's *The Emergence of the American University*.[23] The standard history of the French universities, published at the end of the nineteenth century, is surely not the last word that can be written on the subject.[24] And the histories of many other important educational institutions remain to be written.

Moreover, the study of universities is an ideal theater for historians interested in problems of the *longue durée*. For universities are one of the oldest forms of corporate organization in the West. Few institutions have been at once so fragile and so durable; few have been altered so radically, both internally and in their relationship to the larger society, adding new purposes, allowing others to lapse, and managing to maintain some of those for which they were originally founded. And perhaps because their existence and purpose presuppose an acute sense of the past, universities are rich repositories of information about themselves.

No scholar working alone can expect to take full advantage of these vast sources, nor can he exploit on his own that unique opportunity for the investigation of long-term problems offered by the university as a subject of study. The new institutional history demands collaborative efforts which will press into service the methods of several disciplines as well as the computer.

One such project, under the direction of Allan Bullock and T. H. Aston, is concerned with the social history of Oxford University from earliest times to the present. Another collaborative study, a statistical survey of universities in the West, is under way at the Shelby Cullom Davis Center for Historical Studies of Princeton University. A major goal of the project is to explore the cyclical patterns of expanding and contracting enrollments in Western universities, a phenomenon whose causes are not understood. Universities in England, Spain, and Germany exhibited similar patterns of rising enrollments in the sixteenth and early seventeenth centuries, of rapid decline beginning in the mid-seventeenth century, and of stagnation throughout the eighteenth. English and German enrollments again rose sharply in the nineteenth century. Was there a general decline in university matriculation throughout the West between about 1650 and 1800? If so, what were its causes, and what were its social, cultural, economic, and political consequences? Why did expansion resume in the nineteenth century? How did these cycles affect the pace and character of modernization in the West?

The Davis Center project is also concerned with two other problems: one, patterns in the relationship of university education to social mobility and to recruitment for professional, political, and administrative elites; two, the role of universities as transmitters of culture. The latter problem will consider education both as an intellectual and a socializing process and will ask how the structure, composition, and intellectual activities of the faculty changed over time—how and why the university was eventually able to become the critic of society as well as its servant.

Such collaborative enterprises can make significant contributions to our knowledge of the internal history of universities. But each study will eventually have to face the general problem with which much of this essay has been concerned: the establishment of cause-and-effect relationships between changes in education and changes in other sectors of society. This task, though the most difficult, may also prove the most rewarding.

III

Why has the history of education undergone such extreme change in recent years? The resurgence of interest is in part a consequence of the troubled state of contemporary education. New questions shaped by the dilemmas of our own times require new approaches to the past. The older historiography was found inadequate both because it was too narrow and inward-looking, and because it was ignorant of some essential facts concerning education itself. Long untouched by the great changes that have overtaken historical research in this century, the history of education became one of the last refuges of the Whig interpretation. So long as its practitioners were mainly concerned with searching the past for the antecedents of their own contemporary institutions, they could believe that education in the West had followed an upward linear progression. We now find this view hard to accept. We know, for example, that periods in which formal instruction was fairly widespread have been followed by periods in which it was restricted to small groups. The older historiography could neither accommodate such findings nor answer the questions they raise. Their exploration requires new modes of analysis. To pursue our example, it is clear that any satisfactory explanation of these expansions and contractions will have to take into account changes in demographic patterns and in the family, in the economy, the social structure, and the political system, in beliefs about the nature and purpose of human life. And it will also have to be recognized that education has turned back upon these influences in subtle and complex ways, working changes on its own.

Such a task is clearly beyond the old-style historian of education and the old-style historiography. But the demands of the task will not be satisfied by a new historiography of education as such. It may be doubted whether education, a process so deeply entangled in the life of an entire society, deserves to be called an "area of study" at all. Surely there can be little justification for making education a particular genre of historical scholarship. The history of education touches upon all the varieties of history. It is a task for the generalist, who must bring to the study of education a thorough knowledge of the society of which it is a part.

REFERENCES

1. Bernard Bailyn, *Education in the Forming of American Society: Needs and Opportunities for Research* (Chapel Hill: University of North Carolina Press, 1960), p. 14. I am grateful to my friends and colleagues in the Shelby Cullom Davis Center for Historical Studies of Princeton University, whose comments in a seminar on The University in Society provided suggestions for this essay. They are: Robert Church, Richard Kagan, Tom Laqueur, Sheldon Rothblatt, Henry Smith II, and Lawrence Stone.

2. See, for example, Michel Fleury and Pierre Valmary, "Les progrès de l'instruction élémentaire de Louis XIV à Napoléon III, d'après l'enquête de Louis Maggiolo, 1877-1879," *Population,* 12 (1957), 71-92.

3. For a brilliant example of the analyses now going on see Pierre Bourdieu and Jean-Claude Passeron, *Les héritiers: les étudiants et la culture* (Paris: Editions de Minuit, 1964).

4. For a pioneer effort see J. H. Hexter, "The Education of the Aristocracy in the Renaissance," *Reappraisals in History* (New York: Harper and Row, 1961), pp. 45-70, an earlier version of which appeared in the *Journal of Modern History* (March 1950); also Hester Jenkins and D. Caradog Jones, "Social Class of Cambridge University Alumni of the 18th and 19th Centuries," *British Journal of Sociology,* 1 (1950), 93-116.

5. Lawrence Stone, "The Educational Revolution in England, 1560-1640," *Past and Present,* no. 28 (July 1964), 68.

6. See, for example, François de Dainville, "Effectifs des collèges et scolarité aux XVIIe et XVIIIe siècles dans le nord-est de la France," *Population,* 10 (1955), 455-488; "Collèges et fréquentation scolaire au XVIIe siècle," *Population,* 12 (1957), 467-494; Frank Musgrove, "Population Changes and the Status of the Young in England Since the 18th Century," *Sociological Review,* 11 (1963), 69-93.

7. See, for example, David Ward, "The Public Schools and Industry in Britain after 1870," *Journal of Contemporary History,* 2, no. 3 (1967), 37-52; two studies by Rupert Wilkinson, *Gentlemanly Power: British Leader-*

ship and the Public School Tradition (New York: Oxford University Press, 1964), and with T. J. H. Bishop, *Winchester and the Public School Elite* (London: Faber, 1967). On the French lycée see John E. Talbott, *The Politics of Educational Reform in France, 1918-1940* (Princeton: Princeton University Press, 1969); Paul Gerbod, *La condition universitaire en France au XIXe siècle* (Paris: Presses universitaires de France, 1965).

8. For an early and still useful discussion of the role of primary education in the promotion of nationalism see Carleton J. H. Hayes, *France, A Nation of Patriots* (New York: Columbia University Press, 1930); also Charles E. Merriam, *The Making of Citizens: A Comparative Study of Methods of Civic Training* (Chicago: University of Chicago Press, 1931); for recent work see, for instance, Pierre Nora, "Ernest Lavisse, son rôle dans la formation du sentiment national," *Revue historique*, 228 (July-September 1962), 73-106; Jacques and Mona Ozouf, "Le thème du patriotisme dans les manuels primaires," *Le Mouvement Social*, no. 49 (October-November 1964), 5-32.

9. Donald G. MacCrae, "The Culture of a Generation: Students and Others," *Journal of Contemporary History*, 2, no. 3 (1967), 3.

10. For an early suggestion that the American common school may not have been the spearhead of democracy, see the essay in intellectual history of Merle Curti, *The Social Ideas of American Educators* (New York: C. Scribner's Sons, 1935); more recently, Michael Katz has expressed a similar view from the perspective of social history in *The Irony of Early School Reform: Educational Innovation in Mid-Nineteenth Century Massachusetts* (Cambridge, Mass.: Harvard University Press, 1968).

11. E. P. Thompson, *The Making of the English Working Class* (New York: Vintage, 1963), especially pp. 711-745; also Georges Duveau, *La pensée ouvrière sur l'éducation pendant la Seconde République et le Second Empire* (Paris: Domat-Montchrestien, 1948); R. K. Webb, *The British Working-Class Reader, 1790-1848* (London: Allen and Unwin, 1955); R. D. Altick, *The English Common Reader* (Chicago: University of Chicago Press, 1957); J. F. C. Harrison, *Learning and Living, 1790-1960: A Study in the History of the English Adult Education Movement* (London: Routledge and Kegan Paul, 1961).

12. Edward Shils, "Intellectuals in the Political Development of the New States," *World Politics*, 12 (April 1960), 329-368.

13. See Lawrence Stone, "The Educational Revolution in England, 1540-1640," *Past and Present*, no. 28 (July 1964), 41-80. In a more recent essay Stone has concluded: "More and more it looks as if this educational expansion was a necessary—but not sufficient—reason for the peculiar and ultimately radical course the revolution took." "The Causes of the English Revolution," in Robert Forster and Jack P. Greene, eds., *Preconditions of Revolution in Early Modern Europe* (Baltimore: Johns Hopkins University Press, 1970); Mark H. Curtis, "The Alienated Intellectuals of Early Stuart England," *Past and Present*, no. 23 (November 1962), 25-43; J. H. Elliot, "Revolu-

tion and Continuity in Early Modern Europe," *Past and Present,* no. 42 (February 1969), 35-56; Robert Darnton, "Social Tensions in the Intelligentsia of Pre-Revolutionary France," paper read at the annual meeting of the American Historical Association, December 1969. On the importance of a similar phenomenon in nineteenth-century Spain see Raymond Carr, *Spain, 1806-1939* (Oxford: Oxford University Press, 1966), p. 167; on nineteenth-century Germany see Lenore O'Boyle, "The Democratic Left in Germany, 1848," *Journal of Modern History,* 33 (1961), 374-383; John R. Gillis, "Aristocracy and Bureaucracy in Nineteenth-Century Prussia," *Past and Present,* no. 41 (December 1968), 105-129.

14. David C. McClelland, "Does Education Accelerate Economic Growth?" *Economic Development and Cultural Change,* 14, no. 3 (April 1966), 259.

15. R. S. Schofield, "The Measurement of Literacy in Pre-Industrial England," in Jack Goody, ed., *Literacy in Traditional Societies* (Cambridge, Eng.: Cambridge University Press, 1969), p. 312 and n: "The necessity of literacy as a pre-condition for economic growth is a persistent theme running through many UNESCO publications . . . These measures [established by UNESCO] are very general and throw no light at all on the question of why literacy should be considered essential to economic growth." See also Lawrence Stone, "Literacy and Education in England, 1640-1900," *Past and Present,* no. 42 (February 1969), 69-139; Carlo M. Cipolla, *Literacy and Development in the West* (Baltimore: Penguin, 1969).

16. Ronald P. Dore, *Education in Tokugawa Japan* (Berkeley: University of California Press, 1965), p. 292.

17. David Landes, *The Unbound Prometheus: Technological Change and Industrial Development in Western Europe from 1750 to the Present* (Cambridge, Eng.: Cambridge University Press, 1969), pp. 343-348.

18. One of the few studies of nineteenth-century scientific education is D. S. L. Cardwell, *The Organisation of Science in England* (Melbourne: Heinemann, 1957). On literature on scientific education see Thomas G. Kuhn, "The History of Science," *International Encyclopedia of the Social Sciences,* XIV, 78. John H. Weiss is writing a Harvard University doctoral dissertation on scientific education in nineteenth-century France; Steven Turner is preparing a Princeton University dissertation on scientific education in Germany.

19. For a brief discussion of some of these problems, see Stone, "Literacy and Education in England, 1640-1900," pp. 93-95; Bailyn, *Education in the Forming of American Society,* pp. 75-78. One of the boldest and most widely-heralded inquiries into these questions to have appeared in recent years is Philippe Ariès, *Centuries of Childhood: A Social History of Family Life* (New York: Knopf, 1962). The idea of childhood as a distinct phase of life, Ariès argues, is an invention of the late Middle Ages, when changes in the family and a new concern for education led to the removal of the child from the adult society in which he had formerly been free to roam. This practice, at first limited to the upper classes, gradually permeated the rest

210   JOHN E. TALBOTT

of society. Though Ariès has perhaps done more than anyone to stimulate interest in the historical study of the family, the argument of his book, despite—or because of—his ingenious use of iconographical evidence, is not entirely convincing. For a study that owes much to Ariès but has a great deal more to say about education see Georges Snyders, *La pédagogie en France aux XVIIe et XVIIIe siècles* (Paris: Presses Universitaires de France, 1965). Important historical work on the family is now beginning to appear in the United States, pursuing lines of inquiry established by Edmund S. Morgan and Bernard Bailyn. See, for example, John Demos, *A Little Commonwealth: Family Life in Plymouth Colony* (New York: Oxford University Press, 1970); Philip J. Greven, Jr., *Four Generations: Population, Land, and Family in Colonial Andover, Massachusetts* (Ithaca: Cornell University Press, 1970). Demos has more to say about education. For England see, among the articles of Frank Musgrove, "The Decline of the Educative Family," *Universities Quarterly,* 14 (September 1960), 377-406.

20. For an interesting discussion of functionalism see Olive Banks, *The Sociology of Education* (London: Schocken, 1968). See also Gillian Sutherland, "The Study of the History of Education," *History,* 54 (February 1969), 53-54.

21. Sheldon Rothblatt, *The Revolution of the Dons: Cambridge and Society in Victorian England* (New York: Basic Books, 1968).

22. *Ibid.,* pp. 17-26.

23. Laurence R. Veysey, *The Emergence of the American University* (Chicago: University of Chicago Press, 1965). Veysey follows ground broken by Richard Hofstadter and Walter P. Metzger in *The Development of Academic Freedom in the United States* (New York: Columbia University Press, 1955), which is about much else besides academic freedom. Veysey's study of the movement to redefine the purpose and structure of American higher education in the post-Civil War era also shows how much can be missed by assuming too close a fit between a society's needs and the response of educational institutions to these needs. "During the early years of the American university movement, until about 1890," he contends, "academic efforts burgeoned largely in spite of the public, not as the result of popular acclaim . . . Academic and popular aspirations seemed rarely to meet" (p. 16).

24. Louis Liard, *L'enseignement supérieur en France, 1789-1889,* 2 vols. (Paris, 1888-1894).

FRANK E. MANUEL

The Use and Abuse of Psychology in History

ALMOST A century ago Friedrich Nietzsche, that history-intoxicated son of the German philological school, delivered a tirade against the hypertrophy of history in the life of his times. In appropriating the title of his essay, I confess to a similar ambivalence respecting the modern uses of psychology in historical studies. After some years of history-writing I have begun to fear that I may be losing my way in the jungles of psychologism. In my predicament I could of course appeal to the analytical philosophers and ask them to enlighten me about the implicit assumptions of my work; but having read their interpretations of the writings of my colleagues I am obdurately resistant. Instead, I shall seek a way out of my perplexity by hearkening to the advice of Alfred North Whitehead, who once said that when a man is lost, he should not ask where *he* is, but where the *others* are. And so, advancing behind a chronological shield, I intend to locate myself by passing in critical review the experience of historians and psychologists whenever they have come into close proximity. After skimming over the eighteenth-century origin of their relationships, I shall concentrate on the last hundred years and even more especially on the recent period, when both disciplines have become mammoth academic enterprises, whose cohabitation, some might say, is doomed to sterility from the outset, like the improbable mating of a whale and an elephant. What my presentation lacks in depth and subtlety, I hope it may achieve in breadth. Perhaps at the end I may find a place for myself, and, who knows, others might be willing to join me even if it means standing midstream in rather shallow waters.

My level of discourse will not be hard-nosed and analytical but descriptive of the goals and achievements of those who sensed the rich potentialities of a new field of expression and proceeded to

211

cultivate it. Men have been prospecting for a long time in this region, and I am less interested in the scientific theories they brought with them than in what they have carried back from their expeditions. Though I have not made an actual body count, I suspect that of late there has been more hortatory exposition of what might or should be done than perspective on what has in fact been going on. Commenting on the topos, on the content, of psychological history-writing may prove more illuminating than either dissecting benighted historians who enjoy the *Narrenfreiheit* of blithely going their narrative way, or issuing manifestoes on what would constitute a perfect psychological history.

In the past three centuries major attempts have been made to recover not only the written thoughts of men of other times but their thinking; not only the record of their actions but the secret purposes and hidden, even unconscious, feelings that spurred and accompanied the *res gestae;* not only the literary and artistic objects but the sensibility that was expressed and the emotions aroused in the creators as well as in their contemporary audiences. When there are Pyrrhonists about who question the veracity of recorded history in its most commonsensical usage, how must they regard an undertaking that presumes to re-create inner experiences, which do not usually manifest themselves in clear-cut fashion through specific and forthright documents! And yet this is what psychological history has self-confidently set out to do. Admittedly, this wild intention has always been a minor element in historical narrative since the first Persian chronicles, echoed in the Book of Esther, where we are told what a personage "speaks in his heart." Greek and Roman historians used a variety of devices to disclose the secret purposes and unfulfilled desires animating their protagonists; and the Renaissance historians who imitated them availed themselves of a rich psychological vocabulary in describing the wellsprings of human conduct. It is only since the early eighteenth century, however, that some historians have committed themselves to making the re-creation of inner experience the core of their work, shifting the focus from the deed to the psychic events that transpired in the doer.

I

More and more I see in Giambattista Vico, that lone Italian who lived in Naples from 1668 to 1744, the bold conceptualizer of this novel form of historical consciousness. In its exterior aspect his *Scienza Nuova* was a rather conventional theology of history with a cyclical pattern. But if we look beyond the structure, we are amazed to find that he wrote of "tre spezie di natura," three kinds of human nature, and postulated that in each stage of a *ricorso* men had quintessentially different modes of perceiving reality, that not only the physical conditions but the feeling tone of existence was profoundly different in each one, that the very capacity for expression assumed radically different shapes: signs and emblems at one time the only way for mute humans to externalize feelings; poetry the only speech of barbaric men; and not until the rational epoch the voice of reason in prose. Every stage in the cycle was marked by its own balance between rational faculties and aggressive violence, between terror of death and a desire for convenience, between robust imagination and calculated punctiliousness. In sum, the nature of living—of thinking, feeling, and willing, the three traditional faculties—had undergone revolutions in time. And the changing quality of existence was discernible in the history of language, in literature and laws, and in visual arts like painting.

How was it possible for Vico, a man of the early eighteenth century, to interpret that evidence, to recapture the emotions and spirit of the age of heroic barbarism? His answer was that the cycle of history was imbedded in the human soul. Understanding of the transformations was possible because men in fact themselves lived through the whole of the cycle from primitivism to rationality in the course of their development from earliest infancy through adulthood. And all about in the world there remained vestiges of primitive mentality in savage countries and perhaps in the behavior of women.

The great French romantic historian of the next century, Jules Michelet, translated and commented on the works of Vico when they were hardly known in Western culture. Michelet's voluminous history of France can be conceived as an effort to explore the changing consciousness of Frenchmen in their thousand years of national life. His dramatization of the Renaissance as a new way of perceiving the world was an innovation in the uses of psychology in history entirely in the spirit of Vico's "New Science." By mid-nineteenth century Michelet had at his disposal more refined psychological tools, some inherited from the utilitarian tradition of the Enlightenment, others derived from the works of Jean-Jacques, that great revealer of the previous age, who had made himself transparent and bared his own complex private world as a model for every man.

In the latter part of the eighteenth century the Germans had a parallel to Vico in Herder, who imagined that through the course of world history an infinite number of human aggregates would be fashioned in isolation by the physical and climatic conditions of their living-space and that each one, in a totally unique way, would forge for itself an idiosyncratic balance of sense perceptions which no other *Volk* could imitate. This *Volk*-genius was early embodied in a mythology, a religion, a poetry, in short a *Volk* culture, within the confines of which men of that *Volk* were forever fixed. In the later efflorescence of a culture, elements of reason might appear, but for all time every work of literature, art, and music was in its essence a reflection of the primitive, affective *Volk* psyche. Herder's universe pullulated with *Volk* cultures at different stages in their life-cycles; and though he made feeble efforts to establish connexities among them in an overriding concept of *Humanität*, he was the founder of a particular type of German historicism that emphasized the search for concrete psychological "specificity"— the word is his friend Goethe's—in time and place. For both Vico and Herder the nature of things was hidden in the emotional differences among human collectives.

Hegel's contribution to psychological history does not, in my judgment, lie primarily in his characterization of the stages in the history of spirit, but rather in his power to grasp and present the phenomenological fullness of crucial human relationships—for example, his insightful diagnosis of the contrarieties of the master-slave bond, and his depiction of *Entfremdung*, alienation, which was passed on to Marx and Kierkegaard and has since been inflated as the central psychological distinction of modern consciousness.

II

In the last decades of the nineteenth century, there was a substantive discontinuity in the history of psychological history, a breakthrough. Psychology began to achieve a measure of recognition as an autonomous science in the German academic world. Though it had had a long literary and philosophical past—the name itself was invented by Rudolf Goclenius of Marburg in the sixteenth century—when psychology first appeared as an independent form of knowledge at the university it underwent a crisis of adolescence. What was it? A physical science in quest of uniformities? Or did it belong to humanist studies and could it be subsumed under history? Almost simultaneously with the rise of experimental psychology, new schools of psychiatry were founded, and the unconscious itself was baptized around the 1880's. This date then becomes a convenient starting-point for taking a prospect of the modern relationship of history and psychology.

In the German and French schools there were two early significant moves in the direction of fusing these disciplines, the older one under Wilhelm Dilthey, born in 1833, and another under Lucien Febvre, born in 1878. Dilthey's first important writing was published in 1883, and twenty-five years later he was still at work on a critique of historical reason, some fragments of which appeared posthumously after World War I.[1] A professor of philosophy in Berlin, he strongly influenced Troeltsch and Meinecke, Heidegger, and a whole generation of German academic historians of ideas. He even left his mark on Spengler, who would have spurned any identification with him. Lucien Febvre ultimately became a professor at the Collège de France and one of the founders of *Annales*, a journal that was to propagate his ideas. Though both Dilthey and Febvre were dedicated to exploring the relationship of psychology and history, they were virtually unaware of each other's existence, separated as were their intellectual worlds by a generation gap and by the then insuperable barrier of the Rhine. And they meant rather different things by psychology. Both, of course, were totally untouched by such outrageous novelties as the doctrines of their contemporary, Sigmund Freud. As for the historical forays of Freud himself and his immediate disciples, they rarely came within the purview of the academic historians of any country at this period. (Preserved Smith, of Cornell University, was one of the exceptions.) Dilthey and Febvre represent two different versions of an initial stage in the emergence of psychological history in recent times.

Though Dilthey's testament remains unfinished, his essays on the towering figures of western European thought, above all his Schleiermacher and his young Hegel, leave no doubt about his purposes.[2] He would have had all studies of man absorbed into intellectual history and would have allowed no independent status to either psychology or sociology. Rejecting the feasibility of any connected world history in a traditional sense and scornful of the Rankean state as the primary object of historical knowledge, Dilthey was convinced that the history of man could best be presented as a series of psychological world outlooks, more significantly emotive than rationalist, embodied mainly in the writings of literary, religious, and philosophical geniuses. For all his ambition to seize the essence—in a phenomenological sense—of entire ages and to interrelate economico-social and philosophico-religious trends, he always seemed most comfortable with biographical studies of creative men in whom he saw the various psychic currents of an age criss-cross and ultimately assume a manageable structure. His heroic figures are vessels for the dominant passions, cosmic attitudes, and deep-rooted beliefs of a whole epoch. Through the study of the historical varieties of human psychic experience he found an affirmation of freedom, an emancipation from dogmatism, a humanist deliverance. Though he belittled Nietzsche, it is now easy to recognize that with a far less arresting rhetoric and with none of Nietzsche's moral fervor, Dilthey was developing a parallel conception of monumental world personages the expression of whose spiritual, form-imprinting natures was the stuff of history. Resurrecting and consorting with these overmen was virtually the sole justification for historical knowledge.

Rarely, if ever, did Dilthey descend from the heights of exalted intellectual history sprinkled with affects. In theory he was committed to relating the individual psychological natures of his heroes with the grand world outlooks which they had evolved, to lay before us the fullness of his subject's lived experience. But it is always lived experience as a closeted Wilhelmine professor of philosophy conceived it. His histories are elitist dramas of the passions of great men's souls. Dilthey studied the manuscripts of his protagonists and provided us with glimpses of their social status, of their intellectual friendships, occasionally of a great love. Their search for God is always apprehended with a deep sympathy and understanding of the intricacies of the Western religious tradition. But nothing below the navel was mentionable. Economic and social reality may penetrate his narrative, but only as part of a world-view, and political revolutions are quickly transformed into abstract ideas. Incapable of grappling with total psychic breakdown, when confronted by Hölderlin's madness Dilthey dissolves into utter banality and depicts the dying poet as sitting in Tübingen, his mind "wandering, wandering."[3] If this is *Erlebnis,* it is the

Erlebnis of soap opera. On the other hand, the nuanced description of Schleiermacher's religious experience attains universality.
Dilthey was aware of the depths of the unconscious, but for him it
was accessible only in the form of an artistic creation.

Dilthey has testified to the impression made upon him by Hüsserl's phenomenology, and in his turn Heidegger in *Sein und
Zeit,* which historicized the categories of cognition, described his
view of the historical world as dependent on the philosophical
implications of Dilthey's writings. To the extent that pure intellectual
biography is still being written and there are still attempts to present *Weltanschauungen* in literary psychological terms, Dilthey
endures as a living if limited influence. Karl Jaspers, who began his
career as a student of psychiatry as practiced in Germany in the
first decade of the twentieth century, untouched by Freud, was
less restrictive in his studies of Swedenborg, Hölderlin, Strindberg, and Van Gogh, in which he combined a phenomenological
psychology with an attempt to communicate the varieties of world
historical outlooks.[4] His pathographies were even intended to show
the neurotic drives of his characters as allies in their creative
achievements, an insight which Freudian psychohistorians have
sometimes claimed as their unique discovery. But when he sought
to encompass the whole psychic universe in his *Psychologie der
Weltanschauungen* of 1919, a work that caused quite a stir in its
day, his typologizing remained on the same intellectualist plane as
Dilthey's.[5]

The French historical tradition since Michelet has been rich in
the study of religious and other forms of emotional expression; but
it was not until Lucien Febvre that a declaration was made on the
centrality of *histoire psychologique.* Febvre summoned his colleagues to devote themselves to histories of *mentalité* and *sensibilité.* I would loosely translate *mentalité* in this context as what was
"thinkable" in a human collective at a given moment of time. While
the Germans tended to be impressionistic in their psychological
portraits, Febvre insisted on great technical, one might say positivistic, rigor.

The heritage he bequeathed is nonetheless problematic. After
we have been assured in the opening of his *Luther* that the underlying preoccupation of his study was the relationship between the
individual and the mass, between personal initiative and public
necessity, we are left dangling. Whether or not one agrees with
the conclusions of Erikson's *Luther,* published as a study in psycho-

history thirty years later, it does propose answers to the initial query set by Febvre, whose *histoire psychologique* flatly refused to engage with what he dismissed as the hypothetical Luther of the youthful period. "Let us frankly abandon the effort to reconstruct Luther's early surroundings; their effect on his ideas and sentiments could never be estimated . . . It is better even to hold out against the seductions of the psychoanalysts for whose taste no theory is too facile . . . A Freudian Luther is so easy to imagine that one feels not the least curiosity or wish to prosecute the acquaintance when an investigator undertakes to delineate him. For, in fact, might one not with an equal facility conjure up a Lutheran Freud, and observe how completely the illustrious father of psychoanalysis exemplifies permanent traits of the German national genius, of which Luther in his day was so notable an exponent?"[6] This is the voice of a French nationalist of the twentieth century, relying on a fatuous, *ad hominem* argument against Freud, with whose writings he had only the most casual acquaintance.

Febvre's *Rabelais* is the work in which his particular skill in communicating what another epoch "willed, felt, and thought" established the school's prototype of *histoire psychologique,* its virtues as well as its limitations. When Febvre concentrated upon an interpretation of his subject's religious beliefs, he was able to demonstrate with a plethora of empirical evidence that Rabelais' *plaisanteries courantes* and *malices d'Eglise* could be read as proof of atheism only by committing the historical sin of sins—anachronism.[7] Febvre moved in ever-extending circles to define the limits of what was thinkable and what could have been experienced in one's relationship to the supernatural in sixteenth-century Europe. Far from a herald of the new rationalism, Rabelais appears as a kind of Erasmian Christian, as do his giants. In passing, Febvre developed a character for the age in standard literary psychological terms, and he proposed the identification of the discrete elements of a collective historical psychology as the historian's primary mission. But the "mental structure" of the age is confined to the conscious level—the manifest content of ideas and beliefs, the style of their expression, where the line was drawn between the natural and the divine, or the intensity in the externalizing of emotion as compared with men of the twentieth century. In the world of the sixteenth he found imprecision, lack of historical awareness, absorption with the senses of smell and hearing rather than sight. This sort of workmanlike history of ideas and sensibility is still

practiced in France both in the literary and in the historical faculties, and is yielding a steady flow of respectworthy Gargantuan
dissertations on subjects like the idea of nature or of happiness in
various epochs.

But Febvre pointed out one of the greatest obstacles in the way
of any attempt to define the history of sensibility in a segment of
past time. In the course of a review of Johan Huizinga's *Waning of
the Middle Ages*, he asked skeptically whether in fact it could ever
be determined that some periods were characterized by more love,
fear, cruelty, or violence than others in their over-all feeling tone,
and he cautioned against reading into other epochs a psychology
derived from contemporary sensibility. How would it be possible, he
wondered, to apply psychological models of the comfortable
twentieth century to ages that knew endemic famine, awoke and
went to sleep with the sun, suffered extremes of heat and cold as
a norm. He mocked biographies of Pharaohs that were merely
portrayals of moderns gotten up in the stage costumes of ancient
Egyptians. Cooperative research in which historians and psychologists would be joined—and he referred to French academic
psychologists like Dr. Henri Wallon—was the only safeguard he
could propose against such follies. But though conscious of the
pitfalls, Febvre held to the very end that capturing the unique
sensibilité of a past age was the ultimate goal of the historian to
which all his other efforts were subordinated. "It is true that to
presume to reconstitute the emotive life of a given epoch is a task
at once extraordinarily seductive and terrifyingly difficult. But what
of it? The historian does not have the right to desert."[8] Stirring
declamation, *de l'époque*.

One of Febvre's disciples, Robert Mandrou, who adheres to
the pure tradition, spent years in the detailed study of the judicial
aspects of witchcraft in seventeenth-century France, and has
recently produced an exhaustive history to show the transformation in the mentality of the judges of the *Parlement* of Paris that
made a belief in witchcraft, still acceptable to so sophisticated an
intelligence as Jean Bodin's early in the century, virtually impossible
by the end.[9] This is a classical, multifaceted diagnosis of an important change in the mentality of a ruling group and of the
political, social, and scientific forces that effectuated the revolution. Mandrou is a superb craftsman, who does not presume to
plumb lower depths. His methodology is positivistic and its conclusions hardly to be faulted, except for neglect of the general

question—which may be the critical one for a historian with a psychological bent in 1970—of what the change signified on an unconscious psychic level. Recent American studies of white racism, perhaps an analogous phenomenon, which sometimes call themselves psychohistorical and may be pretentious and methodologically sloppy, nevertheless give an inkling of how a historian might explore collective obsessions related to excremental and oedipal fantasies.[10] Such ideas are untouchable in the purist French school of *histoire psychologique,* though there has been a growing intrusion of psychoanalytic concepts in recent issues of *Annales.*

When the elaborate outside scaffolding of Michel Foucault's theoretical model is stripped away, there still remain elements of Febvre's original program in Foucault's brilliant and well-documented definitions of seventeenth- and eighteenth-century concepts of madness and reason, and perhaps even in his attempts, in *Les mots et les choses,* to grasp the content of mental structures of various epochs.[11] His analysis is more intricate and formally constructed, if less readily demonstrable, than Febvre's approach to a historical mentality. Freud, who belatedly made the scene in France after World War II, has forced Foucault's generation to peer into the underground recesses that were still forbidden to the previous one. Though I frequently lose Foucault along the way of his argument, I find his work the most exciting new event in French *histoire psychologique,* though not as unrelated to the original master of the school as might be imagined.

III

Apart from the continuation of the Dilthey and Febvre traditions, the years between the World Wars brought novelty in two important respects. First, a number of brilliant young Frenchmen of the Ecole Normale, military class of 1905, Raymond Aron and Jean-Paul Sartre among them, in the most daring intellectual adventure since Mme. de Staël's, traveled to faraway Berlin and submitted themselves to the influence of German sociology and the phenomenological philosophy. At about the same time, the advent of Hitler and a Jewish exodus from Central Europe brought to America men of the generation of around 1900 who had in various ways come within the orbit of Freud's doctrines. I refer to thinkers like Herbert Marcuse and Erik Erikson, not to speak of a large contingent of psychoanalysts who made the United States the world center of Freudian thought and practice. Then, in the loose, free-wheeling intellectual atmosphere of the post-World War II period in America, a host of theories were formulated with an intimate though problematic link to Freud. Marcuse tried to amalgamate a philosophical interpretation of Freudian texts—often excerpted ruthlessly without regard to the main body of the work—with a Marxist-Hegelian world-view that on the face of it is totally alien to Freud. Erikson, joining forces with Freudian ego psychologists, struck off in a truly new direction of psychological history, and in the sixties popularized the term "psychohistory." And in the same postwar period Sartre attempted a monumental syncretism in which phenomenological philosophy, Marxist dialectical materialism, and, of late, Freudian psychoanalysis—*quelle galère*—are made to lie together in existential unhappiness. His *Critique de la raison dialectique*, now a decade old, does not yet seem to have made a breach in the historical ramparts of either Europe or America.[12] In France a new generation of structuralists writes about him as if he has long since been, as they say, transcended; but the announcement of his demise is premature.

When Freud finally married the unconscious after the long flirtations conducted by other men (the *mot* is his), the ground was laid for a fundamental innovation in the employment of psychological concepts in history, though, as I have indicated, virtually no historian was aware of it at the time. The therapeutic technique devised by Freud resulted in the accumulation of literally hundreds of thousands of personal histories. Perhaps Erik Erikson exaggerated when he once said that in the twentieth century we have learned more about individual human development than in all previous ages put together; but the clinical histories have surely provided us both with new types of data and with a flood of material that are not of the same order as the literary and philosophical reflections of the past. After all, every classical analysis produces about 10,000,000 words that in some fashion reveal the inner life of a man. From now on out, human conduct can no longer be explained in terms of plain utilitarian motives, as it was by nineteenth-century writers, and even Augustinian churchmen are today willing to complicate the war of the two cities by adopting tactical suggestions on the ways of the devil from the great disbeliever.

Freud himself made a number of applications of psychoanalysis to history. Though he retained a certain diffidence, shying away from the interpretation of Descartes' famous dreams, for example,[13] at times he boldly ventured brief psychobiographical hypotheses about creative men, as in his essays on Leonardo and Dostoevsky, where paintings and novels were used as illustrative documents.[14] In this manner he could support his conceptions with objective materials that were public property and did not require disguise, as did his own self-analysis and the case histories of his patients. Aside from his interpretations of literary documents, he invented for us a macrohistorical myth on the origin of civilization; he advanced an extravagant psychological hypothesis about the beginnings of Jewish monotheism (he once called his *Moses and Monotheism* a "historical novel"[15]); and he interspersed his writings with analogies between primitive and neurotic behavior. The identification of phylogeny and ontogeny was axiomatic with Freud. The psychological history of civilized mankind probably did not differ substantively from one period to another. Wars and revolutions, whatever their genesis, could be viewed in general terms as changing opportunities for the manifestation of aggression. From time to time there were massive social outbursts against the excesses of instinctual repression in civilized society. But history as a whole meant only the recurrent, eternal conflict of Eros and death.

While Freud's historical essays were attacked for errors in detail, his analytic method of gaining access to the unconscious opened a vast new area to historical inquiry. The followers of Freud, in imitation of the master, but often without his reticence, or at least ambivalence, proliferated psychobiographies. In the beginning their efforts were devoted almost exclusively to the pathography of literary figures—an example would be Marie Bonaparte's *Poe*, which enjoyed the imprimatur of the master in a few introductory remarks.[16] The writings of poets and novelists lent themselves to plausible readings as symbolic representations of the inner states of their authors, their deep loves and hates, their longings and terrors. Fictional incidents were analyzed as disguised materials or fantasy wish-fulfillment of neurotic drives, all by analogy to the dream-work of patients. A similar method of symbolic interpretation was extended to painters by Ernst Kris, a psychoanalyst who was trained as an art historian, and to composers by Editha and Richard Sterba.[17] Except for obiter dicta, until very recently it has not been attempted with physical scientists—though some of us may be creeping up on them, casting doubt on the autonomous development of science itself. The effect of all this on historical evidence in the traditional sense is disconcerting, and sometimes constrains the more hide-bound professionals to avert their eyes from the glass, like the eminent contemporaries of Galileo. Henceforth the plainest affirmations in memoirs, dispatches, letters, and secret confessions may require intricate psychological interpretation in the light of the Freudian model. The unconscious demands a hearing and will not be silenced.

Though some psychoanalytic biographers formulated hypotheses about the nature of creativity as a universal phenomenon, in general their artistic subjects were approached as self-contained little monads sufficient unto themselves. This kind of discrete treatment was superseded, however, when political scientists and historians, trying to explain historical developments on the grand scale, applied Freudian personality theory to world-historical actors. An American professor of political science, Harold Lasswell, was one of the first to come up with a formula relating the individual and the collective, something to the effect that the great politician displaces private affects upon public objects.[18] The merit of the political studies has varied enormously; Woodrow Wilson has received a sophisticated treatment at the hands of Alexander and Juliette George and a vulgar one in William Bullitt's analysis, which Freud may or may not have approved.[19] Despite scandalous instances of overinterpretation, immense new vistas have been opened up on the behavior of the monumental figures of world history; and if one is repelled by the grossness of some analyses, one has only to look back on such pre-Freudian compilations as Augustin Cabanès' *Grands névropathes, malades immortels* to appreciate the enormous strides that have been taken.[20]

This, I believe, is the perspective from which to examine the work of Erik Erikson. With Erikson, who has written both programmatic statements and two biographical studies of politico-religious figures, the analytic method applied to history has received its most subtle exemplification.[21] Yet the basic problem raised by Lucien Febvre remains unresolved. We are obliged to ask: Is the ideal psychological model of human development in eight stages, constructed by Erikson, universally applicable? Is this not a summary of twentieth-century psychoanalytic experience, whose relevance to other cultures and periods is open to question?

Clearly, in epochs where the composition of the family, its spiritual and economic character, and life expectancy are very different from ours, definitions of the successive crises of life would have to vary. Erikson might say they would need modification. But a historian confronted, for example, with data on Florence 1426-1427 indicating that the average age differential of husband and wife was twenty years and that fathers died early in their children's lives could feel that in this instance the schema would have to undergo drastic alteration.[22] A historian may hold with Plato and Aristotle, Locke and Descartes, yes, and Freud and Erikson that the earliest experiences are far and away the most potent (we remember Descartes' analysis of his predilection for cock-eyed girls based on an early fixation). And he will surely welcome Erikson's shift from exclusive emphasis on infancy and the early family romance to a more extensive view of ego development including periods of life that are better documented and hence more accessible to historical treatment. But can he accept without debate the proliferation of later "crises" in the Eriksonian design, or Erikson's assignment of weight to each of eight crises? The historian should be warned that the selection of materials to fill the boxes of the eight stages may make of the schema a self-fulfilling prophecy. I find wholly credible the crises of adolescence and what early nineteenth-century psychiatrists like Philippe Pinel called the male climacteric, for these are vocal, articulate periods whose anguish is attested by cries and confessions. The rest of the eight stations of life appear rather arbitrary; the traditional divisions of the Church Fathers or Dante's four or Vincent de Beauvais' six may be quite enough. Before I can seriously evaluate the Eriksonian model as a historical tool, I feel that the history of the epigenetic cycle itself, diversified in time and place, needs to be written—and initial soundings in this direction have been made.[23] These reservations aside, however, Erikson's stress upon the total epigenetic cycle, whatever its form, seems to me a permanent acquisition of historical consciousness.

In the two studies of men he calls politico-religious geniuses, Luther and Gandhi, Erikson found a motive drive to heroic action in the need of the sons to outstrip their fathers and compensate for their failures. When he generalizes these conjectures about a small and special sample to all geniuses, he is speaking as a theorist of psychoanalysis, eager to find uniformities, and a historian's judgment must remain suspended. His catalogues of the common characteristics of geniuses—a secret foreboding that a curse lies upon them, a tie to the father which makes open rebellion impossible, a sense of being chosen and carrying a superior destiny, a feeling of weakness and shyness and unworthiness, a precocious conscience in childhood, an early development of ultimate concerns, a brief attempt to cast off the yoke of their fate, and a final settling into the conviction that they have a responsibility for a segment of mankind—is troubling even to a historian who has wandered far from the all-too-commonsensical positivists. As a description of Gandhi's and perhaps Luther's experience, yes; as a historical typology, no.

In his *Gandhi*, Erikson closely scrutinized the manner in which a group of followers resonated to their hero, identified with him in terms of their own life cycles. The skill and imagination with which he handles their recollected dreams, fantasies, and symbolic acts is unmatched in contemporary psychological history-writing. On the other hand, the general relationship between the world historical figure and his age is not advanced much beyond Hegel's lectures. There is no theory of social change in Eriksonian psychology, any more than in Freud's, except for the assumption that each new generation strives to surpass the older one, to innovate upon its works, risking oedipal ambivalence in the process. Erikson does not offer us any help in comprehending either the tempo or the direction of change beyond the categorical assertion that at certain moments mankind is prepared for epoch-making transformations—an epochal identity vacuum is created, he tells us[24] —and the hero comes along and sounds the clarion-call. Each such moment has its potentialities for new creation and redemption from historical psychic blocks that inhibit a society from embarking on a course for which it is ripe and which it desires in its innermost being. The genius leader first releases himself from psychic bondage or points the way to a release for others which he may not have personally achieved.

There is too much of the sacred drama for me in this model of the historical moment. That the hero responds sharply to forces in his world, that he has antennae in his head giving him prescience, foreknowledge, is metaphoric language that German *Zeitgeist* historians have resorted to for many decades. Though he does not mention him, I cannot help hearing the overtones of Hegel's world-historical person, who incarnates the ongoing history of absolute spirit. I am left unenlightened as to what brought about the historical crisis and unconvinced that the hero's prescience is the force that resolves it. On occasion there is a prophetic quality to

Erikson's heralding of the next stage in world history, with its ever-broadening area of common identities, that leaves the agnostic behind. The austere and rigorous criteria for "psychohistorical evidence" that he set forth in a theoretical statement are not always observed in practice.[25]

Deriving from a totally different tradition is Sartre's existentialist amalgam of psychology and history. He has at least one thing in common with Eriksonian psychohistory, and that is a humanist emphasis upon personality in history and the freedom of, shall we say, ego-will—though Sartre is now prepared to give greater weight to the fetters of inherited psychological conditioning than he was previously.

Sartre renders existential the legacy of a psychologized Marxist framework, fills in the interstices in the history of socioeconomic development with choices of human wills as he presumes Marx would have done, and subjects the action of these wills to psychological analysis. A general Marxist class determinism is postulated, but, in addition, he believes that a humanist history can show how it is possible for individuals with a variety of class and psychic identities to sacrifice their lives in common historic actions. He has fleshed out a Marxist historical dialectic based on production relations and class structure with an existential account of how men who in an inert state have a relationship of mere seriality to one another—like people waiting in a queue—come, in a given historical crisis, to assume ties that entail responsibilities of life and death in action. His convoluted argument is less interesting for a historian than the kinds of questions he addresses to his materials. Rereading histories of the French Revolution, the Revolution of 1848, and the Commune, he asks: What really happens when a crowd moves on an objective? What is the nature of the secret psychological commitments and pacts they have made with one another? How in fact does collective historical action come about? Though Sartre's passion for phenomenological totalization will put many of us off, historians may be able to adapt to other times and places his method of extracting the full existential implications of isolated events. In his treatment of individuals, Sartre has created prototypes for the fusion of social and psychological knowledge. The published fragments of his Flaubert, a work in progress, are a brilliant synthesis of Marxist and Freudian insights.[26]

The penetration of the outer social and ideological world into the intimacy of the family and the psychological history of the individual in this primary field of confrontation are for Sartre the first and perhaps most significant of a whole sequence of developments. In the introduction to his *Critique de la raison dialectique,* he criticized his Marxist friends for concerning themselves solely with adults: "Reading them one would believe that we are born at the age when we earn our first wages . . . Existentialism, on the contrary, believes that it can integrate the psychoanalytic method which discovers the point of insertion for man and his class—that is, the particular family—as a mediation between the universal class and the individual."[27] I have considerable sympathy for this viewpoint. At the present time writers who call themselves psychohistorians are forced to use, *faute de mieux,* crude and misleading affirmations about both the economy and the interpsychic relationships of the Western family. A measure of our poverty is the frequency with which Philippe Ariès' history of childhood is cited as Holy Writ.[28] Whenever I have tried to interpret the family relations of historical figures I have felt on shaky ground in relying on old-hat, impressionistic utterances about this nuclear institution. But the possibilities for research are open and the materials cry for exploitation. There seems to be a consensus among social historians, prosopographers, and historians with an interest in psychological phenomena that the history of the family represents a gaping lacuna in our knowledge to which a new generation of historians should give significant priority.

History can now be individuated and particularized in a way that Leopold von Ranke never dreamed of. The economic and social existence of individuals and aggregates today can be seen reflected in the family alongside the psychic pattern set by this primal reality at a crucial period in life. The insights of Marx and of Freud can thus be brought together not in the sibylline macro-historical rhetoric of Herbert Marcuse or Norman Brown but in concrete historical works where life situations are depicted.

IV

A certain imperialistic character attaches to a major intellectual discovery such as psychoanalysis. When a new instrument for the study of man is developed, believers in its potency tend to conceive of it as a panacea, a solution to a wide range of problems, ultimately including the historical. If it is a successful and persuasive technique that wins assent in one area of the study of man, why should it not be introduced elsewhere? Proclamations are issued raising high hopes and staking out large claims. The new technique is often applied with a heavy hand. Revolutionary results are awaited, as it pretends to answer questions for which there already exist explanations more elegant and plausible or more nuanced. It becomes totalitarian. Under attack the proponents of the new technique may withdraw from their most advanced outposts: their position was misunderstood, their theory was not meant to be all-embracing. It is only the most important interpretive device and does not quite account for everything. The original formulation has been misrepresented, misconstrued.

The initial negative reaction of official historians—and there is such a body of academic mandarins in every country—to a new method like psychoanalysis in history is equally fervid. The new technique is based on a series of false assumptions; it is not acceptable even in its own discipline; depending upon it is leaning upon a weak reed. Psychology and history are declared to be different in their essence—as if either of them had an "essence" that enjoys even a partial consensus. The human phenomena that psychological analyses are presumed to illuminate are too elusive, or if they can be grasped they are insignificant and irrelevant as far as the true vocation of the historian is concerned. The evidence brought forth by these techniques is obfuscatory, raising more problems than it resolves—as if the opening up of new problems were not in itself a virtue instead of a fault.

As studies multiply—good, bad, and indifferent—the proponents cite the best as examples and the opponents the most ill-conceived and outlandish specimens. With time, however, both extreme positions are eroded. The imperialists of the new technique pull in their horns, and the absolute deniers of its usefulness permit it a humble place in the republic of knowledge. Eventually the new perceptions insinuate themselves into the most normative orthodox history-writing, often without the author's awareness, and the controversy joins the ranks of those "appearance problems" that at intervals have shaken the intellectual world and that one later reads about with some incredulity. This has been the historical fortune of Marxist conceptions and seems a fair prognosis of what will happen to Freudian ideas in the process of their assimilation by historians.

Despite serious misgivings about some of the uses of psychology in history, I feel we have come a long way from the intellectualist psychological history of the earlier part of the century. I still cast my lot with the Freudian "psychologizers." A historian can scarcely compose a narrative line without committing himself, implicitly or explicitly, to some theory of personality and motivation. In various periods since the late seventeenth century there have been dominant psychologies, like those of Locke and Descartes, that seeped into the literary language as well as into everyday speech, and through these media constrained the historian to employ their motivational terminology. Today a historian must feel at least some uneasiness about adhering to the traditional nineteenth-century patterns of motivation. A skeptic may rightly be uncertain that the more novel systems are intrinsically superior or truer in an absolute sense than those handed down by the past; but it is eccentric in 1970 to go about in satin knee-breeches or wear a Prince Albert frock-coat, even if one likes the style. The historian is probably always obliged to accept and express himself in the psychological language of his times; and thus, as I see it, there is no escape from Freud's conceptions in some form, orthodox or heterodox.

Although there may have been a general appreciation of the long interdependency of history and psychology in a wide variety of shapes and forms, on both a theoretical and a practicing level, most members of the American historical profession, positivists and relativists alike, were nevertheless ill-prepared for the bombshell that fell into their midst on December 29, 1957, when William Langer in his presidential address before the American Historical Association in New York announced that the historian's next assignment was an application of the findings of psychoanalysis to history. There were visible stirrings among members of the audience that a behavioral scientist of any school would have identified as consternation. This was the most unkindest cut of all, from a scholar who had produced an impressive array of impeccably solid works of diplomatic history. Since then, there are indications that the stubborn resistance of a phalanx of historians generally suspicious of what they considered random psychological associations is being overcome. Papers dealing with psychology and history, presented at a number of recent meetings of the American Historical Association, have attracted large audiences. In 1963 Bruce Mazlish assembled an impressive group of theoretical statements on psychoanalysis and history, and urged the historian to acquaint himself with the relevant texts.[29] Stuart Hughes reiterated the general sense of Langer's manifesto and added a programmatic statement of his own in *History as Art and as Science* (1964), where he called for historical research into the "shared anxieties and aspirations [of various epochs] which may be all the more decisive for being only partially conscious." Experiences such as these, he maintains, cut across the conventional delimitations of class or elite groups, and he has voiced confidence in the feasibility of arriving at valid historical generalizations about "deep-seated fears and ideal strivings."[30] While it is probable that the American historical profession has produced in the last decade more articles about the desirability of establishing a bridge between history and psychology than works animated by the new ideas, that there has been far more talk about the subject than actual performance, some younger historians are beginning to incorporate the findings of the new psychology into the body of their work. For example, the June 1970 issue of the *American Historical Review* contained an article by a young historian, John Demos, "Underlying Themes in the Witchcraft of Seventeenth-Century New England," that was informed by psychoanalytic concepts judiciously introduced.[31] In this respect, however, American historians have lagged behind the political scientists, who have more eagerly embraced the new ideas in their studies of dominant contemporary political figures—witness the *Dædalus* issue on "Philosophers and Kings" (Summer 1968).

The collaborators of the French *Annales*, which has lately shown itself hospitable to articles on psychoanalysis and history, are beginning to explore the psychological aspects of demography, of which they are today the outstanding school in the world. The Russians for Marxist ideological reasons and the official English historians for traditionalist ones are likely to hold out longest against the new trend.

Any contemporary use of psychology in history must postulate the existence of the unconscious, a belief that the unconscious of past epochs has left behind visible traces, and a conviction that these traces are decipherable. About the interpretation of the documentary vestiges of psychic experience there will inevitably be controversy, as there has been over the reading of dead and forgotten languages, and at present the historian is faced with rival and contradictory theories of human development from among which he must choose an initial hypothesis if he is to avail himself of the new techniques. The lack of consensus among psychologists and psychoanalysts is bound to perplex him. Once even a tentative commitment is made, however, to some psychoanalytic theory—and the historian may permit himself the luxury of being eclectic and pluralist—the results can vastly enrich our understanding of historical experience. The investigation of psychological phenomena in past epochs not only will alter historical conceptions about other ages, but could lead to an appreciation of the historical dimensions and limitations of present-day psychological doctrines.

Accusations of dilettantism are commonly made against those who are introducing modern psychology into history, and the problem of professional training in two disciplines, psychology and history, is admittedly nettlesome. Yet is it not precisely at the crossroads of two forms of knowledge that the most fertile conceptions in present-day historiography are emerging? The idea of an *équipe,* of the teaming of a psychologist and a historian, is a too-facile solution; an ultimate synthesis must take place within the mind of the historian if the work is to have a wholeness.

On the use of a specialized vocabulary and the borrowing of technical terminology, as contrasted with concepts, my position is rather conservative. I find the psychological jargon, with infrequent exceptions, too ugly for narrative history, and am convinced that one can adopt the concepts without the nomenclature, which derives from a parochial scientistic tradition. After all, no therapist worth his salt will resort in his consultation room to technical terms because of the obvious danger that they may be confused with common and vulgar usage. If the historian eschews technical words, he is less likely to be seduced into dogmatism. His explanations of historical phenomena can be ambiguous, multifaceted, possible, or probable; he can write suggestively, propose solutions by indirection. Psychological labels are unnecessarily restrictive; historical figures are not patients admitted to a hospital who have to be categorized for housekeeping convenience.

Acceptance of psychoanalytic concepts in history-writing presupposes, of course, a somewhat different set of criteria for historical proof than those to which traditional historians are accustomed. For some, the evidence is not concrete enough, and the element of conjecture more obtrusive than they can countenance. While the quantitative school of history continues the Galilean tradition of mathematicizing knowledge with the instruments of a new technology congenial to our age, psychology in history still has a tendency toward the sample of one and the search for uniqueness. Any prospect of quantification seems remote, though not entirely to be excluded as an element in analyses of the behavior of groups.[32]

On the whole I feel that psychological knowledge is at this stage more useful in description than in explanatory system-making. When two disciplines are locked into the same cage, the historical keepers tell me, cannibalistic tendencies well up from their unconscious and they sometimes try to devour each other. Recent attempts to merge psychology and history in a clumsily labeled psychohistorical process do presume the sort of grand monist thesis to which history has always been refractory. Since so many historico-psychological problems have not been mapped even in a crude manner, I am reluctant to embrace elaborate theoretical structures. In the end I conceive of psychology as playing a more modest role, adding a set of vivid psychedelic colors to the historian's palette, offsetting the mournful black-and-white of structure and number that in this technological age will inevitably suffuse a large part of the historical.

The new psychologies can open up whole areas of inquiry by encouraging the historian to ask some direct, perhaps impertinent questions. The restriction of the method to biography, where it has enjoyed at least partial acceptance, should not be a lasting confinement. Historians will have to wrestle anew with symbolic representation on a broad scale. There are central problems in the history of ideas that cannot be treated adequately on an intellectualist and conscious level of expression alone and that invite the use of new psychological tools: the history of feelings about time, space, utopia, myth, love, death, God. The "unconscious mental habits" that Arthur Lovejoy hoped to analyze in his history of ideas had little or nothing to do with Freud's unconscious. Perhaps the fundamental shortcoming of his work and that of the Febvre school was their exclusive intellectualism. We all know that the experience of love and death and aggression has changed through the centuries. If a professor dared to propose a course on the history of love he would certainly take a ribbing from his colleagues. Yet this emotion has been as protean in its forms and as vital to human existence as, let us say, shipping or banking, whose respectability as subjects for historical treatment in university teaching is quite unchallenged. When a psychologist investigating contemporary attitudes toward death looks for historical comparisons, we can only provide him with impressions and isolated, sparse instances. Particularly dramatic intrusions of death, such as great plagues, have been studied by historians in their psychological as well as their economic, political, and artistic consequences; Millard Meiss's study of the Black Death is a prototype.[33] But there is need for an exploration of the long-term, changing meaning of death on the unconscious as well as on the conscious level. Death in the eighteenth century had its special character, but I think we know far less about it than we do about the diplomatic relations between Parma and Venice in that period.

The particular forms of psychic repression have a history and so do the forms of sublimation—their instrumentalities differ widely in time and place. The overt manifestations of neuroses have changed, as any sampling of case histories over the past seventy years will show. As far back as 1913 Karl Jaspers in a section of his *General Psychopathology* entitled "Social and Historical Aspects of the Psychoses and the Personality-Disorders" recognized that "the neuroses in particular have a contemporary style."[34] Few historians have yet coped with the intricacies of presenting to their readers the varying patterns of libidinal satisfaction in different epochs. You can read that grand masterpiece of provincialism, the *Cambridge Modern History*, in its newest version, without even suspecting the existence of these transformations.

The histories of fashion, clothes, sexual and marital customs, punishments, style, and a hundred other questions which have traditionally belonged to *la petite histoire* and to the antiquarians need to be explored for their symbolic content. Freud's second most important legacy to a historian may well be the dissolution of a hierarchy of values among historical materials. If all things can become vehicles of expression for feelings and thoughts, then the state document, grand philosophical affirmation, and scientific law may lose some of their prestige to other more intimate records of human experience. The day of Dilthey's elitist psychological history is over. Conversely, classical psychoanalysis, with a dubious future as a therapy, might be reborn as a historical instrumentality. The dead do not ask to be cured, only to be understood.

A great expansion in our comprehension of the past might be effected through the rereading of old or neglected documents with a different apperception. Notebooks and scribbles that seemed destined for the ashheap of history may be rescued and made to live again—as exciting a reconquest of the past as a new archaeology. A great body of dream literature and of fantasies of past ages is unexplored. In Western Europe and in America there are voluminous materials—legal, political, medical, literary—in manuscript and print, to say nothing of representations by the plastic arts, that have not been researched for their psychological meaning. The questions have not been asked, and therefore historians have not been on the *qui vive* for the answers that lie concealed in the texts.

Economic history has become respectable, and who would now demean the history of labor, or the history of consumption patterns? I merely advocate adding to them a history of other needs and expressions of living. In defense of his idealist history of Spirit as the definition of human existence, Hegel once wrote with utter contempt of nutritive history. Now that we have, in despite of Hegel, recognized the claims of hands and stomach to a share in human history, let us make ready to welcome the other more secret and hidden parts of man into the temple.

An earlier version of this essay was presented as the Rabbi Irving M. Levey Lecture at Princeton University, April 29, 1970.

REFERENCES

1. Wilhelm Dilthey, *Einleitung in die Geisteswissenschaften: Versuch einer Grundlegung für das Studium der Gesellschaft und der Geschichte* (Leipzig: Duncker and Humblot, 1883), I (no more volumes published). A second edition with additions from unpublished manuscripts forms vol. I, ed. Bernhard Groethuysen (1923), of Dilthey's *Gesammelte Schriften* (Leipzig: Teubner). With the exception of vol. II, *Weltanschauung und Analyse des Menschen seit Renaissance und Reformation* (1914), the collected works appeared from 1921 to 1936. *Der Aufbau der geschichtlichen Welt in den Geisteswissenschaften. Studien . . . .*, pt. I, was published in the *Abhandlungen der Königlich Preussischen Akademie der Wissenschaften: Phil.-hist. Klasse* for 1910; a new edition with additions from unpublished manuscripts forms vol. VII, ed. Bernhard Groethuysen (1927) of the *Gesammelte Schriften.*

2. Wilhelm Dilthey, *Die Jugendgeschichte Hegels,* which appeared in the *Abhandlungen der Königlich Preussischen Akademie der Wissenschaften* in 1905, now vol. IV, ed. Herman Nohl (1921) of the *Gesammelte Schriften; Leben Schleiermachers,* published with *Denkmale der inneren Entwicklung Schleiermachers, erläutert durch kritische Untersuchungen* (Berlin, 1870), I (no more volumes published).

3. Wilhelm Dilthey, *Das Erlebnis und die Dichtung,* 13th ed. (Stuttgart: Teubner, 1957; original ed., 1905), p. 289.

4. Karl Jaspers, *Strindberg und Van Gogh: Versuch einer pathographischen Analyse unter vergleichender Heranziehung von Swedenborg und Hölderlin* (Bern: E. Bircher, 1922).

5. Karl Jaspers, *Psychologie der Weltanschauungen* (Berlin: J. Springer, 1919; 4th ed., 1954).

6. Lucien Paul Victor Febvre, *Un destin: Martin Luther* (Paris: Rieder, 1928); quotation is from *Martin Luther: A Destiny*, trans. Roberts Tapley (New York: E. P. Dutton, 1929), pp. 33, 35.

7. Lucien Febvre, *Le problème de l'incroyance au XVIe siècle: La religion de Rabelais* (Paris: A. Michel, 1947; original ed., 1942), p. 163.

8. Lucien Febvre, *Combats pour l'histoire* (Paris: A. Colin, 1953), p. 229.

9. Robert Mandrou, *Magistrats et sorciers en France au XVIIe siècle: Une analyse de psychologie historique* (Paris: Plon, 1968).

10. See, for example, Joel Kovel, *White Racism: A Psychohistory* (New York: Pantheon, 1970).

11. Michel Foucault, *Histoire de la folie à l'âge classique* (Paris: Plon, 1961); *Les mots et les choses* (Paris: Gallimard, 1966).

12. Jean-Paul Sartre, *Critique de la raison dialectique, précédé de Questions de méthode* (Paris: Gallimard, 1960).

13. Sigmund Freud, "Brief an Maxim Leroy über einen Traum des Cartesius" (1929), in *Gesammelte Schriften*, XII (Vienna: Internationaler Psychoanalytischer Verlag, 1934), pp. 403–405; for English translation, see the *Standard Edition of the Complete Psychological Works of Sigmund Freud*, ed. James Strachey with the collaboration of Anna Freud (London: Hogarth Press), XXI, 203-204.

14. Sigmund Freud, *Eine Kindheitserinnerung des Leonardo da Vinci* (Leipzig: F. Deuticke, 1910; for English translation see *Standard Edition*, XI, 63-137); *Der Wahn und die Träume in W. Jensen's "Gradiva"* (Vienna: F. Deuticke, 1907; English translation in *Standard Edition*, IX, 3-95); "Dostojewski und die Vatertötung" (1928), published as a preface to *Die Urgestalt der Brüder Karamasoff* (a supplementary volume in the German edition of Dostoevsky's works by René Fülöp-Miller and F. Eckstein) and republished in the *Gesammelte Schriften*, XII, 7-26 (English translation in *Standard Edition*, XXI, 177-196).

15. Sigmund Freud, *Der Mann Moses und die monotheistische Religion, Drei Abhandlungen* (Amsterdam: A. de Lange, 1939; parts 1 and 2 published in German in *Imago* in 1937; English translation by Katherine Jones, *Moses and Monotheism*, New York: Knopf, 1939); Ernst L. Freud, ed., *The Letters of Sigmund Freud and Arnold Zweig*, trans. Elaine and William Robson-Scott (New York: Harcourt Brace and World, 1970), p. 91, Freud to Zweig, September 30, 1934.

16. Marie Bonaparte, *Edgar Poe: Etude psychanalytique*, 2 vols. (Paris, 1933).

17. Ernst Kris, *Psychoanalytic Explorations in Art* (New York: International Universities Press, 1962; original ed., London: Allen and Unwin, 1953); Editha and Richard Sterba, *Beethoven and His Nephew: A Psychoanalytic Study of Their Relationship*, trans. Willard R. Trask (London: Dennis Dobson, 1957).

18. Harold D. Lasswell, *Psychopathology and Politics* (Chicago: University of Chicago Press, 1930), pp. 75–76.

19. Alexander L. George and Juliette L. George, *Woodrow Wilson and Colonel House: A Personality Study* (New York: John Day, 1956); Sigmund Freud and W. C. Bullitt, *Thomas Woodrow Wilson, Twenty-Eighth President of the United States: A Psychological Study* (Boston: Houghton Mifflin, 1967).

20. Augustin Cabanès, *Grands névropathes, malades immortels,* 3 vols. (Paris: A. Michel, 1930–1935).

21. Erik H. Erikson, *Childhood and Society* (New York: Norton, 1950); *Young Man Luther* (New York: Norton, 1958); *Identity and the Life Cycle: Selected Papers* (New York: International Universities Press, 1959); *Insight and Responsibility* (New York: Norton, 1964); *Gandhi's Truth* (New York: Norton, 1969).

22. D. Herlihy, "Vieillir au Quattrocento," *Annales: économies, sociétés, civilisations* (November–December 1969), pp. 1338-1352.

23. Creighton Gilbert, "When Did a Man in the Renaissance Grow Old?" *Studies in the Renaissance,* 14 (1967), 7–32, is an example of what needs to be done on a broad scale.

24. Erikson, *Insight and Responsibility,* p. 204.

25. Erik H. Erikson, "On the Nature of Psycho-Historical Evidence: In Search of Gandhi," *Dædalus* (Summer 1968), pp. 695–730.

26. Jean-Paul Sartre, "La conscience de classe chez Flaubert," *Les Temps Modernes,* 21st year, no. 240 (May 1966), 1921–1951, and no. 241 (June 1966), 2113–2153; "Flaubert: Du poète à l'artiste," *Les Temps Modernes,* 22nd year, no. 243 (August 1966), 197–253; no. 244 (September 1966), 423–481; no. 245 (October 1966), 598–674.

27. Jean-Paul Sartre, *The Problem of Method* (prefatory essay of *Critique de la raison dialectique*), trans. Hazel E. Barnes (London: Methuen, 1963), p. 62.

28. Philippe Ariès, *L'enfant et la vie familiale sous l'Ancien Régime* (Paris: Plon, 1960).

29. Bruce Mazlish, ed., *Psychoanalysis and History* (Englewood Cliffs, N.J.: Prentice-Hall, 1963).

30. H. Stuart Hughes, *History as Art and as Science* (New York: Harper and Row, 1964), pp. 61, 62.

31. John Demos, "Underlying Themes in the Witchcraft of Seventeenth-Century New England," *American Historical Review,* 75 (1970), 1311–1326.

32. An interesting attempt to deal with the psychology of a social aggregate that raises the problem of quantification is Marc Raeff, *Origins of the*

Russian Intelligentsia: The Eighteenth-Century Nobility (New York: Harcourt, Brace and World, 1966).

33. Millard Meiss, *Painting in Florence and Siena after the Black Death* (Princeton: Princeton University Press, 1951).

34. Karl Jaspers, *General Psychopathology,* trans. J. Hoenig and Marian W. Hamilton (Chicago: University of Chicago Press, 1963; original German ed., *Allgemeine Psychopathologie,* 1913), p. 732.

ROBERT DARNTON

Reading, Writing, and Publishing in Eighteenth-Century France: A Case Study in the Sociology of Literature

Non numerantur sed ponderantur.
—Marc Bloch[1]

HISTORIANS HAVE always taken what a society writes, publishes, and reads as a guide to its culture, but they have never taken all its books as guidebooks. Instead, they select a few works as representative of the whole and settle down to write intellectual history. Of course those select few may not deserve to serve as cultural attachés. If chosen without proportional representation, they may give a distorted view of reading habits in the past. Nowhere is the culturomorphic distortion produced by miscast classics more at issue than in the study of the French Enlightenment, a subject located at the crossroads between the traditional history of ideas and more recent trends of social history.

Social historians tend to see the Enlightenment as a social phenomenon—one of the forces of "innovation" opposing "inertia" in the Old Regime (to use the vocabulary of the *Annales* school). They attempt to situate the Enlightenment within a general cultural context rather than to explicate its texts. And they study culture quantitatively, often working from statistics of authorship or book production. This essay will survey their work in order to see what conclusions can be drawn concerning writing and reading in eighteenth-century France and will then attempt to show how that work might be supplemented by an investigation of eighteenth-century publishing. Publishing was an activity where social, economic, and cultural forces naturally converged. But it cannot be understood, in the eighteenth century, without reference to political factors. So a final section will deal with politics and publishing as an aspect of the prerevolutionary crisis.

238

I

The quantitative study of eighteenth-century culture goes back to an article published sixty years ago by Daniel Mornet. Mornet tried to measure literary taste under the Old Regime by tallying up titles in five hundred catalogues of private libraries, which had mostly been printed for auctions in the Paris area between 1750 and 1780. He found one lonely copy of Rousseau's *Contrat social.* Eighteenth-century libraries contained a surprisingly small percentage of the other Enlightenment classics, he discovered. Instead their shelves bulged with the works of history's forgotten men and women: Thémiseul de Saint-Hyacinthe, Mme. de Graffigny, and Mme. Riccoboni. Eighteenth-century booklovers divided French literature into "before" and "after" Clément Marot. When they read the philosophes, it was the Voltaire of *La Henriade* and the Rousseau of *La nouvelle Héloise.*[2]

Coinciding ironically with the "great books" approach to the study of civilization, Mornet's research seemed to knock out some of the pillars of the Enlightenment. He made a gap, at least, in the view that the *Social Contract* prepared the way for Robespierre, and his followers have been trying to widen the breach ever since.[3] Meanwhile, the Rousseauists have repaired some of the damage in a counterattack on Mornet's evidence.[4] Why should private libraries important enough to have printed catalogues be taken as an indication of a book's appeal to ordinary and impecunious readers? they ask. They point out that the message of the *Social Contract* could have reached the general reading public through the version of it in book five of Rousseau's highly popular *Emile,* through numerous editions of his collected works, or through editions that came out during the momentous last decade of the Ancien Régime, which Mornet's study did not cover.[5] So Mornet's case remains unproved, either right or wrong.

Nonetheless, Mornet raised some fundamental problems that have only begun to be faced: What was the character of literary culture under the Old Regime? Who produced books in the eighteenth century, who read them, and what were they? It will be impossible to locate the Enlightenment in any cultural and social context until those questions are answered, and they cannot be answered by traditional methods of research.

The most influential attempt to formulate a new methodology has been Robert Escarpit's *Sociologie de la littérature* (Paris, 1958).[6]

As his title suggests, Escarpit, now director of the Centre de sociologie des faits littéraires at Bordeaux, wanted to define the objects and methods of a new branch of sociology. He treated books as agents in a psychological process, the communication of writer and reader, and also as commodities, circulating through a system of production, distribution, and consumption. Since the author plays a crucial role in both the psychological and the economic circuits of exchange, Escarpit concentrated on the study of writers. They constitute a distinct segment of the population subject to normal demographic laws, he argued, and on this assumption he produced a demographic history of authorship.

In order to survey the literary population, he began with the back pages of the *Petit Larousse,* moved on to bibliographies and biographical dictionaries, and emerged with a list of 937 writers born between 1490 and 1900. He then worked this material into a two-page graph, where the "fait littéraire" appeared in terms of the rise and fall of writers under the age of forty. Escarpit observed that the proportion of young writers rose after the deaths of Louis XIV, Louis XV, and Napoleon. The Edict of Nantes also coincided with an upsurge of youth, which was cut short first after the triumph of Richelieu and then following the collapse of the Fronde. To Escarpit the conclusion was clear: political events determine literary demography. He confirmed this interpretation by reference to England, where the Armada produced a "vieillissement" among writers that was only overcome by the death of James I.

It is a stirring spectacle, this adjustment of the literary population to battles, edicts, revolutions, and the birth of sovereigns. But it leaves the reader confused. Is he to believe that a kind of intellectual contraception took hold of the republic of letters? Did writers limit their population out of loyalty to Good Queen Bess (and Victoria, too), or was *vieillissement* their curse on the queens? Did young men start writing in England in order to make life more difficult for Charles I, or did they stop in France in order to show disaffection for Louis XIV? If one should discount any conscious motivation, why did young writers decrease in numbers after the accession of Louis XIV and increase after the accession of Louis XV and Louis XVI? And why should the birth and death of rulers have such demographic importance—or so much more than the revolutions of 1789 and 1848, which do not disturb the undulations of Escarpit's graph, although 1830 appears as a great turning point?

The answers to these questions might be found among the deficiencies of Escarpit's statistics. To take 937 writers over 410 years is to spread the sampling pretty thin—an average of 2.3 writers a year. Adding or subtracting a single man could shift the graph by 5 per cent or more, yet Escarpit hung some weighty conclusions on such shifts—his distinction, for example, between a youthful romantic movement and the middle-aged character of literary life under the Empire. More important, Escarpit had no idea of how many writers went uncounted. He evidently believed that a few dozen men (Lamartine and twenty-three others in the case of the early romantics) could represent, demographically, an entire literary generation. A few individuals could, to be sure, represent a new stylistic trend or cultural movement but not the phenomena that can be analyzed demographically, like generational conflict and the adjustment of population to resources.

Escarpit attributed the sociological differences between eighteenth- and nineteenth-century writing to two other factors: "provincialization" and professionalization. He detected a rhythmic "alternance Paris-province" by tracing the geographical origins of his preselected authors. But the geographical argument suffers from the same statistical fallacies as the demographical, and so Escarpit fails to prove that the Paris of Balzac dominated French literature any more than the Paris of Diderot. In the case of professionalization, Escarpit's conclusions seem sounder. He produced two statistical tables to show that there were more middle-class professionals, or writers who lived entirely from their pens, in the nineteenth than in the eighteenth century. But his argument is not helped by the fact that the percentages in the table of eighteenth-century writers add up to 166 per cent.[7]

In this instance, Escarpit drew his statistics from *The French Book Trade in the Ancien Régime* by David Pottinger, another example of the quantitative study of authorship. Pottinger proceeded by combing biographical dictionaries for information about six hundred "writers" who lived between 1500 and 1800. He then sorted his men into five social categories—the clergy, nobility of the sword, high bourgeoisie, middle bourgeoisie, and petty bourgeoisie—and apparently concluded that the authors of the Old Regime belonged predominantly to the nobility of the sword and the high bourgeoisie. Again, the conclusion is more convincing than the statistics, because Pottinger destroyed the representativeness of his sample by eliminating 48.5 per cent of the writers on the grounds that he could not identify their social background. That stroke of statistical surgery left an average of one author a year to support a social analysis spread out over three centuries. Moreover, Pottinger apparently misfiled many individuals like Restif de la Bretonne, who went into the category of the First Estate because he had a brother who went into the church. Most of the sixteen others in that category either had relatives or protectors who were clergymen. But who in the Old Regime, excepting peasants, did not? Pottinger's other categories are not much more solid. He placed all writers who served in the army or navy with the nobility of the sword and placed teachers, apothecaries, architects, and anyone "whom we can identify with the law or with semilegal positions in the State"[8] in the high bourgeoisie. That kind of admissions policy would put at the top of society many lowly writers who lived like the Neveu de Rameau but called themselves lawyers and even registered with the Paris bar. In any case, it is almost impossible to delimit strata of high, middle, and low bourgeois, because social historians have struggled vainly for years to reach agreement on a meaningful definition of the "bourgeoisie"; and definitions of social stratification in the sixteenth century may not be applicable to the eighteenth.

What then can one conclude from quantitative history's attempts to analyze authorship? Nothing at all. Neither Escarpit nor Pottinger produced evidence to prove that the handful of men they chose to represent the entire literary population of a given period was in fact representative—and neither could possibly do so, because it would first be necessary to have a census of all the writers of the Old Regime. No such census can be contrived, for what, after all, is a writer? Someone who has written a book, someone who depends on writing for a living, someone who claims the title, or someone on whom posterity has bestowed it? Conceptual confusion and deficient data blighted this branch of sociocultural history before it bore its first fruit. But the sociology of literature need not stand or fall on the first attempts to put it in practice. And statistics on reading should be more fruitful than those on writers— if Mornet can be modernized.

II

Mornet showed that a primary obstacle to understanding the culture of the Old Regime is our inability to answer the fundamental

question: What did eighteenth-century Frenchmen read? The answer eludes us because we have no best-seller lists or statistics on
book "consumption" for the early modern period. Quantitative historians therefore have taken soundings in a variety of sources,
hoping to tap enough information to reconstruct the general outline of eighteenth-century reading habits. Their predilection for
statistics does not imply any belief that they can reduce the reader's
internal experience to numbers, or measure quality quantitatively,
or produce a numerical standard of literary influence. (Newton's
Principia would score low on any crude statistical survey.) The
quantifiers merely hope to get an over-all view of reading in
general and by genre. An enormous amount of data has already
been compiled in monographic articles and books by François
Furet, Jean Ehrard, Jacques Roger, Daniel Roche, François Bluche
(using the work of Régine Petit), and Jean Meyer.[9] Each drew on
one of three kinds of sources: catalogues of private libraries, book
reviews, and application to the state for authorization to publish.
So the reading problem has been heavily attacked on three sides.
If it has been cornered, if those long hours in the archives and
those laborious calculations have extracted a common pattern from
the data, then one can hope to watch the general contours of
eighteenth-century literary culture come slowly into focus. Before
seeing whether all of the monographs can be synthesized, it is
necessary to explain the character of each, because each has special
strengths and weaknesses.

François Furet surveyed the Bibliothèque Nationale's registers
of requests for permission to publish books. The requests fell into
two categories: *permissions publiques* (both *privilèges* and *permissions de Sceau*) for books processed formally through the state's
censoring and bureaucratic machinery, and *permissions tacites* for
books that censors would not openly certify as inoffensive to morals,
religion, or the state. Furet expected that a traditional cultural
pattern would show up in the first category and an innovative pattern in the second, because, thanks to Malesherbes' liberal director-
ship of the book trade, the *permissions tacites* became a paralegal
loophole through which many Enlightenment works reached the
market during the last half of the century. But what works? How
many of them? And in what proportion to the total number of
books that can be identified with innovation? Furet could not say.
He acknowledged that an unrecorded mass of books circulated
with *permissions simples, permissions de police,* and mere *tolér-*

ances according to the Old Regime's carefully graduated scale of quasilegality. Furthermore, the French stuffed unknown quantities of completely illegal "mauvais livres" into their breeches, the false-bottoms of their trunks, and even the coach of the Parisian lieutenant-general of police. So the official list of *permissions tacites* may not take one very far in identifying innovation.

The identification problems thicken when it comes to classifying the titles entered in the registers. Furet adopted the classification scheme of eighteenth-century catalogues: five standard headings —theology, jurisprudence, history, "sciences et arts," and "belles-lettres"—and a profusion of subcategories that would produce bedlam in any modern library. To rococo readers, travel books belonged under history, and "économie politique" rightly came after chemistry and medicine and before agriculture and agronomy, all happy neighbors in "sciences et arts." But the modern reader is bewildered upon learning that early works on politics (of the *permissions publiques* variety) were "presque tous des manuels de technique commerciale."[10] How can statistics on "économie politique" satisfy his desire to know whether French reading became increasingly political as the eighteenth century progressed? Framing twentieth-century questions within the confines of eighteenth-century categories can be misleading, especially for the researcher trying to fit the Enlightenment into the over-all picture of reading in the Old Regime.

Finally, Furet faced the problem of incomplete data. The requests to print books do not indicate how many copies were printed or the number of volumes, dates, places, and social groups involved in sales. Except in the case of privilege renewals, they give best-sellers the same numerical value as failures—the value of one. They do not even indicate whether a request resulted in an actual publication. And of course they tell nothing about the connection between buying and reading books.

To compensate for these deficiencies, Furet made a broad statistical sweep of the 30,000 titles registered between 1723 and 1789. His analysis of six samplings from the data was thorough enough for him to map out some general trends without professing a detailed knowledge of the eighteenth century's literary topography. He reduced his findings to bar graphs divided into the eighteenth-century categories. The graphs reveal a decline in theological and an increase in scientific writing, which is enough to carry Furet's main conclusion about the "désacralisation" of the world. They also reinforce Mornet's belief that the traditional, classical culture inherited from the seventeenth century outweighed the enlightened elements of the eighteenth. But those elements are scattered too haphazardly throughout the graphs to provide any quantitative profile of the Enlightenment.

By quantifying book reviews, Jean Ehrard and Jacques Roger tried to measure eighteenth-century reading by a standard that could not be applied to Furet's data. They attempted to show which kinds of writing had most vogue, as indicated by the number of books reviewed and the length of the reviews in two serious, "quality" periodicals, the *Journal des savants* and the *Mémoires de Trévoux*. They gathered their statistics from approximately the same periods and fit them into the same categories as Furet did, and they came up with complementary conclusions about the rise of interest in science (they locate it earlier in the eighteenth century), the decline of theology, and the "persistance des formes traditionnelles de la littérature."[11] Unfortunately, they made no similar effort to measure their results against Mornet's. Mornet himself had made a careful study of reviews in the *Mercure* and concluded that they bore no relation whatsoever to the real popularity of novels.[12] His findings might be corroborated by more consultation of literary evidence, because eighteenth-century journalism frequently reflected the interests of journalists rather than those of their readers. The journalists of the Old Regime scratched and clawed their way through a world of *cabales, combines,* and *pistons* (to use terms that necessity was obliged to invent in the rough-and-tumble French Republic of Letters), and their copy bore the marks of their struggle for survival. Thus the *Journal des savants* featured medical articles very heavily in the early eighteenth century, not because of any great interest among its readers—who actually ceased buying "ce triste répertoire de maladies"—but because the government in effect had taken it over and then surrendered it to a *cabale* of doctors, who used it to propagate their own views on medicine.[13]

Ehrard and Roger tried to cushion their statistics against the shock of such incidents by analyzing a large number of reviews—reviews of 1,800 books in the case of the *Journal des savants*. But it is difficult to winnow conclusions from such data and to coordinate them with other studies. What, for example, can be made of the fact that the *Journal des savants*, a predominantly scientific periodical, reduced its scientific reviewing by almost a third in the late eighteenth century? Its reviews showed a decline in the whole category "sciences et arts," while the category "belles-lettres" rose spectacularly. It would be rash to conclude that the public lost interest in science, because the *permissions tacites* showed precisely the opposite trend, according to François Furet. Moreover, a recent study of three other journals by Jean-Louis and Maria Flandrin produced results that contradict both those of Furet and those of Ehrard and Roger.[14] Periodicals do not seem to be a good source for quarrying statistics about the tastes of the reading public.

The catalogues of private libraries, as Mornet originally indicated, might serve quantitative history better. But they present difficulties of their own. Few persons read all the books they own, and many, especially in the eighteenth century, read books they never purchased. Libraries were usually built up over several generations: far from representing reading tastes at any given time, they were automatically archaic. And eighteenth-century libraries were censored for all illegal books before being put up for auction. The censoring may have been imperfect (Mornet found forty-one copies of Voltaire's forbidden *Lettres philosophiques*), but it may also have been influential enough to exclude much of the Enlightenment from the auction catalogues.

Despite these difficulties, Mornet's work remains the most important of its kind, because it covered so many (five hundred) libraries, and because Mornet was able to trace the social position of so many of the owners. He found that they came from a variety of stations above the middle middle-class (a great many doctors, lawyers, and especially state officials, as well as clergymen and nobles of the robe and sword) and that reading tastes did not correlate closely with social status. Louis Trenard got similar results from a nonquantitative investigation of libraries in Lyons.[15] But the most successful applications of Mornet's methods have occurred in studies of a single social group. Daniel Roche's research on the library of Dortous de Mairan actually was limited to the reading of a single man. But Roche made a convincing case for Mairan's typicality as a second-rank savant of the mid-eighteenth century; so his results suggest the general character of reading habits in the influential milieu of lesser academicians. Drawing on the research of Régine Petit, François Bluche studied the libraries of thirty members of the Parlement of Paris, which were catalogued between 1734 and 1795. He worked his findings into a convincing picture of parlementary culture, but not as it evolved over time.

His comparison of catalogues taken from 1734-1765 and from 1766-1780 does not reveal a declining interest in law and an increased interest in *belles-lettres* and *sciences et arts,* as he maintained, because the statistical differences are trivial—not more than 1 per cent. Nonetheless, Bluche's conclusions correspond quite closely with those of Jean Meyer, who studied the libraries of twenty members of the Parlement of Brittany. Meyer based his statistics on posthumous inventories of property (*inventaires après décès*), which usually are more reliable than auction catalogues as sources. He found a preponderance of "traditional" literature in contrast to a small proportion of enlightened works, and he also noted a decline in the incidence of legal and religious works and an increase in contemporary literature as the century progressed. Quantitative history thus seems to have been instrumental in defining the culture of the high nobility of the robe.

But has it succeeded in measuring the reading habits of France as a whole? There is hope for success in the complementary character of the monographs. Where one is weak, another is strong. Furet surveyed the whole terrain but gave equal weight to every title and did not get near the eighteenth-century reader; Ehrard and Roger got nearer, but their measure of reading incidence seems faulty; Mornet, Roche, and Bluche entered right into eighteenth-century libraries, but only the sections of those libraries that reached public auctions. If each monograph covered the exposed portions of another, the entire topic may be considered safely under wraps. Are the results mutually reinforcing or mutually contradictory? The issue seems important enough to be put graphically (see page 224).[16]

No consistent pattern, unfortunately, can be extracted from this confusing mosaic of graphs. Some of the inconsistencies can be explained away: law naturally shows strongly on the graphs of the *parlementaires,* science on Dortous de Mairan's graph, and theology among the *permissions publiques* as opposed to the *permissions tacites.* But standard categories like *belles-lettres,* history, and science vary enormously; and the proportions are wildly different. By imagining each bar graph as a girl and each black stripe as part of her two-piece bathing suit, one can see what a misshapen, motley crowd of monographs we must live with.

There is some relief from this bikini effect in considering how the monographs spread their proportions over time. They all agree that the French read a great deal of history—so much as to make

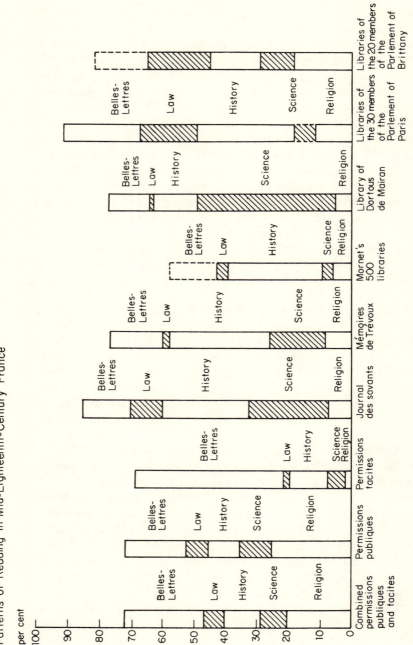

Patterns of Reading in Mid-Eighteenth-Century France

For explanation, see note 16.

untenable the already discredited myth about an "ahistorical" eight-eenth century—and read a consistent amount of it throughout the century. The monographs also indicate that the French read less religious literature as time went on. Scientific reading probably increased, although it may have remained constant. And, in general, some "désacralisation," as Furet put it, took hold of the reading public. This tendency, however, might represent an acceleration of a secularizing trend that had begun in the Middle Ages; acknowledging it does not help to refine any generalizations about the Age of the Enlightenment, and no other generalizations can be extracted from the quantitative studies.

Perhaps it is impossible to generalize about the over-all literary culture of eighteenth-century France because there might not have been any such thing. In a country where something like 9,600,000 people had enough instruction by the 1780's to sign their names,[17] there could have been several reading publics and several cultures. In that case, quantitative historians would do better to avoid macroanalysis of reading and to concentrate instead on studies of specific groups like the *parlementaires* of Bluche and Meyer. When used carefully, in conjunction with other kinds of evidence and in reference to clearly-defined segments of the population, this kind of quantitative history has proved to be a valuable tool. But it has not provided answers to the broad questions raised by Mornet, and there is no reason to expect that those answers will emerge from the continued multiplication of monographs.

Just as this essay was going to press, two more statistical studies of eighteenth-century reading were published.[18] They contain another whole series of bar graphs, which are as rich in mutual contradictions as the earlier series. The problem in trying to fit them all into one coherent picture of the Old Regime's literary culture is that they cover different ranges of data: some refer to the reading habits of particular milieux, others to reading throughout France as revealed by different sources. The contradictions are more serious in the second kind, but all of the monographs suffer from deficient data; and the deficiencies will not disappear if more official records and more periodicals are subjected to quantification. The run of graphs could be extended indefinitely. But where will it all lead? Perhaps back to Mornet. No later research has done much either to discredit or refine his emphasis on the mountainous deposits of traditional culture in contrast to the few rivulets of modernity in the literary habits of the eighteenth century.

But even Mornet's interpretation calls for further proof, because none of the sources examined by him or his successors was likely to contain the most modern works, and none of the categories used for the examining could be considered commensurate with the Enlightenment. The problem of measuring "inertia" against "innovation" in reading during the Old Regime always comes down to a problem of data: to sift statistics through administrative sources, censored journals, or censored library catalogues is to eliminate much of the Enlightenment. No wonder the quantitative historians found the weight of the past so heavy, when so much of the present was excluded from their balance. It may be cruel to conclude that all this laborious quantification has not advanced us far beyond Mornet, but the fact remains that we still do not know much about what eighteenth-century Frenchmen read.

III

If the sociology of literature has failed to develop a coherent discipline of its own, and if its commitment to quantification has not yet produced answers to the basic questions about reading and writing in the past, nonetheless the sociologists and quantifiers have demonstrated the importance of interpreting the Old Regime's literary culture in more than merely literary terms. Books have a social life and an economic value. All the aspects of their existence —literary, social, economic, and even political—came together with the greatest force in the publishing industry of the eighteenth century. So sociocultural history (or the sociology of literature, if the term must be retained) might gain a great deal from the study of publishing. To suggest some of the possible gains, it seems best to draw on material in the papers of publishers and other related sources in order to develop three hypotheses: what Frenchmen read was determined in part by the way in which their books were produced and distributed; there were basically two kinds of book production and distribution in the eighteenth century, legal and clandestine; and the differences between the two were crucial to the culture and politics of the Old Regime.[19]

The differences emerge clearly by a comparison of documents in official archives and those in the papers of clandestine publishers. The bookdealers of Lyons, for example, filled the *Direction de la librairie* with letters and memoranda about their devotion to the law,[20] while addressing the foreign publishers who supplied them with illegal books in terms like the following (A. J. Revol, a Lyonnais dealer, is arguing that he did not overcharge the Société typographique de Neuchâtel for his smuggling services):

Nous avons exposé liberté, vie, santé, argent et réputation.

Liberté, en ce que sans nos amis, nous aurions été enfermé par lettre de cachet.

Vie, en ce qu'ayant été en différentes fois aux prises avec les employés des fermes et les avoir forcés, les armes à la main, à nous restituer les balles qu'ils nous avaient saisies (à cette époque il y en avait douze à votre maison qui auraient été perdues pour vous, sans ressource.)

Santé, combien de nuits avons-nous passé, exposés à toutes les intempéries des saisons, sur la neige, traversé les rivières débordées et quelquefois sur les glaces.

Argent, quelle somme n'avons-nous pas donnée en différentes fois, tant pour faciliter l'exportation que pour éviter les poursuites et calmer les esprits.

Réputation, en ce que nous avions acquis celle de contrebandiers.[21]

Hundreds of men like these operated the underground system for supplying French readers with prohibited and pirated works, the kind that could never qualify for *permissions tacites.* They were colorful characters, these literary buccaneers: the obscure mule-drivers who hauled crates of books over tortuous trails in the Juras for 12 livres the quintal and a stiff drink; the merchants on both sides of the border who paid off the drivers and cleared paths into France for them by bribing agents of the General Tax Farm;[22] the waggoners who took the crates to stockpiles in provincial clearing houses like the Auberge du Cheval Rouge outside Lyons; the provincial bookdealers who cleared the crates through their local guilds (at 5 livres a quintal in Revol's case) and relayed them to entrepôts outside Paris; the entrepôt keepers like Mme. La Noue of Versailles—to all the world a garrulous, warmhearted widow, to her customers a shrewd businesswoman, "passablement arabe"[23] and full of professional pride ("je me flatte que lon sait me randre justice par les precaution que je prand pour cest sorte de marchandises,"[24] she wrote to a client in her semiliterate hand); the colporters like Cugnet et femme, "bandits sans moeurs et sans pudeur"[25] as they were known in the trade, who smuggled the books from Versailles to Paris; and deviate Parisian distributors like Desauges père et fils, who were well acquainted with the Bastille,[26] and Poinçot, "bien avec la police"[27] but "l'être le plus acariâtre que je connaisse,"[28] according to J. F. Bornand, one of the many literary secret agents in Paris who did odd jobs for the foreign publishers and completed the circuit by supplying them with manuscripts and best sellers to pirate.[29] An enormous number of illegal books passed through these slippery hands, greasing palms as they went. Their importance in relation to legal and quasilegal literature cannot be calculated until the clandestine import records are compiled. But one nonquantitative conclusion seems significant at the outset: underground publishing and legal publishing operated in separate circuits, and the underground operation was a complicated affair, involving a large labor force drawn from particular milieux. Far from having been lost in the unrecorded depths of history, the individuals who processed clandestine books can be found and situated socially. They had names and faces, which show up vividly in the papers of eighteenth-century publishers. And their experience suggests that underground publishing was a world of its own.

How different was the world of legal publishing. The thirty-six master printers and one hundred or so master booksellers of Paris lived in pomp and circumstance, parading behind their beadle, dressed splendidly in velvet trimmed with gold lilies, on ceremonial occasions; celebrating solemn masses before the silver statue of their patron, Saint John the Evangelist, in the Church of the Mathurins; feasting at the sumptuous banquets held by their confraternity; initiating new members into their guild, a matter of ritualistic oaths and examinations; participating in the Tuesday and Friday inspections of legally imported books delivered to the guild-hall by "forts" from the customs and city gates; and minding their own businesses. As businessmen, they kept closed shops. Elaborate regulations—at least 3,000 edicts and ordonnances of all kinds in the eighteenth century alone[30]—specified the qualifications and limited the number of everyone connected with legal publishing, down to the 120 ragged colporters who divided up the official monopoly of hawking almanacs and proclamations in the streets and wore leather badges to prove membership in their corps. Corporateness, monopoly, and family connections tied down every corner of the trade. In fact the cornering of the market dated from a seventeenth-century crisis. In 1666 Colbert had settled a trade war between the Parisian and provincial publishers by, in effect, ruining provincial printing and placing the industry under the control of the Communauté des imprimeurs et libraires de Paris. By ruling this guild, a few families of master printer-booksellers dominated legal French publishing throughout the eighteenth century.

The guild spirit shows clearly through the major edicts on publishing issued in 1686, 1723, 1744, and 1777. The edict of 1723, which laid down the law throughout most of the eighteenth century, communicates an attitude that might be called "mercantilistic" or "Colbertist," for it codified the reorganization of the trade produced in the 1660's by Colbert himself. Condemning capitalistic "avidité du gain,"[31] it stressed the importance of maintaining quality standards, which it defined in great detail. The type-face of three "l"s must be exactly the same in width as one "m," and the "m" must conform precisely to a model "m" deposited with the syndics and deputies of the guild, who were to inspect the thirty-six printing shops once every three months in order to make sure that each contained the requisite minimum of four presses and nine sets of type, both roman and italic, in good condition. Strict requirements regulated the advancement of apprentices to masterships, which were limited in number and tended to become family possessions—for at every point the edict favored widows, sons, and son-in-laws of the established masters. These privileged few enjoyed an air-tight monopoly of book production and marketing. Non-guild members could not even sell old paper without facing a 500 livres fine and "punition exemplaire."[32] The guild was elaborately organized and favored with "droits, franchises, immunités, prérogatives et privilèges."[33] Not only did it monopolize its trade, but as a corps within the university it benefited from special tax exemptions. Books themselves were tax-exempt. Each contained a formal "privilège" or "permission," granted by the king's "grâce" and registered in the chancellery and in the guild's Chambre syndicale. By purchasing a privilege, a guild member acquired an exclusive right to sell a book, thereby transforming a "grâce" into a kind of commodity, which he could divide into portions and sell to other members. So monopoly and privilege existed at three levels in the publishing industry: within the book itself, within the guild, and as an aspect of the guild's own special status within the Old Regime.

This third level deserves emphasis, because the guild's special position involved a policing as well as an economic function. The state had not often shown an enlightened attitude in its attempts to police the printed word before 1750, when Malesherbes became *Directeur de la librairie.* In 1535 it responded to the discovery that books could be seditious by deciding to hang anyone who printed them. In 1521 it had tried to tame the new industry by subjecting it to the surveillance of a medieval body, the university. And in 1618, it tried again, this time by confining publishers within the guild, another rather archaic kind of organization. In addition, the state attempted to bring books under control by developing its own apparatus—at first within the chancellery and the Parisian *lieu-tenance-générale de police,* later under the *Direction de la librairie*—and by holding its own against rival book-inspectors in the Parlement of Paris, the General Assembly of the Clergy, and other influential institutions. This bureaucratic entanglement did not choke the power of the guild; on the contrary, the guild continued to hunt out "mauvais livres" until the Revolution. The edicts of 1723 and 1777 reaffirmed its authority to search for illegal printing and to inspect books shipped to Paris. This policy made perfect sense: the state created a monopoly with a vested interest in law enforcement, and the monopolists maintained their interest by crushing extra-legal competition. Although some guild members dabbled in underground publishing, most of them wanted to stamp it out. It robbed and undersold them, while the guild existed to protect their privileges. Well-protected privileges meant secure profits, which looked more attractive than the risky business of illegal publishing, especially since illegality exposed them to a double danger: punishment for the particular infraction and then expulsion from the magic circle of monopolists. A printer-book-seller's mastership really belonged to his family. He could not risk it lightly. Better to buy the privilege on a prayer book and to collect a certain but limited profit than to wager everything on a clandestine edition of Voltaire. Such an attitude suited a "traditional" economy, where even merchant adventurers dropped out of trade as soon as they had made enough to invest in *rentes*—or borrowed at 5 per cent to buy land that yielded 1-2 per cent of its purchase price in annual profits.[34]

It would be a mistake, therefore, to underestimate the economic element in the Old Regime's legislation on publishing. P. J. Blondel, an old-fashioned abbé who had no love for philosophes, fulminated against the edict of 1723, even though it tightened the restrictions on philosophic works, because he saw it as a purely economic measure: an extension of the guild's monopoly.[35] Actually, the political and economic aspects of the edict complemented each other. Strengthening the guild seemed to serve the interests of the state as well as those of the privileged publishers. But the reform movement modified the state's view of its interests, and the publishing code of 1777, promulgated soon after Turgot's attacks on the six great commercial guilds of Paris, shows a shift away from the old "Colbertism." Instead of condemning "avidité du gain," the king now repudiated any intention of favoring "monopole," praised the effects of "concurrence," and relaxed the rules governing privileges in order to "augmenter l'activité du commerce."[36] He did not undercut the notion of privilege; in fact he confirmed its character as a "grâce fondée en justice"[37] rather than as a kind of property, but he modified it in favor of authors and at the expense of the bookdealers. The guild had tried to prevent such a blow long before it actually struck by getting an author to present its case. The result, Diderot's *Lettre sur le commerce de la librairie*, reiterated the old arguments about maintaining quality by restricting productivity in contradiction to Diderot's own liberal principles and Malesherbes' *Mémoires sur la librairie*, which had partly inspired the reform project. Apparently dismissing Diderot's *Lettre* as the work of a hired hack, Malesherbes' liberal successors, especially Sartine and Le Camus de Néville, pushed through the edicts of 1777 and so somewhat loosened the guild's stranglehold on the publishing industry.[38]

But the controversial item in the code of 1777 concerned the relations of guild members and authors: privilege was now clearly derived from authorship and belonged to the author and his heirs perpetually or expired after his death, if he had ceded it to a bookdealer and the dealer had had it for at least ten years. This provision brought many works into the public domain and provoked bitter complaints by the guild members, but it did not really undermine their monopoly.[39] The code reinforced their power to police the book trade and repeated in the strongest possible terms that no one outside the guild could engage in publishing. So the dynasties of printer-booksellers continued to dominate their industry until the Revolution. The greatest of them, Charles-Joseph Panckoucke, operated as a sort of combination press baron and minister of culture: "sa voiture le portait chez les ministres du roi, à Versailles, qui le recevaient comme un fonctionnaire ayant un portefeuille."[40]

There had never been any question of creating a free trade in books by abolishing the guild as Turgot had abolished the six great *jurandes*. The economic issue took another form; it arose from the ancient enmity between Parisian and provincial bookdealers. Provincial printing had not recovered since the trade war of the seventeenth century, but provincial booksellers survived in large numbers throughout the eighteenth century, and they drew much of their stock (often in the form of exchanges, measured in page gatherings) from outside France, where hundreds of enterprising printers turned out cheap pirated editions of French works. The state inadvertently produced a boom in this illicit trade in the 1770's by levying a tax on paper, a much more costly item in the budget of eighteenth-century printers than it is today.

Printer's *papier blanc* had been taxed from time to time, notably in 1680 and 1748, but not at a ruinous rate and not much, if at all, outside Paris—until March 1, 1771, when the abbé Terray, trying desperately to cut the deficit accumulated during the Seven Years' War, taxed it 20 sous per ream. In August 1771 he increased that rate by 10 sous as a result of the across-the-board tax of 2 sous per livre. Since exports of French paper went duty free, foreign printers and their provincial allies gained an enormous advantage. A ream of good white *papier d'Auvergne* cost 11 livres in Paris and 8 livres in Switzerland, according to one estimate.[41] To right the balance, Terray placed a duty of 60 livres per quintal on imports of French and Latin books on September 11, 1771. But this measure massacred the exchange trade between provincial dealers and foreigners.

Seized by panic, publishers like the Société typographique de Neuchâtel suspended all shipments to France and cast about desperately for ways of cracking the tariff barrier while their tough customers in the provinces, men like Jean Marie Bruysset and Périsse Duluc of Lyons, agitated for the repeal of the duty.[42] The agitation paid: on November 24, 1771, the tax was reduced to 20 livres; on October 17, 1773, it went down to 6 livres 10 sols; and on April 23, 1775, Turgot withdrew it altogether. But this reversal of policy again tipped the economic balance in favor of the foreign publishers. An unsigned memorandum to the ministry reported: "C'est depuis ce moment que les Suisses, ayant senti qu'ils pouvaient donner nos livres à 50% meilleur marché que nous, ont pillé et ravagé notre librairie, et en effet ils donnent nos livres a trois liards ou un sol de France la feuille, et comme aux frais de l'impôt sur le papier, du haut prix de l'impression et du tirage en France, il faut joindre l'achat des manuscrits, on ne peut souvent pas trouver de bénéfice en vendant cette même feuille deux ou trois sols." As an example, the writer said that Panckoucke's new *Encyclopédie méthodique* would have to sell at 11 livres a volume for Panckoucke merely to cover production costs, while a pirated

Swiss edition could sell in Paris at 6 livres a volume and produce a 40-50 per cent profit.[43]

Until mid-1783 the business of foreign publishers and provincial dealers seems to have flourished at the expense of their Parisian rivals, but on June 12, 1783, Vergennes, the foreign minister, destroyed it with a stroke of the pen. He issued orders to the General Tax Farm requiring that all book imports—garnished with the usual seals, lead stamps, and *acquits à caution*—be transmitted to the Chambre syndicale of the Parisian guild for inspection before being delivered to their final destination. Without tampering further with the taxation system or passing through formal, legal channels like the earlier edicts, this measure at once restored the guild's domination of the book trade. It meant that a crate of books sent from Geneva to Lyons now had to pass through the hands of the guild officials in Paris, which gave the Parisians an opportunity to weed out pirated editions and saddled the Lyonnais with a detour that would cost more than the books were worth. Even the extra trip from Rouen to Paris and back would ruin his business, a desperate Rouennais wrote.[44] Booksellers in Lille reported that they had no choice but to let imports pile up and rot in their damp customs house.[45] The Lyonnais claimed that they had suspended all book imports—a matter of 2,000 quintals a year—and were in danger of suspending payments.[46] And while protests from provincial dealers flooded the *Direction de la librairie*, frantic letters flew around the circuit of publishers who fed the provincials from across France's borders. Boubers of Brussels, Gosse of The Hague, Dufour of Maestricht, Grasset of Lausanne, Bassompierre of Geneva, and dozens of others, all trembled for their commercial lives. The Société typographique de Neuchâtel sent out an agent, J.-F. Bornand, to inspect the damage done to its supply lines. Bornand reported that the "malheureux arrêt" had stopped all book traffic in Savoy and Franche-Comté. A side trip to Grenoble showed him that the southern route was "hérissée de gardes, au point qu'au bureau de Chaparillan on m'a saisi tous mes livres dans ma malle . . . en nous faisant voir l'ordre du roi qui leur enjoint de ne laisser passer aucune librairie quelconque."[47] The bookdealers in Lyons told Bornand such gloomy stories that he concluded, "Il faut renoncer à la France."[48] They believed that Panckoucke was behind the crackdown, because he wanted to destroy his Swiss competitors, notably Heubach & Cie, of Lausanne, whose pirating had cut deeply into the sales of his edition of Buffon's *Histoire naturelle.* Bornand reported the same rumor from Besançon; and when he arrived in Paris, the booksellers turned their "air de mépris" on him with full force. One threatened to cause him "tout le mal possible, et c'est un pacte formé entre les libraires de Paris contre les libraires étrangers et même contre ceux de province."[49] By mid-1785, the Neuchâtelois still found it impossible to get their books to the great clandestine trade center of Avignon,[50] and they abandoned attempts to reach Paris through smugglers stationed in Geneva, Besançon, Dijon, Châlons-sur-Saône, and Clairvaux. Their booming business in France had been cut to a trickle. It never recovered, because, as they explained to a Parisian confidant, "Nous ignorons de quelle voie se servent les autres imprimeurs d'ici, de Lausanne et de Berne; nous ne connaissons point d'autre que d'expédier sous acquit à caution pour Paris . . . Toute autre voie nous est interdite, parce que nous ne voulons pas courir des risques, ni nous exposer à la confiscation et à l'amende."[51] Vergennes had cut the lifeline linking foreign producers and provincial distributors.

According to the provincial protests, Vergennes' orders would decimate the legal foreign trade in books. By making imports impossibly expensive, the new rules would produce an inevitable decline in exports, especially since the import-export business was usually conducted in exchanges of so many page-gatherings rather than in money. The state saw the orders as a new policing technique, aimed at the destruction of pirated and prohibited books—the bread and butter of underground publishing. Both views may have been correct, but the clandestine trade probably suffered the most. The monopolistic practices of the Parisians had forced the provincials to seek shelter underground. There they formed alliances with foreign publishers, who sent them illegal works under cover of an *acquit à caution,* a customs permit that protected book shipments from all inspection between the border and their points of destination within France, where they were to be examined by the nearest official bookdealer. He would certify their legitimacy by endorsing the back of the *acquit* and returning it, by the driver who had delivered the books, to the border station where it had been issued. A dealer collaborating with an illegal publisher could either market the books himself (instead of impounding them), or he could relay them on toward Paris and collect a commission. Since domestic book shipments were never inspected en route, they could reach an entrepôt outside Paris, usually in Versailles, without risk and then could be smuggled in small quantities into the capital. The system worked quite well as long as provincial dealers could discharge the *acquits à caution*. But by placing that function in the hands of the Parisian guild, Vergennes undercut the whole operation. Of course there were other ways of reaching the market, but it was no easy task to thread one's way through the internal customs barriers and to dodge the roaming inspectors of the General Farm, who received a reward and a portion of the goods after every confiscation. What the drivers and clandestine agents wanted was legal camouflage so they could send whole wagonloads rumbling down the middle of France's splendid highways to provincial guildhalls and to the very palace of the king. The clandestine trade was a matter of calculating risks and profit margins. Too chancy, too elaborate a system of smuggling would not pay. So when Vergennes changed the rules of the game, the foreign suppliers and provincial dealers faced disaster. If the papers of the Société typographique de Neuchâtel indicate the general reaction to the order of June 12, 1783, the whole underground industry fell into a depression that lasted for at least two years and perhaps until 1789.[52] As far as foreign publishing was concerned, the French government had finally committed itself to a policy of laissez faire but not laissez passer.

Curiously, the graphs of legal French book production constructed by Robert Estivals and François Furet also show a spectacular drop in 1783, the low point of a slump extending roughly from 1774 to 1786.[53] Why this slump occurred is difficult to say. It does not seem to be related to Labrousse's prerevolutionary economic crisis or the Labrousse-like "cycles" that Estivals somehow sees in his statistics. Could it be connected with Vergennes' orders of June 12, 1783? The purpose of the orders stands out clearly in the text: to put an end to "la multitude de libelles imprimés dans l'étranger et introduits dans le royaume."[54] Even the petitions from the provincial bookdealers acknowledged that "le motif de l'ordre est d'empêcher l'introduction des libelles qui viennent de l'étranger."[55] And a glance at Vergennes' correspondence with his ambassadors shows how much the *libelles* concerned him. In 1782 and 1783 he wrote as many letters to England about the need to suppress a smut factory run by émigré French "libellistes" as he did about the diplomatic preliminaries to the Treaty of Paris. He sent secret agent after secret agent (a bizarre collection of bogus barons and one police inspector disguised as an umbrella salesman) to buy off or kidnap the *libellistes*. No details of their fantastic, rococo intrigues were too trivial for Vergennes' attention, for he feared the effect of the *libelles* on public opinion in France. Well before the Diamond Necklace Affair, he exhorted the French chargé d'affaires to stamp out political pornography: "Vous connaissez la malignité de notre siècle et avec quelle facilité les fables les plus absurdes sont reçues."[56] The orders of June 12, 1783, must have been part of this campaign, and they must have been fairly successful, judging from the consternation they produced in the world of underground publishing and the large collection of works like *Les amours de Charlot et Toinette* and *Essais historiques sur la vie de Marie-Antoinette* that the revolutionaries gleefully inventoried in the Bastille after 1789.[57]

There is no reason to connect the campaign against *libelles* with the drop in legal book production. Nonetheless, it seems possible that Vergennes was so determined to shut off the flow of *libelles* from outside France that he dammed up the channels of legitimate imports, too. His action could have created repercussions in the legal system of publishing, exactly as the provincial dealers argued. It would have forced even the most honest provincial booksellers to retrench, because it would have increased their expenses drastically and destroyed their exchange trade. It would also have eliminated their roles as middlemen (an important business in Lyons) in commerce between northern and southern Europe. As always, the Parisians might have profited from the provincials' losses. But provincial dealers drew some of the stock that they used for foreign exchanges from Paris. So Vergennes' offer also could have damaged part of the Parisians' market. It certainly reduced book imports on a national scale and, owing to the crucial importance of exchanges in the book trade, probably produced a corresponding drop in exports. Over-all French book production therefore would have suffered, just as it suffered from the buffeting given it since 1771 by the succession of taxes and tariffs. If these hypotheses are correct, they suggest that underground and legal publishing were not so separate and so inimical that they could not be injured by a common blow. A certain symbiosis might have attached segments of the two circuits. Each circuit relied heavily on injections of foreign books, and that foreign element must be measured if there is to be more exact knowledge about the circulation of ideas in the Old Regime. At this prestatistical stage, however, it seems legitimate to insist on one point: far from flourishing as a result of virtual freedom of the press, as is usually maintained, French publishing underwent a severe crisis on the eve of the Revolution, a crisis that has not been noticed by historians, because it did not manifest itself in formal documents, like the edicts on the book trade.[58]

The publishing crisis seems especially worthy of notice, because its economic and intellectual aspects were related in a way that reveals aspects of the prerevolutionary crisis. Economically, legal and clandestine publishing stood for antithetical ways of doing business. Faithful to the old "Colbertist" methods, the Parisian Communauté des libraires et imprimeurs produced a limited number of quality goods according to official specifications. It turned out traditional books for a traditional market, which it controlled by virtue of an official monopoly. It ran no risks, because it owed its profits to its privileges; and its privileges were family treasures, handed down from father to son and husband to widow. Furthermore, the guild fortified its monopoly by a share in the repressive power of the state. In publishing, as in so many other cases, the Old Regime was eaten away by privilege—not the juridical privileges dividing nobles from commoners, but the privilege of vested interests, which devoured the state like a cancer. In its last years, the government tried to rally and reform. But its efforts reactivated the century-old conflict between provincial and Parisian bookdealers, and the book duties of 1771-1775 followed by Vergennes' order of June 12, 1783, represented the final triumph of the Parisian publishing dynasties.

But this triumph was limited by the limitations of an archaic production system. Despite the flexibility introduced through the use of *permissions tacites* and the adventurous policies of a few guild members, privileged publishing failed to satisfy the demand created by an enlarged readership and by changing literary tastes. The reading patterns of the past weighed heavily in the traditional sector of publishing, as the statistics of Mornet and Furet demonstrate; and the reluctance of most traditional publishers to deviate from those patterns is perfectly understandable. Why should they abandon their privileges, risk their special status, and endanger their families' livelihood by producing new literature of uncertain legality? "Innovation" came through the underground. Down there, no legalities constrained productivity, and books were turned out by a kind of rampant capitalism. Not only did the state's misguided fiscal policies make it cheaper to produce new works outside

France, but foreign publishers did a wild and woolly business in pirating old ones. As soon as their agents reported that a book was selling well in Paris, they began setting type for a counterfeit edition. Some of them also printed prohibited, hard-core "mauvais livres." They were tough businessmen who produced anything that would sell. They took risks, broke traditions, and maximized profits by quantity instead of quality production. Rather than try to corner some segment of the market by a legal monopoly, they wanted to be left alone by the state and would even bribe it to do so. They were entrepreneurs who made a business of Enlightenment.

The enlightened themes of the books they produced—individualism, liberty, and equality before the law as opposed to corporatism, privilege, and "mercantilist" restrictions—suited their way of doing business. A Marxist might argue that the modes of production determined the product—an extravagant interpretation, but one that might serve as an antidote to the conventional history of ideas.[59] Books are economic commodities as well as cultural artifacts; and as vehicles of ideas, they have to be peddled on a market. The literary marketplace of eighteenth-century France calls for closer analysis, for its books—whether privileged or philosophic, traditional or innovative—epitomized the character of the Old Regime.

IV

Since the Old Regime was a political as well as a social and economic system, a socioeconomic interpretation of its publishing ought to take account of political factors. What, in fact, were those books that Vergennes wanted so desperately to keep out of France? They were listed in handwritten catalogues entitled "livres philosophiques," which circulated secretly and offered such delicious forbidden fruit as:[60]

Vénus dans le cloître, ou la religieuse en chemise, figures
Système de la nature, 8°, 2 vol. 1775 très belle édition
Système social, 8°, 3 vol. 1775
Fausseté des miracles
La fille de joie, 8°, figures
Contrat social par Jean-Jacques Rousseau 12°
Journal historique des révolutions opérées en France par M. Maupeou, 3 vol. 8°
Mémoires authentiques de Mme. la comtesse Du Barry, 1775
Margot la ravaudeuse, 12°, figures

Lettres de l'abbé Terray à M. Turgot
Les droits des hommes et leurs usurpations

The same underground publisher also circulated a formal printed catalogue, openly advertising its name, address, and items like the following:[61]

Bélisaire, par Marmontel, nouvelle édition augmentée, 8°, figures, Lausanne, 1784: 1 livre.
Bible (la Sainte), 8°, 2 vol., Neuchâtel, 1771: 6 livres.
Bibliothèque anglaise, ou recueil des romans anglais, 14 vol., 12°, Genève, 1781: 15 livres.
Bonnet (M. Charles), ses oeuvres complètes de physique et d'histoire naturelle, 4°, 8 vol., figures, Neuchâtel, 1782: 81 livres.

The books in the second catalogue may have been legal or pirated, but they did not offend religion, morality, or the French state. Those in the first catalogue offended all three and therefore earned the title "livres philosophiques"—a very revealing trade name, which recurs constantly in the commercial correspondence of underground publishers.

How offensive actually was this "philosophy"? *Les amours de Charlot et Toinette,* a work that was high on Vergennes' list of *libelles,* began with a description of the queen masturbating and then moved on to an account of her supposed orgies with the comte d'Artois, dismissing the king as follows:[62]

> On sait bien que le pauvre Sire,
> Trois ou quatre fois condamné
> Par la salubre faculté,
> Pour impuissance très complète,
> Ne peut satisfaire Antoinette.
> De ce malheur bien convaincu,
> Attendu que son allumette
> N'est pas plus grosse qu'un fétu;
> Que toujours molle et toujours croche,
> Il n'a de v . . . que dans la poche;
> Qu'au lieu de f . . . il est f . . .
> Comme le feu prélat d'Antioche.

Crude stuff, but no less ineffective for its gross versification. A similar work, which pretended to defend the queen, and various courtiers and ministers as well, by refuting the calumnies against her in minute, scabrous detail, explained that the *libelles* circulated through several strata of society:[63]

Un lâche courtisan les ["ces infamies"] met en vers en couplets, et, par le ministère de la valetaille, les fait passer jusqu'aux halles et aux marchés aux herbes. Des halles elles sont portées à l'artisan qui, à son tour, les rapporte chez les seigneurs qui les ont forgées, et lesquels, sans perdre de temps, s'en vont à l'Oeil-de-Boeuf se demander à l'oreille les uns aux autres, et du ton de l'hypocrisie la plus consommée: Les avez-vous lues? les voilà. Elles courent dans le peuple de Paris.

No doubt one could pick up some smut from the gutter at any period in the history of Paris, but the gutters overflowed during the reign of Louis XVI; and the inundation worried Louis' chief of police, J.-C.-P. Lenoir, because, as Lenoir put it, "Les parisiens avaient plus de propension à ajouter foi aux mauvais propos et aux libelles qu'on faisait circuler clandestinement, qu'aux faits imprimés et publiés par ordre ou permission du gouvernement."[64] Lenoir later reported that his attempt to suppress the circulation of *libelles* "furent combattus par des hommes de la cour qui faisaient imprimer ou protégeaient l'impression d'écrits scandaleux. La police de Paris ne pouvait atteindre que les marchands et colporteurs les vendant et débitant. On faisait enfermer les colporteurs à la Bastille, et ce genre de punition ne mortifiait pas cette classe de gens, pauvres mercénaires qui souvent ignoraient les vrais auteurs et imprimeurs . . . C'est surtout à l'égard des libelles contre le gouvernement que les lois, dans les temps qui ont précédé la révolution, furent impuissantes."[65] The police took the *libelles* seriously, because they had a serious effect on public opinion, and public opinion was a powerful force in the declining years of the Old Regime. Although the monarchy still considered itself absolute, it hired hack pamphleteers like Brissot and Mirabeau to give it a good name.[66] It even attempted to manipulate rumors, for eighteenth-century "bruits publics" produced eighteenth-century "émotions populaires"—riots. A riot broke out in 1752, for example, because of a rumor that the police were kidnapping working-class children to provide a literal blood bath for some royal prince of the blood.[67] It was the primitiveness of such "emotions" and opinions that made the regime vulnerable to *libelles*.

How badly the *libelles* damaged the public's faith in the legitimacy of the Old Regime is difficult to say, because there is no index to the public opinion of eighteenth-century France. Despite the testimony of expert observers like Vergennes and Lenoir,[68] it might be argued that the public found its dirty books amusing, nothing more. *Libellistes* had piled up trash for years without burying anyone. But there also could have been a cumulative effect that produced a deluge after Louis XV. Louis' private life provided plenty of material for the *Vie privée de Louis XV*, which in turn set the tone for a whole series of *Vie privées* about court figures. These scurrilous works hammered at the same points with such ferocity that they probably drove some home, at least in the case of a few leitmotivs: Du Barry's sexual success story (from brothel to throne), Maupeou's despotism (his search for a man to build a machine that would hang ten innocent victims at a time); and the decadence of the court (not merely a matter of luxury and adultery but also of impotence—in the *libelles* the high aristocracy could neither fight nor make love and perpetuated itself by extramarital infusions from more virile lower classes).[69] Louis XVI, notoriously unable to consummate his marriage for many years, made a perfect symbol of a monarchy in the last stages of decay. Dozens of pamphlets like *La naissance du Dauphin dévoilée* (another on Vergennes' list) provided dozens of revelations about the real lineage of the heir to the throne. And then the Diamond Necklace Affair produced an inexhaustible supply of muck to be raked. A king cuckolded by a cardinal: What better finale to a regime that was finished—better even than the rumor of the warming pan that brought public opinion to a boil in England on the eve of 1688.

It is easy to underestimate the importance of personal slander in eighteenth-century French politics, because it is difficult to appreciate that politics took place at court, where personalities counted more than policies. Defamation was a standard weapon of court cabales. And then as now, names made news, although news did not make the newspapers. Rigorously excluded from legal periodicals, it circulated in pamphlets, *nouvelles à la main,* and by *nouvellistes de bouche*—the real sources from which political journalism originated in France. In such crude media, politics was reported crudely—as a game for kings, their courtiers, ministers, and mistresses. Beyond the court and below the summit of salon society, the "general public" lived on rumors; and the "general reader" saw politics as a kind of nonparticipant sport, involving villains and heroes but not issues—except perhaps a crude struggle between good and evil or France and Austria. He probably read his *libelles* as his modern counterpart reads magazines or comic books, but he did not laugh them off; for the villains and heroes were real to him; they were fighting for control of France. Politics was living folklore. And so, after enjoying *La gazette noire's* titillating account of venereal disease, buggery, cuckoldry, illegitimacy, and impotence in the upper ranks of French society, he may have been convinced and outraged by its description of Mme. Du Barry[70]

passant sans interruption du bordel sur le trône, des bras des laquais dans ceux du monarque; culbutant le ministre le plus puissant et le plus redoutable; opérant le renversement de la constitution de la monarchie; insultant à la famille royale, à l'héritier présomptif du trône et à son auguste compagne, par son luxe incroyable, par ses propos insolants, à la nation entière mourant de faim, par ses profusions vaines, par les déprédations connues de tous les roués qui l'entouraient; voyant ramper à ses pieds non seulement les grands du royaume, les ministres, mais les princes du sang, mais les ambassadeurs étrangers, mais l'Eglise canonisant ses scandales et ses débauches.

This was more dangerous propaganda than the *Contrat social*. It severed the sense of decency that bound the public to its rulers. Its disingenuous moralizing opposed the ethics of little people to those of "les grands" on top, because, for all their obscenities, the *libelles* were strongly moralistic. Perhaps they even propagated a "bourgeois morality" that came to full fruition during the Revolution. "Bourgeois" may not be the proper term for it, or for the Revolution either, but the "petits" who rose against the "gros" in the Year II responded to a kind of Gaulois Puritanism that had developed well before 1789. Gullible about the plots and purges of the Terror,[71] they had gullibly assimilated legends from their earlier *libelles*. Thus an aristocratic plot to kidnap bourgeois wives before the Revolution: "Avez-vous une jolie femme? Est-elle du goût de quelque nouveau parvenu, de quelque petit fat en puissance, de quelque talon rouge, par exemple? On vous la séquestre proprement. Voulez-vous raisonner? On vous envoie aux galères."[72] Of course one can only speculate about what went on in the minds of such primitive readers, but it might have been "désacralisation," occurring at levels well below the elite. Without this occurrence, it is hard to understand how the *Père Duchesne* could have had such an appeal or how people brought up to believe in the royal touch could have read about "la tête de véto femelle séparée de son foutu col de grue"[73] without erupting in "émotion populaire." The king had lost some of his mystical touch with the people long before Hébert's harangues about the "louve autrichienne" and her "gros cocu." How great a loss it was, no one can say, but works like *Les rois de France régénérés* made the Bourbons look literally illegitimate. The administration feared those works, because it appreciated their power to make a mockery of the monarchy. The ridiculing of Louis XVI must have done a great deal of damage at a time when nobility was still identified with "liqueur séminale"[74] and when the Salic Law still required that the royal "race" be transmitted through a magical unbroken chain of males. The magic had gone out of the Bourbons by the reign of Louis XVI. Lenoir reported that as the Revolution approached he could not get crowds to applaud the queen by paying them, although they had cheered spontaneously earlier.[75] And in 1789 Desmoulins described a four-year-old being carried around the Palais-Royal on the shoulders of a street-porter, crying out, " 'La Polignac exilée à cent lieues de Paris! Condé idem! Conti idem! d'Artois idem! la reine . . . !' je n'ose répéter."[76] The *libelles* had done their work all too well.

The step from publishing to libeling was easily taken outside the closed circles of the guild because nonguild publishers could only exist outside the law, and law in the Old Regime meant privilege (*leges privatae,* private law).[77] The nuances of legality and illegality covered a broad enough spectrum, however, for many underprivileged bookdealers to do a pretty legitimate business. The underground contained several levels. Its agents near the top may never have touched *libelles,* while those at the bottom handled nothing but filth. The Société typographique de Neuchâtel generally pirated only good, clean books like the works of Mme. Riccoboni, but the neighboring house of Samuel Fauche and his prodigal sons produced the very works that Vergennes tried to suppress in London. Fauche also printed the political and pornographic writings of Mirabeau: *l'Espion dévalisé, Ma conversion ou le libertin de qualité, Erotika Biblion,* and *Lettres de cachet.*[78] And yet when the last ten volumes of the *Encyclopédie* appeared in 1765, they bore the false imprint "A Neufchastel chez Samuel Faulche." The underground genres easily got mixed up, and underground dealers often moved from one level to another. Hard times forced them into lower reaches of illegality; for as they sank deeper into debt, they took greater chances in hopes of greater profits. The crisis of the 1780's might have produced precisely that result. Ironically, Vergennes might have transformed some rather inoffensive pirates into purveyors of *libelles* and actually increased the circulation of "livres philosophiques" by decreasing the relatively above-the-board traffic in *contrefaçons.* The Société typographique de Neuchâtel seems to have done more business in *libelles* after 1783 than before Vergennes' crackdown.[79] As the Revolution approached, provincial dealers who earlier had merely discharged a few false *acquits à caution* may have speculated more on shipments of works like *Les amours de Charlot et Toinette* and passed around more catalogues of "livres philosophiques." Or perhaps their customers' tastes changed in response to episodes like the Diamond Necklace Afair. It is impossible at this point to tell whether supply followed demand fairly neatly or whether demand was influenced by what could be supplied. Reading habits could have evolved as a result of the peculiar conditions determining literary output or could have been the determining factor themselves; or each element could have reinforced the other. Whatever combination of causes was at work, the Old Regime put *Charlot et Toinette*, *Vénus dans le cloître*, d'Holbach, and Rousseau in the same boxes and shipped them under the same code-name. "Livres philosophiques" to the dealers, "mauvais livres" to the police, it made little difference. What mattered was their common clandestineness. There was equality in illegality; Charlot and Rousseau were brothers beyond the pale.

The very way in which these works were produced helped reduce them to the common denominator of irreligion, immorality, and uncivility. The foreigners who printed them felt no loyalty to France, the Bourbons, or, often, the Catholic Church. The dealers who distributed them operated in an underworld of "bandits sans moeurs et sans pudeur." And the authors who wrote them had often sunk into a Grub Street life of quasi-criminality. The arch-*libelliste* Charles Théveneau de Morande was brought up in brothels and educated in prisons, and those mileux provided the material for his writing.[80] Perhaps the underground's impurities rubbed off on the books that passed through it: the message certainly suited the medium. But what a state of affairs! A regime that classified its most advanced philosophy with its most debased pornography was a regime that sapped itself, that dug its own underground, and that encouraged philosophy to degenerate into *libelle*. When philosophy went under, it lost its self-restraint and its commitment to the culture of those on top. When it turned against courtiers, churchmen, and kings, it committed itself to turning the world upside down. In their own language, the *livres philosophiques* called for undermining and overthrowing. The counterculture called for a cultural revolution—and was ready to answer the call of 1789.

REFERENCES

1. Marc Bloch, "Critique historique et critique du témoignage," *Annales: économies, sociétés, civilisations,* 5 (1950), 5; reference supplied by Roberto Vivarelli.

2. Daniel Mornet, "Les enseignements des bibliothèques privées (1750-1780)," *Revue d'histoire littéraire de la France,* 17 (1910), 449-492.

3. Although he carefully qualified the conclusions in his article, Mornet made more sweeping statements in his later work. He wrongly implied that his research on the *Social Contract* was valid for the period after 1780: "De ce livre redoutable, c'est à peine si l'on parle avant 1789," Daniel Mornet, "L'influence de J.-J. Rousseau au XVIIIe siècle," *Annales Jean-Jacques Rousseau,* 8 (1912), 44. See also Daniel Mornet, *Rousseau, l'homme et l'oeuvre* (Paris: Boivin, 1950), pp. 102-106, and Daniel Mornet, *Les origines intellectuelles de la Révolution Française,* 5th ed. (Paris: Colin, 1954), p. 229. Robert Derathé accepted Mornet's interpretation: "Les réfutations du *Contrat Social* au XVIIIe siècle," *Annales de la Société Jean-Jacques Rousseau,* 32 (1950-1952), 7-12. And Alfred Cobban extended it: "Rousseau's *Contrat social* had no ascertainable influence before the Revolution and only a very debatable one during its course"; see his "The Enlightenment and the French Revolution," reprinted in *Aspects of the French Revolution* (New York: Braziller, 1968), p. 22. The latest extension is Joan McDonald, *Rousseau and the French Revolution, 1762-1791* (London: Athlone Press, 1965).

4. See the devastating review article by R. A. Leigh, "Jean-Jacques Rousseau," *The Historical Journal,* 12 (1969), 549-565.

5. Although Rousseau's treatise was too abstruse to provoke the sort of controversy that followed *Emile* and his discourses (except in Switzerland), its influence, like all ideological influence, is difficult to measure. If repression is any indication of importance, it should be noted that the French state never formally condemned the *Contrat social* but did not permit it to circulate freely. The revolutionaries found it locked up with other seditious literature in the *pilon* of the Bastille: Bibliothèque de l'Arsenal, Ms. 10305, "le pilon de la Bastille."

6. Escarpit's book was published in the widely-read "Que Sais-Je" series and has already gone through four editions. As an example of its influence, see Louis Trenard, "La sociologie du livre en France (1750-1789)," *Actes du cinquième Congrès national de la Société française de littérature comparée* (Paris, 1965), p. 145.

7. Robert Escarpit, *Sociologie de la littérature,* 4th ed. (Paris: Presses universitaires de France, 1968), p. 46. It should be noted also that the development of writing as a *métier* in the eighteenth century did not correspond to the sociological phenomenon of professionalization. See the article "Professions" by Talcott Parsons in the *International Encyclopedia of the Social Sciences,* XII, 536-547.

8. David Pottinger, *The French Book Trade in the Ancien Régime, 1500-1791* (Cambridge, Mass.: Harvard University Press, 1958), p. 9.

9. The studies, to be cited henceforth by name of author, are: François Furet, "La 'librairie' du royaume de France au 18e siècle" in *Livre et société dans la France du XVIIIe siècle* (Paris and The Hague, 1965); Jean Ehrard and Jacques Roger, "Deux périodiques français du 18e siècle: 'le Journal des Savants' et 'les Mémoires de Trévoux,' Essai d'une étude quantitative," in the same volume; Daniel Roche, "Un savant et sa bibliothèque au XVIIIe siècle: les livres de Jean-Jacques Dortous de Mairan, secrétaire perpétuel de l'Académie des sciences, membre de l'Académie de Béziers," *Dix-huitième siècle,* 1 (1969), 47-88; François Bluche, *Les magistrats du Parlement de Paris au XVIIIe siècle, 1715-1771* (Paris: Les Belles Lettres, 1960), pp. 291-296, which incorporates the findings of an unpublished study by Régine Petit, *Les bibliothèques des hommes du parlement de Paris au XVIIIe siècle* (1954); and Jean Meyer, *La noblesse bretonne au XVIIIe siècle* (Paris: Imprimerie nationale, 1966), pp. 1156-1177.

10. Furet, p. 19.

11. Ehrard and Roger, p. 56.

12. Mornet, "Les enseignements des bibliothèques privées," p. 473.

13. Quotation cited in Raymond Birn, "Le Journal des savants sous l'Ancien Régime," *Journal des savants* (January-March 1965), p. 28 and in Eugène Hatin, *Histoire politique et littéraire de la presse en France* (Paris, 1859-1861), II, 192.

14. Jean-Louis and Marie Flandrin, "La circulation du livre dans la société du 18e siècle: un sondage à travers quelques sources," *Livre et société,* 2 (Paris, 1970), 52-91. The Flandrins studied three private or at least un-censored literary journals, which discussed philosophic works that could not be mentioned in the pages of quasi-official, heavily-censored periodicals like the *Journal des savants.* But the Flandrins' three journals show the opposite bias from those studied by Ehrard and Roger. They discussed mainly sensational books—books that made news—and thus do not repre-sent the general literary tastes of their readers any more than do the *Journal des savants* and the Jesuit *Mémoires de Trévoux.*

15. Trenard, "La sociologie du livre en France."

16. The main problem in constructing these graphs was to find comparable units and statistics for them in the eight studies under analysis. In order to make comparisons possible, it was necessary to redo some of the mathematics and to reconvert some of the data that appeared in graph form in the two articles published in *Livre et société.* The graphs all refer to the mid-century, although they represent slightly different time spans. The subjects that do not appear on them mostly concern the various "arts" catalogued under the heading "sciences et arts." Because that heading seemed too broad to mean much to the modern reader, it was replaced by the subcategory "sciences." Composed of four subsubcategories—*phy-*

sique, médecine, histoire naturelle, and *mathématiques*—the "sciences" could be computed in every case except those of Mornet and Bluche-Petit. Mornet gave no statistics on mathematical books, but the omission probably concerned much less than 1 per cent of all his titles and so did not affect the general pattern. Bluche did not differentiate "sciences" from "sciences et arts" at all. Athough the subcategory "sciences" varied widely in other cases (from 10 per cent to 70 per cent of the general category), it seemed reasonable to estimate it at half of Bluche's "sciences et arts" or 7 per cent of the total—a rough approximation indicated by broken lines that the reader may prefer to discount. Mornet's figures covered only "romans" and "grammaires" in the category "belles-lettres," which probably left out a little over half that category, judging from the distribution in Furet's *permissions publiques* and *permissions tacites.* The category probably would have occupied between 10 per cent and 20 per cent of Mornet's total and is indicated as 15 per cent by broken lines. Unlike the others, Mornet did not classify travel literature with history, as was the practice in the eighteenth century. Had he done so, his "history" division would have expanded by another 1.5 per cent. Meyer's "belles-lettres" also is approximate and therefore appears in broken lines.

A graph combining Furet's studies of *permissions publiques* and *permissions tacites* was constructed from computations based on his original data, because it was hoped that an over-all picture of literary output would emerge by combining statistics from those two very different sources. Suggestive as it is, this composite bar graph contradicts all the others. For example, it somewhat resembles the graph based on Mornet's statistics, but Mornet would have the French reading far fewer religious works (6 per cent) in relation to science (3 per cent) and especially history (30 per cent) than would Furet, whose combined graph shows 20 per cent religion, 9 per cent science, and 11 per cent history.

Because all eight studies kept close to the eighteenth-century classification scheme, they do not give much help to the modern reader in search of the Enlightenment. Does he associate Enlightenment with "philosophie," one of the eight subcategories under "sciences et arts"? If so, he must contend with four sibling subsubcategories: *philosophie ancienne, logique, morale,* and *métaphysique.* The last two seem promising, but (except in Roche's statistics, which include two additional subsubcategories) the data do not distinguish them from their two predecessors. The four studies that provide statistics on "philosophie" as a whole suggest it comprised a small, stable portion of eighteenth-century reading: the *permissions publiques* fix it at 3 per cent (1723-1727), 3.7 per cent (1750-1754), and 4.5 per cent (1784-1788); the *permissions tacites* at 6 per cent (1750-1759), 5 per cent (1770-1774), and 6 per cent (1784-1788); the reviews in the *Journal des savants* at 3 per cent (1715-1719), 4 per cent (1750-1754), and 5 per cent (1785-1789); and it made up 7 per cent of Dortous de Mairan's library. Not much evidence for the spread of *lumières.* But then the Enlightenment cannot be identified with any of the eighteenth-century categories or their subdivisions.

It would also be possible to express Pottinger's study of two hundred eighteenth-century authors in a bar graph, because he produced a statistical table of their publications, taking Mornet's work as a model. But, as explained above, Pottinger's selection of writers is so arbitrary and his statistics so incomplete and unrepresentative that the graph would not mean very much. Nonetheless, for purposes of comparison, his findings ought to be mentioned (Pottinger, *The French Book Trade,* pp. 30-31): religious works 11 per cent of the total produced by his authors, science 20 per cent, history 20 per cent, law 2 per cent, belles-lettres 10 per cent.

17. This figure is based on the Maggiolo study of literacy as presented by Michel Fleury and Pierre Valmary in "Les progrès de l'instruction élémentaire de Louis XIV à Napoléon III d'après l'enquête de Louis Maggiolo (1877-1879)," *Population* (1957), pp. 71-92, estimating the population at 26 million.

18. Julien Brancolini and Marie-Thérèse Bouyssy, "La vie provinciale du livre à la fin de l'Ancien Régime" and Jean-Louis and Marie Flandrin, "La circulation du livre dans la société du 18e siècle: un sondage à travers quelques sources," both in *Livre et société,* 2 (Paris, 1970). For a detailed discussion of these studies, see Robert Darnton, "In Search of the Enlightenment: Recent Attempts to Create a Social History of Ideas," a review article that will apear in a forthcoming issue of the *Journal of Modern History.*

19. The remainder of this essay is essentially a "work in progress" report based on the first stages of research in the papers of the Société typographique de Neuchâtel in the Bibliothèque Publique de la Ville de Neuchâtel, Neuchâtel, Switzerland, cited henceforth as STN. Other important sources were the papers of Jean-Charles-Pierre Lenoir, *lieutenant-général de police* of Paris from 1774 to 1775 and 1776 to 1785, in the Bibliothèque municipale d'Orléans, Mss. 1421-1423; the Archives de la Chambre syndicale and Collection Anisson-Duperron papers of the Bibliothèque Nationale (especially fonds français, Mss. 21862, 21833, 22046, 22063, 22070, 22075, 22081, 22109, 22116, 22102); the papers of the Bastille and related papers on the book trade in the Bibliothèque de l'Arsenal (especially Mss. 10305, 12446, 12454, 12480, 12481, 12517); and the Ministère des affaires étrangères, Correspondance politique, Angleterre (Mss. 541-549). For information on the underground book route through Kehl and Strasbourg as opposed to Neuchâtel and Pontarlier, the relevant papers in the Archives de la ville de Strasbourg (mainly Mss. AA 2355-2362) were consulted but turned out to be less useful than the others. Research on publishing under the Old Regime by now has made J.-P. Belin, *Le commerce des livres prohibés à Paris de 1750 à 1789* (New York, no date, a Burt Franklin reprint of the original edition, Paris, 1913) somewhat dated. For information about the most important secondary works, see the bibliographies in Nicole Herrmann-Mascard, *La censure des livres à Paris à la fin de l'Ancien Régime, 1750-1789* (Paris: Presses universitaires de France, 1968), and Madeleine Ventre, *L'imprimerie et la librairie en Languedoc au dernier siècle de l'Ancien Régime, 1700-1789* (Paris and The Hague: Mouton, 1958). The present essay was written before the thesis of H.-J. Martin became available, but it relies heavily on his article, "L'édition parisienne au

XVIIe siècle: quelques aspects économiques," *Annales: économies, sociétés, civilisations,* 7 (July-September 1952), 303-318. Another suggestive article is Léon Cahen, "La librairie parisienne et la diffusion du livre français à la fin du XVIIIe siècle, *Revue de synthèse,* 17 (1939), 159-179.

20. A typical example is the memoire of August 2, 1783, by Périsse Duluc, syndic of the Chambre syndicale of Lyons in the Bibliothèque Nationale, Mss. français 21833, fol. 96.

21. Revol to STN, July 4, 1784, STN Ms. 1205.

22. For example, the Société typographique de Neuchâtel received a letter dated October 30, 1783, from François Michaut, its agent on the Swiss side of the French border, which explained, "Votre partie est assez chatouilleuse à raison de la crainte que les porteurs ont qu'en cas de prise ils ne fussent saisis comme introducteurs d'ouvrages qui attaquent la religion ou qui traitent à dénigrer certaines personnes en place . . . Si vous ne voulez introduire que des livres irrépréhensibles par leur contenu, les porteurs vous demanderont votre garantie pour ces faits là, et vous en trouverez dans nos environs qui vous rendront le quintal à 12 livres de France à Pontarlier ou même une lieue plus loin s'il le fallait. Autre quoi il faut encore donner à boire à chaque porteur avant que de partir. Il faut vous observer, Messieurs, qu'à ce prix là les porteurs font pour le mieux sans vous répondre de la marchandise." Michaut observed with some pride that "effectivement ma position est assez avantageuse pour les entrées clandestines" but warned, "l'on trouve le long de la route et dans les villages des employés ambulants, qui malgré que l'on soit en règle arrêtent et épluchent la charge d'un voiturier." He therefore stressed the need of having an agent to dupe or bribe the employees of the General Farm from the French side of the border: "Je ne connais personne de plus propre à cela que le sieur Faivre," STN Ms. 1183. Faivre did not hesitate to recommend himself. On October 14, 1784, he informed the society, "Samedi prochain vos balles entreront. J'ai tant fait et promis à ces porteurs que je leur donnerait de quoi boire et qu'ils seront contents, ce qui les a ranimés à retourner . . . Je suis au moment de traiter avec un employé des fermes pour nous laisser passer librement la nuit et m'indiquer les chemins où l'on doit passer en sûreté," STN Ms. 1148.

23. STN to J.-P. Brissot, April 29, 1781, STN Ms. 1109.

24. Mme. La Noue to STN, September 8, 1782, STN Ms. 1173. Mme. La Noue was sensitive to complaints that she overcharged and underprotected her customers. On December 9, 1780, she wrote to the STN, "Je vous prie M. vouloir bien aitres tranquille sur le sort de vos objet. Lorsquils sòn entre mais mains je ne neglige rien pour le mettre a labry des evenements. Obligé moy davoir confiance en ma façon de travailler." But on January 13, 1783, she confessed that six of its crates had been seized at her doorstep: "Le voituriè etoit suivi au point quil cest trouvè icy a la de charge dudit voituriè 3 personne de la prevotté qui ce sont emparrè des dditte 6 balles et de lettres de voiture que le voituriè na put leurs reffuzè par les menaces quils luy on fait et amoy bien des question pandant quinze jour pour

declarrè les personnes a qui apartenoit les dittes balles et dou elle venoit aquoy je me suis reffuzè," *ibid.*

25. Paul de Pourtalès to STN, June 23, 1784, STN Ms. 1199.

26. See the Desauges dossier in the Bibliothèque de l'Arsenal, Ms. 12446. On April 4, 1775, Desauges père wrote dyspeptically from the Bastille to his son, who had just been released, "il faut prendre son mal en patience. Je t'avouerai franchement que je m'ennuie à la mort." The Desauges dossier in Neuchâtel, Ms. 1141, shows the sharp practices of underground book-dealers at their most cutthroat.

27. Mme. J. E. Bertrand to STN, October 7, 1785, STN Ms. 1121.

28. J.-F. Bornand to STN, August 10, 1785, STN Ms. 1124. Poinçot occasion-ally smuggled books from Versailles to Paris for Desauges at twelve livres the quintal, which apparently was cheap compared with the charges of Mme. La Noue: three livres per "gros objet," which her nephew delivered to appointed hiding places on the outskirts of Paris (see Desauges to STN, November 24, 1783, Ms. 1141 and Mme. La Noue to STN, June 22, 1781, Ms. 1173).

29. Among his tasks, Bornand had to try to cope with the "verbiages" of Mme. La Noue (Bornand to STN, February 19, 1785, Ms. 1124), the ruses of Poinçot and Desauges, and the impecuniousness of authors: "C'est une triste ressource que les auteurs pour l'argent" (Bornand to STN, March 9, 1785, *ibid.*).

30. Giles Barber, "French Royal Decrees Concerning the Book Trade 1700-1789," *Australian Journal of French Studies,* 3 (1966), 312.

31. A. J. L. Jourdan, O. O. Decrusy, and F. A. Isambert, eds., *Recueil général des anciennes lois françaises* (Paris, 1822-1833), XXI, 230.

32. *Ibid.,* p. 218.

33. *Ibid.,* p. 217.

34. George V. Taylor, "Noncapitalist Wealth and the Origins of the French Revolution," *American Historical Review,* 72 (1967), 469-496.

35. P. J. Blondel, *Mémoire sur les vexations qu'exercent les libraires et im-primeurs de Paris,* ed. Lucien Faucou (Paris, 1879); see especially pp. 18-25 and 45.

36. Quotations from *Recueil général des anciennes lois françaises,* XXV, 109, 119, and 110 respectively.

37. *Ibid.,* p. 109.

38. Because of the complicated problems of dating Diderot's *Lettre,* relating it to earlier documents that influenced Diderot's argument, and establishing a correct version of the text, it is important to read the *Lettre* in the critical edition by Jacques Proust (Paris: Colin, 1962). But even the old edition in Diderot's *Oeuvres complètes,* ed. J. Assézat and Maurice Tourneux

(Paris, 1876), XVIII, 6, included a note by someone in the *Direction de la Librairie* (d'Hémery?) which observed that Diderot wrote the *Lettre* "d'apres le conseil des libraires et sur des matériaux que M. Le Breton . . . lui a fournis, et dont les principes sont absolument contraires à la bonne administration des privilèges." Although the *Lettre* contains some heartfelt statements about liberty and the tribulations of authors, its logic is twisted to favor publishers and it reproduces the old arguments advanced by the guild. It is therefore difficult to accept Brunel's claim that Diderot did not write the *Lettre* either as an ally or as a paid propagandist of Le Breton and the other privileged publishers: Lucien Brunel, "Observations critiques et littéraires sur un opuscule de Diderot," *Revue d'histoire littéraire de la France*, 10 (1903), 1-24.

39. The code of 1777 weakened some of the Parisian guild's power by giving authors the right to sell their own works and by providing for two public book sales in Paris every year. It favored provincial publishers by permitting them to print the increasing number of books that it caused to fall into the public domain—an acknowledgment of the fact that they had engaged in illegal activities for lack of "un moyen légitime d'employer leurs presses," *Recueil général des anciennes lois françaises*, XXV, 109. The edicts of 1777 thus attempted to "faire cesser la rivalité qui divise la librairie de Paris et celle des provinces, de la faire tourner au profit de cette branche importante du commerce, et de former de tous les libraires une même famille qui n'aura plus qu'un même intérêt," *ibid.*, pp. 119-120. But this rivalry went too deep to be settled by such small concessions to the provincial dealers, who continued to protest against exploitation by the Parisians throughout the 1780's. The 1777 code also extended and strengthened the guild system in the provinces, because "S.M. a reconnu qu'il serait dangereux de laisser subsister les imprimeries isolées dans un état d'indépendance qui y facilite les abus," *ibid.*, p. 112. So the reorganization of the guilds did not substantially weaken them or impair their policing function.

40. D.-J. Garat, *Mémoires historiques sur la vie de M. Suard, sur ses écrits et sur le XVIIIe siècle* (Paris, 1820), I, 274.

41. Bibliothèque Nationale, Mss. français 21833, foll. 87-88. This account of French tax and tariff legislation is derived from several documents in Ms. 21833, particularly foll. 89-91 and 129-140.

42. The tariff legislation was a constant theme in the commercial correspondence of the Société typographique de Neuchâtel for the first half of the 1770's. The society even sent one of its partners on a business trip through eastern France to sell books, to find new ways of making fraudulent shipments, and to learn as much as possible about tariff policy. According to the instructions in his travel-log, he was to seek out "J. M. Bruysset, homme froid et habile: 1° S'entretenir avec lui de la librairie française en général, savoir de lui si en effet l'impôt sera levé ou diminué," STN, Ms. 1058, "Carnet de voyage, 1773, J. E. Bertrand." The Bruysset house was one of the most effective lobbyists against the tariff, judging from the memoranda in the Bibliothèque Nationale, Mss. français 21833, especially foll. 87-88 and 129-140. The tariff damaged the illegal trade, because pirated works

were usually shipped through legal channels, at least at the border, under false *acquits à caution* and therefore paid duty.

43. Bibliothèque Nationale, Mss. français, 21833, foll. 87-88. This memoire reads as though it were the work of Panckoucke. One sou per gathering was the normal printing charge of the Société typographique de Neuchâtel, whose flourishing business in the late 1770's seems to have resulted from the combination of France's favorable tariff policy and the cheap conditions of printing in Switzerland.

44. *Ibid.*, foll. 111-115. The dealer showed, by a very detailed argument, that a six-hundred-pound crate would cost him 61 livres, 15 sous in extra charges, would cause enormous delays and damage through mishandling, and would make it impossible for him to collect insurance for damaged shipments.

45. *Ibid.*, fol. 70.

46. *Ibid.*, fol. 107: "Les libraires éloignés de Paris, et ceux de Lyon en particulier, ont sur le champ contremandé les envois qu'on devait leur faire, fait rétrograder les ballots qui étaient en route, annulé leurs marchés, et renoncé aux entreprises d'impression pour lesquelles ils se voient maintenant sans débouchés. Enfin, il n'existe déjà plus de correspondance active entre les libraires français et les libraires étrangers."

47. J. F. Bornand to STN, April 12, 1784, STN Ms. 1124.

48. J. F. Bornand to STN, April 9, 1784, *ibid.*

49. J. F. Bornand to STN, February 19, 1785, *ibid.*

50. STN to Garrigan, a bookdealer in Avignon, August 23, 1785: "Nous partageons sans doute bien sincèrement le regret sur l'interruption de notre correspondance que vous voulez bien nous témoigner par l'honneur de votre lettre du 10 de ce mois, mais vous n'ignorez pas que la cause fatale ne peut en être attribué qu'à la rigueur toujours subsistante des ordonnances concernant l'introduction de la librairie étrangère dans le royaume. Les choses sont encore sur un tel pied à cet égard, que nous ne pouvons faire entrer une balle *Libri* par le bureau de notre frontière qu'en prenant un acquit à caution pour Paris, où les vôtres seraient obligés d'aller en faisant ainsi un détour immense et subissant l'examen de la Chambre syndicale Parisienne, ce qui est absolument impraticable," STN Ms. 1110.

51. STN to Mme. J. E. Bertrand, early October 1785, STN Ms. 1110.

52. The archives in Strasbourg, an important center of the clandestine trade, complement those in Neuchâtel in that they show a determined effort by the government to stop traffic in prohibited works. Strasbourg's *préteur royal* received frequent reports from local officials about seizures of illegal shipments from the publishers across the Rhine; and he also received strict orders from his own superior, the *garde des sceaux* (letter of April 26, 1786, in Archives de la Ville de Strasbourg, Ms. AA2356): "La librairie proscrite par nos lois vous environne de toute part; et elle pénétréra par les moyens

que vous ne lui aurez pas interdits, si vous ne les lui interdisez pas tous . . . Je vous exhorte donc fortement, vous et le magistrat de votre ville, à prendre les mesures convenables." Despite this rigor, printers in Kehl seem to have got a great many books—political pamphlets and *libelles* as well as Beaumarchais' Voltaire—through the traps laid for them in Strasbourg. The town's semiautonomy, guaranteed by the capitulations of 1681, may have made it relatively easy to penetrate.

53. See Furet, p. 8, and Robert Estivals, *La statistique bibliographique de la France sous la monarchie au XVIIIe siècle* (Paris and The Hague: Imprimerie nationale, 1965), p. 296.

54. Bibliothèque Nationale, Ms. français 21833, fol. 107.

55. *Ibid.*, fol. 108; see also foll. 99-104.

56. Vergennes to d'Adhémar, May 12, 1783, Ministère des affaires étrangères, Correspondance politique, Angleterre, Ms. 542. The details of "cette machination d'intrigues, de cupidité, et de fourberie," as Vergennes called it (Vergennes to Lenoir, May 24, 1783, *ibid.*)—and which I plan to recount in a later work—can be found in the series 541-549.

57. Bibliothèque de l'Arsenal, Ms. 10305. The inventory also included *Le gazetier cuirassé, L'espion dévalisé, Vie privée de Louis XV, Le diable dans un bénitier*, and other classics of the London School of *libellistes*. It specified that they had been shipped to some of the customers of the Société typographique de Neuchâtel, notably Poinçot, Blaizot, and Mme. La Noue. Poinçot himself drew up the inventory.

58. For the conventional view that the government's policy was severe in theory and permissive in practice, see J.-P. Belin, *Le commerce des livres prohibés à Paris de 1750 à 1789* (New York, no date, a Burt Franklin reprint of the original edition, Paris, 1913) and the restatement of Belin's interpretation in Nicole Herrmann-Mascard, *La censure des livres à Paris à la fin de l'ancien régime, 1750-1789* (Paris: Presses universitaires de France, 1968). Both books dismiss the June 12, 1783, orders in two sentences—the same sentences, curiously, almost word for word (Belin, p. 45; Herrmann-Mascard, p. 102).

59. It also might serve as a corrective to the Marxist tendency to treat the Enlightenment as bourgeois ideology. One version of this tendency argues that ideas such as social contract, individualism, liberty, and equality before the law derived from capitalist methods of exchange, which involve contractual obligations between legally free and equal individuals: Lucien Goldmann, "La pensée des 'Lumières,'" *Annales: économies, sociétés, civilisations*, 22 (1967), 752-770. Considering the multitude of writers who expressed such ideas before the development of capitalism, this argument seems less convincing than its opposite, which relates the Enlightenment to a tradition of aristocratic liberalism: Denis Richet, "Autour des origines idéologiques lointaines de la Révolution française: élites et despotisme," *ibid.*, 24 (1969), 1-23.

60. STN, Ms. 1108.

61. *Ibid.* In contrast, the manuscript catalogue offered the following under the letter "B": "*La belle allemande, ou les galanteries de Thérèse,* 1774; *Bijoux indiscrets* par Diderot, 8° figures; *Le bonheur,* poème par Helvétius; *Le bon sens, ou idées naturelles, opposées aux idés surnaturelles.*"

62. Reprinted in A. Van Bever, *Contes et conteurs gaillards au XVIIIe siècle* (Paris: Daragon, 1906), pp. 280-281. In notes that he assembled for his memoirs, the former lieutenant general of police J.-C.-P. Lenoir associated this work with a widespread outbreak of libeling in the 1780's (Bibliothèque municipale d'Orléans, Ms. 1423): "Les moeurs du successeur de Louis Quinze étant inattaquables, le nouveau roi fut inaccessible de ce côté à la calomnie pendant les premières années de son règne, mais on commença en 1778 à le diffamer du côté de sa faiblesse, et les premières calomnies qui furent ourdies contre sa personne ne préludèrent que de trés peu de mois ceux de la méchanceté contre la reine. M. de Maurepas, qui jusques là avait été fort insouciant touchant des épigrammes et des chansons faites contre lui, M. de Maurepas, qui s'amusait de tous les libelles, de toutes les anecdotes privées et scandaleuses qu'on fabriquait et imprimait avec impunité, eut avis que des écrivains avaient fait entre eux une sorte de spéculation, qu'ils avaient lié une correspondance au moyen de laquelle les uns envoyaient de Paris les histoires courantes et fournissaient des titres et des matériaux à ceux qui les composaient et faisaient imprimer à La Haye et à Londres, d'où ils les faisaient entrer en France en petite quantité par des voyageurs étrangers. Un secrétaire d'ambassade d'Angleterre lui annonça qu'on devait incessament y introduire en France un libelle abominable intitulé *Les amours de Charlot et d'Antoinette.*"

63. *Le portefeuille d'un talon rouge contenant des anecdotes galantes et secrètes de la cour de France,* reprinted under the title *Le coffret du bibliophile* (Paris, no date), p. 22. Lenoir's manuscripts confirm this account (Bibliothèque municipale d'Orléans, Ms. 1422): "Il n'est plus douteux maintenant que c'étaient MM. de Montesquiou, de Créqui, de Champcents, et d'autres courtisans, qui de concert avec Beaumarchais, Chamfort, et autres écrivains vivants encore avaient composé des libelles contre la cour, contre les ministres, et même contre ceux des ministres qui les employaient. Il est plus que probable que Beaumarchais avait composé, porté à Londres, où il a été imprimé, un libelle avec figures gravées intitulé *Les amours de Charlot et d'Antoinette.*"

64. *Ibid.*

65. *Ibid.* Lenoir's remarks might seem to contradict the above interpretation about a crackdown on underground publishing, but they refer primarily to the circulation of *libelles* inside Paris, not to the traffic from outside France to the capital. There seems to have been a considerable domestic production of *libelles,* which survived the police's attempts to impound them because of influential "protection" and the immunities of "lieux privilégiés" like the Palais-Royal, where the police could not penetrate. See *ibid.,* Ms. 1421.

66. See Robert Darnton, "The Grub Street Style of Revolution: J.-P. Brissot, Police Spy," *Journal of Modern History,* 40 (1968), 320-321.

67. Lenoir later tried to investigate the rumor and the riot but without success: Bibliothèque municipale d'Orleans, Ms. 1422.

68. Lenoir developed his observations most fully in an essay entitled "De l'administration de l'ancienne police concernant les libelles, les mauvaises satires et chansons, leurs auteurs coupables, délinquants, complices ou adhérents," *ibid.*

69. [Charles Théveneau de Morande], *Le gazetier cuirassé: ou anecdotes scandaleuses de la cour de France* ("imprimé à cent lieues de la Bastille à l'enseigne de la liberté," 1771), p. 92: "La nation française est si mal constituée aujourd'hui, que les gens robustes sont sans prix: On assure qu'un laquais qui débute à Paris est payé aussi cher par les femmes qui s'en servent qu'un cheval de race en Angleterre. Si ce système prend faveur, une génération ou deux suffiront pour rétablir les tempéraments." In *Le libertin de qualité,* reprinted in *L'oeuvre du Comte de Mirabeau,* ed. Guillaume Apollinaire (Paris, 1910), Mirabeau described aristocratic immorality in great detail. After recounting a depraved duchess' abandonment of her lover, he remarked (p. 232), "Elle l'a remplacé par un prince, et réellement, quant au moral, ils se convenaient; pour le physique, elle eut ses laquais: c'est le pain quotidien d'une duchesse."

70. [Charles Théveneau de Morande], *La gazette noire par un homme qui n'est pas blanc: ou oeuvres posthumes du gazetier cuirassé* ("imprimé à cent lieues de la Bastille, à trois cent lieues des Présides, à cinq cent lieues des Cordons, à mille lieues de la Sibérie," 1784), pp. 194-195.

71. See Richard Cobb, "Quelques aspects de la mentalité révolutionnaire," *Revue d'histoire moderne et contemporaine,* 6 (1959), 81-120, and "The Revolutionary Mentality in France," *History,* 42 (1957), 181-196.

72. *La gazette noire,* p. 7. For a similar example of such rumors about the promiscuous use of police by "gens en place" see M. de Lescure, ed., *Correspondance secrète inédite sur Louis XVI, Marie-Antoinette, la Cour et la ville de 1777 à 1792* (Paris: H. Plon, 1866), II, 157-158.

73. The subheadline of the account of the queen's guillotining in *La Père Duchesne.*

74. Pierre Goubert, *L'Ancien Régime* (Paris: Colin, 1969), I, 152.

75. Bibliothèque municipale d'Orléans, Ms. 1423.

76. Quoted in Frantz Funck-Brentano and Paul d'Estrée, *Les nouvellistes* (Paris: Hachette, 1905), p. 304.

77. Goubert, *L'Ancien Régime,* p. 152. The connection between privilege and monopoly is brought out clearly in the first definition of "privilège" given in the *Dictionnaire de l'Académie française* (Paris, 1778): "Faculté accordé à un particulier ou à une communauté de faire quelque chose ou de jouir de quelque avantage à l'exclusion des autres."

78. See Charly Guyot, *De Rousseau à Mirabeau: pèlerins de Môtiers et prophètes de 89* (Neuchâtel and Paris: Victor Attinger, 1936), chap. 4.

79. Although the increased severity in the policing of the book trade cut down on its business in France, the Société typographique de Neuchâtel still did its best to supply works like the following, which it entered in its "Livre de commission" (STN Ms. 1021, foll. 173-175) after receiving an order from Bruzard de Mauvelain, a clandestine dealer in Troyes, dated June 16, 1784: "6 *Les petits soupers de l'Hôtel de Bouillon;* 6 *Le diable dans un bénitier;* 6 *L'espion dévalisé;* 1 *Correspondance de Maupeou;* 1 *Recueil de remontrances au Roi Louis XV;* 2 *Mémoirs de Madame de Pompadour;* 2 *Vie privée de Louis XV;* 12 *Fastes de Louis XV;* 6 *Histoire philosophique* 8°, 10 vol; 6 *Erotika biblion* 8°; 1 *La Mettrie;* 1 *Boulanger complet, antiquité, Christianisme, et despotisme;* 1 *Helvétius complet;* 6 *Lettres de Julie à Calasie, ou tableau du libertinage à Paris;* 1 *la dernière livraison de Jean-Jacques* 12°; 6 *Chronique scandaleuse;* 6 *Les petits soupers du comte de Vergennes;* 6 *Le passe-temps, d'Antoinette.*"

80. See Paul Robiquet, *Théveneau de Morande: étude sur le XVIIIe siècle* (Paris: A. Quantin, 1882).

M. I. FINLEY

Archaeology and History

Momigliano began his elegant obituary of Mikhail Rostovtzeff by recalling the "unforgettable impression" made on students of his (and my) generation by the publication in 1926 of the *Social and Economic History of the Roman Empire:*

> All seemed, and indeed was, extraordinary in the book. Even the external appearance was unusual. We were accustomed to books on ancient history where the archaeological evidence, if used at all, was never presented and explained to the reader. Here a lavish series of plates introduced us directly to the archaeological evidence; and the caption of each plate really made us understand what one could learn from apparently insignificant items . . . Rostovtzeff delighted and surprised us by what seemed to us his uncanny gift of calling ancient things to life. He guided us through the streets of Rome, Pompeii, Nîmes and Trèves and showed how the ancients had lived.[1]

Half a century later the situation has radically altered in some respects. Although there are still too many books written about ancient history in which the archaeological evidence receives no more than lip service, not merely in the presentation but also in the historian's own study, it is also true that classical and Near Eastern historians, as a whole, are much more conscious of, and knowledgeable about, archaeological evidence than they were when Rostovtzeff's book appeared.[2] If it is hard to think of anyone since who possesses his gift of the illuminating caption, that is sad but not very significant. What is serious is that the demands made by historians of antiquity upon archaeology, and the methods of employing and presenting archaeological evidence in ancient history, have not advanced much beyond what was possible for Rostovtzeff, and often lag behind. Yet in the same half-century archaeology itself, at its best, has advanced immeasurably, and historians ought to have advanced with it.

281

However, it is not my intention in this essay to produce a catalogue of grievances along these lines; it would soon become boring and unilluminating. Looking to the future, there are two central questions, in my judgment. The first is whether current trends in archaeology are departing so far from the kinds of questions historians have traditionally put to archaeologists that the gap between the two will soon be widened rather than narrowed. That will be my concern in the first section; to my mind, at least, there is a close kinship with the problems created by the trend toward "serial history" (by whatever name it is called) dealt with elsewhere in the present volume. Then I shall go to my second question, limited to classical archaeology alone: What is it that the classical historian ought to be asking of archaeological evidence today, and how successfully are the archaeologists, from their side, adjusting their own older aims and techniques to these new demands? Implicit in this discussion is the assumption that contemporary historians, even of antiquity, *are* asking new kinds of questions. Anyone who is happy with kings and battles or with "calling ancient things to life" (I deliberately resort to a caricature) will find the discussion wholly irrelevant.

I

In common with other disciplines in the humanities and social studies, archaeology gives the appearance of being in a crisis. That is attested by the spate of books and articles with such titles as *New Perspectives in Archaeology*.[3] At the simplest level, there is a strong reaction within the discipline against the familiar excursions into prehistoric religion, economics, or art appreciation that are neither grounded in, nor controlled by, theory or adequate knowledge. There is a new mood of austerity, even of pessimism. It may seem "hard doctrine to some people," writes Stuart Piggott, but "the observational data of prehistory seem to me in almost every way to be more ambiguous, and more capable of varied interpretations, than the normal run of material available to historians. What we have at our disposal, as prehistorians, is the accidentally surviving durable remnants of material culture, which we interpret as best we may, and inevitably the peculiar quality of this evidence dictates the sort of information we can obtain from it. Furthermore, we interpret the evidence in terms of our own intellectual make-up, conditioned as it is by the period and culture within which we were brought up, our social and cultural background, our current assumptions and presuppositions, and our age and status."[4]

One example demonstrating the urgent necessity for such "hard doctrine" merits examination—the remarkable fable of the Great Mother Goddess. For Jacquetta Hawkes that goddess was so omnipresent and omnipotent in Bronze Age (Minoan) Crete that the civilization itself is labeled a "predominantly feminine force." The case rests on a group of small Neolithic figurines, averaging less than two inches in height, which she describes as follows: "The material evidences of the religious life of these Stone Age farmers consist very largely of formalized statuettes of women (carved or modelled) which they kept in their homes or sometimes provided with sacred houses of their own. In making these images they called attention to the reproductive function, giving them huge breasts and buttocks, and often the mountainous bellies of advanced pregnancy. Moreover they usually set them in a squatting position, which at that time may have been the accepted position for childbirth."[5] Apart from Miss Hawkes's private fancy about feminine and masculine forces in civilizations, her interpretation of the figurines is a restatement of what had become virtually received doctrine in archaeology.[6] It has now been shattered beyond hope of rescue by the publication of Peter Ucko's book on the figurines.[7]

The total number of Neolithic Cretan anthropomorphic figurines known by 1969 was 103. Of these, only 28 are certainly female, 5 male, and 28 sexless; the remainder cannot be classified, primarily because of their fragmentary state. They sit, stand, kneel, and crouch as well as squat. "The majority of female figures have close-set breasts which are flat and small and which project very little from the body," and anyway the assessment "is almost always largely subjective." Only two figurines have come from houses anywhere in Crete, none from any structure which can be identified as a shrine. Usually the find site can be described only as "general habitation debris." And there are also numerous animal figurines.

The received view is thus an extreme case of the type that D. L. Clarke, a leading Young Turk in the field, criticized when he wrote, "The degree of confidence that we are logically justified in placing in many archaeological generalizations is often undermined by failure to specify the proportion of observed cases, the variety of circumstances or the existence of conflicting examples."[8] The wonder is that no one before Ucko had bothered to examine systematically all the 103 Cretan figurines.[9] Now "archaeologists and students of prehistoric religion" are asked to "overhaul present theories very critically."[10] Beyond doubt they must, but it is not mere *Besserwisserei* to point out that some of us—archaeologists as well as historians and anthropologists—have been challenging the Mother Goddess for years. Even without Ucko's breakdown, other methodological objections had been raised—for instance, that the Mother Goddess devotees made no effort to explain the complete disappearance of these figurines in the Minoan period, and offered no foundation for their vast superstructure other than the vaguest subjective verbiage about the "meaning" of big breasts and heavy buttocks. It should be recorded that Ucko had published his Cretan analysis as early as 1962 in the authoritative official organ of the Royal Anthropological Institute,[11] with little visible impact.

How, then, do we interpret such remains as the anthropomorphic figurines? The archaeological Young Turks reject Piggott's kind of pessimism. "The argument," writes L. R. Binford, "that archaeologists must limit their knowledge to features of material culture is open to serious question; and second, the dichotomy between material and nonmaterial aspects of culture itself and the relevance of this dichotomy for a proposed hierarchy of reliability have also been the subject of critical discussion . . . It is virtually impossible to imagine that any given cultural item functioned in a socio-cultural system independent of the operation of 'non-material' variables. Every item has its history within a socio-cultural system—its phases of procurement of raw material, manufacture, use, and final discarding . . . *There is every reason to expect* that the empirical properties of artifacts and their arrangement in the archaeological record will exhibit attributes which can inform on different phases of the artifact's life history" (my italics).[12]

Of course no one imagines that cultural items function independently, least of all the pessimists whom Binford is attacking. The issue lies in the final sentence I have quoted. Is there any reason to expect what Binford expects, and significantly can offer only as an expectation rather than as a proposition for which there is available evidence? On the contrary, there is sufficient evidence that identical artifacts and arrangements of artifacts can result from different socioeconomic arrangements of procurement, manufacture, or distribution. For example, we know from the chance preservation of accounts inscribed on stone, that the most delicate stone carving on the temple in Athens known as the Erechtheum was produced by free men and slaves working side by side at the end of the fifth century B.C. Nothing in the material remains (the carving itself) could have told us that. On the other hand, the surviving accounts of the temple of Apollo at Epidaurus, built thirty or forty years later, are of such a nature that the labor force is not specified. How does Binford imagine it will be possible to discover whether or not slaves were employed, at the highest skill level, on that temple?[13]

The most radical, elaborate, and sometimes brilliant argumentation will be found in Clarke's *Analytical Archaeology* already mentioned. For Clarke the crisis in archaeology is most obviously exposed by the attempt to produce "imitation history books."[14] His objective is to establish archaeology "as a discipline in its own right, concerned with archaeological data which it clusters in archaeological entities displaying certain archaeological processes and studied in terms of archaeological aims, concepts and procedures . . . The entities, processes, aims, procedures and concepts of archaeology have a validity of their own in reference to the archaeological frame and despite their generation by—and partial correlation with—former social and historic entities."[15] The "fundamental" archaeological entities are "the attribute, artefact, the artefact-type, the assemblage, the culture and the culture group."[16] The major aims of the discipline are (1) "the definition of the fundamental entities"; (2) "the search for repeated similarities or regularities in form, function, association, or developmental sequence amongst the particular entities from every area, period and environment"; (3) "the development of higher category knowledge or principles that synthesize and correlate the material at hand whilst possessing a high predictive value. The development of increasingly comprehensive and informative general models and hypotheses."[17]

We know where we are now; the familiar polemic of the social scientist against history has been carried back into prehistory, though I am unable to discover in his more than six hundred pages what he means by "a general archaeological theory." Insofar as Clarke rests on a tautology—"an archaeological culture is not a racial group, nor a historic tribe, nor a linguistic unit, it is simply an archaeological culture"[18]—his sophisticated statistical procedures, requiring extensive use of computers, will no doubt enhance and refine archaeological inquiry considerably. However, it is apparent that he does not wish to be taken too literally. That is revealed by the way the word "function" creeps into the second of the "aims," and by the conventional admission of social anthropology into the exclusive club.[19] When he speaks of "religious data" and "religious artefacts," and writes a short paragraph about Minoan Crete that includes such phrases as "embalmed within the conservative memory of the religious subsystem," "the later Minoan idealized bull cult," "a religious 'memory' or a cultural 'dream' of such a former trajectory,"[20] one is entitled to protest not only that he has abandoned "archaeological procedures" but that he has descended to the excesses of the Mother Goddess fable.[21]

Furthermore, when Clarke leaves prehistory for periods for which there is some documentation, other than archaeological, he is surprisingly happy if his archaeological analysis seems occasionally to coincide with written documentary evidence. I say "seems to" because it does not always do so as he claims, and because when it does, the coincidence is illusory. Of the former failing, I merely cite the inaccuracy and the misunderstanding of the nature of such Greek sources as Homer, Herodotus, and Eratosthenes, which pervade the paragraph that is supposed to provide literary substantiation of his account of Hallstatt assemblages from the ninth to the fifth centuries B.C.[22] For the second, there is a more significant example. Clarke reports a computerized analysis of more than one thousand "burial assemblages of weaponry and harness artefacts" of Turkic-speaking nomads between about A.D. 900 and 1300. The analysis produced a diachronic classification into four main groups, the transition to the fourth being marked by the replacement of horse gear in the women's graves by "distinctive new Mongolian types . . . earrings, mirrors, birch-bark head-dresses." "Historically," Clarke adds, "and by coin evidence it was possible to associate this change with the period of the Golden Horde invasions."[23] Though the observations are no doubt accurate, the obvious comment is that, granting the Mongolian character of the objects can be established from the objects themselves, no "archaeological procedures" would have revealed the "Golden Horde invasions," as Clarke's own wording concedes. Why, then, does he resort to what he has earlier labeled, pejoratively, a "nostalgic retreat into historiography"? Why does he not leave the final transition as "unhistoriographical" as the other three, for which there appear to be no distracting coins or documents?

These questions raise the fundamental one of the purpose of the exercise. Why expend effort and financial resources to sort out in a time-series some four hundred years of burial assemblages—or to sort out, in any fashion, any group of past phenomena, prehistoric or historic? Is it only in order to achieve a more or less abstract classification of objects? To ask the question is to answer it. No one can make a claim for such a bloodless procedure, beyond the aesthetic one that can equally be made of a game of chess, the claim that elegant precision has value for its own sake. Unless one is prepared, in the study of the past, to abandon all interest in change, growth, evolution, in institutions, events, or the interrelationships among the different aspects of human society, I see no virtue in the insistence that any one type of evidence, or one type of analytical procedure, must be isolated from all other types—no virtue, in short, in Clarke's "validity of their own despite their correlation with social and historical entities." No more do I see any virtue, as I have already said, in the practice of historians who similarly neglect archaeological materials. And perhaps I should repeat that, on all available evidence, it is impossible to infer social arrangements or institutions, attitudes or beliefs from material objects alone.

None of this is an argument against more and better quantification of evidence. But it is an argument against the view, sometimes expressed explicitly, that what cannot be quantified cannot be dealt with at all, that only quantification produces "scientific" (as distinct from "subjective" or "ideological") analysis and results. The objection is simply that large areas of human behavior thereby disappear from the "scientist's" view altogether, including all historical events or series of events. This is the point at which I believe the Young Turks in archaeology and in history meet. Historical demographers are now able to provide complicated graphs of the trends in life expectancy, size of family, illegitimacy over long periods of time. These are important data for the history of the family, but they are not equal to the history of the family, and never will be. Likewise, it is interesting to know that central Asian women took horse gear to the grave with them in one period, and in another preferred earrings and mirrors, but no table of correlations will reveal the thinking and the value judgments behind the habits.[24] Admittedly the latter kind of interest requires speculation, with a low coefficient of reliability, and explanations cannot be verified in the same way as frequency tables can be, but that seems insufficient ground for dismissing serious, disciplined efforts as mere "counterfeit history."

II

It is self-evident that the potential contribution of archaeology to history is, in a rough way, inversely proportionate to the quantity and quality of the available written sources. It is also self-evident that the line between prehistory and history is not a sharp one, that for centuries after the introduction of writing, the historian's evidence remains almost exclusively archaeological, at least for some civilizations, notably the Greek and the Roman. Perhaps the most frustrating example is that of the Etruscans: despite some 10,000 more or less deciphered texts and a considerable, though late and distorted, Roman tradition behind them, assemblages of artifacts remain not only the base of all accounts but nearly the whole of the evidence. An Etruscan tomb is nothing more than an assemblage of artifacts, despite the sophistication of the technology or of the wall-paintings, so long as there is no adequate literary key to the conventions and values represented by the artifacts. Nowhere is Piggott's hard doctrine more necessary, and nowhere is it more systematically ignored in a continuous outpouring of "counterfeit history"—with notable exceptions that need not be named here, though I cannot refrain from noting that what needs to be said in protest against the methods that produce that counterfeit history will be found in Massimo Pallottino's *The Etruscans*.[25]

For the earliest historical periods, an extraordinary complication is introduced by oral tradition and historical legends. The problem is then not simply one of correlating archaeological and literary evidence but of using archaeology to assess whether, and how far, the literature has any worth at all. How difficult that is, and how little agreement has been reached so far, in large part because of unclarity about the canons of discrimination, are clear from the current debates about the Minoan and Mycenaean civilizations and the Trojan War.[26] Apart from the anomalous Linear B tablets, there is no contemporary written evidence for this long period, and it remains the province of the prehistorian rather than of the historian; in the final analysis the work is one of reconstruction from archaeology, even if one is prepared to take more from the legends than I am.

The earliest Roman history presents a different situation, because it began late enough to fall within the period of literacy and because the Roman traditions about their origins, unlike the Greek, have the external appearance of a very detailed history, full of narrative and of constitutional and institutional information ordered in a coherent time sequence. Roman history cannot be said to begin before the period of Etruscan rule, the sixth century B.C., and the contemporary documentation for the following century, the first

period of independence, though scrappy, includes annalistic fragments and the Twelve Tables.[27] The "histories" are of course very
late—the early books of Livy, who died in A.D. 17, and of his contemporary, Dionysius of Halicarnassus, and several lives by Plutarch, still later by about a century—and largely fictitious. However,
Theodor Mommsen and others had already demonstrated, long before there was any relevant archaeology of value, that there are
techniques by which some data could be pulled out, chiefly in the
constitutional, legal, and religious spheres, to which one could with
some confidence attach the name of genuine history. Today we have
available a full synthesis of the archaeology of early Rome and its
environs, unrivaled in Graeco-Roman archaeology in its completeness, and it is important to assess its impact on the received view of
early Roman history.[28] In the first place, by itself it reveals perhaps
less than some had hoped, in broad terms that sixth and fifth century Rome was a fairly primitive village, with strong Etruscan traits,
far removed from the great Livian Rome of the kings and early
Republic, but one that was rising in its material level and its size by
the end of the fifth century. In the second place, archaeology has
confirmed the chronological outlines of the tradition—that is to say,
historians are satisfied that it has, whereas the individual archaeologists most directly involved in the discussion insist, for some reason
I am unable to fathom, that the literary chronology must be down-
dated by about half a century.[29] And in the third place, we are in
all other respects left with no tools of analysis other than those inherited from the nineteenth century, refined, occasionally supplemented by new epigraphic fragments, checked by modern comparative studies, but unchanged in their fundamental nature.

From this particular, pessimistic report it is tempting to draw the
rather paradoxical conclusion that the contribution of archaeology
to history becomes greater as the volume and reliability of nonarchaeological evidence increase (until the latter reaches the volume
and nature of modern, even early modern, documentation). There is
truth in that proposition, I believe, but not the whole truth, as I
shall illustrate in a moment. It would be pointless to catalogue the
many important contributions archaeology has in fact made to our
knowledge of ancient history. Instead, I have selected three further
examples that raise major problems about future possibilities and
needs, examples that fall within the field of economic history.

The first example is at the same time a demonstration of the limits of my paradoxical proposition—the history of what is convention-

ally called Greek "colonization," in reality the history of Greek expansion between about 1000 and 550 B.C., to Asia Minor and the coastal areas surrounding the Black Sea in the east, to southern Italy, Sicily, and along both shores of the Mediterranean in the west. The Greek tradition, scattered in a multitude of writers from Herodotus to Eusebius, consists of a chronological framework (and by the end in very precise dates), anachronistic propaganda on behalf of the Delphic oracle, and anecdotes. No history of colonization was possible on that basis. Archaeology has confirmed the chronological frame, though of course not the precise dates (as with early Rome), but it has also achieved very much more. In combination with the literary materials, it has made possible a kind of history, not a narrative political account but a picture of settlement, growth, and movement, of urban organization, of trade and manufacture, of relations with the native populations, of cults and temples. The picture exists only in broad outlines, it is very incomplete, much is uncertain and controversial, but hardly any of it could be derived from the ancient traditions alone—or from the archaeology alone.[30] The lines of further archaeological exploration are now clear—and so are the difficulties and weaknesses in our methods of interpretation.[31]

The second example is the history of money and coinage in antiquity. Systematic study began in the eighteenth century, but it was dominated, almost monopolized, by the interests of collectors until the last few decades, and that interest still retains a strong hold. However, the function of coins, as distinct from their rarity or their aesthetics, has become an increasingly prominent subject of research, and the results have been considerable. Discussions of money and coinage are uncommon in both Greek and Roman literature; only from the coin finds can significant conclusions be drawn about the volume of minting, for example, or the circulation of coin. As a preliminary step, it was necessary to devise better techniques for dating Greek coins than the aesthetic canons that once prevailed (since the coins lack dates and, before the Hellenistic period, portraits), and this has been achieved by intensive studies of the dies. It was also necessary to appreciate that coin hoards, not excavation coins, are the fundamental source of material; that hoards must therefore be published promptly and completely; that they must be subjected to proper, and not partial, statistical analysis. Other recent advances need not be enumerated. Nor need it be argued that what we now know, or think we know, about monetary history, as about the history of colonization, rests on archaeological evidence but not on "archaeological" analysis. And the interpretation of the archaeological evidence is the point at which the dialogue between historians, numismatists, and archaeologists is still unsatisfactory.[32]

My third example is a curiosity—the perverse refusal by some distinguished experts in the history of technology to permit either the historian or his documentation to make a contribution. They prefer to write the history of technology largely, if not solely, from the artifacts, carrying Clarke's psychology to a *reductio ad absurdum,* without the saving grace of his rigorous techniques. The consequences can be exemplified by comparing the first two volumes of the much praised *A History of Technology,* edited by Charles Singer and others,[33] with the painstaking, often unrewarding, but always more fruitful and more accurate studies during the past decade or so, by scholars who combine the archaeological and documentary evidence in an investigation of agricultural technology in Gaul and other parts of the western Roman Empire.[34]

It will be apparent that much of what I have been calling an advance has been the consequence of a new focus, of new historical interests, and of new questions that the historian had not earlier put to himself, and therefore not to the archaeologists either. What do we now wish from the archaeologist, and, more narrowly, what have the new ways to offer to the ancient historian?

Immediately I must express my belief that the rapid development and application of sophisticated scientific techniques provide only a small part of the answer. Of course they have proved valuable, especially in locating the most promising places to explore. A more interesting example, providing stimulating implications, is the spectroscopic analysis which revealed that the obsidian (volcanic glass) used for tools, by 6000 B.C. at the latest, in a region extending from southern Macedonia to Crete, all came from the island of Melos, where on present evidence there was no settlement for several thousand years after the obsidian mining began.[35] Or, as an example from the historical era, it is not yet possible to determine the source of the marble used in any specific Greek statue or building. The usual, and casual, statements about marble sources in archaeological reports turn out often to have been mere guesses of no value. However, new techniques open up the possibility in the future of answering a complex of questions of the highest interest for social and economic history—questions such as: How much weight was given to costs, especially transport costs, in the decision to select one marble rather than another for any given temple, as against other considerations, political, technological (the preference of the architect and the masons), or aesthetic? Until now the information has been so lacking that it has been pointless to tackle such a question (and indeed no adequate study of quarries in antiquity has ever been undertaken). Now the possibility exists, but its realization will require laborious examination on a large scale of widely scattered artifacts and of marble outcroppings.[36]

A note of caution about carbon-14 dating is also necessary here. It is a familiar complaint of prehistorians that classical archaeologists do not make proper use of this most widely known of all the new scientific techniques—an unjustified complaint. In the first place, the accumulated experience with carbon-14 dating has revealed more eccentricities and complexities in the method than had originally been suspected. "The archaeologist," Clarke warns us, "can rarely, if ever, date excavated strata and their assemblages to precise points in time—all archaeological dates are relative, even the so-called absolute isotope decay datings."[37] Furthermore, relative dates, or dates ±50 or 100 years, are virtually useless for the late Bronze Age, let alone the historical age. They will not help resolve such current controversies as the date of the destruction of Cnossus, the connection between the volcanic explosion at Santorini and the destruction of sites in eastern Crete, the dates of the earliest Greek colonies in southern Italy and Sicily.

In the end, what ancient historians now require of archaeologists is something much simpler, much more primitive—a willingness to devote themselves to precisely formulated historical questions and a far greater consciousness of the value of statistics, for which pencil and paper and elementary numeracy are on the whole sufficient, though a simple computer would do no harm. Rostovtzeff made the point directly a generation ago. In discussing the extraordinary position of Hellenistic Rhodes as the greatest entrepot and financial center, and perhaps the wealthiest city, of the Mediterranean world, he wrote:

We have only slight knowledge regarding the volume and the character of the Rhodian transit trade. I have discussed the evidence which refers to it above and I have mentioned the stamped jar-handles of Rhodes and Cnidus, and the problems connected with them. One of the most important of these problems is that of their respective dates. *A full catalogue of Rhodian stamps will certainly help us to establish their chronology.* Some progress has been made in this direction. We are able to date a considerable group of stamps found at Pergamon (220 to 180). Another group of stamps found at Carthage is certainly earlier than the year of the destruction of the city. Thus we have some indications with regard to those stamps which belong to the period between 220 and 146 B.C. . . . *We require comparative statistics* of the various stamps for each place where Rhodian stamps have been found in order to determine whether modern scholars are right in assuming that the Rhodian stamps of the period 220 to 146 are the most common stamps in all the centers of Rhodian commercial activity. *As things stand, we must confine ourselves to some very general statements* [my italics].[38]

That was published in 1941. We still await the full catalogue and the comparative statistics, and we are still confined to very general statements.[39] The reluctance of archaeologists to embark on such projects (comparable to the analysis of marbles I have already mentioned) deserves sympathetic understanding. Archaeology is an expensive activity; patrons are chiefly attracted by the prospect of museum pieces, or of a public sensation. Presumably that is the psychological explanation of the fact that complete catalogues and comparative statistics are becoming increasingly common for coins, geometric pottery, archaic Greek sculpture, and the like, whereas Gjerstad's catalogue of the archaeology of early Rome remains an exception, the catalogue of Rhodian jar-stamps still a desideratum. Yet it is an explanation the historian cannot accept—and he is not by profession competent to do the work himself.[40] Nor is it the whole explanation. A few years ago Snodgrass collected all the identifiable remains of cutting tools and weapons found in mainland Greece (excluding Macedonia) that could be dated in the period ca. 1050-900 B.C. His tabulation of these finds follows:[41]

	Bronze	*Iron*
Swords	1	20+
Spearheads	8	30+
Daggers	2	8
Knives	0	15+
Axe-heads	0	4

No sensation there, yet this simple table answers a question that had not been posed in quite that way before, while vague statements were based on the Homeric poems and guesswork: How rapid was the shift from bronze to iron, not "in general," but in the decisive weapons and implements? Once the chronological question was formulated that way, the only correct way, no alternative remained, if one wished an answer, to the *total* collection and tabulation of the evidence.

That illustration—and I hasten to add that there are others—explains why I rank an interest in precise historical questions on a par with numeracy and closer attention to statistics in stating what I consider to be the urgent requirement in the immediate future. My own experience suggests that Snodgrass' task was exacerbated by the poor state of the archaeology and the archaeological reporting with respect to graves and grave-goods. I have twice in recent years tried to use such evidence, first for the complicated and ill-understood linguistic situation in Roman Sicily, then for the history of military grave-goods in Greece during the late Bronze Age and the subsequent "Dark Age." Both times I was reduced to impressionistic remarks and to complaints, much like those of Rostovtzeff about the Rhodian jar-stamps. In too few cemeteries have both the excavation and the subsequent publication been systematic and complete.[42] Worse still, it would require a large research project on its own merely to collect the bibliography. Whereas the historian of Anglo-Saxon England has Audrey Meaney's *Gazetteer of Early Anglo-Saxon Burial Sites*,[43] I know of no comparable guide to any district of Greece or any province of the Roman Empire.[44]

We have thus come full circle to Ucko and the Mother Goddess. To multiply examples further would be pointless.[45] But it is necessary to look at the other side, at the historian's needs from the viewpoint of the archaeologist.[46] One common objection can be dismissed out of hand: classification and chronology are still uncertain, it is argued, and until they are fixed more firmly, historical questions must wait. That is nothing but Cornford's Principle of Unripe Time. More serious is the plea that archaeologists are already overworked, that there is so much excavation still to be done, that publication would be even further delayed. There is no answer to that, only a choice of values. Of what use, I should reply, is the vast outpouring of annual reports on the year's work from which nothing emerges except the occasional isolated fact, often canceled or corrected in the next year's work or the third or the fourth year's? Of what use are more and more excavations when so many older ones have not been fully reported, and no small number have not been published at all? And, finally, of what use is archaeology anyway, apart from the museum pieces that sometimes come out of the debris, if it leads to nothing more than reports?

One solution that is being mooted to the genuine difficulty created by overwork, insufficient manpower, and insufficient funds is the employment of good sampling techniques. I must demur. No sampling technique is "good" except in terms of a predetermined range of questions. It would be a bold archaeologist who believed he could anticipate the questions another archaeologist or a historian might ask a decade or a generation later, as the result of new interests or new results from older researches. Computer experience has produced examples enough of the unfortunate consequences, in just this respect, of insufficient anticipation of the possibilities at the coding stage. A similar failure in archaeology is more harmful, because it is in the nature of archaeological excavation literally to destroy—to destroy forever—whatever is dug up and neither fully recorded nor preserved.[47]

There is of course the crushing retort: *tu quoque*. That I accept, as I have already indicated. Ancient historians are also too often satisfied with impressions, too often nonnumerate and nonquantitative, too often imprecise in the questions they put to themselves, about documentary as about archaeological evidence.[48]

III

The Greek city of Akragas (modern Agrigento) in Sicily was famed for its wealth and its conspicuous consumption in the fifth century B.C. The visible symbol that still survives is the number and quality of its stone temples, perhaps ten of which were constructed in that one century. Ten is an extraordinary number and there are interesting social problems to be studied. But what is a fair standard for temple construction in this period? To answer that question today would involve one in a massive research operation, for the reasons I have already given—the absence of gazetters, and, as I discovered when I looked at the question, of easily available summary statistics even for such major cities as Corinth or Miletus. In the absence of literary or epigraphical documentation, only archaeology can provide the figures (with an admitted margin of error), and the archaeologists have not done so. Temples are not paltry grave-goods; they are central to Greek art history and the volume of publications on the subject grows annually, but always by example alone.

I have introduced this illustration in closing not just to introduce one more complaint, but to pile a second paradox onto my earlier paradoxical half-truth. If it is often the case that the usefulness of archaeology to history increases with an increase in documentation, it is also the case that certain kinds of documentation render archaeology more or less unnecessary. If one posed the Akragas question for the Middle Ages, one would find the answer in papal and diocesan records. And one final example. By an ingenious calculation, based wholly on the results of stylistic analysis of remains, R. M. Cook recently arrived at a reasonable estimate of the number of men engaged in the Athenian fine pottery industry in the fifth century B.C.[49] That was an important contribution to economic history. The same question about the English potteries in 1800 would be answered with far greater precision, and with a breakdown by skills and functions which remains out of reach for Athens, simply by going to the pottery archives. It is hardly surprising, therefore, that the relatively new field of industrial archaeology remains a backwater. I should be much more surprised if it ever turns out to be more than that.

REFERENCES

1. Reprinted in A. Momigliano, *Studies in Historiography* (London: Weidenfeld and Nicolson, 1966), p. 91.

2. Throughout this discussion I mean by "archaeological evidence" only artifacts and I exclude documents—papyri, stone or coin inscriptions, leather scrolls—that excavations produce.

3. L. R. and S. R. Binford, *New Perspectives in Archaeology* (Chicago: Aldine, 1968).

4. Stuart Piggott, *Ancient Europe* (Edinburgh: University Press, 1965), pp. 4-5.

5. Jacquetta Hawkes, *Dawn of the Gods* (London: Chatto and Windus, 1968), p. 6.

6. It is perhaps worth noting that Miss Hawkes is one of the most energetic defenders of the romance of archaeology against hard doctrine and the rapidly increasing employment of a battery of scientific tests; see her article, "The Proper Study of Mankind," *Antiquity*, 42 (1968), 255-262. But she is by no means the only one: see, for example, the regret expressed by R. Wauchope, in his introduction to *They Found the Buried Cities* (Chicago: University of Chicago Press, 1965), that "in their published reports, few archaeologists reveal their hardships and adventures, or even their thoughts and emotions."

7. P. J. Ucko, *Anthropomorphic Figurines of Predynastic Egypt and Neolithic Crete* . . . (London: Szmidla, 1968), part II.

8. D. L. Clarke, *Analytical Archaeology* (London: Methuen, 1968), p. 17.

9. This point was made by C. Renfrew in opening his review of Ucko's book in *Man*, 4 (1969), 297-298.

10. *Ibid.*

11. "The Interpretation of Prehistoric Anthropomorphic Figurines," *Journal of the Royal Anthropological Institute*, 92 (1962), 38-54.

12. Binford and Binford, *New Perspectives in Archaeology*, pp. 21-22.

13. A comparable argument, based on Bronislaw Malinowski's Trobriand material, will be found in M. A. Smith, "The Limitation of Inference in Archaeology," *Archaeological News Letter*, 6 (1955), 3-7, the most commonly cited statement of what I have been calling the pessimistic position.

14. Clarke, *Analytical Archaeology*, pp. 11, xiii, 3; cf. A. C. Spaulding in Binford and Binford, *New Perspectives in Archaeology*, p. 33: My "argument turns on (1) the abandonment in effect by both groups [archaeologists and social anthropologists] of the notion of historical explanation as a valid category of intellectual activity and, with even more force, of scientific activity."

15. Clarke, *Analytical Archaeology*, p. 13.

16. *Ibid.*, p. 22.

17. *Ibid.*, pp. 21-22.

18. *Ibid.*, p. 13.

19. See B. G. Trigger, "Major Concepts of Archaeology in Historical Perspective," *Man*, 3 (1968), 527-541. This article and the books by Clarke and Binford and Binford provide full bibliographies on the new perspectives.

20. Clarke, *Analytical Archaeology*, pp. 112-113.

21. The Minoan bull-cult desperately needs the same sort of scrutiny Ucko gave to the Mother Goddess.

22. Clarke, *Analytical Archaeology*, p. 392.

23. *Ibid.*, pp. 618-624. The original study is G. A. Fedorov-Davydov, "On Dating Types of Artefacts from Burial Assemblages," *Sovetskaia Arkheologia*, no. 3 (1965), 50-65, reprinted in English in *Soviet Anthropology and Archaeology*, 5, no. 2 (1966), 22-33.

24. Anyone who believes that it may be easy to draw safe inferences from certain types of objects, at least, will profit from reading P. J. Ucko, "Penis Sheaths: A Comparative Study," in *Proceedings of the Royal Anthropological Institute of Great Britain and Ireland for 1969*, pp. 27-67.

25. A new translation, of the 5th edition, is now in press.

26. See, for example, M. I. Finley and others, "The Trojan War," *Journal of Hellenic Studies*, 84 (1964), 1-20.

27. See E. H. Warmington, ed., *Remains of Old Latin*, III-IV, in the Loeb Classical Library, Harvard University Press.

28. Four volumes of E. Gjerstad's projected six on *Early Rome* have been published so far.

29. See A. Momigliano, *Terzo Contributo alla storia degli studi classici e del mondo antico*, 2 vols. (Rome, 1966), part III, and *Quarto Contributo* . . . (1969), part III; E. Gjerstad, "Discussions Concerning Early Rome," *Historia*, 16 (1967), 257-278.

30. It is fitting that the best general account has been written by an archaeologist: John Boardman, *The Greeks Overseas* (Baltimore: Penguin Books, 1964), a revised edition of which is now in preparation.

31. Attention should be directed to the promising new inquiry now under way, based on the distribution in southern Italy and Sicily of imported Athenian pottery; see the brief report by G. Vallet, with discussion, in *La circolazione della moneta ateniese in Sicilia e in Magna Grecia* (published as a supplement to vols. 12-14 of the *Annali* of the Istituto italiano di numismatica, 1969), pp. 225-237.

32. See my report on classical Greece in *Trade and Politics in the Ancient World*, vol. I of the proceedings of the Second International Conference of Economic History, Aix-en-Provence, 1962 (Paris and The Hague, 1965), pp. 11-35.

33. Charles Singer and others, *A History of Technology* (Oxford: Clarendon Press, 1954-1958). I wrote a harsh review of vol. II in the *Economic History Review*, 2d ser., 12 (1959), 120-125, and I have no reason to retreat in any way. Indeed, my objections are strengthened by the pernicious influence this work continues to exercise; the very recent *Technology in the Ancient World* (London: Allen Lane Penguin, 1970), a popular introduction by an acknowledged expert, H. Hodges, for which the "two main sources" are the Singer volumes and R. J. Forbes's multi-volume *Studies in Ancient Technology* (Leiden: Brill, 1955———), reveals little interest in nonarchaeological evidence, and, it appears from the text, little acquaintance. Forbes, I hasten to add, does not belong to this school of thought.

34. See M. Renard, *Technique et agriculture en pays trévire et rémois* (Brussels: Latomus, 1959); J. Kolendo, "La moissoneuse antique en Gaule romaine," *Annales: économies, sociétés, civilisations* (1960), pp. 1099-1114, and *Postep techniczny a problem sily roboczej w rolnictwie starozytnej Italii* (Polish Academy of Sciences, 1968), with French summary (pp. 184-187 and in *Acta Poloniae Historica*, 18 [1968], 51-62); K. D. White, *Agricultural Implements of the Roman World* (Cambridge, Eng.: University Press, 1967).

35. C. Renfrew and others, "Obsidian in the Aegean," *Annual of the British School at Athens*, 60 (1965), 225-247.

36. See C. Renfrew and J. S. Peacey, "Aegean Marble: A Petrological Study,"

Annual of the British School at Athens, 63 (1968), 45-66. One instance of how historical conclusions were drawn from a false guess about the provenience of a marble slab on which a decree had been inscribed is fully discussed by A. Georgiadès and W. K. Pritchett, "The Koan Fragment of the Monetary Decree," *Bulletin de correspondence hellénique,* 89 (1965), 400-440.

37. Clarke, *Analytical Archaeology,* p. 45.

38. Mikhail Rostovtzeff, *The Social and Economic History of the Hellenistic World,* 3 vols. (Oxford: Clarendon Press, 1941), pp. 775-776.

39. It is only fair to add that the Rhodian catalogue may at last be in sight, thanks to the sustained efforts of Miss Virginia Grace.

40. See P. Courbin in the introduction to a volume he edited, *Etudes archéologiques* (Paris: S.E.V.P.E.N., 1963), pp. 14-16.

41. A. M. Snodgrass, "Barbarian Europe and Early Iron Age Greece," *Proceedings of the Prehistoric Society,* 31 (1965), 229-240.

42. The situation emerges clearly from M. Andronikos' fascicle, *Totenkult,* in *Archaeologia Homerica* (Göttingen: Vandenhoeck, 1968). Whereas his section on inhumation and cremation (pp. 51-76) permits a number of meaningful diachronic tabulations and formulations (though he has not made them himself, preferring the less revealing technique of continuous prose), the much briefer section on grave-goods (pp. 97-102) hardly advances our knowledge.

43. Audrey Meaney, *Gazetteer of Early Anglo-Saxon Burial Sites* (London: Allen and Unwin, 1964).

44. For the Bronze Age an important start has finally been made by the work of W. A. McDonald and R. Hope Simpson in cataloguing sites in the Peloponnese; see *American Journal of Archaeology,* 68 (1964), 229-245.

45. See the details, chiefly for classical Greece, in S. C. Humphreys, "Archaeology and the Social and Economic History of Classical Greece," *La Parola del Passato,* fasc. 116 (1967), 374-400.

46. These are not hypothetical objections; see *ibid.,* pp. 398-400.

47. See Courbin, *Etudes archéologiques,* p. 15: "Working conditions [in archaeology] have very often destroyed the answers before the questions could be posed . . . Why be surprised, under these conditions, that so many excavations turn out to be virtually useless for anything that is not art history?"

48. See my Aix report, cited in note 32 above.

49. "Die Bedeutung der bemalten Keramik für den griechischen Handel," *Jahrbuch des deutschen archäologischen Instituts,* 74 (1959), 114-123.

PIERRE GOUBERT

Local History

WE SHALL call local history that which concerns a village or a few villages, a small or middle-sized town (a large harbor or a capital is beyond the local scope), or a geographical area not greater than the common provincial unit (such as an English county, an Italian *contado*, a German *Land*, a French *bailiwick* or *pays*). Local history, which was practiced long ago with carefulness, zeal, and even pride, was later despised (especially in the nineteenth and the first half of the twentieth centuries) by the supporters of general history. But, since the middle of this century, local history has risen again and acquired new meaning; indeed, some even maintain that only local history can be true and sound.

For a long period—at least until the time when ideas circulated faster (in the eighteenth century) and when men began to move frequently and quickly (during the revolution of the railways in the nineteenth century)—the setting of most Europeans was the parish in the country or the small town and the surrounding district—that is, roughly speaking, the stretch of land covered in a day's walk, from ten kilometers to ten miles, or in a day's ride, about two or three times more. The same laws (local custom) prevailed in this place, as well as the same cultural habits (methods of cultivating the soil, quality of crops, shapes of tools, date of opening for meadows and woods), the same social and economic habits (date of hiring servants, date of weekly markets and quarterly and yearly fairs), the same seignorial rules, the same judicial and administrative area, and the same religious beliefs. Most people never went beyond the boundaries of their districts; their children remained there; a priest, a judge, a seigneur, a notary, and a market were within reach. The cultured part of the population moved about easily: prospective lawyers would take some of their degrees in

300

the neighboring universities, future priests went to diocesan semi-naries when they existed, nobles, when they did not travel far away because of a war, went to their parents' or their suzerains' castles situated outside the bailiwick, or sometimes outside the province itself. There were also vagrants and beggars, of course. But all of them felt they were first of all citizens of their native towns and provinces—from Dijon and Burgundy, from Amiens and Picardy, from Nimes and Languedoc, from Aix and Provence, from Saint-Brieuc and Brittany—and secondly they were French, though they always acknowledged themselves as the king's faithful and obedient subjects. Only small segments of society—the highest stratum and the lowest—could have felt no association with a particular region or place. The great financiers and captains, as well as the gangs of beggars along highways, were not purposely adrift from their homes; all of them knew (especially when the police questioned the beggars) what province, diocese, and parish they came from.

In such a confined life, the intellectual activities of the small minority dealt with either meditations on ancient texts, especially Roman and Greek, or with the history of the region, the region being understood as the land of the family. When they tried to produce histories—as histories were written before Voltaire's *Essai sur les Moeurs*—antiquities, particularities, and the famous exploits of the city or province were emphasized. By the end of the sixteenth century, provincial histories—which were merely lists of noble fami-lies, castles, fiefs, abbeys, and cathedral chapters—or histories of towns and cities—which were enumerations of charters, privileges, famous people, and gossip about the writer's native town—were commonplace. Later, the strongest institutions in the provinces (the Estates, the *parlements*), because of their corporate feelings, and as a way of protecting their interests, published their histories. Monks dedicated to research (for example, the Benedictines) often decided to gather and publish a corpus of documents regarding their own provinces; and such work was frequently carefully done.[1] These generally contained legislative or administrative acts, the founding charters, feudal documents, and other evidences concern-ing the great noble families, the pious priests, and abbots who had been influential. They were sometimes apologies, nearly hagiog-raphies. But they cannot be dismissed, even today. They often re-fer to the text of lost documents and give the only extant version of them.

The nineteenth century, at least in France, was the golden age

of local history. Following and enlarging upon the example given
by provincial academies in the second half of the eighteenth century, many "societies" that called themselves "scholarly" or learned
(and occasionally were so) appeared on the scene, existing sometimes for only a few years. Their members were typical elements
of bourgeois society: magistrates, notaries, priests, spinsters, *rentiers,*
a few teachers, minor nobility. Among thousands of papers and
hundreds of volumes issued in France from the middle of the
nineteenth century, a tenth is perhaps worth glancing through, a
hundredth worth keeping.[2] This "petit bourgeois" social science
would profit from serious sociological and psychological analysis.
The weakness of many of these pseudohistorical works partly explains the contempt with which professional historians of the early
twentieth century regarded local history—a jumble of chance
genealogies, usurped glories, proofless assertions.

Professional historians disdained such local history also because of their own conception of what they chose to see as "general" history. General history was political, military, diplomatic,
administrative, and ecclesiastical. Studying the state involved a
study of statesmen; studying war permitted a study of the military
feats of generals; studying foreign relations involved the publication of ambassadors' memoirs; studying religion led to a recounting
of the achievements of popes and bishops, generally holy and
pious; studying administrative history (written from the records of
offices located in Paris) was represented as being the history of a
whole people. A retrospective psychoanalysis of the historians of
the nineteenth century would probably reveal that many of the
historians who chose to write about monarchy more or less identified themselves with the monarch, that the historian of a particular
minister sometimes imagined he was himself governing the country.
An elementary Freudian interpretation could explain many of the
curious histories that were published.

Yet, the first serious attempts at local history were made by
historians and intellectuals who rank with the best. They understood that a thesis or interpretation, however ingenious, needs to
be supported by precise facts; precise facts have a space as well
as a time dimension. Thus, Sébastien Vauban, pleading for fiscal
reform, used the precise examples of the Vézelay election, his
native *pays,* and Normandy, where he had often been.[3] Thus
Messance, a demographer,[4] rightly opposing the thesis of French
depopulation so brilliantly advanced by intellectuals as famous

though unqualified as demographers as Montesquieu and Voltaire, proved with a strictly regional analysis of numerous parishes in the Lyonnais, Auvergne, and Upper Normandy that the French population had risen markedly between the end of the seventeenth century and the end of the eighteenth. Alexis de Tocqueville, with his great design, which was to understand at the same time the dying Ancien Régime and the French Revolution, used the provincial record offices, particularly in Tours, and illustrated with actual examples the accomplishments of the states of Languedoc.[5] But can a historical form depend upon the work of men of genius?

Alphonse Feillet's technique was more common and more commonly used. Feillet, an often-neglected historian of the misery in France at the time of the Fronde,[6] was a contemporary of Napoléon III. He believed that the French people did not sufficiently know the misdoings of "legitimate" Bourbon monarchies. To support his rather simple thesis, having to do with the misery of the French before, during, and after the Fronde, Feillet used memoirs, letters, monographs, and essays published in large numbers in the nineteenth century: one could always find a French village where somebody was dying of the plague or malnutrition, or where soldiers' violence had created massive disorder in every month between 1640 and 1660. A careful reading of the same documents by a historian who wished to prove the opposite would certainly have been equally compelling. It is quite possible to prove that France was flourishing or that it was miserable during Louis XIII's reign: one needs only to choose one's evidence carefully in the sea of published local histories.

The Feillet method (though Feillet never thought of founding a method; this was still a time when few laid claim to being concerned with methodology) has in fact become very widely used. Any thesis, if it is brilliant, unexpected, or paradoxical, may be supported by selected examples chosen from old scholarly studies of different provinces. History becomes a game where the guiltless amateurs of local history provide others with materials they find useful.

Only in the last twenty years has a new kind of local history become possible. The return to the unexploited archives of a given region and a given period was brought back into fashion by historians who generally were not born in the region studied and were not therefore expressing filial piety. This new trend derived from dissatisfaction with current historical methods, and a concern to establish new kinds of historical questions. Historians of the preceding generation were overwhelmingly preoccupied with the problems of the upper classes. To use French examples, it would be correct to say that the old school was interested in lawmakers and not in law enforcement, in those who governed and not in the governed, in the clergy and not in the faithful, in the memoirs of men of letters describing their countries and not in the realities of the country itself. The return to local history proceeds from a new interest in social history—that is, the history of a whole society, not only the happy few who governed it, judged it, ground it down, or taught it—the history of groups of men, sometimes called orders, classes, *états*, who lived together. This was history as keenly interested in the bodies and minds of the many as in the world-wide plans or profound thoughts of the few; as concerned with the history of bread, oil, and wine as with the history of corporate statutes and military rules. But a history that undertakes all aspects of human life in all classes of men meets first a major obstacle: numbers.

It is not too difficult to study thirty French intendants or twenty ambassadors; trying to study the hundreds of thousands of townsmen and millions of countrymen in all aspects of their lives presents insuperable difficulties. Historians concerned with such matters do not complain of the lack of documents but of their number. Lacking any adequate sampling techniques, and given the state of the archives, historians tried to limit their difficulties by restricting their gaze to a particular geographic region whose records were well gathered and could be analyzed by one man working alone. Lucien Febvre, as early as 1911, did this for the Franche-Comté; Gaston Roupnel did the same ten years later for the Dijon region.[7] These early works went unnoticed, probably because they were too strictly regional. In the French universities of that time (and even of the years following), such history was thought too limited. But these pioneers soon had followers, and they were soon joined by others, so many others that a sort of overproduction of regional history, at least in France, is a real threat today.

Why were these regional monographs important? They established certain proofs, limited in some instances, but proofs nonetheless; their statistics, compiled with a safety-margin, challenged some of the "general" ideas, prejudices, and approximations that had held sway in the absence of more precise investigation.

A few examples may serve to suggest what has been achieved.

It had been common for a long time (and it is still too often common) to oppose unconditionally the nobility of the "sword" to the nobility of the "robe," that is to say, a hereditary nobility to a nobility conferred by appointment to certain important judicial functions. The judges of the French *parlements* were sometimes characterized as bourgeois. The careful thesis of Jean Meyer on the Breton nobility in the eighteenth century[8] proved irrefutably that there was not a single bourgeois and very few former bourgeois in the *Parlement* of Brittany, and that the difference between nobility of the sword and nobility of the robe was nonexistent. The members of the Breton *Parlement* were the descendants of the oldest noble families that had dispensed justice in their province. Obviously, what holds for Brittany may not be equally true of other provinces; the historian's task is to make as painstaking a study of the membership of these other French provincial *parlements* as has been made in Brittany.

To take a very different example, the growth of the seignorial system (which the Marxists call feudal) in France seemed to be quite common; an edict by Louis XIV was sometimes cited to show how the last allodial tenures fared under that king. R. Boutruche, in his study on allodial tenure in the Bordeaux region, has drawn our attention to the fact that completely free lands and peasants sometimes survived the Middle Ages.[9] In his book on the Lower Auvergne, Abel Poitrineau shows, on the basis of notarial documents, that the proportion of allodial tenures sometimes approached 50 per cent in many rural communities of eighteenth-century Auvergne.[10] This phenomenon will probably be found to have been common in other parts of the country as well (mainly in central, eastern, and southern France). The result of these many researches is the inescapable (but unanticipated) conclusion that a part of France during the Ancien Régime (and, by definition, the Middle Ages as well) did not undergo the seignorial system.

It was known that certain feudal customs such as *mortmain* had survived in remote parts of eastern France. Voltaire once spoke of the "serfs du Mont Jura"; the king in the eighteenth century liberated the last serfs who lived on the lands of which he was seigneur. New researches by Abel Poitrineau and Pierre de Saint-Jacob suggest that important groups of peasants subject to *mortmain* were to be found in central France; the study by Régine Robin on northern Burgundy (Auxois) reveals many more of them. It is possible that a fifth of the peasants of this small region lived under a system that was in fact a form of extenuated serfage.[11] Other discoveries of the same nature may be expected for eastern France. This phenomenon was neither known nor understood until minute studies carried on at the village level and seigniorial level were undertaken.

Our image of rural France in this period has been substantially altered by these new insights. Thus, for example, the penetration of Indian corn into Aquitaine in the eighteenth century (an old assertion that even Fernand Braudel thought to repeat recently) is now dated to the seventeenth century. This knowledge is based wholly on the research of young historians who took an interest in the small corn markets of southeast France.[12] The idea, often repeated, that the southern half of France used a biennial rotation system in its corn fields was blasted when a diary of the journeys made by J. F. Henry de Richeprey, an agronomist and officer of the king, was published by a regional learned society.[13] It is now known that biennial rotation was not the rule; all types of rotations were used in the south (and an even greater variety in the west).

The very different attitudes of the peasants with respect to the clergy have been explained by referring to the rate of tithe that existed in a particular region. The tithe was very low in Lower Brittany (3 per cent) and very high in the southeast (from 10 to 12.5 per cent).[14] The clericalism of one region and the anticlericalism of the other has roots that are more ancient than is sometimes realized. One could go on endlessly to indicate what the new researches, local and rural, have contributed to altering our perceptions of Europe's past. It must be said that the researches have not been only those of French historians working on French materials; mention must be made of the renewal of English, Belgian, and Dutch history as a result of the local studies undertaken by W. G. Hoskins on Leicestershire, Joseph Ruwet on the *Herve pays*, and B. Slicher van Bath on Overijssel.[15]

The careful practice of local history and the multiplication of monographs on specific regions may lead much further; they may serve to destroy many of the general conceptions that once seemed so strong and were embodied in so many books, papers, and lectures. Thus, for example, the so-called "crisis" of the seventeenth century and the so-called "agricultural revolution" of the eighteenth century are certain to be reconsidered in the light of the material now being developed.

A whole book would probably be needed to bring out the nuances of, let alone to destroy the myth of the seventeenth-century "crisis," at least in France. The word "crisis" is itself unsuitable; *crise* in French means a violent but brief phenomenon; the use of the term in this sense seems to be disappearing. In my own study of Beauvaisis, I found no justification for the idea that there was a severe crisis in the period previous to the Fronde except for the incidence of epidemics and high mortality attendant on these, common in the seventeenth century (as well as the sixteenth). Population was rising, prices were going up, though slowly, the incomes of landowners were rising, and textile production had reached new levels in Beauvais in the 1630's. It was only in the second half of the century that conditions seemed to deteriorate. It is interesting that subsequent local studies in other areas suggested other patterns. In a thorough study of the northern textile cities, particularly Amiens, Pierre Deyon showed with impressive statistics the character of industrial growth in that area; in doing so, he supported my comments about the "blissful reign" of Louis XIII. After 1660, when Colbert was minister, textile activity came to life again; the industrial "crisis" was put off, and rightly, to the last years of Louis XIV's reign.[16] In his blunt, strange, but substantial thesis, René Baehrel discarded for rural Lower Provence the conception of there having been a crisis in the seventeenth century: he advanced the idea of a general improvement in conditions interrupted by a more difficult period every thirty years.[17] E. Le Roy Ladurie, in his researches focused on the neighboring region of Provence, postponed the coming of a depression till the years following the Holland war—that is, till the 1680's. His new research, especially his methodical use of documents relating to the ecclesiastical tithe, lead him to the conclusion that prosperity continued during Colbert's age, and reached a sort of climax, with greater agricultural production in the years between 1660 and 1680. In southern France the Fronde was never important; as there were no famines in the fifties and sixties, nearly the whole of the seventeenth century—at least until 1680 or 1690—was characterized by expansion.[18] Michel Morineau discovered through his studies in the Dutch record offices and libraries that the American treasures poured more lavishly into Europe in the second half of the seventeenth century than they did in the sixteenth century, so dear to E. J. Hamilton and P. Chaunu.[19] Thus, a series of local studies has led to a serious questioning of the oft-repeated thesis about the general crisis in the seventeenth century. If it occurred, it came at the very end of the century, at least in France. The subject, obviously, is far from exhausted; new researches will perhaps bring new opinions and will revive old ones. It is quite certain, however, that without serious provincial monographs (written by professional historians and not by amateurs) a general revision of the kind suggested would not have been possible.

The "agricultural nonrevolution" associated with Michel Morineau involves a period even closer to us in time. A careful study of the accounts of ecclesiastical tithes and agricultural properties over several centuries allow Morineau to come to a striking set of conclusions: the same agricultural yields are observable in the Middle Ages, the sixteenth, eighteenth, and even nineteenth centuries where the same conditions of climate, political order, and good farming prevail; where, in some periods, outputs decline, there are always easily identifiable reasons: war, bad climatic conditions, social unrest, a closing down of markets. The eighteenth century generally combined fairly favorable conditions, but the outputs were not substantially higher than they had been; they merely reproduced the best outputs of earlier times. A young historian of Sicily, Maurice Aymard, using the same methods in a quite different place, maintains that the yields of good Sicilian corn fields are the same in the eighteenth century as in Cicero's time. An upper and unvarying limit of agricultural output would appear to have existed. No rapid growth can be observed before the nineteenth or the twentieth century. The changes that historians thought they were discovering were changes of short duration, or geographical variances between different regions.[20] Not all historians are ready to accept the rather startling theses propounded by Morineau. They try to discover other regional examples to refute him; often, they are more comparisons of the bad periods of the seventeenth century with the best periods of the eighteenth. The idea of a technological limit appropriate to most regions has certainly to be kept in mind. The slight rise and fall between a maximum and a minimum yield (the one and the other being proper to different regions) probably expresses what was true most of the time. The real agrarian revolution began to "take off" very late— nearly everywhere in the second half of the nineteenth century or even later; sometimes, even more recently.

A now very lively branch of history—historical demography— owes its development to the narrowest type of local history. This field was vegetating, with rumors and proofless theories as its staples, before historians and statisticians became interested in modest, neglected, and widespread documents: parish registers. Using parish registers from Gien (on the Loire River) and from several other places, Jean Meuvret pointed to the link between economic crises and demographic crises in northern France in the seventeenth century and to the weakening of these crises after the middle of the eighteenth. An examination of about thirty parishes in Beauvaisis was the first attempt to make a serious demographic analysis of a whole region. Louis Henry, using the register of Crulai (in Normandy), gave new impulse to the professional use of such data; soon afterwards, he laid down the well-defined rules of method (now unquestioned) that are appropriate for such study. Recognition of the value of parish documents (at a time when, in France, censuses were rare, not well known, and not easy to use) allowed studies to be made of fecundity, marriage, and infantile mortality, with a possibility of accuracy never previously attained. The growing monographic literature soon demonstrated that neither France nor Europe looked like either Crulai or Beauvaisis, but it allowed historians to raise a whole series of new questions: thus, for example, about the beginning of birth control procedures, about nursing practices, about mobility more generally. The problem of illegitimacy and sexual intercourse prior to marriage, with patterns so different as between France and England, and perhaps so typical of a kind of modern mentality,[21] could not have been examined before the arrival of good methodical censuses (1840 in France). Only the parish registers provide the key to all such problems for an earlier period; without them, such problems could not even be tackled.

The success of local and regional historical studies has been considerable in France. The reason for the success is not explicable simply in terms of the methods used. Rather, it must be seen how much of the inspiration for such study has come from the *Annales* school. That school, severely critical of traditional ideas and elitist prejudices, drew attention to new social groups and provided felicitous interdisciplinary associations between historians and scholars in economics, sociology, psychology, biology, and demography. A regeneration of historical studies, with new methods and ideas, was made possible by a new generation that had sufficient talent to make itself heard.

All success brings with it excess. As historical work in France is carried out mainly within universities, it tends to reproduce the faults of the universities. Soon, a servile imitation of innovation establishes a new tradition, or a negative and violent contestation which often ends in reinforcing the thing originally disputed. One can already foresee the birth of yet another novelty, which will owe much to contact between linguistics, psychoanalysis, and history[22] (just as soon as psychoanalysts and linguists agree to study archives, and historians agree to study linguistics and psychoanalysis). A brutal reaction, ideological and political, could also take place, throwing French historians back fifty years or more.

In the most recent period, large numbers of advanced students and young historians devoted themselves to parish monographs. For a year (for the certificate *mémoires de maîtrises*) or for several years (for the thesis of the *troisième cycle,* a kind of Ph.D.), they analyzed, using the archives, different aspects of life in one or several parishes, most frequently in the eighteenth century. That century left abundant archives, they were varied, and they were usually easy to read. The work of novices is generally worth about as much as their authors (and the professor who advised them) are worth. Most often, they simply confirmed what was already known. Some, however, did contain certain new ideas and provided unexpected information—thus, for example, on the early attitude toward birth control of the winegrowers of the Ile de France in the eighteenth century,[23] or on the composition of communities in the villages of Brie (to the east of Paris) in the same century,[24] new information has been provided. It had been thought that the communities of Brie were dominated by rich farm workers; one now finds that several were dominated by the poor, numerous *manouvriers,* who united against the rich peasants through the help of the Intendant General of Paris. Many such parish monographs are poor; they deserve to be forgotten; others are excellent.

Be that as it may, their multiplication approaches overproduction and presents at least three disadvantages. First, it is difficult to find them, read them, or make a synthesis, the more so as the majority of them are not published. Second, an advanced student or a fledgling historian is unlikely to have a sufficient competence to deal with the different elements necessary to good local analysis; law, institutions, economics, demography, sociology, religion are not subjects easily mastered. In the last analysis, there is always the danger of a return to amateurism. Third, even when the monograph is good, the description of an isolated village raises more problems than it resolves: Does the exact information provided have local, provincial, or general significance? To decide such questions, one would need to have other monographs on neighboring parishes as well. The questions and the demands are endless.

The solution, obviously, lies in a systematization of monographic study. In the demographic domain, this systematization is assured by the Société de Démographique Historique in collaboration with the Ecole Pratique des Hautes Etudes, the Institut National d'Etudes Démographiques, and a number of universities; the first two institutions assure publication of the best monographs (or, failing that, of at least a résumé of them). At Aix-en-Provence, the work of advanced students has been directed toward social analysis of the rural communities in the eighteenth century. At Caen, Pierre Chaunu follows the same systematized effort for Normandy. At the Centre de Recherches sur les Civilisations de l'Europe Moderne de Paris, Roland Mousnier has centered the work of his students around several themes: revolts of the seventeenth century, governmental staff of the Ancien Régime, Parisian society during the same period.[25] The difficulty is to achieve genuinely good collaborative publications.

Large provincial studies continue to be undertaken, and many are nearing publication. We expect studies on Anjou, Upper Normandy, the region south of Paris, Lorraine, Dauphiné, Provence, Toulouse, and Gascogne; others will follow somewhat later.[26] These major studies are the only means of verifying the validity of old ideas and propositions, or of discovering new problems and hypotheses. The new trend, in my view a good one, is to examine one or two problems in one or two regions. Thus, for example, the interesting and original work by François Lebrun on men and death in Anjou during the seventeenth and eighteenth centuries is awaited with great impatience. Two of my own best students have recently chosen to concentrate their efforts on the problem of marriage in Champagne and the problem of *metayage* in western France from the sixteenth to the nineteenth centuries. Large provincial studies, concentrating on one important problem, analyzed over a long period (a century or more)—this is perhaps the best course to take for those who wish to remain faithful to the idea of investigating local/provincial history.

I warmly thank my daughter Annie Gresle for her gentle assistance in the English language.

REFERENCES

1. For example, the lawyer Guy Coquille (1523-1603) wrote the *Histoire du pays et duché de Nivernais* (Paris: Vefue A. L.'Angelier, 1612); another lawyer, Antoine Loisel (1536-1617), wrote *Mémoire des pays, villes, comté et comtes, evesché et evesques, pairrie, commune et personnes de renom de Beauvais et de Beauvaisis* (Paris: S. Thiboust, 1617). A provincial history of the seventeenth century is *Histoire du Berry et du diocèse de Bourges* (1689). In the eighteenth century, the most famous provincial histories were: Claude Courtépée and Edmé Béguillet, *Description générale et particulière du duché de Bourgogne,* 7 vols. (Dijon, 1751-1767), and those by Benedictine historians such as Dom Vaissete (Languedoc), Dom Maurice (Bretagne), and Dom Plancher. For a general knowledge of this kind of study, see French bibliographies such as: Henri Hauser, *Les sources de l'histoire de France, XVIe siècle,* 4 vols. (Paris: A. Picard, 1906-1915); Louis André, *Les sources de l'histoire de France au XVIIe siècle,* 8 vols. (Paris: A. Picard, 1913-1935), esp. vol. 8, chap. XIV, "Histoire provinciale et locale."

2. An almost exhaustive bibliography of this literature is in Robert de Lasteyrie· and René Gandilhon, *Bibliographie générale des travaux historiques et archéologiques publiés par les sociétés savantes de la France* (Paris: Imprimerie nationale, 1944-1961).

3. Sébastien Vauban, *Projet d'une dixme royale* (Paris: F. Alcan, 1933); for the memoir on the Vézelay election, see pp. 274-295; for examples in Normandy, see pp. 39-42 (and elsewhere).

4. Messance, *Recherches sur la population des généralités d'Auvergne, de Lyon, de Rouen . . .* (Paris: Durand, 1766); Messance, *Nouvelles recherches sur la population de la France . . .* (Lyon, 1788).

5. Alexis de Tocqueville, *L'Ancien Régime et la Révolution;* see the Appendice, *Des pays d'Etats et en particulier du Languedoc,* especially the last lines.

6. Alphonse Feillet, *La misère au temps de la Fronde et Saint Vincent de Paul* (Paris: Didier, 1862).

7. Lucien Febvre, *Phillipe II et la Franche-Comté* (Paris, 1911), to be republished shortly by the Ecole Pratique des Hautes Etudes and the Maison des Sciences de l'Homme. Gaston Roupnel, *La ville et la campagne au XVIIe siècle, étude sur les populations du pays dijonnais* (1922), 2d ed. (Paris: Colin, 1955, by the Ecole Pratique des Hautes Etudes, Section VI).

8. Jean Meyer, *La noblesse bretonne au XVIIIe siècle,* 2 vols. (Paris: Imprimerie nationale, 1966).

9. Robert Boutruche, *L'alleu en Bordelais et en Bazadais du XIe au XVIIIe siècle* (Paris, 1947).

10. Abel Poitrineau, *La vie rurale en Basse-Auvergne au XVIIIe siècle, 1726-*

1789, 2 vols. (Paris: Presses universitaires de France, 1965), esp. pp. 341-344.

11. Poitrineau, *La vie rurale en Basse Auvergne;* Pierre de Saint-Jacob, *Les paysans de la Bourgogne du Nord au dernier siècle de l'Ancien Régime* (Paris, 1966), pp. 38-40; Regine Robin, *La société française en 1789, Semur-en-Auxois* (Paris, 1970), p. 120: "L'Auxois est terre de mainmorte, 20% des paroisses du bailliage sont mainmortables."

12. Fernand Braudel, *Civilisation matérielle et capitalisme,* I (Paris: Colin, 1967), 126 (Indian corn, eighteenth century); Emmanuel Le Roy Ladurie, *Les paysans de Languedoc* (Paris: Flammarion, 1969), p. 71 (Indian corn, 1637-1678); Georges and Geneviève Frêche, *Le prix des grains, des vins et des légumes à Toulouse, 1486-1868* (Paris: Presses universitaires de France, 1967), esp. pp. 20-22 ("De l'apparition du maïs dans la mercuriale," in 1639 certainly, in 1618 perhaps).

13. *Journal des voyages en Haute-Guienne de J. F. Henry de Richeprey,* in H. Guilhamon, *Archives historiques du Rouergue,* XIX (Rodez, 1952); see especially the cases of Sainte-Eulalie du Larzac, p. 140, of Compeyre, p. 168, and many others.

14. For Brittany, Henri See, *Les classes rurales en Bretagne du XVIe siècle à la Révolution* (Paris: V. Giard et E. Brière, 1906), and some studies by my former students in Rennes, unfortunately not published. For the southeast, see the excellent book by Armand Sarramon, *Les paroisses du diocèse de Comminges en 1786,* in *Collection de Documents inédits sur l'histoire économique de la Révolution Française* (Paris, 1968).

15. W. G. Hoskins, *Studies in Leicestershire Agrarian History* in *Leicestershire Archeological Society* (1949), and *Essays in Leicestershire History* (Liverpool: University Press, 1950). Joseph Ruwet, *L'agriculture et les classes rurales au pays de Herve sous l'Ancien Régime* (Liège, 1943). B. Slicher van Bath, *Een samenleving onder spanning: geschiedenis van het platteland in Overijssel* (Assen: Van Gorcum, 1957).

16. Pierre Deyon, *Amiens, capitale provinciale, étude sur la société urbaine au XVIIe siècle* (Paris and The Hague: Mouton, 1967), esp. chap XIII, and *La production manufacturière en France et ses problèmes,* in *XVIIe siècle,* no. 70-71 (1966), 47-63.

17. René Baehrel, *Une croissance, la Basse-Provence rurale, fin du XVIe siècle–1789* (Paris: S.E.V.P.E.N., 1961).

18. E. Le Roy Ladurie, *Les paysans de Languedoc;* and "Enquêtes en cours, Dîmes et produit net agricole," *Annales: économies, sociétés, civilisations,* 24 (1969), 826-832.

19. Michel Morineau, "D'Amsterdam à Séville, de quelles réalités l'histoire des prix est-elle le miroir?" *Annales: économies, sociétés, civilisations,* 23 (1968), 178-205 (see p. 196 for the figures for 1661-1700).

20. On the agricultural nonrevolution see: M. Morineau, "Y a-t-il eu une révo-

lution agricole en France au XVIIIe siècle?" *Revue historique,* 92 (1968), 299-326; Denis Richet, "Croissance et blocages en France du XVe au XVIIIe siècle," *Annales: économies, sociétés, civilisations,* 23 (1968), 759-787; E. Le Roy Ladurie, quoted above in note 18; M. Morineau, *Révolutions invisibles en France au XVIIIe siècle, agriculture et démographie,* to be published in *Cahiers des Annales* (1970 or 1971).

21. See my article "Historical Demography and the Reinterpretation of Early Modern French History: A Research Review," *Journal of Interdisciplinary History,* no. 1 (1970).

22. Robin, *La société française en 1789,* pp. 229-343, "Le vocabulaire des cahiers de doleances."

23. Michel Tyvaert and Jean-Claude Giacchetti, *Argenteuil, 1740-1790, étude de démographie historique,* in *Annales de démographie historique* (1969), pp. 40-61.

24. Maryvonne Brassens, "Recherches sur les biens communaux a l'Est de Paris," unpublished *mémoire de maîtrise,* Sorbonne, Paris, 1970.

25. See *Annales de démographie historique* (1969), pp. 11-292 (twenty monographical studies); Michel Vovelle, "Etat présent des études de structure agraire en Provence à la fin de l'Ancien Régime," *Provence historique,* no. 74 (1969), 450-484. *Annales de Normandie* and *Cahiers des Annales de Normandie* (studies directed by Pierre Chaunu). Publications of the Centre de Recherches sur les Civilisations de l'Europe Moderne, directed by Roland Mousnier; the most recent publications are Madeleine Foisil, *La révolte des Nu-Pieds et les révoltes normandes de 1639* (Paris, 1970), and Roland Mousnier and others, *Le Conseil du Roi de Louis XII-a la Révolution* (Paris, 1970).

26. To be published soon, thesis on Anjou by François Lebrun; to be published in the coming years, south Paris region by Jean Jacquart, Upper Normandy by G. Lemarchand, Lorraine by G. Cabourdin, Dauphiné by B. Bonnin, Provence by M. Vovelle and R. Pillorget, Toulouse by G. Freche, Gascogne by Anne Zink.

LAWRENCE STONE

English and United States Local History

THE HISTORIOGRAPHY of local history in England in the nineteenth century closely parallels that in France, as described by Professor Goubert. Between 1680 and 1830 there was a remarkable output of county histories, so that by the accession of Queen Victoria most counties were the subject of at least one, and often several, stately folio volumes. In the 1840's there began a rapid proliferation of county archaeological and antiquarian societies, the hobby of landed gentry and clergy with an amateurish interest in the history of their locality. The culmination of this period of activity was the *Victoria County History* which began in 1898 with the intention of providing a scholarly factual history of every parish and town in England. The limitations of this undertaking are now well known, in particular its obsession with manorial descents and the history of the Established Church, and its neglect of the dissenting churches and of the social and economic life of the community. As originally designed, it was basically a history of the upper classes written by the upper classes for the upper classes. The most extravagant example of this state of mind was the history of the Warwickshire parish which solemnly recorded the transmission of the manor from hand to hand but totally failed to mention that at a certain point the village itself was deserted and disappeared.

Between 1920 and 1940 this great enterprise ground almost to a standstill as social changes in the countryside, notably the impoverishment of the gentry and clergy, eroded the basis of its support. For similar reasons the antiquarian societies also fell on hard times, although more and more of them turned their attention to the scholarly publication of local archives. Slowly, a great corpus of printed material was built up, ready for the local historians of

315

the future. The first of the professional historians to use local history to solve national problems were the medievalists, who in the early twentieth century—even before the French had set to work—were establishing the broad outlines of land tenure and field systems in the English countryside. The turning point came, however, in the late 1940's. Local county record offices were established in almost every county, and began to gather in, sort, and catalogue the mass of public and private local archives which had hitherto been almost inaccessible to the scholar. The *Victoria County History* project took a new lease on life, more and more under the direction of professional historians, and displaying increased interest in social and economic history, education, and nonconformist sects—a shift of focus toward the masses of the poor and away from the landed elite. Soon afterwards there emerged what can best be described as the Leicester school of local history, centered around a newly created chair of local history at the University (then University College) of Leicester. The leading figures in this renaissance have been H. P. R. Finberg, W. G. Hoskins, Joan Thirsk, and Alan Everitt (all associated with Leicester) together with J. D. Chambers of Nottingham. This group seems to have owed little or nothing to the French school, although, like the French, its main interest has been in the sixteenth, seventeenth, and eighteenth centuries. This temporal concentration is largely because the source materials are rare and hard to interpret for the Middle Ages, while after 1830 local history tends to become urban history, which is something rather different. The subjects of scholarly investigation have been the traditional English ones of field systems, land tenure, landlord-tenant relationships, and agricultural improvements. This selection of problems is a sensible one, if it is agreed that what above all else distinguished England from the Continent in the early modern period was the disappearance of the peasantry, and the rise in agricultural productivity. This work has mostly been exquisitely small scale, either focusing on a single village or town, or else tackling one specific subject, such as enclosures. A good deal of the best and most important material has appeared in the form of articles rather than books.

The basis of the work has been detailed topographical studies of a microcosm, usually a village, employing a combination of historical records, personal inspection of the terrain, and the new tool of aerial photography, which English historians were among the very first to explore soon after the war. In some cases archaeological excavation has been used, especially on medieval deserted villages and more recently on town dwellings and town churches. Examples are H. P. R. Finberg's work on Anglo-Saxon boundaries, M. Beresford's studies of deserted villages, and M. Biddle's current work on medieval Winchester. From these small-scale village studies there has gradually emerged some larger regional surveys of specific problems, the most notable being the *Agrarian History of England*, currently in progress under the editorship of Dr. Joan Thirsk. Regional studies are also beginning to appear on other topics, for example nineteenth-century education, agricultural economy, and social structure by Margaret Spufford of the Leicester school.

Thus whereas the French jumped right into broad regional studies without prior attempts at detailed topographical inquiry, the English built up slowly from individual examples, and are only now beginning to synthesize their material. As a result the French were the first in the field, where they set standards of the highest quality. The main English contribution as they move to a higher level of synthesis is likely to be a greater awareness of the economic diversity of subregions and smaller districts, which tend to get lost in the broader studies of larger regions favored by the French school.

One of the more curious features of the Leicester school, which is part of both its strength and weakness, has been its provincial and rural bias, which for some of its members takes the form of an overt hostility and suspicion of London, and a nostalgia for pre-industrial, pre-urban England before the nineteenth century. This engaging romanticism is in striking contrast to the hardboiled professionalism with which the modern French historians dissect a provincial society and economy.

In addition to this Leicester school with its well-defined set of problems, the famous "gentry controversy" of the 1950's stimulated a large quantity of local studies, carried on in many different centers, concerning the fortunes of the landed classes in the sixteenth and seventeenth centuries, which were designed to apply a set of general hypotheses to a local situation and to see how they worked. In the last few years there have also appeared a number of important politico-economic studies of towns such as Exeter, Leicester, and Newcastle, particularly in the seventeenth century. It is here that some of the most promising work is likely to be done in the future, particularly since the Leicester school is now moving heavily into this area under the leadership of Professor Everitt, who is working on Northampton. What is still lacking is a full-scale socioeconomic history of London during the early modern period, without which English local history remains a torso without a head, a Hamlet without the Prince of Denmark. At this time, however, two multi-volume studies of London are in preparation, which may ultimately go far toward filling this gap.

All this is very different from the massive assaults on every aspect of a region which are the glory of the French school. One reason is that documentation is poorer in England, which lacks notarial archives, and which has always been grossly underadministered compared to France. Another is that the English local historians have been too modest to aspire to the writing of *histoire totale,* and have lacked a simple tool for historical analysis such as the *structure/conjoncture* dichotomy around which the French have organized their researches. Lastly there is nothing in the English professional career-pattern like the *grande these* which is the main stimulus to force the production of the vast French undertakings. Consequently, although the English school of local history is already a most distinguished one, especially in the field of topography and agrarian history, it has not yet produced a study on the scale of Goubert's *Beauvaisis* or Le Roy Ladurie's *Languedoc.* Nor has it yet devoted as much attention to local subcultures and mental attitudes as it has to economic organization and agricultural output.[1]

In the United States, filio-pietism in the nineteenth and early twentieth centuries along the eastern seaboard led to the publication of a remarkable quantity of local records about the old colonies and their early settlers. But not much use was made of these materials by professional historians before the 1960's, when there suddenly emerged a distinctive New England school of local history, most of whose members were students of Professor Bernard Bailyn of Harvard. This school has so far exclusively concerned itself with New England in the seventeenth and eighteenth centuries, and its focus has been the township rather than either the county or the state, or a particular problem examined on a regional scale. Like the English school, it has begun with the microcosm of the village, although it has been deeply influenced by the recent work of the French school of historical demography, and its offshoot at Cambridge (England). This group of young scholars—J. Demos, P. Greven, K. Lockridge, Chilton Powell, M. Zuckerman—have all concerned themselves with what it is that distinguished life in colonial New England from life in contemporary England. They have identified the principal variables and have set to work to elucidate the complex and changing relationships between them: these variables are the family, with the rise and fall of patriarchy; population, with the shift from scarcity to relative abundance; land, with the shift from abundance to relative scarcity; and government, with the shifting conflicts between oligarchy and democracy, centralization and the dispersion of authority. They have identified the right targets, they have developed a sound methodology, and they have made considerable headway by discovering the evidence to solve the problems they have asked themselves. One of the many tasks of the 1970's will be to extend the number of the samples, and in particular to test the hypotheses which have been formulated for New England in the very different conditions of New Jersey, Pennsylvania, Virginia, and the Carolinas; work on this is just now being undertaken by Philip Greven, Robert Wells, and James Henretta.

REFERENCES

1. In this review of the English literature I have been much assisted by the suggestions of Dr. Joan Thirsk. The value judgments, however, are my own.

STEPHAN THERNSTROM

Reflections on the New Urban History

THE BOUNDARIES of the modern metropolis are elusive. Once the city could be described as "a tightly settled and organized unit in which people, activities and riches are crowded into a very small area clearly separated from its nonurban surroundings," but no more.[1] Instead there is mixture, coalescence, "urban sprawl," which has blurred or erased delineations which earlier seemed meaningful.

The boundaries of the field of urban history today seem equally elusive. The label "urban" is now coming into fashion in history, as in some other disciplines. Courses in the subject have multiplied; texts and readers are being rushed into print; there are urban history newsletters published in both the United States and Britain, and an enormous, monographic literature that professes to be urban history or at least is so considered by some observers. What unites this large and disparate body of work, however, is unclear. Urban history apparently deals with cities, or with city-dwellers, or with events that transpired in cities, or with attitudes toward cities— which makes one wonder what is *not* urban history.

Nearly a decade ago Eric Lampard attempted to bring some order into the chaos by offering a penetrating critique of the existing literature and a series of suggestions for the systematic historical study not of "the city" but of "urbanization as a societal process."[2] Drawing upon recent advances in demography and human ecology, as well as upon his training in economic history, he sketched "a framework for the comparative study of the development and organization of interdependent communities in terms that embrace both westward and urban movements of population, changes in the spatial, occupational and social structures of population, and of sustenance activities." Urban history in this view was not a distinct field but a part of social history; Lampard at one point

320

declared that his aim was to provide "a more certain and systematic foundation for the writing of American social history."

At first it seemed that this advice had fallen upon deaf ears. A discussion of Lampard's manifesto was held at the 1961 American Historical Association meetings; the questioning of the author, according to one observer, "revealed limited understanding of his position and less sympathy for it."[3] Even today we lack much in the way of research that seems to be a direct outcome of Lampard's plea. The broad framework he proposed has not yet been the source of a major book on "urbanization as a societal process."

Lampard's insistence on the relevance of demographic and ecological perspectives, however, prefigured a development that took place in the United States in the 1960's—the emergence of an intellectual tendency that I have called, for want of a better term, "the new urban history."[4]

The label "the new urban history" may have been somewhat misleading in three respects. First, the image it conveyed of a monolithic "old" history was obviously oversimplified. Earlier work by a number of well-established scholars pointed in the direction in which the new urban historians were to move; Oscar Handlin's studies of immigration and assimilation, for instance, were important models.

It did, however, seem that most historical writing about cities and city-dwellers was deficient, not only because it lacked the breadth and analytical rigor which Lampard called for but because it dealt with only a small segment of the population—the visible, articulate elements of the community rather than the masses of ordinary people. The existing literature was based largely upon traditional literary sources, sources which were socially skewed. They revealed relatively little of the social experience of ordinary people, and when they did treat ordinary people they spoke with the accent of a particular class, and too often indicated more about the perceptions of that class than about life at the lower rungs of the social ladder.

This complaint, and consequent appeals for a new "grassroots" history, a history "from the bottom up," had often been heard before.[5] What was somewhat new in this instance was the awareness of readily available and largely unexploited historical sources which could be used for these purposes. The discovery of the parish register as a source of demographic information permitted and stimulated the rich outpouring of work in English and French historical

STEPHAN THERNSTROM

demography in recent years; in similar fashion, the discovery of surviving manuscript schedules of the United States Census, and then of a host of similar materials—city directories, local tax lists, and so forth—provided the base for the new urban history in the United States.

Not that these sources were entirely unknown to previous investigators, any more than the English and French parish registers were.[6] The problem was how to use them to full advantage. The sheer quantity and complexity of the information they contained was bewildering; simply reading the material and turning it over in one's mind would not do at all. It was this pressing need, I think, more than any prior conviction about the desirability of importing the methods of other social sciences into history that made us look to other disciplines for useful concepts, analytical techniques, and data-processing methods. The desire to explore new territory forced the selective borrowing of new methods; we did not make forays across disciplinary boundaries for the sheer joy of seeing what was on the other side.

A second possibly misleading feature of the phrase, "the new urban history," lies with the term "urban," which seems to imply that this is a distinctive specialized field of historical inquiry. I am doubtful about that. The city is a distinctive legal entity, and there are certain phenomena peculiar to it. But the decisive features of urban life in modern times are not spatially distributed in a way that justifies urban history, or for that matter urban sociology, as a special field.[7] The delineation of fields is, of course, largely a matter of convenience, and I do not call for a moratorium on the use of "urban" in course descriptions and the like. It is important, however, to recognize that most of the subjects that have preoccupied the new urban historians—the flow of population from country to city, patterns of social stratification and social mobility, the social consequences of technological change, the distribution of property and power, the position of ethnic and racial groups, and so on—are not confined to the city, and should not be approached as if they were. They involve the workings of the society as a whole, though of course they have different manifestations in communities of varying sizes and types. It is not paradoxical, therefore, that the volume which in a sense marked the beginning of the new urban history— Merle Curti's 1959 study, *The Making of an American Community* —dealt not with a city at all, but with a rural county in Wisconsin.[8] The modern city is so intimately linked to the society around it, and is so important a part of the entire social order that few of its aspects can safely be examined in isolation. The term "urban" in the label "the new urban history" is thus not to be taken as a disavowal of interest in what happens outside cities, nor as a claim that here is a new historical field with a turf of its own from which trespassers should be warned. The ultimate aim of the new urban historian, in my view at least, is to understand how and why the complex of changes suggested by the concept "urbanization" reshaped society. Urban history, in this formulation, lies squarely within the domain of social history, and for the student of modern society it is indeed nearly coterminous with social history.

A final comment on the label "the new urban history" is that although it consciously echoes "the new economic history," the analogy should not be pressed too far. Quantitative evidence plays a greater role in both types of literature than in their traditional counterparts. In both there is less sheer description, and more use of theory. But the differences are important.

The new economic historians are equipped with a theory that purports to represent the workings of a total system and which can be employed to resolve questions about the past as well as the present. The relationship of the new urban historians to theory is quite different. There can be debate over the applicability of modern economic theory to particular historical problems, but there is little question that it is a very powerful tool for dealing with certain kinds of issues. A comparably powerful general social theory which bears upon the matters of prime concern to the urban historian simply does not exist as yet.

There is some reason, indeed, to doubt that it ever will, given the nature of human society. This is not the place to argue the case at length, but there are good grounds for denying the relevance of the universalist model of explanation to historical analysis, and for believing that it is more profitable to strive for theoretical generalizations of a more modest scope, limited in space and time, restricted to certain contexts.[9] I would be the last to argue that it is the business of the historian to concentrate on the ineffable uniqueness of his subject and to refrain from generalization at all. The historian, I think, should generalize as widely as he can, and should strive to "make his conceptualization more explicit, his use of theory more deliberate, his effort to derive further hypotheses for testing bolder and more systematic."[10] But when the desire to abstract, schematize, and universalize leads to the neglect of *essential* features of the historical context, as can be said about a number of efforts to apply imported social science theories to historical problems, we have not advanced knowledge. One principal function of historical research informed by social science concerns is precisely to edit, refine, and enrich theory by identifying and exploring important historical developments which cannot be neatly explained by existing theory.

The relationship of the new urban historian to social science theory, therefore, is critical and eclectic. Instead of applying *a* theory, like the new economic historian, he must draw upon a variety of social sciences, as well as his own historical sense, to identify elements of the historical situation that may have been important and to gain clues as to how these might be measured and analyzed. Perhaps it will some day be possible to develop a model of the process of urbanization which applies equally well to ancient Athens and contemporary Chicago, though I doubt it, but it seems in any event clear that to search for such regularities today, given both the state of existing social science theory and the level of present understanding of the social systems of those two communities, would be unrewarding.

For the present, high priority must go to the careful description and analysis of particular communities and the processes which formed them, for little is known about even some of the most elementary aspects of these matters. As J. A. Banks sensibly observes, "no useful purpose is served by putting forward plausible hypotheses to explain the 'facts' when we do not know what the facts are."[11] There are, of course, facts in abundance in the massive existing literature of American urban history, but they are of little value for two reasons. For the most part, as previously noted, these works focused upon formal institutions and the articulate elements of the community, to the neglect of underlying social processes and mass behavior. Second, earlier investigators typically assumed the uniqueness of the community with which they dealt, and arranged their evidence in categories that precluded systematic comparison with other cities; "the usual shelf of urban history books," Sam B. Warner remarks, "looks like a line of disconnected local histories."[12]

A good many scholars now at work are conscious of both of these failings and are attempting to remedy them. There is growing agreement on the dimensions of past urban life that are most in need of study, and a new awareness of the need to employ categories that will facilitate systematic comparison and contrast. There are, however, important practical difficulties to be overcome. These stem from the character of the available evidence. The United States Bureau of the Census and a host of other governmental and private bodies regularly produce information about the social and economic characteristics of city-dwellers. In some instances the published aggregated data can readily be used to illuminate an important issue, as in a recent study which computed indexes of dissimilarity for nineteenth-century immigrant groups from census data on their distribution by ward and challenged common assumptions about "the ghetto."[13]

Most of the published evidence, however, is not sufficiently rich to supply the details which are analytically strategic. Thus the occupational distribution of Irish immigrants living in American cities in 1870 can be discovered, but not that of the Negroes with whom one would like to compare them. Separate tabulations for blacks were made in subsequent censuses, but never any which distinguished black migrants from the rural South from Negroes born in the North and long familiar with urban culture, information essential to any attempt to determine the extent to which the occupational handicaps of black city-dwellers were attributable to the rural origins of much of the group.

Furthermore, even the most detailed census material provides only a snapshot at one moment in time, when what is needed is an understanding of the dynamics of a process occurring over time.[14] The population registration systems of a few favored European countries supply longitudinal evidence concerning a few basic characteristics; elsewhere the urban historian has to *create* it by painstakingly tracing people over a span of years. Only by following him through subsequent manuscript census schedules, tax records, city directories, and the like can we discover whether the Michael O'Reilly who had fled the Irish potato famine only to find little more to eat for himself and his family as a day laborer in the slums of Boston in 1850 later found a better job, became a homeowner, lived in a better neighborhood, became a pillar of his church and the Democratic party, and was able to educate his children. Only by tracing the experiences of hundreds of Michael O'Reillys and his contemporaries from other backgrounds can one develop systematic knowledge of the dynamics of urban social stratification in the past.

Even in the age of the computer this is a difficult task. The development of electronic data-processing methods has been of crucial significance to historians working in this field, but not because the computer makes it possible to treat dozens of cities simultaneously rather than only one. The computer rather allows the investigator to do in one setting kinds of microscopic social analyses that were previously impossible, except in communities with a very small population.[15] To treat any large city in this fashion entails the manipulation of enormous quantities of data. In my current Boston research I have dozens of items of information about each of nearly 8,000 individual sample members, close to half a million facts to be made sense of. Other ongoing studies of Buffalo and Philadelphia in the nineteenth century treat the total population rather than selected samples, and involve several million items.[16] To collect this mass of evidence is itself a gigantic task, and then there are hard intellectual choices to be made as to coding schemes and analytical procedures. No wonder, then, that at this point one can make only highly provisional generalizations about the process of urbanization in the American past, generalizations based on a scattering of cases that may not be representative. When we possess rather detailed knowledge about the common laborers of Newburyport, Massachusetts, in the late nineteenth century but lack comparable observations about the laborers of New York City, it is risky to generalize about the urban working class of the period.

There is a further important limitation upon what is known at present. Most investigators have done their probing in one brief period, 1850-1880, because the richest source for such studies—the manuscript schedules of the United States Census—are available for only those years. Prior to 1850 the census provided little social data; most of the 1890 schedules were destroyed by fire; and the 1900 and subsequent censuses are still closed to investigators. In fact there are other sources which are nearly as satisfactory for these purposes; for the post-1880 period in Boston I have employed marriage license files, birth certificates, city directories, and assessor's valuation records, for instance, and in states like New York and New Jersey there are manuscript schedules from excellent state censuses which extend into the twentieth century.[17] A number of new demographic studies of colonial New England communities suggest that it may be possible to treat the pre-1850 as well as the post-1880 period satisfactorily.[18] But the first research in the new urban history was stimulated by discovery of the uses of the U. S. Census manuscript schedules, and most of the work published so far is limited in its chronological focus by the availability of those materials.

To emphasize these practical limitations is not, of course, to call for a twenty-year moratorium on generalization and speculation until all the facts are in. As the following examples illustrate, a number of studies already done have corrected significant distortions in our understanding of the past and have shed new light on important issues.[19]

1. *Urban population fluidity*. Nineteenth-century Americans assumed that the supply of free land in the West assured free movement, and that the city was a closed, confining, static environment. Frederick Jackson Turner gave eloquent expression to this view, and it later found seeming confirmation in several studies which disclosed extremely high rates of population turnover on the frontier. Recent research, however, places the matter in a very different perspective, for it appears that the urban population was if anything *more* volatile than the rural population.[20] The burgeoning cities drew into them many more newcomers than rural areas long before the closing of the frontier at the end of the century. What is more, migration to the city was a more complex and dynamic process than has been understood, for only a minority of newcomers permanently settled in the community they first entered. Cities grew rapidly from the heavy volume of net in-migration, but gross in-migration was several times higher than that, for there was massive out-migration at the same time. Boston, for example, then a city of less than half a million, gained some 65,000 new residents from net migration between 1880 and 1890, but more than a million people moved through the city in those years to produce that net gain! The typical urban migrant moved through three or more communities before he settled down around middle age. We have long been aware that cities grew by attracting outsiders into them, but the magnitude of the incessant flow of people into and out of them has never been suspected.

This holds for small communities in the late-nineteenth century—Newburyport, Poughkeepsie—as well as for large ones like Boston, Chicago, Omaha, and Philadelphia, and it applies to southern cities like Birmingham and Atlanta as much as to northern communities. Small cities, indeed, appear to have had somewhat less stable populations than large ones, contrary to stereotype, probably because residents of the metropolis could move a considerable distance (socially as well as physically) and still remain within its boundaries. Despite the automobile, improved national communications, and other developments which have generally been thought to have facilitated the flow of people from place to place, the fragmentary data on the period since 1890 suggest the opposite trend—toward a less volatile population.

2. *Class and ethnic differentials in spatial mobility.* Poor people, immigrants, and blacks were trapped in "slums" and "ghettos," while the middle class was free to move on when opportunity beckoned: such is the prevailing stereotype of the American city of the past. Today there is some grain of truth in this view, for well-educated professionals and managers do indeed move from place to place more often than other occupational groups, and it appears that spatial mobility and economic success are positively correlated. In the nineteenth- and early-twentieth-century city, however, the situation was radically different.[21] Groups low on the social scale were spatially much more volatile than their social betters. There were indeed certain ecological clusterings of poor people in particular neighborhoods, though the prevalence of ghettos in even this sense has been exaggerated. More important, though, is the recent discovery that few of these individuals lived in any one neighborhood for very long. If there was anything like "a culture of poverty" in the American city, it lacked deep local roots, for most of the people exposed to it were incessantly on the move from place to place. In the one community for which information is available over a span of a full century—Boston—it was not until the 1930's that the contemporary pattern began to appear.

Two implications follow from this. One is that, while contemporary migration differentials may plausibly be interpreted in terms of an economic model in which labor mobility yields higher returns, the older pattern hints at the existence of a quite different phenomenon—a permanent floating proletariat, ever on the move physically but rarely winning economic gains as a result of movement. This is speculative, for no one has yet devised a convenient method of systematically tracing past out-migrants and assessing how they fared in other communities,[22] but at least one may note that backward extrapolations from current labor mobility studies seem entirely unjustified. No single issue raised thus far by research in the new urban history is in more need of clarification than this one.

A second conclusion of importance may be drawn from this finding: the extreme volatility of the urban masses severely limited the possibilities of mobilizing them politically and socially, and facilitated control by other more stable elements of the population. It is suggestive, for example, that less than a quarter of the working-class residents of Los Angeles in 1900—but more than 80 per cent of the members of the six middle-class Protestant sects that dominated the city politically and economically—were still to be found there two decades later.[23] In these sharp class differentials in out-migration rates lies a clue, perhaps, to the neglect of ordinary working people in the newspapers, local histories, and so on. The bulk of the citizens who had lived for long in one place and had a wide circle of acquaintances were in fact part of the middle class; they were "the community," while the masses of ordinary workers were transients who could easily be ignored.

3. *Rates and trends in social mobility.* No aspect of urban life in the past is more important than the class structure, and none has received so little serious attention. Implicit assumptions about the functioning of the class system abound in conventional historical accounts, but empirical research into the dynamics of social stratification is rare. Particularly lacking are careful accounts of class as it shapes the life cycle of individuals and their children. The meaning of one's class position depends not only on the advantages or disadvantages it entails today but upon how it affects one's prospects in the future. The study of social mobility, therefore, occupies a central role in the work of the new urban historians.

It is difficult as yet to generalize broadly on the basis of the scattered findings available, for local and temporal variations in opportunity levels were considerable, but it does seem clear that some of my own earlier work—on the laborers of Newburyport—was misleading in its emphasis upon the barriers to working-class occupational achievement. The exceptional sluggishness of the local economy and the large concentration of recent Irish immigrants in the city yielded unduly low estimates of blue collar occupational mobility in general, though even in Newburyport there was impressive social mobility of another kind—advance to home ownership. In other communities, however, the occupational horizon was notably more open.[24] Career mobility a notch or two up the occupational ladder was common, and intergenerational mobility more common still. Four in ten of the sons of the unskilled and semi-skilled workers of Boston attained a middle-class job (though only a minor clerical or sales position in most cases), and another 15 to 20 per cent became skilled craftsmen. Analysis by categories more refined than "skilled," "low white collar," "unskilled," and so on discloses that a great deal of this occupational movement involved only slight changes in status,[25] but the over-all impression of fluidity and openness remains. It is also noteworthy that, despite the old tradition of social criticism which sees the class system becoming more rigid as a result of the spread of factory production, the close of the frontier, the shrinking of class differentials in birth rates, and various other causes, there seems to have been astonishing uniformity in mobility rates over a long span of time.

4. *Immigration and differential opportunity.* Though the social system was impressively fluid, there was enormous variation in the opportunities open to particular ethnic groups.[26] Native Americans of native parentage were generally in a much more advantageous situation than second-generation immigrants of similar class origins, who were in turn better able to advance themselves than their immigrant fathers. As important as these broad differences were variations within these general categories. Poor white rural migrants to Birmingham and Atlanta remained more heavily proletarian than migrants to Boston from rural New England. Particular European groups—the British, the Germans, the Jews—rose quickly, while others like the Irish and the Italians found the environment far more constricted. It may have been the extreme diversity of the experience of particular groups more than general satisfaction with the social system that accounted for the relative absence of militant working-class protest aimed at fundamental social change.[27] With all of the major immigrant groups, however, there was general upward movement with increased length of residence in America.

5. *Negro migrants and European immigrants.* In recent years the clustering of black city-dwellers on the lowest rungs of the social ladder has often been attributed to the continuing influx of uneducated, unskilled migrants from backward rural areas. Earlier European immigrant groups entered American society at the bottom too, the argument runs, because they were unfamiliar with and ill-adapted to urban industrial ways. It took generations for them to rise; Negroes in general have not yet done so because so many are still first-generation newcomers from the southern countryside. A test of the "last of the immigrants" theory in late-nineteenth-century Boston, however, suggests that few of the economic disabilities of black people were attributable to their lack of acquaintance with urban culture.[28] There were some similarities between black newcomers from the South and Irish immigrants; both groups were overwhelmingly concentrated in menial jobs. But the second-generation Irish moved ahead impressively, though more slowly than their counterparts of British or German background, while north-

ern-born blacks were only a shade better off than the rawest black newcomer. Still more striking, Negro males whose *fathers* had been born in the North, and who thus had deep family roots in the free black community of antebellum Boston, were in the same dismal position. Even in what was widely regarded as the most advanced and progressive northern city with respect to race relations, and even by comparison with the European immigrant group which was slowest to rise, the situation of blacks was *sui generis*.

This brief review of some of the findings of recent research in the new urban history is meant to be illustrative, not exhaustive. Fascinating work is now under way on black family structure in nineteenth- and early-twentieth-century cities, work which promises to shatter the conventional wisdom on that subject and to force the rewriting of a major portion of American social history.[29] The family structure of other groups and its relationship to other phenomena is just beginning to receive the scrutiny it so clearly deserves.[30] The texture of neighborhood life and the flow of people between socially distinct sections of the city is coming into focus as another major area for investigation.[31] Institutions like schools, churches, and voluntary associations are coming to be approached in terms of function as well as formal arrangements.[32] The interaction between urban environments and the social organization of work too is beginning to receive serious study.[33]

All this is heartening, but it would be well to conclude on a cautionary note. The emphasis of research in the new urban history thus far has been heavily quantitative. The sources which had been most neglected by previous investigators were peculiarly well-suited to quantitative treatment and seemed to offer a quick pay-off to those willing to attempt it. This was salutary on the whole, I think, because there was a great deal to be learned from even the most simple-minded efforts to measure phenomena which in the past had been discussed on the basis of colorful examples and casual impressions. Andrew Carnegie was a poor boy. Q.E.D.: the typical millionaire of the Gilded Age came from humble origins. (Or, worse yet, Q.E.D.: many poor boys of the era became millionaires.) Some of this work has been superficial, to be sure, or positively misleading. An inadequate formulation of the research problem; the use of categories which blur significant distinctions; employing mathematical techniques ill-suited to the problem at hand: any of these can lead the investigator badly astray. But there are comparable pitfalls for the unwary in every branch of history, and an abundant supply of researchers who will stumble upon them. And it seems to me that the blunders of quantifiers are at least a little more open to exposure and future correction, since the procedure itself forces an investigator to make explicit assumptions which are left implicit in other kinds of work.

There are, however, abuses that eager quantifiers are especially likely to commit, and a word of warning about these is in order. Some enthusiasts appear to assume that the hard evidence that can be gleaned from census schedules, city directories, and the like is the only reliable source of knowledge about past social behavior, and that more traditional sources—newspapers, sermons, manuscripts, novels, and so forth—are so socially skewed as to be quite worthless. What can be counted is real; what cannot is to be left to the storytellers and mythmakers.

This is dangerously obtuse. The descriptive material available in such sources serves several indispensable functions.[34] First, it can provide information essential to arranging harder data in meaningful categories; for instance, instead of imposing an occupational classification scheme derived from research by contemporary sociologists, one may gain clues as to the extent to which division of labor and skill dilution had taken place in particular trades in a given community and develop a scheme more appropriate to the context. Second, such evidence may yield hints of patterns whose existence can be confirmed and explored through statistical analysis; the complaint of a social worker that Irish laborers withdrew their children from school and sacrificed their education in order to accumulate funds to purchase homes suggests a hypothesis worth careful testing. Conversely, descriptive material can assist in the interpretation of relationships that appear in the statistical data by indicating what underlying mechanism produced the observed relationship.

Most important, it is only through such evidence that the investigator may begin to understand the perceptions and emotions of the people he is dealing with. The austerely objective facts uncovered by empirical social research influence the course of history as they are filtered through the consciousness of obstinately subjective human beings. Religion, ideology, cultural traditions—these affected human behavior in the past and shaped the meaning of the demographic and ecological patterns which can be neatly plotted on a map or graph. If we fail to grapple with these dimensions of the past and make no effort to examine them in the light of what we know from harder data, we will have shirked the most difficult but also the most rewarding of challenges.

For valuable criticisms of an earlier draft of this essay I am indebted to those scholars who attended the Rome Conference, and to Stanley Coben of UCLA, Clyde Griffen of Vassar College, and Herbert Gutman of the University of Rochester.

REFERENCES

1. Jean Gottmann, *Megalopolis: The Urbanized Northeastern Seaboard of the United States* (Cambridge, Mass.: M.I.T. Press, 1961), p. 5.

2. Eric E. Lampard, "American Historians and the Study of Urbanization," *American Historical Review,* 67 (October 1961), 49-61. The argument is further extended in two subsequent papers, "Urbanization and Social Change: On Broadening the Scope and Relevance of Urban History," in Oscar Handlin and John Burchard, eds., *The Historian and the City* (Cambridge, Mass.: M.I.T. Press and Harvard University Press, 1963), pp. 225-247, and "The Dimensions of Urban History: A Footnote to the 'Urban Crisis,'" *Pacific Historical Review,* 39 (August 1970), 261-278.

3. Charles N. Glaab, "The Historian and the American City: A Bibliographic Survey," in Philip M. Hauser and Leo Schnore, eds., *The Study of Urbanization* (New York: Wiley, 1965), pp. 53-80.

4. For examples of such work, see Stephan Thernstrom and Richard Sennett, eds., *Nineteenth-Century Cities: Essays in the New Urban History* (New Haven: Yale University Press, 1969), and other specimens cited below. For related developments in Britain, see H. J. Dyos, ed., *The Study of Urban History* (London: Edward Arnold Ltd., 1968), chiefly the papers by Dyos, Armstrong, Dyos and Baker, and Foster, and a forthcoming publication of the Cambridge Group for the History of Population and Social Structure, E. A. Wrigley, ed., *The Study of Nineteenth-Century Society.* Work along somewhat similar lines is going on in France, Sweden, and doubtless other countries as well; on Sweden see Sune Åkerman, "Projects and Research Priorities," in *Särtryck ur Historisk Tidskrift* (1970). My limited knowledge, however, forces me to concentrate on research in American urban history in this paper. In the near future, however, it may by possible to make useful comparative studies of urbanizing communities across national boundaries.

5. See, for instance, the papers by Caroline Ware and Constance M. Green in Caroline Ware, ed., *The Cultural Approach to History* (New York: Columbia University Press, 1940). For that matter, one aim of the New History of the Progressive Era was to "emphasize the experience of the ordinary men and women of the past"; Oscar and Mary Handlin, "The New History and the Ethnic Factor in American Life," *Perspectives in American History,* 4 (1970), 5.

334   STEPHAN THERNSTROM

6. Manuscript census schedules were utilized by Oscar Handlin in *Boston's Immigrants: A Study in Acculturation* (Cambridge, Mass.: Harvard University Press, 1941), and extensively by F. L. Owsley and his students in their investigations of the antebellum South; see *Plain Folk of the Old South* (Baton Rouge: Louisiana State University Press, 1949) and the monographs upon which that synthesis was based. In neither case, however, was there an attempt to use the schedules to trace the changing situation of individuals over time, which has been one of the chief aims of the new urban historians.

7. For a thoughtful appraisal of the state of urban sociology as a field which reaches a similar conclusion, see Robert Gutman and David Popenoe's introduction to *Neighborhood, City and Metropolis: An Integrated Reader in Urban Sociology* (New York: Random House, 1970), pp. 3-23.

8. Curti's work was the first effort to write social history by tracing every resident of a community from census to census for as long as he remained there, and the first to employ mechanical data-processing methods—in this case a counter-sorter rather than a computer—for such purposes. The book was unfortunately conceived as an effort to test Turner's frontier thesis, which was not the most fruitful frame for the data, but the fundamental issues with which it dealt—migration and population turnover, economic and social mobility, the distribution of political power—were precisely the matters the new urban historians sought to explore in other settings.

9. For good statements of this position see Samuel H. Beer, "Political Science and History," in Melvin Richter, ed., *Essays in Theory and History: An Approach to the Social Sciences* (Cambridge, Mass.: Harvard University Press, 1970), pp. 41-73, and William O. Aydelotte, "Notes on the Problem of Historical Generalization," in Louis Gottschalk, ed., *Generalization in the Writing of History* (Chicago: University of Chicago Press, 1963), pp. 163-172.

10. Beer, "Political Science and History," p. 45.

11. J. A. Banks, "Historical Sociology and the Study of Population," *Dædalus* (Spring 1968), p. 399.

12. Sam B. Warner, "If All the World Were Philadelphia: A Scaffolding for Urban History, 1774-1930," *American Historical Review*, 74 (October 1968), 26-43.

13. Sam B. Warner and Colin B. Burke, "Cultural Change and the Ghetto," *Journal of Contemporary History*, 4 (October 1969), 173-187. See also Stanley Lieberson, *Ethnic Patterns in American Cities* (Glencoe, Ill.: Free Press, 1963), and Karl and Alma Taeuber, *Negroes in Cities: Residential Segregation and Neighborhood Change* (Chicago: Aldine Publishing Company, 1965) for further demonstrations of what can be done with aggregated data.

14. For elaboration, see Stephan Thernstrom, *Poverty and Progress: Social*

Mobility in a Nineteenth-Century City (Cambridge, Mass.: Harvard University Press, 1964), passim; Thernstrom, "Notes on the Historical Study of Social Mobility," *Comparative Studies in Society and History*, 10 (January 1968), 162-172.

15. The statistical analysis in *Poverty and Progress* was done by hand tabulation; the drudgery and potential errors were at about the limit of tolerance with even that small city. Five of the nine primarily quantitative projects reported on in *Nineteenth-Century Cities* employed a computer, and in the other four computer analysis is projected for a later stage.

16. The Buffalo study is under the direction of Herbert Gutman of the University of Rochester and Laurence Glasco of the University of Pittsburgh; the Philadelphia project is being done by Theodore Hershberg of the University of Pennsylvania.

17. For a useful guide to these, see Henry J. Dubester, *State Censuses: An Annotated Bibliography of Censuses of Population Taken After the Year 1790 by States and Territories of the United States* (Washington: Library of Congress, 1948).

18. John Demos, *A Little Commonwealth: Family Life in Plymouth Colony* (New York: Oxford University Press, 1970); Philip Greven, *Four Generations: Population, Land, and Family in Colonial Andover, Massachusetts* (Ithaca: Cornell University Press, 1970); Kenneth Lockridge, *A New England Town: The First Hundred Years* (New York: Norton, 1970). Robert Doherty of the University of Pittsburgh will soon be completing a related study, a comparative analysis of urbanization, industrialization, and social change in five New England towns, 1800-1860.

19. Much of what follows is drawn from unpublished sections of my forthcoming study of migration and social mobility in Boston, 1880-1968; unless otherwise indicated, documentation will be found there.

20. For further discussion of population turnover, see Thernstrom and Peter R. Knights, "Men in Motion: Some Data and Speculations on Urban Population Mobility in Nineteenth-Century America," *Journal of Interdisciplinary History*, 1 (Fall 1970), and the literature cited there. Additional confirming details may be found in Paul Worthman, "Working Class Mobility in Birmingham, Alabama, 1880-1914," in Tamara K. Hareven, ed., *Anonymous Americans: Explorations in Nineteenth Century Social History* (Englewood Cliffs, N. J.: Prentice-Hall, 1971); Howard P. Chudacoff, "Men in Motion: Residential and Occupational Mobility in Omaha, 1880-1920," Ph.D. diss., University of Chicago, 1969.

21. Thernstrom and Knights, "Men in Motion."

22. For discussion of one rather inconclusive attempt and its difficulties, see *ibid.*

23. Unpublished research in progress by Gregory Singleton of Northwestern University and Michael Hanson of UCLA.

24. Worthman, "Working Class Mobility"; Chudacoff, "Men in Motion"; Richard J. Hopkins, "Occupational and Geographic Mobility in Atlanta, 1870-1896," *Journal of Southern History*, 34 (May 1968), 200-213.

25. Clyde Griffen, "Problems in the Study of Social Mobility," *Journal of Social History* (1971).

26. Stephan Thernstrom, "Immigrants and WASPS: Ethnic Differences in Occupation Mobility in Boston, 1880-1940," in Thernstrom and Sennett, eds., *Nineteenth-Century Cities;* Clyde Griffen, "Making It in America: Social Mobility in Mid-Nineteenth Century Poughkeepsie," *New York History*, 51 (October 1970); Marc Raphael, "The European Immigrant in Los Angeles, 1910-1928," unpublished seminar paper, University of California, Los Angeles, 1970.

27. As suggested by Norman Birnbaum in his afterword to Thernstrom and Sennett, eds., *Nineteenth-Century Cities*, pp. 421-430.

28. Stephan Thernstrom and Elizabeth H. Pleck, "The Last of the Immigrants? A Comparative Analysis of Black and Immigrant Social Mobility in Late-Nineteenth Century Boston," unpublished paper for the 1970 meetings of the Organization of American Historians.

29. A major study by Herbert Gutman is nearing completion.

30. See, for example, the essays by Richard Sennett and Lynn Lees in Thernstrom and Sennett, eds., *Nineteenth-Century Cities;* Sennett's book, *Families Against the City: Middle-Class Homes of Industrial Chicago, 1872-1890* (Cambridge, Mass.: Harvard University Press, 1970); and the forthcoming study of immigrant working-class families by Virginia McLaughlin of Princeton University.

31. See the Griffen and Blumin essays in Thernstrom and Sennett, eds., *Nineteenth-Century Cities;* Chudacoff, "Men in Motion"; Sam B. Warner, *The Private City: Philadelphia in Three Periods of Its Growth* (Philadelphia: University of Pennsylvania Press, 1968); Warner, *Streetcar Suburbs: The Process of Growth in Boston, 1870-1900* (Cambridge, Mass.: Harvard University Press, 1962).

32. On education, see Michael B. Katz, *The Irony of Early School Reform: Educational Innovation in Mid-Nineteenth Century Massachusetts* (Cambridge, Mass.: Harvard University Press, 1968); on religion, Gregory Singleton, "Religion and Social Change in Los Angeles, 1850-1930," Ph.D. diss. in progress, University of California, Los Angeles.

33. Warner, *The Private City.*

34. For fuller discussion of some of these, see M. Anderson's chapter on "The Study of Family Structure in Nineteenth-Century Britain," in Wrigley, ed., *Nineteenth-Century Society.*

JACQUES LE GOFF

Is Politics Still the Backbone of History?

To A historian trained in what, rightly or wrongly, has been called "the *Annales* school," the title of this essay may in itself seem strange. The *Annales* historian was brought up on the idea that political history was obsolete and out of date. Marc Bloch and Lucien Febvre had said so over and over again. They even invoked the great precursors of modern history. Voltaire, in the *Essai sur les Moeurs et l'esprit des nations*, wrote: "For the last fourteen hundred years, the only Gauls, apparently, have been kings, ministers and generals."[1] Jules Michelet wrote to Charles Sainte-Beuve in 1857: "If I had included only political history in my narrative, if I had taken no account of the various other elements of history (religion, law, geography, literature, art, and so forth), my approach would have been quite different. But I needed a great sweeping movement because all these different elements gravitated together to form one whole."[2] Again, referring to his *History of France*, Michelet said: "Here again I can only say I was on my own. Scarcely anything was ever provided but political history, acts of government, a few words about institutions. No one took any account of what accompanies, explains, and is in part the foundation of political history: social, economic and industrial conditions, the state of literature and thought."[3]

At the same time most historians consciously or unconsciously came under the influence of Marxism, whether to follow it, more or less rigidly, or to challenge it, more or less openly. But too hasty a reading of Marx could suggest that he ranged politics among the superstructures of society, and considered political history an epiphenomenon of the history of production relations. There is the well-known passage in the preface to the *Contribution to a Critique of Political Economy:* "The aggregate of production relations con-

337

stitutes the economic structure of society, the concrete base on which
there rises a legal and political superstructure, and to which certain forms of social consciousness correspond. The mode of production relating to material life determines the pattern of social,
political and intellectual life in general."[4] Without necessarily seeing in Marx's attitude to politics, theoretical and practical (*le
politique* and *la politique*), the fundamental pessimism ascribed
to it by some—usually hostile—commentators,[5] one may still conclude that a conception like the "withering away of the state"
is not likely to enhance the prestige of anything to do with politics,
political history included.

This might be thought a one-sided view, to be found only in a
historian misled by a specifically French tradition and an exaggerated idea of the influence of Marxism. Not at all. Frenchmen
have been among political history's stoutest supporters.[6] And Johan Huizinga, neither a Frenchman nor by any means a Marxist, in
the course of his work gradually moved away from political history. In *The Task of Cultural History*[7] he accords it no more than a
declining ascendancy, based chiefly on the fact that it is both easy
and clear. Since Huizinga was not personally attracted by economic
and social history, though he noted their "irresistible rise,"[8] he soon
turned his main efforts to the establishing of a scientific cultural history.

Economics, society, and culture seem to have monopolized historians' attention for the last half-century. Political history, the in-
sulted and injured, even seems to have been drawn into the epistemological uncertainties arising from the attempt by certain
schools of sociology to blur the distinction between practical and
theoretical politics. To mention only two leading figures in present-
day French sociology, Alain Touraine has recently emphasized the
"two-fold weakness" of political analysis in the social sciences,[9]
and Edgar Morin points out the "crisis" in politics owing to the in-
vasion of its field from all sides by the techniques and sciences.[10] Will
the atomization of politics itself entail a corresponding disintegra-
tion of political history, already driven back on uncomfortable positions within its own discipline? To understand the setbacks suffered
by political history in the twentieth century, we must analyze the
factors that made it flourish before.

Its former ascendancy was doubtless linked to the predominat-
ing form taken on, between the fourteenth and twentieth centuries, first by the society of the Ancien Régime and then by the

society which emerged from the French Revolution. The rise of the monarchical state, of the Prince and his servants, brought to the forefront of the political stage a shadow-show of courtly and government marionettes which bedazzled both historians and people. Aristotelianism in various shapes and forms, especially after the thirteenth century and Aquinas, provided a vocabulary and concepts in which these new realities could be represented. But the triumph of politics and of political history was not immediate. They were adopted rapidly enough in Italy under the stimulus of the rise of the "signorie." But in France, in spite of a step forward under Charles V, the Aristotelian king, who between 1369 and 1374 had Nicole Oresme translate (from a Latin text) Aristotle's *Politics* and *Ethics* and a treatise on economics, it was not until the seventeenth century that the noun *politique* (politics) came into current use, consolidating that of the adjective, which had been established since the sixteenth century. The word *politique* itself probably benefited from the promotion of all the words belonging to the *polis* family. These, together with those deriving from *urbs*— *urbain* (urban), *urbanité* (urbanity), *urbanisme* (town-planning) —between them cover a large part of the semantic field of civilization. It is perhaps through *police* (which did not produce *policé* [organized, civilized] until the nineteenth century) that we arrive at *politesse* (politeness), which appears in the seventeenth century. The realm of *le politique, la politique,* and *les politiques* (theoretical politics, practical politics, and politicians) is thus the realm of the elite, and it is from this that political history derived its nobility. It was part of the aristocratic style. Hence the revolutionary aim of Voltaire, to write "instead of the history of kings and courts the history of men." It looked as if philosophical history would drive out political history. But in fact it usually came to terms with it. One example can be seen in the abbé Raynal's *Histoire philosophique et politique des établissements et du commerce des Européens dans les deux Indes.*[11]

The Revolution of 1789, though it ultimately led in the nineteenth century to the transmission of political power to the bourgeoisie, did not destroy the prerogatives of political history. Romanticism made it totter but did not bring it down. Chateaubriand, who could recognize modernity in history as well as in politics and ideology, though he did so only to reject it, was an isolated case.[12] François Guizot, even more than Augustin Thierry, led history further along the path toward history of civilization,[13] but since

both were primarily concerned with showing the rise of the bourgeoisie, they remained bogged down in political history. But the
"conquering middle classes" not only annexed political history in
all its glory—they also took as much delight as their predecessors in
a historical model which was monarchical and aristocratic: a typical
example of the cultural time-lag which makes a parvenu class affect
traditional tastes. Michelet is a solitary peak.

To take the case of France alone, not until the beginning of the
twentieth century did political history first withdraw and then
succumb before the blows of a new kind of history backed up by
the new social sciences—geography, and especially economics and
sociology. Vidal de la Blache, François Simiand, and Emile Durkheim were, whether they realized it or not, the godparents of this
new history. Its parents were Henri Berr with the *Revue de
synthèse historique* (1901), and even more decisively Marc Bloch
and Lucien Febvre with the *Annales d'histoire économique et sociale*.

Raymond Aron has shown in his essay on Thucydides how
closely political history is linked to narrative and event.[14] The *Annales* school loathed the trio formed by political history, narrative
history, and chronicle or episodic (*événementielle*) history. All
this, for them, was mere pseudohistory, history on the cheap, a
superficial affair which preferred the shadow to the substance.
What had to be put in its place was history in depth—an economic,
social, and mental history. In the greatest book produced by the
Annales school, Fernand Braudel's *La Méditerranée et le monde
méditerranéen à l'époque de Philippe II* (1959), political history
is relegated to part III, which far from being the culmination of
the work is more like the bits and pieces left over. Once the backbone of history, political history has sunk to being no more than an
atrophied appendix: the parson's nose of history.

But political history was gradually to return in force by borrowing the methods, spirit, and theoretical approach of the very social
sciences which had pushed it into the background. I shall try to
sketch this recent comeback by taking medieval history as an example.[15] Sociology and anthropology's first and chief contribution to
political history was to establish as its central concept and aim the
notion of "power" and the facts relating to power. As Raymond
Aron has observed, this notion and these facts apply to all societies and all civilizations: "The problem of Power is eternal,
whether the earth is worked with a pick or with a bulldozer."[16]

It should be noted in this connection that analyses made by political historians in terms of "power" go beyond those in terms of "state" and "nation," whether these are traditional studies or attempts to approach the question from a new angle.[17] It is also worth remembering that Marxism-Leninism, which has been accused of not showing enough interest in political history and theory, has for a long time only concerned itself in this field at the level of state and nation.[18] Lastly, while the word politics suggested the idea of surface and the superficial, the word power evokes center and depth. Surface history having lost its charm, political history becomes history in depth by becoming the history of power. This verbal rehabilitation corresponds to a mental evolution foreshadowed by Marc Bloch, who wrote shortly before his death: "There is a lot to be said about this word 'political.' Why should it always be taken as synonymous with superficial? Is not a history which is centered, as it may quite legitimately be, on the evolution of modes of government and on the fate of the governed, bound to try to understand from the inside the facts it has chosen as the subject of its study?"[19]

The history of political depths started off, however, from the outside, with the signs and symbols of power, as in the work of P. E. Schramm. In a number of studies culminating in the great synthesis *Herrschaftzeichen und Staatssymbolik*,[20] he has shown that the objects which were the characteristic signs of possessors of power in the Middle Ages—crown, throne, orb, scepter, *main de justice*, and so forth—are not to be studied just in themselves. They need to be restored to the context of attitudes and ceremonies of which they formed part, and above all to be seen in the light of the political symbolism from which they derive their true significance.[21]

This symbolism was deeply rooted in a religious semeiology which made the political sphere a province of the religious. Among all the signs and insignia, one in particular lent itself to extensive development, with regard both to politico-religious symbolism and to the institutions in which that symbolism was historically embodied. The whole panorama of medieval politics, linked on one side with the hereditary kingships of antiquity and on the other with the relics of monarchy which have survived into modern times, radiated out from the crown. The symbolic field ranged from the material object itself through the coronation rites to the actual kingdom on one hand and the abstract idea of monarchy on the other. A collection of studies on this political panorama at the end of the Middle Ages is to be found in *Corona Regni: Studien über die Krone als Symbol des Staates in späten Mittelalter.*[22]

Quite recently Georges Duby recalled the multiple symbolism of the medieval crown in connection with the crown of thorns which St. Louis placed in the Sainte-Chapelle in Paris.[23] The reference immediately presents a problem of method. Is this appeal to "political" objects not perhaps due to the nature of the period in question, and to the fact that in the early Middle Ages texts are comparatively rare? Is this not, then, an ad hoc method rather than a really new and generally applicable way of approaching the problem?

Curiously enough, the historians most interested in these aspects of medieval political symbolism seem to accept such objections and to minimize the importance of their own approach. Thus P. E. Schramm writes: "The investigation of the insignia of power must be supplemented by investigation of the symbolism of power in general. This means that historical research, which first had to rely on chronicles, then became more precise through the use of documents, letters, deeds, and so on, still has a very long way to go in systematic development. There are more objects and evidence available than expected, and an adequate critical method has also been evolved. So the already existing picture may be filled out and enriched. For the insignia used by the ruler tell more about his expectations and claims, and tell it more definitely, than other available evidence. *This applies especially to those centuries for which written sources are very limited.*"[24]

Similarly Robert Folz, who thinks he discerns through different kinds of documentation different realities, writes: "Administrative documents, figurative representations, liturgical rites, external signs such as vestments and emblems—all these, together with a few narrative texts, are our essential sources of information for the first part of the Middle Ages, when symbol clearly predominated over theory as the expression of political form. It is only from the twelfth century on, with the revival of legal studies, that argumentation and controversy start providing an increasingly large part of our documentation."[25]

But the new political history, like all other branches of history, must abandon the old prejudice that only *faute de mieux*, that is, in the absence of texts, must it turn to nonwritten documentation. History has to use all the evidence it can get, taking from every kind its own particular contribution and establishing a hierarchy among them all in terms not of the historian's own predilections but of the system of values of the period concerned. This, needless to say, does not prevent him from going on to treat data from the past according to the standards of modern science, and with the help of all its equipment. Every period has a political ceremonial the significance of which it is the historian's job to discern; and this significance constitutes one of the most important aspects of political history. An outstanding result of the recent orientation of political history toward symbolism and ritual has been a revaluation of the significance of kingship within the political system of feudalism. Before, the general opinion had been that monarchy as an institution and the feudal system were antithetical, and that it was out of the decay of feudalism that monarchical power, en route to absolutism, arose at the end of the Middle Ages. According to this view Charlemagne, by his policy of awarding fiefs, which tended to become hereditary estates, as rewards for public service, unconsciously brought into being the force which was to destroy the public authority he himself had tried to recreate, and which was to subdue the royal power that he, by adding to it the dignity of the imperial crown, thought to have made invulnerable. This explanation is now recognized as false in both its terms. It arose from an inability to go beyond the hollow prestige of the state to the study of power itself. But in the new context, with anachronistic concepts of the state abandoned, medieval kingship, particularly that of the Carolingian period, regained its full meaning, and the feudal king was seen to derive his power not despite but within the feudal system.[26]

It was through the methods of comparative history, borrowed from anthropology and the history of religion, that medieval kingship came to have this new significance and that medieval political history was transformed. Various joint publications set the seal on this change. True, the Middle Ages in the West occupied only a small part of the deliberations of the Thirteenth International Conference on the History of Religion in Rome in 1955, the central theme of which was "The King-God and the Sacred Nature of Kingship."[27] This is true also of the volume presented shortly afterwards to Raffaelle Pettazzoni: *The Sacral Kingship—La Regalità Sacra.*[28] But a few years later the *Arbeitskreis für mittelalterliche Geschichte,* led by Theodor Mayer in Constance, devoted a volume of its *Vorträge und Forschungen* to medieval kingship. Meanwhile

the work of Ernst H. Kantorowicz was growing up parallel to that
of Schramm. Kantorowicz, after depicting the greatest sovereign
of the Middle Ages, Frederick II,[29] went on to study medieval worship of rulers through liturgical acclamation.[30] His research cul-
minated in the masterpiece *The King's Two Bodies* (1957), which
restored to its general historical background the conception of political theology which is an essential key to the understanding of the
Middle Ages.[31]

Such were the results, in medieval history, of the trail blazed
by Sir James George Frazer, whose research into the magical origins of kingship[32] probably stimulated the historians' own researches
into medieval kingship, whether or not they were conscious of the
fact or prepared to admit it. One historian at least made no secret
of his debt, though he did not always agree with Frazer and pursued his own studies according to specifically historical methods—
Marc Bloch. His pioneer work, *Les rois thaumaturges,* published in
1924, is still in the forefront of its field. Bloch is not content merely
with describing manifestations of the healing power ascribed to the
kings of France and England, or with tracing its history from its
emergence to its disappearance and explaining the theories behind
it. He also tries to go back to the springs of the collective psychology
involved, studies its "popularity" (book II, chapter I), and attempts to explain *"how* people believed in the royal miracle" (pp.
420-430). In short, he draws up a study model of "political mental
attitudes," which he puts forward simply as a special case—unique
only in terms of its subject—of general forms of mental attitude and
sensibility. But in the vitally important though as yet unexplored
area of the history of mental attitudes, as far as mental attitudes
relating to politics are concerned almost everything still remains to
be done. Naturally there can be no question of applying to the men
of the Middle Ages the opinion poll methods which can contribute
to the study of modern political attitudes. But for the history of
public opinion in the Middle Ages, as for other questions, a problematic, theoretical approach to the problem can be established.[33]

It may be noted at this point that political history and the
sciences which have influenced its recent evolution have sometimes alternated in using one another as stepping stones. Thus, as
we have seen, medieval political history was transformed and enriched by adopting methods borrowed from anthropology: new
light was thrown on medieval kingship by studies in archaic or
primitive kingship. Medieval political history thus seemed to leave

the surface ripples of episodic history for the deep diachronic strata of proto- or para-historical societies.

Meanwhile, conversely, anthropology opened itself to historical approaches, and scholars and researchers increasingly turned to political anthropology.[34] This method recognized, in societies "which have no history," structures of disequilibrium and conflict, and established the theoretical preliminaries necessary for providing them with a political history. In so doing it brought out the fact that dynamic social history is not incompatible with an anthropological view of societies and civilizations. Political history did not necessarily lose its dynamism by turning toward anthropology—it might even rediscover in it the schemas, Marxist or otherwise, of the class struggle.[35] Moreover, the vocabulary and mental attitudes of the Middle Ages lend themselves to the formulation of structures and social behavior in terms which are partly political. The upper strata of society are often designated in medieval texts by the term *potentes*, the powerful, generally in contrast to the *pauperes* or poor; sometimes they are referred to as the *superiores*, as opposed to *inferiores*.[36]

This corroborates researches in various sectors of medieval history which have identified in the basic phenomena a *political* dimension, in the sense of a relationship to *power*. The most striking example is the theory according to which, at various dates but usually around the year A.D. 1000, the *seigneuries foncières*, based on dues levied on land and its economic exploitation, gave place more and more to seigneuries based on the lords' powers of leadership, organization, and justice: these were known as *seigneuries banales*, from *ban*, the name for this kind of feudal power. Thus the whole feudal structure right down to its foundations takes on a coloring which is ultimately political.[37] This conception of feudalism, which does not exclude a final explanation in terms of production relations, has the virtue of emphasizing the importance of political factors, in the widest sense of the term, in the functioning of the feudal system, and the weight exerted by political forms in the dynamics of history.

The political aspect crops up again in cultural history. Education is a power and an instrument of power. The gulf between litterati and illitterati which lay so long between clerics and laymen, whether the latter were otherwise powerful or not, shows social cleavages arising out of demarcations between possession and non-possession of different forms of power, between participation and nonparticipation in these forms. For example, in the case of members of the university a dual relationship with power begins to emerge in the thirteenth century. On the one hand the world of the university tends to form itself into its own kind of supreme power, alongside the power of the church and the king—*studium,* alongside *sacerdotium* and *regnum.*[38] All those who enjoy the privileges of *studium* participate in its power. At the same time, the result—if not the goal—of university studies and distinctions becomes the attainment of some post or function in lay or ecclesiastical society which leads to participation in the other kinds of power.[39] If, in spite of the difficulties involved, a prosopography of university students and masters in the Middle Ages could be worked out,[40] it would be possible to measure the impact of the university group on the organization of medieval society, and there is no doubt that it would emerge in the character and role of a "power elite."

New light could probably also be shed on medieval political history by studying the application, in the Middle Ages, of the Dumézil schema for Indo-European societies. We know the tripartite schema was in use from the end of the ninth century, and that in the eleventh it took on the stereotyped form of *oratores, bellatores, laboratores.* If we knew how and why these ideas reappeared in the Middle Ages, and what was their mental, intellectual, and political effectiveness, we should probably be able to trace more clearly the different aspects of medieval power, their structures, relationships, and functioning. In my view, we should find that this schema was one of the ideological bases of royal power, the latter subsuming and acting as arbiter between the three functions.[41]

Even the realm of art would be illuminated by the application of political analysis in the broad sense. It is not merely a question of measuring the influence of patronage on the form, content, and evolution of art.[42] It is above all a matter of analyzing how the power of works of art is ordered in relation to power in general. It seems to me that Erwin Panofsky took a first step in this direction when he connected the Gothic style, through the multivalent notion of "order" (and hierarchy), with scholastic method; and then related both to a sociopolitical order embodied in the Ile de France around A.D. 1200 by the Capetian monarchy.[43]

Above all Pierre Francastel, in *Peinture et société: naissance et destruction d'un espace plastique, de la Renaissance au cubisme*

(1951), has shown not only that politicians—the Medicis in Florence, the patriciate in Venice—understood "the power of figurative images of space" and made them instruments of their policy[44] ("Botticelli's Venus is a policy made explicit"), but also that the new representation of space in terms of perspective is linked to a mental revolution, to a mythical thought governed by "the social and economic policy of giving."

In the realm of religious history one can cite as an example the underlying links between heretical movements and political parties, a subject in which research has scarcely begun.[45] Similarly, in a context relating at once to geography, sociology, and culture, one could point to many modern studies in urban sociology[46] which show the towns, and especially the town-planning, of the Middle Ages, as both an expression and a vehicle of urban power and its possessors. W. Braunfels has made an initial study of this kind for the cities of Tuscany.[47]

Finally, one can see coming into being—and it would be a good thing if it were hierarchized even farther—a differential political history functioning at various levels, according to what Fernand Braudel has called "the times of history."[48] In the short term there is traditional political history: narrative, episodic, full of movement, but anxious to pave the way for a deeper approach. Every so often it proposes quantitative evaluations; it initiates social analyses; it accumulates evidence for a future study of mental attitudes. In the longer term, to be established according to the model for long-term movements proposed by François Simiand, there will be a history of the phases or trends of political history, in which no doubt, as Braudel hopes, social history in the broad sense will still predominate—political history with a sociological emphasis. In between these two types of history, as in economic history, there would be an area of common ground specially devoted to studying the relationships between secular political trends on the one hand and, on the other, short-term movements and episodic highs and lows: a history of crises, in which structures and their dynamics are revealed in their nakedness by the turmoil of events. Lastly there comes a political history which would be almost immobile if it were not linked, as political anthropology has shown it to be, to the essentially conflictual and therefore dynamic structure of societies —a political history of really long-term structures, comprising both the valid, living part of geopolitics and also analysis based on anthropological models. At every one of all these levels, particular attention would be paid to the study of the various semeiological systems belonging to the science of politics: vocabulary, rites, behavior, mental attitudes.

Although one may, as I did at the beginning of this essay, speak of a certain crisis at present in political history, it is also true that political aspects and approaches are of increasing importance in the human sciences. Not only does the new science of politicology now contribute its concepts, vocabulary, and methods, but geopolitics too, still alive and kicking though somewhat discredited, political sociology, and, as we have seen, political anthropology, all give political history nourishment and support.

I have described it as a new political history, different from the old—dedicated to structures, social analysis, semeiology and the study of power. This is certainly an overoptimistic picture. It is true I have every so often recalled that much or all still remained to be done in certain directions. But the fact is that the new political history I have tried to sketch is as yet a dream rather than a reality.

Worse, the old political history is still a corpse that has to be made to lie down. True, a grammar of political history is and will always remain not only useful but necessary. We cannot do without a chronology of political events or the biographies of great men. In spite of the progress of democracy, political history will always be, not only but also, the history of great men. And now, thanks precisely to politicology and sociology, we know better than before what an event is, and what constitutes the conditioning of a great man.

But there is still a danger that political history in the vulgarized form in which it appears in countless popularizing books and magazines may once again invade the real science of history. There is a danger that historians of economics and culture may be satisfied with producing a political history of economics or culture, that is, a history of economic or cultural politics. The reason for this is still the same as it was when Lucien Febvre first inveighed against pseudohistory as a kind of history which "makes few demands. Very few. Too few."[49] And pseudohistory still seems ready to be happy with half-measures. While it agrees to lift itself up from the level of events and great men (from which one can always sneak in again by the back door to political history) to the level of institutions and environments, it will still stick if it can with outmoded conceptions of government or state. It puts up a poor show against strict juridical conceptions: law, the hope of mankind, is the historian's nightmare. It likes to dabble in the history of ideas and political thought—but often both ideas and politics are superficial. With the best will in the world it remains the most fragile form of history, and the one most likely to succumb to all the old temptations.

I conclude with a fact perhaps worth restating. However much political history may be renewed and regenerated by the other human sciences, it cannot aspire to autonomy. To divide a single branch of learning into separate compartments is more inadmissible than ever in the age of pluridisciplinarity. The comment of Lucien Febvre, cofounder of the *Annales d'Histoire Economique et Sociale,* is truer now than ever: "There is no such thing as economic or social history. There is just history."[50] But it is still true that the models of the new general history must accord the dimension of politics the same place as is occupied in society by the phenomenon of power, which is the epistemological incarnation of politics in the present. To pass from the age of anatomy to that of the atom, political history is no longer the backbone of history but its nucleus.

This article was translated from the French by Barbara Bray.

REFERENCES

1. Cited by Marc Bloch, *Apologie pour l'histoire, ou métier d'historien,* 4th ed. (Paris: Colin, 1961), p. 90.

2. *Ibid.,* p. 78.

3. Cited by P. Wolff, "L'étude des économies et des sociétés avant l'ère statistique," in C. Samaran, ed., *L'histoire et ses méthodes,* Encyclopédie de la Pléiade, 11 (Paris: Gallimard, 1961), p. 847.

4. For example, on page 4 of the introduction to the interesting volume on *Le féodalisme,* a special number of *Recherches internationales à la lumière du marxisme,* no. 37 (June 1963), the editors write "We have primarily included studies dealing with economic and social relations, with a few excursions into the field of institutional or cultural superstructures."

5. For example, the particularly hostile account given by J. Freund in *L'essence du politique* (Paris: Éditions Sirey, 1965), pp. 645ff. According to Freund, political alienation for Marx is alienation supreme, absolute, and irretrievable.

6. Charles Seignobos wrote in 1924, in the preface to his *Histoire politique*

de l'Europe contemporaine, that we must "recognize the degree to which the superficial phenomena of political life dominate the fundamental phenomena of economic, intellectual, and social life" (cited by Wolff, "L'étude des économies," p. 850).

7. "The problems of political history are as a rule immediately obvious." Johan Huizinga, *The Task of Cultural History,* written in 1926, published in Dutch in 1929 and in English translation in *Men and Ideas* (New York: Meridian Books, 1959), p. 27. Again: "The historical forms of political life are already to be found in life itself. Political history brings its own forms: a state institution, a peace treaty, a war, a dynasty, the state itself. In this fact, which is inseparable from the paramount importance of those forms themselves, lies the fundamental character of political history. It continues to enjoy a certain primacy because it is so much the morphology of society par excellence." *Ibid.,* pp. 58-59.

8. For example, in "The Political and Military Significance of Chivalric Ideas in the Late Middle Ages," first published in French in *Revue d'histoire diplomatique,* 35 (1921), 126-138, and translated into English in *Men and Ideas.* Huizinga writes (pp. 196-197): "The medievalists of our day are hardly favorable to chivalry. Combing the records, in which chivalry is, indeed, little mentioned, they have succeeded in presenting a picture of the Middle Ages in which economic and social points of view are so dominant that one tends at times to forget that, next to religion, chivalry was the strongest of the ideas that filled the minds and hearts of those men of another age."

9. A. Touraine, *Sociologie de l'action* (Paris: Editions du Seuil, 1965), chap. VI, "The Political System," p. 298. This two-fold fragility consists partly in the danger that the study of political relationships may be absorbed by structural analysis on the one hand and history on the other; partly in the fact that political theory may be subject either to politics or to political philosophy, itself only a part of the philosophy of history.

10. E. Morin, *Introduction à une politique de l'homme* (Paris: Editions du Seuil, 1965), new ed., 1969, pp. 9-10: *La politique en miettes.*

11. In English the emergence of two terms, "policy" and "polity" (in the fourteenth century the French had tried out *policie,* also copied from the Greek, but it did not take), complicated the field of political science and incidentally that of political history. While the French philosophes of the eighteenth century sought, or accepted, a compromise between philosophical and political history, it may be that in England an even more radical dilemma caused an oscillation between historical and political, at once linked and opposed to each other. This possibility seems suggested by such titles as that published anonymously in London in 1706: *An Historical and Political Essay, Discussing the Affinity or Resemblance of the Ancient and Modern Government.* See J. A. W. Gunn, "The 'Civil Polity' of Peter Paxton," *Past and Present,* 40 (July 1968), 56.

12. The best example is the preface to the *Etudes historiques* (1831).

13. This approach was set out in the *Cours d'histoire moderne: histoire de la civilisation en Europe depuis la chute de l'Empire Romain jusqu'à la Révolution Française* (1828), lecture I. For long passages from Chateaubriand and Guizot, see J. Ehrard and G. Palmade, *L'histoire* (Paris: Colin, 1969), pp. 189-193, 203-207.

14. R. Aron, "Thucydide et le récit historique," *Theory and History,* 1, no. 2 (1960), reprinted in *Dimensions de la conscience historique* (Paris: Plon, 1961), pp. 147-197.

15. As throughout this article, the works quoted on medieval history are meant only as references and examples, not as a bibliography or selection in terms of merit.

16. Aron, "Thucydide et le récit historique," in *Dimensions,* p. 189.

17. An example of a traditional but all the same very pertinent study is F. M. Powicke, "Reflections on the Medieval State," *Transactions of the Royal Historical Society,* ser. 4, XIX (1936). Among new approaches are: B. Guenée, "L'histoire de l'état en France à la fin du Moyen Age vue par les historiens français depuis cent ans," *Revue historique,* 232 (1964), 331-360; "Etat et nation en France au Moyen Age," *ibid.,* 237 (1967), 17-30; "Espace et état dans la France du bas Moyen Age," *Annales: économies, sociétés, civilisations* (1968), pp. 744-758. It will be noted that the word "power" (accompanied, it is true, by an adjective) occurs in the title of the pioneer work by E. Lavisse, "Etude sur le pouvoir royal au temps de Charles V," *Revue historique* (1884), pp. 233-280, which attempts to go beyond the description of institutions to mental realities. Marc Bloch noted the connection between the history of the state and the history of a nation or nations. "It seems to be difficult to separate the history of the idea of the state from the history of the idea of nation, or patriotism." *Revue historique,* 128 (1918), 347.

18. The way Marxists tended to concentrate their interest on the state is apparent from the titles of their works: for example, F. Engels, *Private Property and the State*; V. I. Lenin, *State and Revolution.* On the two senses of "nation" in Marx and Engels (the modern designating "a kind of rising capitalism," and the other the more general Latin sense of ethnic group) see A. Pelletier and J. J. Goblot, *Materialisme historique et histoire des civilisations* (Paris: Editions sociales, 1969), pp. 94ff.

19. Marc Bloch, *Mélanges d'histoire sociale* (1944), p. 120, cited by Guenée, "L'histoire de l'etat en France," p. 345.

20. *Schriften der Monumenta Germaniae Historica,* XIII, 3 vols. (Stuttgart: Hiersemann, 1954-1956).

21. P. E. Schramm summed up the position himself in the résumé of his contribution to the Rome Conference of 1955: "Die Staatsymbolik des Mittelalters," in *X Congresso Internazionale di Scienze storiche* (Rome, 1955), vol. VII, *Riassunti delle communicazioni,* pp. 200-201.

22. M. Hellmann, ed. (Weimar: Böhlau, 1961). Among many studies on the

symbolism of the crown in the Middle Ages, see pp. 336-383, "The Crown as Fiction," in E. H. Kantorowicz, *The King's Two Bodies: A Study in Medieval Political Theology* (Princeton: Princeton University Press, 1957).

23. "It is not by chance that the relic St. Louis brought to Paris and installed in the chapel of his palace is a crown of thorns, doubly symbolic of kingship and of sacrifice." *Le Monde*, April 29, 1970, p. 13.

24. Schramm, "Die Staatsymbolik des Mittelalters," pp. 200-201.

25. Robert Folz, *L'idée d'empire en occident du Ve au XIVe siècles* (Paris: Aubier, 1953), p. 6.

26. On kingship in the early Middle Ages see especially J. M. Wallace-Hadrill, *The Long-Haired Kings* (London: Methuen, 1962), and F. Graus, *Volk, Herrscher und Heiliger in Reich der Merowinger* (Prague, 1965). For the Carolingian period, see the recent study by W. Ullmann, *The Carolingian Renaissance and the Idea of Kingship* (London: Methuen, 1969), which brings out especially well (p. 17) how then, "in conformity to and in accordance with the basic premisses of the ecclesiological theme and the wholeness of view, there was no conceptual distinction between a Carolingian State and a Carolingian Church." Georges Duby stressed the importance of the royal model within the feudal system at the international symposium, *Problèmes de stratification sociale*, 1966, published by R. Mousnier, Publications of the Faculté des Lettres et Sciences Humaines de Paris, Sorbonne, 'Recherches," XLIII (Paris, 1968). See K. Gorski, "Le roi-saint: problème d'idéologie féodale," *Annales: économies, sociétés, civilisations* (1969), pp. 370-376.

27. *Atti dell' VIII Congresso Internazionale di Storia delle religioni* (Florence, 1956).

28. *Studies in the History of Religions*, supplements to NVMEN IV, *The Sacral Kingship: La Regalità Sacra* (Leyden, 1959). Out of fifty-six contributions, only four are devoted to the Middle Ages in the West: M. Maccarrone, "Il sovrano 'Vicarius Dei' nell'alto medio evo," pp. 581-594; M. Murray, "The Divine King," pp. 595-608; L. Rougier, "Le caractère sacré de la royauté en France," pp. 609-619; and J. A. Bizet, "La notion du royaume intérieur chez les mystiques germaniques du XIVe siècle," pp. 620-626.

29. E. H. Kantorowicz, *Kaiser Friedrich der Zweite* (Berlin: Bondi, 1927), and *Ergänzungsband* (Berlin: Bondi, 1931).

30. E. H. Kantorowicz, *Laudes Regiae: A Study in Liturgical Acclamations and Medieval Ruler Worship* (Berkeley and Los Angeles: University of California Press, 1946).

31. E. H. Kantorowicz, *The King's Two Bodies: A Study in Medieval Political Theology* (Princeton: Princeton University Press, 1957). See also the reviews by R. W. Southern in the *Journal of Ecclesiastical History*, 10 (1957), and B. Smalley in *Past and Present*, no. 20 (November 1961).

32. Sir James George Frazer, *The Golden Bough* (London: Macmillan, 1890), part I: "The Magic Art and the Evolution of Kings." Frazer, *Lectures on the Early History of Kingship* (London: Macmillan, 1905).

33. A medievalist, Joseph R. Strayer, wrote an essay on "The Historian's Concept of Public Opinion" in the collection edited by M. Komarovsky, *Common Frontiers of the Social Sciences* (Glencoe, Ill.: Free Press, 1957). Marvin B. Becker, "Dante and His Literary Contemporaries as Political Men," *Speculum* (1966), p. 674, n. 28, calls attention to "the neglected theme of the language and imagery of medieval politics," and quotes the article by E. H. Kantorowicz, "Christus-Fiscus," in *Synopsis: Festgabe für Alfred Weber* (Heidelberg: Schneider, 1948), pp. 225-235.

34. "Anthropologie politique" is the title of an informative essay by Georges Balandier, 1967. He sets out systematically what E. R. Leach has observed to be "contradictory, conflictual, approximate, and externally relative" in societies, developing the theme of E. E. Evans-Pritchard in "Anthropology and History," 1961.

35. Here again there is an incompatibility between the point of view of Freund, *L'essence du politique*, p. 538, according to which "the class struggle is only an aspect of the political struggle," and the Marxist point of view, according to which all forms of political struggle derive from the class struggle. As long as it is not applied too dogmatically and inflexibly, I think the Marxist view is the truer and more fruitful. G. Cracco's stimulating book, *Società e Stato nel medievo veneziano* (*secoli XII-XIV*) (Florence: Olschki, 1967), shows the class struggle functioning normally in the political history of Venice, usually thought to be a world apart. It may be thought, however, that the author is limited by an approach based too much on the idea of the state. F. C. Lane makes reservations of this kind in a generally appreciative review in *Speculum* (1968), pp. 497-501.

36. See especially K. Bosl, "Potens und Pauper: Begriffgeschichtliche Studien zur gesellschaftlichen Differenzierung im frühen Mittelalter und zum 'Pauperismus' des Hochmittelalter," in *Alteuropa und die moderne Gesellschaft: Festschrift für Otto Brunner* (Göttingen: Vandenhoeck and Ruprecht, 1963), pp. 60-87, reprinted in *Frühformen der Gesellschaft im mittelalterlichen Europa* (Munich-Vienna: Oldenbourg, 1964), pp. 106-134. Also J. Le Goff, "Le vocabulaire des catégories sociales chez Saint François d'Assise et ses premiers biographes," in the international symposium organized by the Ecole Normale Supérieure of Saint-Cloud, 1967, on the vocabulary of social classes (in press).

37. G. Duby's conception of *seigneurie banale* is set out in his thesis, *La société aux XIe et XIIe siècles dans la région maconnaise* (Paris: Colin, 1953), and in *L'économie rurale et la vie des compagnes dans l'Occident medieval* (Paris: Aubier, 1962), vol. II, bk. III, "XI-XIIIe siècles: la seigneurie et l'économie rurale." In the legally oriented series, the *Recueils de la Société Jean Bodin*, the volume *Gouvernants et Gouvernés*, XXV (1965), shows a preoccupation with the themes of power which may

derive from Marc Bloch, *La société féodale* (Paris: Michel, 1939), vol. II, bk. 2, "Le gouvernement des hommes." The theme also occurs in J. Dhondt, " 'Ordres' ou 'puissances': l'exemple des états de Flandre," *Annales: économies, sociétés, civilisations* (1950), pp. 289-305.

38. See H. Grundmann, "Litteratus-Illitteratus: Der Wandlung einer Bildungs-norm vom Altertum zum Mittelalter," *Archiv für Kulturgeschichte,* 40 (1958), and his "Sacerdotium-Regnum-Studium: zur Wertung der Wissen-schaft im 13. Jahrhundert," *Archiv für Kulturgeschichte,* 34 (1951).

39. See my *Les intellectuels au Moyen Age* (Paris: Editions du Seuil, 1957), for an attempt to show how, between the end of the twelfth and the four-teenth century, members of the universities moved from a socioprofessional position which was corporative to one which placed them among the possessors of power.

40. The subject proposed by the French delegation to the International Uni-versity Committee on History at the Thirteenth International Conference on Historical Sciences in Moscow, August 1970. I believe Professor Lawrence Stone has a similar project in mind for English universities in the modern era. This revival of interest in the prosopographical method, a method of social history likely to favor the renewal of political history, is evident in various sectors (see the late 1970 number of *Annales: économies, sociétés, civilisations*).

41. Among G. Dumézil's many fascinating studies on the tri-functional ideology of the Indo-Europeans, one of the most recent is *Idées romaines* (Paris: Gallimard, 1969), in which he poses various questions about western Europe in the Middle Ages. Two examples of initial research in this field are J. Batany, "Des 'Trois Fonctions' aux 'Trois Etats'?" *Annales: économies, sociétés, civilisations* (1936), pp. 933-938, and J. Le Goff, "Note sur société tripartie, idéologie monarchique et renouveau économique dans la chrétienté du IXe au XIIe siècle," in T. Manteuffel and A. Gieysztor, eds., *L'Europe aux IX-XIe siècles* (Warsaw, 1968), pp. 63-71.

42. One of the works inspired by this particular question is Joan Evans' inter-esting *Art in Medieval France, 987-1498: A Study in Patronage* (London: Oxford University Press, 1948).

43. E. Panofsky, *Gothic Architecture and Scholasticism* (New York: Meridian, 1957). A more traditional view is given in R. Branner, *St. Louis and the Court Style in Gothic Architecture* (London: Zwemmer, 1965).

44. On the significance of Botticelli's *Primavera* see P. Francastel, *La realité figurative* (Paris: Gonthier, 1965), p. 241, "La fête mythologique au Quattrocentro," and p. 272, "Un mythe politique et social du Quattrocento." See Ernst Gombrich, *Botticelli's Mythologies: A Study of the Neoplatonic Symbolism of Its Circle,* in *Journal of the Warburg and Courtauld Insti-tutes* (1945). P. Francastel has developed these ideas in *La figure et le lieu: l'ordre visuel du Quattrocento* (Paris: Gallimard, 1967).

45. See R. Manselli, *L'eresia del male* (Naples: Morano, 1963), and "Les

hérétiques dans la société italieene du XIIIe siècle," in *Hérésies et sociétés dans l'Europe pré-industrielle, XIe-XVIIIe siècles,* a Royaumont symposium, presented by J. Le Goff (Paris and The Hague, 1968), pp. 199-202. This points out the "very close link between the Catharist heresy and the great political party of the Ghibellines." This study needs to be developed in the direction of a sociological comparison between religious sect and political party.

46. I will limit myself to references to the international symposium in Amsterdam in 1967, "Urban Core and Inner City"; Nelson W. Polsby, *Community Power and Political Theory* (New Haven: Yale University Press, 1963); and the "anti-historicist" works of Manuel Castells, which include "Le centre urbain: projet de recherche sociologique," in *Cahiers internationaux de sociologie* (1969), pp. 83-106, and "Vers une theorie sociologique de la planification urbaine," in *Sociologie du travail* (1969), pp. 414-443. All these deal with the modern period.

47. W. Braunfels, *Mittelalterliche Stadtbaukunst der Toskana* (Berlin, 1953).

48. See especially the preface to F. Braudel, *La Méditerranée et le monde méditerranéen à l'époque de Philippe II* (Paris: Colin, 1949), revised and augmented 2d ed., 1966; the idea is repeated in *Ecrits sur l'histoire* (Paris: Flammarion, 1969), pp. 11-13.

49. L. Febvre, *Combats pour l'histoire* (Paris: Colin, 1953), p. 118 (written in 1947).

50. *Ibid.,* p. 20 (written in 1941).

GORDON A. CRAIG

Political and Diplomatic History

ONE OF the paradoxes of the recent past is the fact that although universities have become politicized to a greater degree than ever before, students have seemed to become progressively less interested in the historical dimensions of politics and, if attracted to the study of history at all, have turned to its economic and social aspects and to the kind of *freischwebende Kulturgeschichte* that discourses on ideas without regard for their national origins or even their place in time. There are still young scholars who believe, as Hegel did, that the state is the proper subject—indeed, the most important subject—of historical investigation. But they seem to be less confident, and certainly less assertive, than those who ring the changes on Herbert Spencer's famous attack upon the state as being irrelevant to the real concerns of mankind.[1] Even when he made it, Spencer's statement was singularly inaccurate, and since his day the functions of the state have proliferated so vastly, and its impact upon almost every phase of its subjects' lives has become so obvious, that one might have expected young historians to be fascinated by this process of aggrandizement and to wish to study it in all its details. Instead, an increasing number act as if the state had somehow or other withered away. Political history—that is, the history of the state or, in a broader sense, of the ways in which men have come together in societies, organized and maintained them, and interacted with other social units—is out of fashion.

The reasons for this are not hard to find. In continental Europe, where schools of national history flourished in the nineteenth century, and where the prevailing tone until the First World War was set by scholars like Lenz and Marcks and Seignobos, Hanotaux, and Lavisse,[2] the patent failure of the national state to fulfill the hopes postulated for it has doubtless stimulated resistance to the

356

older tradition. Thus, in Germany, where veneration of the state was more exaggerated and of longer duration than in other countries, the current intense interest in economic and social history and the tendency to emphasize the negative aspects of German statecraft, while attributing its positive accomplishments to economic or other impersonal forces, must have its psychological roots in disillusionment.

In Great Britain and the United States, where the cult of the state was never very evident, there are other explanations for the shift to new fields. Simply because it has been the principal form of the discipline for so long, political history seems to many scholars to be old-fashioned and is assumed to be predictably dull and unlikely to yield anything very new in the way of results. Moreover, compared with economic and social history, which have availed themselves of techniques of measurement and analysis used by the social scientists, it appears to be deplorably unmethodical, the more so because it insists upon giving importance to the play of contingent factors, to the imponderables, to accident and the individual. Finally, since so much of its emphasis is placed upon the ways in which men and nations have sought and exercised power, and since this has often involved violence and bloodshed, it strikes some as being distinctly unedifying.

In this last respect, the popularity of political history has doubtless suffered from the revulsion against violence caused by the war in Vietnam. Recently a newspaper columnist who is much admired by the academic left launched an emotional attack upon the writing of history. "Think of the heroes our history books gave us!" he wrote. "Hannibal, Caesar, Charlemagne, Napoleon, and even Genghis Khan and Tamerlane! Here was glory! Here was greatness! Here were the values in which you and I were steeped from the days we first learned to read! . . . And yet where in our history books was the blood? Where was the agony? Where was the pain? . . . Now that the end of the human race is no further away than the flick of a switch, we can no longer afford false values."[3] One suspects that the preference of some scholars for economic and social history and the history of ideas is due in part to the fact that they basically agree with this and feel that the political historians have delighted so much in slaughter that they have contributed to the moral debauching of Western society.

That power has the ability to corrupt is doubtless true, but one would have thought that this was reason for studying it rather than the reverse. When Friedrich Meinecke accused Treitschke of having seduced people into overestimating the importance of power in state life,[4] he was not for a moment denying the legitimacy of the historian's interest in power, which was, of course, the subject not only of his own biography of Hermann von Boyen but also of his two greatest works, *Weltbürgertum und Nationalstaat* and *Die Idee der Staatsräson*. In a world in which power is the most inescapable of realities simply because it is always there, to be used for good or for evil, for the protection or destruction of liberty, its varied dimensions, its uses and abuses, and the responsibilities that attach themselves to it deserve more critical historical study than they received in an earlier age when the accumulation of material power was admired for its own sake.[5] This may not attract all historians, but those who turn to it should not feel guilty or be subjected to moral reprobation.

Nor should it be assumed that, because historians devote themselves to the traditional forms of historical research—administrative and constitutional history, the history of diplomacy and military affairs—they are choosing roads already too well traveled to yield exciting new vistas or lead into territory yet unexplored. The truth is that in these conventional areas there is no dearth of important problems that have not yet been investigated, and this is not always because they are of such recent origin that the materials have not yet become available to scholars. Periods and subjects that have attracted researchers for scores of years are still replete with questions not only unanswered but often unasked. If, for example, the proper subject of political history is power, the historian who deals with it must be thoroughly conversant with the instrumentalities that translate it into action. Yet administrative history has not always been treated with the imagination that it demands, and we know much less about institutions than we sometimes think we do. G. R. Elton has recently noted that this is true even of such a well-known body as the English Parliament. "Ever since English constitutional history came of age, in the day of William Stubbs," he writes, "Parliament formed its chief and sometimes its sole object. Acres of paper have been covered with analyses of its growth and development, with discussions of its composition and membership, with high theories about its place in the body politic. It does seem quite incredible that there should be anything further to say. Yet it would not be far wrong to assert that, at least before the nineteenth century and in measure even after, we know just about everything about Parliament except what it did and how it worked. When one asks the obvious first question of any part of its history, almost no answer comes forth; just what went on and why? . . . After a century of intensive study, . . . Parliament remains essentially unknown, because historians have not yet studied it administratively, as an institution rather than a constitutional symbol."[6] In large measure, the same can be said of the German Reichstag after 1871, and doubtless of other similar institutions.

Nor are the possibilities restricted to the most specialized aspects of political history. In one sense, those who have accused the political historians of being unduly preoccupied with violence have right on their side, for the aspects of political history that have been subjected to the closest scrutiny have been rivalries for power, conspiracies, plots, revolutions, civil wars, and other manifestations of political instability. J. H. Plumb has reminded us recently that similar attention has not been lavished on the subject of stability in politics, although it poses some intriguing problems for the historian.[7] We know much less about how societies come to accept a pattern of political authority and the institutions that are required to give it governmental form than we do about symptoms of political disaffection and the anatomy of revolution; as long as this continues to be true, it is idle to pretend that political history is less challenging than those branches of the discipline that seem to be currently fashionable.

It is, of course, true that the political historian is apt to show less respect for the abstract formulations and the generalizations of the behavioral scientists than his colleagues in nonpolitical fields and that he is reluctant to consider a model as a real thing. But this should seem superficial only to those who believe that institutions can work by themselves or ideas exist without minds to hold them. The competent political historian is aware of the usefulness of social analysis and ideological explication, but he has chosen to deal with the things that are analyzed and explained in their active rather than their abstract forms. He agrees with Federico Chabod's insistence that "history, at least up to the present, has been made by men, and not by automata, by doctrines or so-called structures which, by themselves, from the point of view of historical evaluation, are pure abstractions; these acquire the value of a historical force only when they succeed in dominating the minds of men—of individuals and of masses—that is to say, when ideology and social relations become a moral fact," capable of bringing men together "in this political

party or that, behind this or that banner" to fight for specific objectives.[8] The translation of ideas into action and theory into practice and the subtle ways in which they are modified and transformed
in the process by the play of circumstance, chance, and individual
idiosyncrasy is one of the most difficult problems that confronts the
historians of any age. Its solution is not much facilitated by generalizations or by the construction of models, but only by the fascinating process of studying ideas in their particularized and
changing forms—which is, of course, the political historian's stock
in trade.

With the exception of specialists in military affairs, who have
always been the second-class citizens of the historical profession,[9]
none of the practitioners of political history have been charged
more often with myopic vision and analytical superficiality than
those who have taken the world of diplomacy as their province.
Much of this criticism has been justified. Thirty-five years ago,
when G. M. Young wrote that "the greater part of what passes for
diplomatic history is little more than the record of what one clerk
said to another clerk,"[10] he could have proved his point, if he had
wished to do so, by citing any number of arid monographs that had
been literally copied out of the bound volumes of Foreign Office
papers in the Public Record Office, tricked out with Latin tags
(*sub spe rati, rebus sic stantibus,* and the like) and impressive footnotes (FO France/1749; from Lyons, no. 249, very confidential,
March 4, 1869), and sent forth to grace the lower shelves of university libraries. Even so, his formulation was drastic, leaving the
impression, not only that diplomatic history was not being done
very well, but also that the materials of diplomatic history—what
the clerks and their superiors wrote to each other—were not worth
reading.
    Since the crisp authority of Young's dictum won wide acceptance
for this idea, and since it encouraged any number of scholars in the
field of international relations to attempt to write about foreign
affairs without reading the documents, it needs to be corrected. The
diplomatic historian's first duty is to construct a clear record of the
formal relations between states that have dealings with each other,
a record of what actually happened between them, of how they
communicated, and with what result. For this purpose, a nation's
diplomatic archives, which include the official communications between it and other governments, the circular memoranda and de-

tailed instructions sent by its foreign ministry to the various missions abroad, and the political, economic, military, and other reports received from the ambassadors and envoys resident in the countries with which it has formal relations, are an indispensable source of information. It is here and here alone that the historian can find a detailed and documented record of the execution of a particular line of policy or the day-by-day account of a particular set of negotiations: it is these papers that enable him to see the problems of foreign affairs in their most concrete form and to observe the exact manner in which—to use Satow's words—intelligence and tact are applied (or, as the case may be, *not* applied) to the conduct of official relations between the governments of independent states.[11]

In addition to the information that he finds here about the operational aspects of foreign affairs, and the aesthetic pleasure of discovering that diplomatic reports have some literary distinction (witness, for example, Bismarck's reports from Frankfurt in the 1850's, and those of Horace Rumbold and Eric Phipps from Berlin in the 1930's),[12] the scholar who immerses himself in the diplomatic archives is sure to acquire a good deal of incremental knowledge and a considerable amount of insight into the judgments upon which the tactics and even the strategy of policy were based. No one can read the dispatches to Berlin from the German embassy in Washington in the late 1930's without gaining a new understanding of the reasons for Hitler's overestimation of the strength of American isolationism and without learning something about the nature and weaknesses of totalitarian diplomacy. No one can read the printed volume of German diplomatic correspondence on the Spanish Civil War without sensing a connection between the maladroitness of German agents in Spain at that time and Franco's behavior toward Hitler at Hendaye in 1940. What more striking illustration can be found of the illusions that were to produce the policy of appeasement than the protocols of the conversations between Hitler, Anthony Eden, and Sir John Simon in March 1935? What more revealing account of the developing differences between Austria and Prussia than Bismarck's dispatches to Otto von Manteuffel in the 1850's, a correspondence in which the basic features of Bismarck's future policy as Foreign Minister were limned lightly but unmistakeably? This sort of thing is hard to come by in other sources, nor is there a better way of gaining an appreciation of the feel of a situation or of the psychology of those called upon to deal with it than reading what they wrote about it at the time.

As for official communications between states, they are important to the historian for what they say, what they do not say, and how they say it. The future historian of the Berlin crisis of 1958-1962 will have to expend the same degree of analytical skill on the Soviet note of November 1958 as did the officials in the State Department when it arrived; but in reaching a judgment of Soviet motives and objectives he will be aided by knowledge that was not at their disposal and by the ability to compare the first note with subsequent ones and to reflect upon differences of content and emphasis. Future historians of the diplomacy of Italian Fascism may be less interested in the content of Mussolini's messages to other governments than in their style, which tells much about the Duce's pathetic attempt to make a policy and a reputation out of rhetoric and about his failure to comprehend that power is a reality rather than a vocable.

So much for the importance of diplomatic communications, the official ones and, when they can be found, those that were private.[13] Yet, as William L. Langer pointed out as early as 1931, "the study of diplomacy, if it is to lead to anything worthwhile, must go beyond the mere digest or analysis of documents and negotiations."[14] It has to deal not only with the operational aspects of policy but also with policy itself, as an expression of all of the vital forces of a nation, including its moral and intellectual assumptions about foreign policy, the desires of its political parties and economic interest groups, and the influences exerted by the bureaucratic structures that give form to its public life.[15]

To establish the relationship between ideas and foreign policy is always a difficult task, and it is no accident that it has attracted so few historians.[16] It is safe to say that every organized society has some fundamental assumptions about its relations with other states and about its place in the international order, and that some nations include intellectuals who, individually and in schools, think about policy and draw up prescriptions for its success. Sometimes the theories and the assumptions combine in curious ways and acquire enough force to influence policy-makers, although for this to become true some external pressure is often required. In the first chapter of a book that has often been described as a model of what diplomatic history should be,[17] B. H. Sumner has given an account of the way in which Panslavism influenced Russian foreign policy during the great eastern crisis of the 1870's. He describes how this rather formless philosophy, which began as an inchoate bundle of religious and intellectual strivings on the part of small groups of Muscovite landowners, was transformed into an extreme form of Great Russian nationalism, because its most gifted spokesmen knew how to appeal to the religious convictions of the unlettered masses and to the desire of the educated classes for national recognition and their "reaction against the claim of western European civilization to set up as the one true civilization." But he stresses the fact that it was only after "events abroad gave the requisite shock" that Panslavism in its altered form was able to divert and, for a time, to direct the policy of the tsar and his immediate advisers.[18] The process that Sumner describes can hardly be applied generally; even so, the manner in which ideas become expressed in foreign policy is rarely less complicated than this.

Ideas are elusive and chameleonlike, characteristics that are apt to leave the historian who seeks orderly and direct connections and influences frustrated and bewildered, like Musil's General Stumm von Bordwehr, who sought vainly to marshal all the great ideas of his time into disciplined and controllable columns and was left feeling as if he had been traveling in a second-class carriage in Poland and had caught fleas. "It is the filthiest feeling of helplessness that I know," the general says. "When you spend too much time with ideas, you itch in every part of your body, and you find no relief even when you've scratched yourself bloody!"[19]

What is worse, when they encounter resistance, ideas about foreign policy are likely, not only to produce their opposites, but also to cohabit with them in incestuous relationships that are sources of continuing embarrassment to the statesmen who seek to use them.[20] Thus, the utopian idealism that marked early American assumptions about foreign policy yielded, in the first diplomatic contacts that the Republic had with the Old World, to the cynical realism of classical diplomacy,[21] and subsequently, in George Washington's great political testament, combined with it in an ambiguous association that was to complicate the definition of American policy aims for generations. Not the least important consequence of this has been that, although Americans pride themselves upon their practicality, they can be inspired to great efforts in foreign affairs less easily by arguments of strategic advantage or *raison d'état* than by sentimental and ideological appeals, and that, even when their statesmen are acting with a ruthlessness equal to that of Bismarck or Metternich, they have to be assured that their motives are nobler and their hearts purer than those of other peoples. Woodrow Wilson, Franklin Roosevelt, John Foster Dulles, and John Kennedy adjusted their diplomatic styles to this awkward marriage between idealism and realism, and the limitations that necessary lip-service to the former imposed upon their freedom of action deserve more attention from historians than they have received.

Finally, ideas about foreign policy are apt to captivate the minds of statesmen (who are not invariably good historians) only after they have become obsolete or obsolescent. Thus, Neville Chamberlain's reading of Harold Temperley's *Canning* apparently gave him one more reason for not opposing Hitler, since Canning had argued that England's role in continental embroilments must always be that of a mediatorial power.[22] A more lamentable example of the failure to understand that the passage of time can invalidate prescriptions that once were sound could hardly be found, were it not for the memory of Dean Rusk's Munich fixation and his insistence on applying the lessons of 1938 to situations for which they were inappropriate. The foreign policies of great powers have been guided as often by stereotypes from the past as by visions of the future, another theme for historical reflection.

In addition to dealing with the impact of ideas upon policy, the diplomatic historian is called upon to address himself to the relationship between foreign policy and domestic and economic forces. This is particularly important today, for, as if in belated response to an older breed of diplomatic historians who believed in the primacy of foreign policy and wrote about it as if it had no domestic roots, there is a tendency among contemporary historians who are interested in foreign affairs to assert a *Primat der Innenpolitik*. Notable among the productions of this school is Helmut Böhme's study of Germany's unification and consolidation,[23] a book that is avowedly revisionist and seeks in its early chapters to diminish the part played by Bismarck's diplomacy and the victories of Prussian arms in creating the German empire, attributing the greatest influence in this process to the movement of economic forces. The attempt does not succeed, partly because of the author's cavalier dismissal of parts of the story that do not fit his thesis as insignificant and partly because of the indisputable fact that, in the critical days when the struggle for German hegemony came to a head, economic interest did not prejudice political decisions in states like Saxony and Hannover, which, despite the importance of their economic ties with Prussia, fought against her in 1866. As Lothar Gall has written, whatever may be said about the movement of economic forces, "there is no getting around the fact that the decision over the further development [of the German question] was made only on the battlefield of Königgrätz and not in the area of economic and commercial policy."[24]

Böhme's mistake is to claim too much,[25] a criticism that can also be leveled against a much more sophisticated example of this genre, Hans-Ulrich Wehler's book on Bismarck and imperialism.[26] This impressive work brings a broad spectrum of economic, sociological, and sociopsychological theories and techniques to bear upon the still perplexing problem of Germany's reasons for inaugurating a policy of overseas expansion in the years 1883-1885. In it Wehler argues, first, that the drive for colonies was essentially the result of an ideological consensus in favor of their acquisition, on the assumption that they were necessary to correct the problems posed by the economic growth crisis of the 1870's and to avert social disruption and the possibility of political revolution. Second, he states that Bismarck responded to this by mounting an elaborate "manipulative social imperialism" to shore up his own position and to maintain the authoritarian social order. Wehler's book is a formidable demonstration of the inadequacies of the traditional methods of dealing with this kind of a subject, and it should be studied seriously by historians. But, there is no doubt that its view of Bismarck's imperialism is flawed by its author's revisionist zeal. His insistence that the chancellor's policy always functioned under the primacy of domestic factors takes little account of the external circumstances that influenced his initial moves in colonial policy—namely, the provocatively excessive claims made by the British in South West Africa—and it fails to explain why, if colonial acquisition was so necessary to support the social order, Bismarck lost interest in it so quickly.[27] To underestimate the way in which Bismarck, at every stage of his career, adjusted his policy to the opportunities offered or denied by the state of international politics is as great a delinquency as to view his policy solely from its diplomatic aspect. Students of foreign affairs should make every effort to avail themselves of the new tools of analysis that Wehler uses with such skill, but they should remember that such techniques are more profitable when they are regarded as means of complementing the more traditional methods of the political historian rather than as means of replacing them.[28]

They should bear in mind also the advice given by Federico Chabod in his great history of Italian foreign policy, that it is dangerous to attempt to draw a distinct line between domestic and foreign policy and to think in terms of the primacy of one or the other.[29] The lessons of history and our own experience should convince us that the two spheres are so intimately connected as to represent a fusion of factors that exert varying pressures in different circumstances. Recently, Arno J. Mayer has suggested that the internal causes and purposes of war in the period after 1870 deserve more rigorous analysis than they have hitherto received and, to start things off, has hypothesized that *raison d'état*, that concept so beloved by diplomatic historians, can serve as a guide to statesmen only in times of political stability. When the legitimacy of a regime is threatened by the operation of internal economic and social forces, political parties and other groups are likely to substitute their own selfish desires for any objective view of state interest and, depending upon whether they are in favor of change or maintenance of the status quo, are likely to speculate upon the uses of war for the promotion of their domestic goals.[30] This is not an entirely original suggestion—in a cruder and more polemical form it is to be found in Charles A. Beard's article "Giddy Minds and Foreign Quarrels"[31]—and the mind leaps immediately to examples that appear to contradict it. If, for instance, one considers the period immediately antecedent to that chosen by Mayer for his "research assignment," how does his hypothesis fit the war of 1866, which was certainly fought in conditions of great political instability inside Prussia, since the forces of organized liberalism were challenging the whole structure of the authoritarian state? Not very well, one must conclude, for the liberals, the forces of movements, were singularly unenthusiastic about the war, whereas their opponents, who did seek the test of arms, were not, in the first instance, thinking about its domestic effects. When Moltke spoke of the war's being fought for an ideal end, the acquisition of power, he was thinking of Prussia's European position.[32] There is no good reason to doubt the sincerity of Bismarck's statement: "Even if the government found itself at peace with the country, [I] would have advised in favor of war . . . Domestic reasons do not make a war necessary, but they are, indeed, additional reasons for making it seem advantageous."[33]

Even so, Mayer's suggestion is valuable, the more so because of the terms in which it is stated, which are fully in accord with Chabod's cautionary prescription. "The calculus of the internal political effects of intensified external conflict or war," Mayer writes, "is more likely either to deter or to encourage recourse to war in a revolutionary era and under conditions of internal instability than in times of domestic and international equipoise."[34] The last adjective should be noted. Internal forces which, other things being equal, would call for a policy of aggressive action may be controlled by the configuration of the international scene, as they were, for instance, during the near eastern crisis of 1838-1841, when those domestic interests in France that desired war were prevented from having their way by the forces for stability in the international system. Conversely, the dangerous nature of the foreign situation may force the acceptance of war at a time when no party can anticipate material advantage from fighting it. The historian who is intent upon demonstrating domestic influences on the determination of foreign policy must, in short, constantly bear in mind the kind of limitations that are imposed by forces beyond the water's edge.

Nor should he forget the decisive influence that is often exerted by the instrumentalities of the state itself. Foreign policy in the modern era responds not only to the pressures that are brought to bear upon it by organized interest groups in the private sector but also to those wielded by agencies of the government which, despite their official nature, may put a high valuation on the protection of parochial interests. The way in which policy debates in time of crisis are influenced by institutional affiliation and bureaucratic rivalries has been little studied, although, for instance, it is well known that differences between the Treasury and the Foreign Office played a role in the victory of appeasement in Great Britain in the years 1937-1938 and although Graham T. Allison has demonstrated that the views of President Kennedy's advisers during the Cuban missile crisis of 1962 were related to their positions in the government.[35] Still less has been done to investigate the institutional responses of even the greatest of great powers to the changing conditions of international diplomacy that have resulted, since 1920, from such things as the breakdown of the homogeneity of the traditional international system, the emergence of new nations without experience in foreign affairs or a diplomatic tradition of their own, the appearance of international corporations that play their own power game according to their own rules,[36] and the existence of formal international agencies.

With all this to be looked into, it is clear that diplomatic history must broaden its focus and turn its attention to the ideas, the interest groups, and the institutions that help to mold the policies that the diplomat in the field seeks to execute. In making this adjustment, the diplomatic historian need not abandon his faith in the role of the individual or be less insistent that "in a given situation the work of the individual statesman always intervenes incisively in the course of events, whether he allows himself weakly to be submerged by their flow or, greatly, succeeds in channeling them somehow, making them follow one rhythm or another, directing them to this goal or that, slackening their pace or quickening it."[37] What he does have to do is to devote more thought than some of his predecessors have devoted to the difficult problem of determining the relationship between structures—whether ideological, socioeconomic or institutional—and personality in history.[38]

REFERENCES

1. "Perpetually, governments have thwarted and deranged . . . growth, but have in no way furthered it, save by partially discharging their proper function and maintaining social order . . . It is not to the State that we owe the multitudinous useful inventions from the spade to the telephone; it was not the State which made possible extended navigation by a developed astronomy; it was not the State which made the discoveries in physics, chemistry and the rest which guide modern manufacturers; it was not the State which devised the machinery for producing fabrics of every kind, from transferring men and things from place to place, and for ministering in a thousand ways to our comforts. The world-wide transactions conducted in merchants' offices, the rush of traffic filling our streets, the retail distributing system which brings everything within easy reach and delivers the necessaries of life daily at our doors, are not of governmental origin. All these are the results of the spontaneous activities of citizens, separate or grouped. Nay, to these spontaneous activities governments owe the very means of performing their duties. Divest the political machinery of all those aids which Science and Art have yielded it—leave it with those only which State-officials have invented—and its functions would cease." Herbert Spencer, *Man versus the State* (1884), as quoted from the 1914 edition in Donald O. Wagner, ed., *Social Reformers* (New York: Macmillan, 1939), pp. 347-348.

2. See John Higham, Leonard Krieger, and Felix Gilbert, *History* (Englewood Cliffs, N. J.: Prentice-Hall, 1965), p. 344.

3. Arthur Hoppe, "Farewell to Glory,". *San Francisco Chronicle,* November 16, 1970.

4. Friedrich Meinecke, *Die Idee der Staatsräson in der neueren Geschichte,* ed. Walther Hofer (Munich: Oldenbourg, 1963), pp. 467-468.

5. For examples of what can be done with the subject, see Leonard Krieger

and Fritz Stern, eds., *The Responsibility of Power: Historical Essays in Honor of Hajo Holborn* (Garden City, N. Y.: Doubleday, 1967).

6. G. R. Elton, *Political History: Principles and Practices* (New York: Basic Books, 1970), pp. 33-34.

7. J. H. Plumb, *The Growth of Political Stability in England, 1675-1725* (London: Macmillan, 1967), pp. 12-13.

8. Federico Chabod, *Storia della politica estera italiana dal 1870 al 1896,* vol. I: *Le premesse* (Bari: Laterza, 1951), p. xii.

9. See Sir Charles Oman, "A Plea for Military History," in his *On the Writing of History* (New York: E. P. Dutton and Company, n.d.), pp. 159ff; and Gordon A. Craig, *War, Politics and Diplomacy: Selected Essays* (New York: Praeger, 1966), pp. 86-87.

10. G. M. Young, *Victorian England: Portrait of an Age* (Garden City, N. Y.: Doubleday, 1954), p. 155; originally published in 1936.

11. Sir Ernest Satow, *A Guide to Diplomatic Practice,* ed. Sir Nevile Bland, 4th ed. (London: Longmans, 1957), p. 1.

12. Bismarck's Splendid Dispatch *(Prachtbericht)* of 1856 is always cited in this respect. See Bismarck, *Die gesammelten Werke,* 15 vols. (Berlin: O. Stollberg and Company, 1924-1935), II, 142ff. For an example of the lighter vein, see Phipps's report on a visit to Goering's hunting lodge in 1934, which was widely circulated in London at the time. E. L. Woodward and Rohan Butler, eds., *Documents on British Foreign Policy, 1919-1939* (London: H. M. Stationery Office, 1949———), 2d ser., VI, 749-751.

13. For the policy of Napoleon III one has to go beyond the official documents printed in *Les origines diplomatiques de la guerre de 1870-1871,* for the Emperor liked to operate through a network of secret agents and private correspondents. Similarly, in the years 1916-1918, Austrian Foreign Minister Czernin was not content to rely on his official envoys to influence German policy, but availed himself of the good offices of politicians, businessmen, and officials in German state governments to carry his ideas to Berlin. On the latter case, see Robert Hopwood, "Interalliance Diplomacy: Count Czernin and Germany, 1916-1918," Ph.D. dissertation, Stanford University, 1965.

14. William L. Langer, *European Alliances and Alignments,* 2d ed. (New York: Knopf, 1950), p. vii.

15. Chabod speaks of foreign policy bearing the imprint of "tutta la vita di un popolo, nelle sue aspirazioni ideali e nelle ideologie politiche, nelle condizioni economiche e sociali, nelle possibilità materiali come nei contrasti interni d'affetti e di tendenze." Chabod, *Storia della politica estera,* p. x.

16. On this weakness of diplomatic history, see Peter Paret, "Assignments New and Old," *American Historical Review,* 76 (February 1971), 119-126.

17. B. H. Sumner, *Russia and the Balkans, 1870-1880* (Oxford: Clarendon Press, 1937). Even such an acerbic critic as A. J. P. Taylor has called this "a wonderful book." A. J. P. Taylor, *The Struggle for Mastery in Europe, 1848-1918* (Oxford: Clarendon Press, 1954), p. 597.

18. Sumner, *Russia and the Balkans,* pp. 56-80.

19. Robert Musil, *Der Mann ohne Eigenschaften,* ed. Adolf Frisé (Hamburg: Rowohlt, 1952), p. 374 (bk. I, pt. 2, chap. 75).

20. General Stumm formulates this in military terms: "Aber du bemerkst wohl . . . wenn du eine der heute im Gefecht stehenden Gedankengruppen betrachtest, dass sie ihren Nachschub an Kombattenten und Ideenmaterial nicht nur aus ihrem eigenen Depot, sondern auch aus dem ihres Gegners bezieht; du siehst, dass sie ihre Front fortwährend verändert und ganz unbegründet plötzlich mit verkehrter Front, gegen ihre eigene Etappe kämpft; du siehst andersherum, dass die Ideen ununterbrochen überlaufen, hin und zurück, so dass du sie bald in der einen, bald in der anderen Schlachtlinie findest: Mit einem Wort, man kann weder einen ordentlichen Etappenplan, noch eine Demarkationslinie, noch sonst etwas aufstellen, und das Ganze ist, mit Respekt zu sagen—woran ich aber andererseits doch wieder nicht glauben kann!—das, was bei uns jeder Vorgesetzte einen Sauhaufen nennen würde!" *Ibid.*

21. The alliance between France and America, concluded in 1778, "was not a document of a 'new diplomacy'; it was a political alliance pure and simple, conceived and written in terms of old-style diplomacy." Felix Gilbert, *To the Farewell Address: Ideas of Early American Foreign Policy* (Princeton: Princeton University Press, 1961), p. 85.

22. See Keith Feiling, *Life of Neville Chamberlain* (London: Macmillan, 1946), p. 321.

23. Helmut Böhme, *Deutschlands Weg zur Grossmacht: Studien zum Verhältnis von Wirtschaft und Staat während der Reichsgründungszeit 1848 bis 1881* (Cologne: Kiepenheuer & Witsch, 1966).

24. Lothar Gall, "Staat und Wirtschaft in der Reichsgründungszeit," *Historische Zeitschrift,* 209 (1969), 621-622. See also Otto Pflanze, "Another Crisis Among German Historians?" *Journal of Modern History,* 40 (1968), 118-129. It is not intended here to deny the merits of Böhme's study, particularly for the period after 1871, where he presents a mass of new material to illustrate the rise of modern industry, the emergence of new pressure groups, and the part they played in Bismarck's "refounding" of the Reich in 1879.

25. If one can judge from the judicious evaluation of data in Theodore S. Hamerow's *The Social Foundations of German Unification, 1858-1871: Ideas and Institutions* (Princeton: Princeton University Press, 1969), and particularly the author's measured calculation of the political weight of organized groups, his second volume, which will deal with the political story, will not make the same mistake.

26. Hans-Ulrich Wehler, *Bismarck und der Imperialismus* (Cologne and Berlin: Kiepenheuer & Witsch, 1969).

27. See Wolfgang J. Mommsen's review in *Central European History,* 2 (December 1969), 366-372.

28. This is essentially the argument of Otto Brunner, "Das Problem einer europäischen Sozialgeschichte," in *Neue Wege der Sozialgeschichte* (1956), pp. 7ff, and Werner Conze, *Die Strukturgeschichte des technisch-industriellen Zeitalters als Aufgabe für Forschung und Unterricht* (Arbeitsgemeinschaft für Forschung des Landes Nordrhein-Westfalen, Geisteswissenschaften, 66 [1957]).

29. Chabod, *Storia della politica estera,* p. xi.

30. Arno J. Mayer, "Internal Causes and Purposes of War in Europe, 1870-1956: A Research Assignment," *Journal of Modern History,* 41 (September 1969), pp. 291-303.

31. Charles A. Beard, "Giddy Minds and Foreign Quarrels," *Harper's,* 179 (September 1939), 337-351.

32. "The war of 1866 was entered on not because the existence of Prussia was threatened, nor was it caused by public opinion and the voice of the people. It was a struggle long foreseen and calmly prepared for, recognized as a necessity by the Cabinet, not for territorial aggrandizement, for an extension of our domain, or for material advantage, but for an ideal end—the establishment of power." H. von Moltke, *Gesammelte Schriften und Denkwürdigkeiten* (Berlin: E. S. Mittler und Sohn, 1891-1893), III, 426.

33. Bismarck, *Gesammelte Werke,* V, 372.

34. Mayer, "Internal Causes and Purposes of War in Europe," p. 296.

35. Graham T. Allison, "Conceptual Models and the Cuban Missile Crisis," *American Political Science Review,* 63 (1969), 689-713. An excellent study of the influence of civil servants on policy formulation is Zara S. Steiner's *The Foreign Office and Foreign Policy, 1898-1914* (London: Cambridge University Press, 1969).

36. See Henry Pachter, "The Problem of Imperialism," *Dissent* (September-October 1970), p. 478.

37. Chabod, *Storia della politica estera,* p. xiv.

38. See Theodor Schieder, "Strukturen und Persönlichkeiten in der Geschichte," *Historische Zeitschrift,* 195 (1962), 265-296.

PETER PARET

The History of War

UNTIL RECENTLY, war was a major subject of historical analysis, if not for its own sake, then as a constant of political history. Accounts of armed conflict written after the Middle Ages lost much of their mythological and symbolic quality, gained in precision, and became more analytic. By the eighteenth century, historians had become adept at employing a variety of sources in tracing the diplomatic events leading to war, the course of military operations, and the negotiations leading to the reestablishment of peace. But their work still suffered from a lack of appreciation of differences in economic, social, and political conditions that might exist between antagonists—between Sweden and Russia, for instance, or the Hapsburg and Ottoman Empires—or differences between former ages and their own times. On the whole they interpreted the military institutions and policies of earlier generations according to their own conditions and ideals. They regarded Caesar and Condé as contemporaries, and judged both by the practices of Frederick the Great.

Nor did they inquire systematically into the relationship between military and political institutions, or analyze the interaction of strategic policy and battle. Voltaire's history of Charles XII, for instance, devotes a great deal of attention to military events without ever departing far from a straight narrative whose single unifying principle appears to be the author's concern with the effect that a ruler's psychology may have on policy. Even the detailed description of a major encounter such as the Battle of Poltava, though derived from eyewitness accounts and set down in paragraphs of elegant clarity, leaves the reader puzzled about much that occurred.

Toward the end of the Enlightenment this historiographical mold was broken. In 1797 Gerhard Scharnhorst published a history

372

of the War of the First Coalition whose purpose was to identify and understand the apparently crucial differences between the monarchies and revolutionary France. Unlike other writers who sought the key to the French successes in specific techniques, such as the *levée en masse* or skirmishing, Scharnhorst took note of the advantages that France enjoyed: a more favorable strategic position, superior numbers, unified political and military command, and greater incentive. But he also analyzed the innovations in the French army's organization and methods, tried to trace their historical development, explained the strategy of the revolutionary commanders by the military and political situation, and pointed beyond military institutions to the greater energies that could be generated in a society that was more free than his own. "The reasons for the defeat of the allied powers must be deeply enmeshed in their internal conditions and in those of the French nation," he said, adding that he referred to psychological as well as physical elements.[1]

A few years later, his pupil Carl von Clausewitz extended the liberation of military history from the principles of cabinet diplomacy and maneuver strategy to the study of earlier conflicts. In his work on the Thirty Years' War, written between 1803 and 1805, Clausewitz made a point of criticizing those scholars who could treat the war only with a sense of horror and superiority as a formless, brutish struggle, which they would have preferred to ignore altogether. The men of the early seventeenth century, Clausewitz wrote, acted in accordance with their economic and technological condition, their political and religious concerns, and their psychology. It was an anticipation of the conservative motif of historicism for Clausewitz further to suggest that modern standards not only did not apply to the 1630's but that the energy and idealism of the generation of Gustavus Adolphus and Wallenstein might well have been superior to that of their descendants.[2]

In the historiography of the nineteenth century, political and military elements were generally closely connected. Sir John Seeley's proposition that the degree of a state's internal freedom was determined in reverse proportion by the degree of military and political pressure on its borders illustrates the interpretive reach of the time, though detailed explorations of political and military interdependence were perhaps more often found in the work of Continental scholars. Even Ranke, when he addressed himself to writing the history of Prussia during the French Revolution and the Napoleonic era, alternated as a matter of course between internal and foreign affairs, between the description of military planning and military action. Nor did historians whose work ordinarily lay in other fields hesitate to study themes that were predominantly military in character—as Friedrick Meinecke did in his biography of Boyen, when he integrated military history with the history of ideas and political attitudes. Toward the end of the century some scholars began to apply the speculations of the early sociologists about military elites and organized violence to their research into the nature and development of political institutions.

In the writings of Otto Hintze this fusion carried the history of war to a new level of methodological and interpretive significance. His long essays combined political, social, and economic history and the study of bureaucracies with comparative analysis; he firmly placed the military factor into a newly comprehensive approach to constitutional and institutional history. The armed forces served as a central element of his interpretations, not only in treatments of a particular episode—"Prussian Reform Attempts Before 1806," for instance—and in comparative explorations—such as "The Armed Forces and the State," which sought universal factors and regularities in the interaction of war and society over the course of Western civilization—but also in his many studies of such topics as feudalism, constitutional government, and imperialism. When Hintze wrote in 1906 that comparative history had established beyond question that "every political organization is originally an organization for war," he was not alluding to a prime mover that historians of later periods could safely ignore.[3] He was putting forward a programmatic statement. But although Hintze's work never lost its vitality—indeed, the strength of his method is only now becoming fully recognized—his immediate influence was limited.

Few historians took up his search for the specific links between institutional and constitutional development on the one hand and military force, its organization and employment, on the other. Nor can it be said that the historical profession in general was receptive to those scholars who wished to devote their work largely or exclusively to the study of the military theories, institutions, and policies of the past. History, as a discipline, continued to be dominated by political history,·which, indeed, the epigoni of the idealistic school tended to treat more narrowly than had their masters. Efforts to develop new fields, such as social or economic his-

THE HISTORY OF WAR

tory, met vigorous opposition; acceptable specialization was still limited to the auxiliary historical sciences, to philology, and to a few periods and national categories. Academics particularly interested in the study of war were further handicapped by the sizeable organizations of historians dealing specifically with military affairs that had been established in France, Germany, Austria, Russia, and elsewhere in the historical sections of the various armed services. These official bodies to some extent preempted the field through their control of the archives and through their technical expertise, the importance of which was increasing with the industrialization of war. Their interpretations, particularly in Germany and France, came to exert a profound effect on civilian scholarship. Some of the official historians—for example Jean Colin of the *Section historique* —were independent and original scholars; but too often the service publications had an apologetic or policy-oriented character that could only compromise the view in which the historical profession held the study of war. The antagonism that often existed between civilians and soldiers in Europe may also have played a part; it was simple enough to scoff at a professor as a *Zivilstratege* or, on the other hand, to dismiss the writings of nonacademic staff officers as the *Kultur der Kulturlosen.*

The failure of the European nation-state in our time has made the European historian more critical of his society's record of wars, without lessening his interest in it. Such works as Gerhard Ritter's *Staatskunst und Kriegshandwerk,* Rudolf Stadelmann's superb essays on Gerhard Scharnhorst, Émile Léonard's *L'armée et ses problèmes au xviiie siècle,* or Raoul Girardet's *La société militaire dans la France contemporaine,* which take a synoptic view of political, military, intellectual, and social history, or apply economic data to the analysis of social and military development, as Otto Büsch does in his *Militärsystem und Sozialleben im alten Preussen,* are exceptional for their level of achievement, but otherwise not unusual in modern French and German historiography. The years since 1945 have also brought increasing sophistication to the treatment of strategic decisions and actual operations. An example is Andreas Hillgruber's *Hitlers Strategie,* in which extensive interlocking studies explore the political, diplomatic, military, and psychological background of the Russo-German war.

Equally innovative studies have been written by contemporary English historians, who in general seem less interested in treating ideas on war and their connection with political concepts than in exploring civil-military relations and the development and execution of strategy—a preference in which they may find themselves at one with American scholars. Their work, which has generated considerable new knowledge on how societies and governments arm themselves, and how they fight, is accompanied by a vast output of books which, in Michael Howard's description, skillfully blend reputable history with wide public appeal.[4] While this popular literature has little or nothing to say to the scholar, it appears to possess as much justification as do textbooks addressed to the college audience—indeed, the educational functions of the two genres are not dissimilar. Military history is, in fact, frequently popular history. It seems to respond to a demand for colorful gore and for the vicarious experience of crime and punishment—appetites whose apparent universality may have something to say about the intractability of the subject with which these books are concerned. Possibly the mass of historical belles lettres, which is as prevalent on the Continent as it is in England, acts as a brake to change in the field, or at least limits the influence of innovation; but it does not prevent the history of war and of military institutions in general from occupying a secure if no longer a major place in the range of European historiography.

This is not its position in the United States. Good strategic and operational histories—mainly of the Second World War—are being written by American scholars, as are some valuable essays on military institutions, and a good many reinterpretations of American policy in the twentieth century, in which military considerations are on the whole treated with a notable lack of understanding. But there have been few books that combine the necessary technical and institutional knowledge with original work in other fields of history and the methodological sophistication found in the works of men such as Ritter or Girardet. At a time when many of the conventional categories of research and teaching in history are no longer deemed tenable, the history of military institutions and of war in America appears to be firmly encapsulated, in the eyes of most of its practitioners as well as to many historians with other specialties. I am not suggesting that this separation, even isolation, is entirely an American phenomenon; traces can be detected in other countries as well. But it is very striking in American historiography, and it is worthwhile to try to understand why this should be so. A more detailed review of the conditions of military history in one country may help clarify its problems and opportunities in general.

I

Far too much military history is being written in America. In this respect, at least, its condition does not differ from that of other fields of history. But with few exceptions, the character of the work produced is extremely conventional—descriptive history, centering on leading figures, campaigns, and climactic battles, often with a strong antiquarian bent.[5] Few enterprising minds are interested in war and in military institutions for their own sake.

Some years ago, in a critique of the kind of military history written in America, I suggested that the field was marked by enormous methodological confusion. More accurately, I should have said that the field was characterized by indifference to problems of methodology, most writers being content to jog along in the old narrative ways. Confusion does exist, but it relates more directly to purpose. In 1961, in the pamphlet *Military History* written for the American Historical Association's Service Center for Teachers, Walter Millis divided American military literature into three categories: the literature of recall, with which he designated memoirs, unit histories, and personal reminiscences; the analytic study of war as an institution, by which, oddly enough, Millis meant strategic and operational analysis; and works such as Emory Upton's *The Military Policy of the United States,* in which military history was used "not simply to teach battlefield tactics but as a foundation for broad national policy."[6] It is suggestive that such an intelligent and able writer as Millis, whose contribution to our understanding of the American military past is considerable, could see military history as purely utilitarian—except for the instruction and vicarious pleasure that may be derived from reading the memoirs of General Sherman or General MacArthur.[7] His argument belongs, of course, to a vigorous tradition that is far from being exclusively American. For example, when Sir Frederick Maurice, in his London inaugural lecture in 1929, spoke on "The Uses of the Study of War," he stated that the first use, "which most concerns the citizen, is to promote peace by promoting an understanding of the realities of war and of the problems which may lead to war. The second, which most concerns the professional, but also does or should concern the citizen, is to ensure that war, if it comes, is waged in the best possible way."[8] The desirability of these purposes need not be denied, but by themselves they are hardly adequate guides for research. They appear threadbare in their pragmatic exclusiveness

when they are compared with Delbrück's nearly simultaneous statement in the introduction to the fourth volume of his *Geschichte der
Kriegskunst im Rahmen der politischen Geschichte:* "Recognition of
the reciprocal effects of tactics, strategy, political institutions, and
politics throws light on the interconnections in universal history, and
has illuminated much that until now lay in darkness or was misunderstood. This work was not written for the sake of the art of war,
but for the sake of world history. If soldiers should read it and find
it stimulating, I shall be delighted and honored; but the book is
written for friends of history by a historian."[9] Once or twice, to be
sure, Millis' pamphlet suggests that aspects of the military past
might be studied for their own sake, but these are digressions that
do not affect his main argument that the writing and study of
military history has two functions: "to train professional military
men in the exercise of their profession and on the other hand to
educate governments and peoples in the military requirements of
today." With this as his premise, Millis naturally enough concludes
that since the strategy and tactics of the Civil War or even of
the Second World War can no longer serve as models for the
nuclear age, "military history as a specialty has largely lost its function." In a brief final paragraph, he urges military history, if it is to
regain its usefulness, to "turn away from a study of past wars to the
study of war itself in its broadest possible terms."[10]

No one can disagree with the proposal that military historians
make greater use of other disciplines—a suggestion to which I want
to return—but Millis' argument that the history of war "would have
to become less military and more civilian" contains at the very least
a dangerous ambiguity. Research in civil-military relations obviously
responds to his suggestion; but most recent work of this genre concentrates not on the two partners or protagonists, but on the relations between them, or deals primarily with the civilian side. Indeed, one of the marks of military history in America today is that
surprisingly few historians working on topics with a military
dimension are in fact studying that dimension. In much of the
literature that is considered military history, the services are
treated—often quite appropriately so—as agencies of the executive
without characteristics of their own, supporting players in what is
in effect political or diplomatic history. When historians do deal
directly with the peculiar features of war and its institutions, they
more often than not write as critics rather than historians. The
literature is full of vigorous second-guessing, of corrections and

condemnations, possibly at the expense of energy that might have gone into posing problems of historical interpretation and into their analysis. Compared to this, the fact that certain scholars, agreeing with Millis, aspire to influence policy through their books, seems a less serious if equally naïve defect.

Before considering the position assumed by the historical profession as a whole, which is both one of the causes of the difficulties in which military history finds itself and a reaction to its inadequacies, we should look briefly at the single most important institutional influence in the field: official military history.

The most extensive of the United States government's historical programs have been and continue to be the research and publication projects concerning America's military experience. They began with the publication in the last decades of the nineteenth century of the *Official Records of the War of the Rebellion* and with other documentary series on the Revolutionary War and on America's participation in the First World War. More recently emphasis has shifted from the publication of records to scholarly interpretive history, which produced such important series as *The United States Army in World War II*, the largest cooperative effort in historical writing yet undertaken in this country. These projects involved—and helped train—many civilian historians; one series, Samuel Morison's fifteen-volume history of the *United States Naval Operations in World War II*, though sponsored by the Navy, was published commercially. Some of the research techniques used were innovative. The most interesting seems to me to have been S. L. A. Marshall's teams of interviewers, who accompanied units into action, and, through observation and comprehensive interviews, sought to establish exactly what occurred during an engagement. In general, the quality of the official histories is high; at the very least they provide a reliable base line for the work of other scholars, and will influence interpretations for a long time to come.[11] But it is questionable whether they provide satisfactory models for interpreting more recent wars.

A flaw in the official projects has always been the absence of informed treatment of the highest planning and decision-making levels; America has nothing comparable to the United Kingdom's War Cabinet history or the integrated Canadian Defense Historical Program. This defect has been rendered more serious by organizational changes in the defense establishment since 1947. The individual services now play a far smaller role in over-all strategic planning, and consequently their historical sections are largely excluded from treating policy and politics, which in the wars in Korea and Vietnam mesh particularly closely with events in the field. In a session on contemporary history and war at the American Historical Association meetings in 1967, the Army's project for writing the history of its operations in Vietnam was criticized on this score—the Army historians cannot, of course, be held responsible for the change—as well as for certain methodological weaknesses of the project: it did not appear sound to develop a hypothesis on the nature and scope of a war in progress, and then turn this hypothesis into a scheme for writing the history of this war. Rather than considering broad integrative history, the Office of the Chief of Military History seemed to regard its subject in a narrow operational and tactical context.[12] This is only one of the problems. The primary purpose of the historical teams presently in Vietnam, on whose work subsequent interpretations will strongly depend, is to identify tactical and operational lessons learned, and to assist in determining the validity of current service concepts and doctrine.[13]

Undoubtedly the policy orientation of the current official service projects helps account for the distrust of military history among American historians, or for their indifference to it. As in Europe before 1914 and between the wars, the academic shortcomings of these programs confirm already existing prejudices and fashions. Changes may be taking place in the intellectual styles that dominate historical studies generally, but military history still tends to be thought of in narrow compartments to which service history projects lend a convenient definition, and it is not highly thought of.

It is tempting to seek the reasons for this negative attitude in the history of the United States. Though the country's past has been as violent as that of many European and Asian societies, the professional military establishment did not play a major role in America until technological developments compromised the security that geography had always provided. Throughout most of their history Americans could cherish the assumption that civilians were able to overcome not only the peacetime challenges of their country, but also that more than a few specialists in organized violence were not really needed. American historians, too, experienced difficulties in studying something that seemed to them to be undeniably wrong and that had no future. They were hard put to understand that bonds might exist between the American experience and the past of foreign societies—other, perhaps, than that of the English. Though they might know better, they felt or wanted to believe that America's wars had in general been caused by foreign transgression, and both politically and ideologically were defensive in character. The few obvious exceptions—the war with Mexico, for instance—were too insignificant to weaken their faith, while that unique cataclysm, the Civil War, seemed less a war to them than a phase in the nation's self-education and growth to maturity. Perhaps for this reason the Civil War required no special pleading on the part of military historians. On the contrary. Evidently neither American scholars nor their students felt uncomfortable immersing themselves in this conflict. In their view of the American world and of its past, the Civil War might be described as an intellectual zone of free security: its exploration obliged no one to regard war in general other than with disdain or indifference.

The Cold War, Korea, and especially Vietnam have rendered it unnecessary to insist that war is, after all, important, and have stimulated fresh, more encompassing inquiries into the nature and development of American political society—and thus into the martial side of American history. Some questions that potentially may be the most rewarding are just beginning to be asked; but scholars have already succeeded in so shattering the sense of the United States as a peaceful giant that it will require years of different national policies before the image can safely reappear. Not that it has been completely blotted out. In the universities resentment over the current war is certainly affected by the unhappiness with which some academics are at last compelled to recognize that historical and contemporary America contains many of the same tendencies that can be found elsewhere, that America the Beautiful has also always been America the Bellicose. Indeed, some continue to interpret the present situation as exceptional—an aberration. But who can doubt that those historians who saw themselves as guardians of the country's past and conscience, and scorned military history as un-American, have been overtaken by events.

The weakness of their intellectual position is accentuated by the fact that other disciplines, notably political science and sociology, have never evinced a comparable reluctance to investigate war and military institutions. But even among those historians who have worked on military topics, or who are showing a new interest in them, few have yet sufficiently appreciated the possibly relevant techniques, approaches, and findings of their sister disciplines. To sum up, American history is still suffering from the longstanding

indifference of American scholars to military history, and their
ignorance of it. At the same time, too much of the military history
that is being written is the work of conventional and unenterprising
minds that have never adequately distinguished the task of the
historian from that of the critic and debunker and show little concern with problems of theory and with methodological experimentation.

II

If we survey the historical literature on war in America and in
Europe, we find much detailed reconstruction and some general
statements, but few middle-range propositions. Here possibly is
another reason for the critical view that some scholars take of military history: it lacks a broad monographic base offering hypotheses
in a variety of contexts that can stimulate and structure discussion.
The analysis of military operations, which continues to make up the
bulk of the literature, is hardly conducive to the development of
creative historical hypotheses. Other areas of research appear far
more promising.

The study of war offers the greatest opportunities to those historians who, whether or not primarily interested in military problems, are prepared to range outside their own discipline. History
has always borrowed heavily from other fields of scholarship and
from the arts. Today many of us are trying to bring our research
into a closer and less haphazard relationship to the social and
behavioral sciences. The work of social scientists is of course
strongly committed to the present and future, and it would be a
mistake simply to assume that violence in our time, in any of its
many forms, is related or similar in kind to violence of the past.
But there are constants, and even in those areas where fundamental
differences seem to exist, research into contemporary issues can be
instructive.

The systematic analyses of general phenomena and the construction of models represent the most valuable contributions of
the social sciences to history. As long as historians believe in the
uniqueness of the human actor and of his condition they will hardly
work consistently within these patterns, but models can be useful
nevertheless. They support the categorizing, systematic tendencies
that are pronounced in some historical writing today, and make it
easier for the historian to distinguish the general from the specific

in the tasks that faced men in the past. Obviously the literature on misperception in crises or on theories of international relations has something to offer the historian of war, and yet how many of them draw on the kind of research that is published, for instance, in the *Journal of Conflict Resolution?* When I study collective violence in the Napoleonic era, and the attempts of men of that time to cope with it politically and psychologically, I can only benefit from the exploration of such scholars as Bernard Brodie or Alexander George into stress in political decision-making and into the character of coercive strategies, or from Klaus Knorr's analyses of military potential and military power. But, to repeat, a given model need structure neither research nor interpretations. More likely its generalizations act simply as additional flares that help light up the past. No doubt some behavioral scientists would consider a subjective exploitation of that kind disappointing, and obviously it is no better than the political scientists' use of historical data, which tends to be crude.

Besides the social scientist's model, some of his techniques for formulating and carrying out research—quantification, game theory, simulation, and role-playing—may benefit the historian of war. The methods will need to be adapted to his purposes, which means collaborating with colleagues in other disciplines. Among examples of other interdisciplinary work is the current Social Science Research Council seminar on state- and nation-building in Western Europe, whose members are addressing themselves to such topics as bureaucratization, taxation and social structure, food supply and public order, and the social and political functions of armed forces. Sociology, which since Spencer and Weber has shown great interest in war, continues to be heavily engaged in this field—a case in point being the Inter-University Seminar on Armed Forces and Society and its publication program, which involves members of several disciplines.

The application of the history of war to research in other fields of history constitutes another kind of opportunity. There may be considerable advantages in exploring nonmilitary problems from a new direction, and much military history has been written with this ultimate purpose, or lends itself to this use. An example is the extensive research that David Bien is presently conducting on the background and careers of the students of the *École Militaire* before the Revolution. In a collateral essay Bien has suggested that the emphasis on mathematics in the school's curriculum was not so much a response to scientific and technological change as a reaction against the larger culture of French society, whose character seemed to prevent the growth of a professional officer corps.[14] Mathematics rather than literature and rhetoric was the core around which a new military style developed. We do not yet adequately understand this shift, nor do we know enough about its effects on military education in other countries; but among the possibilities that emerge are not only a greater understanding of the French army as well as of French society, but also new and precise insights into the diverging paths of Germany and France. In Prussia, the addition of mathematical and technical instruction to the training of officers in the nonscientific branches of the service did not proceed, as in France, in interaction with a rich, if occasionally overblown, culture; instead, creative technical military expertise was developed before society as a whole had become fully saturated with the values of the Enlightenment.

Research such as this suggests that there is a limit to the usefulness of categorizing history as "social," "intellectual," or "military" according to the topic on which the historian is working. Of equal importance appear to be his interpretive goals, and the design of his research and analysis. The social and moral motives for the new curriculum in Paris are as much a concern for the history of war as the battles and campaigns with which it is usually identified— just as historians of education, for example, might find it useful to study the somewhat earlier discussions in the Hanoverian army over personnel policy and training, which were one of the main factors leading to the foundation of the University of Göttingen.

That the various genres of history are dependent on one another is a commonplace, but if the history of war is to achieve a value to other fields of history that is commensurate to the importance of its subject it needs to expand its efforts in several directions. Both economists and historians are showing new interest in applying economic theory to the history of war, and in studying the economic aspects of the management and expenditure of force, but this still remains the most overlooked side of military history. A related area of study concerns the interaction of war with science and technology.[15] We have not really moved very far beyond Hintze in defining the role played by military institutions and war in the history of political institutions. The history of ideas relating to war remains surprisingly old-fashioned. The study of strategic theory developed largely around commanders and writers of the first magnitude—Machiavelli, Frederick II, Napoleon, Friedrich Engels, Alfred T. Mahan are representative examples—and we still know little about their progenitors, less prominent contemporaries, critics, and epigoni, or about the growth and decline of entire strategic systems. We are even less well informed on the general ideas about war held by various generations. Works such as Karl-Ernst Jeismann's study of views on preventive war in the Bismarck era or Sir George Clark's analysis of the ethical and social values of war in the seventeenth century are as significant as they are rare. Finally historians of war need to go much farther in the exploration of the central element of military history: violence.

III

War is policy expressed in extreme forms of organized violence. The historian of war must obviously consider the numerous nonviolent phenomena that are constituent elements of his topic, as well as violent and partly violent motives that have been translated into activities that are violent in their eventual but not in their immediate expression—the drafting of strategic plans for instance. But all these ideas and actions derive their substance from the presence or the potential of violence alone. In many contexts it is appropriate, indeed essential, to analyze violence as simply another form that policy may take—one of many that are available to society—with its own theories, institutions, and techniques. But it is equally necessary to recognize that this policy is, after all, of a very special, primary character: it postulates the intimidation and killing of human beings by other human beings. We must also inquire how far each specific war is the tool of policy—that is, to what extent political considerations create and direct it—or whether the evolutionary process is not reversed to greater or lesser degree. Policy, if it results in war, may give great scope to aggressive instincts; it may also be generated by them.

It is not difficult to dismiss theories that seek the basis for war and for its conduct in irrational behavior, in psychological aberrations. Theories postulating that wars are products of exceptional circumstances fly in the face of most historical and contemporary evidence; they seem to attract some people because they remove the need to search for broader, more ordinary factors in individual and group violence. More sophisticated explanations of war as the work of special interests, or of the anarchic condition of the state

system, or of capitalism, nevertheless have certain affinities with
the simplistic psychological approach: they share with it an
unwillingness to acknowledge objective conflicts of interest, which
might obtain under any variety of political and social arrangements,
and they doubt or deny the presence of politically influential aggressive forces in the rational individual. A recent special issue on
conflict of the *Journal of International Affairs* concluded that "there
can be no purely psychological theory of war or of international
relations, . . . there can only be psychological factors within a general theory."[16] For the political scientist and the historian such a
theory would have to be built around the central political processes
of the society under investigation. But by the same token there can
be no adequate theory—or history—of war that ignores psychological forces.

The most precise and reliable devices for exploring the structure and dynamic of human aggression that are available to us
have been developed by psychoanalysis. Historians whose work
deals with organized violence should, if it is at all possible, avail
themselves of these insights. On the basis of considerable clinical
evidence and observational data, psychoanalysis argues that hatred,
sadism, and destructiveness are elemental forces in human nature.
It is the degree and manner in which these elements are fused
with more unifying forces of love and sex in the broadest sense,
brought under rational control, rechanneled constructively, or even
transformed altogether, that to a large extent accounts for differences between individuals, cultures, and subcultures. From earliest
childhood on, the modes of dealing with the inner world and external reality evolve and tend to become habitual. But regardless
how effective and healthy the individual or group, vast residues of
primitive aggression are retained. In whatever form they may take,
these forces cannot be brought under control unless their existence
is first recognized. A genuine acceptance of their existence is also
essential for the historical interpretation of their effects. It is hardly
necessary for me to add that the psychoanalytic views are not universally accepted, that there is great disagreement among psychiatrists and psychologists on the nature of human aggression; but
one need not adhere to one specific school and reject all others in
order to acknowledge the presence in man of extremely crude,
violent drives, or at least of aggressive reactions—often furthered
and trained by society.[17]

So much has been written on psychoanalysis and history that

it would be absurd for me to pretend to discuss the subject here, so to speak, in passing. But rather than leave my suggestion to military historians in mid-air, let me briefly state what I take to be some basic practical considerations.

The application of psychoanalysis to history is delimited by the fact that psychoanalytic theory generically is a therapeutic theory, and that clinical work remains its central concern. Psychoanalytic therapy depends for its effectiveness on the patient's recognition that he needs help, on his readiness to enter into the analytic process, and on his ability to participate actively in it. Furthermore, the data unearthed in analysis are less significant than the understanding and attitudes that emerge in the analysand through interaction with his analyst, and in the continuing, often unexpressed, process of self-analysis on the part of the patient during analysis and after its formal conclusion. Historians, by contrast, are dealing with the dead past. They can approach it with whatever psychological knowledge and insight they possess; but they must apply these qualities to something that is inanimate (if we exclude Friedrich Theodor Vischer's *Tücke des Objekts*) and impervious to change. At best, the historian's work may be compared to a preliminary diagnosis. No psychoanalytically influenced historical interpretation can equal the many-faceted structure of insights that is constructed in the course of a successful therapeutic analysis. Unlike the analysand, the past does not want to be helped. The historian may wish to affect the present by his interpretation of the past, but he is hardly involved in a therapeutic process. Finally, his effectiveness as a scholar is dependent on the extent to which his readers can accept the theoretical and methodological concepts underlying his work.

This last consideration imposes special problems on the historian who employs psychological concepts. The number and variety of psychological theories is considerable. They are often contradictory, and a historian who rigidly and explicitly adheres to a particular doctrine would seem to limit his audience. Even if he does not arouse his readers' unwillingness to follow the arguments of the school of psychology to which he adheres, he very likely still faces a deep fund of misunderstanding and ignorance. Some writers have attempted to overcome this difficulty by prefacing their interpretations with an outline of the psychological theories by which they were guided. But psychological theories are not understood by reading a textbook discussion of them.

It seems to me that the great value of psychological theory to the historian consists in its ability to sensitize him to psychological forces, and to teach him something about them. This is particularly true for those of us who have actually worked in the discipline, have themselves been analyzed, or have received psychoanalytic training. But even we would do best not to introduce chunks of theory and terminology to our writings that are addressed to a general historical audience. Such an approach would arouse resistance in many of our readers, while very possibly weakening our interpretations through an easy reliance on technical phrases and hypotheses.

The diffusion of Freud's ideas through our culture has been accompanied by an exceptional amount of vulgarization, but the widespread receptivity to his ideas has also enabled laymen to make responsible use of them. Some of the most enlightening and productive applications of psychoanalytic concepts to history have occurred in the work of scholars whose knowledge of psychoanalysis has not exceeded that of the serious amateur. Among recent examples is John Shy's attempt to understand the contemporary military behavior of American society by identifying major elements in the manner in which Americans, since they first settled this country, have perceived and interpreted outside threats, and in the character of their responses.[18] Shy develops a historical explanation for present policy rather than one based on the country's socioeconomic structure or on accident, an interpretation that "measures time less in years than in centuries; . . . action not in terms of struggles that divide society, but in terms of the shared attitudes that unite it. By measuring long-run continuity and broad consensus, rather than change or conflict, [this interpretation] defines the extent to which we may regard American society as a living organism whose behavior reveals an internal consistency." Two peculiarities common to all military activity are postulated: Violence and intermittence. The episodic character of warfare, the endless alternation of war and peace, lends great significance to society's military memory, whose selective working guides future behavior: "A remembered American military past has always more or less constrained both action in the present and thinking about the future." The seventeenth and eighteenth centuries he sees as a formative period of serious military troubles, in which the high military potential of the colonies was joined by a fairly low capacity for effective self-defense. Warfare was therefore thought of, and experienced, less in terms of immediate self-defense than in terms of retaliation and retribution, attitudes which were reinforced by the experiences of the nineteenth century. Then, gradually at first, all public issues come to be touched by the growing consciousness of military problems. American strategic doctrines since 1890 —sea power, strategic air attack, and limited war or flexible response—in a sense represent a shift from an earlier outlook, but "the elements of continuity are still most impressive: new ideas were absorbed and reshaped by old, deeply embedded modes of thinking about war." These not only expressed national policy, but themselves created it: an absolute conception of security, the feeling that effective military action must be total. The doctrine of limited war, which at first sight may appear as a retreat from the ideal of slow but finally total response, is predicated on the related belief that *all* unfriendly action is a danger to American security. Shy concludes that "amidst rapid military and social change . . . American society has been able to find—unconsciously of course— the intellectual and psychological means to preserve much of an older response to military problems, and to preserve that response in something like its primary force."

The continuity of historical forces sometimes impedes their analysis. In the United States today the legitimacy of the state's use of violence and its authority to compel participation by the citizen are questioned more widely than ever before. Some recent historical writing certainly reflects this questioning. The dangers that are created when contemporary concerns invade the study of history are well known; but if the present can be kept from dominating, it may prove useful to history. Experiences in this century have taught Europeans to be more critical of military power, while Americans have gained a new awareness of the close connection that exists between politics and war. On both sides of the Atlantic, the events of the past decades may help an increasing number of scholars to take a more balanced and penetrating view of the role that military theory, institutions, and policy have played in history.

In writing this paper I have benefited from observations by Felix Gilbert, Maurice Matloff, Walter Rundell, Jr., John Shy, and my former student Major Edward Vallentiny, U.S.A.F.

REFERENCES

1. Gerhard Scharnhorst, "Entwicklung der allgemeinen Ursachen des Glücks der Franzosen in dem Revolutionskriege," in C. v. d. Goltz, ed., *Militärische Schriften von Scharnhorst* (Dresden, 1891), pp. 195, 203.

2. Carl von Clausewitz, "Gustav Adolphs Feldzüge von 1630-1632," in *Hinterlassene Werke* (Berlin, 1837), IX, 18, 19-21, 101-106.

3. Otto Hintze, "Staatsverfassung und Heeresverfassung," *Gesammelte Abhandlungen* (Göttingen: Vandenhoeck & Ruprecht, 1962), I, 53. Compare this to the statement in Sir Lewis Namier's book, *England in the Age of the American Revolution* (London: Macmillan, 1930), p. 7: "The social history of nations is largely moulded by the forms and development of their armed forces, the primary aim of national organisation being common defence." The opening section of Namier's book, "The Social Foundations," seems to me to contain a number of direct reflections of Hintze's thought.

4. Michael Howard, "The Demand for Military History," *Times Literary Supplement,* November 13, 1969.

5. Incidentally it might be noted that, official histories apart, even the standards of technical knowledge are not demanding, so that books on the War for Independence that repeat hoary legends of the American rifleman, or biographies of Civil War generals that betray ignorance of the operational practice of their commands, are nevertheless well received. It is as though institutional historians were to deal solely with ministerial decisions, while having no idea how position papers are drafted or how a subordinate administrative office actually functions. In which case one might ask, why bother?

6. Walter Millis, *Military History* (Washington, D. C.: Service Center for Teachers of History, 1961), pp. 5-7; see also pp. 10-11.

7. As Frank Craven pointed out in his lecture "Why Military History," U. S. Air Force Academy, 1959, Millis' own work takes a far broader approach than his policy-oriented categories would imply.

8. Quoted in Michael Howard, "Military Power and International Order," *International Affairs,* 40 (July 1964), 397.

9. Hans Delbrück, *Geschichte der kriegskunst im Rahmen der politischen Geschichte* (Berlin: G. Stilke, 1920), IV, unpaginated introduction.

10. Millis, *Military History,* pp. 16, 17-18.

11. The Army series readily accommodated different and even opposing points of view. Compare, for instance, the essays by Kent Roberts Greenfield and Robert R. Palmer in the first volume of the series (on the Army ground forces), or the respective volumes on the Mediterranean campaign by Maurice Matloff and R. M. Leighton.

12. See the paper "Official History and the War in Vietnam," by Charles

MacDonald, and the comments by Leonard Krieger, Peter Paret, John Shy, and C. P. Stacey in *Military Affairs*, 32 (Spring 1968).

13. In the words of a member of one of these groups: "Lessons from complex, involved situations are difficult to grasp, hence there seems to be a tendency to narrow in on clearly identifiable points, and to view them in a kind of isolation from related problems. There are a number of difficulties with following this course, not the least of which can be the unconscious (or conscious, depending upon one's cynicism) inclination to impart a considerable degree of logic and orderly flow to the arrangement of events and factors, where little may actually have existed." Documentation and analysis of the war itself, or even of the conduct of a particular operation, has a lower priority, and is often severely handicapped. In many cases primary documents are destroyed after operational information has been extracted. The teams working in the field include few men with advanced professional training in history. Their reports are reviewed by higher authority, whose professional interests may be affected by them. In September 1968 I was asked to serve on an ad hoc History Advisory Committee of the Air Force, which was to evaluate the various historical activities of the service. I was unable to join the group, but submitted the following memorandum, which elicited no response at the time but may be of interest here:

1. It is my impression that like the Army, Air Force units in S.E. Asia no longer collect and record all data on a particular operation, but instead compress and edit the data into reports on lessons learned. While this may benefit combat efficiency, it leads to the permanent loss of information, some of which may be more important from a historian's point of view than the matter that is preserved. It should be possible to retain all data for future use by historians.

2. The men who work up accounts of operations are exposed to pressure and censorship by officers who participated in these operations. Since their studies are read at a higher level, and since historians are at least as fallible as most human beings, the operational commanders would be saints if they did not seek to control the tone and conclusion of the historians' work. On the other hand, responsible history cannot be produced under such conditions. It is true that in later years it may be possible to reconstruct and analyze an operation more objectively on the basis of the original study and its supporting documents; but even if this were not such a difficult task, think of the time that is wasted in bringing out the first glossy, pussyfooting account. The historical sections working in S.E. Asia should have greater independence. Their potential for damaging a man's career might be reduced if their work were not circulated, even on a restricted basis, for a number of years, and if the imperfect nature of our discipline were clearly admitted.

Both of these points bear on the issue that must be basic to the committee's considerations: the conflict that always exists between the operational requirements of the service, the personal interest of officers whose actions are narrated and dissected, and the scholar's need to be free.

14. David Bien, "Military Education in Eighteenth-Century France: Techni- cal and Non-Technical Determinants," *Proceedings* of the Third Annual Military History Symposium at the U.S.A.F. Academy.

15. After the First World War it was occasionally suggested that the enormous advances in science and technology, on which armed forces had become entirely dependent, invested civilian scholars with a new competence in analyzing war. It is more likely, however, that the concurrent growth of a specifically military technology worked against any advantage the academic historian might have gained. A somewhat familiar situation arose after 1945. Civilians now play a far more important role than ever before in developing strategic theory; but although this has probably stimulated a wider interest in history among some social scientists, there is no indication that it has been of special benefit to the civilian historian of war.

16. Unsigned "Editor's Foreword," *Journal of International Affairs,* 21 (1967), xiv.

17. An excellent treatment of this subject by two British psychoanalysts, which deserves a new edition, is E. F. M. Durbin and J. Bowlby, *Personal Aggres- siveness and War* (New York: Columbia University Press, 1939). Ex- cerpts of their discussion are reprinted in L. Bramson and G. W. Goethals, eds., *War: Studies from Psychology, Sociology, and Anthropology* (New York: Basic Books, 1964).

18. I am quoting from manuscript since the paper has not yet been published at the time of writing. It will appear in *Journal of Interdisciplinary History,* I, no. 2.

ARTHUR SCHLESINGER, JR.

The Historian as Participant

AFTER A marked recession in the nineteenth century, "eyewitness history"—history written by persons who themselves took part in the events they record—has undergone a revival in the later twentieth century. This revival has met with a certain skepticism and resistance from professional historians. Yet it may well be related to deeper tendencies within modern society; and, since these tendencies will only intensify in the foreseeable future, we may expect eyewitness history to continue to spread among us for some time to come. For this reason the phenomenon deserves examination.

Let us begin with some distinctions. The term eyewitness history, I have suggested, covers historical accounts written by those who directly observed at least some of the events described. Such observation may take place at a high or a low level. Plainly the historian who participates in decisions at the summit will have one kind of knowledge; but it is an error, I think, to suppose that the historian who served, say, as an infantryman in the Second World War was not affected by that experience and would not write, as a historian, about the war with insight he might not otherwise have had. Eyewitness history is obviously a branch of that larger field, contemporary history, by which one means historical accounts written by persons alive in the time in which the events take place.

Eyewitness history must be distinguished from memoirs, which are eyewitness accounts *not* written from the historical viewpoint. There is something distinctive, one assumes, about the historical temperament and the historical approach; the historian surely brings to the observation and analysis of events a perspective different from that brought by the nonhistorian. Bernal Diaz, Saint-Simon, Boswell, Caulaincourt, U. S. Grant, for example, were all formidable participant-observers or memoirists, but they cannot be said to have perceived events as historians would have perceived them. Memoirs are part of the raw material of history, but they are written for their own purposes—to set down one man's experience or to chronicle notable events or to discharge vanities or rancors— rather than to discern causation in the flow of events over time. Thus memoirs were produced in steady volume through the nineteenth and early twentieth centuries, while eyewitness history, on the other hand, rose and fell, and now has risen again.[1]

For there is nothing new, of course, in the idea that historians should write from their own direct experience. "Of the events of the [Peloponnesian] war," observed Thucydides, "I have described nothing but what I either saw myself, or learned from others of whom I made the most careful and particular enquiry." Confident that the war "would be great and memorable above any previous war," Thucydides, he tells us, began work on his history when the Athenians and the Peloponnesians first took up arms against one another. As an Athenian, he was soon swept up in the conflict him- self; and it seems unlikely that he would have carried his history as far as he did had it not been for his failure as a commander in the field. The twenty year exile imposed by his native city after the dis- aster of Amphipolis liberated him to visit battlefields, interview veterans, verify or disprove second-hand tales, and reconcile con- flicting testimony; "the task was a laborious one, because eye-wit- nesses of the same occurrences gave different accounts of them, as they remembered or were interested in the actions of one side or the other."[2]

It would be wrong to conclude that only failed soldiers could become effective eyewitness historians; Xenophon and Caesar are contrary examples. It would also be wrong to suppose that most classical history was contemporary history. The eyewitness historian Flavius Josephus of Jerusalem (another failed soldier, who collected the materials for his history of the Judaeo-Roman war during his years as a Roman captive) complained that the later Hellenic his- torians had ignored the events of their own country and age, turn- ing instead to the remote history of Assyria and Media. Josephus much preferred their predecessors who had "devoted themselves to writing the history of their own times, in which their personal par- ticipation in events gave clarity to their presentment and every falsehood was certain of exposure by a public that knew the facts."[3]

When the Renaissance revived traditions of secular history, historians felt free to write about the present as well as the past. Nor was there prejudice against participants. Guiccardini and Machiavelli were eyewitness historians of sixteenth-century Florence, as was Clarendon of seventeenth-century England. When historians could not take part in the events they were writing about, they often took part in such events as were available to them and believed that such participation benefited them as historians. "The discipline and evolution of a modern battalion," wrote Gibbon, "gave me a clearer notion of the phalanx and the legions, and the captain of the Hampshire grenadiers (the reader may smile) has not been useless to the historian of the Roman empire."[4] Until the later nineteenth century, most of the great historians were, in one way or another, captains of the Hampshire grenadiers—from Bacon and Raleigh to Macaulay, Tocqueville, Guizot, Carlyle, Bagehot, Bancroft, Parkman, Henry Adams. They were all involved in the public world; they were not men just of the study and the lamp.

In the later nineteenth century, however, a new question arose, I think for the first time—the question whether participation in public events might not disqualify the participant from writing about these events as a historian; whether, indeed, experience in the public world might not be incompatible with the ideal of historical objectivity. Such questions were a direct consequence of the professionalization of history. Historians were now increasingly segregated in universities, enshrined in academic chairs, surrounded by apprentices; and the crystallization of this distinct and specific status brought with it a tendency to reject, first, historians who participated in the events they described and, soon, historians who participated in anything beyond the profession of history. Indeed, it may have been unconsciously felt that eyewitness history, by involving the historical profession in ongoing conflicts, might raise threats to the hard-won new status. As Sir Walter Raleigh, one of the few historians to suffer the ultimate criticism of the executioner's ax, had warned two and a half centuries before, "Whosoever, in writing a modern history, shall follow truth too near the heels, it may haply strike out his teeth."[5]

Professionalization conceived historical research and writing as a self-sufficient, full-time, life-long vocation. Felix Gilbert has recalled to us Meinecke's heartfelt statement:

We must be aware of the inner difficulties with which a rising historian has to struggle today. At first, he will have to concentrate on studies in

a very narrow and isolated area. He is confronted by tasks and problems of a professional character and he must tackle them in a prescribed
manner. Editions and specialized documentary studies—usually not
chosen by himself but assigned to him or recommended to him—will
usually absorb the first decade of his scholarly life. Today scholarship,
having become an organized large-scale enterprise, presses most heavily
on the individual scholar in the most susceptible years of his development.[6]

Professionalization meant rigorous training in the techniques of the
craft; it meant specialization; it meant bureaucratization; it meant
a stern insistence on critical methods as the guarantee of objectivity;
it meant a deep pride in the independence and autonomy of the
historical guild and an ardent conviction that the new professional
techniques were winning history unprecedented new successes.
"The historians of former times," wrote Acton, "unapproachable
for us in knowledge and in talent, cannot be our limit. We have the
power to be more rigidly impersonal, disinterested and just than
they."[7]

Such severe standards created the image of the historian as a
monastic scholar, austerely removed from the passing emotions and
conflicts of his own day. From this viewpoint, participation in the
public world meant the giving of hostages—to parties, to institutions, to ideologies. In retrospect, it seemed that Macaulay was too
deeply a Whig, Bancroft too deeply a Jacksonian, Henry Adams too
deeply an Adams. The view arose that not only participant-his-
torians but even historians who wrote about contemporaneous
events were too deeply compromised to fulfill the pure historical
vocation.

As late as the days before the Second World War, a professional
historian who carried his lectures up to his own time was deemed
rash and unhistorical; a professional historian who wrote on contemporary events was considered to have lapsed into journalism;
a professional historian who took part in events and wrote about
them later was a rarity. Most scholars still felt that a generation or
so was required before current affairs underwent the sea change
into history. Today, however, few American universities would
hestitate to offer courses which start with the Second World War
and end with yesterday's newspaper. Only the most ascetic scholars
now object to attempts to write serious accounts of the very recent
past. And contemporary history has inevitably brought along with
it eyewitness history as a vital component.

How to account for this unexpected emergence of contemporary history into academic respectability? The fundamental explanation lies, I think, in the acceleration of the rate of social change—an acceleration produced by the cumulative momentum of science and technology. Each decade generates both more innovations and more effective ways of introducing innovations into the social process. This acceleration, which Henry Adams was first among historians to understand, has meant, among other things, that the "present" becomes the "past" more swiftly than ever before in the history of man. If Rip Van Winkle had made a habit of coming back from the Catskills every twenty years, he would find each new visit more perplexing and more incredible. This steady increase in the velocity of history inevitably affects the psychology of the historian. What historians perceive as the "past" is today chronologically much closer than it was when historical change was the function, not of days, but of decades. In the twelfth century, the historian's "past" was centuries back; in the nineteenth century it was a generation or two back. Now it is yesterday.

At the same time, the emergence of a more extensive educated public than the world has ever known has increased the popular demand for knowledge about the problems that torment modern man—especially when, with the invention of nuclear weapons, these problems, if not brought under control, might rush civilization on to the final catastrophe. History becomes an indispensable means of organizing public experiences in categories conducive to understanding. And the popular appetite for knowledge is further whetted by the development of television, bringing with it new experiences and new stimuli as well as creating the unprecedented situation in which history-in-the-making is now made, or at least observed, in every living room. Moreover, the fear of dehumanization so pervasive in the high-technology society, the felt threats to individual identity, also doubtless invite the effort to rehumanize the historical process produced by eyewitness history.

Along with these developments, there have been novel happenings within the historical field itself. Great manuscript collections, in the United States, at least, now tend to be open to scholars sooner than ever before. Franklin D. Roosevelt, in leaving his papers to the National Archives of the United States and providing for their early accessibility to students, set a salutary example which all subsequent Presidents have followed. Where the Adams papers, for example, were closed for decades, where the papers of even so

recent a President as Herbert Hoover were impounded for a generation, the Roosevelt precedent will make it difficult for public men of
the future—again, at least in the United States—to lock up their
manuscripts indefinitely. Hereafter the presumption will surely be
in favor of making papers available to scholars as speedily as pru-
dent standards of security and discretion permit. The alternative
presumption will be that the deponent has something to hide.

Yet the very accessibility of contemporary manuscript collections
has had another and somewhat paradoxical effect: it has demonstrated to scholars the inadequacy of documents by themselves
as sources for twentieth-century history. In the early nineteenth
century, if a public figure had a message to send, paper was the
only means, save face-to-face conversation, of communication.
Moreover, quill pen in hand, he could write only a limited number
of letters. Historians studying these good old days can relax fairly
comfortably in the archives, confident that the documents will not
only be competent sources but will not be too numerous to be read
by a single student.

Those days, alas, are gone forever. The revolution in the
technology of communications—especially the invention of the
typewriter and the telephone—has depreciated the value of the
document. While the typewriter has increased the volume of
paper, the telephone has reduced its importance. Far more documents are produced, and there is far less in them. If a contemporary
statesman has something of significance to communicate, if speed
and secrecy are of the essence, he will confide his message, not to a
letter, but to the telephone. Until the Federal Bureau of Investigation opens up its library of wire taps, we must assume that these
vital historical moments will elude the documentary record.

Ironically the rise of contemporary history has itself doubtless
contributed to the condition of documentary impoverishment.
The growing insistence that papers should, as a matter of right,
be immediately opened to scholars may lead to a dilution and
distortion of the written record. Public officials, fearing next
decade's graduate students, become reluctant to put in writing
the real reasons behind some of their actions. Theodore Roosevelt
was not the last politician to take the precaution of writing memoranda for the files or letters to friends in order to present his own
version of public events or decisions. Yet this very condition of
documentary impoverishment serves as a further stimulus to contemporary history; for, if the eyewitness is part of the cause, he

can also be part of the cure. As Flavius Josephus pointed out nearly two thousand years ago, a primary justification of the eyewitness historian is the evidence he preserves. "To place on record events never previously related and to make contemporary history accessible to later generations," Josephus wrote, "is an activity deserving of notice and commendation. Genuine research consists not in the mere rearrangement of material that is the property of others, but in the establishment of an original body of historical knowledge."[8]

This variety of factors helps explain the comeback this century of the historian who writes out of his own direct experience. The revival began outside the guild when participants who lacked the professional badge but possessed the historical temperament began to write the history of events they themselves had witnessed. Winston Churchill's *The World Crisis* (1923-1929) was an early and influential example, followed, of course, by *The Second World War* (1948-1954). In the meantime the two world wars brought professional historians themselves into the public arena, whether as soldiers, diplomats, intelligence analysts, political advisers, or official historians; and many were tempted to apply their craft to the dramatic events unfolding before their eyes. Some even may have had the illusion they could influence affairs; Johannes von Müller was not the last historian in search of a hero.

Yet the traditional case of the professional historian against contemporary history remained. That case derived essentially from the ancient proposition *veritas temporis filia*. Truth was seen as the daughter of time: written history became better the farther away the historian was from the events he was describing. So Sir Herbert Butterfield analyzed the stages of historiographical growth:

If we consider the history of the historical writing that has been issued, generation after generation, on a given body of events, we shall generally find that in the early stages of this process the narrative which is produced has a primitive and simple shape. As one generation of students succeeds another, however, each developing the historiography of this particular subject, the narrative passes through certain typical stages until it is brought to a high and subtle form of organisation.[9]

History, in this view, regularly passed from the "heroic" phase, in which contemporary writers portrayed personal goodness and badness as dominant motives and employed melodrama as the dominant tone, into the "technical" phase, when later historians could at last see men as trapped in a structural predicament with right and wrong on both sides and the dominant tone one of tragedy.

The technical historian, recollecting in tranquility, was presumed to have solider knowledge, clearer perspective, and surer freedom from emotion and prejudice. "That history which is most liable to large-scale structural revision," Professor Butterfield argued, "is contemporary history—the first version of events as they appear from the special platform of particular actors in the drama, often indeed a version used for militant purposes in the conflicts of the time." When historians studied the conflicts of the past, they should therefore give little credence to "the contemporary ways of formulating that conflict."[10] And, of all forms of contemporary history, eyewitness history logically contained more pitfalls than any other, was more vulnerable to interest, bias, illusion, and wishful thinking.

There is plainly great force in this argument. It seems plausible that historians coming along later should have access to a wider range of materials than eyewitness historians could have had. It seems plausible that they should be more free of passion and prepossession. It seems plausible that, with their knowledge of the way things have come out, they could more accurately identify the critical factors in the process. One can see the evolution described by Professor Butterfield at work today, for example, in the movement from "heroic" to "technical"—from melodramatic to tragic—renditions of the origins of the Cold War.

The traditional argument for the inferiority of contemporary history, and especially of eyewitness history, thus rests on alleged deficiencies in both the collection and the interpretation of historical facts. But is this all there is to be said? Certainly if eyewitnesses are going to write an increasing amount of modern history, it is perhaps appropriate to reexamine this traditional case.

One may start by inquiring whether the superiority supposedly possessed by the technical historian in the collection of historical facts is all that self-evident. Guiccardini's caution—"Documents are rarely falsified at the start. It is usually done later, as occasion or necessity dictates"[11]—suggests one advantage enjoyed by the eyewitness historian: he has the chance of seeing evidence before it is cooked. Probably Guiccardini's warning has less application in the xerox age, where the ease of immediate duplication complicates the task of subsequent falsification. But one can never be sure, as when one hears President Johnson read Walter Cronkite a memorandum claiming to direct the Defense Department in February 1968 to prepare alternatives to further escalation in Vietnam—a document directly contrary in sense to the one that the Secretary of Defense says he then received from the White House.

Moreover, personal participation in a historical episode may well make the historian more critical of his materials. In writing about the past, the technical historian often is tempted to use letters, diaries, memoranda, newspapers as if they were reliable forms of evidence. When such evidence is construed under the pressure of direct experience, however, it may become more apparent that *A's* letters are his own self-serving versions of events, that *B's* diaries are designed, consciously or not, to dignify the diarist and discredit his opponents, that *C's* memoranda are written to improve the record and that the newspapermen recording the transactions had only the dimmest idea what was really going on.

The technical historian is inevitably the prisoner of the testimony that happens to survive. He cannot, like Thucydides, cross-examine witnesses; nor, like Flavius Josephus, does he expose himself to a public that knows the facts. Mr. Dooley well summed up the truth of the matter: "Th' further ye get away fr'm anny peeryod th' betther ye can write about it. Ye are not subject to interruptions be people that were there."[12] Hence one vital importance of eyewitness history for the future technical historian: it can, as Josephus suggested, help meet the need to supplement documents if we are to recover the full historical transaction.

Tocqueville, in the notes for his unwritten second volume on the French Revolution, discriminates between facts available to technical historians and facts reported by eyewitness historians:

We are still too close to these events to know many details (this seems curious, but it is true); details often appear only in posthumous revelations and are frequently ignored by contemporaries. But what these writers know better than does posterity are the movements of opinion, the popular inclinations of their times, the vibrations of which they can still sense in their minds and hearts. The true traits of the principal persons and of their relationships, of the movements of the masses are often better described by witnesses than recorded by posterity. These are the necessary details. Those close to them are better placed to trace the general history, the general causes, the grand movements of events, the spiritual currents which men who are further removed may no longer find.[13]

Tocqueville's point about the grand movements applies equally to people. "It is not true," said Santayana, "that contemporaries misjudge a man. Competent contemporaries judge him . . . much better than posterity, which is composed of critics no less egotistical, and obliged to rely exclusively on documents easily misinterpreted."[14] Charles Francis Adams made a related point in this introduction to his grandparents' letters. "Our history," he wrote, "is for the most part wrapped up in the forms of office . . . Statesmen and Generals rarely say all they think." They are seen for the most part "when conscious that they are upon a theatre," and in their papers "they are made to assume a uniform of grave hue."

The solitary meditation, the confidential whisper to a friend, never meant to reach the ear of the multitude, the secret wishes, not blazoned forth to catch applause, the fluctuations between fear and hope that most betray the springs of action,—these are the guides to character, which most frequently vanish with the moment that called them forth, and leave nothing to posterity but those coarser elements for judgment, that are found in elaborated results.[15]

Moreover, the controversy produced by exercises in what has been acrimoniously called "instant history"—the claims and counterclaims made by participants while they are still around—indispensably enrich the historical record.

It may further be the case that eyewitness historians often have a more realistic judgment about the operative facts. Practical experience may yield qualities of insight hard to achieve in the library; historians who *know* how laws are passed, decisions made, battles fought are perhaps in a better position to grasp the actuality of historical transactions. Thus Woodrow Wilson, praising Tocqueville and Bagehot, remarked that they were great analysts because they "were not merely students, but also *men of the world,* for whom the only acceptable philosophy of politics was a generalization from actual daily observation of men and things."[16]

Participation may not only sharpen the historian's judgment; it may also stimulate and amplify what might be called the historian's reconstructive imagination. To take part in public controversy, to smell the dust and sweat of conflict, to experience the precariousness of decision under pressure may help toward a better understanding of the historical process. When I was a very young historian, a so-called revisionist school used to write about the coming of the American Civil War on the assumption that the burning emotions of the day, especially those seizing the abolitionists, were somehow artificial and invalid. But personal immersion in a historical experience leaves the historian no doubt that mass emotions are realities with which he no less than statesmen must deal. Far from being gratuitous and needless, as the revisionist historians once tried to tell us, the way people think and feel is an organic part of history.

This is something that the technical historian misses, as Professor Butterfield has noted: "The reader of technical history learns too little from it of the hopes and fears of the majority of men, too little of their joy in nature and art, their falling in love, their family affection, their spiritual questings, and their ultimate vision of things." Since this is so, Professor Butterfield himself has wondered "whether technical history can claim to give us the mirror of life any more than modern physics provides us with an actual picture of the universe."[17] If technical history cannot claim to give us the mirror of life, can one be so certain about the advantages allegedly provided by the stages of historiographical growth? If I may cite a personal example, I have no question that, by writing *A Thousand Days* the year after President Kennedy's death, I was able to suggest something about the mood and relationships of the Kennedy years which no future historian could ever get on the basis of the documents—indeed, which I myself could not have reproduced, with the fading of memory, the knowledge of consequences, and the introduction of new preoccupations and perspectives, had I tried to write the book ten or twenty years later. Page Smith (in *The Historian and History*) argues persuasively that, for historians writing years after the fact, "the difficulty of re-creating faithfully the events and their causes will be greater and demand a more powerful effort of the will and the creative imagination than that demanded of the participant-historian."[18]

The case against the eyewitness historian in the domain of facts thus seems on examination less compelling than the arguments of the technical historian at first suggest. Against the doctrine that truth is the daughter of time one may perhaps place Emerson's dictum: "Time dissipates to shining ether the solid angularity of facts."[19]

Are the traditional arguments against eyewitness history in the domain of interpretation any more satisfactory? The theory of the stages of historiographical growth assumes the purifying effects of the passage of time, with distance steadily removing distortions of interest and emotion until a final version can be attained, or at least approached. Professor Butterfield has well stated the ideal: "I should not regard a thing as 'historically' established unless the proof were valid for the Catholic as well as the Protestant, for the Liberal as well as the Marxist."[20]

But little appears more wistful in retrospect than the confidence of technical historians that the deepening of research and the lengthening of perspective will ineluctably produce scholarly consensus on the large historical questions. It is not obvious in practice that time has been, in fact, the father of truth, if by truth we mean the agreement of historians. We know now that time cannot be counted to winnow out prejudice and commitment and leave the scholar, all passion spent, in tranquil command of the historical reality.

The passage of time does not, for example, liberate the historian from his deepest values and prepossessions. Posterity, in Santayana's phrase, is "composed of critics no less egotistical." "Historians of every period," David Butler has well said, "seem able to acquire equally deep emotions about their subject matter," and he recalls that his grandfather, A. F. Pollard, the noted scholar, "expressed far more vehement views about Martin Luther than I have ever ventured about any contemporary politician."[21] The major difference on the question of bias is that the bias of the eyewitness historian is infinitely easier to detect and thus to discount. Wherever vital issues are involved, whether the events are as close to us as the war in Vietnam or as remote as the fall of the Roman Empire, distance will not insure convergence. All interesting historical problems may be said to be in permanent contention; that is why they are interesting. One comes to feel that historians agree only when the problems as well as the people are dead.

As long as the problems are still alive, the passage of time only offers new possibilities for distortion. The present, as historians well know, re-creates the past. This is partly because, once we know how things have come out, we tend to rewrite the past in terms of historical inevitability. And it is partly because each new generation in any case projects its own obsessions on the screen of the past. But, despite E. H. Carr, hindsight may not be the safest principle on which to base the writing of history. What Hamilton in the 70th *Federalist* called "the dim light of historical research"[22] is not always an x-ray beam, penetrating to the underlying structure of reality; it is more often a flickering candle, revealing only those surfaces of things a time-bound historian is able to see.

"Every true history," said Croce, summing up the epistemological issue, "is contemporary history."[23] So a religious age interprets political conflicts in religious terms and an economic age interprets religious conflicts in economic terms, and so on until one must conclude that, if truth is the daughter of time, it takes a wise father to know his own children. In the words of Dewey, "We are committed to the conclusion that all history is necessarily written from the standpoint of the present, and is, in an inescapable sense, the history not only of the present but of that which is contemporaneously judged to be important in the present."[24] One must ask forgiveness for summoning high authority to labor so elementary a point, except that the point is all too rarely applied to the validity of eyewitness history. If eyewitness history lacks perspective, so does technical history and in much the same sense.

If history thus provides an infinite regression of historical interpretations, how then are we to say that one interpretation is "truer" than another?—if truth is to mean more than felt relevance to a climate of opinion. And, if there is no obvious answer to this question, can it be that eyewitness history not only offers an essential supplement to technical history but may—at least in some ways and certain circumstances—supply a more satisfying and enduring version of events?

Far from historical truth being unattainable in contemporary history, it may almost be argued that in a sense truth is *only* attainable in contemporary history. For contemporary history means the writing of history under the eye of the only people who can offer contradiction, that is, the witnesses. Every historian of the past knows at the bottom of his heart how much artifice and extrapolation go into his reconstructions; how much of his evidence is partial, ambiguous, or hypothetical; and how safe he is in his speculations because, barring recourse to spirit mediums, no one can easily say him nay, except other historians, and all they have to put up is other theories.

Once men are dead, the historian can never really know whether his reconstruction bears much relation to what actually happened. As Lionel Trilling observed in an essay on Tacitus, "To minds of a certain sensitivity 'the long view' is the falsest historical view of all, and indeed the insistence on the length of per-

spective is intended precisely to overcome sensitivity—seen from
sufficient distance, it says, the corpse and the hacked limbs are
not so very terrible, and eventually they even begin to compose
themselves into a 'meaningful pattern.' "[25] "*Restored* history," wrote
Ruskin in *The Stones of Venice*, "is of little more value than restored painting or architecture . . . The only history worth reading
is that written at the time of which it treats, the history of what
was done and seen, heard out of the mouths of the men who did
and saw."[26]

To reject the testimony of men and women as to the significance
of their own actions and lives, to say that, while they *thought*
they were acting on such-and-such motives, we, so much wiser,
know they were acting on quite other motives, is to commit the
sin of historical reductionism. It is, as Page Smith well says, to
"deprive these lives of their meaning by judgments imposed long
after the event," and this is "to deny our forebears their essential
humanity." In doing this, we not only diminish them; we diminish
ourselves. We tie ourselves to reductionist theories which subsequent generations have every right to turn against us. We sur-
render, Page Smith warns, "our belief in ourselves, in the integrity
of our own lives."[27]

Professor Butterfield himself has made much this same point in
his brilliant critique of Sir Lewis Namier for draining "the intellectual content out of the things that politicians do" and for refus-
ing to realize the operative force of ideas" and thereby divesting
history of "the ideas and intentions which give [policies] so much
of their meaning."[28] The denial that people in the past understood
why they were doing things can lead only to the conclusion that
we don't know why we are doing things either; and the difficulty
of sustaining this position may well be an important reason for the
failure of a great deal of historical revisionism. After much theo-
rizing through the years, American historians today (like Bernard
Bailyn) have come to a position about the causes of the American
Revolution not too far from that taken in 1789 by David Ramsay in
his *History of the American Revolution*; so historians today, instead of dismissing the rhetoric of Jacksonian democracy as
"campaign claptrap" (the phrase is Lee Benson's),[29] are returning
to the view that the Jacksonians may have meant what they said;
so historians today, after a long pursuit of other causes, generally
agree with those who personally fought the American Civil War
that it was more "about" slavery than about anything else. Of

course these current historical judgments are time-bound too and undoubtedly will be revised; but one feels that historians will return more often to contemporaneous interpretations than to subsequent reinterpretations. If the actors themselves gave lucid and urgent testimony as to why they lived, struggled, died, is it not a form of intellectual arrogance for historians to come along later and pretend to know better?*

This argument assumes, of course, the reality of a certain measure of human choice and self-determination. It rejects philosophies of historical determinism. This does not imply extravagant claims about the extent of human freedom. One may accept Tocqueville's formulation of the problem: "It is true that around every man a fatal circle is traced beyond which he cannot pass; but within the wide verge of that circle he is powerful and free."[30]

In short, the insight generated by participation is not confined to perceptions and interpretations of specific episodes. It goes, I would argue, to very general conceptions of history. For historians

---

* This argument is, of course, incomplete. There are some things the future historian *can* know better; and the problem of the conflict between contemporaneous consciousness of reality and the facts as determined later is too much a digression to go into at length here. A couple of examples, however, may suggest the issue. Thus Bernard Bailyn has argued that a major cause of the American Revolution was the theory held by leading colonists that George III was carrying out a conspiracy against the English constitution—a theory which Sir Lewis Namier has shown to be an illusion. Or consider the question of the profitability of slavery in the United States. The new economic historians, especially Alfred Conrad and John Meyer, employing refined tools of economic analysis, have demonstrated persuasively that—contrary to the contemporaneous impression—the slavery system was profitable. The contemporaneous impression had important historical consequences, but it was apparently wrong.

In other words, contemporaneous perceptions may well be misperceptions, which is doubtless why Professor Butterfield warns against yielding to "the contemporary ways of formulating . . . conflict." Still the misconceptions of the American colonists in the 1770's or of the slaveholders in the 1850's are a vital segment of the historian's story; and, while it is part of the historian's job to test the validity of contemporaneous perceptions, he must always take care not to replace the categories of the actors by his own latter-day categories when he discusses the motives of action. Full historical reconstruction requires attention to Sorel's reminder in *Reflections on Violence*: "We are perfectly aware that the historians of the future are bound to discover that we laboured under many illusions, because they will see behind them a finished world. We, on the other hand, must act, and nobody can tell us today what these historians will know; nobody can furnish us with the means of modifying our motor images in such a way as to avoid their criticisms." Georges Sorel, *Reflections on Violence* (New York: Collier Books, 1961), p. 149.

are frequently the victims, if more often in a small than a grand way, of what James has called "our indomitable desire to cast the world into a more rational shape in our minds than the shape into which it is thrown there by the crude order of experience." The historian's compulsion is the passion for pattern. Reconstructing events in the quiet of his study, he likes to tidy things up, to find interconnections and unities. "The form of inner consistency," to borrow James's language, "is pursued far beyond the line at which collateral profits stop."[31]

If, however, the historian has taken part in great events, he has learned that things rarely happen in a tidy, patterned, rational way. General George Marshall used to say that battlefield decisions were taken under conditions of "chronic obscurity"—that is, under excessive pressure on the basis of incomplete and defective information. This is probably the character of most critical decisions in the field of public policy. The eyewitness historian tends to preserve the felt texture of events and to recognize the role of such elements as confusion, ignorance, chance, and sheer stupidity. The technical historian, coming along later, revolts against the idea of "chronic obscurity" and tries to straighten things out. In this way, he often imputes pattern and design to a process which, in its nature, is organic and not mechanical. Historians reject the conspiratorial interpretation of history; but, in a benign way, they sometimes become its unconscious proponents, ascribing to premeditation what belongs to fortuity and to purpose what belongs to accident.

Participation may, of course, breed its own deformations. Again we may look to Tocqueville to suggest the appropriate distinctions:

I have come across men of letters, who have written history without taking part in public affairs, and politicians, who have only concerned themselves with producing events without thinking of describing them. I have observed that the first are always inclined to find general causes, whereas the others, living in the midst of disconnected daily facts, are prone to imagine that everything is attributable to particular incidents, and that the wires they pull are the same that move the world. It is to be presumed that both are equally deceived.

For himself, Tocqueville added, he detested those "absolute systems" which represented all events as depending on first causes and linked by the chain of fatality—systems which, as it were, "suppress men from the history of the human race." Many important facts, he continued, can only be explained by accidental circumstances; many others remain totally inexplicable. "Chance, or rather that tangle of secondary causes which we call chance, for want of the knowledge how to unravel it, plays a great part in all that happens on the world's stage; although I firmly believe that chance does nothing that has not been prepared beforehand."[32]

This is an accurate account of the play of events as eyewitness historians tend to see it; and it is why such historians would probably agree with a couple of Emerson's aphorisms (and urge that they be framed above every historian's desk):

In analysing history, do not be too profound, for often the causes are quite superficial.

And:

I have no expectation that any man will read history aright who thinks that what was done in a remote age, by men whose names have resounded far, has any deeper sense than what he is doing today.[33]

History infused by this spirit has its own distinctive character. Without prolonged philosophical digression, one can refer to James's insistence in "The Dilemma of Determinism" on the reality of the idea of chance and the argument against historical inevitability developed so brilliantly in our own day by Isaiah Berlin. My impression is that the experience of participation tends to inoculate historians against what James called "a temper of intellectual absolutism, a demand that the world shall be a solid block, subject to one control."[34] The inoculation does not always take; Marx—a contemporary historian and a participant in events if never an eyewitness historian—remains a monumental exception. But, in the main, historians who have been immersed in the confusion of events seem less inclined to impose an exaggeratedly rational order on the contingency and obscurity of reality.

I am not contending that eyewitness history, or contemporary history in general, are "better" than technical history, whatever such a judgment might mean. Obviously we need both, and the dialectic between them is a major part of the historical exercise. I would only suggest that the conventional reasons for professional disdain may not be so impressive as historians once thought—that eyewitness history has its own and distinctive strengths and advantages.

In any case, eyewitness history appears to meet significant intellectual and social needs and therefore will be with us for some time to come. If this is so, then let eyewitness historians abide by the highest standards of their peculiar trade and write always in the spirit of Clarendon:

And as I may not be thought altogether an incompetent person for this communication, having been present as a member of Parliament in those councils before and till the breaking out of the Rebellion, and having since had the honour to be near two great kings in some trust, so I shall perform the same with all faithfulness and ingenuity, with an equal observation of the faults and infirmities of both sides, with their defects and oversights in pursuing their own ends; and shall no otherwise mention small and light occurrences than as they have been introductions to matters of the greatest moment; nor speak of persons otherwise than as the mention of their virtues or vices is essential to the work in hand: in which as I shall have the fate to be suspected rather for malice to many than of flattery to any, so I shall, in truth, preserve myself from the least sharpness that may proceed from private provocation or a more public indignation; in the whole observing the rules that a man should, who deserves to be believed.[35]

REFERENCES

1. As a practitioner in this doubtful area, I must declare an interest. In *The Age of Roosevelt* I am attempting what is essentially contemporary history. *A Thousand Days: John F. Kennedy in the White House* was part personal memoir, part eyewitness history, part contemporary history in the more general sense. Such a mixture is no longer uncommon.

2. Thucydides, *History of the Peloponnesian War,* trans. Benjamin Jowett (Oxford: Clarendon Press, 1900), I, 1, 16.

3. Flavius Josephus, *The Jewish War,* in A. J. Toynbee, ed., *Greek Historical Thought* (New York: New American Library, 1952), p. 62 (Mentor Books).

4. Edward Gibbon, *Autobiography,* ed. D. A. Saunders (New York: Meridian Books, 1961), p. 134.

5. Sir Walter Raleigh, *History of the World, Works* (Oxford: University Press, 1829), II, lxiii.

6. Felix Gilbert, "European and American Historiography," in John Higham and others, *History: The Development of Historical Studies in the United States* (Englewood Cliffs, N. J.: Prentice-Hall, 1965), p. 331.

7. Lord Acton, "Inaugural Lecture on the Study of History," in *Lectures on Modern History* (London: Collins, 1961), p. 41 (The Fontana Library).

8. Toynbee, ed., *Greek Historical Thought,* p. 62.

9. Sir Herbert Butterfield, *History and Human Relations* (London: Collins, 1951), p. 10.

10. *Ibid.,* pp. 210, 15.

11. Francesco Guicciardini, *Maxims and Reflections of a Renaissance States-man* (New York: Harper & Row, 1965), p. 71 (Harper Torchbooks).

12. [Finley Peter Dunne], "On Heroes and History," in *Mr. Dooley on Making a Will and Other Necessary Evils* (New York: Scribner's, 1919), pp. 105-106.

13. Alexis de Tocqueville, *The European Revolution,* ed. John Lukacs (Garden City, N. Y.: Doubleday, 1959), p. 32.

14. Quoted in W. H. Auden and Louis Kronenberger, eds., *The Viking Book of Aphorisms* (New York: Viking Press, 1962), p. 237.

15. Charles Francis Adams, ed., *Familiar Letters of John Adams and His Wife Abigail Adams* (New York, 1875), pp. v-vi.

16. Woodrow Wilson, "On the Study of Politics," *The Papers of Woodrow Wilson,* ed. Arthur Link and others (Princeton: Princeton University Press, 1966——), V, 397.

17. Sir Herbert Butterfield, *Man on His Past* (Cambridge, Eng.: University Press, 1955), p. 137.

18. Page Smith, *The Historian and History* (New York: Knopf, 1964), p. 205.

19. R. W. Emerson, *Essays,* "History."

20. Butterfield, *Man on His Past,* p. 139.

21. David Butler, "Instant History," *New Zealand Journal of History* (October 1968), p. 108.

22. Alexander Hamilton and others, *The Federalist Papers,* No. 70.

23. Benedetto Croce, *History: Its Theory and Practice* (New York: Harcourt, Brace, 1921), p. 12.

24. John Dewey, *Logic: The Theory of Inquiry* (New York: Holt, 1938), p. 235.

25. Lionel Trilling, *The Liberal Imagination* (Garden City, N. Y.: Doubleday Anchor Books, 1950), p. 195.

26. John Ruskin, *The Stones of Venice* (Everyman), III, Appendix 9, p. 201.

27. Smith, *Historian and History,* pp. 206-207.

28. Sir Herbert Butterfield, *George III and the Historians* (London: Collins, 1957), pp. 211, 219, 60.

29. Lee Benson, *The Concept of Jacksonian Democracy* (Princeton: Princeton University Press, 1961), p. 81.

30. Alexis de Tocqueville, *Democracy in America,* ed. Phillips Bradley (New York: Vintage Books, 1959), II, 352.

31. William James, "The Dilemma of Determinism," in *Essays on Faith and Morals,* ed. R. B. Perry (Cleveland: World Publishing Company, 1962), p. 147 (Meridian Books).

32. Alexis de Tocqueville, *Recollections,* ed. J. P. Mayer (New York: Meridian Books, 1959), pp. 63-64.

33. E. W. Emerson and W. E. Forbes, eds., *Journals of Ralph Waldo Emerson* (Boston: Houghton Mifflin, 1909-1914), IV, 160; Emerson, *Essays,* "History."

34. James, *Essays on Faith and Morals,* pp. 157-158.

35. Edward, Earl of Clarendon, *The History of the Rebellion and Civil Wars in England* (Oxford: Clarendon Press, 1888), I, 3.

JAN VANSINA

Once Upon a Time: Oral Traditions as History in Africa

"Our books are in our heads."
—Mbope Louis (Congo, 1953)

MOST PRECOLONIAL African civilizations were "oral civilizations."
Our own European or American contemporary societies are "literate civilizations." Inevitably, the attitudes of two such different societies toward words and speech differ radically. For the Dogon of
the Sudan the world was created when speech was created: "in
the beginning was the word."[1] The Tio of Brazzaville use the same
word to designate "navel" and "personal name" and believe that if
one knows the name of a person one has knowledge of the essence
of that person and can bewitch him. What is in a name? To these
people, everything. All oral cultures distinguish between important
words and banale speech. Most commonly, these important words
are inherited from forefathers: the oral traditions. The attitude of
members of an oral society toward speech is similar to the reverence
members of a literate society attach to the written word. If it is hallowed by authority or antiquity, the word will be treasured.

Members of literate societies find it difficult to shed the prejudice
of contempt for the spoken word, the counterpart of pride in writing and respect for the written word. Any historian who deals with
oral tradition will have to unlearn this prejudice in order to rediscover the full wonder of words: the shades of meaning they convey
to those who ponder them and learn them with care so that they
may transmit the wisdom they contain as the culture's most precious
legacy to the next generation.

Another difference between modern historians and members of

413

the oral societies they study is the ease with which the written word can be multiplied; we literally live in a sea of written messages. The historian is in a hurry and counts on understanding the message of a text by reading additional texts, by the redundancy built into the very repetition of texts. Africans chide us for hurrying, for not lingering over an oral communication to savor its bouquet, to meditate about it, to make it part of one's intellectual personality, rather the way one savors poetry. We must learn to do this if we want to use oral traditions as sources for history; we must learn to slow down.

Because most societies in Africa south of the Sahara were oral, even if they used writing marginally, historians who study them must confront the question of the validity of oral traditions as sources for history. To go by our experience of what sources survived orally in Europe, for example, in the nineteenth century, is to go wrong. For centuries all data felt to be socially important were written down; only trivia remained unrecorded. Thus, in his survey of oral tradition Ernst Bernheim cited only song and tale, saga, legend, anecdote, *geflügelte Wörter,* and proverbs.[2] Quite a contrast with Africa, where all the principal political, legal, social, and religious texts were transmitted orally. Indeed, for every functional type of written source in Europe one can find an equivalent oral source in Africa. For instance, most African courts had archivists, who learned by rote the royal genealogy—which legitimized the position of the ruler—and the history of the state—which was its unwritten constitution. Typically, when such an oral civilization moves to become literate, the first items recorded are the texts felt to be most important, just as the first printed book in Europe was the Bible. When Sultan Njoya of the Bamum in the Cameroons invented a script, the first materials written down were the royal chronicle and a code of the customary law and the local pharmacopoeia.[3]

Historians faced with the problem of reconstructing the past of oral societies such as the African ones did not rely solely on a study of oral traditions. They sought help from other sources, primarily archaeology, linguistics, ethnographic data, biological facts, as well as written data from visitors to the society. Despite the fact that oral tradition played the role of written documentation in literate societies, they were not interchangeable. Oral tradition does have a specificity of its own. This specificity includes limitations on its use as a source for history, limitations which often can be overcome by recourse to other data.

I

"We are telling from a tale
That the Babuya have told long ago."
—Rureke[4]

This verse tells us what oral tradition is: *oral testimony trans-mitted verbally, from one generation to the next one or more.* This excludes accounts by eyewitnesses which are oral data. It excludes rumor which is oral but is not transmitted from one generation to the next, since rumor is gossip and "hot news," soon to be forgotten. But on occasion rumor can be transmitted and thus become a source for tradition. The time factor in the definition is not arbitrary but crucial, for it changes the whole character of the communication. Oral tradition is presented as the respected lore of the past; it has a tradition, whether it purports to tell specifically what happened in the past (historical traditions) or merely to take delight in the per-formance of oral wisdom, wit, or beauty of the past (literary tradi-tions). Thus religious hymns, proverbs, and animal stories are just as much oral tradition as are lists of kings or royal chronicles.[5]

Written records and oral traditions differ in two essentials: the verbal character and the mode of transmission of the latter. The usual canons of the historical method can and must be applied to oral sources just as to written documents. It would seem sufficient to sketch the effects of the verbal character and the modes of trans-mission on oral tradition. Yet, it is also necessary to discuss the meaning and social role these traditions exhibit because African oral tradition is flowering in societies and cultures so foreign to our own.

A written document is an artifact; it is a manuscript. There are no problems as to what the testimony is. A verbal account is not so clearly presented, for a witness frequently gives several successive accounts of the same set of events. Are all of these separate testi-monies? It is best to consider all the declarations of one person con-cerning one referent as a single testimony, provided the witness has not acquired any new knowledge in the interval between his first and his last statement.

Furthermore, there is a crucial difference between a testimony and a tradition. A witness can mix data from several traditions in a single testimony, which happens most often with the most learned informants. Tradition can originate in several ways: as an eyewit-ness account of events or the invention of a literary statement, for example, a tale; as a fabrication of historical events or a literary work that is a mix of several other literary works; as a rumor. Plagiarism is common. The initial testimony is then transmitted along a chain of witnesses, generation after generation, until it reaches the last witness. The historian must ascertain what in a testimony belongs to a tradition, whether the tradition really goes back to its supposed point of origin in time and space, and what distortions may have occurred between the first testimony and the last. Contrary to expectation, this often can be done with a reasonable amount of precision.

The form of the oral account must be examined first. Two basic principles are involved in determining form: first, an account can be learned by rote or not, and second, the account has either a rigid or a flexible formal structure. If the account is learned by rote, as in a poem, the words themselves belong to the tradition; otherwise they do not. If the formal structure is rigid, as in epics, the structure belongs to the tradition. The combination of the two principles yields four basic forms of accounts.[6]

	wording frozen	wording free
rigid form	poetry	epic
free form	formula	narrative

Narrative, with free form and free wording, presents the most serious problems in investigating last testimony and its relation to tradition. The last narrative—in fact, every stage of the transmission —may represent several traditions. To disentangle this, one begins by determining the actual author of the last testimony. A person can speak for himself, he can speak for a whole collectivity, he can be prompted by questioning, and he can testify during a confrontation. In the first case he is the sole author of his testimony; in the second case he presents the minimum on which the group agrees, but it is likely that traditions may include more than the testimony indicates; in the third case there are two authors, the one who asks the questions and the one who answers them; and in the fourth case the situation of confrontation often leads to a situation of compromise among several authors. If one knows under which circumstances the testimony was recorded, it becomes possible to evaluate the influence of coauthors. Once this is done, the best way to disentangle several traditions behind one narrative is to examine variants of the narrative in other testimonies.

Starting with the last witness, one must work back along the chain of witnesses to come to the original author of a tradition. Oral tradition about the Koran, the *hadīth*, is important in Islam. Hence Muslim scholars developed a technique of assessing the value of each of the links in the chain of testimonies (*isnād*) and will not accept any tradition for which data about the chain are not extant and reasonably complete.[7] This technique can be followed only in cases where information about the links is also transmitted orally, a rare occurrence outside of Islam, or when the tradition is shallow enough for the links to be identified, as with family traditions. In a general way, however, it is possible to investigate in what milieu a tradition was transmitted, in what manner this was done, and whether checks existed to ensure that the transmission was accurate.

A careful examination of the social and geographical milieu of the tradition will tell a great deal. How was the account given and with what frequency? The climate in which traditions are told influences their content. For instance, there may be a performance[8] in which artistic value is far more important than accuracy of transmission, or traditions may be short or long because the situation demands it. In Burundi, traditions were short because most of them were told at informal gatherings and everyone had to have his say during the evening; in the neighboring society of Rwanda many narratives were spun out because a one-man professional had to entertain his patron for a whole evening. In both cases accuracy of transmission was not the foremost concern of the witnesses. On the other hand, in Rwanda[9] transmission of esoteric lore was done in seclusion, the verses were learned by rote in a systematic fashion, mnemotechnic controls were used, every production was checked by fellow specialists, and errors in reproduction were punishable. Obviously, in such cases one can surmise that the transmission was essentially correct.

Formal instruction and the use of checks and mnemotechnical devices were practiced in many African societies, most often with official political traditions, genealogies, or other traditions that functioned as "social charters." But these checks were used for poetry and songs as well. In these cases the prestige of the troubadour and the benefits of his position made it worth his while to learn his texts well. In the case of popular songs, correction by others was an important check on production. Some traditions were recounted frequently, others rarely. The royal genealogy among the Bushoong of Kasai (Congo) was recited formally only at installations of kings, and in West Africa among the Dogon certain rituals and texts that went along with the rites were recited in public only once every sixty years. In the last case the possibility of error through forgetting becomes great, depending upon frequency of instruction. In cases of very frequent recitation, the multiplication of the reproduction itself could make for the introduction of variants faster than otherwise.

Frequently, glosses or commentaries are present as a parallel tradition to explain obscure points in the major one. Archaisms and imagery allusion in poetry, in particular, could not be understood directly; they elicited questions from the audience. As the reciter answered these questions he established a parallel line of commentary. Often a person learned a tradition but did not understand the meaning of its content. In the next generation, the pupil asked the master what such and such meant. He did not want to tell the apprentice that he himself forgot to ask his master, so he made up an explanation and thus started a spurious commentary. Therefore, one must distinguish carefully between the main tradition and commentary. A commentary is most frequent with poetry but it occurs to some extent with practically every type of tradition. In a story about migrations, for example, the whereabouts of the place-names are often elicited by commentary.

Distortions during transmission—either willed or unconscious—can be at least suspected from an examination of the aims of the tradition in relation to the interests of the milieu in which transmission occurs. A chiefdom whose traditions acknowledge that it lost a battle is a rare thing. When such a tradition is acknowledged, it is probably true because it runs counter to the interest of glorification. In the opposite case, one should record a claim for victory with the observation that this type of tradition is natural in an official milieu.

To evaluate the accuracy of the transmission, all variants that still exist about a tradition should be analyzed. When traditions are popular there are many variants, whose range of variation may be broad or narrow. If the range of variation is broad, the transmission was obviously not very careful. The range should be established through testimony gathered from independent witnesses, that is, people who did not know each other at the time of recording. This method can be followed for many popular traditions.

When accounts are inherited by specialists or have an official character, there may be few or no variants. Often, all the witnesses know each other and have discussed the contents of the tradition, or, as frequently happens in this case, there is only one or perhaps two or three witnesses. We have a paradox: official traditions, which are obviously most tampered with for social reasons, are best preserved, but there are few variants to check on the state of preservation; popular traditions, though not so much tampered with for official reasons, are often transmitted in a slipshod fashion and can be altered profoundly for aesthetic reasons, as is evident from the multiple variants. Between these two extremes lie a number of intermediate cases.

It is not always possible to reconstruct the original tradition from variants. When the wording is frozen, textual analysis can lead to the construction of an archetype. If the tradition has a rigid form but the wording is free, as in the case of an epic, only part of an archetype can be reconstructed because the wording does not belong completely to the tradition. In the case of a narrative, there is no archetype at all.[10] A comparison of variants in those cases is invaluable, however, because it casts light on the origins of the narrative. If it stems from only one tradition, its plot, episodes, sequence of episodes, setting, and cast should correspond, and in the absence of an archetype a major outline of the original story can be given. But often such narratives, especially literary traditions, originate wholly in borrowings from other texts. When such narratives or parts of narratives pretend to tell what happened in the past but are shown to be derived from fictional stories, the value of the testimony is negligible. There are five major traditions dealing with the origin of the last dynasty to rule over Burundi. By showing how parts and wholes were related to fictional narrative, it was possible to eliminate four of the five traditions and to show for the fifth which parts were fictive. One could show that some fiction traditions already existed when this dynasty was founded around 1700 and thus also indirectly date literary traditions.[11]

Whether the chain of a tradition really goes back to the time of the supposed occurrence of the events in it can generally be assessed only by determining whether the milieu in which the account was transmitted existed at that time. This method applies to most cases and eliminates automatically stories of creation and chaos. When a tradition is shown to be derived from other traditions, as in the case of Burundi just mentioned, it follows that it does not go back to the purported eyewitness and first author. In other cases it can be shown that the tradition goes back to rumor rather than to eyewitness accounts. This will often be the case when the tradition is popular, widespread, and appears in areas away from the historical places where events were supposed to have happened. In a Rundi case of the early twentieth century, "the death of Maconco," some variants occur only near the places where the action happened. They form a tradition stemming from eyewitnesses. In other areas, other versions form traditions stemming from rumor current at the time of Maconco's demise. They are untrustworthy about the events themselves but are sources about public sentiment in these parts of the kingdom. Therefore, even traditions which go back to rumor can be of interest to the historian.[12]

Other cases in which it can be shown that traditions were invented are aetiological narratives derived from folketymology and iconatrophy. The latter case is frequent in Africa. Present populations find artifacts of people who lived in their location once. They automatically attribute them to certain populations who, according to oral tradition, lived there before them. This is logical but often incorrect since many populations may have succeeded one another in a given area and all remnants are not necessarily from the last one that is remembered. Other cases of iconatrophy, rarer in Africa, derive a story from speculation about the builders of a still visible monument. When archaeological finds are correlated with tradition, one must be wary not to take the local assertions as Gospel. It is important to know what the traditions were *before* the discovery was made, and *only* in cases where the site was invisible and unsuspected by the local inhabitants. The spurious commentaries already mentioned are another class of invented traditions.

The effects of the verbal character of the tradition and its transmission on its contents can be gauged. It is clear, however, that the collection of traditions must provide the materials for the evaluation. The collector must perform the difficult task of providing information on his witnesses, the chain and the milieu of the transmission, the existence of mnemotechnic devices, and the frequency of recitation. Above all it is important to find *all* the variants of a given tradition, just as one strives to unearth all the manuscript copies of a written text if the original is lost. These requirements, and those necessary to assess the reliability of a given tradition by applying the canons of the historical method, presuppose a thorough knowledge of the languages involved and a great intimacy with the society and culture in which the traditions flourish.

Undoubtedly, African historians who study their own societies hold an incalculable advantage over outsiders. One can foresee that collecting and analyzing oral traditions will be more and more one of the special concerns of African historians. Even they need a real familiarity with linguistic, literary, and anthropological techniques and concepts. E. J. Alagoa associated himself with a linguist to transcribe and translate the traditions he recorded in his own language. These difficulties help explain why so few text editions of bodies of traditions have been published. Those that have were usually the result of collaboration between a linguist and an anthropologist, rather than a historian.[13] For the present far too few text editions exist and most collections made before the 1960's, and many since then, remain of limited value because variants were not considered.[14]

Having dealt with the specific elements which distinguish oral traditions from written data it remains to sketch briefly the variety of traditions that can be encountered. The following table sets up a typology for historians. Its criteria are those facts that affect the content of a tradition as well as its form: verbal character, formal structure, manner of transmission, purpose, and significance. This is not a literary or sociological typology; it is rather a listing of kinds of sources in terms of historical interest.

As most of the types listed are familiar, I will restrict comment to the unusual ones. Personal poetry is often elegiac or deals with death. Lyrical, intensely personal poetry is rare in the extreme; both love and the beauties of nature are rarely sung. Liturgical and ceremonial poetry correspond to rubrics in written books on the mass or other services. These rules for procedure along with the formulae to be recited are put in verse and learned by rote by the specialists who have to perform the rites. The Rwanda example[16] is the only detailed case known so far.

Epics in the European sense—that is, with free wording but bound by formal rules—are uncommon at best. Most African epics are narrative, interwoven with song and poetry, and do not fall into this type. In structure they are like narrative but are longer and exhibit an *Epische Breite* that other tales lack. They belong to the artistic tales. All narratives except personal memories, usually transmitted within a family, are myths for the anthropologists, although a category myth would encompass properly only the aetiological narrative. Since the word "myth" is so protean in meaning, it is avoided as a type, but I use it in its anthropological sense.

Auxiliary commentary is prompted by the need to explain another text; its transmission is intimately linked with the main text it

A Historical Typology of Oral Traditions[15]

Category	Subcategory	Type
Formulae		Names
		Titles
		Slogans
		Didactic formulae (e.g., proverb)
		Ritual formulae
Poetry (including song)	official	Historical
		Panegyric
		Liturgical and ceremonial
	private	Religious
		Personal
Epics		Epics
Lists		Place-names
		Personal names (e.g., genealogy)
Narrative	mythical[a] { historical	General
		Local
		Familial
	didactic	Aetiological
	artistic	Artistic
	personal	Personal memory
Commentaries	legal	Precedents
	auxiliary	Explanations and glosses
	sporadic	Occasional note

[a] All narrative except personal narrative is considered "myth" by anthropologists.

explains. Sporadic commentary is not elicited by another tradition and consists of more or less haphazard questions. Its transmission is quite erratic. For example, a boy and his grandfather walk along the field and the boy *may* ask "Where do beans come from?" and the old man *may* know and say "From X or Y." Such traditions are often all the more valuable because they seem so unimportant to those who tell them. They often include data which should have been forgotten by "structural amnesia," as the anthropologists call the process of letting a tradition that has no more practical use fall into oblivion. But they were saved thanks to natural curiosity. Much of the information on the origins of crops, the practices of trade, changes in style of dress, and so on derives from this humble source.

Most historians have collected only historical narratives to the neglect of many other types, especially commentaries and literary data such as poetry. Yet, these can and do contribute to our knowledge of the past. For concrete examples one can turn to Alagoa's discussion of these in the framework of Nembe (Nigeria) history.[17]

Having described the specific characteristics of traditions and sketched their scope and variety, let us turn to their African character and the linguistic and anthropological problems posed when we try to apply the historical method to them.

II

> *La pensée sauvage* (the untutored
> mind; the wild pansy).
> —Lévi-Strauss (1962)

The translator of *La pensée sauvage* called it *The Savage Mind* and missed the meaning. I call attention to this example, not only to emphasize the problem of multiple meaning, but also to draw attention to a major work of an author who stresses the unconscious symbolic meaning of narrative in "oral societies." *La pensée sauvage* is a motto for the historian who probes into the meaning and background of traditions in order to assess their value as documents.

Traditions should be recorded in the language in which they were transmitted. This is usually done for most kinds of oral transmission, with the exception of narratives, commentaries, and epics. Indeed, it has been suggested that historians rely on instantaneous translations for immediate understanding of narratives,[18] but those who have recorded "live" traditions in the original would not agree with this suggestion. In a translation the linguistic "markers," the exact shadings or nuances, the multiple meanings of the original narration, the whole literary climate of the performance is lost. With that loss, the impact of the language on the content of the tradition will remain largely undetected.

A linguistic and literary analysis is essential to understanding the meaning of traditions. First, the formal structure of the text must be established. If the form is rigid, its rules must be found. This sort of analysis has, as yet, not been pursued to any great extent, not even by linguists. The pioneering work for different genres of poetry is that of T. Kamanzi and A. Coupez.[19] For the different varieties of Rwanda poetry they established the formal norms; the linguistic markers, such as uncommon uses of linguistic features of the type referred to as "poetic license"; and the patterns of expected evolution in content. But all literary genres recognized by the people themselves have different formal characteristics. Therefore, the historian must determine how each group classifies its own literature and must study samples of every genre to define the formal structure of each.

Each verbal expression also contains an internal structure. Any utterance has such a structure, but it is most visible in narratives. This internal structure includes a plot, a sequence of episodes, the building-in of one or more climaxes, parallelisms, repetitions, and transformations of episodic material. All these points must be analyzed before the narrative can be used, for the requirements of the internal structure may well have distorted the content. When, for example, the Rundi rebel is killed just in the sight of the messengers who are running to the spot bringing pardon, one sees immediately that some rearrangement of the actual events may have been involved. This type of internal structure has been called the morphology of the text.[20] It gives access to an understanding of the dynamics of growth of the text, especially if variants are available. For instance, H. Scheub showed that the Xhosa *intsomi* narratives are built around kernels of proverbs or songs. Episodes built around these kernels are then strung together to make up a tale. Obviously, the dynamic evolution of such a genre allows for reordering combinations of kernels, dropping some, adding others. These are artistic tales, yet their techniques have influenced historical narratives as well. Indeed, famous sayings are the proverbs around which pseudo-historical episodes are often constructed.[21] Beyond the internal structure and an analysis of its dynamics there is yet another level of structure, the symbolic structural level. The techniques for discovering it have been refined by Lévi-Strauss.[22] Its impact on the contents of tradition can readily be seen by anyone who analyzes the symbolic meaning of the "images d'Epinal," or popular imagery, in history.

The internal structure of an account is the key to understanding its different meanings. There are three levels of meaning: the literal, the intended, and the symbolic, the latter being largely unconscious. To understand the literal meaning special attention is paid to items such as archaisms, esoteric language, foreign expressions, and key cultural terms, just as is done for written texts. Understanding key words is complicated by the fact that they are part of a foreign culture. In addition, the semantic fields of the terms may have changed in time, and they are, in any case, so broad that the context dictates the meaning. Extensive scholarly dictionaries are not available for most African languages, and a simple gloss may only cause confusion. In Burundi the word *ganwa* refers to the royal lineage, the aristocracy. But it can also designate anyone who is in a position of authority, aristocrat or not. The context may tell which meaning must be chosen. Some key terms such as "witchcraft," "conquest," "brother," and so forth require a profound understanding of the society and the culture involved. These words are often false friends, for a first reading of the account may not seem to pose any problem of interpretation at all. Such terms are comparable to the word *justitia* in medieval Latin documents or "democracy" in more recent times.

The intended meaning of an account corresponds to its internal structure. Literary devices, including playing with words, are usually responsible for the difference between literal and intended meaning. These devices are those proper to each literary genre— allegory, poetic allusion, explicit symbol—all found in written documents as well. The fondness for stereotypes in oral societies is great, whether these are simple stock sentences or complex episodes used as *topoi* (clichés) or even complete *Wandersagen*.[23] To understand why a complex cliché or a *Wandersage* is used is not always easy. First the cliché must be recognized, which can be done only in reference to a corpus of data including those of many other societies besides the one studied. Unfortunately for the Africanist, no reliable reference work on this subject exists. The folk-motiv index is of little use,[24] and the work by H. Baumann, completed in 1936, deals with only a fraction of such clichés.[25]

Clichés do mask some facts handed down by tradition. For example, J. S. Boston found two stereotypes current among the Igala to explain why a community was founded. In one the founder was a hunter; in the other the founder was a member of the royal house. The hunter cliché meant, Boston suggests, that the founder came from outside the established framework of authority. He did not necessarily migrate from another society; he may have merely assumed leadership without previous legitimation.[26]

If working with clichés and *Wandersagen* involves again a real familiarity with the literature and the society of the people who tell the tradition, an understanding of the unconscious symbolic

meaning of a text is even more of a challenge. In the parlance of
Lévi-Strauss and the anthropologists who followed him, most narratives are myths. Any myth refers to a dualistic structure of basic
symbols which express, not only the fundamental values cherished
by that particular society, or indeed any human society, but also
the working of the human mind itself. The human mind must
organize, before it can grasp and communicate, raw data, and its
basic principle of organization is a binary system of parallels and
oppositions involving transformation of propositions by shift of
terms or inversion. There is no doubt that such a level of meaning
really exists. To explain what it is or may be does not, however,
necessarily invalidate the whole content of a tradition, as T. O.
Beidelman would like to have it.[27] Serious distortion of the events
in the account can be expected, but the events may have happened.
Because the popular accounts of the Mayflower are highly complex
symbolic statements does not mean that there never was a Mayflower. In addition, the discovery of the unconscious message concealed in all texts leads only to a probability that is often less than
the probabilities historians are wont to consider valid. There are two
approaches, both involving a great deal of personal interpretation
of symbols by the anthropologist. One is the method used by V.
Turner, who links symbols to each other—verbal symbols to symbols
in ritual and symbols in one society to those operating elsewhere.[28]
The other approach is exemplified by Lévi-Strauss in his massive
work on myths. The structure of one myth becomes clearer by the
analysis of other myths, whether they belong to the same culture
or to historically related cultures. His studies deal with South
America and in order to explain his reference myth, a tale of the
Bororo, he must range over the whole mythology of both Americas.[29]

How can the historian take this into consideration when he tries
to establish the validity of an account? In theory, the unconscious
message can be the most insidious factor of distortion during the
transmission, realigning the original statement of the eyewitness to
make it conform more and more to a given system of symbols. An
effective approach is to start from the internal structure, list all
symbols that may appear, and see how these fit into a system by
analyzing the ritual and ceremony of the culture involved. Again
the historian must be an anthropologist.

He must also have a sense for literary analysis. We have considered most of the questions dealt with in literary analysis, with
the exception of the crucial one: What alternatives are open to

performers to make an account more beautiful or to make it dull? What is banale, what is original, what has strong appeal, what bores? Among a set of variants, which one is a work of art and which is a pedestrian rendering? Only members steeped in the culture itself, and sometimes only the more sensitive among them, can give an answer to this. This is yet another reason why it is preferable that study of traditions be entrusted to people who belong to the society itself. But outsiders can ask the audiences who have listened to the performances which of several variants are preferred and why, thus recording the prevailing tastes. This is what the historian must know, for it is the force that distorts the original message most. Moreover, many oral literary data are remembered only for their aesthetic appeal. Their beauty may have distorted the message, but at the same time it has been responsible for the very preservation of the poem or song.

Once the meaning of traditions is understood, one must determine why they have been transmitted. What are their functions and purposes? Have these purposes distorted an original or led to the fabrication of a spurious tradition? Just as for written sources, one first determines if a tradition is official or private, if the testimony is voluntary or unconscious. Most oral literary data give unconscious information since they do not purport to tell what happened in the past. Official traditions range the gamut of politics and social interests: royal genealogies and dynastic histories providing legitimation for a regime and a line of rulers; local traditions "proving" rights over land; family traditions showing aristocratic precedence or prestige. A tradition can be official with respect to one group and private when it deals with another group. A family tradition may be the official account of its ancestors but it is a private account when it deals with the history of the state because the family is only a tiny part of the state and does not have authority to speak officially on state history.

Every tradition has some use, even if it is merely fulfilling an aesthetic or didactic function. Since one tradition may serve several purposes, or its role may have changed during the transmission because the society changed, the assessment of distortions induced by social pressures is sometimes difficult to estimate. A common situation is one where genealogies are manipulated and altered to explain why social groups *now* exhibit the relationships they have to other social groups *now*. They are an explanation of society, especially when society is based entirely on principles linked with descent. Unimportant ancestors are forgotten and the genealogy is "telescoped." The reverse happens as well. This sort of situation has led some anthropologists such as J. Goody to argue that there is a homeostatic relationship between a society and its oral inheritance. What is conflicting with changed norms or new institutions is altered or dropped and at any given time the corpus of traditions in an oral society corresponds entirely to its composition, its structures, and its functions. Inconvenient traditions are simply forgotten by a process of "structural amnesia": "In oral societies the cultural tradition is transmitted almost entirely by face-to-face communication; and changes in its content are accompanied by the homeostatic process of forgetting or transforming those parts of the tradition that cease to be either necessary or relevant."[30]

Professor Goody exaggerates. If this process were so complete, why would one encounter archaisms, obscure passages, and above all traditions which exhibit a conflict of interests born from changes in the society?[31] Moreover, the more popular and less specialized a tradition is, the less affected it will be by changes in social structure.[32] One does well to remember that most traditions deal with relatively shallow time depths. The changes in African societies during the nineteenth century can be documented and their impact on official and other traditions assessed.

A tradition also embodies values and ideals, as it is the product of a given set of basic categories in the Kantian sense. Each society expresses its beliefs, values, and ideals in its literature and stereotypes. From the corpus of traditions it is easy to deduce which ideals, which virtues, and which vices are exemplified by different heroes in the narratives (and allow for estimation of distortion). Formulae and poetry, more than any other kinds of tradition, yield this type of information.

Categories, inculcated during the childhood years, prior to experience by the senses, include the basic notions about space, time, cause, historical truth, color, and so on—a constellation of basic notions that form the framework for all cognition. These must be known to the student of tradition, for their effect on the perception, the interpretation, and the transmission of events is paramount. If people hold that causal chains cannot exist but that each present-day phenomenon derives directly from an original cause, they negate the concept of change as a set of antecedents leading to a set of consequences and this attitude colors all their traditions. Or again, if they believe in recurring cyclical time from a golden age through a period of quietness to further military glory and then collapse back to the golden age, their historical traditions will be arranged so as to fit the pattern, at least in the most obvious places. All of this is true for written data as well.

After reading the recital of all the factors that may influence or distort the original account, one may well wonder if oral tradition can be used at all. Yet it does work. First, it is not uncommon for a tradition to be corroborated by other independent traditions or by data from other disciplines or written records. Such a coincidence establishes a high degree of probability for the historical reality of such information. Then it must be remembered that *all* history is a matter of evaluation and of probabilities. Even if the probabilities remain lower than one could wish for, the data can be used to recreate the past as long as their strengths and weaknesses are made clear and as long as they are the best evidence available. In any case, the cardinal rule for all sources remains true: they must be used in conjunction with all other available evidence. It remains to be seen what other sources can be used, how oral tradition compares to them, and whether traditions have been, in fact, valuable for reconstructing African history.

III

A comparison between oral tradition and other sources available to the historian of Africa indicates best what uses can and should be made of tradition. The other data are written documents, archaeological artifacts, cultural material, and linguistic information.[33] All these data, with the exception of written texts, are studies by specialists other than the historian. Interpretation, therefore, requires at least some familiarity with the other disciplines involved—an understanding of the reasoning used by other scholars and the validity of their deductions.

Written documents in Africa were done by outsiders who misunderstood the workings of the society and the culture they were dealing with. The older the document, the more this is true. But the dictum applies even to the majority of writings which originated during the colonial period. Proponents of oral traditions emphasize that they give an inside view that corrects the perspective of the writings. There is a great measure of truth to this allegation. But written documents are precious because of their precise chronology, because they are often less distorted than traditions, and because most writings are originals.[34] Before the colonial period written sources yield information about trade, accounts of major political developments, and vague descriptions of items dealing with social structure, religion, or art. Oral traditions, on the other hand, cover virtually every aspect of society and culture barring two blind spots: quantitative data and unconscious gradual change, especially in religion, value systems, and ideology. But oral tradition can be used for all sociopolitical information, economics, religion, art, and such fields as demography, population movements, and material culture.

Both traditions and written data in Africa have increased in quantity, from a handful starting around the fifteenth century to a plethora of documents by 1900. For many places, especially after 1750 or 1800, oral traditions and written documents can be used jointly. Large parts of Africa remain undocumented in the written record before 1850 and later, although in the lower Congo and Angola a fair quantity of writings survives from the sixteenth century onward. Thus in the tropical forest or in the interior of Tanzania oral tradition is the major source until almost 1880, while the history of the former kingdom of Kongo has been reconstructed almost entirely from written records.

Relations between oral traditions and writing can be intimate. Professor William A. Brown found an occasional nineteenth-century letter surviving in Masina (Mali). Its contents were explained by reference to a whole set of correspondence now lost but remembered only because of the surviving letter. The letter served as a mnemotechnic device to give a reason and some help for retaining the tradition. More recently one finds that information learned from books is fed back into the tradition. The more traditions have been collected and published, the more the danger of such a process exists. It is often easy to detect if the collector is aware of the problem, and is really no different from the problem of phony traditions picked up from radio or television.

Archaeology is the other major source for reconstructing the past of the dark continent. For periods before A.D. 1400 it stands almost alone. It remains crucial for the recovery of data until well into the eighteenth century, and if archaelogists were sensitive to the needs of historians, they would even investigate many nineteenth-century sites as well. Archaeology yields a reasonably good chronology until the end of the seventeenth century,[35] its data have no cultural bias, it testifies directly from the artifacts. From these much can be deduced about economics, nutrition, environment, pattern of settlement, rank (grave goods), a scale of political organization, and art. This is much less than what some have recently claimed.[36] The relationship between archaeology and oral tradition is also intimate. Often the collection of tradition helps to locate sites and sites throw light on the validity of traditions, whether they confirm or invalidate. In a recent case, a grave that should have been dated around A.D. 1650 according to tradition turned out to be circa A.D. 400. The Rwanda dynasty, from which the tradition stemmed, had probably annexed the hallowed grave sites of much earlier ages for its own, no doubt to legitimize its own position. Even if a tradition is shown to be wholly untrustworthy, as has happened, the new problem becomes to know why, when, and by whom the tradition was fabricated, itself a fact of history.

The danger of iconatrophy or backfeeding from a site to tradition and then back has been mentioned. Before the dig begins, traditions about a site should be collected and careful record should be made of anything visible on the site before the excavation. Given this precaution, it is obvious that the confrontation of sites and traditions is most fruitful. The notorious chronological weakness of the traditions can be strengthened by the archaeologist, who can also check if the general picture provided for a given period by the traditions is likely or not. The traditions, on the other hand, fill in the picture of the culture uncovered by the spade with regard to intangible items.

Traditions also exist for certain objects, such as the famous fifteenth-century Dogon (Tellem) statuettes. The objects can be dated sometimes by the tradition and sometimes by the art style, as with the royal portraits of the Kuba. These objects were never buried and thus never became artifacts for the archaeologist. They are—in strict historical parlance—monuments, and occupy a position halfway between archaeological and ethnographic data. Ethnographic data is divided into tangible artifacts and intangible "behavior." Distributions through space provide clues to diffusion of the objects or practices. But this technique has run into serious problems and the quality of the evidence is often marginal. It is therefore best to combine it with linguistic research into the presence of loan words. Ethnographic evidence can also be used in other ways, for instance to reconstruct the evolution of a set of societies *known* to be related from a common ancestral society.[37] Oral tradition has not yet been used often in conjunction with this type of data.

Linguistics, also, has not been used extensively in relation to traditions, beyond its contribution in translating the language in which the traditions are told. Historical linguistics that deals with a very remote past has no possible overlap with oral tradition, but loan words, whose potential historical significance is just being grasped, make it possible to compare evidence thus adduced with the record of the tradition. A Kuba tradition says that the royal family came from the Mongo area. Certainty is provided when it is found that the word *boolo* (strong) in the royal salutation is unknown elsewhere in Kuba speech, but is a typical Mongo word. Linguistics, like ethnographic data, is extremely weak in chronology, its most serious drawback. Only when loan words can be dated in relative sequence, or when evidence about internal evolution within a language can be given in sequence, will this handicap disappear.

Other disciplines occasionally contribute some historical evidence to oral tradition. Biology, for example, contributes knowledge of the origins of domesticated plants and animals, even if it cannot as yet tell us much about the development of different strains of animals, plants, and human populations. On some occasions oral traditions are considered in connection with this type of evidence.[38]

Obviously, then, oral tradition is one of the three main sources of African history. It suffers from a major weakness, however: an uncertain chronology, the backbone of history. African historians have had to come to terms with this problem in various ways. It is well known that each society has its own concept of time, a time related to biological or structural phenomena: a day, a month, a year, a generation, an age-class, a length of reign. Most oral literary data do not even contain an internal sequence of relative time and would be undatable and unusable were it not for information from outside the account. Often, dating can be accomplished by a study of distribution, comparison with historical accounts that borrowed from literary materials, and so on. But the dating remains rough. In fact, no one so far has even attempted a chronology for these materials in any part or for the whole of Africa.

Many narrative sources have a relative chronology—"A followed B"—and the problem is to convert the local narrative sequence into a universal chronology. In fact, the problem is not only one of time but also one of space. A tradition refers to a "universe" that may be quite small: a few settlements, a lineage, a small chiefdom. To make it meaningful it must be put into a set of traditions related to the neighboring elements in space. This solves the problem of limitation in space, but not in time.[39]

Dating by reference to a sun eclipse or other meteorological occurrence is possible when these have been observed.[40] Astronomers can date the time of day and date of every eclipse of the sun that has occurred or will occur. Since more than one past eclipse has generally occurred in the area where a tradition is remembered, a rough calculation of the time elapsed since the eclipse of the tradition happened, working in terms of generations or lengths of reign or age-grades backwards, is necessary to find which one of the possible eclipses is the correct one. If the time of day is mentioned by tradition, the possibility of error in identifying the correct eclipse becomes minimal. The use of other meteorological phenomena is rarer, but the occurrence of some meteors or other celestial phenomena have helped to date specific events on occasion. It was highly likely that a Kuba (Congo) king, Mbakam, ruled in 1680 when there was a sun eclipse. Confirmation comes from the fact that tradition remembered it had once snowed during his reign, an occurrence almost miraculous 4° south of the equator. *Spectrum of Time*, a service of the British astronomical association, was able to tell us that the only cold wave in southern Africa strong enough to produce snow occurred between 1690 and 1693, thus confirming the choice of the eclipse date over an alternative choice of 1619.

Almost equally strong chronology can be obtained by direct correlation between a tradition and written data or an archaeological date. But most of the time one must work with very rough indicators of structural time age-sets, genealogies, and lengths of reign. For age-sets, nineteenth-century practice learned what fixed intervals of time elapsed between two initiations so that a chronology can be constructed from that. These intervals are quite regular, generally every eight, ten, or fifteen years.

The situation is quite different for lengths of reign or a generation span, as a measure of the time elapsed between the birth of a man and that of his oldest child. It has been shown[41] that the variability of averages of generations and lengths of reign from one culture to another is quite significant. The formula often used in Africa—twenty-seven to thirty years to the generation—is completely unsound. There are only two ways in which one can convert these relative time measurements on an absolute scale. The first way consists of calculating the averages in each case for portions of the time span which can be determined by other means and then extrapolating the average for the portions backward to the beginning of the time scale in the tradition. Dated portions of lists exist for most of nineteenth-century Africa. It is obvious that the method is still rough because it presupposes that general sociopolitical conditions remained unchanged over the whole period and that the average length of reign or generation was not affected by such conditions. Knowledge of an average age or reign does not allow one to determine easily when a particular generation or a particular king lived. The second approach, using an extremely large sample of known dynasties and genealogies pertaining to aristocracies in the literate world, will eventually make it possible to state probabilities for both length of generation and length of reign given certain conditions of descent system, marriage, succession, and environment. It will thus be possible to detect improbabilities in traditions.

David Henige, who is now conducting such a study, discovered that it is extremely rare for a father-son succession to continue undisturbed beyond the sixth or seventh generation. One will be able to assess the effect of the founder (long or short reign) on average reign length and other similar data. Once these tables of probabilities become available, it will be possible to state that in case A ten generations represent x years with a probability of 70 per cent or more, the most accurate way this kind of information can be assessed.

Another method for converting relative into absolute chronology is through the use of synchronisms. This technique, first developed to cope with ancient Mesopotamian chronology, is now applied in Africa to the fairly small number of cases where adjacent kingdoms allowed for its use. From the Middle Eastern experience it is known that synchronisms between reigns through more than one intermediary often become spurious and should be rejected. One can, however, rely on synchronism between three units. If it is known that A ruled when B ruled and B ruled when C ruled, then one can accept that A ruled when C ruled. In practice, traditions are scrutinized first to determine whether the synchronisms come early or late in the reigns of the rulers mentioned and the putative synchronisms may be adapted by taking this into account.

By using these techniques to convert relative into absolute dating, most oral traditions can be assigned a valid chronology. Once the results of research in progress become available, the degree of validity should become much greater than the one standard deviation of the radiocarbon chronology used in archaeology.

Oral traditions have been used intensively and are being used more and more in reconstructing Africa's history. This trend is evident in the *Journal of African History*. Since its inception in 1960, the journal has had at least one article a year involving oral tradition. Three recent general histories of East Africa rely mainly on oral tradition for the period between 1500 and 1850, especially for the interior. A remarkable feature of programs to collect oral tradition in Tanzania has been the systematic search for family traditions and even eyewitness accounts of events from the early colonial period—the dramatic *maji maji* rising of 1905-1907, for example.[42] In Central and West Africa oral tradition is also used intensively. Even in the literate areas of the Sudan, such research is so valued that the Niger Republic set up a special center for the collection and preservation of oral tradition.[43] It is therefore no longer a question of whether oral traditions should be used. They are. It is not a question of whether they can be valid. How valid are they? This depends on the careful collection and analysis of the data. We must regret, along with many anthropologists and archaeologists, that much shoddy work is still being done. There is room for considerable improvement in our practices, especially in collecting. But one must not condemn the documentation because it is not well handled by some. Even as things stand, imperfect as they are, no one can imagine any longer a history of Africa reconstructed without any recourse to oral traditions. They have proved too valuable. That is why it is worth tackling the intricate problems involved in gathering and evaluating traditions. Much of what they have to say no other voice can tell.

REFERENCES

1. Marcel Griaule and Germaine Dieterlen, *Le renard pâle* (Paris: Institut d'ethnologie, 1965).

2. Ernst Bernheim, *Einleitung in die Geschichtswissenschaft* (Sammlung Göschen) (Berlin: W. de Guyter and Company, 1920), pp. 97-108, for the most easily accessible edition. His handbook on historical method has been the source of all general handbooks since 1889.

3. Engelbert Mveng, *Histoire du Cameroun* (Paris: Présence Africaine, 1963), pp. 235-236.

4. Daniel Biebuyck and Kahombo Mateene, eds. and trans., *The Mwindo Epic* (Berkeley: University of California Press, 1969), p. 17. Rureke told the epic as recorded in this book.

5. The following discussion is based upon but amends Jan Vansina, *De la tradition orale* (Tervuren: Musée Royal de l'Afrique Centrale, 1961); page references are to the translation, *Oral Tradition* (Chicago: Aldine Publishing Company, 1965). On oral tradition in Africa, recent statements were made by H. Moniot, "Les sources orales," in Hubert Deschamps, *Histoire de l'Afrique* (Paris: Presses universitaires de France, 1970), I, 131-138; J. A. Kieran, "Oral Tradition," in B. A. Ogot and J. A. Kieran, *Zamani: A Survey of East African History* (Nairobi: E.A.P.H. and Longmans, 1968), pp. 9-12, and H. Deschamps, "Histoire et ethnologie," in J. Poirier, *Ethnologie générale* (Paris: Gallimard, 1968), pp. 1439-1444, as typical statements.

6. This corrects Vansina, *De la tradition orale*, pp. 26, 51, 56-57 especially.

7. H. A. R. Gibb, *Mohammedanism,* 2d ed. (New York: Oxford University Press, 1962), pp. 74-87, as an introduction to *hadith.*

8. "Performance" is the name given to most oral accounts in their original setting. The term rightly stresses the acting which accompanied many accounts. See H. Scheub, "The Ntsomi: A Xhosa Performing Art," Ph.D. dissertation, University of Wisconsin, 1969, I, 19-57.

9. Marcel d'Hertefelt and A. Coupez, *La royauté sacrée de l'ancien Rwanda* (Tervuren: Musée Royal de l'Afrique Centrale, 1964) is the text edition for these.

10. Contrary to Vansina, *De la tradition orale*, p. 137.

11. Jan Vansina, *La légende du passé: traditions orales du Burundi,* forthcoming (Tervuren).

12. *Ibid.*

13. Such as d'Hertefelt and Coupez, *La royauté sacrée.* Other text editions for Rwanda were made by a linguist and an African from the culture. See A. Coupez and T. Kamanzi, *Récits historiques rwanda* (Tervuren: Musée Royal de l'Afrique Centrale, 1962); A. Coupez and T. Kamanzi, *Littérature de Cour au Rwanda* (Oxford: Oxford University Press, 1970); Biebuyck and Mateene, *Mwindo Epic,* a text edition resulting from a combination of anthropologist and African linguist. There are a few exceptions to the pattern, but they confirm it. Thus the numerous text publications of G. Hulstaert in the 1960's are the work of a linguist who spent thirty years in the same area and also wrote anthropological works.

14. The oldest great collection was perhaps F. Callet, *Tantara ny Andriana eto Madagascar,* 4 vols. (Antananarivo, 1875-1902).

15. Supersedes Vansina, *De la tradition orale*, p. 144.

16. M. d'Hertefelt and A. Coupez, *La royauté sacrée.*

17. E. J. Alagoa, "The Use of Oral Literary Data for History," *Journal of American Folklore*, 81 (1968), 235-242; E. J. Alagoa, "Songs as Historical Data," *Research Review* (Legon), 5 (1968), 1-16. Literary data begin to be published in text editions in series such as the Oxford Library of African Literature.

18. P. Curtin, "Field Techniques for Collecting and Processing Oral Data," *Journal of African History*, 9 (1968), 367-386.

19. Coupez and Kamanzi, *Litterature de Cour au Rwanda.*

20. Vladimir Propp, *Morphology of the Folktale*, ed. Svatava Pirkova-Jakobson (Bloomington: Indiana University Center in Anthropology, Folklore, and Linguistics, 1958), trans. from Russian by Laurence Scott.

21. H. Scheub, "The Ntsomi," pp. 203-262.

22. C. Lévi-Strauss, *Mythologiques*, 3 vols. (Paris: Plon, 1964-1969). There is wide disagreement over the way in which this level can be found; for example, F. W. Young, "A Fifth Analysis of the Star Husband Tale," *Ethnology*, 9 (1970), 389-413. Five anthropologists arrived at five different conclusions using five different methods to analyze one text. One easily finds other approaches, such as T. O. Beidelman, "Myth, Legend and Oral History: A Kaguru Traditional Text," *Anthropos*, 65 (1970), 74-97.

23. For example, L. Bynon, "Comparison thematique d'un conte kerewe et d'un conte rundi," *Africa-Tervuren*, 9 (1963), 1-10, for an example in the interlacustrine area and a way to handle *Wandersagen.*

24. John Greenway, *Literature Among the Primitives* (Hatboro, Pa.: Folklore Associates, 1964), pp. 289-292, and the scathing but correct criticism, p. 292.

25. Hermann Baumann, *Schöpfung und Urzeit des Menschen im Mythus der afrikanischen Völker* (Berlin: Verlag von Dietrich Reimer/Andrews und Steiner, 1936).

26. J. S. Boston, "The Hunter in Igala Legends of Origin," *Africa*, 34 (1964), 116-125.

27. Beidelman, "Myth, Legend and Oral History," has been the most violent critic of historians because narrative traditions do have symbolic meaning.

28. V. W. Turner, *The Forest of Symbols* (Ithaca: Cornell University Press, 1967) and his *The Drums of Affliction* (London: International African Institute, 1968).

29. Lévi-Strauss, *Mythologiques.*

30. John R. Goody, ed., *Literacy in Traditional Societies* (Cambridge, Eng.: University Press, 1968), p. 67. See pp. 27-67 for the argument.

31. See R. G. Willis, "Traditional History and Social Structure in Ufipa," *Africa*, 34 (1964), 340-351, for a case where two different political groups with opposing interests each preserved their traditions. One had ousted the

other from the leadership over Ufipa. The case is remarkably frequent in Africa.

32. Vansina, *De la tradition orale*, pp. 164-169, shows that popular traditions were least affected by the differences in sociopolitical structures of Rwanda and Burundi.

33. For this section see Daniel McCall, *Africa in Time-Perspective*, II (New York: Oxford University Press, 1969) and C. Gabel and N. R. Bennett, eds., *Reconstructing African Culture History* (Boston: Boston University Press, 1967).

34. Not all are originals. In fact, the major printed seventeenth-century source, O. Dapper, *Naukeurige beschrijvinge der Afrikaensche gewesten* (Amsterdam: J. van Meurs, 1676) is a compilation of written reports by others which have been lost. The problems of authorship for any section of this book are among the most formidable that can be encountered.

35. Radiocarbon dating is usually unreliable for dates after the middle of the seventeenth or the beginning of the eighteenth century.

36. Sally R. Binford and Lewis R. Binford, *New Perspectives in Archeology* (Chicago: Aldine Publishing Company, 1968).

37. E. Sapir, *Time Perspective in Aboriginal American Culture: A Study in Method* (Ottawa, 1916), reprinted in David G. Mandelbaum, ed., *Selected Writings in Language, Culture, and Personality* (Berkeley: University of California Press, 1963), pp. 398-462, is the standard account for the historical use of both ethnographic and linguistic data in history. See also Jan Vansina, "The Use of Ethnographic Data as Sources for History," in T. O. Ranger, ed., *Emerging Themes of African History* (Nairobi: East African Publishing House and Northwestern University Press, 1968), pp. 97-124.

38. Physical anthropology has not yet advanced far enough to be more than of incidental use now. See J. Hiernaux, *La diversité humaine en Afrique subsaharienne*, 2 vols. (Brussels: Université libre de Bruxelles, 1968). Eventually human biology will be of considerable assistance in checking data from traditions, especially when the traditions make claims about human migrations.

39. See S. Saberwal, "The Oral Tradition, Periodization and Political Systems," *Canadian Journal of African Studies* (1967), pp. 155-162, for a discussion of the relation between political system and size of area controlled by it and periodization.

40. For Africa see R. Gray, "Eclipse Maps," *Journal of African History*, 6 (1965), 251-262, and R. Gray, "Annual Eclipse Maps," *ibid.*, 9 (1968), 147-153.

41. *Journal of African History*, 11 (1970), 161-268, deals entirely with these problems of dating.

42. Ogot and Kieran, *Zamani;* Andrew Roberts, ed., *Tanzania Before 1900* (Nairobi: East African Publishing House, 1968); G. S. Were and D. A. Wilson, *East Africa Through a Thousand Years* (Nairobi: East African Publishing House, 1970). G. C. Gwassa and J. Iliffe, *Records of the Maji Maji Rising,* Parts, I, II (Nairobi: East African Publishing House, 1968, 1969). A. Robert published a small guide for the collection of oral traditions, "Recording East Africa's Past," *African Journal,* 3 (1967), 23-25.

43. Robert S. Smith, *Kingdoms of the Yoruba* (London: Methuen, 1969), pp. ix-xiii, sketches the uses of oral traditions in West African history. The book is largely based on oral traditions as are most recent works dealing with West Africa before 1900. Jan Vansina, *Kingdoms of the Savanna* (Madison: University of Wisconsin Press, 1966) and B. A. Fagan, ed., *A Short History of Zambia* (Lusaka, London: Oxford University Press, 1966) illustrate the situation for parts of Central Africa.

BENJAMIN I. SCHWARTZ

A Brief Defense of Political and Intellectual History . . . with Particular Reference to Non-Western Cultures

I SHALL begin with a confession. In my efforts to study the history of one non-Western civilization—China—I find that I have tended to focus on two areas of history—political and intellectual (as I understand these terms)—which do not currently enjoy high esteem in many sectors of the historical profession. Owing to certain considerations which are not entirely methodological, my interest in political history has largely focused on contemporary China, while my concern with intellectual history has involved both traditional and modern China. There has, however, been a considerable interaction between both interests. In reflecting on the common denominators which may underlie these two areas of interest, it occurs to me that both are, to a considerable extent, involved with the realm of man's conscious life—with his conscious relationship to the situation in which he finds himself and to his conscious behavior within that situation. To the extent that politics involves ideology, policy, decision-making, and even power relations, it involves conscious intention and conscious activity. In this view, even power relations as they appear in political life are power relations as perceived by the actors.

In struggling to achieve a conception of political history, I find myself somewhat in sympathy with the current tendency to downgrade emphasis on the history of political institutions and constitutional history. In the case of those structures known as political institutions, there has emerged a realization of how problematic and complex are the relations between formal structure and the human realities which they supposedly condition and constrain. Certainly, any effort to make sense of the political history of mainland China in the last twenty years could hardly depend entirely on the history of institutions, constitutions, and formal organizations, and yet we

440

are dealing with a history in which there is considerable truth in the assertion that "politics are in command." If this phrase has any meaning within the context of contemporary China, it must refer not simply or even primarily to institutions but to categories such as policy, decision-making, power relations, and the interplay between ideas and political action.

At the same time the notion that political institutions are in some sense less real or fundamental than all those institutions and structures called social seems to me to be based on questionable assumptions. If it derives from the view that political institutions are often created and shaped by conscious intention and conscious activity while social and economic institutions are the products of deep, unconscious impersonal forces "independent of the wills of men," it seems to me that the contrast is overdrawn on both sides. Many American political scientists of the more scientific persuasion are as ardently bent on proving that the structures of political life and models of political development are as independent of the wills of men as any of the structures described by the economists, sociologists, and anthropologists. If one is prepared to believe Lévi-Strauss's assertion that "myths think themselves out in men,"[1] one can perhaps say that constitutions and political institutions think and act themselves out in men. On the other hand, the notion that conscious purpose and conscious activity are absent in such preeminently "objective" areas as economics, the history of technology, or anthropology simply rests on unthinking dogma. A close look at the history of extended lineage structures in South China would indicate that the maintenance of lineages over time was by no means due simply to the preexistence of unconscious *gemeinschaftliche* kinship structures, but to the highly conscious, organizational efforts of enterprising clan leaders.[2]

Nevertheless, one need not deny that in the case of political institutions, the role of conscious activity is often close to the surface. In China we are able to follow quite closely and with comparative clarity the collective deliberations which led to the formation of the Chinese Communist party and to the creation and destruction of various organizations which have emerged since 1949. This fact neither adds to nor subtracts from the reality of such institutions. Political institutions are neither less real nor less pervasive in their effects than other institutions, but they by no means provide the sole, or even the primary, substance of political history.

If political history involves conscious activity, it is, of course, by no means conscious activity in a vacuum, but conscious activity set within the framework of all the problems, pressures, and constraints imposed by the objective situation. In China one can hardly begin to discuss the programs, policies, decisions, and disputes of the political actors without constant reference to such factors as the overwhelmingly agrarian nature of China's economy, the crushing weight of its population, the persistence of cultural patterns inherited from the past, the contingencies of China's relations with the outside world, and so on. The political historian must welcome all the aid which economists, demographers, anthropologists, and others can provide to help him to understand the situation within which political action takes place. It is by no means demonstrated, however, that the responses of the political actors are the only obviously necessary effects of any or all these forces. It is thus quite clear that during the years 1960-1965 sharp differences of perspective developed within the Chinese Communist leadership concerning the policies to be pursued relative to the socioeconomic and cultural situation which had emerged after the Great Leap Forward. One might, of course, explain these divergent perspectives wholly in terms of power struggles within the leadership. Even if one were entirely prepared to settle for this account of the motivation of the various parties involved, the fact remains that power interests became indissolubly linked to different policy perspectives and that these perspectives in turn reflect divergent images, perceptions, and hopes on the part of the political actors involved. To assert that Mao Tse-tung's Cultural Revolution was the only obvious response to the imperatives of the objective situation of the early sixties is simply to indulge in spurious hindsight.

I am not here trying to prove the case for the freedom of political actors in the philosophic sense. If their actions are not clearly determined by the external objective processes, they may still be determined by internal structures and processes. The social backgrounds of the political actors, their personal biographies, their personality structures, and even the role of ideology as myth in Lévi-Strauss's sense may all be brought in to explain their conscious acts and decisions. One may psychoanalyze Mao Tse-tung. The point is that these forms of determinism are mediated through the conscious political acts of the political actors. This leaves quite open the possibility of the relative autonomy of the political sphere. It also leaves open the possibility that political acts and decisions may substantially affect the course of history.

Here, however, we confront another ground for asserting the superficiality of political history—namely, that political history places undue stress on the acts of tiny groups of people or even on the acts of single individuals. It thus lends aid and comfort to the "great man theory of history" and is elitist in its very essence. It is an offense to both populist sentiment and to science—to populist sentiment in that it denies that the important movements of history are the cumulative effects of the behavior of vast masses of men[3] and to science because the general "laws of history" must manifest themselves through vast masses of instances.

It is, of course, entirely true that the data on princes and prime ministers is infinitely more accessible than data on the political history of provinces and villages. This does not mean, however, that there is no political history of villages. Patrice Higonnet has written a dissertation on the social and political history of the village of Pont de Montvert in southern France which indicates a complicated political life within the village as well as a complicated dialectic of relationships between the political and intellectual history of the village and of the nation as a whole. Frederick Wakeman has written a study of the political life of eastern Kwangtung province in the wake of the Opium War which lifts the veil on the enormous complexity of the local political history of one small area of China.[4] Here we find an amazingly intricate web of political relations between local officialdom, clan politics, secret societies, local gentry, and interethnic rivalries. Other young scholars in the field of modern Chinese history have turned their attention to the political history of provinces and cities during the period before the 1911 Revolution and emerged with extraordinarily circumstantial and lively accounts of local political history. All of these accounts combine political history with social history. The authors must make an effort to reconstruct the physiognomy of local social life but it is the dynamic and conscious life of local political history which reveals the concrete human reality of these social relations. There is no reason to think of political history as simply the history of the policies of kings or courts. It may just as well involve the frustration and deflection of policies of leaders in the capital by local power constellations and the local politics of villages. The policies associated with the Cultural Revolution in China were undoubtedly initiated by Mao Tse-tung and a small group of his supporters, but the turbulent evolution of China during the last three years has been as much due to the unanticipated deflection of these policies by various political forces as to the will of the leader himself.

To be sure, even though the web of political history is spread wide, it may be asserted that for the larger part of human history the masses of mankind have not participated in political life and that the political actors, whether they are monarchs or local clan leaders, are almost by definition part of the ruling class. Much, of course, depends on what one means by participation. If one concedes that political acts and political events may have profound and even devastating effects on the lives of men, then the masses certainly have participated in political history at least as victims. In fact, they have participated in many other ways. The stereotype of the Chinese peasant village that lives a timeless life while the waves of political history flow over it may have a certain partial truth for certain times and certain remote places, but it is essentially not true. All of us know—at least in the abstract—about the vast peasant rebellions which periodically swept China affecting and involving vast populations. We also know about conscription of vast hordes of men for military activities and corvée labor far from home. We know of banditry and secret societies and of the voluntary and involuntary participation of even humble peasants in the bitter feuds of local political life. We also know that peasants did not necessarily remain immured in their villages but were frequent visitors to market towns where they undoubtedly exchanged information concerning local political situations and perhaps even concerning the state of the empire. We know about many of these things in the abstract but, at least in the case of China, what we need if we are to clothe these abstractions with flesh is much more attention to the much despised *histoire événementielle,* to the extent that the Chinese sources are able to supply us with materials. While it is true that all of these sources may be limited from the point of view of certain kinds of questions which we would like to address to them, the fact is that we have hardly begun to exploit what they do contain.

The fact that political history tends to be closely associated with history as story—with the history of events—is, of course, another ground for asserting its superficiality. It is quite true that much political history has been concerned with the main events and the actions of the most visible actors, but presumably even a comprehensive political history which would provide an account of all political actions and events down through every province, city, and village would still be superficial in this view because it would still be a history of surface events rather than of the secular movement of deep, underlying, unconscious structures. I shall not dwell here at length on the procedures by which the variables which enter into these accounts of deep, impersonal forces are assigned an independent life of their own as the prime movers of history. It is thus possible to collect all the statistics available on a certain network of trade over a given period of time (no doubt this is a very valuable enterprise from many points of view), to suppress all considerations of political events, military events, shifts in mentalities, and other variables which may have profoundly affected this statistical series, and to emerge with the view that this pattern of trade is an absolutely independent "infrastructural" variable.

Similarly, one way of dealing with the history of mainland China in the last twenty years is to assert that the only significant fact is the fact that China is undergoing a "process of modernization," operating, as it were, behind the backs of all the participants, and that all the shifts of political history are simply surface eruptions of this process or, if not, essentially insignificant. I shall not dwell here on the obscurities of the concept of modernization. It is based on the assumption that there exists an all-encompassing and apparently stable structure of something called "modern society" which provides the clear and unmoving target of all developing societies (since all development is development toward something). One need not deny that all societies now called modern share certain features in common, the most indisputable being a highly industrialized economy. Yet the notion that the differences between these societies are insignificant or the notion that these societies have achieved a kind of plateau of essential stability which will preclude sweeping unpredictable transformations in the future is part of what might be called the ideology of modernization. The target itself is neither clear nor unchanging. Modern societies of the twenty-first century may exhibit features which run entirely counter to the dominant trends of the mid-twentieth century. Without denying for a moment that the political leaders of China are interested in many of the elements which we tend to subsume under the category of modernization, the question of how China will modernize holds many obscurities and uncertainties for the leadership itself. The question of how to modernize becomes a political question and the political decisions of the leaders may have a profound effect on the nature and tempo of China's modernization.

The Bolshevik seizure of power in October 1917 was a political act and part of the history of events. Can one contend that this event had no effect on the history of the Soviet Union during the last fifty years? One need, of course, assume that the intentions of the original actors have been realized. Political intentions and political acts like ideas may have unintended consequences. Yet even the unintended consequences are inconceivable without the original action. At this point in time, it seems to me entirely reasonable to say that the political act of 1917 was one factor of enormous importance in shaping the history of the Soviet Union. Whether it will have any significance whatsoever a thousand years from now is a moot point. It is just as unclear, however, whether our present constellations of demographic, economic, and sociological trends will have any significance a thousand years from now. In the time scale of millennial history, single political acts and policies may shrink in significance, but this leads us to the question of whether the type of history which deals in millennia is necessarily more profound than the type of history which deals with the time scale of a generation or two. In the latter scale, political history retains its perennial significance. To men who happen to live in the time scale of one generation, politics are always with us.

There is in fact one way of regarding political history (and other forms of history as well) which runs quite counter to nineteenth- and twentieth-century historicism and reflects certain older ahistorical ways of looking at history. Political history is here regarded not as a single irreversible process but as a reservoir of instances of political experience. It provides the possibility for a kind of diachronic metahistorical and transcultural comparative politics in which it no longer is heretical to compare something in ancient Roman history to something in modern Chinese history provided that this is done with due deference to the insights which arise out of the "modern sense of history." Thus political actions and political events are significant not only for their place in some single world historic drama but also as comparative material for the study of man in politics in various times and places. This is not to deny the emergence of genuine novelty or the possibility of progress. It is simply to insist that together with novelty one also has the constant recurrence and recombination of problems and motifs of perennial politics.

Turning from political to intellectual history, as already stated, a common element linking the two interests seems to me to be the concern with the realm of man's conscious life. The English term "intellectual history" is most unfortunate since it seems to imply an exclusive concern with the intellect in the narrow sense of the term and hence also seems to imply an exclusive concern with the history of those called intellectuals. Intellectual history, as we conceive of it, involves the totality of man's conscious life—the life of the intellect, the emotions, the imagination, and every variety of sensibility—and not simply the realm of conceptualization. Furthermore, we are by no means exclusively concerned with the intellectual life of man as a self-subsistent realm—as the so-called "history of ideas"—but with human consciousness as related to the historic situations in which men find themselves. To use Merleau-Ponty's trenchant phrase, "To be conscious is, among other things, to be elsewhere."[5] Ideas themselves may be concerned with matters which are entirely material. This view of intellectual history by no means precludes the history of ideas. It cannot be denied that the intellectually articulate in relating to their life situations tend to relate not only to life in its unreflective immediacy but also to the ideas of others about life. One must always understand their thought in relation to the thought of both their predecessors and contemporaries.

Like political history, intellectual history has been subject to the charge of elitism, although in my own view with even less justification. While political action may be confined to small groups, even though the actions themselves affect the society as a whole, the conscious life of man is omnipresent wherever men are to be found. I am, of course, entirely aware of the academic conventions which assign the study of collective mentalities of the masses to sociology or cultural anthropology or social history. It is indeed possible to subsume even the intellectual history of intellectuals under these categories. Thus Lévi-Strauss is quite prepared to treat some of the ideas of his great contemporary Sartre under the category of anthropology.[6] Yet even those who concede a certain autonomy of intellectual history as the history of the ideas of reflective intellectuals, insist on appropriating the mentalities of the masses for the social sciences. Presumably one basis for this assignation is that any phenomenon which is collective must seek its aetiology in sociology or some social science, although Norman Cohn and other psychohistorians have felt it quite possible to explain collective mentalities in Freudian psychological terms. More important, however, is the assumption that, whatever may be the case for intellectuals, the minds of the broad masses may be thought of as passive receptacles which are only able to reflect the mentalities produced in them by vast impersonal societal and cultural forces. Lévi-Strauss assigns a considerable causal weight to collective mental structures but the point is again that these structures, like language, are objective autonomous realities which manifest themselves through the essentially passive receptacle of the individual mind. To be sure, in the case of Lévi-Strauss, it is by no means easy to pigeonhole his thought. In his recoil from Sartre's contrast between the modern dialectical thinker (like Sartre) who is actually able to think and the primitive man whose conscious life is wholly controlled by preestablished structures, he tends to deny the distinction on both sides and points to the broad anthropological evidence concerning "primitive philosophers" who are quite capable of thinking through and justifying in their own terms the traditions of their tribe on a highly conscious level. If this is true of primitive men, it need not be less true of the mentalities of the masses of men in the so-called higher civilizations. The notion that the mentalities of the masses as opposed to the reflections of intellectuals are wholly passive and nonreflective and easily explained in terms of the social models which we impose upon them is not based on any genuine evidence. Whatever the claims of sociology, anthropology, or economic history, there is no reason whatever why the study of the conscious life of the masses should not also be subsumed under the category of intellectual history. It is quite true that intellectual historians of China have so far devoted far too little attention to movements of popular religion, to the "ideologies of rebellion," to the interweavings of mythology and cosmological thinking on the popular level, and a host of other subjects, but they should certainly consider research in these areas as part of their task.

Indeed, one of the barriers to a broadly conceived intellectual history of this type both in China and elsewhere has been the facile acceptance of the distinction between "folk culture" or "little culture" and "high culture." The distinction no doubt has validity as a heuristic device, but the notion that there has anywhere been an iron wall dividing the two has been most misleading, particularly in the case of China where, ever since the eighteenth century, there has been a tendency in the West to contrast the cool rationalistic Confucianism of the literati to the irrational superstitions and primitive folk religion of the masses. In fact, a closer look reveals that the literati most often shared in the superstitions and magical beliefs of the masses and were indeed able to provide a kind of rational basis for these beliefs in their highly developed cosmological theories (as in the case of geomancy). To a greater or lesser degree, they also shared in and were able to provide rationales for their participation in various aspects of so-called popular religion. On the other hand, popular literature, proverbs, and other more immediate sources of evidence would indicate that the ideas of the so-called high culture circulated widely among the masses. The ideologies of rebellion are by no means simple products of the folk mind. They were most often fashioned by literati or semiliterati but were, of course, quite accessible to the masses. As in the case of the rise of Christianity or the Reformation, there have been vast movements of the spirit which have cut across the whole society. To be sure, the modalities of acceptance of these movements by various strata and groups within the society could differ most markedly. The same religious and ethical concepts could be part of Establishment culture and also figure in the ideology of rebellions. To be sure, Buddhist philosophic scholasticism and Neo-Confucian scholasticism, like all scholastic refinements of doctrine everywhere, remained the preserve of the monk and literatus, but this does not mean a priori that there was nothing in common between the religion of the monk, the literatus, and the peasant.

One reason for assigning the collective mentality of the peasant village to the anthropologist is the assumption that peasant villages like primitive tribes have at some point in time reached a stasis of cultural forms which makes both political and intellectual history largely irrelevant. This, again, is an unproved assumption. There is thus considerable evidence that during the T'ang dynasty, when Buddhism was a vital encompassing force in Chinese life, the life of a large part of village China was dominated in all its aspects by Buddhist beliefs, festivals, and the institutions of Monastic Buddhism, while in later centuries, when Buddhism had retreated as a vital force, although one still finds definite Buddhist elements in the diversified folk culture of China, the spirit of popular culture had changed.

However, while intellectual history as here conceived in principle lays as much claim to the mentalities of nonintellectuals as to the ideas of intellectuals, the fact remains that we have most easy access to the ideas of the literate and the articulate. Nor can there be a denial of the fact that for the greater part of human history (including the present) the literate and intellectually articulate

BENJAMIN I. SCHWARTZ

have belonged to the relatively more privileged sectors of society. One may say that they have more or less belonged to the Establishment (particularly in the case of China's gentry—scholar-officials) or at least been appended to it, as in the case of modern academic intellectuals. Hence, it can always be alleged in a quasi-Marxist spirit that their ideas either consciously or unconsciously reflect the interests of the ruling class. It is also frequently alleged that the intellectuals tend to concern themselves with matters which are of exclusive concern to themselves and not to the bulk of mankind. But intellectuals, unless they are blatant propagandists, have always regarded themselves as being engaged in a truth-seeking or truth-proclaiming enterprise designed to cope with the mysteries of man and the universe. They have thus always implicitly attributed to their own conscious efforts a certain degree of transcendence over the various class interests, psychological motives, and other factors which can be viewed as the hidden springs of their behavior. Indeed, most of them have tended to assume that their ideas could even have effects on the world surrounding them.

This, of course, is no place to attempt to confront the enormous philosophic problems involved in giving an account of man which tries to pay due deference to objective forces, to interest motives, and to psychological motives while taking seriously his claims as a truth-seeking animal. All I would suggest is that we ourselves are as deeply involved in these dilemmas as any of our predecessors and that the devices used to separate our own intellectual enterprises from theirs will simply not bear scrutiny. One such device is to assume that at a given point in the historic process, it suddenly becomes possible for certain types of men to free themselves from the trammels of genetic conditioning and to confront the truth in all its fullness. To Hegel, the self-realization of the World Spirit coincides with his own lifetime. To Marx, the rise of the proletariat as a class which will finally overcome all the false consciousness of the past confirms the truth of his doctrine, while to Karl Mannheim his own life witnesses the final emergence of a free-floating intelligentsia whose views are no longer distorted by partial interests. Many American social scientists are convinced that they achieved the happy state of scientific objectivity in the affluent fifties. The procedures here are almost too transparent to require comment.

Another way to achieve this appearance of transcendence is to lay claim to the precious mantle of science. Lévi-Strauss would have us believe that the purity and rigor of his science somehow lifts him above the cultural structure in which he is involved. What is claimed now is that certain theories, ideas, and hypotheses have finally been, or are about to be, verified by the facts, thus placing these theories and hypotheses in an entirely different category from all the ideologies and theories of the past. A historian must, of course, be committed to the supreme value of concrete empirical data. He must insist that all models and theories be constantly confronted with the richness of concrete experience. He must be committed to the view that concrete facts may kill a given generalization or challenge the universal claims of a given model. He is convinced that only a confrontation with concrete experience can deepen and broaden our ideas. One might say that one of the main tasks of history is not so much to confirm given theories and models as to see whether they are falsifiable. It is, however, infinitely easier to falsify than to verify. The notion that certain sweeping hypotheses have been "scientifically" verified by certain types and quanta of facts will be infinitely more convincing to those who accept the models to begin with than those who do not. The fact that one can find a high correlation between two series of statistics may represent a very local relationship and not a law of history. There still remains no royal road to verification in all the larger matters of human history and we have not lifted ourselves out of the dilemmas which confronted our intellectual ancestors. If their intellectual gropings and fumblings inevitably and exclusively reflected the interests of the ruling class, the structures of their culture, or their childhood traumas, then so do ours (as many of the young so vehemently insist).

The notion that the ideas and preoccupations of those who write and leave records are most often of concern only to priests, monks, religious visionaries, scholars, intellectuals, or effete ruling classes is based on what might be called a patronizing humanitarianism. In this view, masses who live in poverty should be properly concerned only with their poverty. Yet as Lévi-Strauss and others have pointed out, the Australian primitives who subsisted on berries and grubs developed vast mythologies, theologies, and cosmologies. There may be certain kinds of scholastic developments and certain kinds of learned jargon which are truly the preserve of the learned and inaccessible to the masses. This is by no means peculiar to traditional society. Both Marxist social science and American varieties of social science have developed precisely this type of scholasticism and learned jargon to an exaggerated degree, yet the practitioners of these scholasticisms remain firmly convinced that they are dealing with matters which are of universal concern. In short, the ideas of thinkers and intellectuals in the past must be taken seriously because they represent efforts quite as serious as our own to cope with the human condition in various times and places. Without assuming that these ideas are the embodiment of a *Weltgeist*, they nevertheless represent preoccupations which may reflect matters of concern even to the illiterate masses.

I have not, however, provided a justification for the particular concern with political and intellectual history in dealing with a non-Western culture in the face of the strong current within the profession to stress "objective" "social scientific" history. In his *Pensée sauvage* Lévi-Strauss states that the ultimate goal of the human sciences is "not to constitute but to dissolve man,"[7] that is, to dissolve him into the various impersonal structures, biological, societal, anthropological, and so forth, which make up his being. Within the French context this undoubtedly represents a reaction against certain forms of existential humanism with their strong stress on subjectivity and a strong reassertion of the pathos of objective scientism. However, in attempting this undertaking in the West, one does so in the face of a vast and profound literature concerned with "constituting man." Any effort to force Rousseau into someone's behaviorial scientific scheme must face a vast battery of Rousseau experts who know their Rousseau much better than the schematizer, while Jean-Paul Sartre is quite capable of defending himself against efforts to fit him into someone's anthropological scheme.

In the case of China, however, the effort to establish the human reality of China across the centuries, of seeing Chinese responding consciously to the political and human situations which confront them, is a task which has still not advanced very far, at least in the West. This makes it far easier to impose our models and pre-established structures onto China. The Chinese will not contradict us because we know so little of what they have said. As John Habakkuk states in a paper submitted to the conference for which this essay was written, "Where the data are sparsest, one has to rely most heavily on reasoning based on a model." He might have added that where the data are sparsest, it becomes easiest to impose the model. China has already suffered far too much from premature structuralism. It is to the credit of Lévi-Strauss that he has on the whole refrained from attempting to impose totalizing structures on the so-called higher civilizations, perhaps because of his suspicion that cultures which occupy such vast areas of time and space do not in fact possess one all-embracing structure.

It may, of course, be urged that a good deal of Western sinology has concerned itself with Chinese thought, hence with the conscious life of the Chinese. In his *Pensée chinoise* Marcel Granet has in fact provided us with a kind of image of the timeless essence of Chinese thought. Written under the influence of Emile Durkheim's conception of "collective representations," it attempts to provide us with the "deep structures" of Chinese thought in Lévi-Strauss's sense. The latter has, in fact, acknowledged his debt to Granet. If there have been synchronic and diachronic tensions and conflicts within Chinese thought, Granet dismisses these as "secondary manifestations."

Now what Granet does—and he does it with consummate skill— is provide us with an account of a certain kind of Chinese cosmology which has indeed been a dominant and persistent strand of Chinese thought. It was, moreover, a brand of cosmology which was not displaced by any rival type of cosmology until modern times. Yet the fact remains that although this cosmology held the center of the stage in the former Han dynasty, in the latter Han dynasty there was a distinct reaction against it. There is the fact that the Confucius of the Analects, while seemingly accepting elements of this cosmology,[8] refuses to place it at the center of his concerns. In the thought of many of the so-called Neo-Taoists of the Wei-chin period it was quite marginal, while there are many aspects of the history of popular religion which bear no particular relationship to the cosmological scheme although efforts were made to fit them into the Procrustean bed. To Granet the range of possibilities covered by Chinese thought may seem to be "secondary manifestations." To the participants, the conflicts and issues may have been quite as fundamental as the issues dividing Lévi-Strauss from Sartre or French Marxists from American liberals even though it can be maintained that the latter both share important general notions in common. An intellectual history of China, as here conceived, would be concerned not simply with "Chinese thought" but with Chinese thinking and thinking within the framework of their historical situations. Similarly, a political history of China would involve not simply a reconstruction of the timeless institutional structures of the Chinese state (crucial as this undertaking may be) but a history of the living politics of the men involved in these structures. In-

BENJAMIN I. SCHWARTZ

deed, the evolution of the structure itself can hardly be understood apart from the context of concrete political situations.

It is, of course, not my intention to anathemize any method of historic investigation. Any kind of research procedure which porvides us with new significant data is relevant to any interpretation of history. It is rather my intention to defend against prevailing fashion an interpretation of history which is still concerned with "constituting man" rather than "dissolving him."

To some this concern with man's conscious life may seem to be a manifestation of a peculiarly tender-minded view of the human situation. While not particularly concerned to establish credentials for tough-mindedness, it seems to me that a concern with conscious attitudes and activities has no necessary connection with any facilely optimistic view of man's destiny. One may indeed contend that conscious attitudes, orientations, and visions of reality have more often than not played a devastatingly tragic role in human affairs.

REFERENCES

1. Claude Lévi-Strauss, "Overture to le Cru et le Cuit," cited in "Structuralism," *Yale French Studies* (October 1966).

2. See M. Freedman, *Lineage Organization in Southeastern China* (London: Athlone Press, 1958).

3. In actuality the theories of history that stress vast impersonal forces do not really ascribe any truly creative role to the masses of mankind. The masses are simply the units of psychological energy through which the large structures and processes manifest themselves.

4. Frederic Wakeman, *Strangers at the Gate: Social Disorder in South China, 1839-1861* (Berkeley: University of California Press, 1966).

5. Maurice Merleau-Ponty, *Eloge de la philosophie et autres essais* (Paris: Gallimard, 1965), p. 325.

6. See chap. 9, "History and Dialectic," in C. Lévi-Strauss, *The Savage Mind* (Chicago: University of Chicago Press, 1966).

7. *Ibid.*, p. 247.

8. The question of how developed this cosmology had become in Confucius' time remains a matter of dispute but there is a tendency to interpret the statement in the Analects that T'ien tao (the way of heaven) was one of the matters which the master seldom discussed as a reference to this type of cosmology.

Notes on Contributors

GORDON A. CRAIG, born in 1913, is J. E. Wallace Sterling Professor of Humanities, Stanford University. Mr. Craig is the author of *The Politics of the Prussian Army, 1640-1945* (Oxford, 1955), *From Bismarck to Adenauer: Aspects of German Statecraft* (Baltimore, 1958), *The Battle of Königgrätz* (Philadephia, 1964), *Europe since 1815* (New York, 1961, 1966; 3d ed., 1971), and *War, Politics and Diplomacy: Selected Essays* (New York, 1967). He edited, with E. M. Earle and Felix Gilbert, *Makers of Modern Strategy: Military Thought from Machiavelli to Hitler* (Princeton, 1943) and, with Felix Gilbert, *The Diplomats, 1919-1939* (Princeton, 1953).

ROBERT DARNTON, born in 1939, is assistant professor of history at Princeton University. He is the author of *Mesmerism and the End of the Enlightenment in France* (Cambridge, Mass., 1968).

PAUL DUMONT, born in 1945, is a research assistant at the Ecole Pratique des Hautes Etudes, Section VI.

M. I. FINLEY, born in 1912, is professor of ancient history and Fellow of Jesus College, University of Cambridge. Mr. Finley is the author of *Land and Credit in Ancient Athens* (New Brunswick, 1952), *The World of Odysseus* (New York, 1954), *The Ancient Greeks* (New York, 1963), *Aspects of Antiquity* (New York, 1968), *Ancient Sicily to the Arab Conquest* (New York, 1968), vol. I of a three-volume history of Sicily with Denis Mack Smith, and *Early Greece: The Bronze and Archaic Ages* (New York, 1970). He is the editor of *Slavery in Classical Antiquity* (Cambridge, Eng., 1960), *The Greek Historians* (New York, 1958), and *Josephus* (New York, 1965).

FRANÇOIS FURET, born in 1927, is director of the Centre de Recherches of the Ecole Pratique des Hautes Etudes, Section VI. He is the co-author of *Structures et relations sociales à Paris au milieu du XVIIIe siècle* (Paris, 1961), *La Révolution française,* 2 vols. (Paris, 1964-1965), and *Livre et société dans la France du XVIIIe siècle,* 2 vols. (The Hague, 1965-1970).

FELIX GILBERT, born in 1905, is professor in the School of Historical Studies at the Institute for Advanced Study, Princeton. Mr. Gilbert is coauthor of *History* (Princeton, 1953) and author of *To the Farewell Address* (Princeton, 1961), *Machiavelli and Guicciardini* (Princeton, 1965), and *The End of the European Era, 1890 to the Present* (New York, 1970).

PIERRE GOUBERT, born in 1915, is professor of early modern history at the University of Paris (Sorbonne) and at the Ecole Pratique des Hautes Etudes, Section VI. He is the author of *Beauvais et le Beauvaisis de 1600 à 1730* (Paris, 1960), *Louis XIV et 20 millions de français* (Paris, 1966; New York, 1970), and *L'Ancien Régime* (Paris, 1969).

JOHN HABAKKUK, born in 1915, is principal, Jesus College, Oxford. He is the author of *British and American Technology in the Nineteenth Century* (Cambridge, Eng., 1962). He was editor of *Economic History Review*, 1950-1960, and of *Cambridge Economic History*.

E. J. HOBSBAWM, born in 1917, is professor of economic and social history at Birkbeck College, the University of London. He is the author of *Primitive Rebels* (Manchester, 1959), *Age of Revolution* (London, 1962), *Labouring Men* (London, 1964), *Industry and Empire* (London, 1968), *Bandits* (London, 1969), and, with G. Rudé, *Captain Swing* (London, 1969).

THOMAS S. KUHN, born in 1922, is M. Taylor Pyne Professor of the History of Science at Princeton University. He is the author of *The Copernican Revolution* (Cambridge, Mass., 1957), *The Structure of Scientific Revolutions* (Chicago, 1962; rev. ed., 1969), and *Sources for History of Quantum Physics* (Philadelphia, 1967), with J. Heilbron, P. Forman, and L. Allen.

JACQUES LE GOFF, born in 1924, is director of studies at the Ecole Pratique des Hautes Etudes, Section VI. He is the author of *Marchands et banquiers du Moyen Age* (Paris, 1956), *Les intellectuels au Moyen Age* (Paris, 1957), *La civilisation de l'Occident Médiéval* (Paris, 1964), and *Das Hochmittelalter* (Frankfurt am Main, 1965).

EMMANUEL LE ROY LADURIE, born in 1929, is professor of history at the University of Paris. He is author of *Les paysans de Languedoc* (Paris, 1966) and *Historie du climat depuis l'an mil* (Paris, 1967).

FRANK E. MANUEL, born in 1910, is Kenan Professor of History at New York University. He is the author of *The New World of Henri Saint-Simon* (Cambridge, Mass., 1956), *The Eighteenth Century Confronts the Gods* (Cambridge, Mass., 1959), *The Prophets of Paris* (Cambridge, Mass., 1962), *Isaac Newton, Historian* (Cambridge, Mass., 1963), *Shapes of Philosophical History* (Stanford, 1965), and *A Portrait of Isaac Newton* (Cambridge, Mass., 1968). Mr. Manuel is editor of the *Dædalus* Library volume on *Utopias and Utopian Thought* (Boston, 1966).

PETER PARET, born in 1924, is professor of modern European history at Stanford University. Mr. Paret is the author of *Guerrillas in the 1960's* (New York, 1962), with John Shy; *French Revolutionary Warfare* (New York, 1964); and *Yorck and the Era of Prussian Reform* (Princeton, 1966). He is editor and translator of Gerhard Ritter, *Frederick the Great* (Berkeley, 1968).

ARTHUR SCHLESINGER, JR., born in 1917, is Albert Schweitzer Professor of the Humanities, The City University of New York. His publications include *Orestes A. Brownson: A Pilgrim's Progress* (Boston, 1939), *The Age of Jackson* (Boston, 1946), *The Age of Roosevelt* (Boston, 1957——), *A Thousand Days: John F. Kennedy in the White House* (Boston, 1965), *The Bitter Heritage: Vietnam and American Democracy, 1941-1966* (Boston, 1967), *Violence: America in the Sixties* (New York, 1968), and *The Crisis of Confidence: Ideas, Power and Violence in America* (Boston, 1969).

BENJAMIN I. SCHWARTZ, born in 1916, is professor of history and government at Harvard University. His publications include *Chinese Communism and the Rise of Mao* (Cambridge, Mass., 1951), *In Search of Wealth and Power: Yen Fu and the West* (Cambridge, Mass., 1964), and *Communism and China: Ideology in Flux* (Cambridge, Mass., 1968).

LAWRENCE STONE, born in 1919, is Dodge Professor of History and director of the Shelby Cullom Davis Center for Historical Studies at Princeton University. He is the author of *Sculpture in Britain: The Middle Ages* (London, 1955), *An Elizabethan: Sir Horatio Palavicino* (Oxford, 1956), and *The Crisis of the Aristocracy, 1558-1641* (Oxford, 1965).

JOHN E. TALBOTT, born in 1940, is assistant professor of history at Princeton University. He is the author of *The Politics of Educational Reform in France, 1918-1940* (Princeton, 1969).

STEPHAN THERNSTROM, born in 1934, is professor of history at the University of California, Los Angeles. He is the author of *Poverty and Progress: Social Mobility in a Nineteenth-Century City* (Cambridge, Mass., 1964) and *Poverty, Planning and Politics in the New Boston* (New York, 1969), coeditor with Richard Sennett of *Nineteenth-Century Cities: Essays in the New Urban History* (New Haven, 1969), and coeditor with Charles Tilly of the Harvard Studies in Urban History.

JAN VANSINA, born in 1929, is African Studies Research Professor at the University of Wisconsin. His publications include *De la tradition orale* (Tervuren, 1961), *Le royaume kuba* (Tervuren, 1964), *L'évolution du royaume rwanda des origines à 1900* (Brussels, 1962), *Kingdoms of the Savanna* (Madison, 1966), *Introduction à l'ethnographie du Congo* (Kinshasa, 1967), and *Geschiedenis van de Kuba* (Tervuren, 1963). Mr. Vansina has done field work in history and anthropology among the Kuba of Kasai Congo Kinshasa, 1953-1956; Rwanda and Burundi, 1957-1960; and the Tio (Bateke) of Brazzaville, 1963-1964.

Acton, Lord, 396
Adams, Charles Francis, 402
Adams, Henry, 396, 397
Administrative history, 358
Age of Roosevelt, The, 410n
Agrarian History of England, 317
Alagoa, E. J., 421, 423
A la recherche du temps perdu, 118
Allardt, Eric, 22
Allison, Graham T., 367
Amours de Charlot et Toinette, Les, 260, 263, 268
Analytical Archaeology, 285
Angeville, A. D. d', 62, 80
Annales/Annales school, viii, 3, 215, 220, 230, 309, 337, 340
Anthropology, 4, 15, 17, 19, 20, 285, 340, 343, 344, 345, 347, 353n, 447, 448; *see also* Social sciences
Aquinas, Thomas, 339
Arbeitskreis für mittelalterliche Geschichte, 343
Archaeology, 430–31, 438n; *see also* Social sciences
Archaeology, history and: classical historian, archaeological evidence and, 287–96; general discussion, 281–82; observational data, interpretation and quantification of, 282–87
Ariès, Philippe, 227
Aristotelianism, 339
Armée et ses problèmes au xviii siècle, L', 375
Aron, Raymond, 220, 340–41
Ashton, T. S., 190n
Assayer, 163
Aston, T. H., 205
Aymard, Maurice, 308

Bacon, Sir Francis, 146–47, 163, 167–68, 171, 172, 175, 176, 179, 189, 190
Baconian movement, *see* Bacon, Sir Francis

Badian, E., 117
Baehrel, René, 58, 307
Bagehot, Walter, 402
Bailyn, Bernard, 152, 193, 318, 406, 407n
Bancroft, George, 396
Banks, J. A., 324
Baran, Paul, 9
Barry, Brian, 37
Bath, B. Slicher van, 306
Baumann, H., 425
Beard, Charles, 110–11, 112, 113, 115–16, 366
Beauvaisis, 318
Béguillet, Edmé, 312n
Beidelman, T. O., 426
Benson, Lee, 406
Beresford, M., 317
Berlin, Isaiah, 409
Bernheim, Ernst, 414
Berr, Henri, 157n, 340
Bertin, M., 67
Bertolet, C. L., 174
Biddle, M., 317
Bien, David, 383–84
Binford, L. R., 284
Blache, Vidal de la, 340
Black, John B., 144
Bloch, Marc, viii, 3, 5, 12, 23, 238, 337, 341, 344
Bluche, François, 243, 246–47, 249
Bodin, Jean, 219
Böhme, Helmut, 364–65
Bohr, Niels, 165
Boltzmann, Ludwig, 165
Bonaparte, Marie, 222
Bonlard, Canon, 67
Bonnin, B., 314n
Bornand, J. F., 251–52, 257–58
Boston, J. S., 425
Boutruche, R., 305
Boyd, Julian, xii
Boyen, Hermann von, 358, 374
Boyle, Robert, 190n

Brahe, Tycho, 169
Braudel, Fernand, 5, 10, 306, 340, 347
Braun, Rudolf, 21
Braunfels, W., 347
Bray, Barbara, 60, 349
Bresciani-Turroni, Constantino, 29
Bretonne, Restif de la, 242
Brodie, Bernard, 383
Brown, Norman, 227
Brown, T. M., 188
Brown, William A., 430
Bullitt, William, 223
Bullock, Allan, 205
Burckhardt, Jakob, xvi, 148, 152
Burtt, E. A., 164
Büsch, Otto, 375
Business Cycles, 29
Butler, David, 404
Butterfield, Sir Herbert, 124–26, 163, 179, 189, 399, 400, 403, 404, 406, 407

Cabanès, Augustin, 223
Cabourdin, G., 314n
Caesar, Julius, 394
Cambridge Modern History, 233
Canning, 364
Carnot, Sadi, 173, 190
Carr, E. H., 404
Cartography, *see* Military archives, French
Cassirer, Ernst, 178
Centre de Recherches sur les Civilisations de L'Europe Moderne de Paris, 311
Chabod, Federico, 145, 359, 365–66
Chambers, J. D., 316
Chambers, Robert, 169
Chamla, M. C., 75
Charles V of France, 339
Charles XII (Voltaire), 372
Chateaubriand, François René, vicomte de, 339
Chaunu, Pierre, 47, 307, 311
Childe, V. Gordon, 23
Church, Robert, 207n
Churchill, Winston, 399
Civilization of the Renaissance in Italy, 148
Clapham, J. H., 3, 29
Clarendon, Earl of, 146, 395, 410
Clark, Sir George, 385
Clarke, D. L., 283, 285–87, 291, 292
Classes and social groups, history of, 16–18

Clausewitz, Carl von, 373
Cobban, Alfred, 269n
Cohn, Norman, 447
Colin, Jean, 375
Comparative history, x, 10, 343
Comparative Studies in Society and History, 3
Comte, Auguste, 147, 177
Condorcet, Marie Jean, marquis de, 147
Conjectural history, 10
Conrad, Alfred, 36, 407n
Constitutional history, 440
Contemporary history, *see* Eyewitness history
Contrat social, 239, 269n
Contribution to a Critique of Political Economy, 337–38
Cook, R. M., 296
Copernican Revolution, The, 185
Coquille, Guy, 312n
Corona Regni: Studien über die Krone als Symbol des Staates in spaten Mittelalter, 342
Cosmopolitanism and the National State, 143, 145
Coulanges, Fustel de, 5
Coupez, A., 423
Courtépée, Claude, 312n
Couturier, Marcel, 49
Craig, Gordon A., 356–71, 455
Craven, Frank, 390n
Critique de la raison dialectique, 221, 227
Croce, Benedetto, 405
Cultural history, 134, 345
Curti, Merle, 322, 334n

Dædalus, 194
Dahl, Robert, 116
Dance to the Music of Time, A, 118
Darnton, Robert, 238–80, 455
Darwin, Charles, 169–71, 189–90n
Darwinism, Social, 114
Daumard, Adeline, 16
Da Vinci, Leonardo, 222
Delbrück, Hans, 378
Demography, 12, 14–15, 46, 56, 230, 240, 308–9, 321–22
Demos, John, 230, 318
Descartes, René, 163, 189, 222, 224, 229
Description générale et particuliere du duché de Bourgogne, 312n
Desmoulins, Camille, 267

Determinism, historical, 407
Devon, Pierre, 307
Dewey, John, 405
Dickens, A. G., 128
Dictionary of National Biography, 110, 111
Diderot, Denis, 255, 274–75n
Dijksterhuis, E. J., 164
"Dilemma of Determinism, The," 409
Dilthey, Wilhelm, 144, 151, 215, 220, 233
Dionysius of Halicarnassus, 289
Diplomatic history, 39; *see also* Political and diplomatic history
Discourse on Method, 163
Doherty, Robert, 335n
Dostoevsky, Fyodor, 222
Dore, Ronald, 201
Duby, Georges, 342
Dumézil, G., 346
Dumont, Paul, 62–106, 455
Dupront, Alphonse, 19
Durkheim, Émile, 63, 340, 453

Ecole Pratique des Hautes Etudes, 132, 311
Econometrics, 37–38, 46
Economic Growth in France and Britain, 1851–1950, 41
Economic history, 2–3, 4–5, 9, 21, 46, 58–59, 234, 323, 338, 347, 350n, 357
Economic history, economic theory and: 27–44; assumptions, quantification of variables and empirical validity of, 33–35, 36; deducing information, 31–33; development in use of theoretical models, 27–30; equilibrium theory, 34–36, 39, 44n, 46, 56–57; five stages of theoretical application, 30–31; fortuitous and systematic elements, 38–39; growth theory, 37; quantification, intuition, and, 40–41; theory, less rigorous use of, 42–43; variables, identification of and relationship between, 35–41
Economic History of Modern Britain, 29
Economics, 3, 4–5, 9–10, 24n, 26n, 200–201; *see also* Economic history; Social sciences
Education, history of: 156n; economy, the, education's relationship to, 200–201; family, role of in educa-
tion, 202, 209–10n; general discussion, 193–95, 206–7; historical process, education's role in, 202–3; institutional history, 203–6, 210n; literacy, problem of, 200–201, 209n; popular education, political implications of, 198–200; society/ social structure, education's relationship to, 195–206
Ehrard, Jean, 243, 245–46, 247
Einstein, Albert, 165
Elton, G. R., 358
Emergence of the American University, The, 204
Emerson, Ralph Waldo, 403, 409
Emile, 239
Eminent Victorians, 115
Encyclopédie, 267
English Social History, 2
Erasmus, 169
Erikson, Erik, 114–15, 217–18, 220, 221, 223–26
Erotika Biblion, 267
Essais historiques sur la vie de Marie-Antoinette, 260
Escarpit, Robert, 239–42, 269n
Espion dévalisé, L', 267
Essai sur les Moeurs et l' esprit des nations, 337
Estivals, Robert, 259
Ethics, 339
Etruscans, The, 288
Etudes galiléenes, 163–64
Euler, Leonhard, 165
Everitt, Alan, 316
Eyewitness history: background and definition of, 393–95; collection and judgment of facts, 400–403; drawing general concepts through, 407–10; historical objectivity, question of, 395–96, 399–400; interpretation of facts, passage of time and, 403–7; revival of, factors affecting, 397–99; truth and contemporary history, 405–7

Family, history of, 227
Febvre, Lucien, 3, 215, 217–19, 220, 223, 232, 304, 337, 340, 348, 349
Feillet, Alphonse, 303
Féral, Pierre, 72
Feudal Society, 12
Federalist, 404
Finberg, H. P. R., 316–17
Finley, M. I., 191n, 281–99, 455

Flandrin, Jean-Louis, 246, 270n
Flandrin, Maria, 246, 270n
Flaubert, Gustave, 226
Fogel, Robert, 31, 32, 36, 42
Folz, Robert, 342
Foster, John, 21
Foucault, Michel, 220
Francastel, Pierre, 346–47
Frazer, James George, 344
Freche, G., 314n
*French Book Trade in the Ancien Ré-
gime,* 241–42
French History, xv
Freud, Sigmund, 114, 215, 217, 218,
220–23, 225, 227, 228, 229, 232,
233, 388
*From the Closed World to the Infinite
Universe,* 163
Furet, François, viii, ix, 45–61, 243–
45, 246, 247, 249, 259, 261, 455

Gandhi, Mohandas, 224, 225
Galileo, 163
Gall, Lothar, 364–65
Gardiner, S. R., 113
*Gazetteer of Early Anglo-Saxon Burial
Sites,* 294
Gelzer, M., 112
General Psychopathology, 233
Genetic method, 151, 152
Geo-politics, 348
George, Alexander, 223, 383
George, Juliette, 223
*Geschichte der Kriegskunst im Rahmen
der politischen Geschichte,* 378
*Geschichte der Lage der Arbeiter
unter dem Kapitalismus,* 17
Gibbon, Edward, 395
"Giddy Minds and Foreign Quarrels,"
366
Gilbert, Felix, 141–58, 389, 395, 455
Girard, L., 17
Girardet, Raoul, 375, 376
Glasco, Laurence, 335n
Goclenius, Rudolf, 214–15
Goethe, Johann Wolfgang von, 214
Goody, J., 428
Gossman, Lionel, 144–45
Goubert, Pierre, 58, 300–314, 315,
318, 456
Graffigny, Mme. de, 239
Grande Peur, 19
*Grands névropathes, malades immor-
tels,* 223
Granet, Marcel, 453

Greer, D., 122
Gresle, Annie, 311
Greven, Philip, 318, 319
Guerry, A., 62
Guicciardini, Francesco, xi, 146, 495,
400
Guizot, François, 339
Gutman, Herbert, 335n, 336n
Gutridge, George, 182

Habakkuk, John, 27–44, 452, 457
Hagen, Everett, 7
Hahn, Roger, 188
Hamilton, Alexander, 404
Hamilton, E. J., 307
Handlin, Oscar, vii, 321
Hanson, Michael, 335n
Hawkes, Jacquetta, 283, 296n
Hébert, Jacques René, 266
Hegel, Georg, 147, 214, 215, 234, 356,
450
Heidegger, Martin, 215
Heilbron, J. L., 188
Henige, David, 434
Henretta, James, 319
Henry, Louis, 309
Herder, Johann Gottfried von, 214
Hermeticism, 186–87
Herrschaftzeichen und Staatssymbolik,
341
Hershberg, Theodore, 335n
Hicks, Sir John, 7, 37
Higonnet, Patrice, 443
Hill, J. E. C., 129
Hillgruber, Andreas, 375
Hintze, Otto, 374, 384
*Histoire du Berry et du diocèse de
Bourges,* 312n
*Histoire du pays et duché de Niver-
nais,* 312n
"Histoire et Longue Durée," 10
*Histoire philosophique et politique des
établissements et du commerce
des Européens dans les deux Indes,*
339
Historia artium et literarum, 146–47
Historia ecclesiastica, 146, 147
Historia ethnica, 146
Historia scholastica, 146, 147, 157n
Historian and History, The, 403
Historian as participant, *see* Eye-
witness history
History as Art and as Science, 229–30
*History of English Thought in the
Eighteenth Century,* 142

History of France, 337
History of the American Revolution, 406
History of the American Tariff, 29
History of the Reformation, xv
History of Technology, A, 291
Hitlers Strategie, 375
Hobsbawm, Eric, viii, 1–26, 456
Hoffman, Stanley, 8
Hölderlin, Johann, 216, 217
Hoover, Herbert, 398
Hoskins, W. G., 306, 316
Housman, A. E., 40
Howard, Michael, 376
Hudson, Liam, 191*n*
Hughes, Stuart, 229–30
Huizinga, Johan, 219, 338, 350*n*
Hüsserl, Edmund, 217

Ibn Khaldun, 23
Ideas, history of, 447; *see also* Intellectual history
Idee der Staatsräson, Die, 358
Industry and Trade, 28
Institut National d'Etudes Demographiques, 311
Intellectual history, 6, 117, 134, 238; biographies of intellectual figures, 151–52, 153; concepts, interconnectedness of, 143; development of through 18th century, 146–48; group intellectual features, analysis of, 152–53; Marx and philosophical idealism, 148–49; methodical procedures, 153–54; political history and, 149–50, 157*n;* politics, influence of ideas on, 145; scholarship, development in branches of, 143–45; science, history of and, 164–71; social history and, 150–51, 154–55; subject matters under sphere of, 142–43; term, origins and acceptance of, 141–42; *see also* Political and intellectual history, defense of
Interest and Prices, 29
Inter-University Consortium for Political Research, 131
Inter-University Seminar on Armed Forces and Society, 383

Jacquart, Jean, 314*n*
Jaeger, Werner W., 193
James, William, 408, 409
Jaspers, Karl, 217, 233

Jeismann, Karl-Ernst, 385
Jevons, William S., 30
Jordan, W. K., 133
Josephson, Matthew, 115
Josephus, Flavius, 394, 399, 401
Journal des savants, 245–46
Journal of African History, 435
Journal of Conflict Resolution, 383
Jugendgeschichte Hegels, 151

Kagan, Richard, 207*n*
Kaldor, N., 34, 37
Kamanzi, T., 423
Kantorowicz, Ernst H., 344
Kapital, Das, 10
Kepler, Johannes, 169, 173
Keynes, John Maynard, 29
Kierkegaard, Sören, 214
Kindleberger, Charles, 42
King's Two Bodies, The, 344
Kinship structure, 14–15
Kirsteller, Paul, 181
Knorr, Klaus, 383
Koran, 417
Koyré, Alexandre, 163–64, 178
Kris, Ernst, 222
Kuczynski, Jürgen, 16–17
Kuhn, Thomas S., 159–92, 456

Lagrange, Joseph-Louis de, 165
Lampard, Eric, 320–21
Landes, David, 201
Langer, William L., 229, 362
Languedoc, 318
La Noue, Mme., 251, 273–74*n*
Lapouge, Vacher de, 63
Laqueur, Tom, 207*n*
Lasswell, Harold, 223
Lattimore, Owen, 23
Lavoisier, Antoine Laurent, 174
Law, history of, 191*n*
Leavis, F. R., 183
Leben Schleiermachers, 151
Lebrun, François, 311, 314*n*
Lefebvre, Georges, 5, 19
Le Goff, Jacques, 337–55, 456
Leicester, University of, 316
Lemarchand, G., 314*n*
Lenoir, J.-C.-P., 264, 267
Léonard, Émile, 375
Le Roy Ladurie, Emmanuel, 16, 18, 56, 62–106, 307, 318, 456
Lettres de cachet, 267
Lettres philosophiques, 246

Lettre sur le commerce de la librairie,
     255, 274–75*n*
Lever, Harold, 41
Lévi-Strauss, Claude, 9, 423, 424, 426,
     441, 442, 447, 448, 450–51, 452–
     53
Liebig, Justus von, 176
Literature, sociology of (reading,
     writing and publishing in 18th-
     century France): authorship,
     quantitative study of, 239–42,
     269*n*, 271–72*n*; general discussion,
     238; publishing: censorship, po-
     litical factors involved, 262–68,
     278–80*n passim*, clandestine, 250–
     52, 254, 256–60, 261–62, 272–74*n*,
     275–77*n*, legal, 252–62, 272–73*n*,
     275–76*n*; reading habits, quantita-
     tive study of, 243–50, 270–71*n*
Livy, 289
Local history: American, 318–19;
     British, 315–18; French, 300–11,
     315, 317, 318; historical demo-
     graphy and, 308–9, 318; Leicester
     school of, 316, 317; social history
     and, 303–4
Locke, John, 229
Lockridge, Kenneth, 318
Loisel, Antoine, 312*n*
Lollards and Protestants in the Dio-
     cese of York, 128
Louis, Mbope, 413
Lovejoy, Arthur, 178, 232
Luther (Erikson), *see Young Man*
     Luther
Luther (Febvre), see *Martin Luther:*
     A Destiny

Macaulay, T. B., 148, 396
McClelland, David, 200
McFarlane, K. B., 117
Machiavelli, Niccolò, 395
Ma conversion ou le libertin de qua-
     lité, 267
Mairan, Dortous de, 246, 247
Maitland, F. W., 113
Making of an American Community,
     The, 322, 334*n*
Making of the Modern Mind, 188–89*n*
Malthus, Thomas R., 28, 169
Manchester school, 59
Mandrou, Robert, 219–20
Mannheim, Karl, 450
Manuel, Frank, 185, 211–37, 456
Marcuse, Herbert, 220, 221, 227

Marot, Clément, 239
Marshall, Alfred, 28, 29
Marshall, George, 408
Marshall, S. L. A., 379
Martin Luther: A Destiny, 217
Marx, Karl, 3, 9–10, 18, 23, 116, 118,
     148–49, 151, 158*n*, 173, 214, 327–
     38, 409, 450
Marxist school/Marxism, 3, 4, 7, 8, 23,
     24*n*, 59, 63, 115–16, 129, 187, 226,
     227, 228, 262, 277*n*, 337–38, 341,
     349*n*, 351*n*, 353; *see also* Marx,
     Karl
Matloff, Maurice, 389
Maurice, Dom, 312*n*
Maurice, Sir Frederick, 377
Maxwell, James Clerk, 165
Mayer, Arno J., 366–67
Mayer, Theodor, 343
Mazlish, Bruce, 229
Meaney, Audrey, 294
Mechanization of the World Picture,
     164
Medieval Ideologies of the Enlighten-
     ment, 144–45
Méditerranée et le monde méditer-
     ranéen a l'époque de Philippe II,
     340
Meinecke, Friedrich, xvi, 143, 145,
     215, 358, 374, 395–96
Meiss, Millard, 232–33
Melanchthon, Philipp, 146
Mémoire des pays, villes, comté et
     comtes, evesché et evesques,
     pairrie, commune et personnes de
     renom de Beauvais et de Beau-
     vaisis, 312*n*
Mémoires sur la librairie, 255
Menger, Carl, 30
Mentalities, history of, 18–20
Mercure, 245
Merleau-Ponty, Maurice, 447
Merton, R. K., 111, 112, 116, 117,
     118, 167, 168, 179
Messance, 302–3
Metaphysical Foundations of Modern
     Physical Science, 164
Meuvret, Jean, 309
Meyer, Jean, 243, 247, 249, 305
Meyer, John, 36, 407*n*
Michaut, François, 273
Michelet, Jules, xvi, 213–14, 217, 337,
     340
Michels, R., 116
Michigan, University of, 131

Militärsystem und Soziallleben im alten Preussen, 375

Military archives, French, quantitative and cartographical exploitation of: absentees, 74; artisans, 70; calculation, method of, 65–67; carters, 70–71; document used, 64–65, 83n; cartwrights, 71; elite and priests, 67–69, 83n; exemptions, 76; fingers, loss of, 75; general discussion, 62–64; general statistics, 76–81; harnessmakers and saddlers, 71–72; health, 79–80, 85n; height, 75–76, 84n; laborers, 69; lameness, 69; map illustrations, 86–106; masons and stonecutters, 77; metalworkers, 73; methodological critique, 81–83; rentiers, 73–74; shoemakers, 72; tailors, 72; volunteers, 78–79; woodworkers, 72–73

Military history, 360; American contemporary studies in, 376, 377–82, 388–89, 390n; application of to other historical research, 383–84; contemporary studies in, 375–76; development of, 372–74; historical profession and, 374–75, 382; official projects, American, 379–80, 391n; popular history and, 376; social sciences and, use of theoretical models, 382–83; unexplored areas relating to, 384–85; violence, psychology of, 385–89

Military History, 377, 378

Military Policy of the United States, 377

Mill, John Stuart, 28

Miller, Perry, 141, 143, 153

Millis, Walter, 377, 378, 379, 390n

Mirabeau, Honoré Gabriel Riquetti, comte de, 267

Modernization, 445

Momigliano, A., 116, 124, 281

Mommsen, Theodor, xv, xvi, 289

Montesquieu, Charles de Secondat, baron de, 303

Morande, Charles Théveneau de, 268

Morin, Edgar, 338

Morineau, Michel, 307, 308

Morison, Samuel, 379

Mornet, Daniel, 239, 242–43, 245, 246, 247, 249, 250, 261, 269n

Mosca, G., 116

Moses and Monotheism, 222

Mots et les choses, Les, 220

Mousnier, Roland, 190n, 311

Müller, Johannes von, 399

Münzer, F., 112

Musil, Robert, 363

Naissance du Dauphin dévoilée, La, 265

Namier, Sir Lewis, 111, 112, 113–14, 116, 117–18, 124–25, 131, 133, 306, 307n

Narrative history, ix, x, 54–55, 340

Nationalism, 22–23

Neale, Sir John, 117, 133

New Antiquarianism, 132

New Cambridge Modern History, 141–42

New England Mind, 141, 143

Newton, A. P., 111, 112

Newton, Sir Isaac, 190

Nietzsche, Friedrich, 211, 216

Nouvelle Héloise, La, 239

Novum Organum, 163

Official Records of the War of the Rebellion, 379

Oral tradition: accounts, basic forms of, 416; ascertaining validity and accuracy of, 416–21; basic cultural notions, effect of on, 428–29; chronology, problems of, 432–35; defined, 415; functions and purposes of, 427; general discussion, 413–14; linguistic and literary analysis of, 423–27; other available sources: anthropology, 430–31, ethnographic data, 431, linguistics, 432, written documents, 429–30; social pressures, distortions induced by, 427–28; testimony and tradition, difference between, 415–16; types of, 421–23

Oresme, Nicole, 339

Origins of Modern Science, 163

Oxford English Dictionary, 141

Pagel, Walter, 186

Paideia, 193

Pallottino, Massimo, 288

Panofsky, Erwin, 181, 346

Paret, Peter, 191n, 372–92, 456

Pareto, V., 116

Peinture et société: naissance et destruction d'un espace plastique, de la Renaissance au cubisme, 346–47

Pensée chinoise, 453

Pensée sauvage, La, 423, 452
Petit, Régine, 243, 246
Pettazzoni, Raffaelle, 343
Philosophy, history of, 180, 182
Piggot, Stuart, 282–83, 284, 288
Pigou, Arthur C., 29
Pillorget, T., 314n
Pinel, Philippe, 224
Plancher, Dom, 312n
Plumb, J. H., 359
Plutarch, 289
Poe, 222
Pointrineau, Abel, 305
Political history, 143, 146, 147, 149–50, 157n, 199, 230, 372, 374; *Annales* school and, 337, 338; art, political analysis and, 346–47; comparative history methods, application of, 343–44; dangers threatening, 348–49; differential, functioning at various levels, 347–48; Dumezil schema, application of, 346; education, concept of power and, 345–46; Marxist thought and, 337–38, 341; new social sciences and, 338, 340, 344–45, 348; origins and former ascendancy of, 338–40, 350n, 351n; political anthropology and, 345, 347; politico-religious symbolism, medieval studies and, 341–43; power as central concept of, 340–43, 345–47, 349; *see also* Political and diplomatic history; Political and intellectual history, defense of
Political and diplomatic history: broader focus, need for, 367–68; diplomatic communications, treatment of, 360–62, 369n; foreign policy: domestic/economic forces and, 364–67, 370n, ideology and, 362–64, state instrumentalities and, 367; power and the state, 357–58, 359; research, traditional, present usefulness of, 358–59; state, shift from study of to economic and social factors, 356–57; theoretical models and, 359–60
Political and intellectual history, defense of: collective mentalities, study of, 437–38, 439; comparative politics, 446; folk culture and high culture, 448–49; "great man theory of history" and, 443–44; history of ideas and, 447; ideology and politics, link between, 440, 446–47; intellectual and scientific transcendence, question of, 450–51; literate and articulate, social classification of, 449–50; modernization, concept of, 445; narrative history and, 444–46; new scholasticism and learned jargon, 451–52; politics, conscious intention and activity in, 440–42; social scientific theory, 451, 452–54
Political Argument, 37
Political economy, 46–47, 55
Political science, 21, 131, 153; *see also* Social sciences
Politicology, 348
Politics, 339
Pollard, A. F., 404
Portrait of Isaac Newton, 185
Positivist history, 47
Pottinger, David, 241–42, 271–72n
Powell, Antony, 118
Powell, Chilton, 318
Principles, 28
Problem of Fall, The, 164
Progress, teleological history of, 59
Prosopography: achievements in, 126–31; American/European studies compared, 131–32; computer technology and, 131, 132–33; data, *see* limitations and dangers; definition and origins, 107–13, 134–35n; elitist school, 108, 109, 113; intellectual roots, 113–18; limitations and dangers: general discussion, 118, 133, deficiencies in data, 119–21, errors in data classification, 121–22, errors in data interpretation, 122–28, historical understanding, limitations of, 123–26; mass school, 108–9, 112–13
Proust, Marcel, 118
Psephology, 112–13, 131
Psychohistory, 221
Psychological history: Dilthey's work in, 215–17; 18th-century contributors to, 212–14; Erikson's work in, 221, 223–26; Febvre's work in, 215, 217–19, 220; Foucault's work in, 220; Freudian school/Freud's work in, 220–27; general discussion, 211–12; history and psychology, relationship between, 227–34; Mandrou's work in, 219–20; psychology, rise of in 19th century,

214–15; Sartre's work in, 221, 226–27

Psychologie der Weltanschauungen, 217

Psychology, 114–15, 134, 386–88; *see also* Freud, Sigmund; Psychological history; Social sciences

Puffendorf, Samuel, 146

Quantitative history, xvii, 45–61, 231; demographic and economic series, use of, 56–59; econometrics and, 46; facts, 54–60; methodology and technique, revolution in, 49–50; nature of, other social sciences and, 45–48; political economy and, 46–47; "politico-ideological" society, 59–60; serial history and, 47–48; sources, 48–54; *see also* Military archives, French

Rabb, Theodore, 122
Rabelais, 218
Radcliffe-Brown, Alfred R., 4
Railroads and American Economic Growth, 42
Raleigh, Sir Walter, 395
Ramsay, David, 406
Randall, J. H., 188–89n
Ranke, Leopold von, xv, xvi, 147, 227, 373–74
Rashdall, Hastings, 193
Raynal, Abbé, 339
Reflections on Violence, 407n
Regalità Sacra, La, 343
Religious history, 343, 347
Research, collective, 133
Revol, A. J., 251
Revue de synthèse historique, 340
Ricardo, David, 28
Riccoboni, Mme., 239
Richeprey, J. F. Henry de, 306
Ritter, Gerhard, 375, 376
Robber Barons, The, 115
Robertson, D. H., 28
Robin, Régine, 305
Robinson, James Harvey, 141
Roche, Daniel, 243, 246, 247
Roger, Jacques, 243, 245–46, 247
Rois de France régénérés, Les, 266
Rois thaumaturges, Les, 344
Rokkan, Stein, 22
Roman Revolution, 111, 124
Roosevelt, Franklin D., 397–98
Roosevelt, Theodore, 398

Rostovtzeff, Mikhail, 281, 292–93, 294
Rostow, W. W., 7
Rothblatt, Sheldon, 203–4, 207n
Roupnel, Gaston, 304
Rousseau, Jean-Jacques, 239, 269n, 452
Rundell, Walter, Jr., 389
Rureke, 415
Ruskin, John, 406
Russell, Bertrand, 178
Ruwet, Joseph, 306

Sainte-Beuve, Charles, 337
Saint-Hyacinthe, Thémiseul de, 239
Saint-Jacob, Pierre de, 305
Santayana, George, 402, 404
Sarton, George, 177
Sartre, Jean-Paul, 220, 221, 226–27, 447, 448, 452
Satow, Sir Ernest, 361
Scharnhorst, Gerhard, 372–73, 375
Scheub, H., 424
Schleiermacher, 215
Schlesinger, Arthur, Jr., 393–412, 457
Schofield, R. S., 201
Scholarship: historical, vii–viii, xi–xxi, 142, 143–44; model historians and, xv–xvi; modern technology and, xii–xv, xix, xx; new trends, xvi–xx
Schorski, Carl, 180, 188
Schramm, P. E., 341, 342, 344
Schulz, Henry, 30
Schumpeter, J. A., 28–29
Schwartz, Benjamin I., 440–54, 457
Science, history as, ix, xvii
Science, history of, 156n; criticism in science and the arts, 189n; general discussion, 159–60; historians and scientists, hostility between, 182–86; historiography of, contribution to separatism problem, 176–79; intellectual history, problems of, 164–71; law, history of and, 191n; neglect of by historical profession, 179–82; separatism question, intellectual and pedagogic consequences, 160–64; socioeconomic history, problems of and, 171–76; technology, cleavage between science and, 171–75
Science, Technology and Puritanism in Seventeenth Century England, 111
Second World War, The, 399
Seeley, Sir John, 373
Seignobos, Charles, 349–50n

Sein und Zeit, 127
Serial history, 47–48, 50, 54, 55, 56, 58, 63
Shanin, Theodore, 17–18
Shy, John, 388–89
Simiand, François, 340, 347
Singer, Charles, 291
Singleton, Gregory, 335n
Smelser, Neil, 7, 39
Smith, Adam, 27, 28, 169, 200
Smith, Henry, II, 207n
Smith, Page, 403, 406
Smith, Preserved, 215
Snodgrass, A. M., 293
Snow, C. P., 183
Social and Economic History of the Roman Empire, 281
Social history, viii, ix, 63, 150–51, 154–55, 238, 304, 320–21, 323, 330, 338, 345, 347, 350n, 357, 443; classes and social groups, 16–18; conflict and transformation, 20–23; demography and kinship, 14–15; development and emancipation of, 1–5; economics and, 2–3, 4–5, 9–10; guidelines for writing, 10–13; mentalities, history of, 18–20; practice of, general discussion, 13–14; progress to date, 23–24; province of, 5–6; social sciences and, 6–10; urban studies, 15–16; *see also* Education, history of
Social Science Research Council, 383
Social sciences, 63, 117, 382, 451, 452; historicization of, 4–5, 6–10; intellectual history and, 150–51; prosopography and, 108–9, 118; quantitative history and, 45–47; synchronic/diachronic dispute, 57; urban history and, 324; *see also* individual sciences
Social Teachings of the Christian Church, 143
Société de Démographique Historique, 311
Société féodale, La, 23
Société militaire dans la France contemporaine, La, 375
Society, history of, *see* Social history
Socioeconomic history, 164, 171–76
Sociologie de la littérature, 239–42
Sociology, 4, 8, 9, 45–46, 131, 134, 153, 338, 340, 348, 383; *see also* Social sciences
Solow, R. M., 34

Sommerfeld, Arnold, 181
Sorel, Georges, 407n
Spanish Monarchy, xv
Spencer, Herbert, 169, 356, 368n
Spengler, Oswald, 149, 215
Spufford, Margaret, 317
Staatskunst und Kriegshandwerk, 375
Stadelmann, Rudolf, 375
Stages of Economic Growth, The, 7
Stephen, Leslie, 142
Sterba, Editha, 222
Sterba, Richard, 222
Stone, Lawrence, 16, 107–40, 196, 207n, 315–19, 354, 457
Storia della politica estera Italiana dal 1870 al 1896, 145
Strachey, Lytton, 115
Strindberg, August, 217
Structure of Politics at the Accession of George III, 111, 124
Stubbs, C. W., 113
Study of Industrial Fluctuations, 28
Sumner, B. H., 362–63
Swendenborg, Emanuel, 217
Syme, Sir Ronald, 111, 112, 113, 116, 123, 124, 125

Talbott, John E., 193–210, 457
Task of Cultural History, The, 339, 350n
Taussig, Frank W., 29
Tawney, R. H., 4, 129
Taylor, L. R., 117
Temin, P., 35
Temperley, Harold, 364
Thernstrom, Stephan, 320–26, 457
Thierry, Augustin, 339
Thirsk, Joan, 316, 317, 319n
Thompson, Edward P., 16, 19, 199
Thousand Days, A, 403, 410n
Thucydides, 340, 394, 401
Tilly, Charles, 7, 52
Tocqueville, Alexis de, xvi, 303, 401–2, 407, 408–9
Touraine, Alain, 338, 350n
Tout, T. F., 113
Toynbee, Arnold, 149
Transformation, societal, 20–23
Treatise on Money, 29
Treitschke, Heinrich von, 358
Trenard, Louis, 246
Trevelyan, G. M., 2
Trevor-Roper, Hugh R., 123, 125, 129
Trilling, Lionel, 405–6
Troeltsch, Ernst, 143, 215

Tücke des Objekts, 387
Turner, Frederick Jackson, 327
Turner, Steven, 209*n*
Turner, V. W., 426
Two New Sciences, 163

Ucko, Peter, 283, 284, 294
"Underlying Themes in the Witchcraft
    of Seventeenth-Century New Eng-
    land," 230
*United States Army in World War II,
    The,* 379
*United States Naval Operation in
    World War II,* 379
*Universities of Europe in the Middle
    Ages, The,* 193
Unwin, George, 3
Upton, Emory, 377
Urban history, new: 15–16, 25*n;* base
    for, sources comprising, 321–22;
    boundaries of, 320; class and
    ethnic differentials in spatial mo-
    bility studies, 328–29; computer
    technology and, 325–26, 335*n;*
    economic history and, 323; immi-
    gration and differential opportunity
    studies, 330; Negro migrants and
    European immigrants, studies of,
    330–31; population fluidity studies,
    327–28; quantitative research,
    dangers of exclusive use of, 331–
    33; rates and trends in social mo-
    bility studies, 329–30; social his-
    tory and, 320–21, 323, 331; sources
    available, limitations of, 324–27;
    term, definition and drawbacks of,
    321–23; theory, relationship to,
    323–24; urbanization as societal
    process, 320–21

Vaissete, Dom, 312*n*
Vallentiny, Major Edward, 389
Van Gogh, Vincent, 217
Vansina, Jan, xix, 413–39, 457
Vauban, Sébastien, 302

Vendée, 7
Veysey, Laurence R., 204
Vico, Giambattista, 147, 212–13, 214
Victoria County History, 315, 316
Vie privée de Louis XV, 265
Vilar, P., 58
Vischer, Friedrich Theodor, 387
Voltaire, 144, 147, 246, 303, 305, 337,
    339, 372
Vorträge und Forschungen, 343
Vovelle, M., 314*n*

Wakeman, Frederick, 443
Walcott, Robert, 125
Wallon, Henri, 219
Walras, Léon, 30
Waning of the Middle Ages, 219
War, history of, *see* Military history
Warner, Sam B., 324
Wealth of Nations, The, 27
Weber, Max, 118, 143
Wehler, Hans-Ulrich, 365
Weiss, John H., 209*n*
Wells, Robert, 319
Weltbürgertum und Nationalstaat, 358
Weltgeschichtliche Betrachtungen, 152
Whitehead, Alfred North, 211
Wicksell, Knut, 29
Wilson, Woodrow, 223, 402
Wolf, Eric, 7
Wolff, P., 72
Woodward, C. Vann, vii
World Crisis, The, 399

Xenophon, 394

Yates, Frances, 186
Young, G. M., 360
Young Man Luther, 217–18, 224, 225
Young, R. H., 189–90*n*

Zhosa *intsomi* narratives, 424
Zink, Anne, 314*n*
Zuckerman, M., 318